Nutrition for Fitness and Sport

Third Edition

Nutrition for Fitness and Sport

Melvin H. Williams
Old Dominion University

Wm. C. Brown Publishers

Book Team

Editor *Chris Rogers*
Developmental Editor *Scott Spoolman*
Production Coordinator *Jayne Klein*
Permissions Editor *Karen Storlie*

 Wm. C. Brown Publishers

President *G. Franklin Lewis*
Vice President, Publisher *Thomas E. Doran*
Vice President, Operations and Production *Beverly Kolz*
National Sales Manager *Virginia S. Moffat*
Group Sales Manager *Eric Ziegler*
Executive Editor *Edgar J. Laube*
Director of Marketing *Kathy Law Laube*
Marketing Manager *Pam Cooper*
Managing Editor, Production *Colleen A. Yonda*
Manager of Visuals and Design *Faye M. Schilling*
Production Editorial Manager *Julie A. Kennedy*
Production Editorial Manager *Ann Fuerste*
Publishing Services Manager *Karen J. Slaght*

WCB Group

President and Chief Executive Officer *Mark C. Falb*
Chairman of the Board *Wm. C. Brown*

Cover photo © George Obremski/The Image Bank

Cover design and interior design Jeanne M. Regan

Copyedited by Lillian R. Rodberg

Consulting Editor Aileene Lockhart/Texas Women's University

Library of Congress Catalog Card Number: 90–86157

ISBN 0–697–10145–2

Printed in the United States of America by Wm. C. Brown Publishers,
2460 Kerper Boulevard, Dubuque, IA 52001

10 9 8 7 6 5 4 3

Contents

Preface

Even in the 1990s, America's love affair with fitness and sports continues to grow. We are no longer a nation of spectators; more of us are becoming participants in physical activities such as aerobic dancing, walking, running, bicycling, swimming, tennis, and a host of other recreational activities and sports. Improvement in health and fitness is one of the major reasons that more and more people initiate an exercise program. But many also are finding the joy of athletic competition, such as participation in a local 10-kilometer road race.

Research has shown that adults who become physically active also become more interested in other aspects of their life-styles—particularly nutrition—that may affect their health in a positive way. Moreover, individuals who compete athletically are always looking for a means to improve performance, be it a new piece of equipment or an improved training method. In this regard, nutrition may be an important factor in improving both health and physical performance.

Nutrition is the study of foods and their effects upon health, development, and performance of the individual. The science of human nutrition has made a significant contribution to our knowledge of essential nutrient needs during this century. However, because most nutritional studies with humans cannot be controlled under exacting laboratory conditions, human nutrition science is not as precise as other scientific areas of study such as chemistry and physics. Given the basic physiological drives for food and fluid and the psychological overtones that surround our eating behaviors, certain individuals and commercial organizations have exploited this imprecise nature of human nutrition science for financial gains by distorting nutritional facts. Quackery represents fraudulent misrepresentation, and the area of nutrition is filled with numerous nutritional products that may be classified as fraudulent.

Physically active individuals are major targets for those who market and sell nutritional supplements. Magazines for active people are filled with advertisements extolling the virtues of various supplements that are said to do everything from preventing aging to improving athletic performance. Some of these supplements include calcium, chromium, special amino acid compounds or athletic vitamin packs, bee pollen, vitamin B_{15}, and vitamin E.

One purpose of this book is to help dispel the myths and misconceptions associated with nutrition for physically active individuals.

This book uses a question–answer approach, which is convenient when you may have occasional short periods to study such as riding a bus or during a lunch break. In addition, the questions are arranged in a logical sequence, the answer to one question often leading into the question that follows. Where appropriate, cross-referencing within the text is used to expand the discussion. No deep scientific background is needed for the chemical aspects of nutrition and energy expenditure, as these have been simplified.

Chapter 1 introduces you to the concept of healthful nutrition and sports nutrition, while Chapter 2 focuses upon energy, the key to all physical activities.

Chapters 3 through 8 deal with the six basic nutrients—carbohydrate, fat, protein, vitamins, minerals, and water—with emphasis on the needs of the physically active individual. Chapters 9 through 11 review concepts of body composition and weight control, with suggestions on how to gain or lose body weight through diet and exercise, as well as the implications of such changes for health and athletic performance. Chapter 12 represents a summary of sound guidelines relative to nutrition for optimal health and physical performance. Numerous appendixes complement the text, providing data on caloric expenditure during exercise, selected diets, and other information pertinent to physically active individuals.

Key concepts are presented at the beginning of each chapter. These can be used for previewing the chapter and for reinforcement once the chapter has been completed. Key terms also are listed at the beginning of the chapter and highlighted when they are first defined in the text. A thorough glossary includes the key terms as well as other terms warranting definition.

The bibliographic references are of three types. Books listed provide broad coverage of the major topics in the chapter. Review articles are detailed analyses of selected topics, usually involving a synthesis and analysis of specific research studies. The specific studies listed are primary research studies. The reference lists have been completely updated for this third edition and provide the scientific basis for new concepts or additional support for those concepts previously developed. These references provide greater in-depth reading materials for the interested student.

Your involvement in practical activities is encouraged. There are a number of opportunities for the reader to get actively involved: estimation of your percent body fat, estimation of the number of Calories to maintain body weight, designing a 1,200-Calorie diet, calculating the caloric expenditure for a given exercise, or initiating a sound exercise program based upon contemporary principles of exercise prescription.

This book is designed primarily for the physically active individual interested in the nutritional aspects of physical and athletic performance. Those who may desire to initiate a physical training program may also find the nutritional information useful, as well as the guidelines for initiating a training program. This book may serve as a handy reference for coaches, trainers, and athletes. With the tremendous expansion of youth sports programs, parents may find the information valuable relative to the nutritional requirements of their active children.

A special note of appreciation is extended to Professors Lloyd L. Laubach (The University of Dayton), Roberta L. Pohlman (Wright State University), Barbara Reynolds (College of the Sequoias), Robert E. Salois (Trenton State College), and Sharon Dinkel Uhlig (University of Montana), for their very helpful reviews of the manuscript.

Melvin H. Williams
Virginia Beach, VA

Nutrition for Fitness and Sport

Key Terms

Basic Four Food Groups

ergogenic aids

epidemiological research

essential nutrient

experimental research

Estimated Safe and Adequate
Daily Dietary Intake
(ESADDI)

Food Exchange System

Healthy American Diet

malnutrition

nonessential nutrient

nutrient

nutrition

quackery

Recommended Dietary
Allowances (RDA)

sports nutrition

United States Recommended
Daily Allowances
(USRDA)

Key Concepts

Success in sports is primarily dependent upon genetic endowment and proper training, but nutrition also can be an important contributing factor.

The principal purposes of the food we eat are to provide energy, build and repair body tissues, and regulate metabolic processes in the body.

More than forty specific nutrients are essential to life processes. They may be obtained in the diet through consumption of the six major nutrient classes: carbohydrates, fats, proteins, vitamins, minerals and water.

The Recommended Dietary Allowances (RDA) should not be construed to be an ideal diet plan, but they can provide us with sound information about our nutritional needs. The United States Recommended Daily Allowances are based upon the RDA.

The RDA represent a set of standards; if individuals in a given population consume foods in amounts adequate to meet their RDA, there will be very little likelihood of nutritional inadequacy or impairment of health.

Consuming a wide variety of natural, wholesome foods from the Basic Four Food Groups or the Food Exchange System will help provide you with the RDA for all essential nutrients.

Basic guidelines for the Healthy American Diet include maintenance of proper body weight and consumption of a wide variety of natural foods high in complex carbohydrates and low in fat.

Probably the most prevalent ergogenic aids in sport are those classified as nutritional, for theoretical nutritional aids may be found in all six classes of nutrients.

A number of recent surveys have reported athletes to be consuming less than the RDA for several nutrients, particularly those athletes attempting to lose weight for competition.

There appears to be no sphere of nutrition in which faddism, misconceptions, ignorance and quackery are more obvious than in athletics.

Nutritional quackery persists in sports for a variety of reasons, including the imitation of dietary practices of star athletes, misleading articles in sports magazines, inadequate nutritional knowledge of coaches, and direct advertising.

The best means to counteract nutritional quackery in sports is to possess a good background in nutrition.

Prudent nutritional recommendations for enhancement of health or athletic performance are based upon reputable research.

Introduction to Sports Nutrition
1

Introduction

Webster's Encyclopedic Unabridged Dictionary defines sport in a variety of ways, using such terms as "pleasant pastime," "entertainment," "recreation," "diversion," "amusement," "play," and "athletic contest." Defined as a pleasant pastime or play, sport has been an integral part of everyday life from time immemorial. But as societies developed, sport eventually evolved into more serious forms of athletic contests. Sport is now most commonly defined as a competitive athletic activity requiring skill or physical prowess, for example, racing, baseball, basketball, soccer, football, wrestling, tennis, and golf.

Success in sport is based primarily upon superior athletic ability, which in turn depends mostly on two major factors: natural genetic endowment and state of training. To be successful at high levels of competition, the athlete must possess the appropriate biomechanical, physiological, and psychological genetic characteristics associated with success in a given sport, and these genetic characteristics must be developed maximally through proper biomechanical, physiological, and psychological coaching and training.

Athletes at all levels of competition, whether for an Olympic gold medal or an age-group award in a local road race, are always interested in ways to improve their performance and gain an edge on the competition. In regard to the two major factors influencing athletic ability, there is nothing an athlete can do to modify his or her genetic endowment, but training programs have become more intense and individualized, and significant performance gains have resulted. In addition to training methods, sport and exercise scientists have investigated a number of means to improve athletic performance, and one of the most extensively investigated areas has been the effect of nutrition.

Proper nutrition is an important component in the total training program of the athlete. Certain nutrient deficiencies can seriously impair performance, while supplementation of other nutrients may help delay fatigue and improve performance. Over the last two decades, research has provided us with many answers about the role of nutrition in athletic performance, but unfortunately some of the research findings have been misinterpreted or exaggerated so that a number of misconceptions still exist.

Proper nutrition also is an important component in a healthy life-style for both athletes and non-athletes. In recent years many Americans have shifted their life-styles in an attempt to improve their health and fitness. This movement toward preventive health, or wellness, has focused upon life-style changes, such as stress management, smoking cessation, and moderation in alcohol consumption, which may help prevent or delay the development of certain chronic diseases. Two of the major components of such a healthy life-style receiving the most attention are exercise and nutrition. Millions of individuals have initiated aerobic exercise programs and modified their diets as recommended by health authorities. Unfortunately again, as with nutritional advice for athletic performance, some exaggerations about the health benefits of nutritional supplements have been made by certain entrepreneurs.

The purpose of this chapter is to provide a broad overview of the role that nutrition may play relative to health, fitness, and sport. More detailed information is provided in the following chapters where appropriate.

Healthful Nutrition

What is nutrition?

Nutrition usually is defined as the sum total of the processes involved in the intake and utilization of food substances by living organisms, including ingestion, digestion, absorption, and metabolism of food. This definition stresses the biochemical or physiological functions of the food we eat, but the American Dietetic Association notes that nutrition may be interpreted in a broader sense and be affected by a variety of psychological, sociological, and economic factors as well.

Although our food selection may be influenced by these latter factors, particularly economic ones in the case of many college students, the biochemical and physiological roles in the body of many different types of food are similar. From a standpoint of health and athletic performance, it is the biochemical and physiological role or function of the food that is important.

What are the functions of the food we eat?

The primary purpose of the food we eat is to provide us with a variety of nutrients, a **nutrient** being a specific substance found in food that performs one or more physiological or biochemical functions in the body. There are six major classes of nutrients: carbohydrates, fats, proteins, vitamins, minerals, and water.

These nutrients perform three major functions. First, they provide energy for human metabolism (see Chapter 2). Carbohydrates and fats are the prime sources of energy, and although protein may also provide energy, this is not usually its major function. Vitamins, minerals, and water are not energy sources. Second, nutrients are used to build and repair body tissues. Protein is the major building material for muscles, other soft tissues, and enzymes, while certain minerals such as calcium and phosphorus make up the skeletal framework. Third, nutrients are used to help regulate body processes. Vitamins, minerals, and proteins work closely together to maintain the diverse physiological processes of human metabolism. For example, hemoglobin in the red blood cell (RBC) is essential for the transport of oxygen to the muscle tissue via the blood. Hemoglobin is a complex combination of protein and iron, but other minerals and vitamins are needed for its synthesis and for full development of the RBC.

"You are what you eat" is a popular phrase, and we are becoming increasingly aware of its implications for both health and athletic performance. Careful selection of wholesome, natural foods will provide you with the proper amount of nutrients to optimize energy sources, tissue building and repair, and regulation of body processes. However, as we shall see in later chapters, poor food selection with an unbalanced intake of some nutrients may contribute to the development of significant health problems. Moreover, although the three major functions of food are important to the sedentary individual, they become increasingly important to the athlete who may increase metabolic activities more than ten-fold through exercise, and maintain that high rate for an hour or more. For example, a number of studies have shown that physical performance may be hampered seriously by inadequate nutrition. On the other hand, as will be noted generally throughout this book, supplemental feeding of nutrients above the recommended dietary intake to individuals who are in nutritional balance generally has not been shown to increase physical performance capacity. The key point is to ensure that you are receiving an adequate amount of Calories (a measure of energy defined in Chapter 2) and specific nutrients as recommended by current knowledge of nutritional requirements. This amount may be modified by the type and amount of physical activity that you do.

What essential nutrients must I obtain from food?

As noted above, six classes of nutrients are considered necessary in human nutrition: carbohydrates, fats, proteins, vitamins, minerals, and water. Within several of these general classes, notably protein, vitamins, and minerals, are a number of specific nutrients necessary for life. For example, more than a dozen vitamins are needed for optimal physiological functioning.

In relation to nutrition, the term **essential nutrients** describes a nutrient that the body cannot produce or cannot produce in adequate quantities. Thus, essential nutrients must be obtained from the food we eat. Essential nutrients also are known as indispensable nutrients. Those nutrients that may be formed in the body are known as **nonessential nutrients,** or dispensable nutrients. A good example of a nonessential nutrient is glucose. Although we may obtain glucose from food, the body can also manufacture glucose from protein and parts of fats when necessary. As we shall see later, glucose is a very important nutrient for energy production during exercise, and although the body may produce some glucose during exercise, the rate of production is not adequate to meet the energy demands during moderate to heavy exertion. Thus, glucose may be a very essential nutrient for certain types of physical activity, but dietary glucose is not essential for life. A wide variety of other nonessential nutrients, such as carnitine, and even naturally occurring antinutrients, such as oxalates, are present in foods we eat. They are discussed in later chapters where relevant.

Table 1.1 lists the specific nutrients currently known to be essential or probably essential to humans. Some of the nutrients listed have been shown to be essential for various animals and are theorized to be essential for humans. It is possible that this list may be expanded in the future as more accurate analytical methods are developed to study the effects of certain minerals in human nutrition. Although carbohydrate is not an essential nutrient in the strictest sense, many nutritionists consider dietary fiber, which is primarily carbohydrate, a specific necessity in the diet for prevention of certain health problems.

Some foods, such as whole wheat bread, may contain all six general classes of nutrients, whereas

Figure 1.1.
Three major functions of
nutrients in food.

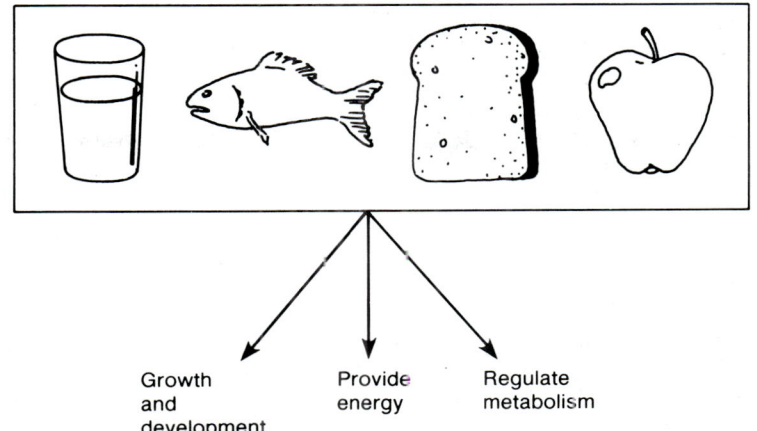

Growth
and
development

Provide
energy

Regulate
metabolism

Table 1.1   Nutrients essential or probably essential to humans

Carbohydrates
Fiber

Fats (essential fatty acids)
Linoleic fatty acid

Protein (essential amino acids)

Histidine	Phenylalanine
Isoleucine	Threonine
Leucine	Tryptophan
Lysine	Valine
Methionine	

Vitamins

Water soluble	Fat soluble
B₁ (thiamin)	A (retinol)
B₂ (riboflavin)	D (calciferol)
Niacin	E (tocopherol)
B₆ (pyridoxine)	K
Pantothenic acid	
Folacin	
B₁₂ (cyanocobalamin)	
Biotin	
C (ascorbic acid)	

Minerals

Major	Trace	
Calcium	Chromium	Molybdenum
Chloride	Cobalt	Nickel
Magnesium	Copper	Selenium
Phosphorus	Fluorine	Silicon
Potassium	Iodine	Tin
Sodium	Iron	Vanadium
Sulfur	Manganese	Zinc

Water

others, such as table sugar, contain only one nutrient. However, whole wheat bread cannot be considered a complete food because it does not contain a proper balance of all essential nutrients.

Essential nutrients are necessary for human life. An inadequate intake may lead to disturbed body metabolism, certain disease states, or death. Conversely, an excess of certain nutrients may also disrupt normal metabolism and may even be lethal.

What are the RDA?

As noted in Table 1.1, humans have an essential requirement for more than forty specific nutrients. A number of countries as well as the Food and Agriculture and World Health Organizations (FAO/WHO) have calculated the amount of each nutrient that individuals should consume in their diets. In the United States, the amounts of certain of these nutrients have been established by the Food and Nutrition Board, National Academy of Sciences–National Research Council. The **Recommended Dietary Allowances** (RDA) represent the levels of intake of essential nutrients considered in the judgment of the Food and Nutrition Board on the basis of available scientific knowledge to be adequate to meet the known nutritional needs of practically all healthy persons in the United States. However, the RDA are not appropriate for individuals with special nutrient needs. RDA have been established for energy intake (Calories), protein, eleven vitamins and seven minerals. Although technically not an RDA, **Estimated Safe and Adequate Daily Dietary Intakes** (ESADDI) have been developed for two additional vitamins and five minerals. The current RDA and ESADDI are found in Appendix A, the tenth revision issued in 1989; the first edition appeared in 1943.

It should be noted that the RDA are based on the median heights and weights for specific age groups. The average male aged 25–50 weighs 174 pounds or in metric terms, 79 kilograms (kg). One kg equals 2.2 pounds. The average female aged 25–50 weights 138 pounds, or 63 kg. Hence, in general, adults who weigh more than these average weights will require a slightly higher RDA, while those who weigh less will require a slightly lower amount. RDA established for children of various ages would also have to be adjusted accordingly.

An individual does not necessarily have a deficient diet if the full RDA for a given nutrient is not received daily. The daily RDA should average over a five- to eight-day period, so that one may be deficient in iron consumption one day but compensate for this one-day deficiency during the remainder of the week. Nutritionists generally become concerned when the dietary intake of a specific nutrient is consistently below 70 percent of the RDA.

The RDA are a set of standards designed to ensure adequate nutrition. If individuals in a population consume foods in amounts adequate to meet their RDA, there will be very little likelihood of nutritional inadequacy or impairment of health. In fact, the RDA are not minimum recommendations, but actually exceed the requirement of most individuals because a safety factor is incorporated in the RDA for protein, vitamins, and minerals.

The RDA are not designed to be used for the requirements of specific individuals. Only a clinical and biochemical evaluation of an individual can reveal his or her nutritional status in regard to any specific nutrient. Nevertheless, comparison of an individual's nutrient intake to the RDA over a sufficient period may be useful in estimating that individual's risk for deficiency.

What should I eat to obtain the RDA?
Years ago nutritionists attempted to design a simple guide to eating that could be understood by the average American, and that also would provide a basis for obtaining the RDA of all essential nutrients. In essence, foods that had similar nutrient content were grouped into categories. Because we will be discussing the concepts of the Basic Four Food Groups and the Food Exchange System throughout this book, it appears important to introduce these concepts at this time.

The most popular grouping used in the United States is the **Basic Four Food Group** approach. Foods of similar nutrient value are placed in either the milk group, meat group, bread/cereal group, or fruit/vegetable group. A fifth group, the fats, sweets, and alcohol group, is often listed; this latter group usually is high in Calories but low in nutrients. The basic premise underlying the Basic Four approach is that by eating a wide variety of foods from each of the four foods groups you will receive the RDA for all essential nutrients. Table 1.2 highlights some of the major nutrients found in each of the four food groups.

An extension of the Basic Four Food Group approach is the **Food Exchange System,** a grouping of foods developed by the American Dietetic Association, American Diabetic Association, and other professional and governmental health organizations. Foods in each of the given exchanges contain approximately the same amount of Calories, carbohydrate, fat, and protein. As with the Basic Four Food Groups, eating a wide variety of foods from the six food exchanges will help guarantee that you receive the RDA for essential nutrients. The basic content of each food exchange is presented in Table 1.3. A detailed list of common foods in the various exchanges may be found in Appendix H.

Although the use of the Basic Four Food Groups or the Food Exchange System is a valuable means to achieve the RDA for essential nutrients, there may be some problems if foods are not selected wisely. It is easily possible to select the least nutritious foods from each group or list, which could lead to a nutrient deficiency. In addition, an individual may select foods that might not be considered the most healthful choices on the basis of current nutritional knowledge.

The RDA are a rather cumbersome tool for planning your daily diet, but they can be a useful guide to securing an adequate amount of nutrients in the food we eat. As a matter of fact, the **United States Recommended Daily Allowances** (USRDA), which are used as a standard for nutritional labeling to provide information about daily intakes, are based on the RDA; however, the USRDA are slightly higher for several nutrients. These and other factors that are important in the design of a healthier diet are covered in detail in Chapter 12.

What are some general guidelines for healthful eating?
As already noted, consuming your RDA for various nutrients does not mean that your diet is healthy. During the 1980s, in response to the need for healthier diets, a variety of public and private health organizations developed some general guidelines for the American public, but there were usually some differences in their recommendations. Recently, ten of these organizations held what amounted to a "food summit" to generate some degree of consensus on

Table 1.2   Major nutrients found in the Basic Four Food Groups

Meat group	Milk group	Bread/cereal group	Fruit/vegetable group
Protein	Calcium	Thiamin	Vitamin A
Thiamin	Protein	Niacin	Vitamin C
Niacin	Riboflavin	Riboflavin	
Iron	Vitamin A	Iron	
		Protein	

Table 1.3   Carbohydrate, fat, protein, and calories in the six food exchanges

Food exchange	Carbohydrate	Fat	Protein	Calories
Milk				
Skim	12	Trace	8	90
Low fat	12	5	8	120
Whole	12	8	8	150
Meat				
Lean	0	3	7	55
Medium fat	0	5	7	75
High fat	0	8	7	100
Starch/bread	15	Trace	3	80
Fruit	15	0	0	60
Vegetable	5	0	2	25
Fat	0	5	0	45

Carbohydrate, fat, and protein in grams (g).
1 g carbohydrate = 4 Calories
1 g fat = 9 Calories
1 g protein = 4 Calories

recommendations for a healthy diet. In addition, the National Research Council recently released its voluminous report entitled *Diet and Health: Implications for Reducing Chronic Disease Risk,* while the Surgeon General's office released the *Surgeon General's Report on Nutrition and Health,* and the U.S. Department of Agriculture and U.S. Department of Health and Human Services released the third edition of *Nutrition and Your Health: Dietary Guidelines for Americans.* The following dozen guidelines represent the essence of the recommendations emanating from these reports, which might be called the **Healthy American Diet.**

1. Achieve and maintain a healthy body weight by balanced food intake and physical activity.
2. Eat a nutritionally adequate diet consisting of a wide variety of natural, wholesome foods.
3. Maintain adequate calcium and iron intake. This is important for both sexes and all ages but is particularly important to women and children.
4. Maintain protein intake at a moderate yet adequate level.
5. Choose a diet with plenty of complex carbohydrates and fiber, such as starches, legumes, fruits, and vegetables, especially dark green and yellow vegetables and citrus fruits.
6. Use sugar in moderation.
7. Choose a diet low in total fat, saturated fat, and cholesterol.
8. Use salt and sodium only in moderation.
9. Children and others susceptible to tooth decay should obtain adequate fluoride and consume less sugar.
10. Avoid taking dietary supplements in excess of the RDA in any one day.
11. Eat fewer foods with questionable additives.
12. If you drink alcoholic beverages, do so in moderation. Pregnant women should not drink any alcohol.

A more detailed discussion of these concepts is presented in appropriate chapters throughout the book, especially in Chapter 12. You may wish to take the brief inventory in Appendix L to provide you with a general analysis of your current eating habits.

Sports Nutrition

What is sports nutrition?

Sports nutrition is a relatively new area of study involving the application of nutritional principles to enhance sports performance. Although investigators have studied the interactions between nutrition and various forms of sport or exercise for more than a hundred years, it is only recently that extensive research has been undertaken regarding specific recommendations to athletes. Several factors suggest that the emerging field of sports nutrition is a viable career opportunity. Probably the most important factor is the amount of research conducted in the 1970s and 1980s concerning the interactions of nutrition and exercise. It is through such well-controlled research—the numerous studies conducted at Ball State University by David Costill and his associates, for example—that answers are provided relative to optimal nutrition for the athlete.

A second factor is the formation of a subsection within the American Dietetic Association concerned with sports nutrition and known as SCAN, for Sports and Cardiovascular Nutritionists. A number of registered dieticians have taken special courses and are advertising their services as sports nutritionists. Still another factor is the development of courses in sports nutrition at many U.S. colleges and universities to help prepare future coaches, athletic trainers, and other sports medicine personnel to better advise athletes on sound nutritional practices.

Finally, the published literature about nutrition for sport has become voluminous. Numerous magazines have been developed for specific groups of athletes pursuing almost every kind of sport, such as runners, swimmers, triathletes, and weight lifters. Invariably each issue contains a nutrition-related article, and several magazines such as *Runner's World* employ nutrition editors with a Ph.D. in the subject. In addition, many books have been written on sports nutrition, and one was even on the best-seller list for a short period (although some of its content has been justifiably criticized by reputable sports nutritionists). Sports nutrition as we know it today has a relatively short history, but it appears to be an important aspect in the total preparation of the athlete.

Are athletes today receiving adequate nutrition?

The dietary habits of athletes may vary tremendously, particularly when different sports are compared. Surveys conducted with several different groups of athletes reveal that some athletes may be obtaining an adequate intake of nutrients while others may not. An excellent review is presented by Sarah Short of Syracuse University. The usual method in these studies was to obtain a three- to seven-day record of the food intake of the athletes and then use computer analyses to compare their intake with the RDA for a variety of nutrients. Although not all studies are in agreement, certain athletic groups, such as football players and strength athletes, appear to obtain adequate nutrition, while inadequate nutrient intakes have been reported in other athletic groups, including ballet dancers, basketball players, body builders, gymnasts, runners, skiers, swimmers, triathletes, and wrestlers.

These nutrient deficiencies were noted in athletes of abilities ranging from the high school level to Olympic caliber. Females were much more likely than males to incur nutrient deficiencies. The most significant nutrient deficiency in most studies was iron, although zinc, calcium, protein and several of the B vitamins also were found to be deficient by several investigators. In many of these reports, the nutrient deficiencies were due to a very low caloric intake. Several studies also noted that the percentage of Calories derived from carbohydrate was lower than that recommended for endurance athletes.

The athletic groups most susceptible to a nutrient deficiency are those attempting to lose weight for sports competition, notably dancers, gymnasts, body builders, runners, and wrestlers. In one nationwide survey of the nutritional habits of elite athletes, the investigators noted that in sports in which body weight and composition are important, such as gymnastics and ballet, nutrient intake may be marginal. In addition, several studies have revealed a high incidence of eating disorders in these groups of athletes as they adopted bizarre techniques in attempts to control body weight. This topic is addressed in Chapter 9.

This brief review does indicate that some athletic groups are not receiving the RDA for a variety of essential nutrients. It should be noted, however, that these surveys have only analyzed the diets of the athletes in reference to a standard, such as the RDA, and have not analyzed performance capacity or the effects that the dietary deficiency exerted on athletic performance. The RDA for vitamins and minerals incorporates a safety factor, so an individual with a dietary intake of essential nutrients below the RDA will not necessarily suffer a true nutrient deficiency. On the other hand, if the athlete does develop a nutrient deficiency, then athletic performance may deteriorate, and some deficiencies may lead to injuries.

A number of reasons may contribute to why many athletes do not appear to be getting adequate nutrition. As noted by Short, several studies have shown that the nutritional knowledge of athletes is relatively poor; hence, the athlete may not have the basis to select and prepare nutritious meals. Other constraints, such as finances and time, may limit food selection and preparation. Moreover, athletes may not be receiving sound nutritional information from their coaches or trainers. Several surveys cited by Short revealed that many coaches at the high school and college levels have poor backgrounds in nutrition, with approximately 60 to 90 percent of the coaches noting that they had not had a formal course in nutrition or were in need of a better background. However, with the introduction of courses in sports nutrition at the college level, this situation should change for the better in the near future.

How important is nutrition to athletic performance?

As mentioned previously, the ability to perform well in an athletic event is dependent primarily upon two factors: genetic endowment and state of training. First and foremost is genetic endowment. The individual athlete must possess the characteristics that are necessary for success in his or her chosen sport. For example, a world class male marathoner must have a high aerobic capacity and a low body fat percentage in order to run over 26 sub-five-minute miles. However, unless he has undergone a strenuous training program and maximized his genetic potential, the performance will be suboptimal. The state of training is the most important factor differentiating athletes of comparable genetic endowment. The better-trained athlete has the advantage. No matter at what level the athlete is competing, be it for a world championship or in a high school swimming meet, genetic endowment and state of training are the two most critical factors determining success. Nevertheless, the nutritional status of the athlete may also exert a significant impact upon athletic performance. An internationally renowned Olympic sports medicine physician, L. Prokop, has noted that again and again he has seen a minor, seemingly negligible mistake in the diet ruin many months and years of hard training at the critical moment.

Malnutrition represents unbalanced nutrition and may exist as either undernutrition or overnutrition, that is, an individual does not receive an adequate intake (undernutrition) or consumes excessive amounts of single or multiple nutrients (overnutrition). Either condition can hamper athletic performance. As noted previously, the three major functions of foods are to supply energy, regulate metabolism, and build and repair body tissues. Thus, an inadequate intake of certain nutrients may impair athletic performance owing to an insufficient energy supply, an inability to regulate exercise metabolism at an optimal level, or a decreased synthesis of key body tissues or enzymes. On the other hand, excessive intake of some nutrients may also impair athletic performance, and even the health of the athlete, by disrupting normal physiological processes or leading to undesirable changes in body composition. In general, athletes who consume enough Calories to meet their energy needs and who meet the RDA for essential nutrients should be obtaining adequate nutrition.

What should I eat to help optimize my athletic performance?

The importance of nutrition to your athletic performance may depend on the particular sport in which you participate. For example, the nutrient needs of a golfer or baseball player may vary little from those of the nonathlete, whereas those of a marathon runner or ultraendurance triathlete may be altered significantly during training and competition.

The opinions offered by researchers in the area of exercise and nutrition relative to optimal nutrition for the athlete run the gamut. At one end, certain investigators note that the daily food requirement of athletes is quite similar to the nutritionally balanced diet for everyone else, and therefore no special recommendations are needed. On the other extreme, some state that it is almost impossible to obtain all the nutrients the athlete requires from the normal daily intake of food, and for that reason nutrient supplementation is absolutely necessary. Other reviewers advocate a compromise between these two extremes, recommending the importance of a nutritionally balanced diet but also stressing the importance of increased consumption or supplementation of specific nutrients to athletes under certain specific situations.

The review of the scientific literature presented in this book supports the latter point of view. Although a nutritionally balanced diet is still the keystone of sports nutrition, some athletes may benefit from dietary modifications. Specific examples are provided throughout the remainder of this book.

Although proper nutrition is important to the athlete to ensure optimal physical performance, unfortunately some of the research findings relative to the effects of specific nutrients upon performance have been misinterpreted. In a number of cases, most often in magazines targeted for specific athletic groups but also in leading sports nutrition books, certain nutrients have been ascribed magical qualities which, if the nutrient is ingested in adequate amounts, would improve physical performance. The next section discusses nutritional quackery and the possible ergogenic effects of food.

Nutritional Quackery in Health and Sports

What is nutritional quackery?

According to the Food and Drug Administration (FDA), **quackery,** as the term is used today, refers not only to the fake practitioner but also to the worthless product and the deceitful promotion of that product. Untrue or misleading claims that are deliberately or fraudulently made for any product, including food products, constitute quackery.

Knowledge relative to all facets of life, the science of nutrition included, has increased phenomenally in recent years. Thousands of studies have been conducted, revealing facts to help unravel some of the mysteries of human nutrition. Certain individuals may capitalize on these research findings for personal financial gain. For example, isolated nutritional facts may be distorted, or the results of a single study will be used, to market a specific nutritional product. Health hustlers will use this information to capitalize on people's fears and hopes, be it the fear that the nutritional quality of our food is being lessened by modern processing methods or the hope of improved athletic performance capacity.

Quackery is big business. It has been estimated that over twenty-five billion dollars a year are spent on questionable health practices in the United States. A substantial percentage of this amount has been for unnecessary nutritional products. Authorities in this area have noted that the amount of misinformation about nutrition is overwhelming, and it is circulated widely, particularly by those who may profit from it. Although we may still think of quacks as sleazy individuals selling patent medicine from a covered wagon, the truth is quite different. Nutritional quacks today are super salespeople, using questionable scientific information to give their products a sense of authenticity and credibility and using sophisticated advertising and marketing techniques. The result is that many people end up buying a product they do not need.

Although quackery is widespread throughout the general population, J. V. Durnin, an international authority in nutrition and exercise, has stated that there is still no sphere of nutrition in which faddism, misconceptions, ignorance, and quackery are more obvious than in athletics. Studies reveal that athletes at all levels of competition consume a wide variety of nutritional supplements as an adjunct to training or in hope of gaining a competitive edge. These supplements are often referred to as ergogenic aids.

What is an ergogenic aid?

As mentioned previously, the two key factors important to athletic success are genetic endowment and state of training. At certain levels of competition, the contestants generally have similar genetic athletic abilities and have been exposed to similar training methods, and thus they are fairly evenly matched. Given the emphasis placed on winning, many athletes in training for competition are always searching for the ultimate method or ingredient to provide that extra winning edge over their opponents. Indeed, one report suggested that two of the key factors leading to better athletic records in recent years are an improved diet and **ergogenic aids.**

The word ergogenic is derived from the Greek word ergo, and is usually defined as *to increase potential for work output.* In sports, various ergogenic aids have been used for their theoretical ability to improve performance. There are several different classifications of ergogenic aids, grouped according to the general nature of their application to sport. Listed below are several major categories with an example of one theoretical ergogenic aid for each.

Mechanical aids. Lightweight racing shoes may be used by a runner in place of heavier ones so that less energy is needed to move the legs and the economy of running increases.

Psychological aids. Hypnosis, through posthypnotic suggestion, may help remove psychological barriers that may limit physiological performance capacity.

Physiological aids. Blood doping, or the infusion of blood into an athlete, may increase oxygen transport capacity and thus increase aerobic endurance.

Pharmacological aids. Anabolic steroids, drugs that mimic the actions of the male sex hormone, testosterone, may increase muscle size and strength. The potential dangers of anabolic steroids, as well as several other dugs, are discussed in later chapters.

Nutritional aids. Probably the most used ergogenic aids are those that are classified as nutritional. Because athletes may believe that certain foods possess magical qualities, it is no wonder that a wide array of nutrients or special food preparations have been used since time immemorial in attempts to run faster, jump higher, or throw farther.

There are theoretical nutritional ergogenic aids in each of the six major classifications of nutrients, and athletes have been known to take supplements of almost every nutrient in attempts to improve performance. For example, special carbohydrate compounds have been developed to facilitate the absorption and utilization of carbohydrates during exercise. Certain drugs have been taken to increase the use of fat as an energy source during exercise and thus spare the utilization of carbohydrate. Special mixtures of protein have been developed and advertised to be natural anabolic steroids to stimulate muscle growth and strength development. A number of different vitamins and even "nonvitamin vitamins" have been ascribed ergogenic qualities ranging from increases in strength to improved vision for sport. Mineral supplementation has been advocated to improve oxygen transport and utilization in the body as well as to possibly help prevent stress fractures. There are even some special waters that have been developed for athletes.

As noted in Chapters 3 through 8, there may be some justification for nutrient supplementation or dietary modification in certain athletes under specific conditions, particularly in cases where deficiencies may occur. However, for the most part nutrient supplementation above and beyond the RDA is not necessary for the vast majority of athletes. With a few exceptions, consumption of specific nutrients above the RDA has not been shown to exert any ergogenic effect on human physical or athletic performance.

Why is nutritional quackery so prevalent in athletics?

As with nutritional quackery in general, hope and fear are the motivating factors underlying the use of nutritional supplements by athletes. They hope that a special nutrient concoction will provide them with a slight competitive edge over their opponent, and they fear losing if they do not do everything possible to win. In this regard, there are four factors within the athletic environment that help nurture these hopes and fears.

First, eating behavior may be patterned after some star athlete who is successful in a given sport. If Olympic champions or professional athletes were to suggest that part of their success was due to a vegetarian diet, to sauerkraut juice, or to the milk of a cow in heat, you may be assured these dietary practices would be adopted by some aspiring young athletes.

Second, many coaches may suggest to their athletes that certain foods or food supplements are essential to success. Surveys reveal that many athletes still receive nutritional information from their coaches, but these surveys also reveal that many coaches have poor backgrounds in nutrition. Thus, misconceptions learned by coaches in the past may be perpetuated in their athletes. Fortunately this situation may be rectified as more colleges and universities preparing future coaches and athletic trainers require courses in nutrition.

Third, misinformation also may be found in leading sports magazines and books, which often present articles on nutrition for the athlete based upon very questionable research. For example, a recent issue of a magazine for body builders published a study suggesting that amino acid supplements would help individuals lose body fat and gain muscle mass. Unfortunately, the study design contained too many flaws to allow such a conclusion. One training manual for health food products notes that books are a silent sales force. If you sell a box of bee pollen to an athlete, you have satisfied the customer's immediate need. If you sell the athlete a book, you create a whole new set of needs.

Fourth, and probably the most significant factor contributing to nutritional quackery in sports, is direct advertising of nutritional products marketed specifically for the athlete. Literally hundreds of nutritional supplements are advertised for athletic consumption. As just one example, a leading runners' magazine carried an advertisement indicating that one tablespoon of the advertised product, mixed with your favorite unsweetened fruit juice, would improve energy and endurance. It was described as the ultimate food formula for ultimate energy. The major ingredient was dried potassium-rich bananas, and the cost was approximately $12 per pound—rather expensive bananas. And, incidentally, fresh bananas are also potassium-rich.

Figure 1.2.
Simulated nutritional
supplement advertisement for
athletes.

To get an **ENERGY EDGE** on the competition
all athletes need

SUPERMIN

A balanced mixture of 20 minerals

Selenium
Utopium
Phosphorus
Ergonium
Radium
Magnesium
Iron
Nickel
and 12 other minerals

SUPERMIN contains all the essential minerals to
help your energy systems exercise in high gear.
MORE POWER. RUN FASTER. LEAP HIGHER.
CONTAINS *NO* KRYPTONITE
HURRY! ORDER YOUR SUPPLY TODAY!

ONLY $50.00 FOR A MONTH OF SUPER ENERGY

Direct advertising is often combined with several of the methods above for perpetuating nutritional information. Often star athletes are hired to advertise a particular product. One advertisement pictured one of America's leading marathoners with the name of a nutritional supplement emblazoned across his running shirt and the statement that this product was an important part of his training program. Also, many sports magazines will run articles on the ergogenic benefits of a particular nutrient, and in close proximity to the article place an advertisement for a product that contains that nutrient. Freedom of speech guaranteed by the First Amendment permits the author of the article to make sensational and deceptive claims about the nutrient. However, freedom of speech does not extend to advertising, so that fraudulent or deceptive claims may be grounds for prosecution by the FDA. Thus, by cleverly positioning the article and the advertisement, the promoter can make the desired claims about the value of the product to athletic performance and yet avoid any illegality. Classic examples of this technique may be found with protein and amino acid supplement advertising in magazines for body builders.

Most of these advertised products are economic frauds. The prices are exorbitant in comparison to the same amount of nutrients that may be obtained in ordinary foods. Besides being an economic fraud, these products are an intellectual fraud, for there is very little scientific evidence to support their claims. Simple basic facts about the physiological functions of the nutrients in these products are distorted, magnified, and advertised in such a way as to make one believe they will increase athletic performance. Unfortunately, in the area of nutrition and sport, it is very easy to distort the truth and appeal to the psychological emotions of the athlete. Dr. Robert Voy, former chief medical officer of the United States Olympic Training Center, has noted that we have abandoned athletes to the hucksters and charlatans. Athletes are wasting their money on worthless and even harmful substances.

How do I recognize nutritional quackery in health and sports?

It is often difficult to differentiate between quackery and reputable nutritional information. Promoters of nutritional supplements can be rather sophisticated. They may appear to be legitimate with imposing titles and degrees listed after their names, but these usually have been obtained from a diploma mill or through their own accrediting agencies. Refer to the brief review by Kleiner and the excellent books by S. Barrett and V. Herbert for a thorough discussion of health quackery and how to recognize it. Specific questions may be addressed to the National Council against Health Fraud, P.O. Box 33008, Kansas City, MO 64114.

The following may be used as guidelines in evaluating the claims made for a nutritional supplement or nutritional practice advertised or recommended to athletes and others. If the answer to any of these questions is yes, then one should be skeptical of such supplements and investigate their value before investing any money.

1. Does the product promise quick improvement in health or physical performance?
2. Does it contain some secret ingredient or formula?
3. Is it advertised mainly by use of anecdotes, case histories, or testimonials?
4. Are currently popular personalities or star athletes used in its advertisements?
5. Does it take a simple truth about a nutrient and exaggerate that truth in terms of health or physical performance?
6. Is it advertised in a health or sports magazine whose publishers also sell nutritional aids?
7. Does it use the results of a single study or dated and poorly controlled research to support its claims?
8. Is it expensive, especially when compared to the cost of equivalent nutrients that may be obtained from ordinary foods?
9. Is it a recent discovery not available from any other source?
10. Is its claim too good to be true?

Where can I get sound nutritional information to combat quackery in sports?

The best means to evaluate the claims of nutritional supplements or other nutritional practices for athletes is to possess a good background in nutrition and a familiarity with quality research conducted in sports nutrition. Unfortunately, most coaches and athletes and many athletic trainers and physicians have not been exposed to such an educational program, so they must either take formal course work in nutrition or sports nutrition, develop a reading program in sports nutrition, or consult with an expert in the field.

This book has been designed to serve as a text for a college course in sports nutrition, but it may also be read independently. It is an attempt to analyze the available scientific literature in the area of sports nutrition and provide an interpretation relative to athletic performance. It should provide the essential information you need to plan a nutritional program for athletes or other physically active individuals and to evaluate the usefulness of many nutritional supplements or practices. Other reliable sources that focus primarily upon the applications of nutrition to physical performance include *Sports Nutrition for the '90's: The Health Professional's Handbook* by Berning and Steen, *Food for Sport* by Smith and Worthington-Roberts, *Eating for Endurance* by Coleman, *Eat to Compete* by Peterson and Peterson, *Sports Nutrition Guidebook* by Clark, and *Nutrition for Sport Success* by the National Association for Sport and Physical Education and other organizations. A more technical coverage is provided in *Nutritional Aspects of Human Physical and Athletic Performance* by Williams and *Nutrition in Exercise and Sport* by Hickson and Wolinsky.

Many scientific journals publish reputable findings about nutrition and exercise, but unfortunately these journals may not be readily available in public libraries and may be too technical for some. Examples of such publications include *Medicine and Science in Sports and Exercise*, the *Journal of the American Dietetic Association*, *The American Journal of Clinical Nutrition*, and the *International Journal of Sports Nutrition*.

Articles in popular health and sports magazines may or may not be accurate. The credentials of the author, if listed, should be a good guide to an article's authenticity. Unfortunately, a Ph.D. listed after the author's name may not guarantee accuracy of the content in the article. Be wary of publications emanating from organizations or publishers that also sell nutritional supplements.

Other accurate information is often published by governmental agencies such as Councils on Physical Fitness and Sports, health professional groups such as the American Heart Association, consumer groups such as Center for Science in the Public Interest, and other groups such as the National Dairy Council. Several manufacturers of sports drinks, such as Ross Laboratories (Exceed) and the Gatorade Sport Science Institute, publish information based upon reputable research.

Another source of information is the nutritional consultant. Such consultants should have a solid background in nutrition, particularly sports nutrition if they are to advise athletes. The consultant should be a registered dietician (R.D.) or clinical nutritionist (C.N.). He or she should be a member of a reputable organization of nutritionists, such as the American Dietetic Association, the American Institute of Nutrition, or the American

Society for Clinical Nutrition. As mentioned previously, the American Dietetic Association has a section of dieticians specializing in sports nutrition (SCAN), and your state or local chapter of the ADA should be able to provide you with an appropriate contact. You may also contact SCAN with a toll-free number, (800)877–1600.

What is the basis for the dietary recommendations presented in this book?

How do we know what effect the food we eat will have upon our health or athletic performance? To find answers to specific questions of concern to us, we should rely on the findings derived from scientific research. As a sophisticated science, nutrition has a relatively short history. Not too long ago, nutrition scientists were concerned primarily with identifying the major constituents of the foods we eat and their general functions in the human body. More recently, however, numerous scientists have turned their attention to the possible health benefits of certain foods, and in the case of sport scientists, the possible applications to athletic performance. These scientists are not only attempting to determine the effect of the total diet upon health and performance but are also investigating the effects of specific nutrients at the cellular level to determine possible mechanisms of action to improve health or performance in sport.

Since this book makes a number of nutritional recommendations relative to sports and health, it is important to review briefly the nature and limitations of nutritional research with humans. Several research techniques have been used to explore the effect of nutrition on health or athletic performance, but the two most prevalent have been epidemiological and experimental research. **Epidemiological research** involves studying large populations to find relationships between two or more variables. For example, several epidemiological studies reported that individuals who consumed a diet high in fat were more likely to develop heart disease. Such research findings help scientists identify important relationships between nutritional practices and health. However, one should note that such research does not prove a cause and effect relationship. Although these studies did note a deleterious association between a diet high in fat and heart disease, they did not actually prove that fat consumption (possible cause) leads to heart disease (possible effect), but only that some form of relationship between the two existed.

Epidemiological research is useful in identifying relationships between variables, but **experimental research** is essential to establishing a cause and effect relationship. In such studies an independent variable or variables (cause) is manipulated so that changes in a dependent variable or variables (effect) can be studied. If we continue with the example of fat and heart disease, a large (and expensive) clinical study could be designed to see whether a low fat diet could help prevent heart disease. Two groups of subjects would be matched on several risk factors associated with the development of heart disease, and over a certain time, say ten years, one group would receive a low fat diet (cause) while the other would continue to consume their normal high fat diet. At the end of the experiment, the differences in the incidence of heart disease (effect) between the two groups would be evaluated to determine whether or not the low fat diet was an effective preventive agent. If the results of such a study showed that consumption of a low fat diet had no effect upon the incidence rate of heart disease, should you continue to consume a high fat diet? Not necessarily!

It is important to realize that the results of one study with humans does not prove anything. Studies need to be repeated by other scientists and a consensus developed. Unfortunately, such a consensus is often lacking in recommendations about specific nutritional modifications for improved health or enhanced athletic performance. For example, some sport scientists may recommend that marathon runners consume caffeine prior to their event, others may recommend that marathoners abstain from caffeine, while still others may note that it makes no difference if marathoners consume caffeine or not. Who is right? As we shall see in Chapter 4, possibly all—depending upon the individual athlete and the environmental conditions associated with the race.

It is very difficult to conduct nutritional research about health and athletic performance with human subjects. For example, many diseases such as cancer and heart disease are caused by the interaction of multiple risk factors and may take many years to develop. It is not an easy task to control all of these risk factors in freely living human beings so that we could isolate one independent variable, such as dietary fat, to study its effect on the development of heart disease over ten to twenty years.

Numerous physiological, psychological, and biomechanical factors also influence athletic performance on any given day. Why can't athletes match their personal records day after day? Because their physiology and psychology vary from day to day, and even within the day. To study the effect of a specific nutrient or dietary manipulation upon athletic performance, the investigator must try to control all extraneous factors that may affect performance. The ideal experiment usually involves a double-blind placebo (a substance known to have no effect) crossover treatment. In such a study, neither the investigator nor the subject knows the difference between the experimental treatment and the placebo, and all subjects take both the treatment and the placebo so that each subject serves as his or her own control. The study should also involve athletes or subjects who would benefit from the nutrient. For example, endurance athletes may be expected to benefit from carbohydrate intake during performance, whereas a golfer would not. Most experienced contemporary investigators generally use similar sophisticated research designs to generate meaningful data.

Within the lifetime of many students a tremendous amount of both epidemiological and experimental research has been concerned with the effect nutrition may have upon health and athletic performance. Although in many cases we still do not have absolute proof that a particular nutritional practice will produce the desired effect, we do have sufficient information to make a recommendation that is prudent, meaning that it is likely to do some good and cause no harm. Thus the recommendations offered in this text should be considered prudent; they are based upon a careful analysis and evaluation of the available scientific literature, including specific studies or comprehensive reviews of the pertinent research by individuals or public and private health or sports organizations.

Nevertheless, remember that we all possess biological individuality and thus might react differently to a particular nutritional intervention. For example, relative to health, some individuals are very sensitive to salt intake and will experience a significant rise in blood pressure with increased dietary salt. Relative to athletic performance, some individuals experience gastrointestinal distress when they ingest certain forms of carbohydrate before performing. Such individual reactions have been noted in some research studies and are discussed where relevant in the following chapters.

References

Books

Barrett, S. (Ed.). 1980. *The Health Robbers.* Philadelphia: Stickley.

Berning, J., and Steen, S. N. 1991. *Sports Nutrition for the '90s: The Health Professional's Handbook.* Gaithersburg, MD: Aspen Publishers.

Clark, N. 1990. *Nancy Clark's Sports Nutrition Guidebook: Eating to Fuel Your Active Lifestyle.* Champaign, IL: Leisure Press.

Coleman, E. 1988. *Eating for Endurance.* Palo Alto, CA: Bull Publishing.

Editors of Consumer Reports Books. 1980. *Health Quackery.* Mt. Vernon, NY: Consumers Union.

Eisenman, P., Johnson, S., and Benson, J. 1989. *Coaches Guide to Nutrition and Weight Control.* Champaign, IL: Leisure Press.

Herbert, V. 1980. *Nutrition Cultism.* Philadelphia: Stickley.

Hickson, J., and Wolinsky, I. 1989. *Nutrition in Exercise and Sport.* Boca Raton, FL: CRC Press.

Horton, E., and Terjung, R. 1988. *Exercise, Nutrition and Metabolism.* New York: Macmillan.

National Association for Sport and Physical Education et al. 1984. *Nutrition for Sport Success.* Reston, VA: American Alliance for Health, Physical Education, Recreation and Dance.

National Research Council. 1989. *Diet and Health: Implications for Reducing Chronic Disease Risk.* Washington, DC: National Academy Press.

National Research Council. 1989. *Recommended Dietary Allowances.* Washington, DC: National Academy Press.

Peterson, M., and Peterson, K. 1988. *Eat to Compete.* Chicago: Year Book Publishers.

Smith, N., and Worthington-Roberts, B. 1989. *Food for Sport.* Palo Alto, CA: Bull Publishing.

U.S. Department of Agriculture and U.S. Department of Health and Human Services. 1990. *Nutrition and Your Health: Dietary Guidelines for Americans.* Washington, DC: U.S. Government Printing Office.

U.S. Department of Health and Human Services, Public Health Service. 1988. *The Surgeon General's Report on Nutrition and Health.* Washington, DC: U.S. Government Printing Office.

Williams, M. 1985. *Nutritional Aspects of Human Physical and Athletic Performance.* Springfield, IL: C. C. Thomas.

Williams, M. 1989. *Beyond Training! How Athletes Enhance Performance Legally and Illegally.* Champaign, IL: Leisure Press.

Yetiv, J. 1986. *Popular Nutritional Practices: A Scientific Appraisal.* Toledo, OH: Popular Medicine Press.

Review Articles

American Dietetic Association. 1987. Position of the American Dietetic Association: Nutrition for physical fitness and athletic performance. *Journal of the American Dietetic Association* 87:933–39.

American Dietetic Association. 1988. Identifying food and nutrition misinformation. *Journal of the American Dietetic Association* 88:1589–91.

Applegate, L. 1988. Fad diets and supplement use in athletes. *Sports Science Exchange* 1(9):1–4.

Beaton, G. 1988. Criteria of an adequate diet. In: *Modern Nutrition in Health and Disease,* eds. M. Shils and V. Young. Philadelphia: Lea & Febiger.

Brotherhood, J. 1984. Nutrition and sports performance. *Sports Medicine* 1:350–89.

Bucci, L. 1989. Nutritional ergogenic aids. In: *Nutrition in Exercise and Sport,* eds. J. Hickson and I. Wolinsky. Boca Raton, FL: CRC Press.

Burfoot, A., et al. 1989. In search of a magic bullet. *Runner's World* 24:73–77, October.

Durnin, J. V. 1967. The influence of nutrition. *Canadian Medical Association Journal* 96:715–20.

Grandjean, A. 1989. Macronutrient intake of US athletes compared with the general population and recommendations made for athletes. *American Journal of Clinical Nutrition* 49:1070–76.

Harper, A. 1986. Recommended dietary allowances in perspective. *Food & Nutrition News* 58:7–10.

Herbert, V., and Barrett, S. 1990. Twenty-one ways to spot a quack. In: *Nutrition 90/91,* ed. C. Cook. Guilford, CT: Dushkin.

Kleiner, S. 1990. Beware of nutrition quackery. *Physician and Sportsmedicine* 18:46–49.

Kris-Etherton, P. 1990. The facts and fallacies of nutritional supplements for athletes. *National Coach* 25:6–9, Spring.

Leaf, A., and Frisa, K. 1989. Eating for health or for athletic performance. *American Journal of Clinical Nutrition* 49:1066–69.

Loosli, A. 1990. Athletes, food and nutrition. *Food and Nutrition News* 62:15–18, May/June.

Murphy, P. 1986. Longer, higher, faster: Athletes continue to reach new heights. *Physician and Sportsmedicine* 14:140–46, August.

National Dairy Council. 1980. Nutrition and human performance. *Dairy Council Digest* 51:13–18.

Proceedings. 1989. First international conference on nutrition and fitness. *American Journal of Clinical Nutrition* 49:909–1140.

Prokop, L. 1989. International Olympic Committee Medical Commission's policies and programs in nutrition and physical fitness. *American Journal of Clinical Nutrition* 49:1065.

Renner, J. 1989. Knowledge best defense against health fraud. *Food and Nutrition News* 61:1–3, September/October.

Short, S. 1989. Dietary surveys and nutrition knowledge. In: *Nutrition in Exercise and Sport,* eds. J. Hickson and I. Wolinsky. Boca Raton, FL: CRC Press.

Sienkiewicz, F., and De Bruyne, L. 1988. Nutrition for sport: Knowledge, news, and nonsense. *Nutrition Clinics* 3:1–24.

Telford, R. 1987. Nutrition and intense training. *Excel* 3:3–8, June.

Thornton, J. 1990. Feast or famine: Eating disorders in athletes. *Physician and Sportsmedicine* 18:116–22.

Voy, R. 1989. Ergogenic aids. In: *The Theory and Practice of Athletic Nutrition: Bridging the Gap,* eds. K. Wheeler, A. Grandjean, and J. Storlie. Columbus, OH: Ross Laboratories.

White, P., and Mondeika, T. 1988. Food fads and faddism. In: *Modern Nutrition in Health and Disease,* eds. M. Shils and V. Young. Philadelphia: Lea & Febiger.

Williams, M. H. 1989. Nutritional ergogenic aids and athletic performance. *Nutrition Today* 24:7–14, January/February.

Yesalis, C. 1990. Winning and performance-enhancing drugs—Our dual addiction. *Physician and Sportsmedicine* 18:161–67, March.

Specific Studies

Barr, S. 1987. Nutrition knowledge of female varsity athletes and university students. *Journal of the American Dietetic Association* 87:1660–64.

Bassarre, T., et al. 1986. Incidence of poor nutritional status among triathletes, endurance athletes and control subjects. *Medicine and Science in Sports and Exercise* 18:S90.

Bedgood, B., and Tuck, M. 1983. Nutrition knowledge of high school coaches in Texas. *Journal of the American Dietetic Association* 83:672–77.

Benson, J., et al. 1989. Relationship between nutrient intake, body mass index, menstrual function, and ballet injury. *Journal of the American Dietetic Association* 89:58–63.

Chen, J., et al. 1989. Nutritional problems and measures in elite and amateur athletes. *American Journal of Clinical Nutrition* 49:1084–89.

Corley, G., et al. 1989. Nutrition knowledge and dietary practices of college coaches. Journal of the American Dietetic Association 90:705–09.

Douglas, P., and Douglas, J. 1984. Nutrition knowledge and food practices of high school athletes. *Journal of the American Dietetic Association* 84:1198–1202.

Ellsworth, N., et al. 1985. Nutrient intake of elite male and female Nordic skiers. *Physician and Sportsmedicine* 13:78–92, February.

Hickson, J., et al. 1987. Nutritional intake from food sources of high school football athletes. *Journal of the American Dietetic Association* 87:1656–59.

Huber, L., et al. 1986. Nutritional status of college female gymnasts and cross-country runners. *Medicine and Science in Sports and Exercise* 18:S64–65.

Johnson, A., et al. 1985. Psychological, nutritional and physical status of Olympic road cyclists. *British Journal of Sports Medicine* 19:11–14.

Keith, R., 1989. Dietary status of trained female cyclists. *Journal of the American Dietetic Association* 89:1620–23.

Krowchuk, D., et al. 1989. High school athletes and the use of ergogenic aids. *American Journal of Diseases of Children* 143:486–89.

Kurtzman, F., et al. 1989. Eating disorders among selected female student populations at UCLA. *Journal of the American Dietetic Association* 89:45–53.

Lamar-Hildebrand, N., et al. 1989. Dietary and exercise practices of college-aged female bodybuilders. *Journal of the American Dietetic Association* 89:1308–10.

Loosli, A., et al. 1986. Nutrition habits and knowledge in competitive adolescent female gymnasts. *Physician and Sportsmedicine* 14:August, 118–30.

Nieman, D., et al. 1989. Nutrient intake of marathon runners. *Journal of the American Dietetic Association* 89:1273–78.

Nowak, R., et al. 1988. Body composition and nutrient intakes of college men and women basketball players. *Journal of the American Dietetic Association* 88:575–78.

Parr, R., et al. 1984. Nutrition knowledge and practice of coaches, trainers, and athletes. *Physician and Sportsmedicine* 12:127–38, March.

Peters, A., et al. 1986. Diets of endurance runners competing in a 20-day road race. *Physician and Sportsmedicine* 14:63–70, July.

Pratt, C., and Walberg, J. 1988. Nutrition knowledge and concerns of health and physical education teachers. *Journal of the American Dietetic Association* 88:840–41.

Rosen, L., et al. 1986. Pathogenic weight-control behavior in female athletes. *Physician and Sportsmedicine* 14:79–86, January.

Saris, W. 1989. Nutrition and topsport. *International Journal of Sports Medicine* 10:S1–S76.

Steen, S. N. 1991. Precontest strategies of a male bodybuilder. *International Journal of Sport Nutrition* 1:69–78.

van Erp-Baart, et al. 1989. Nationwide survey on nutritional habits in elite athletes. *International Journal of Sports Medicine* 10:S11–S16.

Van Handel, P., et al. 1984. Nutritional status of elite swimmers. *Journal of Swimming Research* 1:27–31.

Key Terms

adenosine triphosphate (ATP)

aerobic

anaerobic

ATP–PC system

Calorie (kilocalorie)

Basal metabolic rate (BMR)

brown adipose tissue (BAT)

calorimeter

dietary-induced thermogenesis (DIT)

electron transfer system

energy

exercise metabolic rate (EMR)

fatigue

glycolysis

joule

Krebs cycle

lactic acid system

maximal oxygen uptake

metabolic aftereffects of exercise

metabolism

METS

mitochondrion

onset of blood lactic acid (OBLA)

oxygen system

phosphocreatine (PC)

power

resting energy expenditure (REE)

resting metabolic rate (RMR)

steady-state threshold

thermic effect of food (TEF)

work

Key Concepts

Energy represents the capacity to do work, and food is the source of energy for humans.

The Calorie, or kilocalorie, is a measure of chemical energy stored in foods; this chemical energy can be transformed into heat and mechanical work energy in the body.

Carbohydrates and fats are the primary energy nutrients, but protein may also be an energy source. In the human body one gram of carbohydrate = 4 Calories, one gram of fat = 9 Calories and one gram of protein = 4 Calories. Alcohol is also a source of Calories, one gram = 7 Calories.

The potential energy sources in the body include: ATP and PC; serum glucose; glycogen in the liver and muscle; serum free fatty acids (FFA); triglycerides in the muscle and in adipose tissue; and muscle protein.

Three human energy systems have been classified on the basis of their ability to release energy at different rates of speed; they are the ATP–PC, lactic acid, and oxygen systems.

Human metabolism represents the sum total of all physiological processes in the body, and the metabolic rate reflects the speed at which the body utilizes energy.

The basal metabolic rate (BMR) represents the energy requirements necessary to maintain physiological processes in a resting, postabsorptive state.

The resting metabolic rate (RMR) is the BMR plus the energy associated with dietary-induced thermogenesis. The terms BMR and RMR are often used interchangeably because of small differences between them.

A number of different factors may affect the RMR, including body composition, drugs, climatic conditions and prior exercise.

The exercise metabolic rate (EMR) provides us with the most practical means to increase energy expenditure.

The metabolic rate during exercise is directly proportional to the intensity of the exercise, and the exercise heart rate may serve as a general indicator of the metabolic rate.

Activities that use the large muscle groups of the body, such as running, swimming, bicycling, and aerobic dance, will facilitate energy expenditure.

The ATP–PC and lactic acid energy systems are used primarily during fast, anaerobic, power-type events, while the oxygen system is used primarily during aerobic, endurance-type events.

The utilization of carbohydrates and fats is approximately equal at low levels of exercise intensity, but carbohydrates begin to be the preferential fuel as the exercise intensity increases.

A sound training program and proper nutrition are important factors in the prevention of fatigue during exercise.

Human Energy

2

Introduction

As noted in Chapter 1, the body uses the food we eat to provide energy, to build and repair tissues, and to regulate metabolism. Of these three functions, the human body ranks energy production first and will use food for this purpose at the expense of the other two functions in time of need. Energy is the essence of life.

Through technological processes, humans have harnessed a variety of energy sources such as wind, waterfalls, the sun, wood, and oil to operate the machines invented to make life easier. However, humans cannot use any of these energy sources for their own metabolism, but must rely on food sources found in nature. The food we eat must be converted into energy forms that the body can use. Thus, the human body has developed a number of metabolic systems to produce and regulate energy for its diverse needs, such as synthesis of tissues, movement of substances between tissues, and muscular contraction.

Sport energy! The underlying basis for the control of movement in all sports is human energy, and successful performance depends upon the ability of the athlete to produce the right amount of energy and to control its application to the specific demands of the sport. Sports differ in their energy demands. In some events, such as the 100-meter dash, success is dependent primarily upon the ability to produce energy very rapidly. In others, such as the 26.2 mile marathon, energy need not be produced so rapidly as in the 100-meter dash but must be sustained for a much longer period. In still other sports such as golf, the athlete need not only produce energy at varying rates (compare the drive with the putt) but must carefully control the application of that energy. Thus each sport imposes specific energy demands upon the athlete.

A discussion of the role of nutrition as a means to help provide and control human energy is important from several standpoints. First, inadequate supplies of necessary energy nutrients, such as muscle glycogen or blood glucose may cause fatigue. Fatigue also may be caused by the inability of the energy systems to function optimally because of a deficiency of other nutrients, such as selected vitamins and minerals. In addition, the human body is capable of storing energy reserves in a variety of forms, including body fat and muscle tissue. Excess body weight in the form of fat or decreased body weight due to losses of muscle tissue may adversely affect some types of athletic performance.

One purpose of this chapter is to review briefly the major human energy systems and how they are used in the body under conditions of exercise and rest. The following six chapters discuss the role of each of the major classes of nutrients as they relate to energy production in the human body, with the primary focus on prevention of fatigue caused by impaired energy production. Another purpose of this chapter is to discuss the means by which humans store and expend energy. Chapters 9 through 11 focus on weight control methods and expand on some of the concepts presented in this chapter.

Measures of Energy

What is energy?

For our purposes, **energy** represents the capacity to do work. **Work** is one form of energy, often called mechanical energy. When we throw a ball or run a mile, we have done work; we have produced mechanical energy.

Energy exists in a variety of other forms in nature, such as the light energy of the sun, nuclear energy in uranium, electrical energy in lightning storms, heat energy in fires, and chemical energy in oil. The six forms of energy—mechanical, chemical, heat, electrical, light, and nuclear—are all interchangeable according to various laws of thermodynamics. We take advantage of these laws every day. One such example is the use of chemical energy of gasoline to produce mechanical energy, or the movement of our cars.

In the human body, four of these types of energy are important. Our bodies possess stores of chemical energy that can be used to produce electrical energy for creation of electrical nerve impulses, to produce heat to help keep our body temperature at 37° C (98.6° F) even on cold days, and to produce mechanical work through muscle shortening so that we may move about.

The sun is the ultimate source of energy. Solar energy is harnessed by plants, through photosynthesis, to produce either plant carbohydrates, fats,

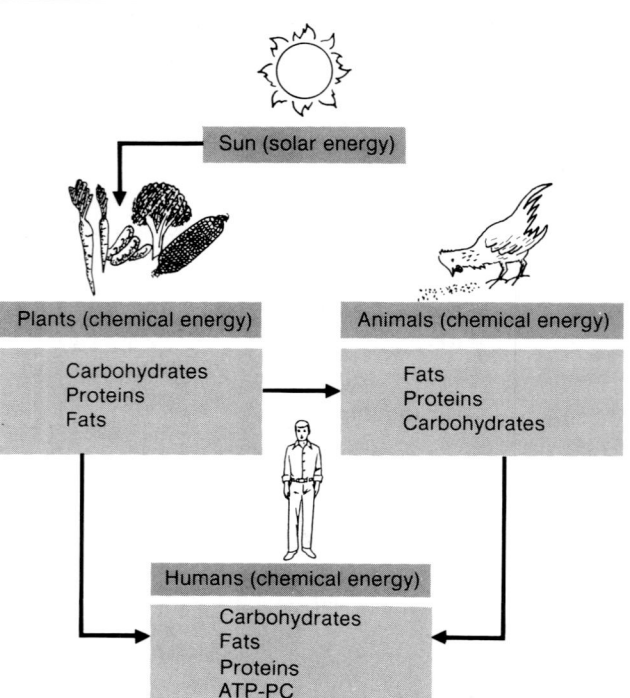

Figure 2.1.
Through photosynthesis, plants utilize solar energy from the sun and convert it to chemical energy in the form of carbohydrates, fats, or proteins. Animals eat plants and convert the chemical energy into their own stores of chemical energy—primarily fat and protein. Humans ingest food from both plant and animal sources and convert the chemical energy for their own stores and use.

or proteins, all forms of stored chemical energy. When humans consume plant and animal products, the carbohydrates, fats, and proteins undergo a series of metabolic changes and are utilized to develop body structure, to regulate body processes, or to provide a storage form of chemical energy (Figure 2.1).

The optimal intake and output of energy is important to all individuals, but especially for the active person. To perform to capacity, body energy stores must be used in the most efficient manner possible.

How do we measure work and energy?
Energy has been defined as the ability to do work. According to the physicist's definition, work is simply the product of force times vertical distance, or in formula format, $W = F \times d$. When we speak of how fast work is done, the term **power** is used. Power is simply work divided by time, or $P = W/t$.

Two major measurement systems have been used in the past to express energy in terms of either work or power. The metric system has been in use by most of the world, while the United States has used the English system. In an attempt to provide some uniformity in measurement systems around the world, the International Unit System (SI) has been developed. It is very similar to the metric system. The SI is used in most scientific journals today, but the other two systems appear in older journals. Terms that are used in each system are presented in Table 2.1.

Legislation has been passed by Congress to convert the United States to the SI, and terms such as gram, kilogram, milliliter, liter and kilometer are becoming more prevalent, but it appears that it will take some time before this system becomes part of our everyday language. For our purposes in this text, we shall use the terms foot-pound and kilogram-meter (KGM) to express work, but if you read scientific literature you should be able to convert values among foot-pounds, KGM and joules if necessary. For example, if you weigh 150 pounds and climb a 20-foot flight of stairs, you have done 3,000 foot-pounds of work. One KGM is equal to 7.23 foot-pounds, so you would do about 415 KGM. One **joule** is equal to about 0.74 foot pounds so you have done about 4,054 joules of work. Some basic interrelationships among the measurement systems are noted in Table 2.2. Other equivalents may be found in Appendix B.

In essence then, to measure work we need to know the weight of an object and the vertical distance through which it is moved. This is fine according to the formal definition of work, but are you doing work while holding a stationary weight out in front of your body? According to the formal definition, the answer is no, because the distance moved is zero. How about when you come down stairs as compared with going up? It is much easier to descend the stairs, and yet according to the formula you have done the same amount of work. Also, how

Table 2.1 Terms in the English, metric, and international systems

Unit	English system	Metric system	International system
Mass	slug	kilogram (kg)	kilogram (kg)
Distance	foot (ft)	meter (m)	meter (m)
Time	second (s)	second (s)	second (s)
Force	pound (lb)	Newton (N)	Newton (N)
Work	foot-pound (ft-lb)	kilogram-meter (kgm)	joule (J)
Power	horsepower (hp)	watt (W)	watt (W)

Table 2.2 Some interrelationships between work measurement systems

Weight	Distance	Work
1 kilogram = 2.2 pounds	1 meter = 3.28 feet	1 KGM = 7.23 foot pounds
1 kilogram = 1000 grams	1 meter = 1.09 yards	1 KGM = 9.8 joules
454 grams = 1 pound	1 foot = 0.30 meter	1 foot pound = 0.138 KGM
1 pound = 16 ounces	1,000 meters = 1 kilometer	1 foot pound = 1.35 joules
1 ounce = 28.4 grams	1 kilometer = 0.6215 mile	1 joule = 1 newton meter
3.5 ounces = 100 grams	1 mile = 1.61 kilometers	1 kilojoule = 1000 joule
	1 inch = 2.54 centimeters	1 megajoule = 1,000,000 joule
	1 centimeter = 0.39 inch	1 joule = 0.102 KGM
		1 joule = 0.736 foot pound
		1 kilojoule = 102 KGM

Figure 2.2.
A bomb calorimeter. The food in the calorimeter is combusted via electrical ignition. The heat (Calories) given off by the food raises the temperature of the water, thereby providing data about the caloric content of specific foodstuffs.

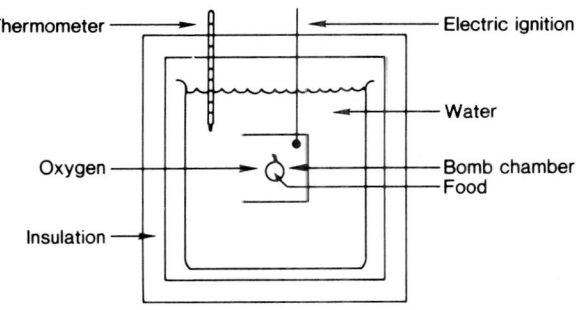

about when you run a mile? You know you have worked, but most of the distance you covered was horizontal, not vertical. Therefore, we need to have means to express the energy expenditure of the human body other than simply the amount of work done.

The other means of measuring energy in the body deal with chemical and heat energy. Without going into much detail, look briefly at two different methods for measuring energy production in humans. First, a device known as a **calorimeter** may be used to measure the energy content of a given substance. Figure 2.2 shows how a bomb calorimeter works. For example, a gram of fat contains a certain amount of chemical energy. It may be placed in the calorimeter, oxidized completely, and the heat

it gives off recorded. We then know the heat energy of one gram of fat and can equate it to chemical or work units of energy if needed. Large, expensive calorimeters are available that can accommodate human beings and measure their heat production under differing conditions of exercise.

A second, more commonly used method of measuring energy is to determine the amount of oxygen an individual consumes. The volume of oxygen one uses is usually expressed in liters (L) or milliliters (ml); one L is equal to 1,000 ml. One liter is slightly larger than a quart. In general, humans need oxygen, which helps metabolize the various nutrients in the body to produce energy. It is known that when oxygen combines with a gram of carbohydrate, fat, or protein, a certain amount of energy

Eight ounces of orange juice will provide enough chemical energy to enable an average man to produce enough mechanical energy to run about one mile.

(David Corona)

is released. If we can accurately measure the oxygen consumption (and carbon dioxide production) of an individual, we can get a pretty good measure of energy expenditure. The amount of oxygen used can be equated to other forms of energy, such as work done in foot-pounds or heat produced in Calories.

What is the most commonly used measure of energy?

Although there are a number of different ways to express energy, the most common term used in the past and still most prevalent and understood in the United States by most people is **Calorie.** This term is used as the energy requirement in the 1989 RDA.

A calorie is a measure of heat. One small calorie represents the amount of heat needed to raise the temperature of one gram of water 1° Celsius; it is sometimes called the gram calorie. A large Calorie, or kilocalorie, is equal to 1,000 small calories. It is the amount of heat needed to raise 1 kg of water (1 L) 1° Celsius. In human nutrition, because the gram calorie is so small, the kilocalorie is the main expression of energy. It is usually abbreviated as kcal, kc, or C, or capitalized as Calorie. Throughout this book, *Calorie* or *C* will refer to the kilocalorie.

According to the principles underlying the first law of thermodynamics, energy may be equated from one form to another. Thus, the Calorie, which represents thermal or heat energy, may be equated to other forms of energy. Relative to our discussion concerning physical work such as exercise and its interrelationships with nutrition, it is important to equate the Calorie with mechanical work and the chemical energy stored in the body. As will be explained later, most stored chemical energy must undergo some form of oxidation in order to release its energy content as work.

The following represents some equivalent energy values for the Calorie in terms of mechanical work and oxygen utilization. Some examples illustrating several of the interrelationships will be used in later chapters.

1 C = 3,086 foot-pounds
1 C = 427 KGM
1 C = 4.2 kilojoules (kj) or 4200 joules
1 C = 200 ml oxygen (approximately)

Through the use of a calorimeter, the energy contents of the basic nutrients have been determined. Energy may be derived from the three major foodstuffs—carbohydrate, fat and protein, plus alcohol. The caloric value of each of these three nutrients may vary somewhat, depending on the particular structure of the different forms. For example, carbohydrate may exist in several forms—as

Figure 2.3.
The Calorie as a measure of energy.

1 teaspoon sugar = 5 grams carbohydrate = 20 Calories

1 teaspoon salad oil = 5 grams fat = 45 Calories

glucose, sucrose or starch—and the caloric value of each will differ slightly. In general, one gram of each of the three nutrients, measured in a calorimeter, yields the following Calories:

1 gram carbohydrate = 4.30 C
1 gram fat = 9.45 C
1 gram protein = 5.65 C
1 gram alcohol = 7.00 C

Unfortunately, or fortunately if one is trying to lose weight, humans do not extract all this energy from the food they eat. The human body is not as efficient as the calorimeter. For one, the body cannot completely absorb all the food eaten. Only about 97 percent of ingested carbohydrate, 95 percent of fat, and 92 percent of protein are absorbed. In addition, a good percentage of the protein is not completely oxidized in the body, with some of the nitrogen waste products being excreted in the urine. In summary, then, the caloric value of food is reduced somewhat in relation to the values given above. Although the following values are not exactly precise, they are approximate enough to be used effectively in determining the caloric values of the foods we eat. Thus, the following caloric values are used throughout this text as a practical guide:

1 gram carbohydrate = 4 C
1 gram fat = 9 C
1 gram protein = 4 C
1 gram alcohol = 7 C

For our purposes, the Calories in food represent a form of potential energy to be used by our bodies to produce heat and work (Figure 2.3). However, the fact that alcohol and fat have about twice the amount of energy per gram as either carbohydrate or protein does not mean they are better energy sources for the active individual. These important issues are discussed in later chapters when we talk of the efficient utilization of body fuels.

Human Energy Systems

How is energy stored in the body?

The ultimate source of all energy on earth is the sun. Solar energy is harnessed by plants, which take carbon, hydrogen, oxygen, and nitrogen from their environment and manufacture either carbohydrate, fat, or protein. These foods possess stored energy. When we consume these foods, our digestive processes break them down into simple compounds that are absorbed into the body and transported to various cells. One of the basic purposes of body cells is to transform the chemical energy of these simple compounds into forms that may be available for immediate use or other forms that may be available for future use.

Energy in the body is available for immediate use in the form of **adenosine triphosphate (ATP)**. It is a complex molecule constructed with high-energy bonds, which, when split by enzyme action, can release energy rapidly for a number of body processes, including muscle contraction. ATP is classified as a high-energy compound and is stored in the tissues in small amounts. Another related high-energy phosphate compound, **phosphocreatine (PC)**, is also found in the tissues in small amounts. Although it cannot be used as an immediate source of energy, it can rapidly replenish ATP.

ATP may be formed from either carbohydrate, fat, or protein after those nutrients have undergone some complex biochemical changes in the body. Figure 2.4 represents a basic schematic of how ATP is formed from each of these three nutrients. PC is actually derived from excess ATP.

Because ATP and PC are found in very small amounts in the body and can be used up in a matter of seconds, it is important to have adequate energy stores as a backup system. Your body stores of carbohydrate, fat, and protein can provide you with ample amounts of ATP, enough to last for many weeks even on a starvation diet. The digestion and

Figure 2.4.

Simplified schematic of ATP formation from carbohydrate, fat, and protein. All three nutrients may be used to form ATP, but carbohydrate and fat are the major sources via the aerobic metabolism of the Krebs cycle. Carbohydrate may be used to produce small amounts of ATP under anaerobic conditions, thus providing humans with the ability to produce energy rapidly without oxygen for relatively short periods.

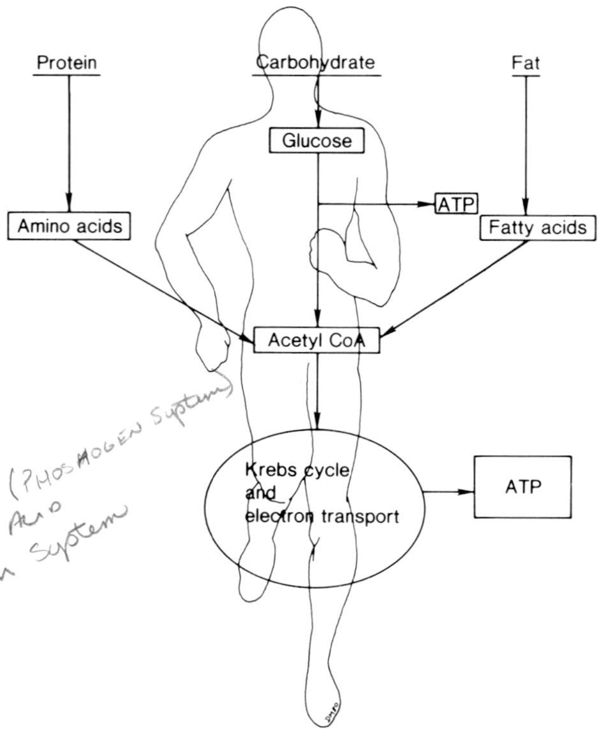

metabolism of carbohydrate, fat, and protein are discussed in their respective chapters, so it is unnecessary to present that full discussion here. However, you may wish to preview Figure 2.10 in order to visualize the metabolic interrelationships between the three nutrients in the body.

It is important to note that parts of each energy nutrient may be converted to the other two nutrients in the body under certain circumstances. For example, protein may be converted into carbohydrate during prolonged exercise, whereas excess dietary carbohydrate may be converted to fat in the body during rest.

Table 2.3 summarizes how energy is stored in the human body as carbohydrate, fat, and protein. The total amount of energy, represented by Calories, is approximate and may vary considerably between individuals. Carbohydrate is stored in limited amounts as blood glucose, liver glycogen, and muscle glycogen. The largest amount of energy is stored in the body as fats. Fats are stored as triglycerides in both the muscle tissue and adipose (fat) tissues; triglycerides and free fatty acids (FFA) in the blood are a limited supply. The protein of the body tissues, particularly the muscle tissue, is a large reservoir of energy but is not used under normal circumstances. The role of each of these energy stores during ex-

Table 2.3   Major energy stores in the human body with approximate total caloric value in humans*

Energy source	Major storage form	Total body Calories
ATP	Tissues	1
PC	Tissues	4
Carbohydrate	Serum glucose	20
	Liver glycogen	400
	Muscle glycogen	1,500
Fat	Serum free fatty acids	7
	Serum triglycerides	75
	Muscle triglycerides	2,500
	Adipose tissue triglycerides	80,000
Protein	Muscle protein	30,000

*These values may have extreme variations depending on the size of the individual, amount of body fat, physical fitness level, and diet.

ercise is an important consideration that is discussed briefly in this chapter and more extensively in their respective chapters.

Figure 2.5.
ATP, adenosinetriphosphate. (1) ATP is stored in the muscle in limited amounts. (2) Splitting of a high-energy bond releases energy, which (3) can be used for many body processes including muscular contraction. The ATP stores are used for fast, all-out bursts of power that last about one second. ATP must be replenished from other sources for muscle contraction to continue.

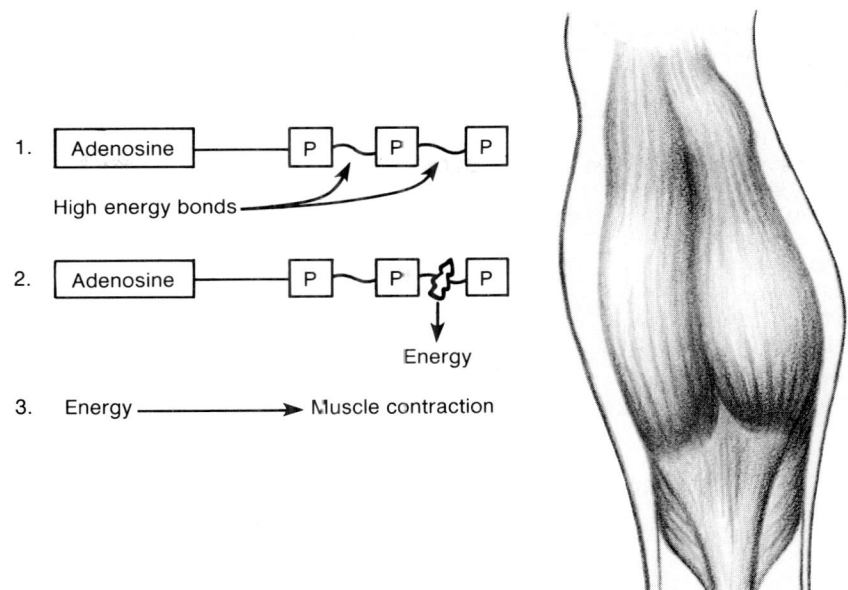

1. Adenosine — P ⌒ P ⌒ P

   High energy bonds

2. Adenosine — P ⌒ P ⌐ P

   Energy

3. Energy ⟶ Muscle contraction

What are the human energy systems?

Why does the human body store chemical energy in a variety of different forms? If we look at human energy needs from an historical perspective, the answer becomes obvious. Sometimes humans needed to produce energy at a rapid rate, such as when sprinting to safety to avoid dangerous animals. Thus, a fast rate of energy production was an important human energy feature that helped ensure survival. At other times, our ancient ancestors may have been deprived of adequate food for long periods, and thus needed a storage capacity for chemical energy that would sustain life throughout these times of deprivation. Hence, the ability to store large amounts of energy was also important for survival. These two factors—rate of energy production and energy capacity—appear to be determining factors in the development of human energy systems.

One need only watch weekend television programming for several weeks to realize that a diversity of sports are popular throughout the world. Each of these sports imposes certain requirements on humans who want to be successful competitors. For some sports, such as weight lifting, the main requirement is brute strength, while for others such as tennis, quick reactions and hand/eye coordination are important. A major consideration in most sports is the production of energy, which can range from the explosive power needed by a shot-putter to the tremendous endurance capacity of an ultramarathoner. The physical performance demands of different sports require specific sources of energy.

As noted above, the body stores energy in a variety of ways—in ATP, phosphocreatine, muscle glycogen, and so on. In order for this energy to be used to produce muscular contractions and movement, it must undergo certain biochemical reactions in the muscle. These biochemical reactions serve as a basis for classifying human energy expenditure by three systems: the ATP–PC system, lactic acid system, and the oxygen system.

The **ATP–PC system** is also known as the phosphagen system because both adenosine triphosphate (ATP) and phosphocreatine (PC) contain phosphates. ATP is the immediate source of energy for almost all body processes, including muscle contraction. This high-energy compound, stored in the muscles, rapidly releases energy when an electrical impulse arrives in the muscle. No matter what you do, scratch your nose or lift 100 pounds, ATP breakdown makes the movement possible. ATP must be present for the muscles to contract. The body has a limited supply of ATP and must replace it rapidly if muscular work is to continue. See Figure 2.5 for a graphical representation of ATP breakdown.

PC, which is also a high-energy compound found in the muscle, can help form ATP rapidly as ATP is used. PC is also in short supply and needs to be replenished if used. PC breakdown to help resynthesize ATP is illustrated in Figure 2.6.

The ATP–PC system is critical to energy production. Because these phosphogens are in short supply, any all-out exercise for 5–6 seconds could deplete the supply in a given muscle. Hence, they

Figure 2.6.
Phosphocreatine (PC). (1) PC is stored in the muscle in limited amounts. (2) Splitting of the high-energy bond releases energy, which (3) can be used to rapidly synthesize ATP. ATP and PC are called phosphagens and together represent the ATP–PC energy system. This system is utilized for quick, maximal exercises lasting about one to six seconds, such as sprinting.

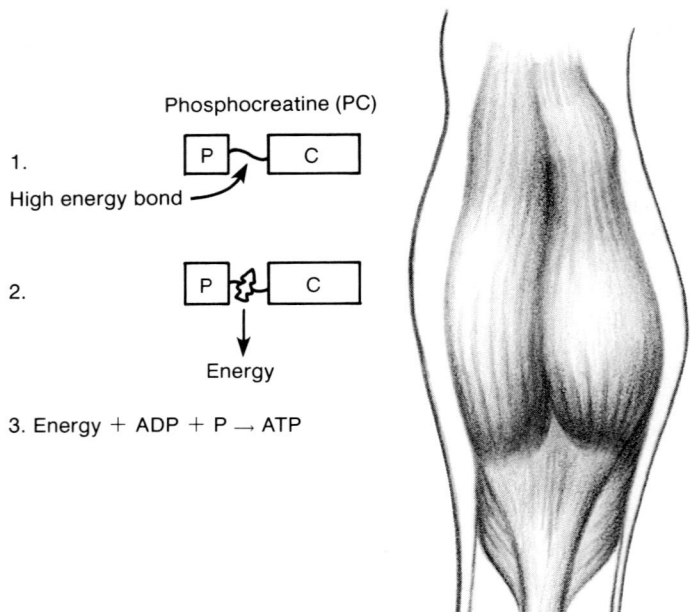

Phosphocreatine (PC)

1.

High energy bond

2.

Energy

3. Energy + ADP + P → ATP

must be replaced, and this is the function of the other energy sources. We cannot eat ATP–PC, but we can produce it from the other nutrients stored in our body. PC replenishment will not be discussed per se, but keep in mind that when ATP is being regenerated, so is some PC. In summary, the value of the ATP–PC system is its ability to provide energy rapidly.

The **lactic acid system** cannot be used directly *1-3 minutes* as a source of energy for muscular contraction, but it can help replace ATP rapidly when necessary. If you are exercising at a high intensity level, the next best source of energy besides ATP–PC is muscle glycogen. To be used for energy, muscle glycogen must be broken down in a series of reactions to eventually form ATP. This process is called **glycolysis.** One of the major factors controlling the metabolic fate of muscle glycogen is the availability of oxygen in the muscle cell. In simple terms, if oxygen is available, a large amount of ATP is formed. This is known as **aerobic** glycolysis. If little or no oxygen is available, then little ATP is formed and lactic acid is a by-product. This is known as **anaerobic,** or without oxygen, glycolysis. The lactic acid system is diagrammed in Figure 2.7.

The lactic acid system has the advantage of producing ATP rapidly. Its capacity is limited in comparison to aerobic glycolysis, for only about 5 percent of the total ATP production from muscle glycogen can be released. Moreover, the lactic acid produced as a by-product may be involved in the

PH ↓ actually causes pain

onset of fatigue. The lactic acid releases a hydrogen ion that increases the acidity within the muscle cell and disturbs the normal cell environment. The processes of energy release and muscle contraction in the muscle cell are controlled by enzymes whose functions may be impaired by the increased acidity in the cell. The lactate present after loss of the hydrogen ion still has considerable energy content, which may be used by other tissues for energy or converted back into glucose in the liver.

The third system is the **oxygen system.** It is also known as the aerobic system. Aerobics is a term used by Dr. Kenneth Cooper in 1968 to describe a system of exercising that created an exercise revolution in this country. In essence, aerobic exercises are designed to stress the oxygen system and provide benefits for the heart and lungs. Figure 2.8 represents the major physiological processes involved in the oxygen system. The oxygen system, like the lactic acid system, cannot be used directly as a source of energy for muscle contraction, but it does produce ATP in rather large quantities from other energy sources in the body. Muscle glycogen, liver glycogen, blood glucose, muscle triglycerides, blood FFA and triglycerides, adipose cell triglycerides, and body protein all may be ultimate sources of energy for ATP production and subsequent muscle contraction. To do this, glycogen and fats must be present within the muscle cell or must enter the muscle cell as glucose, FFA, or amino acids. Through a complex series of reactions they combine with

Figure 2.7.
The lactic acid energy system. Muscle glycogen can break down without the utilization of oxygen. This process is called anaerobic glycolysis. ATP is produced rapidly, but lactic acid is the end product. Lactic acid may be a major cause of fatigue in the muscle. The lactic acid system is utilized during exercise bouts of very high intensity, those conducted at maximal rates for about one to three minutes.

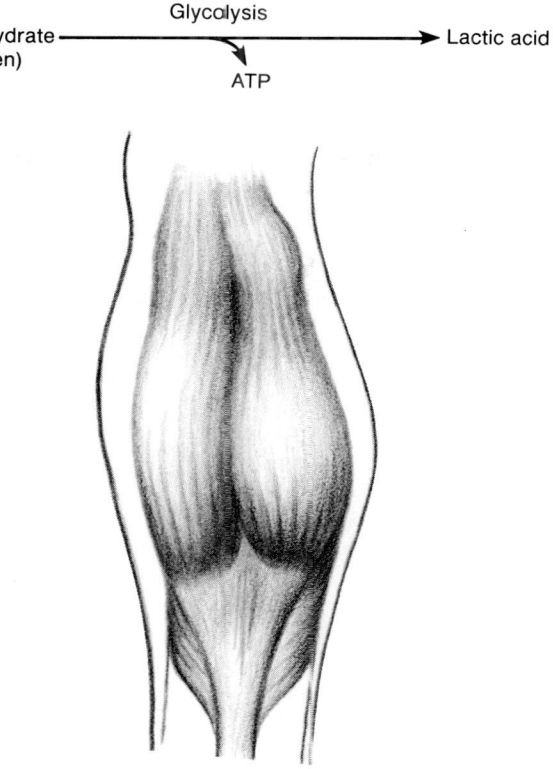

Carbohydrate (glycogen) → Glycolysis → Lactic acid
↓
ATP

oxygen to produce energy, carbon dioxide, and water. These reactions occur in the energy powerhouse of the cell, the **mitochondrion.** The whole series of events of oxidative energy production primarily involves aerobic processing of carbohydrates and fats (and small amounts of protein), the **Krebs cycle,** and the **electron transfer system.** The oxygen system is depicted in Figure 2.9. The Krebs cycle and the electron transfer system represent a highly structured array of enzymes designed to remove hydrogen, carbon dioxide, and electrons from substrate such as glucose. At different steps in this process energy is released and ATP is formed. The hydrogen and electron eventually combine with oxygen to form water.

The major advantage of the oxygen system is the production of large amounts of energy in the form of ATP. However, oxygen from the air we breathe must be delivered to the muscle cells deep in the body and enter the mitochondria to be used. This process may be adequate to handle mild and moderate levels of exercise but may not be able to meet the demand of very strenuous exercise.

Figure 2.10 presents a simplified schematic reviewing the three human energy systems.

What nutrients are necessary for the operation of the human energy systems?

Although the energy for the formation of ATP is derived from the energy stores in carbohydrate, fat, and sometimes protein, this energy transformation and utilization would not occur without the participation of the other major nutrients—water, vitamins, and minerals. These three classes of nutrients function very closely with protein in the structure and function of numerous enzymes, many of which are active in the muscle-cell energy processes.

Water is used to help break up and transform some energy compounds by a process known as hydrolysis.

Several vitamins are needed for energy to be released from the cell sources. For example, niacin and thiamin serve important functions in glycolysis, while riboflavin is essential to forming ATP through the Krebs cycle and electron transfer system. A number of other B vitamins are also involved in facets of energy transformation within the cell.

Minerals, too, are essential for cellular energy processes. Iron is one of the more critical compounds. Aside from helping deliver oxygen to the muscle cell, it is also a component of myoglobin and

Figure 2.8.
Physiological processes
involved in oxygen uptake.

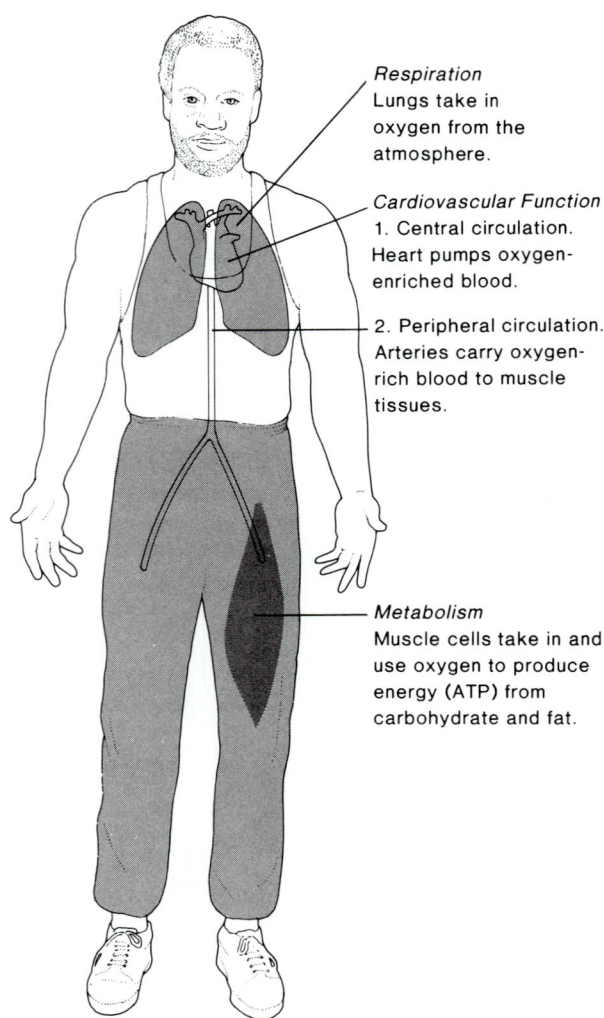

Respiration
Lungs take in
oxygen from the
atmosphere.

Cardiovascular Function
1. Central circulation.
Heart pumps oxygen-
enriched blood.

2. Peripheral circulation.
Arteries carry oxygen-
rich blood to muscle
tissues.

Metabolism
Muscle cells take in and
use oxygen to produce
energy (ATP) from
carbohydrate and fat.

the cytochrome part of the electron transfer system. It is needed for proper utilization of oxygen within the cell itself. Other minerals such as zinc, magnesium, potassium, sodium, and calcium are involved in a variety of ways, either as parts of active enzymes, in energy storage, or in the muscle-contraction process.

Proper utilization of body energy sources requires attention not only to the major energy nutrients but also to the regulatory nutrients—water, vitamins, and minerals.

Human Energy Metabolism during Rest

What is metabolism?

Human **metabolism** represents the sum total of all physical and chemical changes that take place within the body. The transformation of food to energy, the formation of new compounds such as hormones and enzymes, the growth of bone and muscle tissue, the destruction of body tissues, and a host of other physiological processes are parts of the metabolic process.

Metabolism involves two fundamental processes, anabolism and catabolism. Anabolism is a building-up process, or constructive metabolism. Complex body components are synthesized from the basic nutrients. For the active individual, this may mean an increased muscle mass through weight training or an increased amount of cellular enzymes to better use oxygen following endurance-type training. Energy is needed for anabolism to occur. Catabolism is the tearing-down process. This involves the disintegration of body compounds into their simpler components. The breakdown of muscle glycogen to glucose and eventually CO_2, H_2O, and energy is an example of a catabolic process. The energy released from some catabolic processes is used to support the energy needs of anabolism.

Figure 2.9.
The oxygen system. The muscle stores of glycogen and triglycerides, along with blood supplies of glucose and free fatty acids (FFA), as well as small amounts of muscle protein and amino acids, undergo complex biochemical changes for entrance into the Krebs cycle and the associated electron transfer system (ETS). In this process in which oxygen is the final acceptor to the electron, small amounts of muscle protein and amino acids may also be used for energy production. When they eventually combine with oxygen, large amounts of ATP may be produced. The oxygen system is utilized during endurance-type exercises, those lasting longer than four or five minutes.

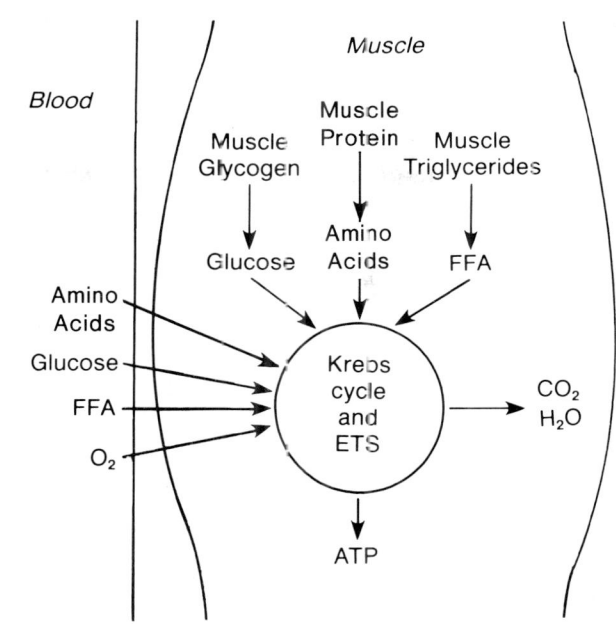

Figure 2.10.
Simplified flow diagram of the three energy systems. Following digestion, the major nutrients and oxygen are transported to the cells for energy production. In the muscles, ATP is the immediate source of energy for muscle contraction. (1) The ATP–PC system is represented by muscle stores of ATP and phosphocreatine. (2) Glucose or muscle glycogen can produce ATP rapidly via the lactic acid system. (3) The oxygen system can produce large amounts of ATP via the aerobic processes in the Krebs cycle.

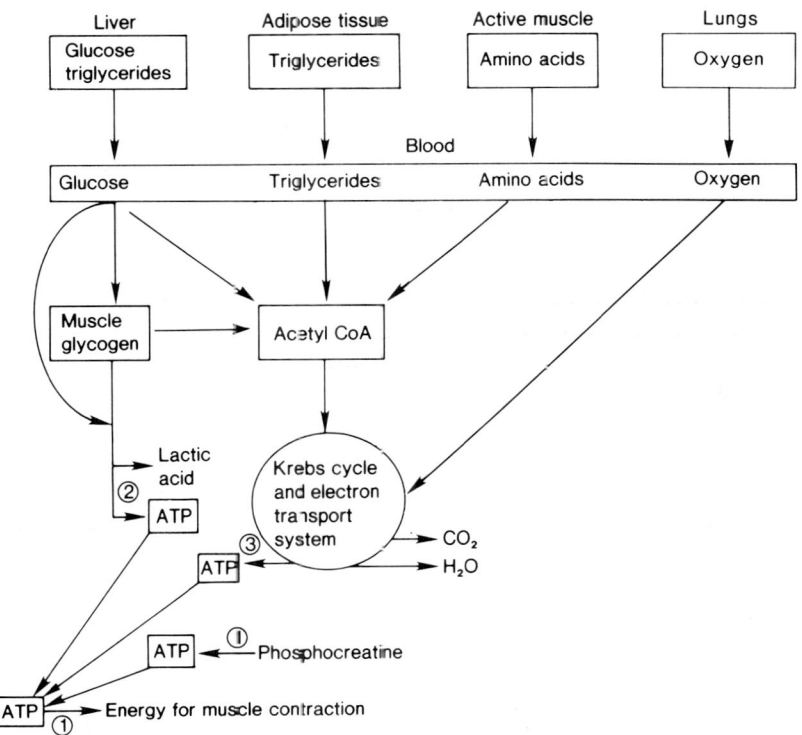

Metabolism is life. It represents human energy. The metabolic rate reflects how rapidly the body is using its energy stores, and this rate can vary tremendously depending upon a number of factors, the most influential one being exercise.

What is the basal metabolic rate (BMR) and the resting metabolic rate (RMR)?

The body is constantly using energy to build up and tear down substances within the cells. Certain automatic body functions such as contraction of the heart, breathing, secretion of hormones, and the constant activity of the nervous system also are consuming energy. The term used by the National Research Council to account for these energy processes at rest is **resting energy expenditure (REE),** which may be subdivided into basal and resting metabolic rates.

Basal metabolism, or the **basal metabolic rate (BMR),** represents the energy requirements of the many different cellular and tissue processes that are necessary to continuing physiological activities in a resting, postabsorptive state throughout most of the day. Other than sleeping, it is the lowest rate of energy expenditure. The determination of the BMR is a clinical procedure conducted in a laboratory or hospital setting. The individual fasts for twelve hours. Then, with the subject in a reclining position, the individual's oxygen consumption and carbon dioxide production are measured. Through proper calculations, the BMR is determined.

The **resting metabolic rate (RMR)** is slightly higher than the BMR. It represents the BMR plus the additional energy expenditure associated with the digestion of food. The significant elevation of the metabolic rate that occurs after ingestion of a meal was previously known as the specific dynamic action of food but is now often referred to as **dietary-induced thermogenesis (DIT)** or **thermic effect of food (TEF).** This elevation is usually highest about one hour after a meal and lasts for about four hours. The increase in the BMR caused by DIT accounts for approximately 5–10 percent of the total energy consumed in the meal so that according to the National Research Council, the BMR and RMR differ by less than 10 percent. Consequently the terms are often used interchangeably.

How can I estimate my daily RMR?

There are several ways to estimate your RMR, but whichever method is used, keep in mind that the value obtained is an estimate. To get a truly accurate value, a standard BMR test along with the calculation of your DIT would be needed. However, a

Table 2.4   Estimation of the daily resting metabolic rate

Age (years)	Equation
Males	
3–9	(22.7 × body weight) + 495
10–17	(17.5 × body weight) + 651
18–29	(15.3 × body weight) + 679
30–60	(11.6 × body weight) + 879
>60	(13.5 × body weight) + 487

Example
154-lb male, age 20
154 lbs / 2.2 = 70 kg
(15.3 × 70) + 679 = 1750

Females	
3–9	(22.5 × body weight) + 499
10–17	(12.2 × body weight) + 746
18–29	(14.7 × body weight) + 496
30–60	(8.7 × body weight) + 829
>60	(10.5 × body weight) + 596

Example
121-lb female, age 20
121 lbs / 2.2 = 55 kg
(14.7 × 55) + 496 = 1304

To get a range of values, simply add or subtract a normal 10-percent variation to the RMR estimate.
Male example: 10 percent of 1750 = 175
Normal range = 1575–1925 Calories / day
Female example: 10 percent of 1304 = 130
Normal range = 1174–1434
Body weight is expressed in kilograms (kg).

number of formula estimates may give you a good approximation of your daily RMR.

Table 2.4 provides a simple method for calculating the RMR of males and females of varying ages. Examples are provided in the table along with calculation of a 10 percent variability.

Can I change my BMR or RMR?

Your BMR is directly related to the amount of metabolically active tissue that you possess. At rest, tissues such as the heart, liver, kidneys, and other internal organs are more metabolically active than muscle tissue, but muscle tissue is more metabolically active than fat. Changes in the proportion of these tissues in your body will therefore be reflected in changes in your BMR.

Many factors influencing the BMR, such as age, sex, body size and surface area, and to a degree, body composition, are genetically determined. The effect of some of these factors on the BMR is generally well known. Because infants have a large proportion of metabolically active tissue and are growing rapidly, their BMR is extremely high. The BMR declines through childhood, adolescence, and adulthood as full growth and maturation are achieved. Individuals with greater muscle mass in comparison to body fat have a higher BMR; the BMR of women is about 10–15 percent lower than that of men, mainly because women have a higher proportion of fat to muscle tissue. Lean individuals have a higher BMR than do stocky individuals because their body surface area ratio is larger in proportion to their weight and they lose more body heat through radiation. The decline in the BMR that occurs with aging may be attributed partially to physical inactivity with a consequent loss of the more metabolically active muscle tissue and an accumulation of body fat.

Body composition may be the only factor affecting the BMR that can be changed so as to alter it. Reducing body fat and increasing muscle mass may raise the BMR because muscle tissue has a higher metabolic level than fat tissue or because the ratio of body surface area to body weight is increased. On the other hand, losing body weight including both body fat and muscle tissue generally lowers the total daily BMR.

Individuals with a greater amount of brown fat in their body, also known as **brown adipose tissue (BAT),** may have a higher BMR. BAT is a highly metabolically active form of fat that produces heat without the formation of ATP. It is thought to be important in the development of obesity and is discussed further in Chapter 9.

The ingestion of a meal may elicit a significant increase in the RMR, probably because the intestines, the liver, and other tissues need energy to absorb and metabolize the food. The RMR may remain elevated for several hours. As noted previously, this effect is known as DIT, or dietary-induced thermogenesis. The greater the caloric content of the meal, the greater the DIT effect. Also, the type of food ingested may affect the magnitude of the DIT. Protein and carbohydrates significantly increase the DIT, whereas the effect of fat is minimal.

The normal increase in the RMR due to DIT from a mixed meal of carbohydrate, fat, and protein is about 8–10 percent, although some studies have reported increases ranging from 6–16 percent. A number of studies have reported that the DIT is significantly higher in lean subjects compared to obese ones, suggesting that the obese are more efficient in storing fat. The composition of some diets for weight-loss purposes has been based upon this DIT effect, and this topic is discussed in Chapter 10 concerning diets for weight control.

The RMR may be decreased significantly in obese individuals who go on a very low-Calorie diet of less than 800 Calories per day. The decrease in the RMR, which is greater than that which would be due to weight loss alone, may be caused by lowered levels of thyroid hormones. In one study, the RMR of obese subjects dropped 9.4 percent on a diet containing only 472 Calories per day. This topic is also covered in more detail in Chapters 9 and 10.

Although caffeine is not a food, it is a common ingredient in some of the foods we may eat or drink. Caffeine is a stimulant and may elicit a significant rise in the RMR. One study reported that the caffeine in 2–3 cups of regular coffee increased the RMR 10–12 percent.

Smoking cigarettes also raises the RMR. Apparently the nicotine in tobacco stimulates the metabolism similarly to caffeine. This may be one of the reasons why individuals gain weight when they stop smoking.

Climatic conditions, especially temperature changes, may also raise the RMR. Exposure to the cold may stimulate activity of the BAT and muscular shivering, which may raise the RMR by 50 percent. Exposure to warm or hot environments will increase energy expenditure through greater cardiovascular demands and the sweating response.

Many of these factors influencing the BMR or RMR are important in themselves but may also be important considerations relative to weight control programs and body temperature regulation. Thus, they are discussed further in later chapters.

The most important factor that can increase the metabolic rate in general is exercise. As we shall see in a later section, exercise also may exert some effects upon the RMR.

What energy sources are used during rest?
The vast majority of the energy consumed during a resting situation is used to drive the automatic physiological processes in the body. Because the muscles expend little energy during rest, there is no need to produce ATP rapidly. Hence, the oxygen system is able to provide the necessary ATP for resting physiological processes.

The oxygen system can use carbohydrates, fats, and protein as energy sources. However, as noted in Chapter 5, protein is not used as a major energy source under normal dietary conditions. Carbohydrates and fats, when combined with oxygen in the cells, are the major energy substrates during rest. Several factors may influence which of the two nutrients is predominantly used. In general, though, on a mixed diet of carbohydrate, protein, and fat, about

40 percent of the energy expenditure at rest is derived from carbohydrate and about 60 percent comes from fat.

Human Energy Metabolism during Exercise

What effect does exercise have on the metabolic rate?

As noted above, the RMR includes both the BMR and the DIT and is measured with the subject at rest in a reclining position. Any physical activity will raise metabolic activity above the RMR and thus increase energy expenditure. Accounting for changes in physical activity over the day may provide a reasonable, although imprecise, estimate of the total daily energy expenditure. Very light activities such as sitting, standing, playing cards, cooking, and typing all increase energy output above the RMR, but we normally do not think of them as exercise. For purposes of this discussion, the **exercise metabolic rate (EMR)** represents the increase in metabolism brought about by moderate or strenuous physical activity such as brisk walking, climbing stairs, cycling, dancing, running, and other such activities.

Exercise is a stressor to the body, and almost all body systems respond. If the exercise is continued daily, the body systems begin to adapt to the stress of exercise. As we shall see in later chapters, these adaptations may have significant health benefits. The two body systems most involved in exercise are the nervous system and the muscular system. The nervous system is needed to activate muscle contraction, but it is in the muscle cell itself that the energetics of exercise occur. Most other body systems are simply designed to serve the needs of the muscle cell during exercise.

The muscle cell is rather a simple machine in design but extremely complex in function. It is a tube-like structure containing filaments that can slide by one another to shorten the total muscle. The shortening of the muscle moves bones, and hence work is accomplished, be it simply the raising of a barbell as in weight training or moving the whole body as in running. Like most other machines, the muscle cell has the capability of producing work at different rates, ranging from very low levels of energy expenditure during sleep to nearly a ninety-fold increase during maximal, short-term anaerobic exercise.

The most important factor affecting the metabolic rate is the intensity or speed of the exercise. To move faster, your muscles must contract more

rapidly, consuming proportionately more energy. The following represents approximate energy expenditure in Calories per minute for increasing levels of exercise intensity for an average-sized adult male. However, it would be impossible to sustain the higher levels of energy expenditure for a minute, and the highest level could be sustained for only a second or so.

Level of intensity	Caloric expenditure per minute
Resting metabolic rate	1.0
Sitting and writing	2.0
Walking at 2 m.p.h.	3.3
Walking at 3 m.p.h.	4.2
Running at 5 m.p.h.	9.4
Running at 10 m.p.h.	18.8
Running at 15 m.p.h.	29.3
Running at 20 m.p.h.	38.7
Maximal power weightlift	90.0

Although the intensity of the exercise is the most important factor affecting the magnitude of the metabolic rate, there are some other important considerations. In some activities the increase in energy expenditure is not directly proportional to speed, for the efficiency of movement will affect caloric expenditure. Very fast walking becomes more inefficient, so the individual burns more Calories per mile compared to more leisurely walking. A beginning swimmer wastes a lot of energy, whereas one who is more accomplished may swim with less effort, saving Calories when swimming a given distance. Swimming and cycling at very high speeds exponentially increase water or air resistance, so Caloric expenditure also increases exponentially. Moreover, the individual with a greater body weight will burn more Calories for any given amount of work in which the body has to be moved, as in walking, jogging, or running. It simply costs more total energy to move a heavier load.

How is exercise intensity measured?

The intensity of a given exercise may be measured in two general ways. One way is to measure the actual work output or power of the activity, such as foot-pounds per second, kilojoule per second, or horsepower. In some cases this is rather easy to do because some machines, such as bicycle ergometers, are designed to provide an accurate measure of work output. However, the actual work output of a basketball player during a game is more difficult to measure.

Figure 2.11.
Maximal oxygen uptake
(VO_2max). The best way to
express VO_2 max is in
milliliters of oxygen per
kilogram (kg) of body weight
per minute (ml O_2/kg/min).
As noted in the figure, the
smaller individual has a lower
VO_2 max in liters, but a
higher VO_2 max when
expressed relative to weight.
In this case, the smaller
individual has a higher
degree of aerobic fitness, at
least as measured by VO_2
max.

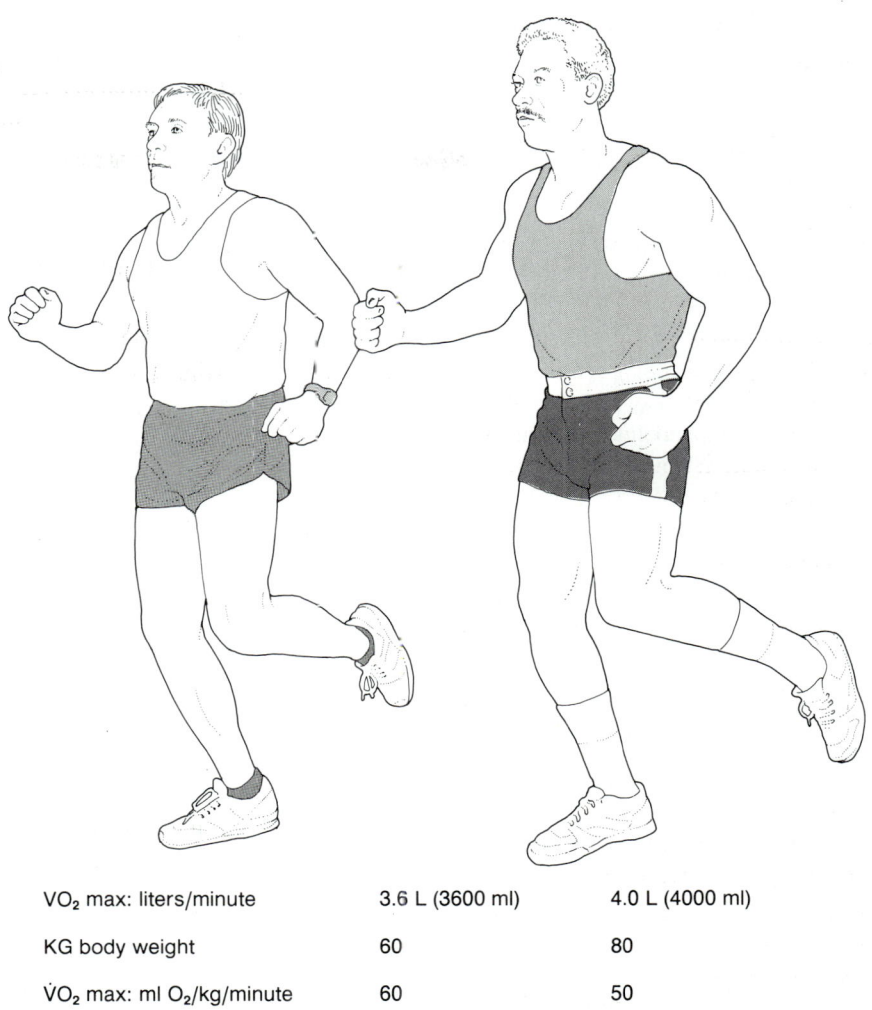

VO_2 max: liters/minute	3.6 L (3600 ml)	4.0 L (4000 ml)
KG body weight	60	80
$\dot{V}O_2$ max: ml O_2/kg/minute	60	50

A second way is to measure the physiological cost of the activity by monitoring the activity of the three human energy systems. There are highly sophisticated laboratory techniques to measure the activity of the ATP–PC system, but they are not commonly used. Laboratory techniques are also available to measure the role of the lactic acid system in exercise, primarily by measuring the concentration of lactic acid in the blood or in muscle tissues.

One measure of exercise intensity is the so-called anaerobic threshold, or that point where the metabolism is believed to shift to a greater use of the lactic acid system. This point is often labeled **OBLA, for onset of blood lactic acid,** or lactate threshold. The anaerobic threshold may also be referred to as the **steady-state threshold,** indicating that endurance exercise may continue for prolonged periods if you exercise below this threshold value. Exercise physiologists disagree about which is the better term, but all terms may be found in scientific literature.

Laboratory tests also are necessary to measure the contribution of the oxygen system during exercise, and this is the most commonly used technique for measuring exercise intensity. The most commonly used measurement is the **maximal oxygen uptake,** which represents the highest amount of oxygen that an individual may consume under exercise situations. In essence, the technique consists of monitoring the oxygen uptake of the individual while the exercise intensity is increased in stages. When the oxygen uptake does not increase with an increase in the workload, the maximal oxygen uptake has been reached. Maximal oxygen uptake is usually expressed as VO_2 max, which may be stated as liters per minute or milliliters per kilogram body weight per minute. An example is provided in Figure 2.11. A commonly used technique to indicate exercise intensity is to report it as a certain percentage of an individual's VO_2 max, such as 50 or 75 percent. In summary, measurement of the three energy

Figure 2.12.
The effect of training upon VO_2 max and the steady-state threshold. Training increases both your VO_2 max and your steady state threshold, which is the ability to work at a greater percentage of your VO_2 max without producing excessive lactic acid—a causative factor in fatigue. For example, before training the VO_2 max may be 40 ml. while the steady-state threshold is only 20 (50% of VO_2 max). After training, VO_2 max may rise to 50 ml, but the steady state threshold may rise to 40 ml (80% of the VO_2 max).

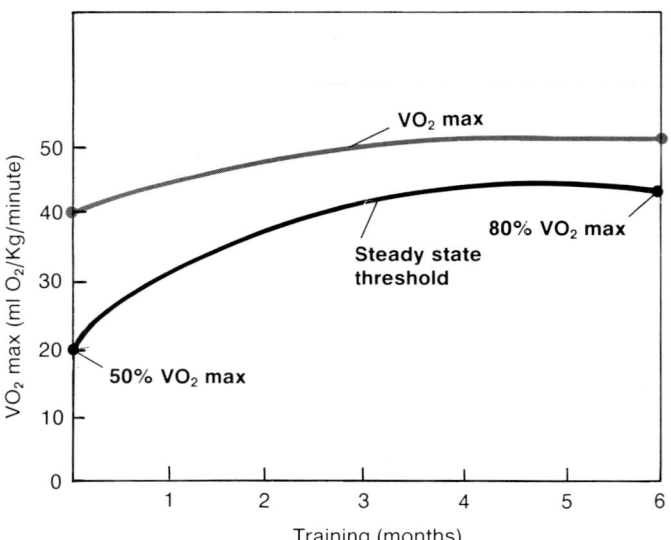

systems during exercise provides us with a measure of the energy cost of the physical activity.

Figure 2.12 illustrates the effects of training on VO_2 max and the steady-state threshold.

How is the energy expenditure of exercise expressed?

A number of research studies have been conducted to determine the energy expenditure of a wide variety of sports and other physical activities.

The energy costs have been reported in a variety of ways, including Calories per minute based upon body weight, kilojoules (kj), oxygen uptake, and METS. The **MET** is a unit that represents multiples of the resting metabolic rate (see Figure 2.13). These concepts are, of course, all interrelated, so an exercise can be expressed in any one of the four terms and converted into the others. For our purposes, we will express energy cost in Calories per minute based upon body weight, as that appears to be the most practical method for this book. However, just in case you see the other values in another book or magazine, here is how you make the conversion. We know the following approximate values:

1 C = 4 kJ
1 L O_2 = 5 C
1 MET = 3.5 ml O_2/kg/min (amount of oxygen
consumed during rest)

These values are needed for the following calculations:

Example: Exercise cost = 20 kJ/minute
To get Calorie cost, divide kJ by the equivalent value for Calories.
20 kJ/min / 4 = 5 C/min

Example: Exercise cost = 3 L of O_2/min
To get Calorie cost, multiply liters of O_2 × Calories per liter
Caloric cost = 3 × 5 = 15 C/min

Example: Exercise cost = 25 ml O_2/kg body weight/min
You need body weight in kg, which is weight in pounds divided by 2.2. For this example 154 lbs = 70 kg. Determine total O_2 cost/min by multiplying body weight times O_2 cost/kg/min
70 × 25 = 1,750 ml O_2
Convert ml to L: 1,750 ml = 1.75L
Multiply liters O_2 × Calories per liter
Caloric cost = 1.75 × 5 = 3.75 C/min

Example: Exercise cost = 12 METS
You need body weight in kg—for this example, 70 kg. Multiply total METS times O_2 equivalent of 1 MET.
12 × 3.5 ml O_2/kg/min = 42.0 ml O_2/kg/min
Multiply body weight times this result.
70 × 42 ml O_2/kg/min = 2,940 ml O_2/min
Convert ml to L: 2,940 ml O_2/min = 2.94 L O_2/min
Multiply liters O_2 × Calories per liter
Caloric cost = 2.94 × 5 = 14.70 C/min

How can I tell what my metabolic rate is during exercise?

The human body is basically a muscle machine designed for movement. Almost all of the other body systems serve the muscular system. The nervous system causes the muscles to contract. The digestive system supplies nutrients. The cardiovascular system

Figure 2.13.

Energy equivalents in oxygen consumption, Calories, Kilojoules, and METS. This figure depicts four means of expressing energy expenditure during four levels of activity. These approximate values are for an average male of 154 pounds (70 kg). If you weigh more or less, the values will increase or decrease accordingly.

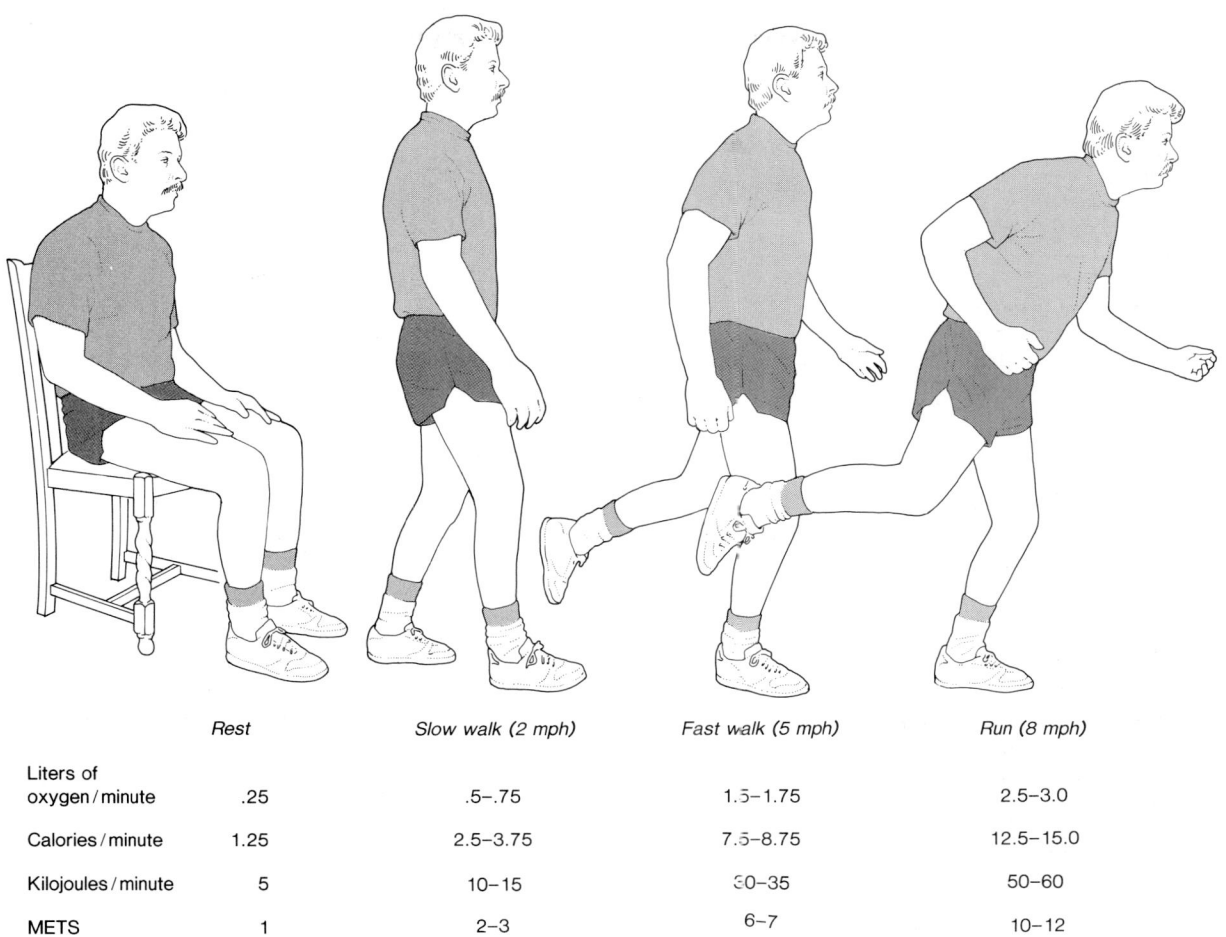

	Rest	Slow walk (2 mph)	Fast walk (5 mph)	Run (8 mph)
Liters of oxygen / minute	.25	.5–.75	1.5–1.75	2.5–3.0
Calories / minute	1.25	2.5–3.75	7.5–8.75	12.5–15.0
Kilojoules / minute	5	10–15	30–35	50–60
METS	1	2–3	6–7	10–12

delivers these nutrients along with oxygen in cooperation with the respiratory system. The endocrine system secretes hormones that affect muscle nutrition. The excretory system removes its waste products. When humans exercise, almost all body systems increase their activity to accommodate the increased energy demands of the muscle cell. In most types of sustained exercises, however, the major demand of the muscle cells is for oxygen.

As noted previously, the major technique for evaluating metabolic rate is to measure the oxygen consumption of an individual during exercise. Unfortunately this is not practical for most of us. However, because of some interesting relationships among exercise intensity, oxygen consumption, and heart rate, the average individual may be able to get a relative approximation of the metabolic rate during exercise.

A more or less linear relationship exists between exercise intensity and oxygen uptake. As the intensity level of work increases, so does the amount of oxygen consumed. The two systems primarily responsible for delivering the oxygen to the muscles are the cardiovascular and respiratory systems. There is also a fairly linear relationship between their responses and oxygen consumption. A simplified schematic is presented in Figure 2.14.

Because the heart rate (HR) generally is linearly related to oxygen consumption (the main expression of metabolic rate), and because it is easy to measure this physiological response during exercise either at the wrist or neck pulse, it may prove to be a practical guide to your metabolic rate. However, a number of factors may influence your specific heart rate response to exercise, such as the type of exercise (running vs. swimming), your level of physical fitness, sex, age, skill efficiency, percentage of

Figure 2.14.
Relationships between oxygen consumption, heart rate, and respiration responses to increasing exercise rates. In general, as the intensity of exercise continues, there is a rise in oxygen consumption, which is accompanied by proportional increases in heart rate and respiration.

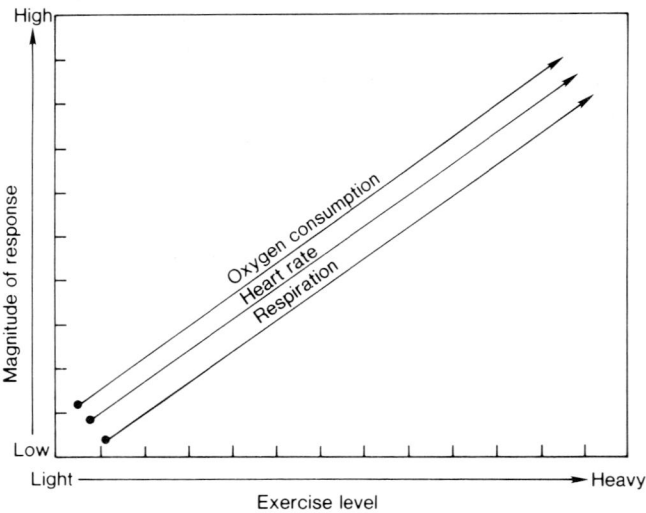

body fat, and a number of environmental conditions. Thus, it is difficult to predict your exact metabolic rate from your exercise HR. As we shall see in Chapter 10, however, the HR data during exercise may be used as a basis for establishing a personal fitness program for health and weight control.

How can I determine the energy cost of exercise?

To facilitate the determination of the energy cost of a wide variety of physical activities, Appendix C has been developed. This is a composite table of a wide variety of individual reports in the literature. When using this appendix, keep the following points in mind.

1. The figures include the RMR. Thus, the total cost of the exercise includes not only the energy expended by the exercise itself, but also the amount you would have used anyway during that same period. Suppose you ran for one hour and the calculated energy cost was 800 Calories. During that same time at rest you may have expended 75 Calories as your RMR. The net cost of the exercise is only 725 Calories.

2. The figures in the table are only for the time you are doing the activity. For example, in an hour of basketball you may exercise strenuously for only 35–40 minutes, as you may take timeouts and rest during foul shots. In general, record only the amount of time that you are actually moving during the activity.

3. The figures may give you some guidelines to total energy expenditure, but actual caloric cost might vary somewhat because of such factors as your skill level, running against the wind or uphill, and so forth.

4. Not all body weights could be listed, but you may approximate by going to the closest weight listed.

5. There may be small differences between men and women, but not enough to make a marked difference in the total caloric value for most exercises.

As one example, suppose we calculate the energy expenditure of a 154-pound individual who ran 5 miles in 30 minutes. You must calculate either the minutes per mile or miles per hour (mph).

1. 30 minutes / 5 miles = 6 min/mile
2. 60 minutes / 6 minutes/mile = 10 mph

Consult Appendix C and find the caloric value per minute for a body weight of 155 lbs and a running speed of 10 mph, a value of 18.8 Calories/minute. Multiply this value times the number of minutes of running, and you get the total caloric cost of that exercise. In this example, 30 × 18.8 = 564 total C expended.

If the activity you do does not appear in Appendix C, try to find one you think closely matches the movements found in your activity. Then check the caloric expenditure for the related activity.

What are the best types of activities to increase energy expenditure?

Activities using the large muscle groups of the body and are performed continuously usually will expend the greatest amount of Calories. Intensity and duration are the two key determinants of total energy expenditure. Activities in which you may be able to exercise continuously at a fairly high intensity for a prolonged period will maximize your total caloric loss. Although this may encompass a wide variety of different physical activities, those that recently have become increasingly popular include walking, running, swimming, bicycling, and aerobic dance. A few general comments about these common modes of exercising would appear to be in order.

Walking and running are popular exercises because they are so practical to do. All you need is a good pair of shoes. As a general rule, the caloric cost of running a given distance does not depend on the speed. It will take you a longer timer to cover the distance at a slower speed, but the total caloric cost will be similar to that expended at a faster speed. However, walking is more economical than running and hence you generally expend fewer Calories for a given distance walking than you do running. Slow, leisurely walking uses about half the number of Calories per mile as compared to running. This does not hold true, however, if you walk vigorously at a high speed. A study by Thomas and Londeree has shown about a 5 percent higher caloric cost jogging at 4.7 mph compared to walking at the same speed. At high walking speeds (above 5 mph), you may possibly expend more energy than if you jogged at the same speed. Fast, vigorous walking, known as aerobic walking, can be an effective means to expend Calories. However, as with other exercise activities, it takes practice to become a fast walker.

Climbing stairs, at home, at work, in an athletic stadium or on step machines is one means to make walking more vigorous. Skipping is also more vigorous but may lead to injuries.

Many individuals use small weights in conjunction with their walking or running programs either by carrying them or strapping them to the ankles or waist. The most popular technique is to carry small weights of 1–3 pounds. A number of research studies have reported that this technique, particularly if the arms are swung vigorously through a wide range of motion during walking, may increase the energy expenditure about 5–10 percent or higher above unweighted walking at the same speed. Increases in energy expenditure greater than 30 percent have been reported with vigorous pumping of one-pound hand weights as compared with just running at the same speed. The heart rate response also increases, and with fast walking is an adequate stimulus to promote a training effect on the cardiovascular system. However, use of hand weights exaggerates the blood pressure response, and thus should be used with caution by individuals with blood pressure problems. Since some researchers have noted that simply walking a little faster without weights will have the same effect on energy cost and heart rate response, this may be a good alternative. Nevertheless, at any given walking speed, hand weights will increase energy expenditure. Addition of weights to the ankle also will increase energy expenditure, but it may also change the normal running style and may predispose one to injury.

Because of water resistance, swimming takes more energy to cover a given distance than does either walking or running. Although the amount of energy expended depends somewhat on the type of swimming stroke used and the ability of the swimmer, swimming a given distance takes about four times as much energy as running. For example, swimming a quarter-mile is the energy equivalent of running a mile.

Bicycling takes less energy, about one third the cost, to cover a given distance in comparison to running on a level surface. The energy cost of bicycling depends on a number of factors such as body weight, the type of bicycle, hills, and body position on the bike (assuming a streamlined position to reduce air resistance). Owing to rapidly increasing air resistance at higher speeds such as 20 m.p.h., the energy cost of bicycling increases at a much faster rate at such speeds. A detailed method for calculating energy expenditure during bicycling is presented in the article by Hagberg and Pena.

For a simplified procedure, you may calculate the approximate caloric expenditure for running a given distance by either one of the following formulas:

Caloric cost = 1 C/kg body weight/kilometer
Caloric cost = 0.73 C/pound body weight/mile

If you are an average-sized male of about 154 lbs (70 kg), or an average-sized female of about 121 lbs (55 kg), you would burn about the following amounts of Calories for a kilometer or a mile.

	Male (154 lbs, 70 kg)	**Female** (121 lbs, 55 kg)
Kilometer	70	55
Mile	112	88

Slow, leisurely walking would burn a little more than half this amount of Calories per mile. Swimming a mile would use approximately four times this amount, whereas bicycling a mile would be about one-third.

Aerobic dance, as now known, has been a popular form of exercise for over twenty years. There are a variety of styles of aerobic dance varying in

Table 2.5   Classification of physical activities based upon rate of energy expenditure*

Light, mild aerobic exercise (< 7 Calories/min)

Archery	Billiards	Horseback riding
Badminton, social	Bowling	Nautilus weight training
Baseball	Dancing, mild square	Swimming (20–25 yards/min)
Bicycling (5–10 mph)	Golf	Walking (2–4 mph)

Moderate to heavy aerobic exercises (8–12 Calories/min)

Badminton, competitive	Handball, moderate	Soccer
Basketball	Paddle ball	Squash
Bicycling (11–14 mph)	Racquetball	Swimming (30–50 yards/min)
Circuit weight training, vigorous	Rope skipping (60–80 rpm)	Tennis, competitive
Dancing, aerobic	Running (5–6 mph)	Volleyball, competitive
Field hockey	Skiing, cross country (4–6 mph)	Walking (4.5–5.5 mph)

Maximal aerobic exercise (> 13 Calories/min)

Bicycling (15–20 mph)	Running (7–9 mph)
Calisthenics, vigorous	Skiing, cross-country (7–9 mph)
Handball, competitive	Swimming (55–70 yards/min)
Rope skipping (120–140 rpm)	Walking (5.8–6.0 mph)

*Calories per minute based upon a body weight of 70 kg, or 154 pounds. Those weighing more or less will expend more or fewer Calories, respectively, but the level of the exercise will be the same. The actual amount of Calories expended may also depend on a number of other factors, depending on the activity. For example, bicycling into or with the wind will increase or decrease, respectively, the energy cost.

Source: Williams, M.H. *Nutritional Aspects of Human Physical and Athletic Performance.* Springfield, IL: CC Thomas, 1985.

intensity and the degree of impact with the floor. Several studies have shown that high-intensity, high-impact aerobic dancing approximates 10 Calories per minute in women, which is indicative of strenuous exercise. Unfortunately, other research has shown that high-impact dancing is more traumatic and may lead to a higher incidence of leg injuries. Thus, the low-impact, or soft-impact, technique was introduced in which one foot usually remains in contact with the floor. Several studies have also shown that if done at a high intensity, low-impact aerobic dance may also use approximately 9–10 Calories per minute and be less likely to induce injuries to the legs.

Table 2.5 provides a classification of some common physical activities based upon rate of energy expenditure. The implications of these types of exercises in weight control programs are discussed later.

Does exercise affect my resting metabolic rate?

Exercise not only raises the metabolic rate during exercise but, depending upon the intensity and duration of the activity, will also keep the RMR elevated during the recovery period. The increase in body temperature and in the amounts of circulating hormones such as adrenaline (epinephrine) will continue to influence some cellular activity, and some other metabolic processes, such as the circulation and respiration, will remain elevated for a limited time. This process, which has been labeled the **metabolic aftereffects of exercise,** is calculated by monitoring the oxygen consumption for several hours during the recovery period after the exercise task. The amount of oxygen in excess of the preexercise RMR, often called excess postexercise oxygen consumption (EPOC), reflects the additional caloric cost of the exercise above and beyond those expended during the exercise task itself.

Some older research had noted that the average amount of additional Calories expended after each exercise session would be about 45–50. However, in a series of more recent studies with more appropriate controls, although most investigators did report an increased RMR following exercise of varying durations and intensities, the magnitude of the response was generally lower. Depending on the intensity and duration of the exercise bout in these studies, the RMR during the recovery period ranged from 4 to 16 percent higher than the preexercise RMR, and it remained elevated for only 15–20 minutes in some studies but up to 4–5 hours in others. Using the oxygen-consumption values presented in these studies, the additional energy expenditure ranged from 3–30 Calories.

Although the metabolic aftereffects of exercise would not appear to make a significant contribution to weight loss, exercise may help mitigate the decrease in the RMR often seen in individuals on very low Calorie diets. This point is explored further in Chapter 10.

Many studies have been conducted to investigate the effect of exercise on dietary induced thermogenesis (DIT). Unfortunately, no clear answer has been found. Some studies have reported an increase in DIT when subjects exercise either before or after the meal, while others revealed little or no effects. Some research even suggests that exercise training decreases the DIT. Other studies have investigated differences between exercise-trained and untrained individuals relative to DIT, and although some preliminary research noted a decreased DIT in endurance-trained athletes, Tremblay and others also noted that it is still unclear if training causes any significant alterations in DIT. In any case, the increases or decreases noted in the DIT due to either exercise or exercise training were minor, averaging about 5–9 Calories for several hours.

What role does the exercise metabolic rate play in my total daily energy output?

Your total daily energy expenditure is the sum of your BMR, RMR, and EMR. For purposes of this discussion, we can assume that the BMR and RMR are similar, and we will refer to them collectively as the RMR. In the new 1989 RDA, the National Research Council has developed a five-category physical activity factor as a means to determine an individual's daily caloric needs. The scale used is based upon an RMR value of 1.0, and increasing levels of physical activity are multiples of the RMR, somewhat comparable to the MET system discussed earlier. For example, an individual doing light activity, such as walking at 2.5 mph, would be expending Calories at approximately 2.5 times the RMR. Table 2.6 briefly summarizes this classification system, although it should be mentioned that this is an arbitrary system and could be affected greatly by factors previously discussed in this chapter. Nevertheless, it is a useful tool to illustrate an answer to the question posed above.

Let us take an example of the 24-hour energy expenditure of two 20-year-old women who have the same body weight, 132 pounds or 60 kg. However, one of the women is a typical sedentary sofa spud, while the other is physically active on her job and as a competitive triathlete. Let us assume that the RMR is the same for both, 1378 Calories per day

Table 2.6 Physical activity factor classification system

Activity	Multiple of RMR
1. **Resting:** Sleeping, reclining while watching TV	1.0
2. **Very light:** Sitting and standing activities, such as driving, playing cards, typing	1.5
3. **Light:** Activities comparable to walking at a leisurely pace, light housework, sports such as golf, bowling, archery	2.5
4. **Moderate:** Walking at a pace of 3.5–4.0 mph, active gardening, sports such as cycling, tennis, dancing	5.0
5. **Heavy:** Faster walking, stair and hill climbing, more active sports such as basketball, soccer	7.0

Adapted from National Research Council. 1989. *Recommended Dietary Allowances.* Washington, DC: National Academy of Sciences.

as calculated from the equation in Table 2.4. Let us further assume that, on average, the sedentary woman sleeps and rests for 12 hours, performs very light activity for 10 hours, and does light activity 2 hours per day. To calculate her total daily energy expenditure, we need to calculate her average daily physical activity quotient. The following example should provide you with the technique:

Resting	12 hours $\times$ 1.00 =	12.00
Very light	10 hours $\times$ 1.5 =	15.00
Light activity	2 hours $\times$ 2.5 =	5.00
Totals	24 hours	32.00

Average physical activity quotient = 32/24 = 1.33

Total daily energy expenditure = 1.33 $\times$ 1378 = 1832 Calories.

A different calculation procedure is presented in Figure 2.15.

For our physically active female, let us assume that she rests 8 hours, does very light activity for 8 hours, does light activity for 4 hours, and performs

Figure 2.15.
Total daily caloric expenditure for a sedentary, 20-year-old female who weighs 132 pounds (60 kg). Based upon calculations from the data presented in the text, she expends approximately 57 Calories per hour during resting activity, 86 Calories per hour during very light activity, and 143 Calories per hour during light activity.

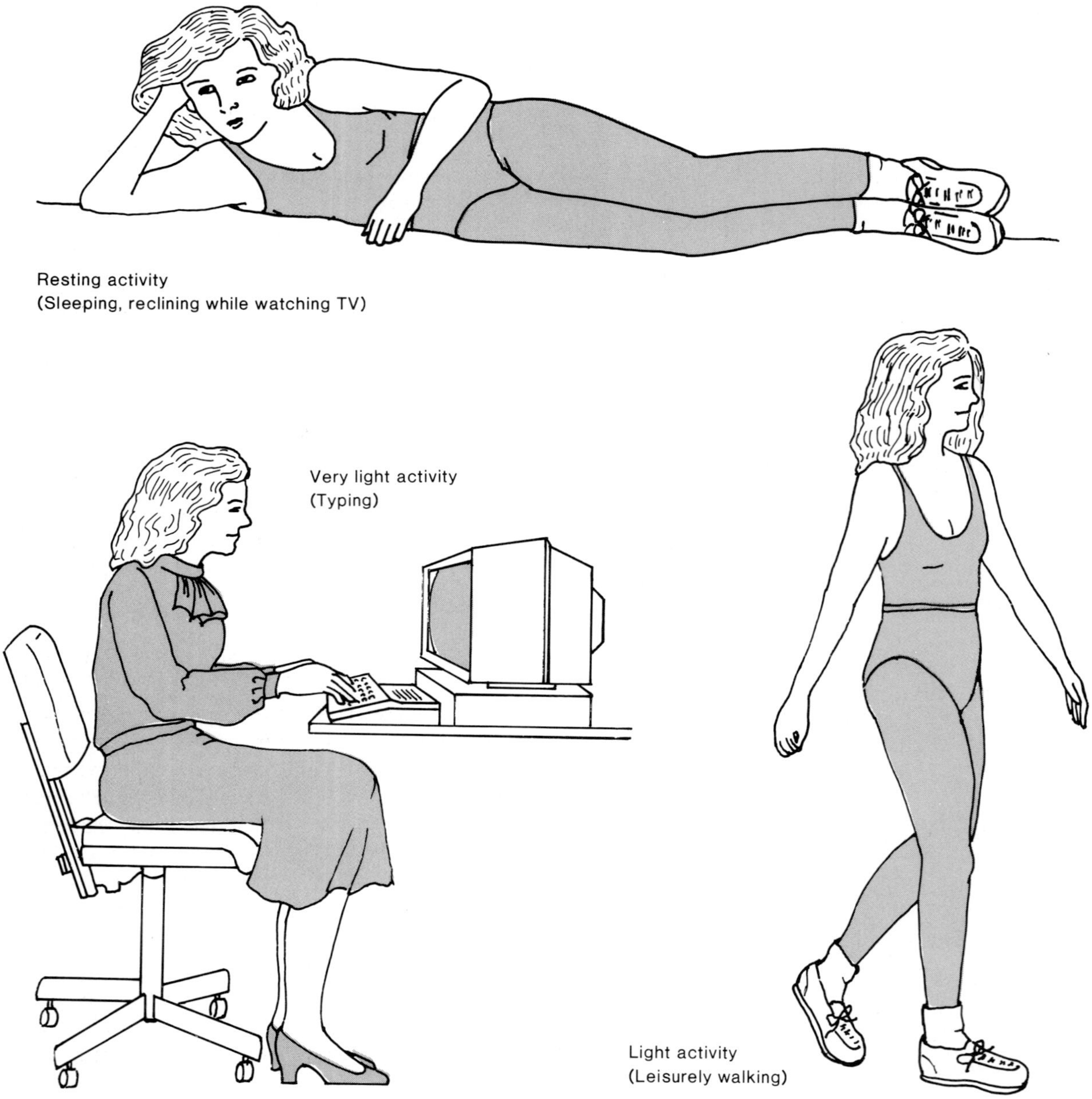

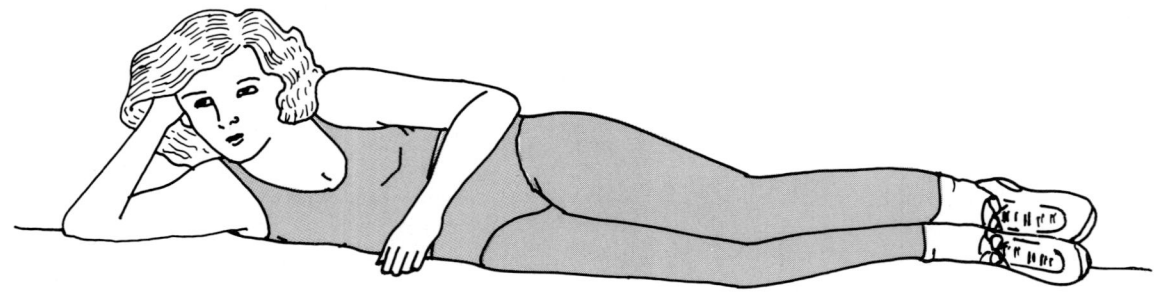

Resting activity
(Sleeping, reclining while watching TV)

Very light activity
(Typing)

Light activity
(Leisurely walking)

12 Hours Resting Activity	=	687 Calories
10 Hours Very Light Activity	=	859 Calories
2 Hours Light Activity	=	286 Calories
Total Calories	=	1832

moderate and heavy exercise for 2 hours each. Following the same procedure, we obtain a value of 3100 Calories.

Resting	8 hours × 1.00 =	8.00
Very light	8 hours × 1.5 =	12.00
Light activity	4 hours × 2.5 =	10.00
Moderate activity	2 hours × 5.0 =	10.00
Heavy activity	2 hours × 7.0 =	14.00
Totals	24 hours	54.00

Average physical activity quotient = 54/24 = 2.25

Total daily energy expenditure = 2.25 × 1378 = 3100 Calories

The total caloric difference between the two women is approximately 1270 per day. It is interesting to note that over 75 percent (1378/1832) of the daily caloric intake of the sedentary woman is accounted for by the RMR, as compared with only about 44 percent in the physically active woman.

As noted above, you may be able to modify your RMR slightly by certain techniques. However, if you are interested in increasing your daily energy expenditure, for all practical purposes your best bet is to concentrate on light, moderate, and heavy physical activities, and incorporate them daily in your life-style.

The importance of such physical activities, particularly exercise, in the design of a proper weight control program is explored in Chapter 10.

Human Energy Systems and Fatigue

What energy systems are used during exercise?

The most important factor determining which energy system will be used is the *intensity* of the exercise, which is the rate, speed or tempo at which you pursue a given activity. In general, the faster you do something, the higher your rate of energy expenditure and the more rapidly you must produce ATP for muscular contraction. Very rapid muscular movements are characterized by high rates of power production. If you were asked to run 100 meters as fast as you could, you would exert maximal speed for a short time. On the other hand, if you were asked to run 5 miles, you certainly would not run at the same speed as you would for the 100 meters. In the 100-meter run your energy expenditure would be very rapid, characterized by a high power production. The 5-mile run would be characterized by low power production, or endurance.

The requirement of energy for exercise is related to a power–endurance continuum. On the power end, we have extremely high rates of energy expenditure that a sprinter might use; on the endurance end, we see lower rates that might be characteristic of a marathon runner. The closer we are to the power end of the continuum, the more rapidly we must produce ATP. As we move toward the endurance end, our rate of ATP production does not need to be as great, but we need the capacity to produce ATP for a longer time.

The human body possesses several different types of muscle fibers, and their primary differences are in the ability to produce energy. Type I is called a slow-twitch red fiber, and it can produce energy primarily by aerobic processes, the oxygen system. It is also referred to as the slow-oxidative fiber (SO). Type IIa is known as a fast-twitch red fiber; it also can produce energy by aerobic processes but in addition can produce energy anaerobically via the lactic acid system. It is also known as the fast oxidative glycolytic fiber (FOG). The third fiber type, IIb, is a fast-twitch white fiber that produces energy primarily by anaerobic processes and is also known as the fast glycolytic fiber (FG). Type II fibers also may use the ATP–PC system at a faster rate than type I fibers.

It should be noted from the outset that all three energy systems—ATP–PC, lactic acid, and oxygen—are used in one way or another during most athletic activities. However, one system may predominate, depending primarily upon the intensity level of the activity. In this regard, the three human energy systems may be ranked according to several characteristics, which are displayed in Table 2.7.

Both the ATP–PC and the lactic acid systems are able to produce ATP rapidly and are used in events characterized by high intensity levels but occurring for short periods, because their capacity for total ATP production is limited. Because both of these systems may function without oxygen, they are called anaerobic. Relative to physical performance, the ATP–PC system predominates in short, powerful bursts of muscular activity such as the short dashes like 100 meters, whereas the lactic acid system begins to predominate during the longer sprints and middle distances such as 400 and 800 meters. In any athletic event where maximal power production lasts about 1–10 seconds, the ATP–PC system is the major energy source. The lactic acid system begins to predominate in events lasting 30–120 seconds, but studies have noted significant elevations in muscle lactic acid in maximal exercise even as brief as 10 seconds.

Table 2.7   Major characteristics of the human energy systems*

	ATP–PC	Lactic acid	Oxygen	Oxygen
Main energy source	ATP; phosphocreatine	Carbohydrate	Carbohydrate	Fat
Intensity level	Highest	High	Lower	Lowest
Rate of ATP production	Highest	High	Lower	Lowest
Power production	Highest	High	Lower	Lowest
Capacity for total ATP production	Lowest	Low	High	Highest
Endurance capacity	Lowest	Low	High	Highest
Oxygen needed	No	No	Yes	Yes
Anaerobic/aerobic	Anaerobic	Anaerobic	Aerobic	Aerobic
Characteristic track event	100-meter dash	400–800 meters	5000-meter (5 km) run	Ultradistance
Time factor	1–10 seconds	10–120 seconds	5 minutes or more	Hours

*Keep in mind that during most exercises, all three energy systems will be operating to one degree or another. However, one system may predominate, depending primarily on the intensity of the activity. See text for further explanation.

The oxygen system possesses a lower rate of ATP production than the other two systems, but its capacity for total ATP production is much greater. Although the intensity level of exercise while using the oxygen system is by necessity lower, this does not necessarily mean that an individual cannot perform at a relatively high speed for a long time. The oxygen system can be improved through a physical conditioning program so that ATP production may be able to meet the demands of relatively high-intensity exercise, as discussed previously and highlighted in Figure 2.12. Endurance-type activities, such as those that last 5 minutes or more, are dependent primarily upon the oxygen system, but the oxygen system makes a very significant contribution even in events as short as 30–90 seconds.

In summary, we may simplify this discussion by categorizing the energy sources as either aerobic or anaerobic. Anaerobic sources include both the ATP–PC and lactic acid systems while the oxygen system is aerobic. Table 2.8 illustrates the percentage contribution of anaerobic and aerobic energy sources, dependent upon the level of maximal intensity that can be sustained for a given time period. Thus, for a 100-meter dash covered in ten seconds, 85 percent of the energy is derived from anaerobic sources. For a marathoner (26.2 miles), with times approximately 130 minutes in international-level competitors, the aerobic energy processes contribute 99 percent. The key point is that the longer you exercise, the less your intensity has to be, and the more you rely on your oxygen system for energy production.

What energy sources are used during exercise?

The ATP–PC system can use only adenosine triphosphate and phosphocreatine, but as noted previously these energy sources are in short supply and need to be replaced by the other two energy systems.

The lactic acid system uses only carbohydrate, primarily the muscle glycogen stores. At high-intensity exercise levels that may be sustained for four to six minutes or less, such as exercising above your VO_2 max, carbohydrate will supply over 95 percent of the energy. However, the accumulation of lactic acid may cause the early onset of fatigue.

On the other hand, the oxygen system can use a variety of different energy sources, including protein, although carbohydrate and fat are the primary ones. The carbohydrate is found as muscle glycogen, liver glycogen, and blood glucose. The fats are stored primarily as triglycerides in the muscle and adipose cells. As we shall see below and in the next three chapters, a number of different factors can influence which energy source is used by the oxygen system during exercise, but exercise intensity and duration are the two most important factors.

Under normal conditions, exercise intensity is the key factor determining whether carbohydrate or fat is used. As you do mild to moderate exercise, say up to 50 percent of your VO_2 max, you will use about 50 percent carbohydrate and 50 percent fat. The muscle glycogen and triglycerides in the muscle, as well as glucose delivered from the liver and free fatty acids from the adipose tissues, are your main sources. As you start to exceed 50 percent of your VO_2 max—

Table 2.8   Percentage contribution of anaerobic and aerobic energy sources during different time periods of maximal work

Time	10 sec	1 min	2 min	4 min	10 min	30 min	60 min	130 min
Anaerobic	85	70	50	30	15	5	2	1
Aerobic	15	30	50	70	85	95	98	99

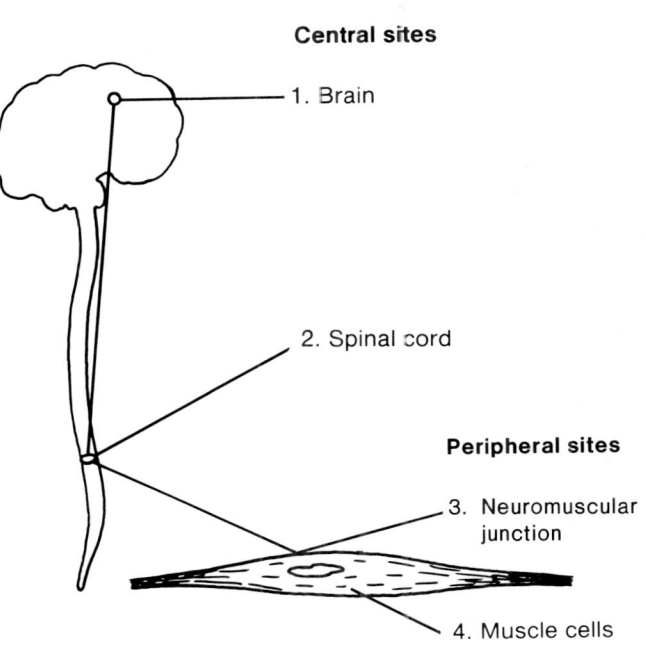

Figure 2.16.
Fatigue sites. The causes of fatigue are complex and may involve central sites such as the brain and spinal cord or peripheral sites in the muscles. Hypoglycemia, or low blood sugar, could adversely affect the functioning of the brain, while the acidity associated with the production of lactic acid could possibly interfere with optimal energy production in the muscle cells.

Central sites
1. Brain
2. Spinal cord

Peripheral sites
3. Neuromuscular junction
4. Muscle cells

that is, as you increase your speed or intensity—you begin to rely more and more on carbohydrate as an energy source. Apparently the biochemical processes for fat metabolism are too slow to meet the increased need for faster production of ATP, and carbohydrate utilization increases. The major source of this carbohydrate is the muscle glycogen. At high levels of energy expenditure, 70–80 percent of VO_2 max, carbohydrates may contribute more than 80 percent of the energy sources. This speaks for the need of adequate muscle glycogen stores when this level of exercise is to be sustained for long periods, say in events lasting over an hour or more.

In events of long duration, when body stores of carbohydrate are nearly depleted, the primary energy source is fat. In the later stages of ultramarathoning events, fat may become the only fuel available. However, protein may become an important energy source in these circumstances. Its role is detailed in Chapter 5.

Other than exercise intensity and duration, a number of different factors are known to influence the availability and use of human energy sources

during exercise. Hormones, state of training, composition of the diet, time of eating prior to competition, nutritional status, nutrient intake during exercise, environmental temperature, and drugs are some of the more important considerations. For example, warm environmental temperatures increase the use of carbohydrates, whereas caffeine may facilitate the use of fats. These considerations will be incorporated in the following chapters where appropriate.

What is fatigue?
Fatigue is a very complex phenomenon. It may be deemed to be psychological in nature as often noted in cases of mental depression, or it may be physiological in nature as seen in the untrained runner during the latter stages of an all-out 400 meter, or quarter-mile, dash. The site of fatigue in the human body may be classified as central, that is, in the brain or spinal cord of the central nervous system, or it may be peripheral, located in the muscle tissue itself or at the junction of the muscle and nerve fibers (see Figure 2.16). The actual psychological or physiological causes of fatigue are also very complex, but

they appear to be related closely to the intensity and duration of the mental or physical tasks to be accomplished. However, most instances of fatigue during exercise are believed to be related to adverse changes in the muscle itself.

For purposes of the present discussion, **fatigue** will be defined as the inability to continue exercising at a desired level of intensity. Relative to this definition, fatigue may be due to a failure of the rate of energy production in the human body to meet the demands of the exercise task. This failure may be due to an inability of the central nervous system to fully stimulate the appropriate muscles, an insufficient supply of the optimal energy source, a reduced ability to metabolize the energy source in the muscle, or inadequate support from body systems, such as blood flow, serving the muscle.

The most important factor in the prevention of fatigue during exercise is training. Athletes must train specifically the energy system or systems that are inherent to their event. However, because fatigue is highly related to the human energy systems, nutrition is an important consideration.

How is nutrition related to fatigue processes?
As noted above in our discussion of the power–endurance continuum, we can exercise at different intensities, but the duration of our exercise is inversely related to the intensity. We can exercise at a high intensity for a short time or at a low intensity for a long time. The importance of nutrition to fatigue is determined by this intensity–duration interrelationship.

In very mild aerobic activities, such as distance walking or low-speed running in a trained ultramarathoner, the body can sustain energy production by using fat as the primary fuel when carbohydrate levels diminish. Because the body has a large storage of fat, energy supply is not a problem. However, low blood-sugar levels, dehydration, and excessive loss of minerals may lead to the development of fatigue in very prolonged activities.

In moderate to heavy aerobic exercise, the body needs to use more carbohydrate as an energy source and thus will run out of muscle glycogen faster. As we shall see later, carbohydrate is a more efficient fuel than fat, so the athlete will have to reduce the pace of the activity when carbohydrate stores are depleted, such as during endurance-type activities lasting over 90 minutes. Thus, energy supply may be critical. Low blood sugar and dehydration also may be important factors contributing to the development of fatigue in this type of endeavor.

In very high-intensity exercise lasting only one or two minutes, the probable cause of fatigue is the disruption of cellular metabolism caused by the accumulation of lactic acid. There is some evidence to suggest that certain nutrients may help reduce this disruptive effect of lactic acid to some extent. Furthermore, a very low supply of muscle glycogen may impair this type of performance.

In extremely intense exercise lasting only 5–10 seconds, a depletion of phosphocreatine, PC, may be related to the inability to maintain a high force production. Although some nutritional practices, such as phosphate loading or gelatin supplements, have been used to increase PC, they have not been regarded to be effective.

In summary, a deficiency of almost every nutrient may be a causative factor in the development of fatigue. A poor diet can hasten the onset of fatigue. Proper nutrition is essential to assure the athlete that an adequate supply of nutrients is available in the diet not only to provide the necessary energy, such as through carbohydrate and fat, but also to ensure optimal metabolism of the energy substrate via protein, vitamins, minerals, and water.

References

Books

CIBA Foundation. 1981. *Human Muscle Fatigue: Physiological Mechanisms.* London: Pitman Medical.

Durnin, J., and Passmore, R. 1967. *Energy, Work and Leisure.* London: Heinemann Educational Books.

Hunt, S., and Groff, J. 1990. *Advanced Nutrition and Human Metabolism.* St. Paul, MN: West Publishing Company.

National Research Council. 1989. *Diet and Health.* Washington, DC: National Academy of Sciences.

National Research Council. 1989. *Recommended Dietary Allowances.* Washington, DC: National Academy of Sciences.

Poortmans, J. 1988. *Principles of Exercise Biochemistry.* Basel: Karger.

Powers, S., and Howley, E. 1990. *Exercise Physiology: Theory and Application to Fitness and Performance.* Dubuque, IA: Wm. C. Brown.

Williams, M. H. 1985. *Nutritional Aspects of Human Physical and Athletic Performance.* Springfield, IL.: C C Thomas.

Review Articles

Bray, G. 1983. The energetics of obesity. *Medicine and Science in Sports and Exercise* 15:32–46.

Consolazio, C. F., et al. 1973. Energy requirement and metabolism during exposure to extreme environments. *World Review of Nutrition and Dietetics* 18:177.

Costill, D. 1984. Energy supply in endurance activities. *International Journal of Sports Medicine* 5:Supplement, 19–21.

Deschenes, M., and Kraemer, W. 1989. The biochemical basis of muscular fatigue. *National Strength and Conditioning Journal* 11(11):41–44.

Durnin, J. 1985. The energy cost of exercise. *Proceedings of the Nutrition Society* 44:273–82.

Essen, B. 1977. Intramuscular substrate utilization during prolonged exercise. *Annals of the New York Academy of Sciences* 301:30–44.

Fitts, R., and Metzger, J. 1988. Mechanisms of muscular fatigue. In: *Principles of Exercise Biochemistry*, ed. J. Poortmans. Basel: Karger.

Gollnick, P. 1988. Energy metabolism and prolonged exercise. In: *Prolonged Exercise*, eds. D. Lamb and R. Murray. Indianapolis, IN: Benchmark.

Hagberg, J., and Pena, N. 1989. Bicycling's exclusive calorie counter. *Bicycling* 30:100–03, May.

Horton, E. 1989. Metabolic fuels, utilization, and exercise. *American Journal of Clinical Nutrition* 49:931–32.

Jequier, E. 1984. Energy expenditure in obesity. *Clinics in Endocrinology and Metabolism* 13:563–80.

Katz, A., and Sahlin, K. 1990. Role of oxygen in regulation of glycolysis and lactate production in humans. *Exercise and Sport Sciences Reviews* 18:1–28.

Kirkendall, D. 1990. Mechanisms of peripheral fatigue. *Medicine and Science in Sports and Exercise* 22:444–49.

Morton, R. 1990. Modelling in human power and endurance. *Journal of Mathematical Biology* 28:49–64.

Newsholme, E. 1988. Application of knowledge of metabolic integration to the problem of metabolic limitations in sprints, middle distance and marathon running. In: *Principles of Exercise Biochemistry*, ed. J. Poortmans. Basel: Karger.

Newsholme, E. 1988. Basic aspects of metabolic regulation and their application to provision of energy in exercise. In: *Principles of Exercise Biochemistry*, ed. J. Poortmans. Basel: Karger.

Rall, J. 1988. Molecular aspects of muscular contraction. In: *Principles of Exercise Biochemistry*, ed. J. Poortmans. Basel: Karger.

Rice, C., et al. 1988. The fibre composition of skeletal muscle. In *Principles of Exercise Biochemistry*, ed. J. Poortmans. Basel: Karger.

Ricquier, D., and Mory, G. 1984. Factors affecting brown adipose tissue activity in animals and man. *Clinics in Endocrinology and Metabolism* 13:501–21.

Ryan, A. 1989. The limits of human performance. In: *Sports Medicine,* eds. A. Ryan and F. Allman. San Diego, CA: Academic Press.

Saltin, B. 1989. Anaerobiosis in exercise: Limitations and implications for performance. In: *Proceedings of the First IOC World Congress on Sport Sciences.* Colorado Springs, CO:USOC.

Sedlock, S. 1990. Status of research in postexercise energy expenditure. *Research Consortium Newsletter* 13(Fall):3.

Stainsby, W., and Brooks, G. 1990. Control of lactic acid metabolism in contracting muscles and during exercise. *Exercise and Sports Sciences Reviews* 18:29–63.

Tremblay, A., et al. 1985. The effects of exercise-training on energy balance and adipose tissue morphology and metabolism. *Sports Medicine* 2:223–33.

Specific Studies

Acevedo, E., and Goldfarb, A. 1989. Increased training intensity effects on plasma lactate, ventilatory threshold, and endurance. *Medicine and Science in Sports and Exercise* 21:563–68.

Allen, T., et al. 1987. Metabolic and cardiorespiratory responses of young women to skipping and jogging. *Physician and Sportsmedicine* 15:109–13, May.

Auble, T., et al. 1987. Aerobic requirements for moving handweights through various ranges of motion while walking. *Physician and Sportsmedicine* 15:133–40, June.

Bernhauer, E., et al. 1989. Exercise reduces depressed metabolic rate produced by severe caloric restriction. *Medicine and Science in Sports and Exercise* 21:29–33.

Bielinsk, R., et al. 1985. Energy metabolism during the postexercise recovery in man. *American Journal of Clinical Nutrition* 42:69–82.

Brehm, B., and Gutin, B. 1986. Recovery energy expenditure for steady state exercise in runners and nonexercisers. *Medicine and Science in Sports and Exercise* 18:205–10.

Bubb, W., and Seay, H. 1990. The effects of various intensities of exercise on post-exercise metabolic rate. *Medicine and Science in Sports and Exercise* 22:S49.

deVries, H., and Gray, D. 1963. Aftereffects of exercise upon resting metabolic rate. *Research Quarterly* 34:314–21.

Elia, M., et al. 1984. Energy metabolism during exercise in normal subjects undergoing total starvation. *Human Nutrition and Clinical Nutrition* 38:355–62.

Fellingham, G., et al. 1978. Caloric cost of walking and running. *Medicine and Science of Sports* 10:132–36.

Forbes, G., and Brown, M. 1989. Energy need for weight maintenance in human beings: Effects of body size and composition. *Journal of the American Dietetic Association* 89:499–502.

Goss, F., et al. 1989. Energy cost of bench stepping and pumping light handweights in trained subjects. *Research Quarterly for Exercise and Sport* 60:369–72.

Graves J., et al. 1987. The effect of hand-held weights on the physiological responses to walking exercise. *Medicine and Science in Sports and Exercise* 19:260–65.

Hagerman, F., et al. 1988. A comparison of energy expenditure during rowing and cycling ergometry. *Medicine and Science in Sports and Exercise* 20:479–88.

Harnischgeger, H., et al. 1988. Incidence of injury following high and low impact aerobics versus running. *Medicine and Science in Sports and Exercise* 20:S88.

Holland, G., et al. 1990. Treadmill vs steptreadmill ergometry. *Physician and Sportsmedicine* 18:79–84, January.

Howley, E., and Glover, M. 1974. The caloric costs of running and walking one mile for men and women. *Medicine and Science in Sports* 6:235–37.

Hufhand, D., et al. 1988. Metabolic responses to low-impact aerobic dance. *Medicine and Science in Sports and Exercise* 20:S88.

Jacobs, I., et al. 1983. Lactate in human skeletal muscle after 10 and 30s of supramaximal exercise. *Journal of Applied Physiology* 55:365–67.

Jung, R., et al. 1981. Caffeine: Its effects on catecholamines and metabolism in lean and obese humans. *Clinical Science* 60:527–35.

Kirkwood, S., et al. 1990. Spontaneous physical activity is a major determinant of 24-hour sedentary energy expenditure. *Medicine and Science in Sports and Exercise* 22:S49.

LeBlanc, J., et al. 1984. Hormonal factors in reduced postprandial heat production of exercise-trained subjects. *Journal of Applied Physiology* 56:772–76.

Lennon, D., et al. 1985. Diet and exercise training effects on resting metabolic rate. *International Journal of Obesity* 9:39–47.

Makalous, S., et al. 1988. Energy expenditure during walking with hand weights. *Physician and Sportsmedicine* 16:139–48, April.

Miller, J., and Stamford, B. 1987. Intensity and energy cost of weighted walking vs running for men and women. *Journal of Applied Physiology* 62:1497–1501.

Otto, R., et al. 1988. The metabolic cost of multidirectional low impact and high impact aerobic dance. *Medicine and Science in Sports and Exercise* 20:S88.

Parker, S., et al. 1989. Failure of target heart rate to accurately monitor intensity during aerobic dance. *Medicine and Science in Sports and Exercise* 21:230–34.

Pendergast, D., et al. 1974. Energy cost of swimming. Paper presented at national American College of Sports Medicine meeting. Knoxville, TN, May 11.

Schwartz, R., Ravussin, E., Massari, M., et al. 1985. The thermic effect of carbohydrates versus fat feeding in man. *Metabolism* 34:285–93.

Sedlick, D., and Cohen, B. 1990. The effect of acute nutritional status on postexercise energy expenditure. *Medicine and Science in Sports and Exercise* 22:S49.

Segal, K., et al. 1985. Thermic effect of food at rest, during exercise, and after exercise in lean and obese men of similar body weight. *Journal of Clinical Investigation* 76:1107–12.

Tesch, P., and Kaiser, P. 1984. Substrate utilization during exhaustive, heavy resistive exercise. *Medicine and Science in Sports and Exercise* 16:174.

Thomas, T., and Londeree, B. 1989. Energy cost during prolonged walking vs jogging exercise. *Physician and Sportsmedicine* 17:93–102, May.

Tremblay, A., et al. 1983. Diminished dietary thermogenesis in exercise-trained human subjects. *European Journal of Applied Physiology* 52:1–4.

Von Hofen, D., et al. 1989. Aerobic requirements for pumping versus carrying .91 kg handweights while running. *Medicine and Science in Sports and Exercise* 21:S7.

Weststrate, J., et al. 1989. Diurnal variation in postabsorptive resting metabolic rate and diet-induced thermogenesis. *American Journal of Clinical Nutrition* 50:908–14.

Williford, H., et al. 1988. The energy cost of different intensities of high and low-impact aerobic dance. *Medicine and Science in Sports and Exercise* 20:S88.

Key Terms

alcoholism

blood alcohol content (BAC)

carbohydrate loading

carbohydrates, simple and complex

cirrhosis

dietary fiber

disaccharide

ergolytic

ethanol

fetal alcohol effects (FAE)

fetal alcohol syndrome (FAS)

fructose

galactose

gluconeogenesis

glucose

glucose-alanine cycle

glucose polymer

glycemic index

hyperglycemia

hypoglycemia

insoluble fibers

insulin

maltodextrin

millimole

monosaccharides

polysaccharide

proof

psyllium

soluble fibers

Key Concepts

Most foods in the bread/cereal and fruit/vegetable groups contain a high percentage of carbohydrates, primarily complex carbohydrates, which should constitute 55–60 percent, or more, of the daily caloric intake for most athletes.

Most ingested carbohydrates are initially converted into blood glucose and used for energy or stored as liver and muscle glycogen, but excess carbohydrates may be converted into fat.

The major function of carbohydrates in human metabolism is to supply energy; blood glucose is essential for optimal functioning of the nervous system, whereas muscle glycogen is essential for endurance exercise.

The three sources of carbohydrate in the body of an average adult male are blood glucose (5 grams; 20 Calories), liver glycogen (75–100 grams; 300–400 Calories), and muscle glycogen (350–400 grams; 1,400–1,600 Calories).

The body can make glucose from certain by-products of protein and fat.

Carbohydrate is the most important energy source for high-intensity exercise, and the only one that can participate significantly in aerobic and anaerobic energy pathways.

Regular training increases the ability of the muscles to store and use carbohydrate for energy production.

Low levels of blood glucose or muscle glycogen may be contributing factors in the early onset of fatigue in prolonged exercise.

Carbohydrate intake immediately before and during prolonged exercise may help delay the onset of fatigue, but such practices will not improve performance in most athletic events of shorter duration.

Glucose, sucrose, and glucose polymers appear to be equally effective as a means to enhance performance, but fructose may be more likely to cause gastrointestinal distress.

Athletes who train intensely on a daily basis should have a diet high in complex carbohydrates to replenish muscle glycogen, in order to maintain the quality of training.

Various carbohydrate-loading techniques may effectively increase muscle glycogen stores, but rest and a high-carbohydrate diet are the essential points.

Carbohydrate loading is not a technique for all types of athletes, but it appears to benefit athletes involved in long-distance competition such as marathoning.

Alcohol is not an effective ergogenic aid, but may actually impair athletic performance, i.e., it is ergolytic.

An increase in the amount of dietary fiber may be helpful as a protective measure against the development of several chronic diseases.

Consumption of alcohol in moderation appears to cause no major health problems for the normal, healthy adult, but may be contraindicated for some, such as during pregnancy. Heavy drinking is associated with numerous health problems.

Carbohydrates: The Main Energy Food

3

Introduction

One of the most important nutrients in your diet, from the standpoint of both health and athletic performance, is dietary carbohydrate. In the past, dietary carbohydrate suffered a poor reputation in the mind of the general public, particularly in those attempting to lose body weight, but it is now considered one of the most important components of a healthful diet, not only for its potential in preventing certain chronic diseases but also as an integral part of a proper diet to lose body fat. The possible health benefits of a diet high in complex carbohydrates and fiber and low in simple refined sugars are presented in this chapter, whereas the role of carbohydrate in a weight control plan will be addressed in Chapter 10.

As noted in Chapter 2, the major role of carbohydrate in human nutrition is to provide energy, and scientists have long known that carbohydrate is one of the prime sources of energy during exercise. Of all the nutrients we consume, carbohydrate has received the most research attention in regard to a potential influence upon athletic performance, particularly in exercise tasks characterized by endurance such as long distance running, cycling, and triathloning. Such research is important to athletes who are concerned about optimal carbohydrate nutrition during training and competition. Indeed, continued research over the past twenty years, both in the United States and abroad, has enabled sports nutritionists to provide more specific and useful responses to athletes' questions. For example, compared to the first edition of this book published in 1983, readers of this third edition will note several significant differences concerning dietary carbohydrate recommendations to athletes.

In this chapter, we explore the nature of dietary carbohydrates, their metabolic fates and interactions in the human body, their possible influence upon health status, and their potential application to physical performance, including the adverse effects of low-carbohydrate diets; the value of carbohydrate intake before, during, and after exercise; the efficacy of different types of carbohydrates; the role of carbohydrate loading; and carbohydrate foods or compounds, including alcohol, with alleged ergogenic properties. Although the role of sport drinks containing carbohydrate, such as Gatorade and Exceed, is introduced in this Exceed, is introduced in this chapter, additional detailed coverage of these fluids and their effect upon performance is presented in Chapter 8: Water, Electrolytes, and Temperature Regulation.

Dietary Carbohydrates

What are the different types of dietary carbohydrates?

Carbohydrates represent one of the least expensive forms of Calories and hence are one of the major food supplies for the vast majority of the world's peoples. They are one of the three basic energy nutrients formed when the energy from the sun is harnessed in plants through the process of photosynthesis.

Carbohydrates are organic compounds that contain carbon, hydrogen, and oxygen in various combinations. A wide variety of different forms exist in nature and in the human body. In general terms, the ones of importance to our discussion may be categorized as simple carbohydrates, complex carbohydrates, and dietary fiber. (Sugars)

Simple carbohydrates, which are usually known as sugars, can be subdivided into two categories: disaccharides and monosaccharides. Saccharide means sugar or sweet. Think of saccharin, a noncaloric sweetener. The three major **monosaccharides** are **glucose, fructose,** and **galactose.** Glucose and fructose occur widely in nature, primarily in fruits, as free monosaccharides. Glucose is often called dextrose or grape sugar, while fructose is known as levulose or fruit sugar. Galactose is found in milk as part of lactose.

The combination of two monosaccharides yields a **disaccharide.** The disaccharides include maltose (malt sugar), lactose (milk sugar), and sucrose (cane sugar or table sugar). Upon digestion these disaccharides yield the monosaccharides as follows:

```
   sucrose (table            lactose
          sugar)
      /     \               /      \
glucose   fructose     glucose   galactose


          maltose
          /     \
     glucose   glucose
```

Figure 3.1.
Glucose polymer. A glucose
polymer is a string of glucose
molecules. Muscle glycogen
is a glucose polymer.
Commercial glucose polymers
also have been developed for
consumption by endurance
athletes.

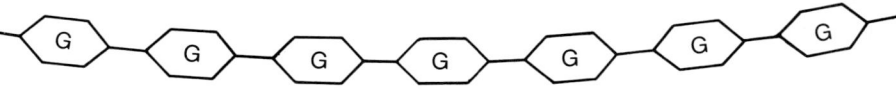

Monosaccharides and disaccharides, such as glucose and sucrose, may be isolated from foods in purified forms known as refined sugars. For example, high-fructose corn syrup, a common food additive, is derived from the conversion of glucose in corn starch to fructose.

Complex carbohydrates, commonly known as starches, are generally formed when three or more glucose molecules combine. This combination is known as a **polysaccharide, or a glucose polymer** when more than ten glucose molecules are combined (Figure 3.1). The vast majority of carbohydrates that exist in the plant world are in polysaccharide form. **Maltodextrin** is a common form of glucose polymer used in sport drinks. Of prime interest to us are the plant starches, through which we obtain a good proportion of our daily Calories along with a wide variety of nutrients, and the animal starch, glycogen, about which we shall hear more later in relation to energy for exercise.

Dietary fiber is the carbohydrate polysaccharide in plant cell walls that is resistant to digestive enzymes and hence leaves some residue in the digestive tract. Dietary fiber exists in two basic forms: water soluble and water insoluble. **Soluble fibers** include gums and pectins, whereas the **insoluble fibers** are cellulose, hemicellulose, and lignin. Although classified as fiber, technically, lignin is not a carbohydrate. Some plant fibers are both water soluble and water insoluble, such as **psyllium.**

What are some common foods high in carbohydrate content?

Of the four food groups, the bread/cereal and fruit/vegetable are the two primary contributors of carbohydrate to the diet. Some foods in the meat and milk groups contain moderate to high amounts of carbohydrate. Dried beans and peas, because their protein content is comparable to meat, may be listed in the meat group. One-half cup of navy beans contains 20 grams of carbohydrate, which is nearly 70 percent of the energy content. A glass of skim milk contains 12 grams of carbohydrate, over 50 percent of the energy content. Table 3.1 shows some foods

in the different food groups that have high carbohydrate content. Complex-carbohydrate foods are accentuated, as they are highly recommended in the Healthy American Diet.

Foods other than those listed in the table may have appreciable amounts of carbohydrates. Seeds and nuts have moderate amounts in general, dried chestnuts having a high content. Miscellaneous foods such as pies, puddings, candy, cookies, cake with icing, maple syrup, and table sugar are high in carbohydrates, but primarily the refined type. The carbohydrate content in sport drinks varies. As one example, Gatorade Light contains 7 grams while Gatorlode contains about 47 grams in 8 ounces of fluid. Sport bars are usually high in carbohydrate; for example, an Exceed Sports Bar contains 53 grams of carbohydrate, about 76 percent of its 280 Calories.

Foods high in dietary fiber include most vegetables and fruits, foods in the bread/cereal group made from whole grains, and dried beans and peas in the meat group. Wheat products are good sources of the insoluble fibers, while oats, beans, dried peas and fruits are excellent sources of the soluble fibers. Because of the purported health benefits of fiber, cereal manufacturers have released new products containing 13–14 grams of fiber per serving. Psyllium, once used primarily as a laxative, is now added to several breakfast cereals. Table 3.2 presents the average fiber content in some common foods. High fiber foods in the six food exchanges are also highlighted in Appendix H.

How much carbohydrate do we need in the diet?

As we shall see below, carbohydrate serves several important functions in human metabolism. However, the National Research Council has not established an RDA for carbohydrate, probably because the body can adapt to a carbohydrate-free diet and manufacture the glucose it needs from parts of protein and fat. Nevertheless, some dietitians contend that carbohydrate is an essential nutrient, and the daily diet should include at least 50–100 grams to

Foods high in dietary fiber.

(David Corona)

Table 3.1 Foods high in carbohydrate content

Bread/cereal group	Fruit/vegetable group	Milk group	Meat group	Sport drinks/ Sport bars
Bagels	Apples	Ice Milk	Kidney beans	Exceed
Biscuits	Applesauce	Skim milk	Navy beans	Gatorade
Bread	Apricots	Yogurt	Split peas	Gatorlode
Cereal	Bananas			Exceed Sports Bar
Cornbread	Blackberries			Power Bar
Crackers	Blueberries			
Grits	Cantaloupe			
Macaroni	Cherries			
Muffins	Corn			
Noodles	Dried fruits			
Pancakes	Figs			
Pasta	Oranges			
Rice	Peaches			
Spaghetti	Pears			
Waffles	Pineapple			
	Plums			
	Potatoes			
	Raspberries			
	Squash, winter			
	Sweet potato			
	Tangerines			

BAILEY- 60-70% CARBOS.   350 - 425 g

Table 3.2 Fiber content in some common foods

Beans	7–9 grams per 1/2 cup, cooked
Vegetables	3–5 grams per 1/2 cup, cooked
Fruits	1–3 grams per piece
Breads and cereals *	1–3 grams per serving
Nuts and seeds	2–5 grams per ounce

*Fiber content may vary considerably in bran-type cereals, ranging up to 13–14 grams per serving.

spare the catabolism of protein. Nutritionists also suggest that fiber is an essential nutrient.

Recent recommendations for increased consumption of carbohydrate have suggested that such a dietary change would have important health benefits. As mentioned in Chapter 1, the Healthy American Diet represents an attempt to change the nutritional habits of most Americans toward a more healthful diet. One of the recommended goals is to raise the carbohydrate content of the diet to 55–60 percent of the total caloric intake. Simple refined sugars should be limited to 10 percent, while the complex carbohydrates should comprise about 45–50 percent. Other diet plans developed for optimal health, such as the Pritikin program, recommend that 80 percent of the dietary Calories be supplied by carbohydrates, mostly complex and unrefined. The current average amount of fiber intake is approximately 12–14 grams per day, and the National Cancer Institute recommends that this amount be doubled, or in the range of 25–40 grams per day. An increased intake of complex carbohydrates would facilitate this goal.

A large percentage of the world's population subsists on such a high-carbohydrate diet. The health implications of a high-carbohydrate diet are discussed later in this chapter.

Sports nutritionists also recommend a high-carbohydrate diet for individuals engaged in athletic training programs. The general recommendation for most athletes parallels the recommended dietary goals noted above. For an athlete consuming 3,000 Calories per day, 55–60 percent from carbohydrate would be 1,650–1,800 Calories, or about 400–450 grams. However, even higher amounts, 70 percent or more of the dietary Calories from carbohydrate, have been recommended for those athletes involved in heavy endurance-type training programs. For an endurance athlete who consumes about 3,500 Calories per day, this would amount to about 2,450 Calories from carbohydrate (70 percent

of 3,500), or about 600 grams per day. However, dietary surveys conducted with athletes, including endurance athletes, often reveal a dietary intake significantly lower than these recommendations.

Metabolism and Function

What happens to dietary carbohydrate in the human body?

Carbohydrates usually are ingested in the forms of polysaccharides (starches), disaccharides (sucrose and lactose), and monosaccharides (glucose and fructose). In addition, special carbohydrate compounds, such as glucose polymers, have been developed for athletes. Although there is very little digestion of carbohydrate in the stomach, the rapidity with which carbohydrate leaves the stomach, and its impact upon the absorption of water, may be important considerations for some athletes and will be discussed below and in Chapter 8.

It is not necessary to explain all the intricate steps of the digestive process here, but essentially what occurs is a breakdown of the polysaccharides and disaccharides to the monosaccharides. The primary site of digestion is the small intestine, and the monosaccharides are then absorbed into the blood. Of the three monosaccharides, glucose is of most importance to human physiology. It is the blood sugar. Fructose and galactose are converted to blood glucose either in the intestinal wall or the liver.

A high-carbohydrate meal will lead to a rather rapid increase in the blood sugar level, usually within an hour. The glycemic index represents the effect a particular food has upon the rate and amount of increase in the blood glucose level. In particular, foods containing high amounts of refined sugars have a high glycemic index because they lead to a rapid rise in the blood sugar. On the other hand, foods high in fiber, such as beans, generally have a low glycemic index. Interestingly, fructose has a low glycemic index, which is one of the reasons its use had been advocated for endurance athletes. We discuss the role of fructose later in this chapter.

The maintenance of a normal blood glucose level is very important for proper metabolism. Thus, the human body possesses a variety of mechanisms, primarily hormones, to help keep blood glucose levels under precise control. The rise in blood glucose, also known as serum glucose, stimulates the pancreas to secrete insulin into the blood. Insulin is a hormone that facilitates the uptake and utilization of glucose by various tissues in the body, most notably the muscles and adipose tissue.

Figure 3.2.

Fates of blood glucose. After assimilation into the blood, glucose may be stored in the liver or muscles as glycogen or be utilized as a source of energy by these and other tissues, particularly the nervous system. Excess glucose may be partially excreted by the kidneys, but major excesses are converted to fat and stored in the adipose tissues.

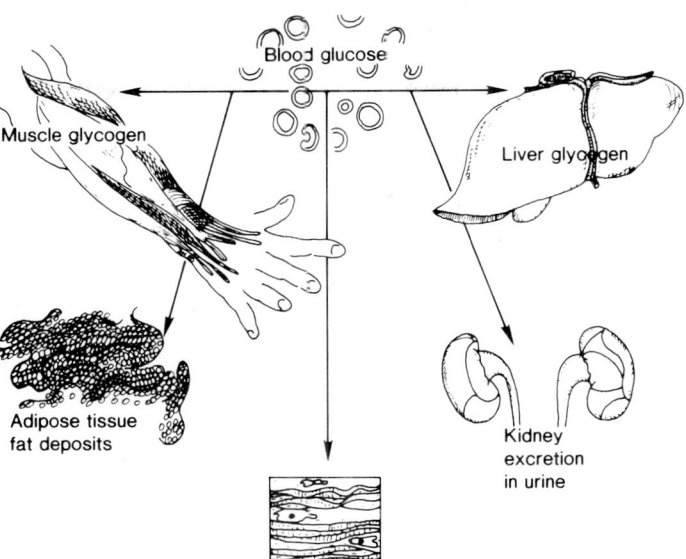

Other tissues CO_2 + H_2O + Energy

Foods with a high glycemic index will lead rapidly to high blood glucose levels, or **hyperglycemia,** which will cause an enhanced secretion of insulin from the pancreas. High serum levels of insulin will then lead to a rapid, and possibly excessive, transport of the blood glucose into the tissues. This may lead in turn to a reactive **hypoglycemia,** or low blood glucose level. This insulin response to carbohydrate intake may be an important consideration for some athletes and is discussed later.

The fate of the blood glucose is dependent upon a multitude of factors, with exercise being one of the most important. In essence, however, the following points represent the major fates of blood glucose. Figure 3.2 schematically represents these fates.

1. Blood glucose may be used for energy, particularly by the brain and other parts of the nervous system that rely primarily on glucose for their metabolism. Hypoglycemia can impair the normal function of the brain. Although hypoglycemia as a clinical condition is quite rare in the general population, transitory hypoglycemia may occur in very prolonged endurance exercise.

2. Blood glucose may be converted to either liver or muscle glycogen. It is important to note that liver glycogen may later be reconverted to blood glucose. However, this does not occur to any appreciable extent with muscle glycogen. In essence, glucose is locked in the muscle once it enters, owing to the lack of a specific enzyme needed to

change its form so it can cross the cell membrane. Most of the muscle glycogen is converted to this locked form of glucose during the production of energy.

3. Blood glucose may be converted to and stored as fat in the adipose tissue. This situation occurs when the dietary carbohydrate, in combination with caloric intake of other nutrients, exceeds the energy demands of the body and the storage capacity of the liver and muscles for glycogen.

4. Some blood glucose also may be excreted in the urine if an excessive amount occurs in the blood because of rapid ingestion of simple sugars.

How much total energy do we store as carbohydrate?

A common method to express the concentration of carbohydrate stored in the body is in millimoles (mmol). A **millimole** is 1/1000 of a mole, which is the term representing gram molecular weight. In essence, a mole represents the weight in grams of a particular substance such as glucose. The chemical formula for glucose is $C_6H_{12}O_6$, so it contains six parts of carbon and oxygen and twelve parts of hydrogen. The atomic weight of carbon is 12, hydrogen is 1, and oxygen, 16. If you multiply the number of parts by the respective atomic weights of each of the elements for glucose [(6 × 12) + (12 × 1) + (6 × 16)], you would get a total of 180. Thus, one mole of glucose is 180 grams, or about six

Figure 3.3.
The millimole concept. The concentration of some nutrients in the body is often expressed in millimoles. See text for explanation.

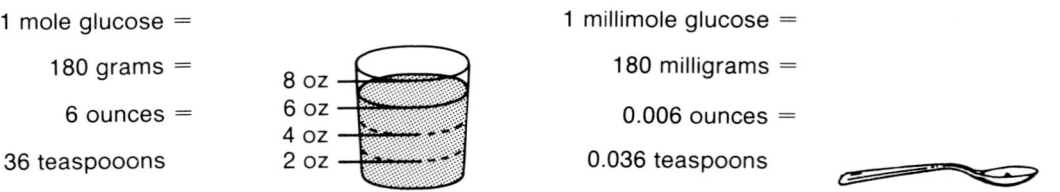

1 mole glucose =	1 millimole glucose =
180 grams =	180 milligrams =
6 ounces =	0.006 ounces =
36 teaspooons	0.036 teaspoons

ounces. One millimole is 1/1000 of 180 grams, or 180 milligrams. (See Figure 3.3.)

As an illustration, the normal glucose concentration is about 5 mmol per liter of blood, or 90 mg/100 ml, (90 mg/dL). To calculate, 5 mmol × 180 mg = 900 mg/liter, which is the same as 90 mg/100 ml. The normal individual has about 5 liters of blood. Thus, this individual would have a total of 25 mmol of glucose in the blood, or a total of 4,500 milligrams (25 × 180), or 4.5 grams.

These calculations have been presented here because this is the means whereby concentrations of glucose, glycogen, and other nutrients are expressed in contemporary scientific literature. A knowledge of these mathematical relationships should help you interpret research more effectively. However, because we are using the Calorie as the measure of energy in this book, and because each gram of carbohydrate equals approximately four Calories, an estimate of the energy content of the major human energy sources of carbohydrate may be obtained.

The body has three energy sources of carbohydrate—blood glucose, liver glycogen, and muscle glycogen. Initial stores of blood glucose are rather limited, totaling only about 5 grams, or the equivalent of 20 Calories (C). However, blood glucose stores may be replenished from either liver glycogen or absorption of glucose from the intestine. The liver has the greatest concentration of glycogen in the body. However, because its size is limited, the liver normally contains only about 75–100 g of glycogen, or 300–400 C. One hour of aerobic exercise uses over half of the liver glycogen supply. It is also important to note that the liver glycogen content may be decreased by starvation or increased by a carbohydrate-rich diet. Fifteen hours or more of starvation will deplete the liver glycogen, while certain dietary patterns may nearly double the glycogen content of the liver, a condition that may be useful in certain tasks of physical performance.

The greatest amount of carbohydrate stored in the body is in the form of muscle glycogen. This is because the muscles compose such a large proportion of the body mass as contrasted to the liver. One would expect large differences in total muscle glycogen content between different individuals because of differences in body size. However, for an average-sized, untrained man with about 30 kg of his body weight consisting of muscle tissue, one could expect a total muscle glycogen content of approximately 360 g, or 1,440 C. This would represent a concentration of about 66 mmol, or 12 grams, per kg of muscle tissue. As with liver glycogen, the muscle glycogen stores also may be decreased or increased, with considerable effects on physical performance. For example, a trained endurance athlete may have twice the amount of stored muscle glycogen that an untrained sedentary individual has.

If we calculate the body storage of carbohydrate as blood glucose, liver glycogen and muscle glycogen, the total is only about 1,800–1,900 C, not an appreciable amount. One full day of starvation could reduce it considerably.

Can the human body make carbohydrates from protein and fat?

Because the carbohydrate stores in the body are rather limited, and because blood glucose is normally essential for optimal functioning of the central nervous system, it is important to be able to produce glucose internally if the stores are depleted by starvation or a zero-carbohydrate diet. This process in the body is called **gluconeogenesis,** meaning the new formation of glucose. A number of different substrates from each of the three energy nutrients may be used and are depicted graphically in Figure 3.4.

Protein may be a significant source of blood glucose. Protein breaks down to amino acids in the body, and certain of these amino acids, notably alanine, may be converted to glucose in the liver. This is referred to as the **glucose–alanine cycle,** which is explained further in Chapter 5. A number of other amino acids also are gluconeogenic. Glucose is essential for the brain and several other tissues. If at

Figure 3.4.
Gluconeogenesis. The liver is the major site for gluconeogenesis in the body. The breakdown products of fats, protein, and carbohydrate from other parts of the body may be transported to the liver by the blood for eventual reconversion into glucose. Glycerol, glucogenic amino acids, lactate, and pyruvate may be important sources for the new formation of glucose.

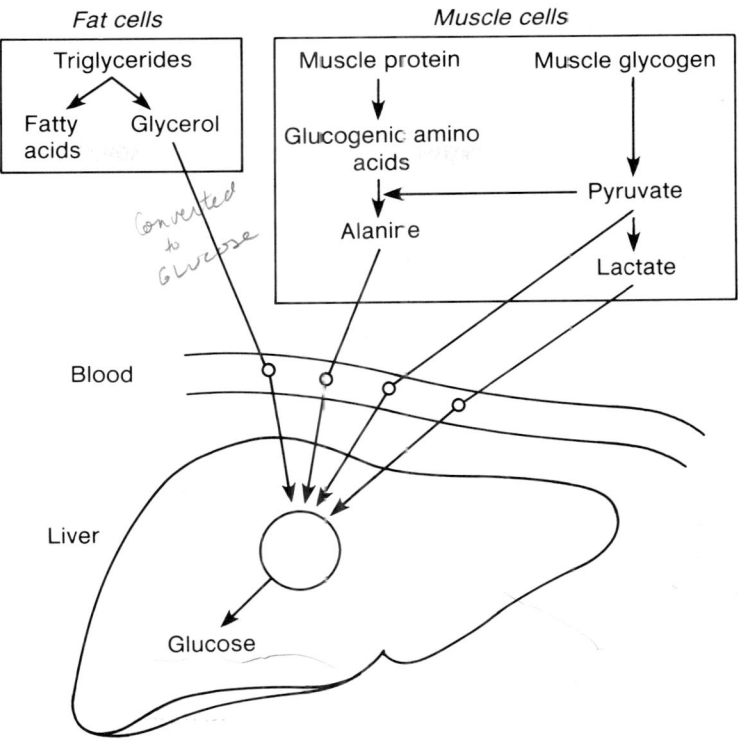

least 50–100 grams of carbohydrate are not consumed daily, then the body will produce the glucose it needs, primarily from protein in the body.

Fats in the body break down into fatty acids and glycerol. Although there is no mechanism in human cells to convert the fatty acids to glucose, the glycerol may be converted to glucose through the process of gluconeogenesis in the liver.

In addition, certain by-products of carbohydrate metabolism, notably pyruvate and lactate, may be converted back to glucose in the liver. Figure 3.5 illustrates some of the interrelationships among carbohydrate, fat, and protein in human nutrition.

What are the major functions of carbohydrate in human nutrition?

The major function of carbohydrate in human metabolism is to supply energy. Some body cells, such as the nerve cells in the brain and retina and the red blood cells, are normally totally dependent upon glucose for energy and require a constant source. Through a series of biochemical reactions in the body cells, glucose is hydrolyzed, eventually producing water, carbon dioxide, and energy. As noted in Chapter 2, carbohydrate can be used to produce energy either aerobically or anaerobically. Recall that in the lactic acid system, ATP is produced rapidly via anaerobic glycolysis, but for this system to continue functioning, the end product of glycolysis, pyruvic acid or pyruvate, must be converted into lactic acid. In the oxygen system, aerobic glycolysis predominates and pyruvic acid is converted into acetyl CoA, which enters into the Krebs cycle and electron transfer system for complete oxidation and the production of relatively large amounts of ATP.

The primary carbohydrate source of energy for physical performance is muscle glycogen, specifically the glycogen in the muscles that are active. As the muscle glycogen is being used during exercise, blood glucose may enter the muscles and also enter the energy pathways. In turn, the liver will release some of its glucose to help maintain blood glucose levels and prevent hypoglycemia.

Since hypoglycemia may disrupt functioning of the central nervous system (brain and spinal cord), the body attempts to maintain an optimal blood glucose level. Exercise itself, like insulin, facilitates the transport of blood glucose into the muscle. Thus, insulin levels normally drop during exercise so as to help maintain normal serum glucose. Other hormones, epinephrine (adrenaline), glucagon, and cortisol, also help maintain, and even increase, blood glucose levels during exercise. Epinephrine is secreted from the adrenal gland during exercise, particularly intense exercise, and stimulates the liver to release glucose; it also accelerates the use of glycogen in the muscle. Glucagon is released from the

Figure 3.5.
Interrelationships between carbohydrate, fat and protein metabolism in humans. All three nutrients may be utilized for energy, although the major energy sources are carbohydrate and fat. Excess carbohydrate may be converted to fat; the carbohydrate structure also may be used to form protein, but nitrogen must be added. Fat cannot be used to generate carbohydrate to any large extent, because acetyl CoA cannot be converted to pyruvate. The glycerol component of fat possibly may form very small amounts of carbohydrate. Fats may serve as a basis for the formation of protein, but again nitrogen must be added. Excess protein cannot be stored in the body but can be converted to either carbohydrate or fat.

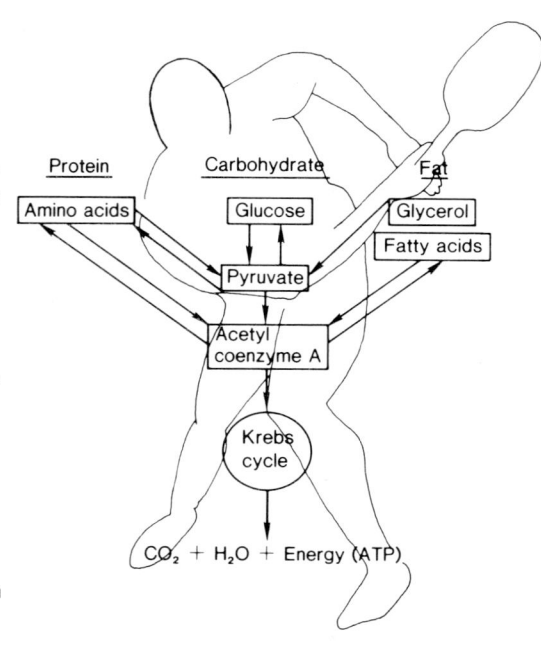

pancreas and generally increases the rate of gluco-neogenesis in the liver. Cortisol is secreted from the adrenal gland and facilitates the breakdown and release of amino acids from muscle tissue to provide some substrate to the liver for gluconeogenesis. The blood glucose normally increases during the initial stages of exercise and is normally well maintained by these hormonal mechanisms, but it does begin to decline in prolonged exercise tasks, sometimes to the point of hypoglycemia.

Carbohydrate is the most important energy food for exercise. Besides being the only food that can be used for anaerobic energy production in the lactic acid system, it is also the most efficient fuel for the oxygen system. If we look at the caloric value of carbohydrate (1 gram = 4 C) and fat (1 gram = 9 C) we might think that fat is a better source of energy. Indeed, this is so if we just look at Calories per gram. However, more oxygen is needed to metabolize the fat, and if we look at how many Calories we get from one liter of oxygen, we will find that carbohydrate yields about 5.05 and fat gives only 4.69. Thus, carbohydrate appears to be a more efficient fuel than fat, by about 7 percent. The metabolic pathways for carbohydrate are also more efficient than those for fat. In essence, carbohydrate is able to produce ATP for muscle contraction up to three times as rapidly as fat.

Carbohydrates have some functions in the body other than energy production. Monosaccharides can be used to form other smaller carbohydrate molecules such as trioses and pentoses. These substances may combine with other nutrients and form body chemicals essential to life, such as glycoproteins. Ribose is a key pentose that is a part of a number of indispensable compounds in the body. One of those compounds is RNA, or ribonucleic acid, which plays an important part in anabolic processes in the cells.

What effect does endurance training have on carbohydrate metabolism?

Since carbohydrate is a primary fuel for exercise, as you initiate an endurance exercise program a major proportion of your energy will be derived from your muscle glycogen stores. Recall that exercise itself exerts an insulin-type effect by facilitating the transport of blood glucose into the muscle both during and immediately following the exercise bout.

As you continue your endurance exercise program, such as running or bicycling, your body undergoes several significant changes that have implications for physical performance and the fuels used. Figure 3.6 schematically represents some of these changes at the cellular level. The following have been noted to occur following several months of endurance training:

Figure 3.6.
Some of the effects of aerobic or endurance training upon skeletal muscle. Increases in glycogen (G) and triglyceride (T) provide a greater energy store, while the increase in mitochondria size and number (M), myoglobin content (My), oxidative enzymes (ox), and slow-twitch muscle fiber size facilitates the use of oxygen for production of energy.

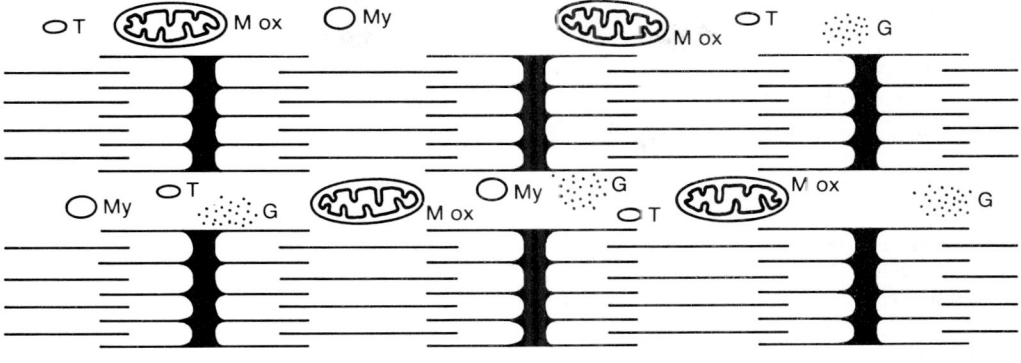

Untrained Muscle

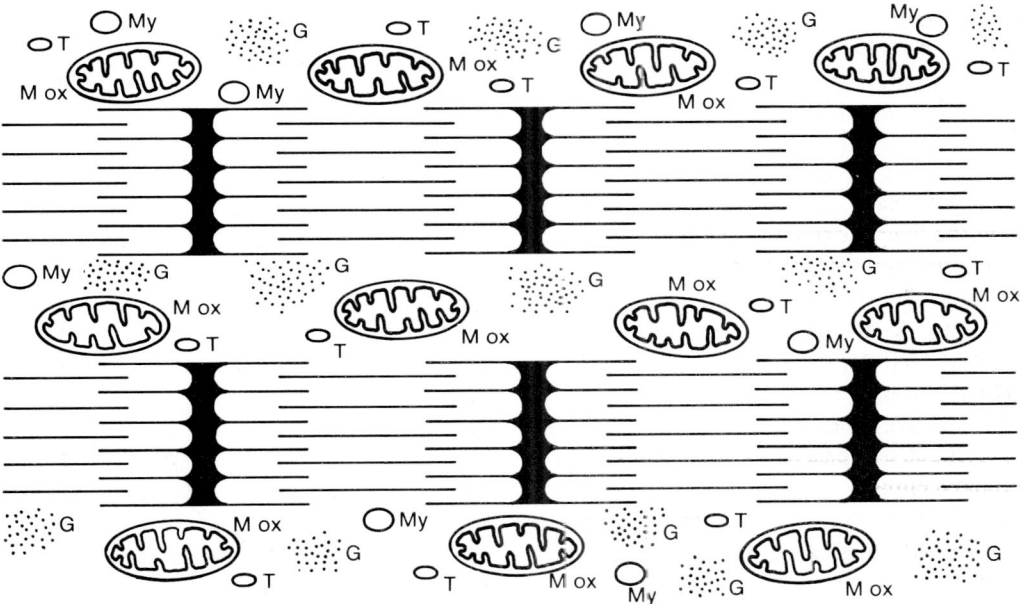

Trained Muscle

1. You will increase your VO_2 max through beneficial changes in your cardiovascular system and the oxygen system in your muscle tissues. This will help your body deliver and utilize more oxygen at the muscle tissue, significantly increasing your endurance capacity.

2. Of equal or greater importance, you will be able to work at a greater percentage of your VO_2 max without fatigue. At the beginning of your training program you may reach your steady-state threshold at about 50 percent of your VO_2 max and start producing lactic acid more rapidly, which may cause an early onset of fatigue. However, after training you may be able to perform at 70 percent or higher of your VO_2 max without lactic acid production. World-class marathoners may operate above 80 percent. You may wish to refer back to Figure 2.12.

3. The enzymes that metabolize carbohydrate in the muscle cells will increase, especially oxidative enzymes associated with the Krebs cycle. This allows your muscles to process carbohydrate more efficiently.

4. More glycogen is stored in the muscle. This means you may maintain an optimal speed for a longer time.

What do all these changes mean? You may be able to run a 10-kilometer (6.2 miles) road race at a 7-minute-per-mile pace instead of 8 minutes. You can cruise in high gear for longer periods because you have increased your ability to produce energy from carbohydrates. As we shall see in the next chapter, training also induces significant changes in the way your body uses fats during exercise, which may help to spare the utilization of your body stores of carbohydrate. This may be very beneficial in prolonged endurance events.

Carbohydrates for Exercise

In what types of activities does the body rely heavily on carbohydrate as an energy source?

Carbohydrate supplies approximately 40 percent of the body's energy needs during rest. As one engages in mild to moderate exercise, carbohydrate use increases to 50 percent or more. When exercise becomes more intense, such as when a person is working at 70–80 percent of capacity, carbohydrate is the preferred fuel. At maximal or supramaximal exercise efforts, it is used almost exclusively. Thus, carbohydrate may be the prime energy source for events lasting from such time frames as less than one minute to over an hour or two.

Carbohydrate use, then, is associated with the intensity level of the exercise. The more intense the exercise, the greater the percentage contribution of carbohydrate. Of course, the more intense the exercise, the sooner exhaustion occurs. A well conditioned person may be able to exercise for many hours at 40–50 percent of VO_2 max, for one to two hours at 70–80 percent of VO_2 max, but only for minutes at maximal or supramaximal levels of VO_2 max. As noted in Chapter 2, the fatigue that occurs in very high-intensity exercise of short duration, such as a minute or two, is probably due to the increased acidity resulting from the rapid production of lactic acid. On the other hand, the fatigue associated with more prolonged exercise may be connected with inadequate supplies of body carbohydrate stores due to inadequate dietary intake or depletion during exercise.

Carbohydrate is most important for prolonged endurance events lasting more than 90–120 minutes. Data from such endurance tasks as the Tour de France, the Daedalus project of human-powered flight over 70 miles across the Aegean Sea, the bicycle Race Across America, and the Ironman triathlon, illustrate the importance of dietary carbohydrate in sustaining high energy output for prolonged periods. Most of the athletes in these events consumed high-caloric diets rich in carbohydrates. A classic example is the ultradistance runner from Greece, Yannis Kouros, who won the Sydney to Melbourne race in Australia, a distance of approximately 600 miles, in 5 days and 5 hours, or about 114 miles of running per day. He consumed up to 13,400 Calories per day, with up to 98 percent being derived from carbohydrates. Data obtained from exercise tasks of lesser magnitude, such as the typical marathon, also provide evidence for the importance of carbohydrate as the prime energy fuel.

The nature of the environment during the event may also influence carbohydrate utilization. Performance at high altitudes and in both warm and very cold environments will increase the utilization of carbohydrate as an energy source.

How do low levels of carbohydrate stores in the body adversely affect performance?

Recall that blood glucose, liver glycogen, and muscle glycogen are the three main energy sources of carbohydrate in the body. The blood glucose is in very short supply, so as it is being used during exercise it must be replenished from the liver glycogen stores. A depletion of liver glycogen may lead to hypoglycemia, resulting in a feeling of weakness. Because muscle glycogen is the primary carbohydrate energy source during exercise, low levels also may lead to impaired performance. Thus, both hypoglycemia and muscle glycogen depletion have been identified as causative factors in the development of fatigue.

Hypoglycemia is known to impair the functioning of the central nervous system and is often accompanied by acute feelings of dizziness, muscular weakness, and fatigue. The normal blood glucose level usually ranges from 80–100 mg of glucose per 100 ml of blood (4.4–5.5 mmol per liter). As this level gets progressively lower, hypoglycemic symptoms may develop. The point usually used to identify hypoglycemia during research studies with exercise is 45 mg per 100 ml, or 2.5 mmol per liter, although some investigators have used higher levels.

Hypoglycemia may be a concern of athletes in several situations. One possibility is a reactive hypoglycemia following the consumption of a high carbohydrate meal 30–60 minutes or more prior to an athletic event. If hypoglycemia developed just prior to or during the early stages of the event, the effect could impair performance. This possibility will be covered under the next question.

Hypoglycemia may also develop during prolonged exercise tasks, but it may be dependent upon the intensity level of the exercise. In low-intensity exercise, such as 30–50 percent of VO_2 max, the primary fuel is fat and hence the use of carbohydrate is minimized. Moreover, at this low-intensity level gluconeogenesis can help maintain blood glucose above hypoglycemic levels. However, in exercise tasks above 50 percent VO_2 max, muscle glycogen use increases, more blood glucose is used, and gluconeogenesis is not rapid enough to replace that which is used.

During the early part of prolonged exercise, muscle glycogen is the major source of energy derived from carbohydrate, although some blood glucose is utilized. However, as muscle glycogen levels get low in the latter stages of an endurance task, blood glucose may account for 75–90 percent of the muscular energy from carbohydrate. At this high rate of blood glucose utilization, the liver glycogen stores become rapidly depleted and thus the blood glucose levels fall toward hypoglycemia.

Whether hypoglycemia impairs physical performance may depend upon the individual. Some earlier research reported that exercise-induced hypoglycemia led to the expected symptoms, including dizziness and partial blackout. However, more contemporary research from three different laboratories has revealed that a number of subjects may become hypoglycemic during the latter stages of a prolonged exercise task to exhaustion at 60–75 percent of their VO_2 max, and yet are able to continue exercising while hypoglycemic, even at levels as low as 25 mg per 100 ml. It appears that the role hypoglycemia plays in the etiology of fatigue in prolonged exercise has not been totally elucidated. Nevertheless, prevention of hypoglycemia is one of the major objectives of carbohydrate feeding during prolonged exercise.

Investigators generally agree that prolonged, moderately high to high intensity aerobic exercise is limited by muscle glycogen stores. The depletion of muscle glycogen seems to be a limiting factor when exercising at 65–90 percent of VO_2 max. A number of studies have shown that physical exhaustion was correlated with very low muscle glycogen levels, but others have shown some glycogen remaining even though subjects were exhausted. Costill has indicated that performance would be adversely affected only when muscle glycogen levels went below 40 mmol/kg of muscle tissue. It may be that complete depletion of muscle glycogen is not necessary for performance to suffer, for glycolysis may be impaired with lower glycogen levels or the glycogen in the muscle fiber may be located where it is not readily available for glycolysis.

The fatigue that develops may be related to the depletion of muscle glycogen from specific muscle fiber types. In prolonged exercise at 60–75 percent of VO_2 max the Type I fibers (red, slow twitch) and Type IIa (red, fast twitch) are recruited during the early stages of the task, but as the muscle glycogen is depleted the athlete must recruit the Type IIb (white, fast twitch) to maintain the same pace. However, it takes more mental effort to recruit the Type IIb fibers, which will be more stressful to the athlete. Type IIb fibers also are more likely to produce lactic acid, increasing the acidity, which may increase the perceived stress of the exercise. What usually happens is that as the muscle glycogen becomes depleted in the red fiber types, the muscle cell will rely more on fat as the primary energy source. Since fat is a less efficient fuel than carbohydrate, the pace will slow down.

Fatigue in very high-intensity, anaerobic-type exercise generally is attributed to the detrimental effects of the acidity in the muscle cell associated with lactic acid production. Research has now shown that maximal high-intensity exercise, lasting only about 60 seconds, is not impaired by a very low muscle glycogen concentration, approximately 30 mmol/kg muscle. However, with somewhat longer anaerobic tasks, approximating three minutes, one laboratory study reported a reduced performance in the time to exhaustion test after four days of a low carbohydrate, high fat diet when compared to a normal, mixed diet and a high carbohydrate diet. Although muscle glycogen levels were not measured, a logical assumption is that they were lower on the low carbohydrate diet.

In addition, field research has suggested that the slower overall sprint speed, such as in the latter parts of prolonged athletic contests like soccer and ice hockey, may be due to muscle glycogen depletion. Muscle biopsies of these athletes revealed very low glycogen levels, which were attributed not only to the strenuous exercise in the contest but also to the fact that these athletes were consuming diets low in carbohydrates. Also, as shall be noted below, low muscle glycogen stores may lead to a decrease in exercise intensity during training.

In summary, low levels of glycogen in the white, fast-twitch IIb muscle fibers may limit performance in intermittent, anaerobic-type exercise tasks. Both hypoglycemia and low glycogen in the red muscle fiber types, most likely a combination of the two, may be contributing factors to fatigue in prolonged endurance exercise.

Will eating carbohydrate immediately before or during an event improve physical performance?

Because hypoglycemia or muscle glycogen depletion may be causes of fatigue during endurance exercise, supplementation with glucose or other forms of carbohydrate before or during exercise may be theorized to delay the onset of fatigue and improve performance. Thousands of studies have been conducted on this topic since carbohydrates were identified as the most efficient energy source for exercise over 70 years ago, and researchers interest in this topic remains unabated today. In recent years the research designs have usually been highly sophisticated as investigators have attempted to provide specific answers relative to the type, amount, and timing of carbohydrate ingestion before and during performance.

The reviewer attempting to synthesize the available research is confronted with a difficult task since the experimental designs varied considerably. The amount and type of carbohydrate ingested, the use of liquid or solid forms, the method of administration (oral ingestion or venous infusion), the time prior to or during the exercise that it was taken, the diet of the subject several days prior to the study, the amount of glycogen in the muscle and liver, the intensity and duration of the exercise, the type of exercise task (running, swimming, cycling, etc.), the fitness level of the subjects, the environmental temperature, and the method used to evaluate blood glucose and muscle glycogen utilization are some of the important differences between studies. Needless to say, not all results were consistent.

Nevertheless, based upon an overall review of these studies with the given limitations, the following generalizations and practical recommendations appear to be logical. More specific information is provided in the following question.

1. If the individual has normal liver and muscle glycogen stores, glucose feedings are unnecessary for continuous exercise work bouts lasting 60–90 minutes or less. Since the body can store carbohydrate in the muscles and liver, the usefulness of glucose or other carbohydrate intake before or during exercise depends on the adequacy of those supplies already in the muscle and liver to meet energy needs. The muscle and liver glycogen stores should be adequate to meet carbohydrate energy needs. The critical point is to consume substantial amounts of carbohydrates the day or two

prior to the event and to decrease the duration and intensity of training to assure ample endogenous glycogen supplies.

The available research has shown that the consumption of glucose, fructose, sucrose, maltodextrin (a glucose polymer), or other carbohydrate combinations immediately prior to events of short or moderate duration has a negligible effect upon performance. Adding a gallon of gas to a full tank will not make a car go faster during a short ride. The same is true of sugar to a muscle already filled with glycogen. Similarly, if the muscle glycogen levels are low and the exercise task is somewhat prolonged, then ingestion of carbohydrate prior to the exercise bout may improve performance.

2. Carbohydrate intake 60–240 minutes prior to prolonged exercise tasks (longer than 90 minutes) may enhance performance. Research emanating from the Exercise Physiology Laboratory at Ohio Sate University, under the guidance of David Lamb and William Sherman, has demonstrated improved performance when adequate carbohydrate was consumed either 1, 3, or 4 hours prior to a prolonged exercise task involving simulated racing conditions during the latter stage. Sherman recently suggested that preexercise carbohydrate feedings may increase performance by delaying the normal decline in blood glucose either by enhanced release of glucose by the liver, by continued gastric emptying and intestinal absorption of the ingested carbohydrate, or both.

3. Individuals who may be prone to reactive hypoglycemia should avoid carbohydrate intake, particularly high glycemic index foods, 15–60 minutes prior to performance. Simple sugars ingested within this time frame may actually impair physical performance in such individuals because of the adverse effects of reactive hypoglycemia, such as muscular weakness. Moreover, this same insulin response may speed up muscle glycogen utilization. This may be a disadvantage to the marathoner, whose glycogen levels may be depleted too early in the race. Several earlier studies showed that run time to exhaustion was shorter by about 20–25 percent after athletes consumed 2–3 ounces of glucose within an hour before the endurance test.

However, not all individuals experience reactive hypoglycemia. In a study by John Seifert, subjects were given various carbohydrate solutions to raise their insulin levels; when their insulin levels peaked, they undertook an exercise task at 60 percent of VO_2 max for 50 minutes. No hypoglycemia developed, nor were there any adverse sensory or psychological responses. In another study from Penn State, candy bars containing either 46 or 92 grams of carbohydrate were consumed 30 minutes prior to a 90-minute cycling task at 70 percent VO_2 max. These investigators did note hypoglycemia about 15 minutes into the exercise bout, but it was transient and glucose levels returned to baseline by 30 minutes. There were no adverse effects on metabolic processes or performance. Other well controlled studies have reported no adverse effects of glucose, fructose, or maltodextrin ingestion 30–45 minutes prior to prolonged exercise. Compared to placebo conditions with artificially sweetened water, the various carbohydrate solutions elicited no significant differences in muscle glycogen utilization or exercise capacity when subjects were exercising at 55–75 percent of VO_2 max.

Although these studies have shown no adverse effect on performance, neither have they shown an improved performance. It may be best to avoid this technique if possible and to use the other recommendations advanced above and below relative to timing of intake. However, for individuals not prone to reactive hypoglycemia and who for one reason or another cannot adhere to the recommended time schedule, the consumption of carbohydrates within 15–60 minutes prior to performance may confer some benefits.

4. Carbohydrate intake immediately prior to (within 5–10 minutes) or during prolonged endurance exercise tasks of two hours or more may help delay the development of fatigue if the athlete is exercising at a level greater than 50 percent VO_2 max, such as 60–75 percent. The majority of the studies, including controlled laboratory investigations and field research involving different types of endurance athletes, support this point of view. Moreover, research has shown that individuals engaged in endurance type contests with intermittent bouts of sprinting, such as soccer, may maintain faster speed levels in the latter stages of the contest with this technique.

At this level of exercise intensity the insulin response to glucose ingestion is suppressed; in addition, the secretion of epinephrine is increased. These two hormonal responses interact to help maintain or elevate the blood glucose level and prevent the hypoglycemic response that typically may occur if more time elapses between the ingestion of the carbohydrate and the initiation of exercise. Carbohydrate ingested during exercise can help maintain blood glucose levels and reduce the psychological perception of effort, as measured by the ratings of perceived exertion, during the latter stages of an endurance task. As the exercise task continues and the muscle glycogen level falls, the amount of energy derived from the ingested carbohydrates increases.

Andrew Coggan and Edward Coyle, in research conducted at the University of Texas, have noted that even a single carbohydrate feeding late in a prolonged exercise bout may help replenish blood glucose levels, increase carbohydrate oxidation, and delay fatigue.

5. Using labeled carbohydrate sources and analyzing the expired carbon dioxide for radioactivity, investigators have shown that the ingested, or exogenous, carbohydrate may be used as an energy source within 5–10 minutes, indicating that it may empty rapidly from the stomach, be absorbed from the small intestine into the blood, and enter into metabolic pathways. A number of studies have shown that the ingested glucose may contribute a significant percentage, as much as 60–70 percent, of the carbohydrate energy source during exercise, particularly as the endogenous liver and muscle glycogen stores become depleted.

6. The precise mechanism whereby glucose ingestion helps delay the onset of fatigue has not been totally elucidated, but the available data suggest the delaying effect may be related to the maintenance of higher blood glucose levels, possibly by sparing liver glycogen, and the prevention of hypoglycemia in susceptible individuals; the blood glucose would be available to enter the muscle and provide a source of energy for aerobic glycolysis. As noted above,

exogenous glucose is used increasingly as the exercise task becomes prolonged. Some research has shown that glucose ingestion could make an endurance task psychologically easier and suggested that the physiological effects of the glucose, either in the brain or in the muscles, reduced the stressful effects of exercise.

Although sparing of muscle glycogen could be another benefit of carbohydrate ingestion before or during exercise, this does not appear to be the case. David Costill has noted that no data are available to support the concept that carbohydrate intake during exercise will reduce the muscle reliance upon muscle glycogen stores. In a recent unique experiment from the University of Texas, subjects received venous glucose infusions to maintain a hyperglycemic state during two hours of exercise at 73 percent of VO_2 max, but the net rate of muscle glycogen utilization was not affected compared to control conditions.

Nevertheless, Costill still notes that our understanding of the mechanisms underlying the enhanced utilization of carbohydrate intake during exercise and improved performance is still unclear.

7. Although glucose ingestion may help delay fatigue during moderately high intensity exercise, it cannot totally prevent the onset of fatigue. It appears that the blood glucose cannot meet the energy demands of the muscle at this intensity level, and therefore when the muscle glycogen stores are reduced to a critical level fatigue will be evident by a reduced pace. Research suggests that the maximal amount of energy that may be derived from the exogenous carbohydrate is approximately one gram per minute, much lower than the energy needs at 65–85 percent of VO_2 max.

8. Research out of Ohio State University has indicated that although the intake of carbohydrate either before or during exercise may separately enhance performance, the best effect was observed when carbohydrate was consumed both before and during exercise.

9. The intake of carbohydrate during prolonged exercise may decrease the reliance upon gluconeogenesis. Recent data indicate carbohydrate intake decreased the catabolism of amino acids during prolonged

exertion. Such an effect may help prevent the use of muscle proteins.

10. Probably the most important recommendation is for the athlete to experiment with different types and amounts of carbohydrate during training before using them in competition. Just as it is important for you to know your optimal race pace for an endurance event, so too must you know how well you can tolerate different concentrations and types of carbohydrates. For example, a highly concentrated sugar consumed just prior to competition may create an osmotic effect and actually hold excess fluid in the stomach or intestines, which may cause gastrointestinal distress and impaired performance. Just as you train your muscles to learn their capacity, you may also be able to train your digestive system to know its limits. Ron Maughan, an internationally respected authority in sports nutrition, indicated that the optimal strategy relative to carbohydrate utilization is to use your own subjective experience.

When, how much, and in what form should carbohydrates be consumed before or during exercise?

The most common athletic events or physical performance activities that may benefit from carbohydrate feedings are those associated with long duration, 90–120 minutes or more, at moderate to high intensity levels. Marathon running, cross-country skiing, and endurance cycling are common sports of this kind. Other sports that require intermittent bouts of intensive activity over a prolonged period, such as soccer, may also benefit. However, the individual participating in these activities, particularly under warm or hot environmental conditions, also needs to replenish fluid losses incurred through sweating. In such cases, fluid replenishment is more critical than carbohydrate. The topic of fluid replacement during exercise is covered in more detail in Chapter 8, but since carbohydrate is one of the contents in the majority of the sport drinks developed as fluid replacements for athletes, its role is discussed briefly here.

Many studies have been conducted in recent years to determine the best carbohydrate feeding regimen to prevent fatigue during prolonged exercise. A number of different variables have been studied, such as the timing of the feeding and the type, amount, and concentration of carbohydrate.

The following points represent the general conclusions and recommendations from the available research for individuals who may be exercising at 60–80 percent of their VO$_2$ max or greater for two hours or longer. But remember, different individuals may have varied reactions to carbohydrate intake, so athletes should experiment in training before using these recommendations in competition:

1. The amount of carbohydrate ingested four hours prior to performance should be based upon body weight. Several studies have used 4–5 grams/kg with good results. For an athlete who weighs 60 kg (132 pounds), the recommended amount would be 240–300 grams. The carbohydrates could be consumed in any of several forms, including fluids such as juices or glucose polymer solutions, or solid carbohydrates such as fruits or starches. The fiber content should be minimized to prevent possible intestinal problems during exercise. Keep in mind that 300 grams of carbohydrate is about 1,200 Calories, a somewhat substantial meal. You may consult Appendix H for an expanded list of foods high in carbohydrate, but use the following for a quick estimate from the two food exchanges high in carbohydrates, plus several sport drinks:

   1 fruit exchange = 15 grams
     1 apple
     1 orange
     1/2 banana
     4 ounces orange juice
   1 bread/starch exchange = 15 grams
     1 slice bread
     1/2 cup cereal
     1/4 large bagel
     1/2 cup cooked pasta
     1 small baked potato
     7–8 ounces = 15 grams
   Sport drinks
     Exceed
     Gatorade

2. If carbohydrate is consumed approximately one hour prior to performance, about 1–2 grams/kg (60–120 grams for a 60-kg athlete) may be recommended, for these levels have been shown to enhance performance in several studies. Both glucose polymers and foods with a low glycemic index have been used successfully. One study using only 12 grams one hour prior to performance has shown no beneficial effect.

3. If carbohydrates are consumed immediately before exercise, i.e., within ten minutes of the start, about 50–60 grams of a glucose polymer in a 40–50 percent solution has been used effectively in some studies. Dry glucose polymers are available commercially, such as Gatorlode (not Gatorade), and Exceed. One teaspoon is 5 grams. To make a 50 percent solution containing 50 grams of the polymer, put 10 level teaspoons of the polymer into 100 milliliters (about 3–4 ounces) of water. To make a 7.5 percent solution containing 15 grams, put 3 teaspoons of the polymer into 200 milliliters (about 7 ounces) of water.

4. During the exercise, feedings every 15–30 minutes appear to be a reasonable schedule. Costill has noted that the maximal amount of carbohydrate that can be ingested, assimilated, and utilized during exercise has not been established. Researchers from the University of Limburg in the Netherlands recently reported that cyclists could assimilate 0.92–3.70 grams/kg body weight of a glucose polymer immediately before and during a two-hour cycling task, but there was a limit to the amount the body could use. They theorized that some of the excess carbohydrate was stored as glycogen in the inactive muscles.

   Reasonable estimates from the research literature suggest that athletes may use approximately 60 grams of ingested carbohydrate per hour, about 1 gram per minute. Therefore, the athlete should attempt to consume a 5–10 percent solution containing about 15–20 grams of carbohydrate every 15–20 minutes during exercise. Consumption of solutions above 10 percent during exercise may delay gastric emptying and cause gastrointestinal distress, but some athletes, such as ultramarathoners who may exercise at a relatively low intensity, may tolerate higher concentrations, ranging from 20–50 percent.

   Probably the most effective protocol would be to use a high concentration immediately before or during the first 20 minutes of the exercise (about 1 gram/kg body weight), and then use the lower concentrations (about 0.2–0.3 gram/kg body weight) at regular intervals. Because of the nature of their sport, soccer players and other such athletes may need to consume a high concentration before the game and during halftime.

5. A number of different types of carbohydrates have been studied, including glucose, glucose polymers, cornstarch, fructose, and sucrose, both individually and in various combinations. Most have been given in a liquid form, but some studies used solid carbohydrates. In general, there appears to be no difference between these different types of carbohydrates as a means to enhance endurance performance when used appropriately. However, there may be some important considerations relative to the use of fructose or the glucose polymers.

Fructose has been theorized to be a better source of carbohydrate than glucose because it is absorbed more slowly from the intestine and hence will not create an insulin response and the potential reactive hypoglycemia. Indeed, research has shown that fructose, compared to glucose, may lead to a more stable blood sugar during the early stages of prolonged exercise when ingested 45 minutes prior to the activity. However, when fructose is ingested immediately before or during exercise, its effect on the blood sugar and carbohydrate metabolism appears to be little different than that of glucose. Moreover, fructose does not spare the use of muscle glycogen any more or less effectively than glucose. In addition, since fructose is absorbed slowly from the intestinal tract, it can create a significant osmotic effect in the intestines leading to diarrhea and gastrointestinal distress in some individuals. A recent study from the Exercise Physiology Laboratory at the Quaker Oats Company indicated that a 6 percent solution of fructose, when compared to similar solutions of glucose and sucrose, caused significant gastrointestinal distress and an impairment in exercise performance. Additional research from France has noted that exogenous fructose was less readily available for oxidation than glucose. On the basis of these findings, the athlete should be cautious in using fructose as the sole source of carbohydrate before or during exercise.

Recall that a glucose polymer is a molecular chain of glucose molecules that is shorter than starch but longer than the simple sugars and is derived via a partial hydrolysis of polysaccharides, such as cornstarch. Its major characteristics include a rapid digestibility and absorption, and a lesser osmotic effect than simple sugars, which permits a more effective absorption of water from the intestinal tract. A recent meta-analysis (a statistical method comparing the findings of a large number of different studies) revealed that glucose polymer solutions, as compared with simple sugar solutions, caused less inhibition of gastric emptying both at rest and during exercise. Thus, glucose polymers can provide both glucose and fluids rather effectively. Many of the studies cited as showing improvements in performance when carbohydrate was ingested immediately before or during exercise used glucose polymers. Although most of the studies that compared different types of carbohydrates consumed during exercise have reported little or no differences among the types relative to performance, the available research suggests that a glucose polymer may be the preferable choice because of its lower osmotic effect compared to glucose and its lesser chance of causing gastrointestinal distress than fructose.

This topic is covered in more detail in Chapter 8, but it is deemed important to reemphasize the point that if water intake is the most important concern, then the concentration of carbohydrate, in any form, in the ingested solution should be reduced.

What is the importance of carbohydrate replenishment after prolonged exercise?

There are several possible applications of this question. One is the athlete who may be involved in a prolonged exercise bout, have a rest period of 1–4 hours, and then must exercise again. A second application is the athlete who trains intensely every day and must have an adequate recovery in the one-day rest interval. A third application, covered in the next section, is the technique of carbohydrate loading.

Several studies have shown that ingesting carbohydrate during the rest interval between two prolonged exercise bouts improves performance in the second bout. This finding is comparable to the beneficial effects of carbohydrate intake during prolonged exercise bouts. The carbohydrate can help restore blood glucose levels but may also be used to resynthesize muscle glycogen. Glucose, sucrose, or glucose polymers would appear to be the preferred source of carbohydrate, for they apparently lead to a faster restoration of muscle glycogen than does a meal high in complex carbohydrates. Research by Blom and his associates in Norway has suggested that a dose of about 0.7 grams of glucose or sucrose per kg body weight every two hours may effectively increase muscle glycogen levels. For a 70-kg athlete, this would be about 50 grams, about 10 level teaspoons of pure carbohydrate. Other research suggests a 20–25 percent solution containing one gram or more of carbohydrate/kg body weight—about 50–100 grams of glucose, sucrose, or glucose polymer—should be consumed immediately after exercise, followed by an additional 50 grams each hour. With this protocol, the rate of muscle glycogen synthesis is about 7 percent per hour. Ingestion of fructose or complex carbohydrates with a low glycemic index results in a much slower rate of resynthesis. It is also probably better to rest during the recovery interval because mild exercise during this time has been shown to impede the resynthesis of muscle glycogen.

Success in athletic competition is contingent upon optimal training, and for the endurance athlete optimal training may be contingent upon adequate nutrition, primarily the ingestion of sufficient carbohydrate intake every day. Some early Scandinavian research showed that the amount of time that an athlete could train at a given pace is dependent upon the amount of glycogen in the muscle at the start of the exercise. The greater the amount, the greater the time the individual could train at a set pace. Unfortunately, many endurance athletes may be consuming much less than the recommended amount. A study of elite cyclists competing in a 12-day road race reported that only 51 percent of the dietary Calories were derived from carbohydrate. David Costill, in several of his many studies on carbohydrate metabolism in athletes, found that runners or swimmers who trained hard every day and consumed a diet inadequate in carbohydrates experienced low levels of muscle glycogen and impaired training ability.

Thus, Costill and other researchers such as Edward Coyle, William Fink, John Ivy, David Lamb, and William Sherman recommend that the endurance athlete who trains for 1–2 hours daily may need about 500–600 grams of carbohydrate in the daily diet to replace muscle glycogen stores and maintain a quality training program. This represents 2,000–2,400 Calories from carbohydrate, or about 65–70 percent of the daily caloric intake of an athlete consuming 3,500 Calories.

The recommendation of Costill and others appears to have merit. For one, research has shown that adequate daily carbohydrate intake helps prevent the catabolism of muscle protein during intensive training, which could impair the proper adaptation to training. Also, although not all research is in agreement, the majority of studies with competitive and recreational athletes have shown that increasing the percentage of daily Calories derived from carbohydrate helped improve performance in exercise tasks during training. How athletes feel psychologically during training, as measured by the vigor and fatigue components of the Profile of Mood States (POMS) questionnaire, may also improve when switching to diets higher in carbohydrate. In general, the normal carbohydrate intake of these athletes was increased from approximately 40–45 percent to 65–70 percent of the daily Calories for a week or more. In one study, the muscle glycogen content of rowers increased and they experienced improved performance in three simulated 2,500-meter race workouts each week. Soccer players improved performance on an intermittent exercise task designed to mimic physical activity in a game, while runners were able to endure longer on a treadmill run to exhaustion. In a study with triathletes, Mindy Millard-Stafford used a glucose polymer to increase the daily carbohydrate intake by 14 percent compared to a placebo period. She reported a significant improvement in treadmill endurance following 30 minutes of swimming, cycling, and running. It appears logical to assume that such enhanced training may equate with improved competitive performance.

Consuming 500–600 grams of carbohydrate per day should help fully replenish muscle glycogen in 20–24 hours. Research by Ivy has suggested that if glucose is consumed within two hours after the training session, muscle glycogen will be synthesized at a faster rate compared to eating at a later time. Zachwieja and others also reported that glycogen resynthesis is faster in muscles that have experienced a greater glycogen depletion. As suggested above, glucose, sucrose, or a glucose polymer in solution form may be a convenient means to consume carbohydrate immediately after exercise. The remaining carbohydrate should be derived from other natural sources in the diet, including both simple carbohydrates in fruits and complex carbohydrates in grains and other foods with adequate dietary fiber. Research has shown that although simple carbohydrates may speed resynthesis of muscle glycogen for the first six hours after exercise, a diet high in complex carbohydrates and fiber resulted in the same muscle glycogen levels 20 hours after exercise. Thus, on a daily basis it is important to include carbohydrates that may also confer some health benefits. Some examples of high carbohydrate diets are given in the following section.

Carbohydrate Loading - 2/yr,

What is carbohydrate, or glycogen, loading?

Because carbohydrate becomes increasingly important as a fuel for muscular exercise as the intensity of the exercise increases, and because the amount of carbohydrate stored in the body is limited, muscle and liver glycogen depletion could be factors that may limit performance capacity in distance events characterized by high levels of energy expenditure for prolonged periods. **Carbohydrate loading,** also called glycogen loading and glycogen supercompensation, is a dietary technique designed to promote a significant increase in the glycogen content in both the liver and the muscles in an attempt to delay the onset of fatigue. It is generally used for 3–7 days in preparation for major athletic competitions.

What type of athlete would benefit from carbohydrate loading?

In general, carbohydrate loading is primarily suited for those individuals who will sustain high levels of continuous energy expenditure for prolonged periods, such as long-distance runners, swimmers, bicyclists, triathletes, cross-country skiers, and similar athletes. In addition, athletes who are involved in prolonged stop-and-go activities, such as soccer, lacrosse, and tournament-play sports like tennis and handball, may benefit. In essence, carbohydrate loading may be effective for athletes engaged in events that use muscle glycogen as the major energy source and that may lead to a depletion of the glycogen in the muscle fibers. Body builders have been reported to carbohydrate load in attempts to appear more muscular owing to increased muscle glycogen levels and associated water retention.

Recall from Chapter 2 that humans have several different types of skeletal muscle fibers. In general, the slow-twitch red and fast-twitch red fibers are used mainly during long, continuous activities and are aerobic in nature, whereas the fast-twitch white fibers are used for short, fast activities and are anaerobic in nature. Consider the differences between a distance runner and a soccer player. The former may run at a steady pace for hours, whereas the latter will constantly be changing speeds, with many bouts of full speed interspersed with recovery

periods of slower running. Research has shown that glycogen depletion patterns of the two different muscle fiber types are related to the type of exercise. Long, continuous exercise depletes glycogen principally in the slow-twitch red and fast-twitch red fibers, whereas fast, intermittent bouts of exercise with periods of rest, actually a form of interval training, primarily deplete glycogen in the fast-twitch white fibers. However, it should be noted that glycogen depletion may occur in all types of fibers in either long continuous or intermittent exercise and may be quite appreciable, depending upon intensity and duration of the exercise bouts. If carbohydrate loading works for the specific muscle fiber involved, then both types of athletes may benefit. Both should have greater glycogen stores in the latter stages of their respective athletic contests.

Although athletes in most sports may benefit from an increased carbohydrate content in the diet, the full procedure of carbohydrate loading is not necessary for the vast majority of athletes. For example, research has shown that it does not increase the speed of runners in events ranging from 10 kilometers to the half-marathon (6.2–13.1 miles) compared to a normal, mixed diet.

How do you carbohydrate load?

As you might suspect, the key to carbohydrate loading is to switch from the normal, balanced diet to one very high in carbohydrate content. The original, classic carbohydrate-loading technique, emanating from earlier Scandinavian research, involved a glycogen-depletion stage induced by prolonged exercise and a restricted diet. For example, a runner might go for an 18- to 20-mile run to use as much stored glycogen as possible, followed by a two- to three-day period when very little carbohydrate was ingested. Exercise is continued during this two- to three-day period to keep glycogen stores low. Following the depletion stage, the loading stage began. During this phase, carbohydrate may contribute 70 or more percent of the caloric input. The intensity and duration of exercise during this phase was reduced considerably. The usual case was to rest fully for two to three days. Thus, the classic carbohydrate-loading pattern involved three stages: depletion, carbohydrate deprivation (high fat–protein diet), and carbohydrate loading. However, this original method may be particularly difficult to tolerate, especially if one tries to exercise at high levels during the depletion phase. The lack of carbohydrate in the diet combined with the exercise bouts may elicit symptoms of hypoglycemia (weakness, lethargy, irritability). Moreover, prolonged exhaustive exercise

Table 3.3 Different methods for carbohydrate loading

A recommended method

1st day:	depletion exercise (optional)
2nd day:	mixed diet, moderate carbohydrate; tapering exercise
3rd day:	mixed diet, moderate carbohydrate; tapering exercise
4th day:	mixed diet, moderate carbohydrate; tapering exercise
5th day:	high carbohydrate diet; tapering exercise
6th day:	high carbohydrate diet; tapering exercise or rest
7th day:	high carbohydrate diet; tapering exercise or rest
8th day:	competition

Original, classic method

1st day:	depletion exercise
2nd day:	high protein-fat diet; low carbohydrate; tapering exercise
3rd day:	high protein-fat diet; low carbohydrate; tapering exercise
4th day:	high protein-fat diet; low carbohydrate; tapering exercise
5th day:	high carbohydrate diet; tapering exercise
6th day:	high carbohydrate diet; tapering exercise or rest
7th day:	high carbohydrate diet; tapering exercise or rest
8th day:	competition

High carbohydrate diet: 500–600 g per day; about 70–80 percent of dietary Calories should be carbohydrate.

may lead to muscle trauma which may actually impair the storage of extra glycogen. This classic, original method is presented in Table 3.3.

Although some early research supported this technique, more recent data suggest that this strict routine may be unnecessary, particularly the total program of depletion. For example, in trained runners, research has shown that simply changing to a very high carbohydrate diet, combined with one or two days of rest or reduced activity levels (tapering), will effectively increase muscle and liver glycogen. Recent well controlled research by Blom, Costill, and Vollestad noted that exhaustive running is not necessary to achieve muscle glycogen supercompensation. It appears to be important to continue endurance training, or other high intensity training specific to the sport, during the 7–14 days prior to competition. Such training will serve to maintain adequate levels of glycogen synthase, the enzyme in the muscle that synthesizes glycogen from glucose. Evidence also suggests that if the total carbohydrate content is consumed over the entire week, in contrast to concentrating it in 2–3 days, there will be little difference in the muscle-glycogen content between the two techniques.

Although there may be a number of variations in the carbohydrate-loading protocol, a generally recommended format is also presented in Table 3.3. The interested athlete may want to experiment with both techniques, and also make adjustments through experience.

The high-carbohydrate diet should contain about 8–10 grams of carbohydrate per kilogram of body weight, or about 400–700 grams per day, depending on the size of the individual, which is not too different from the generally recommended dietary content of carbohydrate for the endurance athlete in regular training. It is important to note that the athlete should not change his or her diet drastically prior to competition. Consuming a high carbohydrate diet during training will condition the body to metabolize carbohydrate properly during this loading phase. Table 3.4 represents a general dietary plan for carbohydrate loading. The total caloric value and grams of carbohydrate should be adjusted to individual needs. They are dependent upon the size of the individual and daily energy expenditure in exercise. It is important not to consume excess Calories, for they may be converted into body fat if in excess of the maximal storage capacity of the muscle and liver for glycogen.

Research by Costill and his associates at Ball State University has revealed that both simple and complex carbohydrates replace muscle glycogen at about the same rate over a 24-hour period. As already noted, glucose or sucrose may be best for rapid resynthesis of glycogen for a 2–6 hour recovery period, but the synthesis rates for simple and complex carbohydrates appear to be equal over a period of 1 to 3 days. Because glycogen loading for long-distance events occurs over two to three days, it would be wise to stress complex carbohydrates in the diet because of their higher nutrient content. However, simple carbohydrates may also be used effectively to increase muscle glycogen stores, as can the high carbohydrate sport drinks such as Gatorlode and Exceed High-Carbohydrate Source. Moreover, the diet should also include the daily requirements for protein and fat.

Most prolonged endurance events begin in the morning. The last large meal should be about 15 hours prior to race time, possibly topped off with a simple carbohydrate snack before retiring for the night. Some athletes use a glucose polymer for the

Table 3.4   Daily food plan for carbohydrate loading

Dietary sources of fats, proteins, and carbohydrates	Amount and Calories	Grams of carbohydrate, protein, and fat
Meat, fish, poultry, eggs, cheese, Select low-fat items	6–8 oz Calories: 330–440	0 grams carbohydrate * 42–56 grams protein 18–24 grams fat
Breads, cereals, and grain products	10–20 servings Calories 800–1600	150–300 grams carbohydrate 24–60 grams protein
Vegetables, high Calorie (such as corn)	4 servings Calories: 280	60 grams carbohydrate 8 grams protein
Fruits	4 servings Calories: 240	60 grams carbohydrate
Fats and oils	2–4 teaspoons Calories: 90–180	10–20 grams fat
Milk, skim	2 servings Calories: 180	24 grams carbohydrate 16 grams protein
Desserts, like pie	2 servings Calories: 700	102 grams carbohydrate 6 grams protein 30 grams fat
Beverages, naturally sweetened	8–24 ounces Calories: 80–240	20–60 grams carbohydrate
Water	8 or more servings Calories: 0	
TOTAL KCAL	2700–3860	

TOTAL GRAMS AND APPROXIMATE % OF DIETARY CALORIES

Carbohydrate	416–606	65%
Protein	96–146	15%
Fat	58–74	20%

Consult Table 3.1 for specific high-carbohydrate foods in each of the food sources.

*Beans are listed in the meat group because of their high protein content; however, they are also low in fat and high in carbohydrates, so they are an excellent selection from this food group. Substitution of beans for meat will increase the total grams of carbohydrate and the percentage of dietary Calories from carbohydrate. Including high carbohydrate drinks, such as glucose polymers, can add significant amounts of carbohydrate to the diet and may substitute for other foods, such as desserts.

Adapted from Forgac, M. 1979. Carbohydrate Loading. A Review. *Journal of the American Dietetic Association* 75:42–5.

last major meal to avoid the presence of intestinal residue the morning of competition. A carbohydrate breakfast such as orange juice, toast, jelly, or other carbohydrates may be eaten three to four hours prior to competition. This overall dietary regimen should help maximize muscle and liver glycogen stores. The athlete should then follow the guidelines presented previously relative to carbohydrate intake before and during performance.

How do I know if my muscles have increased their glycogen stores?

The most accurate way would be to have a muscle biopsy taken (a needle is inserted into the muscle and a small portion is extracted and analyzed), but this is not very practical. However, keeping an accurate record of your body weight, which should be recorded every morning as you arise and after you urinate, may help you determine the answer to this question. Approximately 3 grams of water are bound to each gram of stored glycogen. If your body stores an additional 300–400 grams of glycogen, along with 900–1,200 grams of water, your body weight will increase about 1,200–1,600 grams, or 2.5–3.5 pounds above your normal training weight during the loading phase. The weight gain would be greater with additional glycogen storage. This is indicative that the carbohydrate loading has been effective, since rapid weight gains from one day to another are usually due to changes in body water content.

Does carbohydrate loading work?

As a method of increasing the glycogen stores in the muscles and liver, the answer is yes. Glycogen content in the muscle has been reported to increase two to three times beyond normal, and liver glycogen content nearly doubled. However, such increases do not appear to offer any advantages to the body builder. A study by Horowitz and others found no increase in the girths of seven different muscle groups following a carbohydrate-loading regimen in weight-trained body builders.

As a means of increasing endurance performance, the answer is a qualified yes. Laboratory studies have shown that exercise time to exhaustion is closely associated with the amount of muscle glycogen available or the amount of carbohydrate in the diet. When endurance performance is compared after subjects have been on either a high fat/high protein diet, a mixed, balanced diet, or a high-carbohydrate diet for 4–7 days, performance on the high fat/high protein diet is worse than on the other two. However, research findings comparing a mixed, balanced diet with a high-carbohydrate diet have been equivocal, with some results favoring the high-carbohydrate diet and others revealing no difference between the two. Unfortunately, the performance tests in many of these studies may not have been long enough for the individual to derive the full benefit from carbohydrate loading; they lasted less than two hours. Although one of these latter studies used a well designed double-blind placebo protocol, we still await sound laboratory experimentation to document whether or not the carbohydrate-loading technique will benefit an individual in events for which it has been designed—for example, a 26.2-mile marathon.

On the other hand, several laboratory and field studies with runners and cross-country skiers have shown improved performances with carbohydrate loading. In general, carbohydrate loading, in contrast to a mixed diet, did not enable these athletes to go faster during the early stages of their events, but the high glycogen levels enabled them to perform longer at a given speed. The end result was an overall faster time. Failure to carbohydrate load has also been identified as one of the factors contributing to collapse of runners in an ultramarathon.

Are there any possible detrimental effects relative to carbohydrate loading?

From a performance standpoint, the extra body weight associated with the increased water content may be a disadvantage. In activities where moving the body weight is important, extra energy will be required to lift the extra 2–3 pounds of body water. However, in most performance events for which carbohydrate loading is advocated, the benefits from the energy aspects of the increased glycogen should more than offset the additional water weight. Moreover, if the individual is performing in a hot environment, the extra water could be available as a source of

sweat and may be helpful in controlling body temperature during exercise in the heat. Although one study suggested that the water stored with glycogen did not confer any advantage in regulation of the body temperature while exercising in the heat, the duration of the exercise, only 45 minutes, would not be sufficient to benefit from the increased water levels. Another study conducted in South Africa revealed no beneficial or detrimental effects of carbohydrate loading on body temperature during 2.5 hours of exercise in a moderate environment (70° Fahrenheit; 21° Celsius). However, performance in longer exercise tasks with greater levels of water losses might be benefited.

From a health standpoint there may be some potential hazards to individuals with certain conditions. Although diabetics have been known to carbohydrate load, they should consult their physicians prior to using the technique. Individuals with high blood-lipid or cholesterol levels should avoid the high fat/high protein diet phase of the depletion stage. Blood serum lipids and cholesterol have been reported to rise significantly during this phase. In addition, these individuals should eat mostly complex carbohydrates during the loading phase because an increased intake of simple carbohydrates may raise blood-lipid levels. Furthermore, hypoglycemia may occur during the high fat/high protein phase.

Several laboratory studies and one case study have reported electrocardiographic (ECG) abnormalities in individuals who used the carbohydrate-loading technique. Although no cause and effect relationship was determined, these investigators speculated that hypoglycemia or glucose intolerance may be involved. On the other hand, other well controlled research with marathoners and typical joggers revealed no ECG changes following the classic method of carbohydrate loading.

Several investigators theorized that carbohydrate loading could possibly lead to destruction of muscle fibers by excessive glycogen storage, but no data were presented to support their contentions.

Other potential problems with the high-carbohydrate phase are diarrhea, nausea, and cramping, particularly when the diet is changed drastically or large amounts of simple carbohydrates are consumed. Individuals who wish to carbohydrate load should experiment with such diets during their training and not just before competition.

In general, however, the recommended carbohydrate-loading technique presented in Table 3.3, which at the most is only a seven-day dietary regimen, poses no significant health hazards to the normally healthy individual.

Carbohydrates: Ergogenic Aspects

Throughout this chapter you have learned that carbohydrate intake, in a variety of ways, may be used to enhance physical performance. Truly, carbohydrates represent one of our most important ergogenic nutrients. You have also learned that certain forms of carbohydrate, such as fructose, possess the potential to impair performance in some individuals if consumed in excess. Such an effect may be **ergolytic,** the opposite of ergogenic. In this brief section we shall look at several forms of carbohydrate that might possess either ergogenic or ergolytic properties, including honey, alcohol (a by-product of carbohydrate fermentation), and metabolic by-products of glycolysis.

Is honey more effective than glucose or other carbohydrates?

One of the main foods of athletes over the years has been honey. In a best-seller entitled *Folk Medicine,* Jarvis suggested that honey gives quick energy release and enables athletes who expend energy heavily to recuperate rapidly from exertion. Although he claimed that honey was an excellent source of potassium, iron, calcium, and a host of other nutrients, the amount is actually so small that honey is not considered to be a good nutrient source other than for its carbohydrate content, 40 percent of which is fructose.

One of the main advocates for honey as an ergogenic aid is Percival, who published his experiences with honey relative to athletic nutrition in the *American Bee Journal:* The reader may perceive the implications. Without reporting any experimental design or quantified results, Percival reported that athletes participating in endurance tests, such as distance running and repeated 50-yard sprints and 100-yard swims, performed better when fed two tablespoons of honey thirty minutes prior to testing. Performance also suffered when the honey was withdrawn. Percival concluded that, without reservation, honey is an ideal energy and fatigue-recovery fuel. Unfortunately, no research specifically concerned with the effect of honey upon physical performance has been uncovered, so the lack of experimental data makes it difficult to accept Percival's conclusions. However, the role of honey may be similar to that of glucose and fructose discussed earlier in this chapter. Since it tastes good, it may be a good source of carbohydrate to incorporate into the diet. On the other hand, the high fructose content may cause gastrointestinal problems in some individuals, so experimentation with its use in training is important.

Is alcohol an effective ergogenic aid?

The alcohol produced for human consumption is ethyl alcohol, or **ethanol.** It is a transparent, colorless liquid derived from the fermentation of sugars in fruits, vegetables, and grains. Although classified legally as a drug, alcohol is a component of many common beverages served throughout the world. In the United States, alcohol is consumed mainly as a natural ingredient of beer, wine, and liquors. Although the alcohol content may vary in different types, in general, beer is about 4 to 5 percent alcohol, wine is about 12 to 14 percent alcohol, and typical bar liquor (whisky, rum, gin, vodka) is about 40 to 45 percent alcohol. The term **proof** is a measure of the alcohol content in a beverage and is double the percentage; an 86-proof bottle of whiskey is 43 percent alcohol, while a 150-proof bottle of Caribbean rum is 75 percent alcohol.

One drink of alcohol is the equivalent of one-half ounce of pure ethyl alcohol or the equivalent of about 13 to 14 grams of alcohol. The following amounts of beer, wine, and liquor contain approximately equal amounts of alcohol and are classified as one drink:

12 ounces (one bottle) of beer
4 ounces (one wine glass) of wine
1.25 ounces (one jigger or shot glass) of liquor

Technically, alcohol may be classified as a food because it provides energy, one of the major functions of food. Alcohol contains about 7 Calories per gram, almost twice the value of an equal amount of carbohydrate or protein. Beer and wine also contain some carbohydrate, a source of additional Calories. In general, a bottle of regular beer has about 150 Calories, while a 4-ounce glass of wine or a shot glass of liquor contains about 100 Calories. Table 3.5 provides an approximate analysis of the caloric content of common alcoholic beverages and nonalcoholic beer.

In general, the Calories found in beer, wine, and liquor are empty Calories. Although wine and beer contain trace amounts of protein, vitamins, and minerals, liquor is void of any nutrient value. Alcohol may have a certain value to us as a social beverage, but its value as a food and source of nutrients is virtually nil.

About 20 percent of the alcohol ingested may be absorbed by the stomach; the remainder passes on to the intestine for absorption. The absorption is rapid, particularly if the digestive tract is empty. The alcohol enters the blood and is distributed to the various tissues, being diluted by the water content of the body. A small portion of the alcohol, about 3 to 10 percent, is excreted from the body through the

Table 3.5   Energy content of typical alcoholic beverages

Beverage	Amount	Carbohydrate		Alcohol		Total
		Grams	Calories	Grams	Calories	Calories
Beer, regular	12 ounces	13	52	13	91	150
Beer, light	12 ounces	7	28	11	77	109
Beer, nonalcoholic	12 ounces	12	48	1	7	55
Beer alcohol free	12 ounces	12	48	0	0	48
Wine, table	4 ounces	4	16	12	84	100
Liquor, (80 proof)	1.25 ounces	0	0	14	98	100

The small discrepancies in the calculation of total Calories for beer and liquor may be attributed to a small protein content in beer and trace amounts of carbohydrate in liquor.

Figure 3.7.
Simplified metabolic pathways of ethanol (alcohol) in the liver. Hydrogen ions are removed from ethanol as it is converted to acetaldehyde, which may be released to the blood for transport to other tissues. The excess hydrogen ions may combine with fatty acids to form triglycerides or with pyruvate to form lactate. Excessive accumulation of triglycerides may lead to the development of a fatty liver, and eventually to cirrhosis.

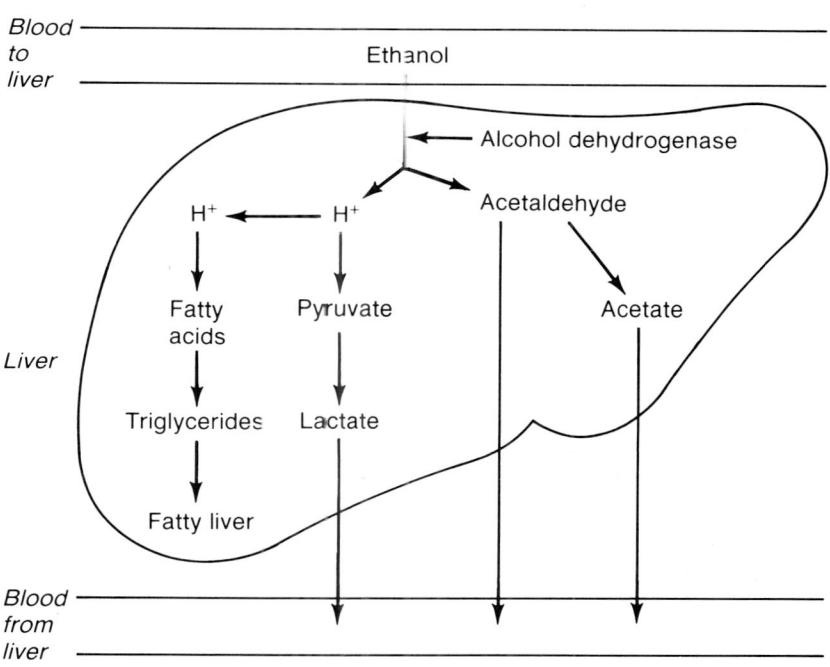

breath, urine, or sweat, but the majority is metabolized by the liver, the organ that metabolizes other drugs. As the blood circulates, the liver of an average adult male will metabolize about one-third ounce (8 to 10 grams) of alcohol per hour, or about the amount of alcohol in one drink.

Although alcohol is derived from the fermentation of carbohydrates, it is metabolized in the body like fat. The liver helps convert the metabolic byproducts of alcohol into fatty acids, which may be stored in the liver or transported into the blood. Several other compounds, such as lactate, acetate, and acetaldehyde, may also be released into the blood. These products may eventually be utilized for energy and converted into carbon dioxide and water. A schematic of alcohol metabolism is presented in Figure 3.7.

As noted above, the liver of a 150-pound male can metabolize only about one-third ounce of alcohol, or one drink, per hour. The rate is lower in smaller individuals and higher in larger individuals. Thus, consumption of alcohol at a rate greater than one drink per hour will result in an accumulation of alcohol in the blood; this is measured as the **blood alcohol content (BAC)** in grams per 100 milliliters of blood. For the average male, one drink will result in a BAC of about 0.025; four drinks in an hour would lead to a BAC of approximately 0.10.

For over a century, athletes have consumed alcohol just prior to or during competition in attempts to improve performance. Alcohol has been alleged to alter energy metabolism, improve physiological processes, or modify psychological factors so as to benefit the athlete. Let us look at the available research to evaluate the truth of these allegations.

Although alcohol contains a relatively large number of calories and its metabolic pathways in the body are short, the available evidence suggests that it is not utilized to any significant extent during exercise. First, the major sources of energy for exercise are carbohydrates and fats, which are in ample supply in most individuals. Alcohol may help form fats, but there is no evidence that it can substitute for other fat sources in the body. Even if it could, this would be of no benefit because the body has more than enough fat to supply energy during prolonged exercise. Second, the by-products of alcohol metabolism that are released by the liver into the blood may enter the skeletal muscles but appear to be of little importance to exercising muscle. Third, even if the energy from alcohol could be used, it would represent an uneconomical source. The amount of oxygen needed to release the Calories from alcohol is greater than for an equivalent amount of carbohydrate and fat. And lastly, the rate at which the liver could metabolize alcohol would limit its use as an energy source during exercise, particularly in an individual working at a high level of intensity. In summary, these four factors suggest alcohol is not utilized during exercise, and even if it were it would not offer any advantages over natural supplies of carbohydrate and fat. In fact, it would be a less economical source.

Research also supports the finding that alcohol in small amounts (one to two drinks) neither improves nor deteriorates physiological processes associated with maximal aerobic exercise, including VO_2 max and maximal heart rate, neither does it affect other indicators of maximal aerobic performance such as exercise tests to exhaustion. Moreover, tests of anaerobic performance such as strength and local muscular endurance also are not affected.

On the other hand, research has revealed that alcohol may interfere with glucose metabolism during exercise. It reduces gluconeogenesis by the liver and glucose uptake by the legs during the latter stages of exercise. In prolonged exercise, such as marathons, these effects could lead to an earlier onset of hypoglycemia or muscle glycogen depletion and a subsequent decrease in performance. Moreover, some studies have reported reduced absorption of vitamin B_1 associated with moderate intakes of alcohol. Theoretically, this could impair physical performance of an endurance nature because vitamin B_1 is involved in the aerobic metabolism of carbohydrate.

Alcohol also has been used as an ergogenic aid for its psychological effects. It is a narcotic, a depressant, that affects the brain. As a depressant, alcohol would not be advocated as a means to improve performance; however, some have contended that increased feelings of self-confidence, reduced anxiety levels, and a perceived decrease in sensitivity to pain may offset any depressant effects and possibly benefit performance. Moreover, alcohol in small doses may exert a paradoxical stimulation effect. Parts of the brain that normally inhibit behavior may be depressed by alcohol, leading to a transitory sensation of excitement.

Although these effects may occur, research does not support the use of alcohol in sports involving psychological processes such as perceptual–motor abilities. Perceptual–motor activities involve the perception of a stimulus, integration of this stimulus by the brain, and an appropriate motor response (movement). The evidence overwhelmingly supports the conclusion that alcohol adversely affects psychomotor performance, such as reaction time, balance, hand/eye coordination, and visual perception, skills that are important in events with rapidly changing stimuli such as tennis.

In one form of athletic competition, such as riflery, pistol shooting, and archery, alcohol may be used to decrease muscle tremor and thereby improve accuracy for competition. Although research generally is not supportive of an improved performance, a recent study with archers revealed a tendency toward reduced tremor with low blood alcohol levels, resulting in a smoother release. However, no actual performance data were revealed; this topic could merit additional research.

Only a limited number of studies have been conducted relative to the effect of social drinking upon physical performance, but there is rather general agreement that light social drinking will not impair performance on the following day. Tests of reaction time, strength, power, and cardiovascular performance were not adversely affected following the consumption of one drink the night before. On the other hand, heavy drinking may impair performance on the following day owing to hangover effects, involuntary eye movements, or dehydration.

The use of alcohol by Olympic athletes had been banned previously by the IOC, but because wine and beer are commonly consumed as a part of many traditional European meals it was removed from the banned list prior to the 1972 Olympics. However, individual sports federations within the IOC still may consider alcohol use during competition as grounds for disqualification. At the present time, only the sports that involve shooting competition ban the use of alcohol.

Do the metabolic by-products of carbohydrate exert an ergogenic effect?

Recall that the primary mechanism in the transformation of muscle glycogen into energy is glycolysis. The end product during aerobic metabolism is normally pyruvate. However, glycolysis leading to the formation of pyruvate involves production of a number of metabolic by-products in a chain of about a dozen sequential steps, each step being controlled by an enzyme. One theory of fatigue is that if one of these steps is blocked by inactivation of an enzyme, glycolysis may not continue at an optimal rate since a necessary metabolic by-product may be in short supply. This blocked step could represent a weak link in the chain, reducing the rate at which ATP could be produced. Thus, a few investigators have studied the effects of several of these metabolic by-products during exercise for their possible bioenergetic effects, which could possess ergogenic potential.

Fructose 1,6-diphosphate (FDP) is a natural metabolic by-product of glycolysis. It has been shown to play an important function in the regulation of glycogen metabolism. Some research has shown that the infusion of exogenous FDP helped prevent glycogen breakdown and stimulate glycogen synthesis in individuals who suffered heart attacks. If such an effect could be produced in healthy individuals, endurance performance might be enhanced. Thus, Myers and his associates recently infused FDP into physically trained subjects to study the metabolic response to exercise during one hour at 70 percent of VO_2 max. However, what may have been effective in diseased individuals with poor metabolic status was not shown to be effective with healthy individuals during exercise. The investigators noted no beneficial effects of FDP upon a wide variety of physiological, metabolic, or hormonal responses during this exercise task.

Dihydroxyacetone phosphate (DHAP) is also a key metabolic by-product of glycolysis. Ron Stanko, of the University of Pittsburgh, has conducted several investigations with dihydroxyacetone and pyruvate (labeled as DHAP), a product that he indicates is currently only being used for research purposes; it is not available in the marketplace. In a well controlled study presented at the 1990 meeting of the American College of Sports Medicine, Stanko and his associates indicated that when added to a high carbohydrate diet for seven days, DHAP significantly improved leg cycling endurance performance by almost 20 percent compared to an identical diet without DHAP. They attributed the beneficial effect to an increased glucose availability to the muscle.

As noted previously, lactic acid is a metabolic by-product of anaerobic glycolysis. We also indicated that although lactic acid is often associated with fatigue, it is the hydrogen ion release that increases the acidity and impairs performance, not the lactate itself. Lactate is actually a small metabolite of glucose; its formula is $C_3H_5O_3$, about half of that of glucose, $C_6H_{12}O_6$. Thus, lactate still possesses considerable energy, and researchers in California have developed a product called polylactate, a combination of lactate and an amino acid. In a study presented at a regional meeting of the American College of Sports Medicine, Larsen and his associates investigated the effect of polylactate upon physiological and psychological responses to a 3-hour bicycle ergometer exercise task at 50 percent of VO_2 max. Compared to a sweetened placebo, they reported that polylactate can help maintain blood glucose, reduce perceived exertion, and enhance blood buffering capacity (lower blood acidity). No performance data were presented. On the basis of these findings, it would appear polylactate is comparable to other carbohydrate supplements, although the potential ergogenic effect of the improved blood buffering capacity may merit additional research.

Since research with all of these metabolic by-products is a relatively recent phenomenon, few data concerning their ergogenic effect are available.

Dietary Carbohydrates: Health Implications

The diet of the typical American appears to be unbalanced. In general, we consume too much fat and refined sugar products and not enough complex carbohydrates. Such a diet may pose several health problems. As we shall see in Chapter 4, excessive consumption of dietary fat appears to be of major concern relative to the development of several chronic diseases and, as is discussed in Chapter 10, a significant contributor to the development of obesity. On the other hand, consuming more carbohydrates, particularly complex carbohydrates, while reducing one's intake of refined sugars and alcohol (a by-product of carbohydrate fermentation) may produce some significant health benefits.

How do refined sugars affect my health?

If you consume the typical American diet, approximately 20–25 percent of your daily caloric intake is derived from refined sugars, such as ordinary table sugar and the high-fructose corn syrup added to numerous processed foods. Over the years, refined sugar has been alleged to contribute to a wide variety of health disorders, such as dental caries, diabetes, cardiovascular disease, obesity, the premenstrual syndrome (PMS), hyperactivity in children, mental illness, and even accelerated aging. Although the role carbohydrates, including refined sugars, may play in the development of several of these health problems is still under investigation, the National Research Council, in its major treatise on *Diet and Health,* stated that with the exception of dental caries, there is minimal evidence linking refined sugar intake per se to specific health problems. Nevertheless, many health organizations around the world have recommended a reduced intake of refined sugars, generally to amounts less than 10 percent of the daily caloric intake. Because refined sugar contains no nutrients, but only Calories, its intake should be limited in any well balanced diet.

Why are complex carbohydrates thought to be beneficial to my health?

To increase consumption of total carbohydrate in the diet while reducing the consumption of refined sugars, one must increase the consumption of complex carbohydrates, a dietary change that will naturally increase the intake of dietary fiber. There is considerable epidemiological evidence, and some experimental evidence, to support the value of adding dietary fiber to the diet of many Americans as a sound preventative health measure. Epidemiological studies have shown that populations with high-fiber diets have lower incidences of colon and rectal cancer and diverticulosis, an inflammatory disorder in the large intestine which may cause rupture leading to serious complications. Epidemiological studies with vegetarians, who consume diets high in complex carbohydrates, have also shown lower levels of obesity and many chronic diseases. Experimental studies have reported reduced cholesterol levels in the blood after a diet high in soluble fibers such as oat bran or brans, a finding that may help us protect against coronary artery disease. High-fiber diets are also being used in the treatment of non-insulin-dependent (adult onset, or type II) diabetes.

Exactly how dietary fiber may be protective is not known, but several mechanisms have been proposed. First, fiber may add bulk to the contents of the large intestine and hence dilute any possible cancer causing agents (carcinogens) that might attack cell walls. Second, the additional bulk stimulates peristalsis and speeds up the transit time of food through the intestines. Thus, any carcinogenic agent present will have less time to function. Third, fiber may bind with carcinogens so that they are excreted by the bowel. Fiber also may bind with and lead to the excretion of bile salts, which contain cholesterol; normally the bile salts are reabsorbed into the body. Fourth, fiber slows down gastric (stomach) emptying and thereby slows glucose absorption in the small intestine. This effect may lead to better control of blood sugar and may also lengthen the sensation of fullness or satiety, which may be important to individuals on weight loss diets. Fifth, diets high in fiber are usually low in fat and cholesterol, which may support these healthful effects. Other independent mechanisms also be functioning. For example, a compound known as glucarate, which has recently been isolated from cruciferous vegetables such as broccoli and cabbage, may interfere with cancer development, at least as shown in laboratory animals.

Although this area is still under investigation, several hypotheses link potential health benefits to the specific type of fiber consumed. Foods that are rich in the water insoluble type of fiber, such as whole wheat products, wheat bran cereals, brown rice, and lentils, are more likely to increase the fecal bulk, maximizing the dilutant effect and speed of transit through the colon, and hence helping prevent diseases of the large intestine and rectum. Foods richer in water soluble fiber, such as apples, bananas, citrus fruits, carrots, and oats, have more of a binding effect and are theorized to be more likely to reduce serum cholesterol. However, it should be noted that research has now shown that oat bran or wheat products added to the diet are equally effective in lowering serum cholesterol. Foods rich in both soluble and insoluble fiber, such as kidney beans, navy beans, and green peas, may provide both benefits.

The National Research Council has cautioned that data relative to a protective effect of fiber per se against the development of certain chronic diseases are inconclusive at present. Nevertheless, the council recognizes the value of the epidemiological data supportive of a protective effect of a diet high in whole grain products, legumes, fruits, and vegetables. Its current recommendation is to obtain approximately 25–40 grams of dietary fiber through the consumption of natural wholesome foods, not fiber supplements. It is important to recognize that the health benefits attributed to fiber may be associated with the form in which the fiber is consumed, as part of a whole, natural food containing other potential health-promoting nutrients such as vitamins, rather than by consumption of a purified supplement form.

There appear to be few or no health disadvantages to such a diet. As we shall see in Chapter 7, there has been some concern that high-fiber diets could lead to increased losses of certain minerals, such as iron and zinc, but research has shown that such concerns are generally unwarranted if one follows the recommendations just given.

What effect can drinking alcohol have upon my health?

Alcohol affects all cells in the body. Many of these effects may have significant health implications. For example, laboratory research has shown that in vitro (that is, in a test tube) alcohol and acetaldehyde cause changes in DNA, the genetic material in body cells, comparable to changes elicited by carcinogens. This finding could be related to the increased risk of certain forms of cancer in those who drink.

Alcohol also has a direct toxic effect on the intestinal walls; it tends to impair the absorption of vitamins such as thiamin (B_1). In addition, alcohol affects liver function in several ways. It may interfere with the metabolism of other drugs, increasing the effect of some and lessening the effect of others. In excess, alcohol may also lead to the accumulation of fat in the liver and eventual destruction of liver cells.

However, the most immediate effects of alcohol are on the brain; often these effects are paradoxical. Although alcohol is a depressant, a small amount often exerts a stimulating effect because it may release some of the normal inhibitory control mechanisms in the brain. For the most part, however, alcohol acts as a depressant, and its effects on the brain are dose-dependent. The effects occur in a hierarchical fashion related to the development of the brain. In general, alcohol first affects the higher brain centers. With increasing dosages, lower levels of brain function become depressed with subsequent disturbance of normal functions. This hierarchy of brain functions, from higher levels to lower levels, and some of the functions affected by alcohol may be generalized as follows:

Thinking and reasoning—Judgment
Perceptual–motor responses—Reaction time
Fine motor coordination—Muscles of speech
Gross motor coordination—Walking
Visual processes—Double vision
Alertness—Sleep, coma
Respiratory control—Respiratory failure, death

If you want to avoid health problems associated with alcohol, abstinence is the simplest approach. There are actually some possible health benefits associated with alcohol consumption in moderation, but health authorities caution that these potential benefits are not sufficient cause to start drinking if you currently abstain. For those who do drink, abstinence is advised under certain conditions. The acute effects of excessive alcohol consumption include impairment of both motor coordination and judgment—two factors that are extremely important in the safe operation of an automobile. At the least, being arrested for drunk driving may have serious social and personal consequences. At the worst, alcohol is involved as a cause of nearly one-half of all automobile fatalities—23,000 to 26,000 deaths per year in the United States alone. As the saying goes, "Don't drink and drive!"

Women who drink should abstain during pregnancy. The term **Fetal Alcohol Syndrome (FAS)** refers to the effects upon the development of a fetus if a mother consumes alcohol while pregnant. The child may experience retardation in growth and mental development as well as facial birth defects. **Fetal alcohol effects (FAE)** may be observed in children when the full-blown FAS syndrome is not present. FAE children are easily distracted and have poor attention spans. Both FAS and FAE are associated with learning disorders in children. No "safe" amount of alcohol during pregnancy has been determined. Thus, the safest approach is abstinence.

There is some controversy as to whether or not light to moderate drinking, the equivalent of about one to three drinks per day, poses a significant health hazard. Most of the research data is epidemiological, although some experimental studies in the laboratory and with humans have been conducted.

On the negative side, the previously mentioned alcohol-related damage to the DNA in the cell nucleus may occur at an alcohol concentration equivalent to one to two drinks. Thus alcohol may be involved in the development of certain cancers. Other research has shown that three or more drinks per day increase the risk of developing high blood pressure and may increase blood lipid levels. Alcohol is also a significant source of Calories, about seven per gram, and may be a contributing factor to obesity. All of these conditions are risk factors for coronary heart disease (CHD).

On the positive side, some epidemiological research has shown that moderate consumption of alcohol (one to three beers or glasses of wine per day) is associated with a lesser chance of developing CHD. The mechanism is not known, but one theory is that the relaxant effect of alcohol may help reduce emotional stress, a risk factor associated with CHD. Another theory has focused upon the effect of alcohol to raise levels of HDL cholesterol, the form of cholesterol that protects against the development of CHD (see discussion on pages 100–102). A number of studies have supported this effect, although the mechanisms have not been determined. Some studies have shown an increase in one form of cholesterol, HDL_2, which is believed to be protective. Other studies note an increase in HDL_3, the effect of which is controversial, although several investigators have reported a protective effect. Additional mechanisms, such as a decrease in platelet aggregability (clotting ability), may be operative.

With some of the exceptions noted above, health professionals generally support the view that alcohol consumed in moderation, along with a balanced diet, should not pose any health problem to the average, healthy individual. But, because of the potential for abuse, addiction, and all types of injuries, prudent consumption or even abstinence is generally recommended by health authorities.

Although drinking in moderation may confer some health benefits, heavy alcohol consumption is a different matter. As already noted, alcohol is involved in a high percentage of automobile injuries and fatalities. It also may be involved in the etiology of breast cancer and is associated with sudden death due to stroke or heart failure. These risks are exacerbated by chronic heavy drinking. Other adverse effects on body tissues have also been reported, such as inflammation of the gastrointestinal tract and increased risk of cancer of the mouth and esophagus.

One of the major body organs affected by alcohol is the liver. Even with a balanced diet high in protein, consuming six drinks a day for less than a month has been shown to cause significant accumulation of fat in the liver. If continued over the years, the liver cells degenerate. Eventually the damaged liver cells are replaced by nonfunctioning scar tissue, a condition known as **cirrhosis.** As liver function deteriorates, fat, carbohydrate, and protein metabolism are not regulated properly; this has possible pathological consequences for other body organs such as the kidney, pancreas, and heart.

Alcohol abuse is the major drug problem in the United States, posing a problem for one in seven males and one in sixteen females, or about one out of every ten drinkers. Excessive intake of alcohol may lead to a disorder known as **alcoholism,** a condition whose etiology is unknown but probably is related to a variety of physiological, psychological, and sociological factors. The National Council on Alcoholism suggests that there is no pat definition for alcoholism; it may be evidenced by a variety of behaviors. The number of behaviors exhibited by the drinker may be related to various stages in the progression toward alcoholism. Appendix D, a questionnaire developed by the National Council on Alcoholism, provides for an assessment of these behaviors.

References

Books

Brody, J. 1985. *Good Food Book: Living the High Carbohydrate Way.* New York: Norton.

Hickson, J., and Wolinsky, I. 1989. *Nutrition in Exercise and Sport.* Boca Raton, FL: CRC Press.

Hunt, S., and Groff, J. 1990. *Advanced Nutrition and Human Metabolism.* St. Paul, MN: West Publishing Company.

Jarvis, D. 1958. *Folk Medicine.* New York: Holt.

Lamb, D., and Murray, R. (eds.). 1988. *Prolonged Exercise.* Indianapolis: Benchmark.

National Research Council. 1989. *Diet and Health: Implications for Reducing Chronic Disease Risk.* Washington, DC: National Academy Press.

National Research Council. 1989. *Recommended Dietary Allowances.* Washington, DC: National Academy Press.

Pritikin, N. 1979. *The Pritikin Program for Diet and Exercise.* New York: Grosset and Dunlap.

Williams, M. H. 1985. *Nutritional Aspects of Human Physical and Athletic Performance.* Springfield, IL.: C C Thomas.

Reviews

American Institute of Cancer Research. 1990. Research update: AICR study finds vegetable compound effective against cancer. *AICR Newsletter* 27:12, Spring.

American Medical Association, Council on Scientific Affairs. 1989. Dietary fiber and health. *Journal of the American Medical Association* 262:542–46.

Anderson, J., et al. 1987. Dietary fiber and diabetes: A comprehensive review and practical application. *Journal of the American Dietetic Association* 87:1189–97.

Applegate, L. 1989. Nutritional concerns of the ultraendurance athlete. *Medicine and Science in Exercise and Sport* 21:S205–S208.

Bennett, B., and Dotson, C. 1990. Effects of carbohydrate solutions on gastric emptying: A meta-analytic investigation. *Medicine and Science in Exercise and Sport* 22:S121.

Costill, D. 1988. Carbohydrates for exercise: Dietary demands for optimal performance. *International Journal of Sports Medicine* 9:1–18.

Costill, D. 1989. Carbohydrate: Fuel for optimal training and performance. *Proceedings of the First IOC World Congress on Sport Sciences.* Colorado Springs, CO: USOC.

Coyle, E. 1988. Carbohydrates and athletic performance. *Sports Science Exchange* 1:1–4, October.

Forgac, M. T. 1979. Carbohydrate loading—A review. *Journal of the American Dietetic Association* 75:42–45.

Friedman, R. 1989. The healthy eater's guide to sugar. *University of California, Berkeley, Wellness Letter* 6:4–5, December.

Geokas, M. (ed.) 1986. Ethyl alcohol and disease. *Medical Clinics of North America* 68:1–246.

Gollnick, P. 1988. Energy metabolism and prolonged exercise. In: *Prolonged Exercise,* eds. D. Lamb and R. Murray. Indianapolis, IN: Benchmark.

Hasson, S., and Barnes, W. 1989. Effect of carbohydrate ingestion on exercise of varying intensity and duration. Sports Medicine 8:327–34.

Hultman, E. 1989. Nutritional effects on work performance. *American Journal of Clinical Nutrition* 49:949–57.

Hultman, E., and Harris, R. 1988. Carbohydrate metabolism. In: *Principles of Exercise Biochemistry,* ed. J. Poortmans. Basel: Karger.

Jacobs, I. 1981. Lactate, muscle glycogen and exercise performance in man. *Acta Physiologica Scandinavica* 495 (Supplement):1–35.

Kyle, C. 1989. The human machine. *Bicycling* 30:196–200.

Maughan, R. 1991. Carbohydrate–electrolyte solutions during prolonged exercise. In: *Ergogenics: Enhancement of Performance in Exercise and Sport,* eds. D. Lamb and M. H. Williams. Indianapolis, IN: Benchmark.

Newsholme, E. 1988. Basic aspects of metabolic regulation and their application to provision of energy in exercise. In: *Principles of Exercise Biochemistry,* ed. J. Poortmans. Basel: Karger.

Newsholme, E. 1988. Application of knowledge of metabolic integration to the problem of metabolic limitations in sprints, middle distance and marathon running. In: *Principles of Exercise Biochemistry,* ed. J. Poortmans. Basel: Karger.

Olson, R. 1986. Eleventh Marabou Symposium: The nutritional reemergence of starchy foods. *Nutritional Reviews* 44:33–91.

Percival, L. 1955. Experience with honey in athletic nutrition. *American Bee Journal* 95:390–93.

Powers, S., et al. 1989. Effect of carbohydrate feedings during high-intensity, short-term exercise. In: *Report of the Ross Symposium on the Theory and Practice of Athletic Nutrition. Bridging the Gap.* Columbus, OH: Ross Laboratories.

Regan, T. 1990. Alcohol and the cardiovascular system. *Journal of the American Medical Association* 264:377–81.

Sandell, R., et al. 1988. Factors associated with collapse during and after ultramarathon footraces: A preliminary study. *Physician and Sportsmedicine* 16:86–94.

Sherman, W. M. 1989. Muscle glycogen supercompensation during the week before athletic competition. *Sports Science Exchange* 2:1–4, June.

Sherman, W. M. 1991. Carbohydrate meals before and after exercise. In: *Ergogenics: The Enhancement of Sports Performance,* eds. D. Lamb and M. H. Williams. Indianapolis, IN: Benchmark.

Sherman, W. M., and Lamb, D. 1988. Nutrition and prolonged exercise. In: *Prolonged Exercise,* eds. D. Lamb and R. Murray. Indianapolis, IN: Benchmark.

Short, S. 1989. Dietary surveys and nutrition knowledge. In: *Nutrition in Exercise and Sport,* eds. J. Hickson and I. Wolinsky. Boca Raton, FL: CRC Press.

Simmons, J. 1990. Is the sand of time sugar? *Longevity* 2:49–51.

Thornton, J. 1989. Carboloading and endurance: A new look. *Physician and Sportsmedicine* 17:149–56, October.

Vuksan, V., et al. 1990. Psyllium. A fiber with comprehensive effects. *The FASEB Journal* 4:A782.

Wheeler, K. 1989. Sports nutrition for the primary care physician: The importance of carbohydrate. *Physician and Sportsmedicine* 17:106–17, May.

Williams, C. 1989. Diet and endurance fitness. *American Journal of Clinical Nutrition* 49:1077–83.

Williams, M. H. 1991. Alcohol, marijuana, and beta-blockers. In: *Ergogenics: The Enhancement of Sports Performance,* eds. D. Lamb and M. H. Williams. Indianapolis, IN: Benchmark.

Winder, W. 1985. Regulation of hepatic glucose production during exercise. *Exercise and Sport Sciences Review* 13:1–31.

Wurtman, R., and Wurtman, J. 1989. Carbohydrates and depression. *Scientific American* 260:68–75, January.

Young, A. 1990. Energy substrate utilization during exercise in extreme environments. *Exercise and Sport Sciences Reviews* 18:65–118.

Specific Studies

Acheson, K., et al. 1988. Glycogen storage capacity and de novo lipogenesis during massive carbohydrate overfeeding in man. *American Journal of Clinical Nutrition* 48:240–47.

Alberici, J., et al. 1989. Effects of preexercise candy bar ingestion on substrate utilization and performance in trained cyclists. *Medicine and Science in Sports and Exercise* 21:S47.

Anderson, D., and Sharp, R. 1990. Effects of muscle glycogen depletion on protein catabolism during exercise. *Medicine and Science in Sports and Exercise.* 22:S59.

Bangsbo, J., et al. 1989. Carbohydrate diet and intermittent exercise performance in soccer players. In: *Proceedings of the First IOC World Congress on Sport Sciences.* Colorado Springs, CO: USOC.

Blair, S., et al. 1980. Blood lipid and ECG response to carbohydrate loading. *Physician and Sports Medicine* 8:69–75.

Blon, T., et al. 1987. The effects of different post-exercise sugar diets on the rate of muscle glycogen synthesis. *Medicine and Science in Sports and Exercise.* 19:491–96.

Bonen, A., et al. 1985. Mild exercise impedes glycogen repletion in muscle. *Journal of Applied Physiology* 58:1622–29.

Borg, G., et al. 1990. Effect of alcohol on perceived exertion in relation to heart rate and blood lactate. *European Journal of Applied Physiology* 60:382–84.

Brewer, J., et al. 1988. The influence of high carbohydrate diets on endurance running performance. *European Journal of Applied Physiology* 57:698–706.

Burgess, M., et al. 1991. RPE, blood glucose, and carbohydrate oxidation during exercise: effects of glucose feedings. *Medicine and Science in Sports and Exercise* 23:353–59.

Callow, M., et al. 1986. Marathon fatigue: The role of plasma fatty acids, muscle glycogen and blood glucose. *European Journal of Applied Physiology* 55:654–61.

Coggan, A., and Coyle, E. 1989. Metabolism and performance following carbohydrate ingestion late in exercise. *Medicine and Science in Sports and Exercise* 21:59–65.

Coggan, A., and Coyle, E. 1988. Effect of carbohydrate feedings during high-intensity exercise. *Journal of Applied Physiology* 65:1703–09.

Costill, D., et al. 1988. Effects of repeated days of intensified training on muscle glycogen and swimming performance. *Medicine and Science in Sports and Exercise* 20:249–54.

Coyle, E., et al. 1986. Muscle glycogen utilization during prolonged strenuous exercise when fed carbohydrate. *Journal of Applied Physiology* 61:165–72.

Davis, J., et al. 1988. Effects of ingesting 6% and 12% glucose/electrolyte beverages during prolonged intermittent cycling in the heat. *European Journal of Applied Physiology* 57:553–59.

Davis, J., et al. 1990. Effects of isocaloric glucose, sucrose and maltodextrin drinks on the physiologic and hormone response to exercise in the heat. *Medicine and Science in Sports and Exercise* 22:S120.

Decombaz, J., et al. 1985. Oxidation and metabolic effects of fructose or glucose ingested before exercise. *International Journal of Sports Medicine* 6:282–86.

DeCosse, J., et al. 1989. Effect of wheat fiber and vitamins C and E on rectal polyps in patients with familial adenomatous polyposis. *Journal of the National Cancer Institute* 81:1290–97.

Demark-Wahnefried, W., et al. 1990. Reduced serum cholesterol with dietary change using fat-modified and oat bran supplemented diets. *Journal of the American Dietetic Association* 90:223–29.

Essen, B. 1978. Glycogen depletion of different fiber types in human skeletal muscle during intermittent and continuous exercise. *Acta Physiologica Scandinavica* 103:446–55.

Flynn, M., et al. 1987. Influence of selected carbohydrate drinks on cycling performance and glycogen use. *Medicine and Science in Sports and Exercise* 19:37–40.

Fogelholm, M., et al. 1989. High-carbohydrate diet for long distance runners—A practical view-point. *British Journal of Sports Medicine* 23:94–96.

Foster, C., Thompson, N., Dean, J., and Kirkendall, D. 1986. Carbohydrate supplementation and performance in soccer players. *Medicine and Science in Sports and Exercise* 18:S12.

Fraenkel-Conrat, H., and Singer, B. 1988. Nucleoside adducts are formed by cooperative reactions of acetaldehyde and alcohols: Possible mechanism for the role of alcohol in carcinogenesis. *Proceedings of the National Academy of Sciences* 85:3758–61.

Greenhaff, P., et al. 1988. Diet-induced metabolic acidosis and the performance of high intensity exercise in man. *European Journal of Applied Physiology* 57:583–90.

Guezennec, C., et al. 1989. Oxidation of corn starch, glucose, and fructose ingested before exercise. *Medicine and Science in Sports and Exercise* 21:45–50.

Hamilton, M., et al. 1990. Carbohydrate utilization during exercise while hyperglycemic. *Medicine and Science in Sports and Exercise* 22:S58.

Hargreaves, M., et al. 1987. Effect of preexercise carbohydrate feedings on endurance cycling performance. *Medicine and Science in Sports and Exercise* 19:33–36.

Hargreaves, M., et al. 1985. Effect of fructose ingestion on muscle glycogen usage during exercise. *Medicine and Science in Sports and Exercise* 17:360–64.

Hartung, G., et al. 1986. Effect of alcohol intake and exercise on plasma high-density lipoprotein cholesterol subfractions and apolipoprotein A-I in women. *American Journal of Cardiology* 58:148–51.

Horowitz, J., et al. 1989. Effects of carbohydrate loading and exercise on muscle girth. *Medicine and Science in Sports and Exercise* 21:S58.

Houmard, J., et al. 1987. Effects of acute ingestion of small amounts of alcohol upon 5-mile run times. *Journal of Sports Medicine* 27:253–57.

Ivy, J., et al. 1988. Muscle glycogen synthesis after exercise: Effect of time of carbohydrate ingestion. *Journal of Applied Physiology* 64:1480–85.

Jacobs, I. et al. 1982. Muscle glycogen and diet in elite soccer players. *European Journal of Applied Physiology* 48:297–302.

Jannson, E., et al. 1986. Epinephrine-induced changes in muscle carbohydrate metabolism during exercise in male subjects. *Journal of Applied Physiology* 60:1466–70.

Jenkins, D. 1981. Glycemic index of foods: A physiological basis for carbohydrate exchange. *American Journal of Clinical Nutrition,* 34: 362–66. ·

Keith, R., et al. 1991. Alterations in dietary carbohydrate, protein, and fat intake and mood state in trained female cyclists. *Medicine and Science in Sports and Exercise* 23:212–16.

Kiens, B., et al. 1990. Benefit of dietary simple carbohydrates on the early postexercise muscle glycogen repletion in male athletes. *Medicine and Science in Sports and Exercise* 22:S88.

Kingwell, B., et al. 1989. Effect of glucose polymer ingestion on energy and fluid balance during exercise. *Journal of Sports Sciences* 7:3–8.

Koivisto, V., et al. 1985. Glycogen depletion during prolonged exercise: Influence of glucose, fructose or placebo. *Journal of Applied Physiology* 58:731–37.

Lamb, D., et al. 1990. Dietary carbohydrate and intensity of interval swim training. *American Journal of Clinical Nutrition* 52:1058–63.

Lamb, D., et al. 1991. Muscle glycogen loading with a liquid carbohydrate supplement. *International Journal of Sport Nutrition* 1:52–60.

Larsen, J., et al. 1988. Effects of ingesting polylactate during prolonged cycling. Paper presented at Southwest Regional Meeting of the American College of Sports Medicine, Las Vegas, NV. December 1988.

Mason, P., et al. 1990. The effect of moderately increased intake of complex carbohydrates (cereals, vegetables, and fruit) for 12 weeks on iron and zinc metabolism. *British Journal of Nutrition* 63:597–611.

Millard-Stafford, M., et al. 1988. Effect of glucose polymer diet supplement on responses to prolonged successive swimming, cycling and running. *European Journal of Applied Physiology* 58:327–33.

Mirkin, G. 1973. Carbohydrate loading: A dangerous practice. *Journal of the American Medical Association* 223:1511–12.

Mitchell, J., et al. 1988. Effects of carbohydrate ingestion on gastric emptying and exercise performance. *Medicine and Science in Sports and Exercise* 20:110–15.

Mitchell, J., et al. 1990. Influence of carbohydrate ingestion on counterregulatory hormones during prolonged exercise. *International Journal of Sports Medicine* 11:33–36.

Murray R., et al. 1989. The effects of glucose, fructose, and sucrose ingestion during exercise. *Medicine and Science in Sports and Exercise* 21:275–82.

Myers, J., et al. 1990. Effect of fructose 1,6-diphosphate infusion on the hormonal response to exercise. *Medicine and Science in Sports and Exercise* 22:102–5.

Noakes, T., et al. 1988. Carbohydrate ingestion and muscle glycogen depletion during marathon and ultramarathon racing. *European Journal of Applied Physiology* 57:482–89.

Okano, G., et al. 1988. Effect of preexercise fructose ingestion on endurance performance in fed men. *Medicine and Science in Sports and Exercise* 20:105–9.

Pallikarakis, N., et al. 1986. Remarkable metabolic availability of oral glucose during long-duration exercise in humans. *Journal of Applied Physiology* 60:1035–42.

Peden, C., et al. 1989. 1 H preexercise carbohydrate meals enhance performance. *Medicine and Science in Sports and Exercise* 21:S59.

Reddy, B., et al. 1988. Biochemical epidemiology of colon cancer: Effect of types of dietary fiber on fecal mutagens, acid, and neutral sterols in healthy subjects. *Cancer Research* 49:4629–35.

Rontoyannis, G., 1989. Energy balance in ultramarathon running. *American Journal of Clinical Nutrition* 49:976–79.

Saris, W. 1989. Study of food intake and energy expenditure during extreme sustained exercise. The Tour de France. *International Journal of Sports Medicine* 10:S26–S31.

Schwellnus, M., et al. 1990. Effect of a high carbohydrate diet on core temperature during prolonged exercise. *British Journal of Sports Medicine* 24:99–102.

Seifert, J., et al. 1990. Glycemic and insulinemic response to preexercise carbohydrate feeding. *Medicine and Science in Sports and Exercise* 22:S121.

Sherman, W. M., et al. 1989. Effects of 4 H preexercise carbohydrate feedings on cycling performance. *Medicine and Science in Sports and Exercise* 21:598–604.

Shutler, S., et al. 1989. The effect of daily baked beans (phaseolus vulgaris) consumption on the plasma lipid level of young, normo-cholesterolaenic men. *British Journal of Nutrition* 61:257–65.

Simonson, J., et al. 1990. Dietary carbohydrate and rowing training. *Medicine and Science in Sports and Exercise* 22:S88.

Snyder, A., et al. 1989. Voluntary consumption of a carbohydrate supplement by elite speed skaters. *Journal of the American Dietetic Association* 89:1125–26.

Stampfer, M., et al. 1988. A prospective study of moderate alcohol consumption and the risk of coronary disease and stroke in women. *New England Journal of Medicine* 319:267–73.

Sole, C., and Noakes, T. 1989. Faster gastric emptying for glucose-polymer and fructose solutions than for glucose in humans. *European Journal of Exercise Physiology* 58:605–12.

Stanko, R., et al. 1989. Effect of dihydroxyacetone and pyruvate on leg endurance. *Medicine and Science in Sports and Exercise* 21:S44.

Swain, J., et al. 1990. Comparison of the effects of oat bran and low-fiber wheat on serum lipoprotein levels and blood pressure. *New England Journal of Medicine* 322:147–52.

Symons, J., and Jacobs, I. 1989. High-intensity exercise performance is not impaired by low intramuscular glycogen. *Medicine and Science in Sports and Exercise* 21:550–57.

Thomas, D., et al. 1990. Influence of the glycemic index of the pre-game meal on carbohydrate metabolism. *Medicine and Science in Sports and Exercise* 22:S121.

Van Horn, L., et al. 1991. Effects on serum lipids of adding instant oats to usual American diets. *American Journal of Public Health* 81:183–88.

Van Zant, R., and Lemon, P. 1990. Effect of fructose and glucose preexercise feedings on muscle glycogen and protein catabolism during exercise. *Medicine and Science in Sports and Exercise* 22:S59.

Vollestad, N., et al. 1984. Muscle glycogen depletion patterns in type I and subgroups of type II fibers during prolonged severe exercise in man. *Acta Physiologica Scandinavica* 122:433–41.

Wagenmakers, A., et al. 1990. Maximal oxidation of oral carbohydrates during exercise. *Medicine and Science in Sports and Exercise* 22:S120.

Wilbur, R., and Moffatt, R. 1991. Influence of glucose polymer ingestion on plasma glucose concentration and performance in male distance runners. *Abstracts, Southeastern Region Meeting of The American College of Sports Medicine,* Louisville, KY, February.

Wilson, G., and Cureton, K. 1984. Effects of glycogen depletion and glycogen loading on anaerobic threshold and distance running performance. *Medicine and Science in Sports and Exercise* 16:190.

Woods, J., et al. 1990. Failure of low dose carbohydrate feeding to affect the plasma glucose and stress response to prolonged cycling exercise. *Medicine and Science in Sports and Exercise* 22:S33.

Wright, D., and Sherman, W. 1989. Carbohydrate feedings 3 H before & during exercise improves cycling performance. *Medicine and Science in Sports and Exercise* 21:S58.

Zachwieja, J., et al. 1991. Influence of muscle glycogen depletion on the rate of resynthesis. *Medicine and Science in Sports and Exercise* 23:44–48.

Key Terms

angina

apoprotein

arteriosclerosis

atherosclerosis

caffeine

carnitine

cholesterol

chylomicron

coronary artery disease (CAD)

coronary heart disease (CHD)

coronary occlusion

fatty acids

fat loading

glycerol

hidden fat

HDL (high-density lipoproteins)

hydrogenated fats

ischemia

ketones

LDL (low-density lipoproteins)

lecithin

lipids

linoleic acid

lipoprotein

monounsaturated fatty acid

myocardial infarct

omega-3 fatty acids

plaque

polyunsaturated fatty acid

risk factor

saturated fatty acid

triglycerides

VLDL (very low-density lipoproteins)

wheat germ oil

Key Concepts

The three major lipids in human nutrition are triglycerides, cholesterol, and phospholipids.

The fat content of foods varies considerably, but generally the fruit/vegetable and bread/cereal groups are good sources of unsaturated fats and are low in total fat, whereas the meat and milk groups have a high total fat and saturated fat content.

Although some fat is essential in the diet as a source of linoleic acid (an essential fatty acid) and the fat-soluble vitamins, these nutrients may be obtained from polyunsaturated fats.

Cholesterol is a non-fat substance vital to human metabolism, and although it may be obtained in the diet only from animal foods, the body can produce its own supply from other dietary nutrients such as saturated fats.

Dietary lipids may be utilized as an energy source, stored in the adipose tissue, or used as part of body-cell structure.

Fats are transported in the blood primarily as lipoproteins, and low-density forms of lipoproteins (LDL) may predispose certain individuals to coronary heart disease whereas high-density forms (HDL) may be protective.

One of the major functions of fat is to provide energy, but it is not the optimal energy source for most athletes.

Fat loading, wheat germ oil, lecithin, glycerol, and carnitine do not appear to be effective ergogenic aids.

Most research suggests that caffeine does not improve performance in events characterized by strength, power, or local muscular endurance. Some evidence does suggest that it may be beneficial in prolonged endurance events, although additional research is needed to clarify this issue.

Diets high in cholesterol and saturated fats may increase the risk of coronary heart disease, so the recommended dietary intake of total fat is 30 percent or less of the total caloric intake with saturated fats at less than 10 percent of the total. The recommended cholesterol intake is less than 300 milligrams per day, or 100 milligrams per 1,000 Calories.

In general, a low-fat diet is recommended for both health and physical performance. One should eat less high-fat meat and dairy products and more fruits, vegetables, and whole-grain products.

Aerobic exercise training increases the ability of the muscles to use fat as an energy source and can be an important adjunct to diet in beneficially modifying the serum-cholesterol level and reducing body fat.

Physicians generally recommend moderation in coffee or caffeine consumption for regular users of these products.

Fat: An Additional Energy Source During Exercise

4

Introduction

From a health standpoint dietary fat is the nutrient of greatest concern to a variety of health organizations, such as the American Heart Association and the American Cancer Society, for excessive consumption of certain types of fat has been associated with the development of a host of pathological conditions, including coronary heart disease, cancer, and obesity. Thus, one of the major recommendations for a healthier diet is to reduce the amount of dietary fat intake to a reasonable level. Part of the rationale for this recommendation and some general guidelines for implementing it are presented in this chapter, but additional information may also be found in Chapters 10 and 12.

Despite its potential hazards, dietary fat contains several essential nutrients that serve a variety of important functions in human nutrition. For the endurance athlete, one of the most important functions of fat is to provide energy during exercise, and researchers have explored a variety of techniques for improving endurance performance by increasing the ability of the muscle to use fat as a fuel.

To clarify the role of dietary fat in health and its possible relevance to sports, this chapter presents information on the basic nature of dietary fats and the associated compound cholesterol, the metabolic fate and physiological functions of fats and cholesterol in the body, the role of fat as a energy source during exercise, the use of ergogenic aids to improve fat metabolism and endurance performance, and possible health problems associated with excessive dietary fat.

Dietary Fats

What are the different types of dietary fats?
What we commonly call fat in our diet actually consists of several substances classified as lipids. **Lipids** represent a class of organic substances that are insoluble in water but soluble in certain solvents like alcohol or ether. The three major lipids of importance to humans are triglycerides, cholesterol, and phospholipids. Although all three have major functions in the body, our concern is primarily with the first two.

The **triglycerides,** also known as the true fats or the neutral fats, are the principal form in which fats are eaten and stored in the human body. Triglycerides are composed of two different compounds—fatty acids and glycerol. (Three fatty acids are attached to each glycerol molecule.) Figure 4.1 is a diagram of a triglyceride.

Fatty acids, one of the components of fat, are chains of carbon, oxygen, and hydrogen atoms that vary in length and in the degree of saturation with hydrogen. Short chain fatty acids contain fewer than six carbons, medium chain fatty acids have six to twelve carbons, long chain fatty acids have fourteen or more carbons. A **saturated fatty acid** contains a full quota of hydrogenated ions so that all of its chemical bonds are full. Unsaturated fatty acids may absorb more hydrogen because they have some unfilled bonds. These latter fatty acids may be classified as **monounsaturated,** capable of absorbing two or more hydrogen ions, and **polyunsaturated,** capable of absorbing four or more hydrogen ions. At room temperature, saturated fats are usually solid, while unsaturated fats are usually liquid. **Hydrogenated fats** or oils have been treated by a process that adds hydrogen to some of the unfilled bonds, thereby hardening the fat or oil. In essence, the fat becomes more saturated. During the hydrogenation process, the normal position of hydrogen ions at the double bond known as *cis,* or same side, may be partly transposed so that hydrogen ions are on opposite sides of the double bond, resulting in a *trans* fatty acid. **Omega-3 fatty acids** are a special class of polyunsaturated fatty acids found mainly in fish oils. Figure 4.2 represents the structural difference between a saturated, an unsaturated, and an omega-3 fatty acid. The health implications of these different types of fats are discussed later in this chapter.

Glycerol is an alcohol, a clear, colorless syrupy liquid. It is obtained in the diet as part of triglycerides, but it also may be produced in the body as a by-product of carbohydrate metabolism. On the other hand, glycerol can be converted back to carbohydrate in the process of gluconeogenesis in the liver.

It may be of interest to note that several dietary fat substitutes have recently been developed. For example, Olestra is composed of sucrose and six to eight fatty acids; the structure of this sucrose

Figure 4.1.
Structure of a triglyceride. Three fatty acids combine with glycerol to form a triglyceride.

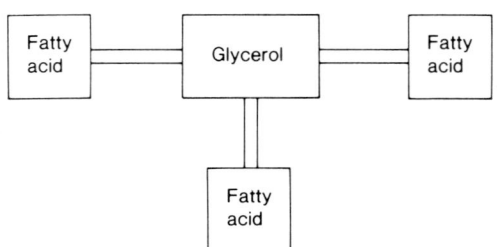

Figure 4.2.
Structural differences between saturated and unsaturated fatty acids. Note the double bonds between carbon atoms in the unsaturated fatty acid, indicating that more hydrogen atoms may be added. In the omega-3 fatty acids, the double bond is located three carbons from the last, or omega, carbon. The R represents the radical, or the presence of many more C—H bonds.

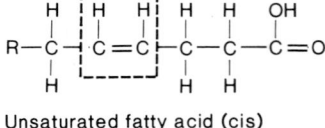

polyester is designed so that it cannot be digested in the intestinal tract, and thus passes through the body unabsorbed. Simplesse is manufactured from milk or egg protein by a microparticulation process so that it has the taste and texture of fat. The caloric value of Simplesse is only 1.3 Calories per gram, compared to 9 Calories per gram of fat. Although a variety of fat substitutes have been developed, currently only Simplesse has been approved for use, and it may be incorporated into a low-Calorie diet for individuals attempting to lose weight, a topic that is detailed in chapter 10.

What are some common foods high in fat content?
The fat content in foods can vary from 100 percent, as found in most cooking oils, to minor trace amounts, less than 5–10 percent, as found in most fruits and vegetables. Some foods obviously have a high fat content: butter, oils, shortening, mayonnaise, margarine, and the visible fat on meat. However, in other foods the content may be high but not

as obvious. This is known as **hidden fat.** For example, whole milk, cheese, nuts, desserts, crackers, potato chips and a wide variety of commercially prepared foods may contain considerable amounts of fat. For example, a 5-ounce baked potato contains 145 Calories with about 3 percent fat, while a 5-ounce serving of potato chips contains 795 Calories, over 60 percent of them from fat. Figure 4.3 presents some examples of hidden fat.

In general, animal foods found in the meat and milk groups are high in fat, particularly saturated fat. However, careful selection and preparation of foods in these groups will considerably reduce fat content. In the meat group, beef and pork products usually contain considerable amounts of fat, although the meat industry is responding to dietary modifications by many Americans and is making low-fat red meats available to consumers. The percentage of fat in meats may vary considerably. Poultry and fish have much lower levels of fat. Trimming the fat from meats or removing the skin from poultry drastically reduces the fat content. Some fish,

Figure 4.3.
Hidden fat. Many of the foods we consume may contain significant amounts of Calories in the form of hidden fat.

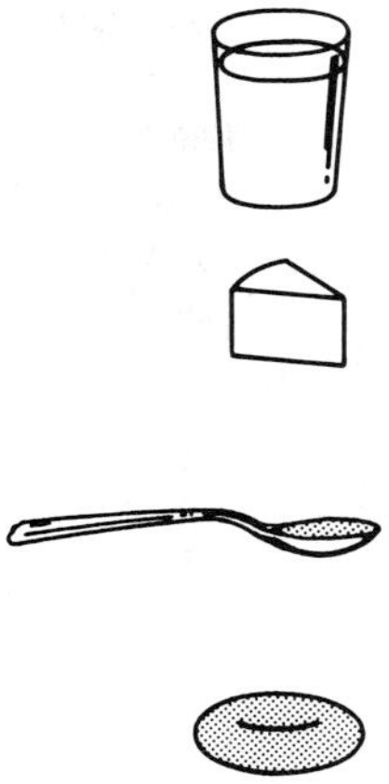

		Calories	Grams of Fat	Percentage Fat Calories
	8 ounces whole milk	150	8	48%
	1 ounce cheddar cheese	115	9	70%
	1 tablespoon peanut butter	95	8	76%
	1 doughnut	100	5	45%

[handwritten note:] HIDDEN FAT REFERS TO the ↑(9 kcal/g) that IS CALCULATED for % fat.

Table 4.1   Approximate percentage of fatty acids in common fats and oils*

Oil/fat	Saturated fat	Monounsaturated fat	Polyunsaturated fat
Beef fat (tallow)	50	43	4
Butterfat	62	30	4
Chicken fat	30	46	22
Cocoa butter (chocolate)	60	33	3
Coconut oil	87	6	2
Canola oil (rapeseed oil)	6	62	30
Corn oil	13	25	60
Cottonseed oil	26	18	53
Margarine (soft tub)	21	48	31
Olive oil	14	74	9
Palm kernel oil	84	12	2
Palm oil	50	38	10
Peanut oil	17	48	33
Pork fat (lard)	40	47	12
Safflower oil	9	12	78
Shortening (animal)	44	48	5
Shortening (vegetable)	26	43	25
Soybean oil	15	24	58
Sunflower oil	11	20	66
Tuna fat	27	26	37
Wheat germ oil	20	16	64

*May not total 100 percent owing to the presence of other fatty substances.

such as flounder and tuna, are remarkably low in fat while others, such as salmon and mackerel, are higher in total fat content, but contain greater amounts of omega-3 fatty acids. In the milk group, whole milk contains about 8 grams of fat per cup; skim milk contains about 0.5–1.0 grams, which is much less than whole milk.

Most plant foods, such as vegetables, fruits, beans, and natural whole-grain products, generally are low in fat content, and the fat they do contain is mostly unsaturated. On the other hand, some plant foods, such as nuts, seeds, and avocados, are very high in fat, but again primarily unsaturated fats. However, coconuts and palm kernels are extremely high in both total and saturated fats.

Since there are some health implications relating to the types of fats we eat, Table 4.1 presents an approximate percentage of the amount of saturated, monounsaturated, and polyunsaturated fatty acids found in some common oils and fats.

How do I calculate the percentage of fat Calories in a food?

It is important to realize that a product advertised as 95 percent fat free (or only 5 percent fat) may contain a considerably higher percentage of its Calories as fat. The advertised percentage refers to the weight of the product, not its caloric content. The product may contain a considerable amount of water, which contains no Calories. Thus, luncheon meat advertised as 95 percent fat free may actually contain more than 40 percent of its Calories from fat depending upon the water weight. Foods with a high water content contain even higher percentages of fat calories. A striking example is whole milk, which is only 3.5 percent fat by weight; however, one glass of milk contains about 150 Calories and 8 grams of fat, which accounts for 48 percent of the caloric content ($8 \times 9 = 72$; $72/150 = 48\%$). Even low-fat milk (2% fat) contains about 37 percent fat Calories.

If you want to calculate the percentage of fat in any foods you eat, simply use the procedure explained in Table 4.2. You need to know the Calories and grams of fat for the food. Both of these values are usually presented in food labels or can be obtained from a food composition table found in most basic nutrition texts. Table 4.3 represents the percentage of food energy that is derived from fat in some common foods; the percentages are indicated for both total fat and saturated fat. Additional information is presented in Chapter 10, where the focus is on reducing high fat foods in the diet.

What is cholesterol?

Cholesterol is one of the lipids known as sterols. It is not a fat, but it is a fat-like pearly substance found in animal tissues. Cholesterol is manufactured naturally in the liver of animals from fatty acids and from the breakdown products of carbohydrate and protein—glucose and amino acids.

What foods contain cholesterol?

Cholesterol is found only in animal products and is not found in fruits, vegetables, nuts, grains, or other non-animal foods. Table 4.4 represents some foods from the meat and milk groups with the cholesterol content in milligrams. Several foods from the bread/cereal group are also included, indicating that the preparation of some bread/cereal products may add cholesterol by including some animal product with cholesterol, mainly eggs.

Table 4.2 Calculation of the percentage of Calories in foods that are derived from fat

Bacon, 2 slices
Food energy = 90 C
Total fat = 8 g
Saturated fat = 3 g
To calculate percentage of food Calories that consists of fat, use caloric value for fat of 1 g = 9 C
Total fat = 8 g $8 \text{ g} \times 9 = 72\text{C}$
$72 \div 90 = .80$
$.80 \times 100 = 80\%$ of the Calories in bacon are supplied by fat.

How much fat and cholesterol do we need in the diet?

Dietary fat is essential to human metabolism, for it provides us with a source of essential fatty acids and a means whereby fat-soluble vitamins are taken into the body. Most fatty acids may be synthesized in the body, but according to the National Research Council, **linoleic acid,** an essential polyunsaturated fatty acid, must be supplied in the diet. Research is continuing to determine whether other fatty acids must also be obtained through the diet, but at the present time, linoleic acid is the only one identified for humans. However, as shall be noted later, other types of fatty acids may confer with some health benefits.

Although no specific RDA has been established for the total amount of fat, the National Research Council recommends a minimum daily adequate amount of 3–6 grams of linoleic acid. Since almost all foods have some fat, sufficient amounts of this essential fatty acid are found in the average diet. Even on a vegetarian diet of fruits, vegetables, beans, and grain products, about 5–10 percent of your total calories would be derived from fat and would provide an ample supply of linoleic acid. Approximately 30 grams of fat from vegetable sources would provide 10 grams of linoleic acid.

Unfortunately, most Americans eat too much fat. The average American consumes about 40 percent of the dietary Calories from fat and about 15 percent from saturated fat, both of which are excessive and conducive to certain chronic diseases. The goals of the Healthy American Diet are to reduce the overall fat consumption to less than 30 percent

Table 4.3   Percentage of total fat Calories and saturated fat Calories in some common foods

Food	% Calories total fat	% Calories saturated fat	Food	% Calories total fat	% Calories saturated fat
Meat group			**Vegetables**		
Bacon	80	30	Asparagus	8	2
Beef, lean and fat (untrimmed)	70	32	Beans, green	7	1.5
Beef, lean only (trimmed)	35	15	Broccoli	12	1.5
			Carrots	4	<1
Hamburger, regular	62	29	Potatoes	1	<1
Chicken, breast (with skin)	35	11	**Fruits**		
			Apples	5	<1
Chicken, breast (without skin)	19	5	Bananas	5	2
Luncheon meat (bologna)	82	35	Oranges	4	<1
Salmon	37	7	**Breads-Cereals**		
Flounder, tuna	8	2	Bread		
Eggs, white and yolk	67	22	White	12	2
			Whole wheat	12	2
Egg, white	0	0	Crackers	30	12
Milk group			Doughnuts	43	7
Milk, whole	45	28	Macaroni	5	<1
Milk, skim	5	2.5	Macaroni and cheese	46	20
Cheese, cheddar	74	47			
Cheese, mozzarella, part skim	56	35	Oatmeal	13	2
			Pancakes, wheat	30	7
Ice cream	49	28	Spaghetti	5	<1
Ice milk	31	18	**Fats and oils**		
Yogurt, partially skim milk	29	14	Butter	99	62
			Lard	99	40
Dried beans and nuts			Margarine	99	21
Beans, dry, navy	4	<1	Oil, corn	100	13
Beans, navy, canned with pork	28	12	Oil, coconut	100	87
			Salad dressings		
Peanuts	77	17	French	95	15
Peanut butter	76	19	French, special dietary low fat	14	<1

<1 = less than 1 percent

of the dietary Calories, with less than 10 percent coming from saturated fats and about 10 percent each from monounsaturated and polyunsaturated fats. Some nutritionists also recommend that the consumption of omega-3 fatty acids, as a form of polyunsaturated fats, be increased through an increased intake of high-fat fishes like salmon.

Cholesterol is vital to human physiology in a variety of ways, so the body needs an adequate supply. Because cholesterol may be manufactured in the body from either fats, carbohydrate, or protein, however, there is apparently little need for us to obtain large amounts in the foods we eat. Also, because a positive relationship has been established between high blood cholesterol levels and coronary heart disease, reduction of dietary cholesterol has been advocated by a number of health-related associations. The goal of the Healthy American Diet

Foods high in cholesterol. Eggs added to flour in some products in manufacturing or preparation (for example, bread and pancake mix) will increase cholesterol content.

(David Corona)

Table 4.4 Cholesterol content, in milligrams for some common foods

	Amount	Cholesterol
Meat group		
Beef, pork, ham	1 oz	25
Poultry	1 oz	23
Fish	1 oz	21
Shrimp	1 oz	45
Lobster	1 oz	25
Eggs	1	220
Liver	1 oz	120
Milk group		
Milk, whole	1 cup	27
Milk, 2%	1 cup	15
Milk, skim	1 cup	7
Butter	1 tsp	12
Margarine	1 tsp	0
Cream cheese	1 tbsp	18
Ice milk	1 cup	10
Ice cream	1 cup	85
Bread/Cereal group		
Bread	1 slice	0
Biscuit	1	17
Pancake	1	40
Sweet roll	1	25
French toast	1 slice	130
Doughnut	1	28
Cereal, cooked	1 cup	0

Fruits, vegetables, grains, and nuts have no cholesterol.

is to reduce the average American intake of 400–500 milligrams or more per day to less than 300, or about 100 milligrams of cholesterol for every 1,000 Calories you eat. Table 4.5 indicates the grams of fat and milligrams of cholesterol that may be consumed daily on a diet containing 30 percent of the Calories as fat and less than 300 milligrams of cholesterol. For lower percentages of fat Calories, say 20 percent, simply multiply the daily caloric intake by the percentage desired and divide by 9 to get the grams of fat allowed per day. For example, 20 percent of 2,500 Calories would permit 500 Calories from fat, or about 55 grams per day.

As we shall see later in this chapter and in Chapter 10, excessive consumption of dietary fat and cholesterol may be linked to a variety of chronic diseases, including heart disease and obesity. In certain individuals with blood lipid abnormalities, the recommended reduction in dietary fats and cholesterol is even greater than the Healthy American Diet, with the total dietary Calories from fat being 20 percent or lower in some diet plans.

Recent dietary surveys also indicate that many athletes consume substantial amounts of fat, ranging from 35–46 percent of the daily caloric intake. High-fat diets may be deleterious to the physical performance in several ways. The fat may displace carbohydrate in the diet, may lead to excessive body weight, and may cause gastrointestinal distress if consumed as part of a pregame meal. All of these factors could possibly impair physical performance.

Table 4.5   Daily allowance for grams of fat and milligrams of cholesterol*

Total Calories	Fat Calories	Grams of Fat	mg of Cholesterol
1,000	300	33	100
1,500	450	50	150
2,000	600	66	200
2,500	750	83	250
3,000	900	100	300

*Based upon a diet containing 30 Percent of calories as fat with 100 milligrams of cholesterol per 1,000 Calories.

Metabolism and Function

What happens to dietary fat in the human body?

The major dietary sources of lipids are the triglycerides, comprising about 95 percent, while the other 5 percent consists mainly of sterols and phospholipids. The ingested lipids are digested primarily in the small intestine by the action of a variety of enzymes (lipases and cholesterases) with the assistance of bile salts. They are broken down into fatty acids (FFA), glycerol, cholesterol, and phospholipids, which are then absorbed into the cells of the intestinal wall. Here they are recombined into a fat droplet called a **chylomicron,** which contains a large amount of triglyceride and smaller amounts of cholesterol, phospholipids, and protein. The chylomicron is one form of a lipoprotein, which by its name you can see is composed of lipids and protein. The chylomicron is then absorbed into the lymph and eventually flows into the bloodstream.

The subsequent fate of this chylomicron depends on the nutritional state of the individual. The enzymes that can catabolize the triglyceride to fatty acids and glycerol are known as lipoprotein lipases and are found in the cell walls of the capillaries in the body tissues, most notably in the liver and adipose (fat) tissues. The chylomicron is removed from the blood mainly by the liver, usually within an hour after ingestion. The liver catabolizes the chylomicron into its components and uses them to synthesize a variety of compounds, mainly the lipoproteins. The chylomicron can also release some of its triglyceride content to the adipose tissues and to the muscles, where the lipoprotein lipase catabolizes the triglyceride to fatty acids and glycerol. The fatty acids are absorbed from the capillary blood and combine with newly formed glycerol in the cells and are stored as triglycerides. The glycerol that was released from the breakdown of the chylomicron travels to the liver for further metabolism, as does the remainder of the chylomicron.

The liver is a clearinghouse in human metabolism. As the blood passes through, its cells take the basic nutrients and convert them into other forms. As mentioned in Chapter 3, it is able to manufacture glucose from a variety of other nutrients, including glycerol. Pertinent to our discussion here is its role in lipid metabolism. In essence, the liver combines fatty acids with glycerol, cholesterol, phospholipids, and protein into different types of lipoproteins.

After the chylomicrons have been cleared from the blood, the lipoproteins constitute approximately 95 percent of the serum lipids. As noted above, the lipoprotein is a complex of lipids and protein, and it is the protein coating that controls the specific function of the lipoprotein. This protein is often referred to as an apolipoprotein or simply an **apoprotein.** Different types of apoproteins, such as alpha and beta, determine the functions of the lipoproteins. A schematic of a lipoprotein is presented in Figure 4.4.

The metabolism of the lipoproteins is complex, for they are constantly being synthesized and catabolized by the liver and other body tissues. As a result, there is an exchange of protein and lipid components between the different classes of lipoproteins, which can lead to the conversion of one form into another.

The classification of the lipoproteins may be determined by several methods. One of the methods is by the type of apoprotein present and its functions, but the most common method is based on the density of the lipoprotein particle.

The chylomicron is one form of lipoprotein, but because it is relatively short-lived, it is not considered a major lipoprotein. For our purposes in this book, the major classifications of lipoproteins along with their suggested composition and function are listed below; a graphical depiction is presented in Figure 4.5. However, it should be noted that a wide variety of lipoproteins exist based upon their specific lipid and protein content. Additionally, their metabolism and complete functions have not been totally elucidated.

Figure 4.4.
Schematic of a lipoprotein. Lipoproteins contain a core of triglycerides and cholesterol esters surrounded by a coat of apoproteins, cholesterol, and phospholipids. The proportion of the protein, cholesterol, triglycerides, and phospholipids varies between the different types of lipoproteins.

Phospholipid

Cholesterol

Cholesterol ester

Triglyceride

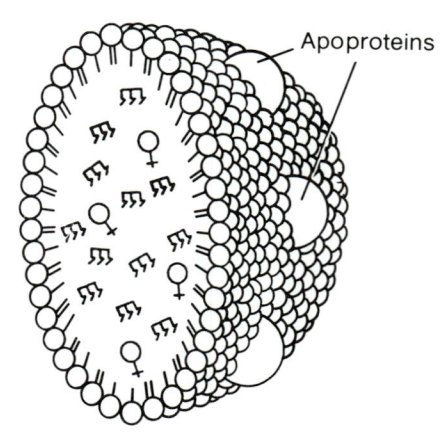

Apoproteins

Figure 4.5.
The approximate content of four different types of lipoproteins.

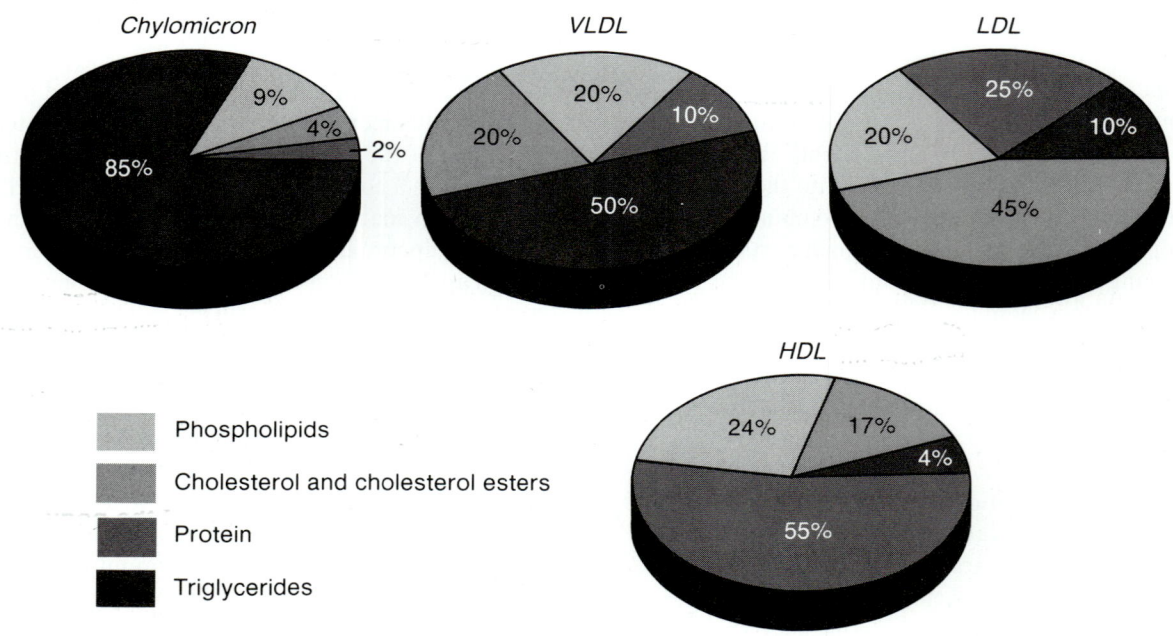

Chylomicron

9%
4%
2%
85%

VLDL

20%
10%
20%
50%

LDL

25%
10%
20%
45%

HDL

24%
17%
4%
55%

Phospholipids

Cholesterol and cholesterol esters

Protein

Triglycerides

VLDL (very low-density lipoproteins). VLDL consist primarily of triglycerides, which are transported to the tissues to provide fatty acids and glycerol. The loss of triglycerides to the tissues will increase VLDL's density to a form called IDL (intermediate-density lipoprotein), which is between VLDL and LDL. Both VLDL and IDL are associated with pre-beta apoproteins.

LDL (low-density lipoproteins). LDL contain a high proportion of cholesterol and phospholipids, but little triglycerides. LDL are formed after the VLDL and IDL release their stores of triglycerides. Recently, a new LDL, small or dense LDL, has been uncovered. LDL are associated with beta apoproteins, often labeled B apoprotein.

HDL (high-density lipoproteins). HDL contain a high proportion of protein, about 50–55 percent, moderate amounts of cholesterol and phospholipids, and very little triglycerides. Several subclasses of HDL have been identified, most notably HDL$_2$ and HDL$_3$. HDL are associated with alpha apoproteins, often labeled A-I apoprotein.

Figure 4.6.

Simplified diagram of fat metabolism. After digestion, most of the fats are carried in the blood as chylomicrons. Through the metabolic processes in the body, fat may be utilized as a major source of energy, used to help develop cell structure, or stored as a future energy source.

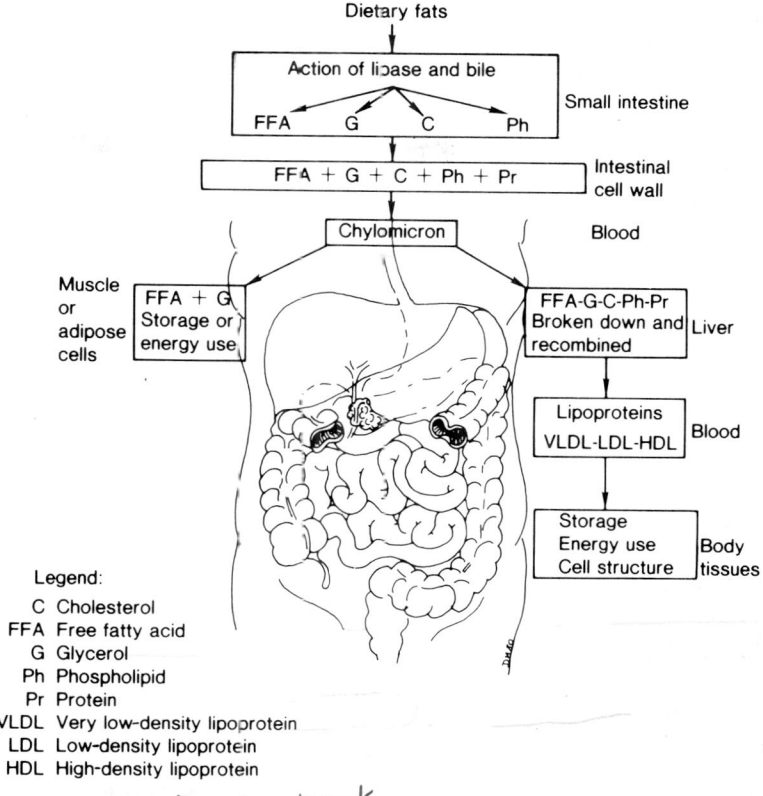

Legend:
C   Cholesterol
FFA   Free fatty acid
G   Glycerol
Ph   Phospholipid
Pr   Protein
VLDL   Very low-density lipoprotein
LDL   Low-density lipoprotein
HDL   High-density lipoprotein

Ketone bodies in book

As the liver metabolizes fatty acids, substances known as ketoacids, or **ketones,** are produced, diffuse from the liver into the blood, and are transported to the body tissues where they can eventually be used as a source of energy. These ketones usually are produced in small amounts, but when the use of fatty acids as an energy source is high (such as with fasting, high-fat diets, and diabetes) the levels in the blood will increase and may cause acidosis.

A simplified schematic of fat metabolism is presented in Figure 4.6.

Can the body make fat from protein and carbohydrate?

You may recall that glycogen is made up of many individual glucose molecules and is a glucose polymer. In essence, fatty acids are polymers of acetyl CoA.

As noted in Figure 3.5, the amino acids of protein may be converted to acetyl CoA, which can then be converted into fat. Carbohydrates also may be converted to fat via acetyl CoA. It is important to understand that the body will take excess amounts of both these nutrients and convert them to fat when caloric expenditure is less than caloric intake. Thus, in general, it is not necessarily what you eat, but rather how much, that determines whether or not you gain body fat. However, as discussed in Chapters 9 and 10, there is some evidence to suggest that dietary fat may be stored as body fat more readily than carbohydrate or protein, and thus may be a factor in the development of obesity.

What are the major functions of the body lipids?

The body lipids are derived from the dietary lipids, but all lipids essential to human metabolism, with the exception of linoleic fatty acid, may be produced by the liver. These body lipids serve a variety of functions, including all three purposes of food; they form body structures, help regulate metabolism, and provide a source of energy.

The structure of virtually all cell membranes, including the nerve membranes, consists partly of lipids, notably cholesterol and phospholipids. The structural fat deposits in the adipose tissues are used as insulators and shock absorbers to protect various organs.

Cholesterol is a component of several hormones, such as testosterone and estrogen, which have diverse effects in the regulation of human metabolism. The majority of cholesterol in the body is used by the liver to produce bile salts, essential for the digestion of fats. Phospholipids are also instrumental for blood clotting.

In general, however, the function of the majority of the body lipids, the triglycerides, is to provide energy to drive the metabolic processes. The majority of the triglycerides in the body are stored in the adipose tissue. They break down to free fatty acids (FFA) and glycerol, which are released into the blood, with the FFA being transported to the tissues and the glycerol going to the liver. In the tissues, the FFA are reduced to acetyl CoA and enter the Krebs cycle to produce energy via the oxygen system. The glycerol is used by the liver to form other lipids or glucose.

During rest, nearly 60 percent of the energy supply is provided by metabolism of fats when the individual consumes a mixed diet.

How much total energy is stored in the body as fat?

The greatest amount of energy stored in the body is fat in the form of triglycerides. Fat is a very efficient, compact means to store energy for several reasons. First, fat has 9 Calories per gram, more than twice the value of carbohydrate and protein. Also, there is very little water in body fat compared to the 3–4 grams of water stored with each gram of carbohydrate or protein. In essence, body fat is about 5–6 times as efficient an energy store as carbohydrate and protein. If the average 154-pound man had to carry all the potential energy of his fat stores as carbohydrate, he would weigh nearly 300 pounds.

Most of the triglycerides are stored in the adipose tissues, approximately 80,000–100,000 Calories of energy in the average adult male with normal body fat. The triglycerides within and between the muscle cells may provide approximately 2,500–2,800 Calories, while those in the blood only about 70–80 Calories. The free fatty acids (FFA) in the blood total about 7–8 Calories. The liver also contains an appreciable store of triglycerides. Thus, you can see that the human body contains a huge reservoir of energy Calories in the form of fat.

Fats and Exercise

Are fats used as an energy source during exercise?

The two major energy sources for the production of ATP during exercise are carbohydrate in the form of muscle glycogen, and fats in the form of fatty acids. In general, a mixture of both fuel sources is used during exercise. As noted in previous chapters,

carbohydrate is the preferred energy source during high-intensity exercise, such as 65 percent of VO_2 max and above. It appears that there is a metabolic limit in the ability of the muscle cell to produce ATP from fatty acids, so that fatty acids alone could not sustain exercise at this intensity. Although fatty acids do provide some of the energy in intense exercise, their contribution diminishes as the exercise intensity increases above 50 percent VO_2 max. However, fatty acids are an important energy source during exercise of mild to moderate intensity (less than 50 percent VO_2 max) and in some situations may constitute the vast majority of the energy available.

The fatty acids for exercise may be derived from a variety of sources, including the chylomicrons and lipoproteins in the plasma. However, the two major sources are the plasma FFA and the muscle triglycerides. The plasma FFA are in short supply, so they must be replenished by the vast stores of triglycerides in the adipose tissues. Hormones such as epinephrine are secreted during exercise and activate enzymes to stimulate the breakdown of these triglycerides and the release of FFA into the blood for transport and entrance to the muscle cell. The muscle triglycerides also are catabolized to fatty acids in the cell. These fatty acids then enter the mitochondria and are degraded to acetyl CoA, which enters the Krebs cycle for ATP production. An enzyme complex using a carrier called **carnitine** is necessary to transport the fatty acid into the mitochondria. (See Figure 4.7.)

During mild to moderate exercise, below 50 percent of VO_2 max, about 30–50 percent of the total energy cost is derived from carbohydrate while the other 50–70 percent comes from fat. The FFA provided by the adipose tissue appear to be the major source of the fat energy during this type of exercise although muscle triglycerides are also used. As the exercise intensity increases toward 60–65 percent VO_2 max, increases in blood lactic acid levels may block FFA release from adipose tissue, so the muscle triglycerides may become increasingly important as the supplier of fatty acids. During prolonged exercise, Holloszy suggests that muscle triglycerides may be the preferential fat source during the early stages, but plasma FFA concentrations may increase during the latter stages and become the primary source. However, as Holloszy and Gollnick note, there is considerable lack of knowledge and debate about the percentile contribution of intramuscular triglyceride as an energy source during exercise.

As noted in previous chapters, the amount of energy that may be obtained from muscle and liver glycogen is rather limited. Hence, within about an

Figure 4.7.

Fat as an energy source during exercise. Free fatty acids (FFA) are an important energy source during endurance exercise. They may be released by the adipose tissue triglycerides and travel by the blood to the muscle cells, and also may be derived from the muscle cell triglycerides. Carnitine is needed to transport the FFA into the mitochondria. The glycerol that is released from the triglycerides may be transported to the liver for gluconeogenesis.

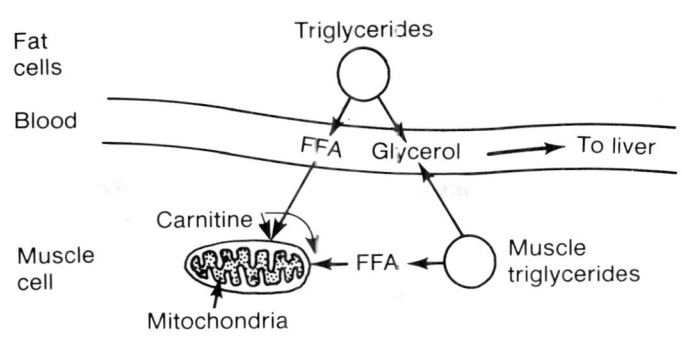

hour or so of high-intensity exercise, glycogen stores approach very low levels and the body shifts to an increasing usage of fatty acids, leading to a decrease in the intensity of the exercise. In such cases, such as prolonged endurance tasks like ultramarathons, fatty acids may provide nearly 90 percent of the energy in the latter stages of the event.

Although ketones may be utilized by the muscle, they do not appear to contribute significantly to energy production during exercise.

Do women use fats more efficiently during exercise than men?

Women possess a greater percentage of body fat than men, and several writers for popular runners' magazines have suggested that women could process this fat more efficiently and thus be more effective in ultramarathon events. However, a number of well controlled studies have shown that when men and women are matched for their aerobic capacity, the utilization of fat as an energy source during prolonged exercise is similar.

What effects does exercise training have on fat metabolism during exercise?

A number of studies have shown that trained athletes use more fat than untrained athletes during a standardized exercise task. For example, if you ran an 8-minute mile both before and after a two-month endurance training program you would use the same amount of caloric energy each time. However, after training, more of that energy would be derived from fat. Hence, training helps you become a better fat burner, so to speak, which may help spare some of the glycogen in your muscles.

Although all of the exact mechanisms have not been identified, several factors may be involved.

Some research indicates that exercise training increases the sensitivity of the adipose cells to epinephrine, which would facilitate the release of FFA into the blood during exercise. Training also increases the muscle triglyceride content. More important, however, exercise training leads to enzyme and other changes in the muscle cells. These changes make muscle cells more efficient in taking up serum FFA and processing fatty acids from both the muscle triglycerides and serum FFA for ATP production. According to Hultman and Harris, the increased content and use of muscle triglycerides may be the primary mechanism underlying the greater capacity of trained muscle to oxidize fatty acids during exercise. As noted previously, however, Gollnick indicates the quantitative role of intramuscular triglyceride use during exercise is still controversial. Nevertheless, increased utilization of fat during exercise is one of the major effects of training.

Although carbohydrate becomes more important as an energy source during high-intensity exercise, Eric Newsholme noted that highly trained endurance athletes may be able to use fats more efficiently at exercise intensity levels greater than 50 percent VO_2 max. In this regard, Dr. David Costill has noted that some highly trained runners could derive as much as 75 percent of their energy from fat even when they were running at about 70 percent  of their VO_2 max. The ability to derive a substantial proportion of the energy demands of intensive exercise from fatty acids is extremely important for athletes such as marathoners who may be able to save some of their muscle glycogen for utilization in the latter stages of the race. The mixture of fatty acids and glycogen for energy will enable them to sustain their pace, whereas the total depletion of muscle glycogen and subsequent reliance on fatty acids as the sole energy supply would force them to slow down. Thus, it is important for the endurance athlete to become a better "fat burner," and a variety of ergogenic aids have been proposed to enhance this effect.

Fats: Ergogenic Aspects

Because exercise training leads to an increased utilization of fatty acids as an energy source and improved performance in endurance events, a variety of techniques or nutritional and pharmacological supplements have been employed in attempts to facilitate this metabolic process during exercise. Among those theorized to be ergogenic in nature are fat loading and supplementation with glycerol, wheat germ oil, lecithin, carnitine, and caffeine.

What is fat loading?

Because the rate at which FFA are oxidized in the muscle is dependent in part upon their concentration in the blood plasma, several different techniques have been tried to increase plasma FFA levels. These may be referred to collectively as **fat loading**. Investigators have theorized that an increased plasma level of FFA might be a means whereby endurance athletes could use fats more efficiently and improve performance.

Medium chain triglycerides (MCTs) have also been suggested to be ergogenic, possibly because they can be absorbed by the portal circulation and delivered directly to the liver instead of via the chylomicron route in the lymph. Although MCTs may increase dietary-induced thermogenesis (DIT), there does not appear to be any evidence to support an ergogenic effect.

Fasting for 24 hours or the consumption of high-fat meals for several days have both been used to increase FFA levels in attempts to produce an ergogenic effect. Unfortunately, such attempts usually impair endurance performance because they reduce muscle glycogen stores or induce hypoglycemia.

High-fat meals also have been given to subjects 1–4 hours prior to exercise performance. Several studies used medium chain triglycerides because they are more water soluble than the long chain triglycerides and thus are more easily digested and absorbed. The usual dose is about 25–45 grams, or about 225–400 Calories. Although high-fat meals may lead to a greater oxidation of fats and a modest sparing of endogenous carbohydrate utilization during exercise, they have not been shown to improve performance. Moreover, in one study comparing equivalent caloric intakes of either fat or carbohydrate ingested one hour prior to a two-hour endurance task at 67 percent of VO_2 max, more endogenous carbohydrate was used following the fat diet. Thus, in agreement with the discussion in the previous chapter, carbohydrate is the preferred fuel to consume prior to endurance exercise. Furthermore, high-fat meals caused gastric distress in some subjects.

When an individual is placed on a low-carbohydrate and high-fat diet for several weeks, the body adjusts its metabolism to use fats more efficiently. In one issue of a highly respected sports medicine journal, a brief article entitled " 'Fat loading' improved endurance performance" reported that some elite cyclists improved their exercise performance after adapting to a high-fat diet over a four week period. However, analysis of the actual study on which this report was based did not support such a conclusion. Although the cyclists did use fats more efficiently during exercise at about 62–64 percent VO_2 max after the four-week diet, there was no increase in endurance capacity. Other experiments using similar procedures suggested that performance at high intensity, about 80 percent of VO_2 max, could actually be impaired with such a technique.

Thus, fat loading by any of these methods does not enhance exercise performance.

Is the glycerol portion of triglycerides an effective ergogenic aid?

As you may recall, glycerol is one of the by-products of triglyceride breakdown. Because glycerol may be converted to glucose in the liver, researchers theorized that it could be an efficient energy source during exercise. However, in well controlled research, glycerol feedings did not prevent either hypoglycemia or muscle glycogen depletion patterns in several prolonged exercise tasks. Apparently the rate at which the human liver converts glycerol to glucose is not rapid enough to be an effective energy source during strenuous prolonged exercise. However, as noted in Chapter 8, glycerol may be used to increase body water stores prior to exercise in the heat and may regulate body temperature more effectively, which could provide ergogenic effects.

Do wheat germ oil supplements enhance athletic performance?

One of the most enduring yet controversial ergogenic foods on the market is wheat germ oil, which has been advertised to improve endurance, stamina, and vigor. **Wheat germ oil** is extracted from the embryo of wheat; it is high in linoleic fatty acid, vitamin E, and octacosanol, a solid white alcohol that has been theorized to be the ergogenic ingredient. It is interesting to note that a product called Octacol 4 appeared on the market and was endorsed by one of the best marathoners in the United States.

Several theories have been advanced about the beneficial physiological effects of wheat germ oil supplements for athletes, such as enhanced glycogen metabolism and increased oxygen uptake. The principal investigator, who studied wheat germ oil for nearly twenty years, stated that the supplements were to be taken in conjunction with training and were beneficial primarily for endurance. However, the research literature does not provide the necessary objective data to actually pinpoint the exact metabolic role of the wheat germ oil or octacosonal in humans that would improve endurance performance. Moreover, a thorough analysis of approximately 35 studies has not supported the contention that wheat germ oil is an effective ergogenic aid. This evidence was used successfully by the Federal Trade Commission to ban advertising claims that wheat germ oil could improve endurance, stamina, and vigor.

How effective are lecithin supplements?

Lecithin is a phospholipid that occurs naturally in a variety of foods, such as beans, eggs, and wheat germ. Because it is an important component of many types of human body tissues, contains choline needed for the synthesis of acetylcholine (an important neurotransmitter), and contains phosphorus, it has been theorized to be ergogenic in nature. Several early German studies conducted over 50 years ago reported increases in power and strength following several days of supplementation with 22–83 milligrams of lecithin. However, these early studies have been discredited because of poor experimental design. In a study with better experimental design, Staton reported no effect of 30 grams of lecithin supplementation daily for two weeks upon grip strength.

Because plasma choline levels have been reported to be significantly lower following exhaustive exercise such as marathon running, a possible reduction in acetylcholine levels at the neuromuscular junction may be theorized to be a contributing factor to the development of fatigue. In a recent study by Burns out of Costill's laboratory, supplementation with lecithin containing either 1.1 or 1.8 grams of choline did increase serum choline levels prior to an endurance exercise task, which consisted of a bicycle ergometer ride at 70 percent VO_2 max for 105 minutes followed by an all-out performance ride for

15 minutes. However, the lecithin supplements did not improve performance compared to the placebo trial.

Although lecithin does not appear to be an effective ergogenic aid, one of its constituents is phosphorus, a mineral that may have ergogenic qualities which will be discussed in Chapter 7.

Can carnitine supplements improve fat metabolism and physical performance?

Discovered in 1905, carnitine has only recently been theorized to enhance physical performance, being recommended as an ergogenic aid by Robert Haas in his book for athletes, *Eat to Succeed*. **Carnitine** is a physiological carrier that facilitates the transport of fatty acids into the mitochondria for oxidation. Theoretically, carnitine would increase the utilization of fatty acids during exercise and spare the use of muscle glycogen. Additionally, carnitine may facilitate the oxidation of certain amino acids and pyruvate, the latter effect possibly reducing the production of lactic acid during exercise. In general, carnitine would theoretically be beneficial for athletes in very prolonged endurance events.

Approximately 90 percent of the body supply of carnitine is located in the muscle tissues. Although Broquist has indicated that carnitine is an extremely important catalyst for metabolic reactions in the muscle, carnitine is not an essential dietary nutrient because it may be formed in the liver from other nutrients, specifically two amino acids, lysine and methionine. Also, carnitine is found in adequate amounts in meat and milk products, so most individuals consume enough carnitine in the daily diet. The body also has an effective conservation system. There is no RDA for carnitine. Although deficiencies are very rare, vegetarians have been reported to have lower plasma levels of carnitine compared to individuals on a mixed diet.

Carnitine supplementation has been used effectively to improve exercise capability in patients with serious diseases. For example, in an Italian study, patients with peripheral vascular disease increased their walking distance on a treadmill after taking 4 grams of carnitine daily for three weeks. Biopsies of the muscle indicated increased levels of carnitine. In another aspect of this study, blood analyses revealed reduced levels of lactic acid during the walking test following the intravenous administration of carnitine.

On the other hand, carnitine does not appear to be an effective ergogenic aid with normal individuals or trained subjects. One field study used carnitine as a component in an energy stimulator that also contained carbohydrate, vitamin C, and several minerals. The blood lactate level was measured in athletes who trained for three hours both with and without the energy stimulator, and the level was found to be lower when the energy stimulant was used. However, there was no control over the actual amount of exercise done by the athletes. In another study, experienced long-distance walkers consumed four grams of carnitine per day for two weeks and were then monitored in a laboratory during a two-hour walk at 65 percent of VO_2 max. Although there was a slight but significant increase in VO_2 max, the data revealed no changes in blood lactate in an anaerobic exercise task, or in utilization of fatty acids as an energy source during prolonged submaximal exercise. Two well controlled double-blind studies from Adelphi University in New York revealed that 500 mg of L-carnitine taken daily for four weeks had no effect upon metabolic functions or use of fats as an energy source at moderate exercise for one hour. Nor did carnitine affect physiological variables during maximal exercise, including VO_2 max, the anaerobic threshold, and exercise time to exhaustion. However, in two other well designed studies using larger doses of 2 grams per day for 2–4 weeks, no significant improvements were noted in VO_2 max, maximal heart rate, or physiological responses and FFA metabolism during submaximal exercise at 50 percent of VO_2 max for one hour. A recent extensive review by Wagenmakers indicated no ergogenic effect of carnitine supplementation.

It should be noted that only L-carnitine should be used for research purposes. One case study with a distance runner suggested that one form of carnitine, D- or DL-carnitine, could be toxic.

Does caffeine improve performance by increasing fat metabolism?

Caffeine is a naturally occurring compound in many of the foods and beverages that we consume every day, such as coffee, tea, colas, and chocolate. Yet caffeine is legally classified as a drug and has some powerful physiological effects on the human body. A normal therapeutic dose of caffeine may range from 100–300 milligrams. Some approximate amounts in the beverages we consume are 100–150 mg in a cup of perked coffee, 20–50 mg in a cup of tea, and 35–55 mg in a glass of cola.

In general, caffeine is a central nervous system stimulant that will increase alertness, but it also stimulates heart function, blood circulation, and release of epinephrine (adrenaline) from the adrenal gland. The epinephrine, also a stimulant, augments these effects and also, in conjunction with the caffeine, stimulates a wide variety of tissues. Together they potentiate muscle contraction, raise the rate of muscle and liver glycogen breakdown, increase release of FFA from adipose tissue, and increase use of muscle triglycerides. One of the most observed effects at rest is an increase in blood levels of FFA. Because some of these physiological effects could be theorized to improve physical performance, the International Olympic Committee (IOC) banned its use as a drug prior to the 1972 Olympics. However, because caffeine is a natural ingredient in some beverages that athletes consume, the IOC removed it from the doping list from 1972–1982. The use of large amounts of caffeine was again banned for the 1984 Olympic games, probably because some recent research had suggested that caffeine could artificially improve performance. Olympic athletes are permitted to consume small amounts of caffeine, but the use of large doses, such as the equivalent of 5–6 cups of strong coffee or only 4 Vivarin tablets in a short time, is grounds for disqualification. About 800 mg of caffeine consumed in 2–3 hours would exceed the legal limit.

Caffeine has been studied for its possible ergogenic effects for nearly 100 years. Early research focused on improvements in strength, power, and psychomotor parameters such as reaction time. However, since research by Costill's laboratory in the late 1970s suggested caffeine could increase endurance, many researchers have investigated the effects of caffeine on fat metabolism as a means to enhance performance of endurance athletes, such as marathoners. In theory, this is what happens. The marathoner relies to a great extent on the muscle and liver glycogen content, which may become depleted during the last six miles or so of the 26.2-mile run. This depletion contributes to fatigue and a reduction in running speed. Caffeine, in conjunction with the increased adrenaline levels, will elevate levels of FFA in the blood and possibly increase their utilization in the muscle as a source of energy during the run. The increased FFA utilization reduces the amount of muscle glycogen used, creating a glycogen-sparing effect, so the marathoner has an ample supply of muscle glycogen to help maintain an optimal speed during the later stages of the race.

Considerable differences exist in the experimental designs of caffeine studies in such aspects as caffeine dosage (3–15 mg per kg body weight), the type of exercise task (power, strength, reaction time, short-term endurance, prolonged endurance) the intensity of the exercise (submaximal exercise, maximal exercise), the training status of the subject (trained, untrained), the preexercise diet (high-carbohydrate, mixed), the subjects' caffeine status (user, abstainer), and individual variability (reactor, nonreactor). These differences complicate interpretation of the results. The following points represent a general summary of the available research.

1. The vast majority of studies revealed that caffeine would not improve performance in events characterized by strength, speed, power, or local muscular endurance, nor in endurance events that last less than 30 minutes. On the other hand, two recent studies have shown that caffeine intake elicited improvement in tests of peak power and peak strength when subjects had abstained from caffeine for four days prior to the test. It should be noted that in both these studies a variety of strength and power tests were administered, and the subjects only improved performance in several of the tests, not all of them. Another recent study with a large dosage (15 mg/kg) did report improved performance in an exercise task to exhaustion which lasted less than 10 minutes.

2. Caffeine can increase alterness, which may improve simple reaction time. Doses of 200 milligrams have been effective, particularly when subjects are mentally fatigued. Larger doses, above 400 milligrams, may increase nervousness and anxiousness, and thus may adversely affect performance in events characterized by fine motor skills and control of hand steadiness, such as pistol shooting.

3. It is well established that caffeine may raise serum FFA levels at rest just before exercise, but there appears to be some controversy regarding serum FFA levels during exercise when trials with and without caffeine are compared. A number of studies that involved subjects who consumed caffeine beverages regularly and that also used a small dose of caffeine (5 mg/kg) have reported no significant differences between caffeine and placebo trials. The most likely reason is that exercise itself, as a stressor, stimulates epinephrine release and raises FFA levels comparably to the small dose. However, other studies that have involved subjects who were not regular caffeine users or who abstained from caffeine use for 4–7 days and which also employed large doses of caffeine (15 mg/kg)

have noted significantly higher levels of FFA during exercise compared to placebo trials. Bucci reported fifteen studies in which caffeine increased FFA over the effect of exercise alone.

4. Even though caffeine may elevate FFA during exercise, whether the use of fat as an energy source is increased during exercise is debatable. Several reviewers have noted an inconsistency in the results when the respiratory quotient (RQ) was used to assess fuel utilization; the RQ may serve as a general guide to the percentage use of carbohydrate and fat during submaximal, mild to moderate intensity exercise. Two groups of investigators performed muscle biopsies as part of their studies, and both studies found a sparing of muscle glycogen. Essig and others noted an increased utilization of muscle triglycerides, while Erickson and associates, even though finding a sparing of muscle glycogen, did not attribute it to increased fat oxidation since the RQ did not change compared to the placebo trial. Unfortunately, neither of these two excellent studies measured performance.

5. As the duration of the endurance event increases to an hour or more, the research data indicates, although not uniformly so, that caffeine may enhance performance. However, the mechanism whereby it may improve performance has yet to be explained. In many studies with improved performance, the psychological effect of caffeine was hypothesized as the cause. A number of studies have shown that caffeine may exert a stimulating effect on psychological processes, such as alterness and mood, which may diminish the perception of effort during exercise and thereby improve performance. A recent well-designed study by Spriet and Graham supports this concept, for caffeine significantly increased epinephrine levels and both running and cycling performance in well-trained, elite runners. The increases in performance were rather phenomenal; for example, mean run time to exhaustion at 85 percent of VO_2 max increased from 49.2 minutes following the placebo to 71.0 minutes after caffeine (9mg/kg body weight), a 44 percent improvement.

6. The glycogen-sparing effect of caffeine has some research support as noted in point 4 above, but it has not been fully tested in the

laboratory or in field research. MacLean and others reported that caffeine (9mg/kg) did spare the use of muscle glycogen during the first 15 minutes of a ride to exhaustion at 78 percent of VO_2 max and significantly improved total ride time by 30 percent compared to the placebo, but few details are available in this brief abstract. Additional research is needed in both the laboratory and the field with prolonged exercise to induce muscle glycogen depletion. It is possible that the stimulating effect of actual athletic competition increases epinephrine secretion and overrides the possible effects of caffeine in a non-competitive setting such as a laboratory.

7. Unfortunately for endurance athletes, research suggests that the practice of carbohydrate loading and having a high carbohydrate breakfast prior to competition may negate the metabolic effects of caffeine. The high carbohydrate levels stimulate insulin release which appears to block the effect of caffeine in raising FFA levels.

8. It should be noted that individuals vary in their responses to any drug. For example, in several of the studies the investigators reported that some subjects had adverse reactions to the caffeine and had an impaired performance.

9. Possibly one of the more important factors determining whether caffeine is an effective ergogenic aid is the caffeine status of the subjects. In a recent well designed study, Tarnopolsky and others gave 6 mg caffeine/kg body weight to highly trained endurance runners who were regular caffeine consumers. The subjects abstained from caffeine for only 15 hours prior to testing. Although the caffeine significantly elevated FFA during exercise, no significant effects were observed in a wide variety of physiological, metabolic, and psychological measurements during a 90-minute treadmill run at 70 percent VO_2 max. Moreover, no significant effects on neuromuscular tests of strength and power were observed. The investigators concluded that caffeine is of no ergogenic benefit to endurance runners who practice normal procedures prior to competition, including carbohydrate intake several hours prior to exercise. Conversely, several studies reported a positive ergogenic effect of caffeine when the subjects had

abstained from caffeine for four or more days. This area is in need of additional research to confirm some of the positive findings.

10. In general, with the exception of some individual subjects, studies have not reported a decrease in performance following caffeine ingestion. Thus, caffeine does not appear to impair performance in most individuals.

If you currently use caffeine and are involved in athletic competition you may desire to experiment with small amounts. Drink 1–2 cups of coffee about an hour prior to some of your workouts. For example, if you are a distance runner, do your long runs periodically with and without the coffee or other caffeine source, and judge for yourself if it works for you. To make it a more valid case study, have someone randomly give you regular or decaffeinated coffee before the runs, but without informing you which type you are drinking until you have done each several times. Try this procedure also after abstaining from caffeine for 4–5 days. Keep a record of your feelings and times after the runs so you may compare differences.

However, there may be conditions in which the use of caffeine is contraindicated. As we shall see in Chapter 8, caffeine may be a possible cause of impaired performance when exercising in a warm or hot environment.

Dietary Fats and Cholesterol: Health Implications

A variety of chronic diseases and health problems are associated with excessive intake of dietary fat or cholesterol, including obesity and the associated incidence of diabetes; cancer of the colon, rectum, prostate, and breast; and several cardiovascular diseases. We shall discuss the relationship of dietary fat to the etiology of obesity in Chapters 9 and 10 and expand upon the Healthy American Diet as a mechanism for cancer prevention in Chapter 12. Because the available evidence relating dietary lipids to cardiovascular diseases is so compelling, however, we shall treat this subject in some detail. Note, that the dietary and exercise recommendations advanced here may also help prevent obesity and cancer.

How does cardiovascular disease develop?
Nearly one out of every two deaths in the United States is due to diseases of the heart and blood vessels. Each year, approximately one million Americans die from some form of cardiovascular disease,

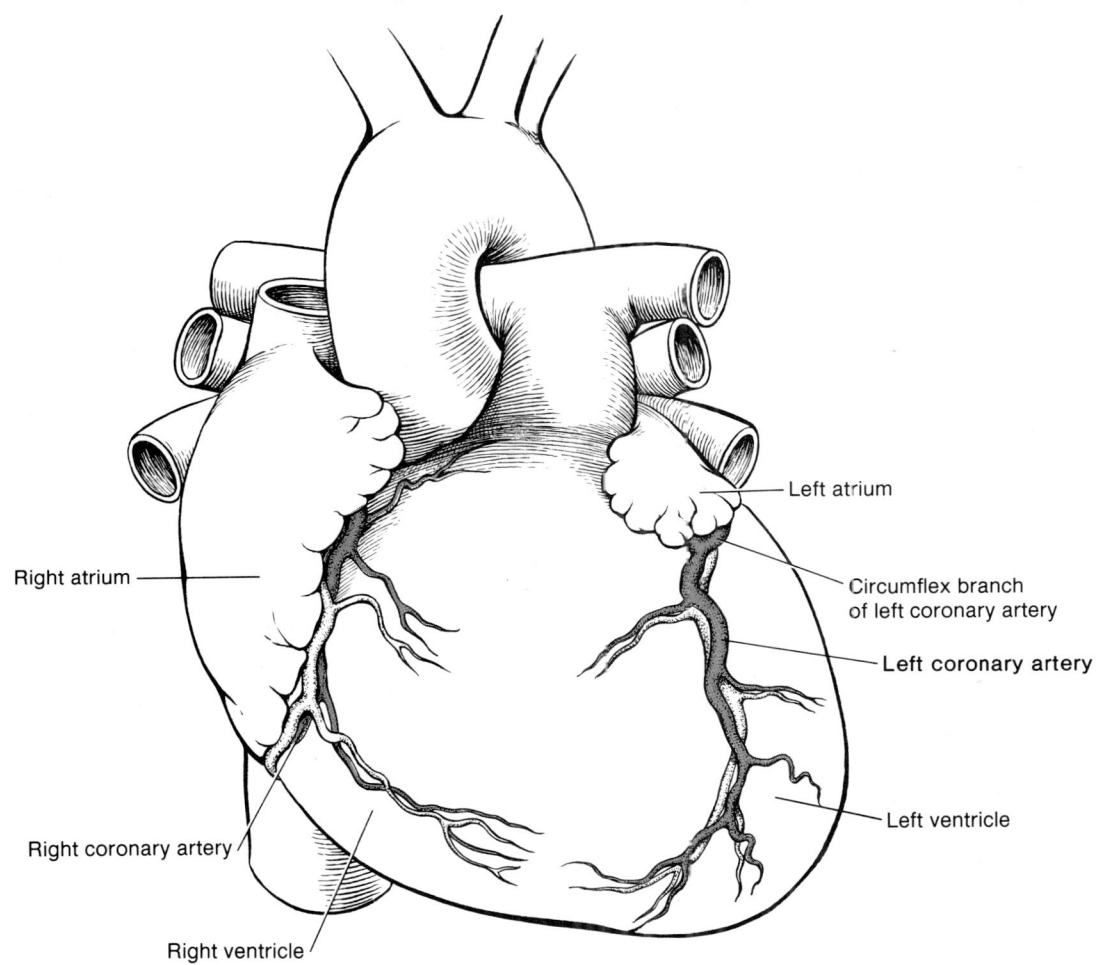

including coronary heart disease, stroke, hypertensive disease, rheumatic heart disease, and congenital heart disease.

Coronary heart disease is the major disease of the cardiovascular system; of the million deaths noted previously, it is responsible for over half. Although the total percentage of deaths due to coronary heart disease has been declining in recent years, it is still an epidemic and the number one cause of death among Americans.

Coronary heart disease (CHD) is also known as **coronary artery disease (CAD)** because obstruction of the blood flow in the coronary arteries is responsible for the pathological effects of the disease. The coronary arteries are illustrated in Figure 4.8. The major manifestation of CHD is a heart attack, which results from a stoppage of blood flow to parts of the heart muscle. A decreased blood supply, known as **ischemia,** will deprive the heart of needed oxygen. In some individuals, ischemia results in **angina,** a sharp pain in the chest, jaw, or along the inside of the arm indicative of a mild heart attack. Other terms often associated with a heart attack include **coronary thrombosis,** a blockage of a blood vessel by a clot (thrombus), **coronary occlusion,** which simply means blockage, and **myocardial infarct,** death of heart cells that do not get enough oxygen due to the blocked coronary artery. The major cause of the blocked arteries is atherosclerosis.

Arteriosclerosis is a term applied to a number of different pathological conditions wherein the arterial walls thicken and lose their elasticity. It is often

Figure 4.9.
The developmental process of atherosclerosis and thrombosis. Deposits of cholesterol, fat, and other debris accumulate in the inner lining of the artery, leading to a decrease or cessation of blood flow to the tissues. Atherosclerosis in the coronary arteries is a major cause of heart disease.

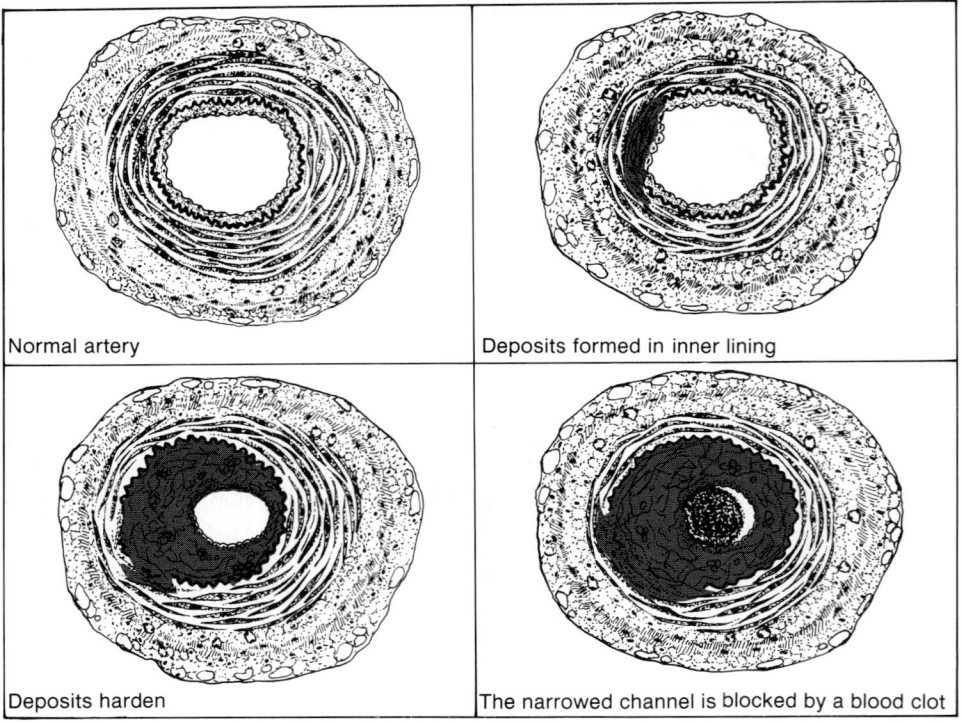

Normal artery

Deposits formed in inner lining

Deposits harden

The narrowed channel is blocked by a blood clot

defined as hardening of the arteries. **Atherosclerosis,** one form of arteriosclerosis, is characterized by deposits of fat, oxidized LDL-cholesterol, macrophages (white blood cells that oxidize LDL-cholesterol), cellular debris, calcium, and fibrin on the inner linings of the arterial wall. These deposits, known as **plaque,** result in a narrowing of the blood channel, making it easier for blood clots to form and eventually resulting in complete blockage of blood flow to vital tissues such as the heart or the brain. Figure 4.9 illustrates the gradual, progressive narrowing of the arterial channel. Figure 4.10 presents a schematic of the content of arterial plaque.

Atherosclerosis is a slow, progressive disease that begins in childhood and usually manifests itself later in life. Because of its prevalence in industrialized society, scientists throughout the world have been conducting intensive research to identify the cause or causes of atherosclerosis and coronary heart disease. The actual cause has not yet been completely identified, but considerable evidence has identified factors that may predispose an individual.

A **risk factor** represents a statistical relationship between two items such as high serum cholesterol and heart attack. This does not mean that a cause and effect relationship exists, although such a relationship is often strongly supported by the available evidence. The three principal risk factors associated with CHD are high blood pressure, high serum cholesterol levels, and cigarette smoking. Other interacting risk factors are heredity, diabetes, diet, physical inactivity, obesity, age, gender, stress, and several others. A guide to assessing your risk factor profile is presented in Appendix K.

How do the different forms of serum lipids affect the development of atherosclerosis?
In atherosclerosis, the plaque that develops in the arterial walls is composed partly of fats and cholesterol. Hence, high levels of blood lipids (triglycerides and cholesterol) are associated with increased plaque formation.

Although high levels of triglycerides are linked to the development of atherosclerosis, the major villain appears to be cholesterol, as depicted in Figure 4.11. Total cholesterol, expressed in milligrams per 100 milliliters of blood, is important. A level below 200 is considered to be desirable, between 200 and 239 is borderline-high, and above 240 is high. (See Table 4.6.) However, you should be aware that there is a rather large standard error of measurement involved in some tests of total cholesterol, being on the

Figure 4.10.
An enlargement of atherosclerotic plaque. Cholesterol, fats, dead cells and other debris collect within or beneath the inner lining of an artery. There is often an ulceration (opening) in the inner layer of the arterial wall through which the cholesterol and other plaque constituents enter.

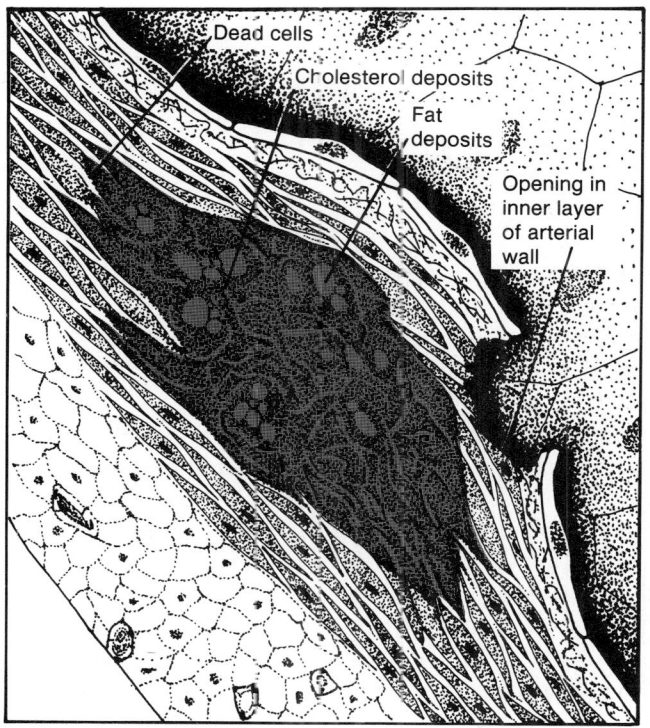

Figure 4.11.
A desirable blood cholesterol is below 200 milligrams per deciliter (mg/dl). The rise of coronary heart disease fatalities increases progressively in individuals with borderline high (200–240 mg/dl) and high blood cholesterol (>240 mg/dl).

Source: U.S. Department of Health and Human Services. Public Health Service. National Institutes of Health. *So you have high blood cholesterol . . .* Washington, DC: U.S. Government Printing Office, NIH Publication, No. 8972922, 1989.

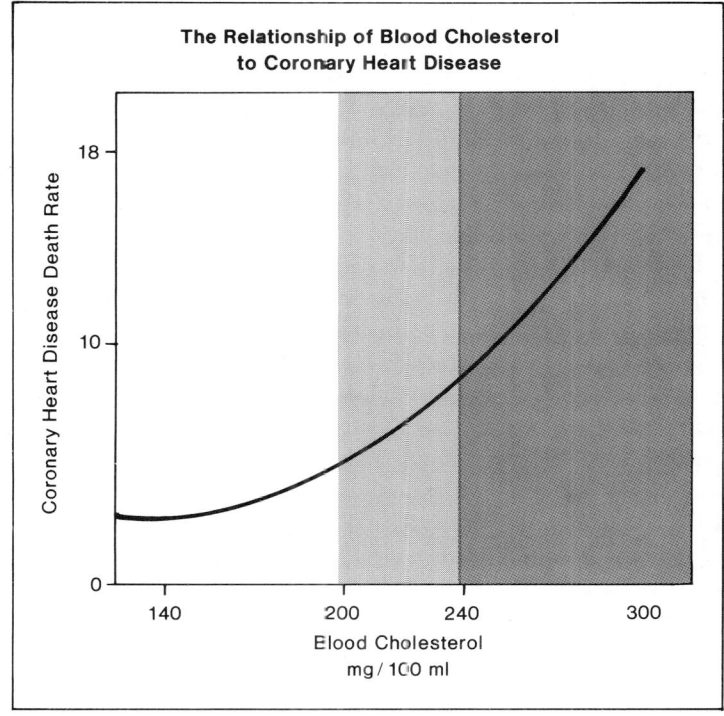

order of 30 milligrams. What this means is that if your blood cholesterol is reported as 220 (border-line-high), it may be possible that you actually have a cholesterol level of 190 (desirable) or 250 (high) if you vary, respectively, one standard error below or above your actual measurement of 220. For this reason, it may be a good idea to have a second test completed if you are concerned with your total cholesterol level.

The means by which cholesterol is transported in your blood may also be related to the development of atherosclerosis. In general, high levels of low density lipoproteins (LDL), particularly a form known simply as dense LDL, associated with beta apoproteins appear to contribute to the development of atherosclerosis by depositing cholesterol in the arterial wall. A current theory suggests the high levels may predispose the LDL to oxidation by macrophages and formation of foam cells for deposition of plaque. Levels of LDL less than 130 are desirable. On the other hand, high levels of high density lipoproteins (HDL), particularly the subfraction HDL_2, associated with alpha apoprotein may be protective against the development of atherosclerosis. Levels of 40 milligrams or more of HDL appear desirable. Research suggests that the HDL acts as a scavenger and picks up cholesterol from the arterial wall and transports it to the liver for removal from the body.

If your total blood cholesterol is borderline or high, a determination of the LDL and HDL levels may be desirable for they provide additional information relative to your risk. One common comparison is the ratio of total cholesterol (TC) to the HDL levels, or TC/HDL. A ratio of 4.5 is associated with an average risk for heart disease, while lower and higher ratios, respectively, are associated with a decreased and increased risk. For example, an individual with a total cholesterol of 200 and an HDL of 60 would have a ratio of 3.33 (200/60), or a lower risk, while someone with the same total cholesterol but an HDL of only 20 would have a much higher risk with a ratio of 10 (200/20). Other ratios, such as the ratio of LDL to HDL, are also used.

Although the health benefits of cholesterol reduction have been challenged in the popular literature by Thomas Moore, his conclusions have been effectively rebutted by several health organizations, including the Center for Science in the Public Interest. High blood triglyceride and cholesterol levels are often treated with drug therapy, particularly in those with genetic causes, but may also be modified favorably by diet and exercise. For many individuals, diet and exercise may be the first form of medical treatment.

Table 4.6 Recommended cholesterol levels of the National Cholesterol Education Program sponsored by the National Heart, Lung, and Blood Institute

	Total cholesterol classification	LDL cholesterol classification
Desirable	<200	<130
Borderline/high risk	200–239	130–159
High risk	>240	>160

What should I eat to modify my serum lipid profile favorably?

Several health organizations, including the American Heart Association, the National Institutes of Health, and the National Heart, Lung, and Blood Institute have recommended a number of dietary modifications that have been shown to lower serum cholesterol or serum triglycerides. Thorough coverage is presented in the review article by Kris-Etherton and others. These are practical recommendations which are based upon the available evidence.

1. Adjust the caloric intake to achieve and maintain ideal body weight. One of the most common causes of high triglyceride levels is too much body fat. In many cases, simply losing body weight or reducing caloric intake will reduce these levels.
2. Reduce the total amount of fats in the diet. As mentioned previously, less than 30 percent of the dietary Calories should be derived from fat. Reducing the total amount of fat will usually reduce the amount of Calories also, but nutrient content will actually improve.
3. Reduce the amount of saturated fat to less than 10 percent of dietary Calories. Saturated fats have been shown to increase blood cholesterol levels, particularly LDL cholesterol associated with development of atherosclerosis.
4. Reduce the consumption of hydrogenated oils or partially hydrogenated oils. They not only become more saturated, but may contain a greater proportion of *trans* unsaturated fatty acids, which are metabolized similarly to saturated fats. Tub type margarine, listing liquid oil first on the ingredient list, is a better choice than stick margarines.

5. Substitute polyunsaturated and monounsaturated fats for saturated fats, but consume only about 10 percent or less of the total dietary Calories in each form.

When substituted for saturated fats, polyunsaturated fatty acids have been reported to reduce serum cholesterol levels, including LDL cholesterol. However, high amounts of polyunsaturated fatty acids in the diet have been associated with the development of cancer of the colon; thus, try to limit the daily intake of polyunsaturated fats to 10 percent of the total Calories, or less. Researchers theorize that the double bonds in these fatty acids are easily oxidized and may produce carcinogenic free radicals. Fortunately, natural vegetable foods that are high in polyunsaturated fatty acids are also high in certain vitamins that have antioxidant properties and help counteract the oxidation of these bonds.

Monounsaturated fats appear to be just as effective as polyunsaturated fats in reducing total and LDL cholesterol without lowering HDL cholesterol. Olive and canola oil are particularly high in monounsaturated fatty acids. Earlier research, primarily with hypercholesteremic individuals, had suggested that polyunsaturated fats would also lower HDL cholesterol, an undesirable effect, while monounsaturated fats would not. However, Dreon and others recently noted no HDL-lowering effect of a polyunsaturated fat–enriched diet, when compared with a monounsaturated fat–enriched diet, in healthy individuals on a low-fat diet. With respect to plasma HDL cholesterol levels, these investigators concluded that there is no apparent advantage in using predominantly monounsaturated rather than polyunsaturated fats if subjects are on the generally recommended healthy diet reduced in fat.

The overall general recommendation is to consume more or less equal proportions of saturated, monounsaturated, and polyunsaturated fatty acids, possibly with a slightly higher proportion of monounsaturated and a lower proportion of saturated fats.

6. Consume foods rich in the omega-3 fatty acids, a special form of polyunsaturated fatty acids. The two principal omega-3 fatty acids are EPA (eicosapentaenoic acid) and DHA (docosahexaenoic acid). They are believed to prevent CHD by reducing serum cholesterol levels. Additionally, they are believed to replace other fatty acids in cell membranes and to modify several metabolic functions in the body. Among their effects may be reducing the viscosity of the blood by making the cell membranes of the red blood cells more fluid and helping prevent the formation of blood clots in the body by making platelets less sticky. They may also be less likely to lead to the production of various eicosanoids (prostaglandins and thromboxanes), metabolic by-products of cell membrane oxidation that act like hormones and may have adverse health effects such as elevated blood pressure. Fish such as salmon, sardines, mackerel, and tuna, as well as wheat germ oil, canola oil, and common varieties of beans have substantial amounts of omega-3 fatty acids.

Although the American Heart Association does recommend an increased consumption of fish, it does not recommend the use of commercial fish oil supplements, for their long-term effectiveness and safety have not been established. They are high in Calories in the dosages recommended, and they may have adverse effects in some individuals, such as prolonged bleeding time.

7. Decrease the amount of dietary cholesterol. Even though only about 35–40 percent of dietary cholesterol is absorbed, blood serum levels go up with increasing amounts in the diet. This is particularly true for cholesterol responders, those individuals with a genetic predisposition whose body production of cholesterol does not automatically decrease when the dietary intake increases. The average U.S. daily intake is approximately 400–500 milligrams or more. It is recommended that this amount be reduced to 300 milligrams per day or less, or 100 milligrams per 1,000 Calories consumed.

The two most significant dietary reductions should be saturated fat and cholesterol. The interested reader is referred to the excellent article by Sonja Conner and others detailing the cholesterol: saturated fat index, a guide to foods that tend to raise or lower serum cholesterol levels.

8. If you consume foods with artificial fats, such as Simplesse, do so in moderation. For

individuals attempting to lose body fat, excessive caloric intake is a major concern, and reducing the dietary fat content is one of the easiest ways to cut Calories. Additionally, reducing the dietary fat content and losing body weight both may contribute to lowering of serum cholesterol. Consuming foods with artificial fats, as substitutes for the regular fat content, will help save Calories. Additionally, in recent research Olestra (a fat substitute pending approval by the Food and Drug Administration), when substituted for dietary fat, has shown a reduction in cholesterol absorption from the intestinal tract.

Nevertheless, experts advise caution in the use of fat substitutes. They note that these substances are not a panacea for obesity, heart disease, or cancer and may actually backfire as Americans rationalize by eating more fat rather than less. Artificial fats may help reduce the total fat content in the diet, but they are not a substitute for the Healthy American Diet focusing upon whole grains, fruits, vegetables, and meat and milk products low in fat.

9. Reduce intake of refined sugars and increase consumption of foods high in starch and fiber. Table sugar provokes higher triglyceride concentrations more than complex carbohydrates do. Again, the value of complex carbohydrates in the diet is stressed, particularly high fiber foods, as a means to help reduce serum cholesterol. Guidelines presented in the preceding chapter are helpful.

10. Nibble food throughout the day. Interestingly, David Jenkins showed a significant reduction in serum LDL cholesterol if subjects consumed their daily Calories, actually the same food, throughout the day rather than in three concentrated meals at breakfast, lunch, and dinner.

In simple practical terms, what do all of these recommendations mean? In essence, eat less butter, fatty meats, organ foods such as liver and kidney, egg yolks, whole milk, cheeses, ice cream, gravies, creamed foods, desserts with animal fats, and refined sugar. Eat more lean meats, fish, poultry, egg whites, skim and low fat milk products, fruits and vegetables, beans, and whole grain products, or the Healthy American Diet.

Can exercise training also elicit favorable changes in the serum lipid profile?

Physical inactivity, or lack of exercise, has been identified as one of the risk factors associated with an increased incidence of atherosclerosis and cardiovascular disease. Hence, exercise programs stressing aerobic endurance-type activities have been advocated as a means of reducing the incidence levels of these conditions. However, the precise mechanism whereby exercise may help reduce the morbidity and mortality of CAD has not been identified. Therefore, many authorities believe that the beneficial effect may not be due to exercise itself, but rather the possible associated effects such as reductions in body weight and blood pressure. Although some investigators believe endurance exercise may have a preventive function independent of these associated effects, it also exerts a significant beneficial influence on the serum lipid profile which, like blood pressure, is one of the major risk factors. A significant brief exercise session, such as a five-mile run, may elicit temporary changes in serum lipids, but our concern here is with the more permanent effects associated with a habitual endurance exercise training program.

Literally hundreds of epidemiological and experimental studies have been conducted in the past decade to address the question posed above. Space does not permit a detailed analysis of each, but several major reviews of the worldwide literature have recently been reported by such prominent authorities as Dufaux, Tran, Murray and others, and by the internationally renowned Stanford University research group, Haskell, Superko, and Wood. These reviews have noted a rather consistent pattern relating exercise and blood lipids. In general, increased levels of exercise are associated with lower plasma levels of triglycerides and LDL, higher levels of HDL, and a lower ratio of total cholesterol to HDL. Research has also indicated that the individuals at greatest risk, those with a total cholesterol over 240, may experience the greatest benefit. Moreover, research has also revealed that the effects of exercise training are additive to a diet modified in fat content, such as substitution of polyunsaturated omega-3 fatty acids for saturated fat.

To bring about significant changes in the serum lipid profile, the endurance exercise equivalent of running 10–15 miles per week, about an additional 1,000 Calories of energy expenditure, appears to be a reasonable estimate of a weekly threshold level. This level must be held for a prolonged period, possibly 3–9 months, before benefits may be noted. Additional caloric expenditure per week may elicit further improvements; Haskell has noted the effect of exercise may be dose related. Lifetime aerobic exercise appears to be the key.

However, in women, excessive exercise that causes amenorrhea may reverse these benefits. The effects of exercise-induced amenorrhea will be discussed further in Chapters 7 and 9, but it appears that the lower levels of estrogen associated with this condition may lead to lower levels of HDL-cholesterol.

Although the precise biochemical mechanisms underlying the beneficial effects of exercise on serum lipids have not been identified, researchers have found that in physically trained males and females, activity levels of several enzymes, such as hepatic lipase and lipoprotein lipase, are modified in such a way as to promote a more rapid catabolism of triglycerides and a greater production of HDL. Exercise may also favorably modify the serum lipid levels by helping the individual lose body fat or influencing changes in other aspects of his or her lifestyle, such as diet.

Is coffee or caffeine harmful to health?

This is one of the most hotly debated questions over the past twenty years. Since the early 1970s a number of epidemiological studies have linked coffee or caffeine consumption with the development of a variety of health problems, including heart disease, high serum cholesterol, high blood pressure, pancreatic cancer, birth defects, and fibrocystic breast disease (painful lumps in the breast tissue). Conversely, other epidemiological studies have shown no relationship between coffee or caffeine consumption and these health problems. Investigators have looked at a variety of factors, including different sources of caffeine such as coffee versus tea, regular coffee versus decaffeinated coffee, and even the method of preparing coffee, such as filtered versus boiled.

The overall general conclusion of most reviewers and health organizations appears to suggest that moderate coffee or caffeine consumption poses few major health risks to the average American. For example, in 1988, the office of the U.S. Surgeon General reported that evidence of the relationship between coffee and heart disease was too weak to warrant recommending a reduction of coffee consumption, while in 1991 the American Heart Association stated that moderate coffee consumption does not appear to be harmful. In 1984, the American Cancer Society concluded that coffee does not increase the risk of cancer.

On the other hand, coffee or caffeine may pose some problems to some individuals. Abstainers or those who consume little caffeine may experience nervousness, irritability, headaches, or insomnia with moderate doses, although long-term consumption of coffee leads to the development of tolerance and reduction of these "coffee nerves" symptoms. Some susceptible individuals experience heart arrhythmias following caffeine consumption, while others experience gastric distress due to increased secretion of acids in the stomach. Thus, individuals with such cardiovascular and gastrointestinal problems should avoid caffeine. Moreover, the association between caffeine and fibrocystic breast disease and birth defects continues to be investigated. Finally, massive doses of caffeine may be fatal. Although rare, death may result from overdoses of caffeine-containing diet or stimulant pills.

Overall, physicians and other reviewers generally recommend moderation in coffee or caffeine consumption for regular consumers of these products, which usually is translated as approximately two to three 6-ounce cups of coffee per day, or about 200–300 milligrams of caffeine. It may be prudent for women who are pregnant or nursing to lower this amount, or abstain.

Caffeine may confer some possible health benefits. It may diminish drowsiness, increase alertness, and promote clearer thinking, all factors that may contribute to safer automobile operation under certain conditions.

References

Books

American Heart Association. 1988. *1988 Heart Facts.* Dallas, TX: American Heart Association.

Berman, M., Grundy, S., and Howard B. (Eds.) 1982. *Lipoprotein Kinetics and Modeling.* New York: Academic Press.

Cooper, K. 1988. *Controlling Cholesterol.* Toronto: Bantam Books.

Cureton, T. 1972. *The Physiological Effects of Wheat Germ Oil on Humans in Exercise.* Springfield, IL: C. C. Thomas.

Haas, R. 1986. *Eat to Succeed.* New York: Rawson Associates.

Hickson, J., and Wolinsky, I. 1989. *Nutrition in Exercise and Sport.* Boca Raton, FL: CRC Press.

Hunt, S., and Groff, J. 1990. *Advanced Nutrition in Human Metabolism.* St. Paul, MN: West Publishing Company.

National Research Council. 1989. *Recommended Dietary Allowances.* Washington, DC: National Academy Press.

National Research Council. 1989. *Diet and Health: Implications for Reducing Chronic Disease Risk.* Washington, DC: National Academy Press.

U.S. Department of Health and Human Services. 1989. *Eating to Lower Your High Blood Cholesterol.* NIH Publication No. 89–2920.

U.S. Department of Health and Human Services. 1989. *Report of the Expert Panel on Detection, Evaluation, and Treatment of High Blood Cholesterol in Adults.* NIH Publication No. 89–2925.

Wadler, G., and Hainline, B. 1989. *Drugs and the Athlete.* Philadelphia: F. A. Davis.

Williams, M. 1985. *Nutritional Aspects of Human Physical and Athletic Performance.* Springfield, IL: C. C. Thomas.

Review Articles

American Heart Association. 1988. Dietary guidelines for healthy American adults. A statement for physicians and health professionals by the Nutrition Committee, American Heart Association. *Circulation.* 77:721A–724A.

Askew, W. 1983. Fat metabolism in exercise. In: *Nutrient Utilization During Exercise,* ed. E. Fox. Columbus, OH: Ross Laboratories.

Bierman, E., and Chait, A. 1988. Nutrition and diet in relation to hyperlipidemia and atherosclerosis. In: *Modern Nutrition in Health and Disease,* M. Shils and V. Young, eds. Philadelphia: Lea & Febiger.

Borenstein, B., and Lachance, P. 1988. Effects of processing and preparation on the nutritional value of food. In: *Modern Nutrition in Health and Disease,* eds. M. Shils and V. Young. Philadelphia: Lea & Febiger.

Broquist, H. 1988. "Vitamin like" molecules (B) Carnitine. In: *Modern Nutrition in Health and Disease,* eds. M. Shils and V. Young. Philadelphia: Lea & Febiger.

Bucci, L. 1989. Nutritional ergogenic aids. In: *Nutrition in Exercise and Sport,* eds. J. Hickson and I. Wolinsky. Boca Raton, FL: CRC Press.

Buchanan, C. 1989. Lecithin supplements: a source of help or hype? *Environmental Nutrition* 12:1, June.

Bulow, J. 1988. Lipid mobilization and utilization. In: *Principles of Exercise Biochemistry,* ed. J. Poortmans. Basel: Karger.

Center for Science in the Public Interest. 1989. The mistaken "cholesterol myth." *Nutrition Action Healthletter* 16:4–7, November.

Conlee, R. 1991. Amphetamines, caffeine, and cocaine. In: *Ergogenics: The Enhancement of Sports Performance,* eds. D. Lamb and M. Williams. Indianapolis, IN: Benchmark.

Conner, S., et al. 1989. The cholesterol–saturated fat index for coronary protection: Background, use, and a comprehensive table of foods. *Journal of the American Dietetic Association* 89:807–816.

Delbecke, F., and Delbackere, M. 1984. Caffeine: Use and abuse in sports. *International Journal of Sports Medicine* 5:179–92.

Dufaux, B. 1982. Plasma lipoproteins and physical activity: A review. *International Journal of Sports Medicine* 3:123–26.

Essen, B. 1977. Intramuscular substrate utilization during prolonged exercise. *Annals of the New York Academy of Science* 301:30–44.

Fuerst, M. 1982. Fat loading improved endurance performance. *Physician and Sportsmedicine* 10:28.

Friedman, R. (Ed.). 1988. Caffeine update: The news is good. *University of California, Berkeley, Wellness Letter* 4:4–5, July.

Goldberg, L., and Elliot, D. 1987. The effect of exercise on lipid metabolism in men and women. *Sports Medicine* 4:307–21.

Gollnick, P. 1988. Energy metabolism and prolonged exercise. In: *Prolonged Exercise,* eds. D. Lamb and R. Murray. Indianapolis, IN: Benchmark.

Goodnight, S. 1989. The vascular effects of omega-3 fatty acids. *Journal of Investigative Dermatology* 53:1025–65.

Gorski, J. et al. 1990. Hepatic lipid metabolism in exercise and training. *Medicine and Science in Sports and Exercise* 22:213–21.

Green, M. 1989. A perspective on dietary fats, plasma cholesterol and atherosclerosis. *Nutrition Today* 24:6–8, May/June.

Grundy, S. 1989. Recent research on dietary fatty acids: Implications for future dietary recommendations. *Food & Nutrition News* 61:1–3, November/December.

Grundy, S., et al. 1989. The place of HDL in cholesterol management. A perspective from the National Cholesterol Educational Program. *Archives of Internal Medicine* 149:505–10.

Haskell, W. 1986. The influence of exercise training on plasma lipids and lipoproteins in health and disease. *Acta Medica Scandinavica* 711 (Suppl):25–37.

Hespel, P., et al. 1988. Effects of training on the serum lipid profile in normal men. *Drugs* 36 (Supplement 2P): 27–32.

Holloszy, J. 1990. Utilization of fatty acids during exercise. In: *Biochemistry of Exercise VII,* eds. A. Taylor et al. Champaign, IL: Human Kinetics.

Hultman, E., and Harris, R. 1988. Carbohydrate metabolism. In: *Principles of Exercise Biochemistry,* ed. J. Poortmans. Basel: Karger.

Jacobson, B., and Kulling, F. 1989. Health and ergogenic effects of caffeine on athletes. *British Journal of Sports Medicine* 23:34–38.

Kantha, S. 1987. Dietary effects of fish oils on human health: A review of recent studies. *Yale Journal of Biological Medicine* 60:37–44.

Kinsella, J. 1989. Dietary polyunsaturated fatty acids, eicosanoids and chronic diseases. *Contemporary Nutrition* 14(1):1–2.

Kris-Etherton, P., et al. 1988. The effect of diet on plasma lipids, lipoproteins, and coronary heart disease. *Journal of the American Dietetic Association* 88: 1373–1400.

Liebman, B. 1990. Trans in trouble. *Nutrition Action Healthletter* 17:7.

Linscheer, W., and Vergroesen, A. 1988. Lipids. In: *Modern Nutrition in Health and Disease*, eds. M. Shils and V. Young. Philadelphia: Lea & Febiger.

Mattson, F. 1989. A changing role for dietary monounsaturated fatty acids. *Journal of the American Dietetic Association* 89:387–91.

Mitchell, D. 1991. Coffee and cholesterol: Grounds for concern? *It's Your Cholesterol!* 3:1–4.

Montogmery, A. 1988. Cholesterol tests: How accurate are they? *Nutrition Action Healthletter* 15(1):4–7, May.

Moore, T. 1989. The cholesterol myth. *The Atlantic Monthly*. September:37–80.

Murray, T., et al. 1989. Regulation of lipids and lipoproteins by diet and exercise. In: *Nutrition in Exercise and Sport*, eds. J. Hickson and I. Wolinsky. Boca Raton, FL: CRC Press.

Newsholme, E. 1988. Application of knowledge of metabolic integration to the problem of metabolic limitations in sprints, middle distance and marathon running. In: *Principles of Exercise Biochemistry*, ed. J. Poortmans. Basel: Karger.

Newsholme, E. 1988. Basic aspects of metabolic regulation and their application to provision of energy in exercise. in: *Principles of Exercise Biochemistry*, ed. J. Poortmans. Basel: Karger.

Olson, R. (Ed.). 1987. Fish oil and the development of atherosclerosis. *Nutrition Reviews* 45:90–92.

Powers, S., and Dodd, S. 1985. Caffeine and endurance performance. *Sports Medicine* 2:165–74.

Shepherd, R., and Bah, M. 1988. Cyclic AMP regulation of fuel metabolism during exercise: Regulation of adipose tissue lipolysis during exercise. *Medicine and Science in Sports and Exercise* 20:531–38.

Smith, S. 1988. "Trans" fatty acids in processed foods . . . Something to worry about? *Environmental Nutrition* 11:6–7. February.

Stamford, B. 1990. What cholesterol means to you. *Physician and Sportsmedicine* 18:149.

Steinberg, D., and Witztum, J. 1990. Lipoproteins and atherogenesis. *Journal of the American Medical Association* 264:3047–52.

Stone, N. 1990. Diet, lipids, and coronary heart disease. *Endocrinology and Metabolism Clinics of North America* 19:321–44.

Superko, H., Haskell, W., and Wood, P. 1985. Modification of plasma cholesterol through exercise. Rationale and recommendations. *Postgraduate Medicine* 78:64–75.

Terjung, R., and Kaciuba-Uscilko, H. 1986. Lipid metabolism during exercise: Influence of training. *Diabetes/Metabolism Reviews* 2:35–51.

Tran, Z., and Weltman, A. 1985. Differential effects of exercise on serum lipid and lipoprotein levels seen with changes in body weight. A meta-analysis. *Journal of the American Medical Association* 254:919–24.

Wagenmakers, A. 1991. L-carnitine supplementation and performance in man. *Medicine and Sport Science: Advances in Nutrition and Top Sport.* F. Brouns (Ed.) 32:110–27.

Watson, R. 1988. Caffeine: Is it dangerous to health? *American Journal of Health Promotion* 2:13–21.

Weinberg, L. 1989. Coffee: Benign beverage or dangerous drink? *Environmental Nutrition* 12:1–3, August.

Wilcox, A. 1990. Caffeine and endurance performance. *Sports Science Exchange.* 3:1–5, May.

Work, J. 1991. Are java junkies poor sports? *Physician and Sportsmedicine* 19:82–88.

Yetiv, J. 1988. Clinical application of fish oils. *Journal of the American Medical Association* 260:665–70.

Yocum, L. (Ed.). 1986. Carnitine toxicity. *Sports Medicine Digest* 8:4, July.

Specific Studies

Bak, A., and Groboee, D. 1989. The effect on serum cholesterol of coffee brewed by filtering or boiling. *New England Journal of Medicine* 321:1432–36.

Brevetti, G., et al. 1988. Increases in walking distance in patients with peripheral vascular disease treated with L-carnitine: A double-bind, cross-over study. *Circulation* 77:767–73.

Burns, J., et al. 1988. Effects of choline ingestion on endurance performance. *Medicine and Science in Sports and Exercise* 20:S25.

Costill, D., et al. 1979. Lipid metabolism in skeletal muscle of endurance trained males and females. *Journal of Applied Physiology* 47:787–91.

Costill, D., et al. 1978. Effects of caffeine ingestion on metabolism and exercise performance. *Medicine and Science in Sports* 10:155–58.

Dougherty, R., et al. 1988. Nutrient content of the diet when the fat is reduced. *American Journal of Clinical Nutrition* 48:570–75.

Erickson, M., et al. 1987. Effects of caffeine, fructose, and glucose ingestion on muscle glycogen utilization during exercise. *Medicine and Science in Sports and Exercise* 19:579–83.

Essig, D., et al. 1980. Muscle glycogen and triglyceride use during leg cycling following caffeine ingestion. *Medicine and Science in Sports and Exercise* 12:109, 1980.

Greig, C., et al. 1987. The effect of oral supplementation with L-carnitine on maximum and submaximum exercise capacity. *European Journal of Applied Physiology* 56:457–60.

Grundy, S. 1986. Comparison of monounsaturated fatty acids and carbohydrates for lowering plasma cholesterol. *New England Journal of Medicine* 314:745–48.

Harris, W., et al. 1990. Effects of fish oils on VLDL triglyceride kinetics in humans. *Journal of Lipid Research* 31:1549–58.

Hurley, B., et al. 1986. Muscle triglyceride utilization during exercise: Effect of training. *Journal of Applied Physiology* 60:562–67.

Ivy, J., et al. 1980. Contribution of medium and long chain triglyceride intake to energy metabolism during prolonged exercise. *International Journal of Sports Medicine* 1:15–20.

Jacobson, B., et al. 1991. Effect of caffeine on delicate motor performance. *Medicine and Science in Sports and Exercise* 23:S76.

Jandacek, R., et al. 1990. Effects of partial replacement of dietary fat by Olestra on cholesterol absorption in man. *Metabolism* 39:848–52.

Jenkins, D., et al. 1989. Nibbling versus gorging: Metabolic advantages of increased meal frequency. *New England Journal of Medicine* 321:929–34.

Lamon-Fava, S., et al. 1989. Effect of exercise and menstrual cycle status on plasma lipids, low density lipoprotein particle size, and apolipoproteins. *Journal of Clinical Endocrinology and Metabolism* 68:17–20.

Lennon, D., et al. 1986. Dietary carnitine intake related to skeletal muscle and plasma carnitine concentrations in adult men and women. *American Journal of Clinical Nutrition* 43:234–38.

Lennon, D., et al. 1983. Effects of acute moderate-intensity exercise on carnitine metabolism in men and women. *Journal of Applied Physiology* 55:489–95.

Lombard, K., et al. 1989. Carnitine status of lactoovovegetarians and strict vegetarian adults and children. *American Journal of Clinical Nutrition* 50:301–306.

Loy, S., et al. 1986. Effects of a 24-H fast on cycling endurance time. *Medicine and Science in Sports and Exercise* 18:S12–S13.

MacLean, D., et al. 1991. Muscle glycogen utilization during exhaustive cycling following caffeine ingestion. *Medicine and Science in Sports and Exercise* 23:S116.

Marconi, C., et al. 1985. Effects of L-carnitine loading on the aerobic and anaerobic performance of endurance athletes. *European Journal of Applied Physiology* 54:131–35.

Masana, L., et al. 1991. The Mediterranean-type diet: Is there a need for further modification? *American Journal of Clinical Nutrition* 53:886–89.

Massicotte, D., et al. 1990. Exogenous 13C-lipids and 13C-glucose oxidized during prolonged exercise in man: A comparison study. *Medicine and Science in Sports and Exercise* 22:S52.

Mattson, F., and Grundy, S. 1985. Comparison of effects of dietary saturated, monounsaturated and polyunsaturated fatty acids on plasma lipids and lipoproteins in man. *Journal of Lipid Research* 26:194–201.

Miller, J., et al. 1983. Effect of glycerol feeding on endurance and metabolism during prolonged exercise in man. *Medicine and Science in Sports and Exercise* 15:237–42.

Nagel, D., et al. 1989. Effects of an ultra-long distance (1000 km) race on lipid metabolism. *European Journal of Applied Physiology* 59:16–20.

Oyono-Enguelle, S., et al. 1988. Prolonged submaximal exercise and L-carnitine in humans. *European Journal of Applied Physiology* 58:53–61.

Sady, S., et al. 1988. Elevated high-density lipoprotein cholesterol in endurance athletes is related to enhanced plasma triglyceride clearance. *Metabolism* 37:568–72.

Satabin, P., et al. 1987. Metabolic and hormonal responses to lipid and carbohydrate diets during exercise in man. *Medicine and Science in Sports and Exercise* 19:218–23.

Scalfi, L., et al. 1991. Postprandial thermogenesis in lean and obese subjects after meals supplemented with medium-chain and long-chain triglycerides. *American Journal of Clinical Nutrition* 53:1130–33.

Spriet, L., and Graham, T. 1991. Caffeine ingestion enhances running and cycling endurance performance in trained runners. *Medicine and Science in Sports and Exercise* 23:S116.

Staton, W. 1951. The influence of soya lecithin on muscular strength. *Research Quarterly* 22:201–7.

Sullivan, V. 1990. Effect of caffeine on anaerobic performance. *Conference abstracts: Southeast Region, American College of Sports Medicine*, Columbia, SC.

Tarnopolsky, M., et al. 1989. Physiological responses to caffeine during endurance running in habitual caffeine users. Medicine and Science in Sports and Exercise 21:418–24.

Turcotte, L., et al. 1990. Differences in kinetics of muscle free fatty acid uptake during exercise in trained and untrained men. *Medicine and Science in Sports and Exercise* 22:S59.

Warhaftig, N., et al. 1990. Effects of caffeine withdrawal on free fatty acid mobilization in caffeine habituated male runners. *Medicine and Science in Sports and Exercise* 22:S85.

Warner, J., et al. 1989. Combined effects of aerobic exercise and omega-3 fatty acids in hyperlipidemic persons. *Medicine and Science in Sports and Exercise* 21:498–505.

Williams, J., et al. 1988. Caffeine, maximal power output, and fatigue. *British Journal of Sports Medicine* 22:132–34.

Williams, K., et al. 1990. The effect of caffeine on muscular strength, power, and power-endurance. *Medicine and Science in Sports and Exercise* 22:S85.

Williams, P. 1990. Weight set-point theory and the high-density lipoprotein concentrations of long-distance runners. *Metabolism* 39:460–67.

Wilt, T., et al. 1989. Fish oil supplementation does not lower plasma cholesterol in men with hypercholesteremia. *Annals of Internal Medicine* 111:900–5.

Wyss, V., et al. 1990. Effects of L-carnitine administration on VO_2 max and the aerobic-anaerobic threshold in normoxia and acute hypoxia. *European Journal of Applied Physiology* 60:1–6.

Key Terms

alanine

alpha-keto acid

amino acids

complementary proteins

complete proteins

deamination

essential (indispensable) amino
    acids

glucogenic amino acids

human growth hormone

incomplete proteins

ketogenic amino acids

lactovegetarian

legumes

limiting amino acid

nitrogen balance

nonessential (dispensable)
    amino acids

ovolactovegetarian

ovovegetarian

protein-sparing effect

proteinuria

purines

semivegetarian

sports anemia

urea

vegan

Key Concepts

Protein contains nitrogen, an element essential to the formation of 20 different amino acids, the building blocks of all body cells.

Essential, or indispensable, amino acids cannot be adequately synthesized in the body and thus must be obtained through dietary protein, whereas nonessential, or dispensable, amino acids may be synthesized in the body. However, all 20 amino acids are necessary for protein formation in the body.

The human body needs a balanced mixture of essential amino acids, and although animal protein provides all of the essential amino acids in the proper blend, a combination of certain plant proteins, such as grains and legumes, will satisfy this dietary requirement.

The RDA for protein is based upon the body weight of the individual, and the amount needed per unit body weight is greater during childhood and adolescence than during adulthood. The adult RDA is 0.8 grams of protein per kilogram body weight, or 0.36 grams per pound body weight.

Dietary protein should comprise approximately 12 percent of the daily caloric intake, and although animal foods in the meat and milk groups have a high protein content, they also may be high in fat.

The major function of dietary protein is to build and repair tissues, hormones, enzymes, and other body compounds, but it also may be used as a significant source of energy under certain conditions.

During exercise, particularly with low carbohydrate stores in the body, muscle protein may supply nearly 5–15 percent of the energy Calories.

Although protein catabolism may occur during exercise, protein synthesis predominates in the recovery period. The type of protein synthesized is specific to the type of exercise program, such as weight training or aerobic endurance.

Several recognized authorities have recommended a protein intake of 1.5–2.0 grams per kilograms per day for athletes attempting to gain weight, and about 1.2–1.5 grams per kilograms per day for endurance athletes.

Although some athletes may benefit from additional protein in the diet, they do not need expensive commercial protein supplements; instead they should obtain the extra protein they need through the increased caloric intake associated with exercise.

Amino acid supplements and other protein-type ergogenic aids are not currently considered to be effective as a means to improve physical performance, although additional research is needed since valid data is sparse.

Dietary deficiencies, as well as dietary excesses of protein and amino acids, may interfere with optimal physiological efficiency, which may lead to impairment of physical performance or health status.

Protein: The Tissue Builder

5

Introduction

Protein is one of our most essential nutrients. It has a wide variety of physiological functions that are essential to optimal physical performance. For example, protein forms the structural basis of muscle tissue, is the major component of most enzymes in the muscle, and can serve as a source of energy during exercise. Because protein is so important to the development and function of muscle tissue, and because most feats of human physical performance involve strenuous muscular activity in one form or another, it is no wonder that protein has persisted throughout the years as the food of the athlete. Indeed, surveys have revealed that the vast majority of high school and college athletes believe that athletic performance is improved by a high-protein diet.

Companies that market nutritional supplements for athletes have capitalized on this belief. Probably the athletic groups most susceptible to the lure of protein supplements are body builders and strength-type athletes, such as weight lifters and football players. Numerous high-protein products have been developed for these athletes in attempts to exploit the protein–muscle strength relationship. In recent years, specific amino acids have been theorized to maximize muscle mass and strength gains and have been advertised extensively in magazines for body builders. Some advertisements even suggest that certain amino acid mixtures have an effect similar to drugs such as anabolic steroids, which have been used to stimulate muscle development.

Protein supplements are marketed for other types of athletes as well. Although protein is not regarded as a major energy source during exercise, research has now suggested that endurance athletes may use some specific amino acids for energy production under certain conditions. It was not long after publication of these findings that a "new protein discovery" designed to replace these amino acids was advertised in magazines for runners.

There is no doubt that a certain amount of dietary protein is essential for all individuals. However, the advertisements directed toward athletes imply that additional protein, usually in the form of protein or amino acid supplements, is necessary to optimal performance. Although some investigators suggest that many athletes may need to increase their protein intake, the usual recommendation is to increase the intake of natural protein sources. On the other hand, other authorities contend that the athlete need only obtain the RDA for protein.

Does the physically active individual need more protein in the diet? The information presented in this chapter should help provide a general answer to this question. Topics to be covered include dietary needs and sources of protein, metabolic fates and functions in the body, the effects of exercise on protein metabolism and dietary requirements, the ergogenic potential of amino acid and other protein supplements, and health aspects of dietary protein.

Dietary Protein

What is protein?

Protein is a complex chemical structure containing carbon, hydrogen, and oxygen—just as carbohydrates and fats do. Protein has one other essential element—nitrogen, which constitutes about 16 percent of most dietary protein. These four elements are combined into a number of different structures called **amino acids**, each one possessing an amino group (NH_2), and an acid group (COOH), with the remainder being different combinations of carbon, hydrogen, oxygen, and in some cases sulfur. There are 20 amino acids (peptides), all of which can be combined in a variety of ways to form the proteins necessary for the structure and functions of the human body. Figure 5.1 depicts the formula of **alanine,** an amino acid discussed later.

Proteins are created when two amino acids link and form a peptide bond; hence, a dipeptide is formed. As more amino acids are added, a polypeptide is formed. Most proteins are polypeptides, combining up to 300 amino acids.

Protein is contained in both animal and plant foods. Humans obtain their supply of amino acids from these two general sources.

Is there a difference between animal and plant protein?

To answer this question, let us first look at a basic difference between two groups of amino acids. Humans can synthesize some amino acids in their bodies but cannot synthesize others. The nine amino

Figure 5.1.
The chemical structure of alanine, an amino acid. The amino group (NH₂) contains nitrogen, while the acid group is represented by COOH.

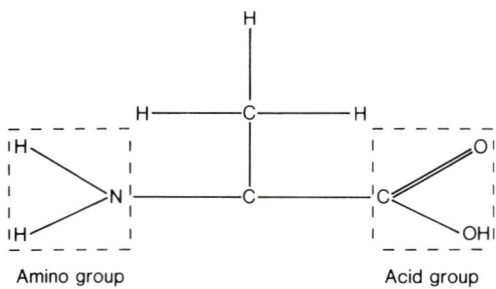

Amino group   Acid group

acids that cannot be manufactured in the body are called **essential,** or **indispensable, amino acids** and must be supplied in the diet. Those that may be formed in the body are called **nonessential,** or **dispensable, amino acids.** Although nutrition scientists prefer the terms indispensable and dispensable, this text uses the terms essential and nonessential, because they are most commonly used.

It should be noted that all 20 amino acids are necessary for protein synthesis in the body and must be present simultaneously for optimal maintenance of body growth and function. The use of the terms essential and indispensable in relation to amino acids is to distinguish those that must be obtained in the diet. Table 5.1 presents the dietary amino acids.

All natural, unprocessed animal and plant foods contain all 20 amino acids. However, the amount of each amino acid in specific foods varies. Over the years a number of different techniques have been used, usually with animals, to assess the quality of protein in selected foods. In general, those foods that contain an adequate content of all nine essential amino acids to support both life and growth are known as **complete proteins,** while those that have a deficiency of one or more essential amino acids and are unable to support life or growth are called **incomplete proteins.** The essential amino acid that is in short supply in a particular food is labeled the **limiting amino acid.**

The proteins ingested as animal products are generally regarded to be of a higher quality than those found in plants. This is not to say that an amino acid found in a plant is inferior to the same amino acid found in an animal. They are the same. When we look at the distribution of all the amino acids in the two food sources, however, we can then see two major reasons why animal protein is called a high-quality protein, whereas plant protein is of lower quality.

First, animal protein is a complete protein because it contains all the essential amino acids. Secondly, it also contains the essential amino acids in

Table 5.1   The dietary amino acids

Essential amino acids	Nonessential amino acids
Histidine	Alanine
Isoleucine	Arginine
Leucine	Asparagine
Lysine	Aspartic acid
Methionine	Cysteine
Phenylalanine	Glutamic acid
Threonine	Glutamine
Tryptophan	Glycine
Valine	Proline
	Serine
	Tyrosine

larger amounts and in the proper proportion. As noted above, all 20 amino acids must be present simultaneously for the body to synthesize them into necessary body proteins. If one amino acid is in short supply, protein construction may be blocked. Having the proper amount of animal protein in the diet is a good way to ensure receiving a balanced supply of amino acids.

Although plant proteins are regarded as being of lower quality than animal proteins, they still may provide you with all the protein and amino acids you need for optimal growth and development. However, proteins usually exist in smaller concentrations in plant foods. For example, two ounces of fish contain about 14 grams of protein, while two ounces of cooked macaroni only have 2 grams; two ounces of beans, which are generally regarded to be good sources of protein, have only 5 grams. In addition, most plant proteins have insufficient amounts of one or more of the essential amino acids. Grain products are usually deficient in lysine, whereas the legumes are low in methionine. An exception to this generality is the protein isolated from soybeans, which is comparable to animal protein. As we shall see in a later section, if vegetables are eaten in proper com-

Foods high in protein include meats, milk, and plants such as legumes.

(David Corona)

binations, the individual may receive a balanced supply of amino acids. Some populations receive most of their protein from plant sources.

What are some common foods that are good sources of protein?

Animal foods in the milk and meat groups generally have substantial amounts of high-quality protein. One glass of milk or its equivalent contains about 7–8 grams of protein, as does one ounce of meat, fish, or poultry. The **legumes,** such as dry beans, lentils, and peas, are relatively good sources of protein. The legumes also are high in carbohydrate and for this reason are currently classified as a starch/bread food exchange. However, because of their relatively high protein content, legumes may be used as a substitute within the meat exchange list. One-half cup contains about 7–9 grams of protein. Nuts contain fair amounts of protein but are high in fat. Fruits, vegetables, and grain products all have some protein, but the content varies; generally speaking, the protein content is low, ranging from less than 1 gram to about 3 grams of protein per serving, although some products may contain more, such as protein enriched pasta, e.g., Superoni.

Table 5.2 and Figure 5.2 present some common foods in each of several food groups, with the number of grams of protein in each. Notice the effect combination-type foods have on protein content: for example, macaroni and cheese versus plain macaroni.

How much dietary protein do I need?

Humans actually do not need protein per se, but rather an adequate amount of nitrogen and essential amino acids. However, because all nine essential

Table 5.2 Protein content in some common foods

Food	Amount	Protein (grams)
Milk List		
Milk, whole	1 c	8
Milk, skim	1 c	8
Cheese, cheddar	1 oz	7
Yogurt	1 c	8
Meat List		
Beef, lean	1 oz	8
Chicken, breast	1 oz	8
Luncheon meat	1 oz	5
Fish	1 oz	7
Eggs	1	6
Navy beans, cooked *	½ c	7
Peanuts, roasted	½ c	18
Peanut butter	1 tbsp	4
Vegetable List		
Broccoli	½ c	2
Carrots	1	1
Fruit List		
Banana	1	1
Orange	1	1
Pear	1	1
Starch/Bread List		
Bread, wheat	1 slice	3
Bran flakes	1 c	4
Doughnuts	1	1
Macaroni	½ c	3
Macaroni and cheese	½ c	9
Peas, green*	½ c	4
Potato, baked*	1	3

Protein (grams) may vary slightly from the food exchange lists since these data were derived from food analyses reported by the United States Department of Agriculture.
*Found in starch/bread list in Appendix H.

Figure 5.2.
Protein in food.

1 glass milk	=	8 grams
1 ounce chicken breast	=	7 grams
1 slice of bread	=	3 grams
½ cup vegetables	=	2 grams
½ cup navy beans	=	7 grams

amino acids and almost all dietary nitrogen are derived from dietary protein, it serves as the basis for our daily requirements.

In the United States, the recommended dietary intake of protein is based upon the RDA. The amount of protein necessary in the diet varies in different stages of the life cycle. During the early years of life, the child is manufacturing protein tissue during rapid growth stages, with the rate of growth (and thus the protein needs) varying from infancy through late adolescence. In young adulthood, the protein requirement stabilizes. Throughout the life cycle, however, the protein requirement established in the RDA is based upon the body weight of the individual. As a person goes through the life cycle, the amount of protein per unit body weight decreases.

Table 5.3 presents the amount of protein needed per kilogram or per pound of body weight for different age groups. To calculate your requirement, simply determine your body weight in kilograms or pounds and multiply by the appropriate figure for your age group. Recall that one kilogram is equal to 2.2 pounds. As an example, compute the protein requirement for a 154-pound, or 70-kg, average 23-year-old male:

0.36 g protein/ pound × 154 pounds = 55.4 or
    56 g protein/day
0.8 g protein/kg × 70 kg = 56 g protein/day

However, the minimum necessary intake of protein is much less than the RDA. If all proteins were the same quality as egg protein, then the RDA would be approximately 0.34 g protein/kg body weight per day. Allowances are made in the RDA for the fact that there exists individual variability in the need

Table 5.3   Grams of protein needed per kilogram body weight during the life cycle

Age in years	Grams/kg body weight	Grams/ pound body weight
0.0–0.5	2.2	1.00
0.5–1.0	1.6	.71
1–3	1.2	.56
4–6	1.2	.56
7–14	1.0	.45
15–18	0.9	.41
19–up	0.8	.36

for protein, that the biologic quality of all dietary protein is not as good as egg protein, and that the efficiency of utilization decreases at higher dietary protein intake levels. Hence, the RDA is adjusted upward to account for these factors.

The RDA for protein, as noted above, is based upon body weight of the individual at different ages. If you would take the recommended energy intake in Calories for each age group, say 2,200 C for the average adult female, and calculate the percentage of this value that the RDA for protein supplies, the values are less than 10 percent for each age group. Mathematically, 56 grams of protein, at 4 Calories per gram, total 224 Calories, which is about 10 percent of 2,200. This value is slightly lower than the generally recommended protein content, i.e., about 12–15 percent of daily caloric intake.

For the average adult, about 10–15 percent of the total protein requirement should consist of the essential amino acids; this amounts to a little over 6

Table 5.4   Estimated RDA for the essential amino acids in an adult male (70 kg)

	RDA (mg/kg)	Total mg
Histidine	8–12	560–840
Isoleucine	10	700
Leucine	14	980
Lysine	12	840
Methionine plus cystine	13	910
Phenylalanine plus tyrosine	14	980
Threonine	7	490
Tryptophan	3.5	245
Valine	10	700
Total		6405–6685

grams. Table 5.4 lists the estimated RDA for these nine amino acids for an adult male. Phenylalanine is an essential amino acid, whereas tyrosine is normally listed as a nonessential amino acid. Both are of similar chemical structure so that when substantial quantities of tyrosine are contained in the diet, the need for phenylalanine will decrease somewhat. The same holds true for the essential amino acid methionine and its chemically related counterpart, cysteine. Although Young and his associates recently suggested that the RDA for essential amino acids are too low and recommended an intake about twice as high, individuals who obtain the RDA for protein should have no problem obtaining even the higher values recommended by Young.

Fortunately we do not need to memorize these amino acids and check our food products to see if they are present. A few general rules can help ensure that we do receive a balanced supply in our diet.

What are some dietary guidelines to insure adequate protein intake?

To answer in one sentence: Eat a wide variety of animal and plant foods. The high-quality, complete proteins are obtained primarily from animal foods. Meat, fish, eggs, poultry, milk, and cheese contain the type and amount of the essential amino acids necessary for maintaining life and promoting growth and development. They are high-nutrient-density foods. Because animal protein is of high quality, you do not need as much of it to satisfy your RDA. For example, although the average male needs about 56 grams of protein per day, he only needs 45 grams if it is animal protein. One glass of milk, with 9 grams of protein, will provide 20 percent of his protein RDA. Two glasses of milk, one egg, and three ounces of meat, fish or poultry will provide 100 percent of

his RDA. In addition, a substantial proportion of daily vitamin and mineral needs will also be supplied in these foods. As noted in Chapter 4, selection of low-fat foods will enhance the nutrient density by reducing Calories.

Plant foods also may provide good sources of protein. Grain products such as wheat, rice, and corn, as well as soybeans, peas, beans, and nuts, have a substantial protein content. However, most plant foods contain incomplete proteins because they lack a sufficient quantity of some essential amino acids. For this reason, the protein RDA for the average adult male is 65 grams per day when plant proteins are the primary source. If certain plant foods are eaten together, they may supply all the essential amino acids necessary for human nutrition and be as complete a protein as animal protein. This topic is addressed later in the chapter.

Metabolism and Function

What happens to protein in the human body?

Dietary protein consists of long, complex chains of amino acids. In the digestive process, enzymes in the stomach and small intestine break the complex protein down into polypeptides and then into individual amino acids. The amino acids are absorbed through the wall of the small intestine, pass into the blood, and then to the liver via the portal vein. The digestion of protein takes several hours, but once the amino acids enter the blood they are cleared within 5–10 minutes. There is a constant interchange of the amino acids among the blood, the liver, and the body tissues. The liver is a critical center in amino acid metabolism. It is continually synthesizing a balanced amino acid mixture for the diverse protein requirements of the body. These amino acids are secreted into the blood and carried as free amino acids or as plasma proteins such as albumin.

The most important metabolic fate of the amino acids is the formation of specific proteins, including the structural proteins such as muscle tissue and the functional proteins such as enzymes. Body cells obtain amino acids from the blood, and the genetic apparatus in the cell nucleus directs the synthesis of proteins specific to the cell needs. The body cells may also use some of the nitrogen from the amino acids to form non-protein nitrogen compounds, such as creatine. For example, the muscle cells will form contractile proteins as well as the enzymes and creatine phosphate necessary for energy production. The body cells will use only the amount of amino acids necessary to meet their protein needs.

They cannot store excess amino acids, although the protein formed may be catabolized to release amino acids back to the blood.

Because the human body does not have a mechanism to store nitrogen, it cannot store amino acids per se. Through the process of **deamination** the amino group (NH_2) containing the nitrogen is removed from the amino acid, leaving a substrate known as an **alpha-ketoacid.** The excess nitrogen must be excreted from the body. In essence, the liver forms ammonia from the excess nitrogen; the ammonia is converted into **urea,** which passes into the blood and is eventually eliminated by the kidneys into the urine.

The alpha-ketoacid that is released may have several fates. For one, it can recombine with another amino group and be reconstituted to an amino acid. It also may be channeled into the metabolic pathways of carbohydrate and fat. The liver is the main organ where this conversion occurs. In essence, some of the amino acids are said to be **glucogenic amino acids,** that is, glucose forming. At various stages of the energy transformations within the liver, the glucogenic amino acids may be converted to glucose. The process is called gluconeogenesis. The **ketogenic amino acids** are metabolized in the liver to ketones, which are eventually converted to fat; this process is called ketogenesis. The glucose and fat produced may be transported to other parts of the body to be used. Thus, although excess protein cannot be stored as amino acids in the body, the energy content is not wasted, for it is converted to either carbohydrate or fat.

Figure 5.3 presents a summary of the fates of protein in human metabolism.

Can protein be formed from carbohydrates and fats?

Yes, but with some major limitations. Protein has one essential element, nitrogen, which is not possessed by either carbohydrate or fat. However, if the body has an excess of amino acids, the liver may be able to use the nitrogen-containing amino groups from these excess amino acids and combine them with alpha-ketoacids derived from either carbohydrate or fat metabolism. A key alpha-ketoacid from carbohydrate is pyruvic acid, while fat yields acetoacetic acid. The net result is the formation in the body of some of the nonessential amino acids using carbohydrates and fats as part of the building materials. Keep in mind that nitrogen must be present for this to occur, and its source is through dietary protein.

What are the major functions of protein in human nutrition?

Dietary protein may be utilized to serve all three major functions of food. Through the action of the individual amino acids, protein serves as the structural basis for the vast majority of the body tissues, is essential for regulating metabolism, and can be used as an energy source. In one way or another protein is involved in almost all body functions. Its individual roles are beyond the scope of this text, so the following discussion represents just some of its major functions of importance to health and fitness.

Protein is the main nutrient used in the formation of all body tissues. This role is extremely important in periods of rapid growth, such as childhood and adolescence. Athletes who attempt to gain weight also need an adequate dietary supply of protein. Certain amino acids, such as the branched-chain amino acids (BCAA) leucine, isoleucine, and valine, constitute a significant amount of muscle tissue.

Protein is critical in the regulation of human metabolism. It is used in the formation of all enzymes, many hormones, and other compounds that control body functions. Insulin, hemoglobin, and the oxidative enzymes in the mitochondria are all proteins that have important roles in regulating metabolism during exercise. Other metabolic roles of protein include the maintenance of water balance and acid-base balance, regulation of the blood clotting process, prevention of infection, and development of immunity to disease. Proteins also serve as carriers for nutrients in the blood, such as the free fatty acids (FFA) and the lipoproteins, and help transport nutrients into the body cells.

Although protein is not a major energy source for humans at rest, it can serve such a function under several conditions. In nutritional balance, the priority use of dietary protein is to promote synthesis of body proteins essential for optimal structure and function. However, as noted above, excess dietary protein may be converted to carbohydrate or fat and then enter metabolic pathways for energy production or storage. On the other hand, during periods of starvation or semistarvation, adequate amounts of dietary or endogenous carbohydrates and dietary fats may not be available. Both dietary protein and the body protein stores are used for energy purposes in such a situation, because energy production takes precedence over tissue building in metabolism. Hence, if the active individual desires to maintain lean body mass, it is essential to have not only adequate protein intake but also sufficient carbohydrate Calories in the diet to provide a **protein-sparing**

Figure 5.3.

Simplified diagram of protein metabolism. Following the digestion of dietary proteins, one of the major functions of the amino acids is the synthesis of body tissues, enzymes, hormones, and antibodies. However, protein also is constantly being degraded by the liver. The excess nitrogen is excreted as urea while the carbon residue may be converted into carbohydrate or fat.

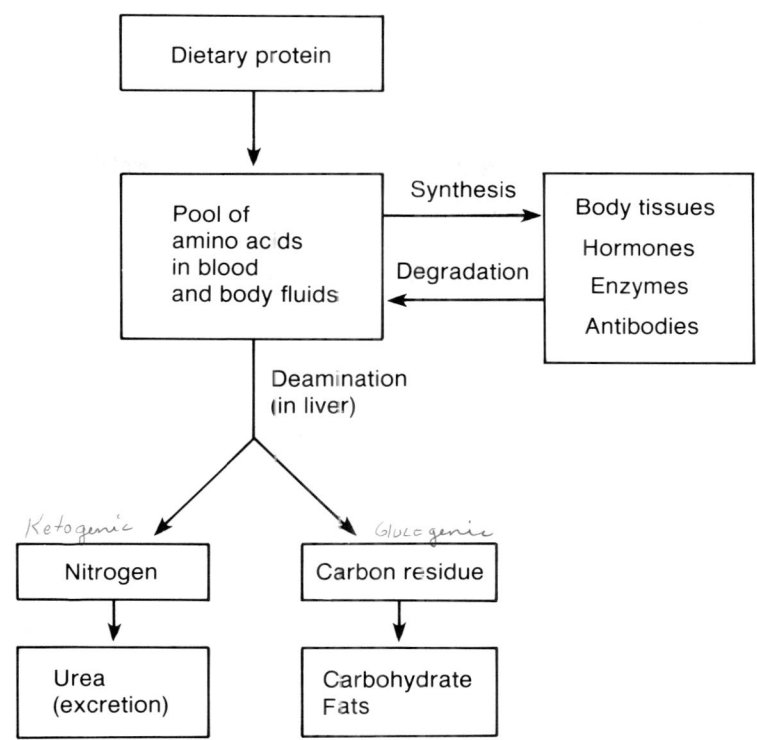

effect. In other words, carbohydrate Calories will be used for energy production, thus sparing utilization of protein as an energy source and allowing it to be used for its more important metabolic functions.

Although body proteins are composed of all 20 amino acids, individual amino acids may have important specific effects in the body. For example, tryptophan and tyrosine are important for the formation of several chemical transmitters in the brain, while the branched-chain amino acids (leucine, isoleucine, and valine) are major components of muscle tissue.

Because of the diverse roles of protein and amino acids in the body, athletes have used protein supplements for years in attempts to improve performance. Amino acid supplements have only recently been introduced for this purpose. The effectiveness of such supplements is evaluated in later sections.

Proteins and Exercise

Are proteins used for energy during exercise?

Protein generally has not been regarded as an important source of energy during exercise because, as noted in the previous two chapters, carbohydrate and

fats serve this purpose quite well. Research has now shown, however, that protein may be a significant source of energy during exercise under certain conditions.

Scientists have used a variety of techniques to study protein metabolism during exercise. Because urea is a by-product of protein metabolism, its concentration in the urine, blood, and sweat has been analyzed. Also, the presence in the urine of a marker for muscle protein breakdown known as 3-methylhistidine, a modified amino acid, has been studied to evaluate protein catabolism. The **nitrogen balance** technique consists of precisely measuring nitrogen intake and excretion to determine whether the individual is in positive or negative nitrogen (protein) balance. Finally, radio-labeled isotopes of amino acids have been ingested or injected to study their metabolic fate during exercise.

Using these techniques, most investigators in this area, including George Brooks, Gail Butterfield, G. Lynis Dohm, William Evans, James Hickson, Peter Lemon, Jacques Poortmans, and Robert Wolfe, have reported that the available data appear to support an increased use of protein, or amino acids, as an energy source during exercise. However, questions still remain concerning the specific protein sources and their proportionate contribution. In the majority of exercise tasks, including strenuous weight training, protein appears to be a relatively minor source of energy and accounts for less than 5 percent of the total energy cost of the activity. As Poortmans has noted, protein may be used to produce significant amounts of ATP in the muscle, but the rate of production is much slower than with carbohydrate and fat, the preferred fuels. On the other hand, Lemon has reported that in the latter stage of prolonged endurance exercise, protein could contribute up to 15 percent of the total energy cost. In this regard, prolonged exercise may be comparable to a state of starvation. As the endurance athlete depletes the endogenous carbohydrate stores, the body catabolizes some of its protein for energy or eventual conversion to glucose. Protein catabolism has been shown to increase significantly even when muscle glycogen is depleted by only about 33–55 percent.

In general, a brief session of exercise lowers the rate of protein synthesis and speeds protein breakdown. The exact mechanisms of protein metabolism during exercise have not been determined, though several mechanisms have been proposed. Parkhouse has reported that exercise, particularly exercise to exhaustion, activates specific proteolytic enzymes in the muscle that degrade the myofibrillar protein. Fitts and Metzger found elevated levels of proteolytic enzymes in fatigued muscle. A number of amino acids released by muscle tissue breakdown could enter the energy pathways, but the major research effort has focused on the fate of leucine, one of the branched-chain amino acids in the muscle. The oxidation of leucine has been shown to increase during exercise. In essence, the by-products of leucine catabolism eventually combine with pyruvate in the muscle cell and are converted to alanine and an alpha-ketoacid. The alpha-ketoacid may enter the Krebs cycle and be used for energy production. The alanine is released into the bloodstream and transported to the liver where it is converted into glucose. The glucose may then be released into the blood to be used by the central nervous system and may eventually find its way to the contracting muscle to be used as an energy source. Alanine appears to be an important means of transporting the amino group to the liver for excretion as urea. This overall process involving gluconeogenesis, known as the glucose–alanine cycle, is depicted graphically in Figure 5.4. Some investigators have noted that during the latter part of endurance exercise, the blood levels of alanine increase, presumably because more is released from the muscle. However, the estimated glucose production approximates only 4

grams per hour, which might be important in mild-intensity exercise but is possibly insignificant during high-intensity exercise when carbohydrate use may approximate 3 grams per minute. Additionally, several investigators have reported an increased release of branched-chain amino acids (BCAA) from the liver during endurance exercise, with subsequent uptake by the muscle cells.

Thus, protein (amino acids) can be utilized during exercise to provide energy directly in the muscle and via glucose produced in the liver, particularly when the body stores of glycogen and glucose are low. A low-carbohydrate diet will facilitate this process. On the other hand, adequate carbohydrate intake before and during prolonged exercise will help reduce the use of body protein for this purpose, because the presence of adequate muscle glycogen appears to inhibit enzymes that catalyze muscle protein. Thus, high carbohydrate diets may have a protein-sparing effect for distance runners.

Although the available evidence suggests that metabolism of protein and its use as an energy source are increased during exercise, the magnitude of its contribution may depend on a variety of factors, such as the intensity and duration of exercise and the availability of other fuels, such as glycogen, in the muscle. This topic is the subject of continuing research.

Does exercise increase protein losses in other ways?

Exercise has been shown to increase protein losses from the body in several other ways. For one, exercise causes an elevated level of protein in the urine, a condition known as **proteinuria.** This condition has been observed following competition in a wide variety of sports, including running, football, basketball, and handball. Research suggests that the greater the intensity of the exercise, the greater the loss of protein in the urine. However, the total amount of protein lost in this manner appears to be rather negligible, amounting to less than 3 grams per day.

Protein also may be lost in the sweat. Several investigators have reported the presence of both amino acids and proteins in exercise-induced sweat. Again, the losses are relatively minor, on the order of 1 gram per liter of sweat in adult males. This avenue could account for 2–4 grams of protein in an endurance athlete training in a warm environment.

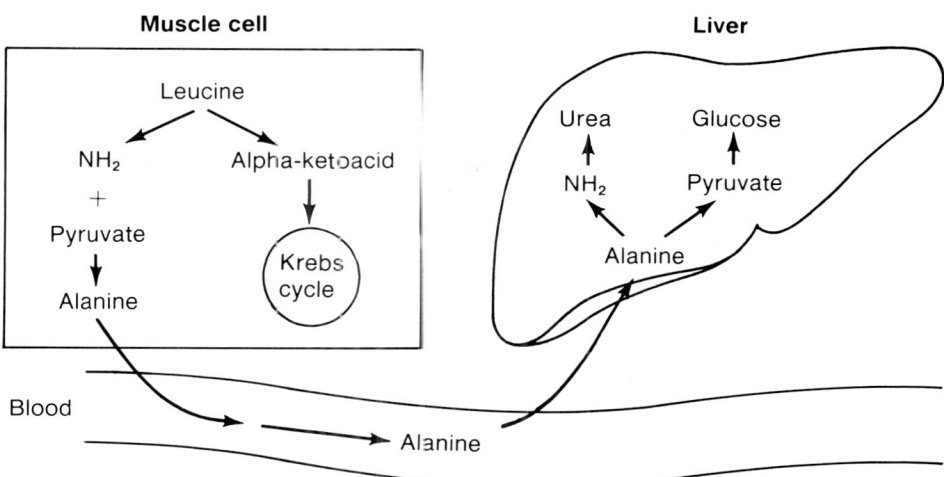

Figure 5.4.
Glucose–alanine cycle. Alanine may be produced in the muscle tissue from the breakdown of other amino acids, most notably leucine. The alanine is then released into the blood and travels to the liver for eventual conversion to glucose through the process of gluconeogenesis.

What effect does exercise training have upon protein metabolism?

This question may be addressed from several perspectives. First, how does training influence protein metabolism during exercise? And second, what happens during the recovery period between training bouts?

As you may recall from the previous chapters, there is substantial research to support the conclusion that aerobic endurance training improves the ability of the muscle cell to use both carbohydrate and fat as energy sources during exercise. Although extensive evidence is not available, some preliminary data suggest that a similar improvement may occur with protein. Recent findings from both animal and human studies suggest an increase in leucine turnover and an increased ability of the muscle cell to oxidize amino acids during exercise following a period of training or when comparing trained to untrained individuals. Moreover, Einspahr and Tharp have reported that after a session of intense exercise at the same relative workload, trained subjects had higher plasma levels of alanine compared to untrained subjects. These researchers suggested this may be physiologically important but noted that other factors require study, such as the measurement of liver extraction and possible conversion to glucose.

These changes in protein metabolism would appear to be contrary to preservation of body protein stores, but they may represent another means whereby the body adapts to endurance training in an attempt to preserve carbohydrate as an energy source. On the other hand, several older studies have suggested that the effects of physical training will lead to a decrease in protein catabolism during exercise. Further research is needed to resolve these conflicting data.

Although protein catabolism may occur during exercise, even following training, the recovery period is marked by an increase in protein synthesis. Numerous studies have found that after exercise, protein balance is maintained or becomes positive. Trained individuals, during rest, have been shown to experience a preferential oxidation of fat and a sparing of protein, as measured by leucine metabolism and the respiratory quotient. The exercise task apparently stimulates the DNA in the muscle cell nucleus to increase the synthesis of protein, and the type of protein that is synthesized is specific to the type of exercise. Aerobic exercise stimulates synthesis of mitochondria and oxidative enzymes, which are composed of protein and are necessary for energy production in the oxygen system. Weight training promotes synthesis of the contractile muscle proteins. These adaptations to training are the key factors in improving performance.

The effect of training in producing a positive nitrogen balance, or a positive protein balance, during the recovery period depends on an adequate dietary supply of protein.

Do individuals in strenuous physical training, including the developing adolescent athlete, need more protein in the diet?

There appears to be a difference of opinion about the answer to this question. For example, the National Research Council, in its 1989 RDA, states there is little evidence that muscular activity increases the need for protein, except for the small amounts needed for the development of muscle during physical conditioning. The council further suggests that in view of the margin of safety in the RDA, no increment is needed during training. One investigator even contends that since exercise training increases the ability of the body to retain protein in the recovery period, athletes in training may need less protein than sedentary individuals if they consume enough Calories to maintain body weight.

On the other hand, many investigators who have studied the protein needs of athletes have recommended that athletes' protein requirements may be increased during periods of heavy physical training. Because weight lifters and body builders are attempting to increase lean muscle mass and strength, the extra protein is recommended to maximize muscle protein synthesis. Additional dietary protein also has been recommended for endurance athletes who may utilize protein as an energy source during exercise, and who also need to synthesize oxidative enzymes and mitochondria. Others have suggested that protein supplementation is particularly important during the early stages of training to help prevent sports anemia. The recommended range of protein varies with the type of athlete, but a review of the literature reveals recommendations ranging from 1.0–3.0 grams of protein per kilogram body weight daily, or higher.

The following is a brief summary of the available research relative to the protein needs of, and the effect of protein supplementation upon, athletes involved in either strength-type or endurance-type activities, including the special condition of sports anemia.

Strength type activities. Individuals involved in these activities include weight lifters, bodybuilders, and football players. They are usually interested in increasing muscle mass and decreasing body fat, as well as improving strength and power. It is unlikely that such athletes use considerable amounts of protein for energy during training. Tarnopolsky and his associates recently reported that one hour of circuit weight lifting did not affect leucine turnover for several hours afterwards, but Pivarnik and others did note increased urinary levels of 3-methylhistidine in untrained subjects after the third day of training, suggesting the skeletal muscle was being degraded through strength-building exercises.

Several studies have attempted to determine the protein requirement for maintaining nitrogen balance during weight lifting. Greg Paul conducted a thorough review of the available literature and reported values of 0.82–1.94 grams of protein per kilogram body weight per day. More recent research by Tarnopolsky suggests a value near the RDA is sufficient to maintain nitrogen balance. In the recent Pivarnik study, there was no indication that the reported breakdown of muscle tissue increased protein requirements, and one of the coinvestigators, James Hickson, was cited as indicating that the RDA was sufficient. These findings may be appropriate for maintaining nitrogen balance but possibly not for creating a positive nitrogen balance, hopefully as muscle mass.

Unfortunately there is very little scientific information about the specific protein requirements for the development of lean muscle mass in weight-training programs. Protein balance is usually positive during these programs, and research studies have suggested that weight lifters could retain between 7 and 28 grams of protein per day. Although it might be assumed this protein would be assimilated as muscle tissue, this has not been determined. A number of respected investigators have recommended that weight lifters and other athletes training to increase muscle mass and strength, particularly the developing adolescent athlete, consume more protein. Peter Lemon, in a 1991 review, recommended between 1.5 and 2.0 grams of protein per kilogram body weight per day. Butterfield recommended a value of twice the RDA plus an additional 200 Calories per day.

Both laboratory and field studies have been conducted to investigate the effect of additional dietary protein upon body weight and composition during physical training. Although the field studies with athletes such as football players were relatively uncontrolled in regard to diet and amount of exercise, most of them reported that increased protein in the form of dietary supplements led to increases in body weight. However, most of these field studies did not evaluate body composition, or the changes in lean body tissue such as muscle versus body-fat changes. Several better controlled laboratory studies have compared the effect of normal protein intake, about 0.8–1.4 grams per kilogram, to higher levels, such as 1.6–2.8 grams per kilogram, on body composition changes during a weight-training program. In general, these studies revealed that although protein balance could be maintained or even be positive with the consumption of a normal amount of protein, the body protein balance was even more positive with the larger amounts. The additional body weight also appears to be in the form of lean body mass. However, in a recent well-designed study using nuclear magnetic resonance to measure leg muscle, Weideman and others reported no significant increase in leg muscle hypertrophy following 13 weeks of weight training with 2.94 grams of protein per kilogram per day.

Another important consideration in weight-gaining programs is sufficient dietary energy in the form of carbohydrate or fat. This topic is covered in Chapter 11.

Although available research suggests that the effects of increased protein intake appear to be beneficial relative to body protein balance during training, the effect upon actual physical performance is very questionable. Field studies that reported increased strength levels following protein supplementation were poorly designed. For example, one study used a milk-protein supplement with elite weight lifters, increasing their daily protein intake from a normal 2.5 grams to 3.5 grams per kilogram body weight. The investigators noted significant gains in both lean body mass and strength following a period of several months when the athletes consumed the supplement, compared to a decrease in these variables after the athletes had consumed a placebo for several months. Although this may appear to be a well designed study, the protein supplement was given during two periods when the athletes were peaking for world championship competition, while the placebo was given during a period of apparently less intensive training between competitions. Thus the effects could be due to the more intensive training presumed to occur in the peak training periods. Several other well designed studies have not revealed any beneficial effects of protein supplementation upon physical performance, even in the model study which used 2.8 grams per kilogram body weight. In the Weideman study cited above, 2.94 grams of protein/kg/day also did not increase strength.

Endurance-type activities. As noted previously, the use of protein as an energy source may increase during prolonged endurance exercise, although the precise source of the protein thus utilized has not been identified. Hickson and Wolinsky, in a recent review, noted that whatever the source of the protein catabolized during exercise, skeletal muscle tissue or otherwise, the fact that it occurs suggests that protein needs may be enhanced with endurance-building activities. Current research appears to support this point of view. Paul reviewed a number of studies involving endurance athletes and found that 0.97–1.37 grams of protein per kilogram per day

were needed to attain nitrogen balance. Other investigators have reported similar findings or recommendations. Friedman and Lemon recently reported values of 1.14–1.39 grams per kilogram per day, and Butterfield concluded from her review that 1.26 grams were necessary, while Poortmans recommended 1.2 grams. But, as Friedman and Lemon have noted, individual endurance athletes can vary greatly in their ability to retain dietary protein, possibly owing to such factors as total energy intake, particularly carbohydrate, and protein quality. In particular, female endurance athletes may need higher values since their energy intakes are usually lower. Friedman and Lemon suggested a greater safety margin when establishing dietary protein recommendations for endurance athletes, and in an earlier review, Lemon and others recommended 1.8–2.0 grams of protein per kilogram per day.

Few data are available regarding the effect of high-protein diets upon endurance performance. One early study did note that low protein intake, only 4 grams per day, did not lower maximal endurance capacity over a ten-day period, but energy intake was adequate. More recently, several studies have emanated from Iowa State University. Sharp and his colleagues investigated the effect of a protein supplement (0.8 g/kg/day) during eight weeks of combined aerobic and anaerobic training on a bicycle ergometer. Although the protein supplement did not increase VO_2 max or mean power output, the subjects were able to generate more work output at the anaerobic (lactate) threshold. These investigators also reported favorable effects of protein supplementation upon anabolic hormones, particularly testosterone, and such an effect could benefit performance. Other investigators have studied the effect of protein supplementation upon possible muscle damage during training, but the results are contradictory. One study reported that 15 grams of protein consumed immediately after exercise enhanced muscle repair, as measured by changes in enzyme status associated with muscle damage. Conversely, another study, using 37.5 grams of protein, showed no facilitation in recovery from muscle damage, as measured by a strength test. It is clear that additional research is necessary before we can make any sound conclusions about the effect of protein supplementation on endurance performance.

Sports anemia. Some investigators have suggested that additional protein be taken during the early stages of an endurance training program to prevent the development of a condition labeled as **sports anemia.** Sports anemia is thought to occur as the body adapts to the exercise in the early stages of the program and uses protein to synthesize myoglobin, mitochondria, and other muscle protein compounds essential for oxygen utilization at the expense of hemoglobin. Thus there is a transitory decline in the serum hemoglobin levels resulting in the appearance of anemia.

Most of the early research relative to protein requirements to prevent sports anemia was conducted in Japan. These studies suggested that 1.5–2.0 grams of protein per kilogram body weight were needed daily for the first month of training to prevent this condition. On the other hand, a more recent report from Japan, although reporting the development of sports anemia in individuals with low protein intake (0.5 grams per kilogram), also stated that normal protein intake of 1.25 grams per kilogram would prevent its development. Other research has suggested that sports anemia is not caused by a loss of hemoglobin but rather by an expansion of the plasma, which simply dilutes the hemoglobin concentration and gives the appearance of anemia. Moreover, sports anemia has not been shown to occur in all subjects initiating a strenuous training program, particularly in those on a balanced diet. Sports anemia also has been associated with iron nutrition and is discussed further in Chapter 7.

What are some general recommendations relative to dietary protein intake for athletes?

Although the available research does not provide us with any definitive data about protein requirements during training, it does suggest that athletes at least need the RDA of approximately 0.8–1.0 grams per kilogram body weight and possibly more to maintain or increase protein balance. The following mathematical presentations are possible scenarios for various athletes who may wish to maintain or increase protein balance. The protein needs are based upon the RDA, a rough estimate of the amount of protein used during strenuous exercise, and additional protein needs for the individual who wants to gain weight.

Let us look first at the young athlete who wants to gain body weight through a weight-training program, preferably in the form of muscle tissue. The protein RDA for an adolescent male is 1.0 grams per kilogram. At moderate activity levels, the average 70-kg adolescent male would be in protein balance with 70 g daily. However, according to the suggested upper recommendation of 2.0 grams per kilogram he would need 140 g daily if involved in a strenuous training program. Is this a reasonable amount?

One pound of muscle tissue is equal to 454 grams, and its composition is approximately 70 percent water, 7 percent lipids, and 22 percent muscle tissue. Hence, one pound of muscle contains about 100 grams of protein (454 × .22). If the desired weight gain is one pound of lean body mass per week, a reasonable goal, then this young male would need an additional 14 grams of protein per day (100 grams/7 days) to supply the amount in one pound of muscle tissue. A gain of two pounds per week, although probably more difficult to accomplish, would require 28 additional grams of protein per day. Let us be liberal and estimate an additional 22 grams of protein per day to cover losses due to exercise. In summary, assuming that a portion of these protein needs are not covered by the safety margin incorporated in the RDA, this young athlete would need approximately 120 grams of protein per day (70 + 28 + 22) to gain two pounds of lean body tissue per week, or about 1.7 grams of protein per kilogram body weight. This value falls within the recommended range and approaches the upper recommended level of 2 grams per kilogram per day.

Endurance athletes are not necessarily interested in gaining weight, but they may need to replenish the protein that may serve as an energy source during training. Running 10 miles per day would expend approximately 1,000 Calories. If 10 percent of this energy cost, or 100 Calories, was derived from protein, then approximately 25 grams of protein (100 Calories/4 Calories per gram of protein) would need to be replaced. With a liberal estimated additional loss of 10 grams of protein in the urine and sweat, the total daily protein requirement for a 70-kg male, again assuming that these additional needs are not accounted for by the safety margin in the RDA, would be 105 grams (70 + 25 + 10), or 1.5 g/kg. Again, this value falls within the recommended range.

These protein needs could be satisfied easily by small adjustments to the normal diet already being consumed in the United States. For example, the average caloric intake for a moderately active young male averages 2,500–3,000 C. This caloric intake may be increased through physical training as more Calories are expended. Thus, caloric intake would be increased to approximately 3,500–4,000 C. It is important to note that adequate energy intake, primarily in the form of carbohydrates, will improve protein balance. In essence, an increased energy intake appears to decrease protein requirements somewhat.

If the protein content of the dietary Calories averaged 12 percent, which represents the approximate intake in the United States, then the intake of protein would approximate 1.5–1.7 grams per kilogram, which parallels the amounts estimated in the examples cited above. Increasing the protein content to 15 percent would provide a value of 1.9–2.1 grams per kilogram body weight.

These values approach the higher amounts recommended by some investigators for individuals in training. The calculations are presented in Table 5.5.

Dietary surveys of athletes have revealed that many strength-type athletes, such as football players, are currently consuming about 2 grams of protein per kilogram per day. On the other hand, athletes such as wrestlers and gymnasts, who are in greater need of protein because of low caloric intake, have been reported to consume less than their RDA. It is important for the athlete to obtain adequate protein nutrition. Wise selection of high-quality protein foods will provide adequate amounts through a balanced diet to meet bodily needs during the early and continued stages of training. It is not difficult to increase the protein content of the diet. For example, 8 ounces of roasted, skinless chicken breast and two glasses of skim milk, a total of less than 600 Calories, will provide over 70 grams of high-quality protein, the RDA for our typical 70-kg adolescent and more than half of the 140 grams that may be recommended for such an athlete attempting to gain muscle mass. Perusal of Table 5.2 and Appendix H will help you select high-protein foods. Additional points on this subject are covered in Chapter 11 under the topic of gaining weight.

Protein: Ergogenic Aspects

Given the potential importance of protein to optimal physical performance, a wide variety of ergogenic aids associated with protein nutrition have been used in attempts to enhance performance, such as special protein foods, amino acids, and by-products of protein metabolism.

Are special protein supplements necessary?

As already discussed, the available research data suggest that athletes involved in weight training to gain weight or in strenuous endurance exercise may need somewhat more than the RDA for protein to maintain or increase protein balance, particularly if energy intake (Calories) in not adequate to meet daily energy expenditure. However, as also noted,

Table 5.5   Calculation of grams protein/ kilogram body weight

Body weight: 70 kg
One gram protein = 4 Calories

Daily caloric intake:	3,500–4,000	3,500–4,000
Percent protein:	15	12
Calories in protein:	525–600	420–480
Grams of protein:	131–150	105–120
Grams protein/kg:	1.9–2.1	1.5–1.7

the ability of protein supplementation to improve physical performance above and beyond the effects of the training program itself is obscure.

To provide additional protein to the diet, investigators have used either powdered protein sources, canned liquid meals high in protein and energy, or special foods and concoctions high in protein content. However, the protein content is actually derived from natural protein, such as milk, egg, or soy protein. As Bucci has indicated, supplements of intact proteins, such as found in these products. offer no advantages over protein found in other food sources, since these supplements are in fact derived from natural foods. In addition, many of these protein supplements are expensive when compared to natural protein that may be obtained easily in high-protein foods such as powdered milk, skim milk, eggs, and chicken. Blending powdered milk into a glass of skim milk, with some vanilla or other flavoring, will provide substantial amounts of high-quality protein, your own personal protein supplement.

Nevertheless, commercial supplements may be a convenient means for some busy athletes to secure additional protein in the diet. Many of these products contain high-quality protein, such as milk or egg protein; provide a balanced mixture of protein, carbohydrate, and fat for additional Calories; and may also contain supplemental vitamins and minerals. Although these products do not contain all of the nutrients of natural foods, they may be useful adjuncts to a balanced diet. Certain brands have been available for years, such as Nutrament, but several companies have recently marketed products specifically for physically active individuals, such as Exceed Sport Nutrition Supplement by Ross Laboratories and Gatorpro (not Gatorade, but pro for protein), by the Quaker Oats Company. Such supplements may also be a less expensive source of protein when compared to expensive meats, including a high-fat, fast food hamburger. It is important to reemphasize the point that these supplements should be used as an adjunct to an otherwise balanced nutritional plan, not as a substitute.

Other protein substances such as spirulina, brewer's yeast, specific enzymes, and even DNA have been advocated as means to improve physical performance. However, there appears to be no research available to support their effectiveness. Spirulina and brewer's yeast are good sources of protein and a variety of vitamins and minerals but convey no magical ergogenic qualities. The enzymes and DNA would be degraded in the digestive process and thus could not be utilized for the purpose for which they were ingested.

Are amino acid supplements effective ergogenic aids?

In recent years amino acid supplements have become popular in certain athletic circles. Weight lifters are consuming arginine in attempts to stimulate the release of growth hormone from the pituitary gland, hoping that the growth hormone will then stimulate muscle development. Certain amino acid mixtures containing arginine have been advertised to have an anabolic-steroid effect. Endurance athletes have been advised to increase their consumption of leucine, primarily because it may be utilized as a fuel during training. Other amino acid mixtures have also been used for weight-control purposes.

Scientific research has shown that individual amino acid supplements may induce specific physiological responses in the body, particularly the formation of certain chemicals in the brain needed for nerve impulse transmission as well as secretion of hormones. However, amino acid metabolism is very complex. It depends upon a variety of factors such as the concentration in the blood, competition with other amino acids, feedback control mechanisms, and the presence in the diet of other nutrients. Consumption of specific amino acid mixtures or even high-protein diets may actually lead to nutritional imbalances, as an overload of one amino acid may inhibit the absorption of others into the body.

Because purified amino acids, known as free form amino acids, have become commercially available for athletes, they have been the focus of increased research activity by sport medicine scientists, although data about their effect upon physical performance still remains limited. The following discussion highlights some of the key findings.

Arginine and ornithine. Research has shown that infusing any of a number of amino acids into the blood potentiates the release of **human growth hormone** (HGH). HGH is released from the pituitary gland into the bloodstream, affecting all tissues. One of its effects is to stimulate the production of another hormone, insulin-like growth factor-1, that spurs growth of tissue, including muscle tissue. Although more than a half-dozen amino acids may stimulate HGH release when injected, the effect of oral supplementation is less clear. However, Jacobson has reported that the oral administration of selected amino acids may lead to HGH release similar to that promoted by infusion. Moreover, Bucci and his colleagues have reported that ornithine at dosages of 40, 100, and 170 milligrams per kilogram of body weight raises HGH levels, but the increase is significant only at the highest dosage. Unfortunately, such a dosage appears to be impractical, since it caused gastric distress in almost all of the subjects.

Arginine and ornithine, two nonessential amino acids, have received the most research attention. They have been advertised in several body-building magazines as being more powerful than anabolic steroids, potent drugs used by some athletes to increase muscle mass. The advertisers apparently are capitalizing on the potential of arginine and ornithine to enhance HGH release.

Three studies have investigated the effect of arginine and ornithine supplementation upon body composition or strength. One report of a poorly controlled study appeared in *Muscle & Fitness,* a popular magazine for body builders. Twenty college students, both males and females, served as subjects. They were apparently nonathletes, although two of them were weight lifters. The subjects were assigned either to a placebo group or the experimental group, which consumed 2 grams of arginine and 2 grams of ornithine for 20 days. Only body composition, as determined by skinfold fat measurements, was recorded. Although the report revealed no significant difference between the groups relative to changes in muscle mass, the tone of the article strongly suggested that amino acid supplements would have favorable effects upon body composition. It is interesting to note that the publishers of this magazine are also in the business of selling amino acid supplements to weight lifters and body builders.

The other two studies, both conducted by Elam, collectively reported that arginine and ornithine supplementation in conjunction with a weight training program reduced body fat, increased lean body mass, and increased strength over a five week period. The dosage was 2 grams per day (one gram each of arginine and ornithine), five days per week. Unfortunately, both studies have been criticized in the literature on the grounds of the statistical procedure by which the experimental and control groups were compared. A different analysis of the same data revealed no significant difference between the experimental and control groups in the first study. The studies have also been criticized for questionable measurement techniques and for making assumptions without adequate supporting data. Hawkins and associates, using experienced male weightlifters as subjects, reported no beneficial effect of oral arginine supplementation on various measures of muscle function, including peak torque and endurance. Warren and others, although using a mixture of amino acids, also reported no effects of the supplements on human growth hormone or strength performance in elite junior weightlifters. Thus, there are currently no sound data supporting an ergogenic effect of arginine and ornithine supplementation.

A detailed discussion of the role of HGH is beyond the scope of this text. It is important to note, however, that extensive research into its effects began only recently when genetically engineered versions of the natural body hormone became available. Available data suggest that in elderly men, who normally have reduced levels of HGH, injections of the hormone modify body composition, decreasing body fat and increasing lean body mass. However, Macintyre, extrapolating from animal data and from studies of adults with acromegaly (a disorder associated with excess secretion of HGH by the pituitary), noted that although the muscles appear larger, they are functionally weaker. He suggested that the increase in muscle bulk may be an enlargement in connective tissue, which does not generate force. In support of these extrapolations, Yarasheski and others recently studied the effect of HGH versus a placebo on adult males who weight-trained for 12 weeks. They reported significant increases in lean body mass in the group receiving HGH, but there were no significant increases in skeletal muscle protein synthesis and size, or in muscular strength, over the effects produced by weight training alone in the placebo group. They suggested that HGH may influence the development of other tissues.

At present, then, there are no data to support an ergogenic effect of HGH on muscle size, strength, or power beyond the effect generated by a proper weight training program. Moreover, the potential adverse health effects of HGH are substantial, and most researchers caution that the long-term health risks of HGH administration, either as genetically engineered HGH or produced by amino acid supplementation, are unknown.

Tryptophan and branched chain amino acids. Although tryptophan is one of the amino acids that may increase the release of HGH, its theoretical ergogenic effect is based upon another function. Two neurotransmitters in the brain, serotonin and 5-hydroxytryptamine, are derived from tryptophan, and both have been implicated in the perception of pain. Segura and Ventura postulated that individuals who show the best tolerance of or resistance to pain may be able to delay the onset of fatigue, and that tryptophan supplementation therefore might improve exercise performance. They had 12 healthy athletes exercise to exhaustion on a treadmill at 80 percent of their VO_2 max under two conditions: A placebo was compared with a dosage of 1,200 milligrams of L-tryptophan consumed in 300-mg doses over the 24 hours prior to testing, the last dose being 1 hour prior to the test. They reported no significant improvement in peak oxygen uptake or heart rate response but did note a significant improvement in time to exhaustion (49%) and a decreased rating of perceived exertion (RPE) following the L-tryptophan trial. Although the times to exhaustion were extremely variable among the individual subjects, ranging from 2.5–18 minutes, the experimental design appeared to be appropriate. Additional research is needed to substantiate the findings of this study, the only one uncovered relative to L-tryptophan supplementation and physical performance.

In contrast, Newsholme has hypothesized that high levels of serum tryptophan may be involved in the etiology of fatigue during prolonged endurance exercise, possibly because of the muscle-relaxing and depressive action of serotonin. Research with animals has shown that high blood levels of the BCAA (leucine, isoleucine, and valine) compete with and limit tryptophan entry into the brain; thus, high levels of blood BCAA may lead to a decreased production of serotonin. Newsholme suggests that serum BCAA levels eventually decrease in endurance exercise, thus possibly facilitating the transport of tryptophan into the brain and increasing serotonin production, leading to fatigue. However, it should be noted that Conlay and others have noted no change in the tryptophan:BCAA ratio in experienced runners immediately following completion of the Boston marathon. Additionally, in a well-designed double-blind placebo, crossover experiment, Galiano and others revealed that the ingestion of BCAA (leucine, isoleucine and valine) in a carbohydrate drink during prolonged exercise at 70 percent VO_2, although increasing serum BCAA levels, had no effect on performance. Vandewalle and others, also studying the effects of BCAA supplementation immediately before and during a progressive bicycle task ending with a ride to exhaustion at 75 percent VO_2 max, first depleted the subjects of muscle glycogen prior to the exhaustive task in order to test Newsholme's hypothesis. Although the serum levels of BCAA increased, there was no effect of the supplement on performance. Both of these studies investigated the effect of supplementation immediately prior to and during the exercise task. In another double blind, placebo, crossover experiment, Richard Kreider, Mary Mitchell, and their colleagues had subjects consume a commercial amino acid supplement or a placebo for fourteen days prior to performing a half Ironman triathlon (2 km swim; 90 km bike; 21 km run). Subjects also consumed the supplement immediately prior to and during the triathlon. Although there were no significant differences between the supplement and the placebo trial for the swim, bike, run, or total time, several favorable metabolic changes occurred and the subjects tended to run the last segment faster (by 12.8 minutes) when on the supplement regimen. Additional research is merited with chronic supplementation with BCAA.

Athletes should be aware, however, that a recent epidemic of eosinophilia–myalgia syndrome (EMS), a neuromuscular disorder characterized by weakness, fever, edema, rashes, bone pain, and other symptoms, has been attributed to consumption of purified L-tryptophan. This epidemic was apparently caused by a contaminant in a specific brand of L-tryptophan, but more than 1,500 cases of EMS have been directly related to L-tryptophan. The interested reader is referred to the article by Teman and Hainline.

Glycine and gelatin. Glycine is a nonessential amino acid. Because it is involved in the formation of creatine phosphate, it could theoretically be an ergogenic aid. Gelatin is derived from a protein substance in connective tissue called collagen, and although it is not a complete protein because it lacks several essential amino acids, it is composed of approximately 25 percent glycine. Several studies conducted a half-century ago suggested a beneficial effect of gelatin supplements upon strength, but the experiments were poorly designed. More contemporary research with proper experimental design and relatively large doses of glycine revealed no beneficial effects upon physical performance. Because gelatin is derived from connective tissue, and because connective tissue degradation is theorized to be a cause of muscle soreness, gelatin supplements have been advocated to prevent the development of soreness following exercise. However, recent experiments have not supported this view.

Aspartates. Potassium and magnesium aspartate are salts of aspartic acid, a nonessential amino acid.

Although the mechanism has not been clearly documented, these substances have been postulated to improve aerobic exercise performance, possibly by enhancing fatty acid metabolism and thereby sparing glycogen, by reducing accumulation of ammonia (metabolic by-product of protein), or simply by improving psychological motivation. The ammonia hypothesis has been tested in several studies since increases in serum ammonia have been associated with muscular fatigue, although the mechanism is not clear.

Research findings relative to the ergogenic effect of aspartates are equivocal. A number of both early and contemporary studies have reported no beneficial effects of aspartate supplementation. For example, Maughan and Sadler had eight males ride to exhaustion on a bicycle ergometer at 75–80 percent of their VO_2 max following either a placebo or 3,000 milligrams each of potassium and magnesium aspartate consumed in 24 hours prior to testing. No beneficial effects upon blood concentrations of energy substrates or ammonia were found, nor were any significant effects on physiological or psychological variables important to aerobic exercise performance.

On the other hand, an equal number of early and contemporary studies have found some beneficial applications of aspartates. Although several of these studies possessed flaws in experimental design, increases in aerobic endurance of 21–50 percent have been reported. More recently, Wesson and others, using a double-blind, placebo protocol, revealed that the ingestion of 10 grams of aspartates over a 24-hour period increased endurance capacity by over 15 percent when subjects exercised at 75 percent of their VO_2 max. These researchers also reported increased blood levels of free fatty acids and decreased levels of blood ammonia.

It appears that additional quality research is needed to evaluate the ability of aspartates to exert an ergogenic effect. Dosage may be a key factor, for dosages of about 10 grams have usually been associated with improved performance.

Inosine. Inosine is not an amino acid but is classified as a nucleoside. It is included for discussion here because it is associated with the development of **purines,** nonprotein nitrogen compounds that have important roles in energy metabolism. On the basis of animal research and studies of blood storage techniques, writers in popular magazines have theorized that inosine may be an effective ergogenic aid for a variety of athletes. Advertisements have suggested that inosine may improve ATP production in the muscle and thus be of value to strength athletes. Additionally, inosine is thought to enhance oxygen delivery to the muscle, thus being beneficial to aerobic endurance athletes.

There are no data to support these claims. No studies investigating the effect of inosine upon strength or power have been uncovered. Research from our laboratory at Old Dominion University has revealed no ergogenic effect of inosine on aerobic endurance, but on the contrary, a possible decrement in performance. Nine highly trained runners consumed either a placebo or 6 grams of inosine prior to several tests of performance, including a peak oxygen uptake test and a 3-mile run on the treadmill conducted to simulate an all-out race. Although there were no differences in 3-mile run performance, peak oxygen uptake, or a variety of hematological and psychological variables, time to exhaustion during the peak oxygen uptake test was longer in the placebo condition. We speculated that inosine may impair the ability of fast twitch muscle to function optimally in very high-intensity exercise, which occurs in the latter stages of tests of maximal or peak oxygen uptake. Thus, on the basis of the available data, inosine does not appear to be an effective ergogenic aid.

In summary, a balanced diet containing 12–15 percent of the Calories as protein will provide amounts of the individual amino acids more than adequate to obtain the estimated RDA, even for those who exercise extensively. For example, some reports suggest that endurance athletes need more leucine because they may use about 850 mg, or 87 percent of the estimated leucine RDA, in a 2-hour workout. One glass of milk contains 950 mg of leucine, while over 5,000 mg are consumed in a normal diet. Similar comparisons could be made with other amino acids.

As Slavin and others have revealed, such supplements purchased in health food stores may be expensive, one small bottle containing arginine, lysine, and ornithine costing over 10 dollars. They also noted the amount of amino acids contained in each tablet appear to be minimal, calculating that an individual would have to consume the entire bottle to obtain the arginine needed to potentially affect HGH.

Whether such individual amino acids confer any ergogenic effect is questionable at best. With the exception of aspartates and glycine, not much research is available relative to the various amino acids theorized to be ergogenic. Additional research is merited, particularly to confirm the reported positive effects of the aspartate salts, the BCAA, and L-tryptophan. However, as noted under the next question, amino acid supplementation may carry some health risks.

Dietary Protein: Health Implications

Although increases in dietary carbohydrate and decreases in dietary fat in the typical American diet may be recommended for health reasons, the general recommendation is to maintain adequate protein intake. Some health problems may be associated with extremes of protein intake, however, as well as with the consumption of individual amino acid supplements.

Does a deficiency of dietary protein pose any health risks?

A short-term protein deficiency (several days) is not likely to cause any serious health problems, but because protein is the source of the essential amino acids, a prolonged deficiency could be expected to cause serious health problems. Such is the case in certain parts of the world where protein intake is inadequate for political, economic, or other reasons. Protein–Calorie malnutrition is one of the major nutritional problems in the world today, particularly for young children. Physical and mental growth may be permanently retarded. Protein deficiency may also occur in individuals who abuse sound nutritional practices, such as drug addicts, chronic alcoholics and extreme food faddists, but adults are more likely to recover fully with adequate nutrition.

Individuals who are on a low-protein diet plan, or young athletes who are on modified starvation diets to lose weight for such sports as gymnastics, ballet or wrestling, may experience periods of protein insufficiency. During this time, the individual may be in negative nitrogen balance; that is, more nitrogen is being excreted from the body than is being ingested. Body tissues such as muscles and hemoglobin may be lost with a possible reduction in strength and endurance capacity. Adequate protein intake is essential for proper physiological functioning, both in the inactive and active individual.

Several major health problems associated with excessive weight loss, both in nonathletes and athletes, are related to both energy and protein balance. These topics are discussed in Chapter 9.

Does excessive protein intake pose any health risks?

The National Research Council, in its recent book *Diet and Health: Implications for Reducing Chronic Health Risk,* reported that the current high protein consumption in the United States appears to be safe, since the human body has a very efficient system for disposal of excess nitrogen. However, the NRC did recommend that individuals consume no more than twice the RDA. Recent surveys in the United States have revealed average protein intakes of more than 100 grams per day, with nearly 70 grams being derived from animal protein. This amount, about twice the RDA, does not appear to be harmful but is on the borderline of the NRC recommendation. On the other hand, some individuals, mainly athletes, are on high-protein diets that may contain over 200 grams of protein per day. One report cited a daily intake of 400 grams of protein in a body builder. Are such diets potentially harmful? Possibly, for several reasons.

One point to consider is that the protein in many foods is often accompanied by substantial quantities of saturated fat and cholesterol. You should be selective in the types of protein foods you eat. For example, a glass of whole milk and a glass of skim milk both have 8 grams of protein, but the whole milk also has 8 grams of fat compared to less than 1 gram in the skim milk. Nutritionally, skim milk is 40 percent protein Calories while the whole milk is 22.5 percent.

Individuals with a personal or family history of liver or kidney problems may be susceptible to adverse reactions from excessive dietary protein. As you may recall, the liver is the major organ involved in protein metabolism. Excess dietary protein may be converted to carbohydrate or fat, with the excess nitrogen being converted to urea for excretion from the body via the kidneys. High-protein diets may also lead to excessive production of ketones, which also must be excreted by the kidney to prevent an increase in blood acidity, known as ketosis. Thus, individuals with inadequate liver or kidney function may experience a host of health problems due to the accumulation of urea or ketones in the blood or other metabolic consequences.

Because both urea and ketone bodies need to be eliminated by the kidneys, dehydration could occur from excessive fluid losses. Such an effect could compromise the ability to deal with warm environmental temperatures, which is discussed further in Chapter 8.

Gout, a painful inflammation of the joints, may be aggravated by high-protein diets containing substantial quantities of purines, which are metabolized to uric acid (not the same as urea). The uric acid may accumulate in the joints and cause the inflammation.

Earlier research had suggested that high levels of protein intake, in the form of purified proteins, would increase the urinary excretion of calcium and possibly lead to decreased bone density. However, the National Research Council and recent reviews have revealed that when protein is consumed with adequate amounts of phosphorus, as in meat and other protein foods in the typical American diet, calcium losses are not increased, even on a diet with over 100 grams of protein daily.

Does the consumption of individual amino acids pose any health risk?

As Slavin and her colleagues have noted, amino acids taken in large doses are essentially drugs with unknown effects. The long-term effects of even moderate doses are also unknown, as noted previously in regard to arginine and its possible effects on HGH. Some evidence from human and animal research indicates such practices may interfere with the absorption of other essential amino acids, suppress appetite and food intake, precipitate tissue damage, contribute to kidney failure, or create unfavorable psychological changes. They may even be fatal.

Do vegetarian diets provide sufficient amounts of protein?

Many Americans have been changing their diets to improve their health. One of the major changes has been a shift toward a vegetarian diet. There are a variety of ways to be a vegetarian. A strict vegetarian, known also as a **vegan,** eats no animal products at all. Most nutrients are obtained from fruits, vegetables, breads, cereals, legumes, nuts, and seeds. **Ovovegetarians** include eggs in their diet, while **lactovegetarians** include foods in the milk group such as cheese and other dairy products. An **ovolactovegetarian** eats both eggs and milk products. These latter classifications are not strict vegetarians, because eggs and milk products are derived from animals.

Others may call themselves **semivegetarians** because they do not eat red meat such as beef and pork products, although they may eat fish and poultry. In practice, then, vegetarians range on a continuum from one who eats nothing but plant foods to someone who eats a typical American diet with the exception of red meat. The concern for obtaining a balanced intake of nutrients depends upon where the vegetarian is on that continuum.

A major concern for the vegetarian is to obtain sufficient amounts of the essential amino acids. This usually is no problem for the ovolactovegetarian, who is able to select foods from all the basic four food groups to get adequate amounts of protein: eggs, milk, and cheese, grain products, legumes, and nuts and seeds. Eggs, milk, and cheese are complete proteins and by themselves can provide all the necessary amino acids. Moreover, the addition of animal protein to plant protein, as in macaroni and cheese, enhances the overall quality of the plant protein.

The strict vegetarian must receive nutrients from breads and cereals, nuts and seeds, legumes, fruits, and vegetables. To receive a balanced distribution of the essential amino acids, the vegan must eat plant foods that possess **complementary proteins.** A vegetable product that is low in a particular amino acid is eaten with a food that is high in that same amino acid. For example, grains and cereals, which are low in lysine, are complemented by legumes, which have adequate amounts of lysine. The low level of methionine in the legumes is offset by its high concentration in the grain products. These types of food combinations are practiced throughout the world. Mexicans eat beans and corn while the Chinese eat soybeans and rice. Through the proper selection of foods that contain complementary proteins, the vegan can get an adequate intake of the essential amino acids. Because all amino acids need to be present for tissue formation, a deficiency of one or two essential amino acids will limit the proper development of protein structures in the body.

In their position statement regarding vegetarian diets, the American Dietetic Association stated that complementary proteins should be consumed over the course of the day. The ADA noted that since endogenous sources of amino acids are available, it is not necessary that complementation of amino acids occur at the same meal. Nevertheless, eating them at one meal will help guarantee that they are utilized by the body.

Table 5.6 provides some examples of combining foods to achieve protein complementarity. Milk is included because it is a common means to enhance the quality of plant protein, but eggs could also be substituted where appropriate. The two most common plant foods that are combined to achieve protein complementarity are grains and legumes. Grains such as wheat, corn, rice, and oats are combined with legumes such as soybeans, peanuts, navy beans, kidney beans, lima beans, black-eyed peas, and chickpeas.

Because a vegetarian diet may be deficient in other nutrients, a more detailed discussion is presented in Chapter 12.

References

Books

Blackburn, G., Grant, J., and Young, V. 1983. *Amino Acids: Metabolism and Medical Applications.* Boston: John Wright PSG.

Garrett, W., and Malone, T. 1988. *Report of the Ross Symposium on Muscle Development: Nutritional Alternatives to Anabolic Steroids.* Columbus, OH: Ross Laboratories.

Table 5.6   Combining foods for protein complementarity

Milk and Grains
Pasta with milk or cheese
Rice and milk pudding
Cereal with milk
Macaroni and cheese
Cheese sandwich
*Cheese on nachos

Milk and Legumes
*Creamed bean soups
*Cheese on refried beans

Grains and Legumes
Rice and bean casserole
Wheat bread and baked beans
*Corn tortillas and refried beans
Pea soup and toast
Peanut-butter sandwich

*Low-fat, low-sodium versions should be selected to minimize excessive saturated fat and sodium intake.

Hickson, J., and Wolinsky, I., eds. 1989. *Nutrition in Exercise and Sport.* Boca Raton, FL: CRC Press.

Hunt, S., and Groff, J. 1990. *Advanced Nutrition and Human Metabolism.* St. Paul, MN: West.

National Research Council. 1989. *Recommended Dietary Allowances.* Washington, DC: National Academy Press.

National Research Council. 1989. *Diet and Health: Implications for Reducing Chronic Disease Risk.* Washington, DC: National Academy Press.

Wadler, G., and Hainline, B. 1989. *Drugs and the Athlete.* Philadelphia: F. A. Davis.

Williams, M. H. 1985. *Nutritional Aspects of Human Physical and Athletic Performance.* Springfield, IL: C C Thomas.

Reviews

American Dietetic Association. 1988. Position of the American Dietetic Association: Vegetarian diets—technical support paper. *Journal of the American Dietetic Association* 88:352–354.

Bannister, E., and Cameron, B. 1990. Exercise-induced hyperammonemia: Peripheral and central effects. *International Journal of Sports Medicine* 11: Supplement 2P, S 129–42.

Benevenga, N., and Steele, R. 1984. Adverse effects of excessive consumption of amino acids. *Annual Review of Nutrition* 4:157–81.

Booth, F., et al. 1982. Influence of muscle use on protein synthesis and degradation. *Exercise and Sport Science Review* 10:27–48.

Brooks, G. 1987. Amino acid and protein metabolism during exercise and recovery. *Medicine and Science in Sports and Exercise* 19:S 150–56.

Bucci, L. 1989. Nutritional ergogenic aids. In: *Nutrition in Exercise and Sport,* eds. J. Hickson and I. Wolinsky, Boca Raton, FL: CRC Press.

Butterfield, G. 1991. Amino acids and high protein diets. In: *Ergogenics: Enhancement of Performance in Exercise and Sport,* eds. D. Lamb and M. Williams. Indianapolis, IN: Benchmark Press.

Clark, N. 1991. How to pack a meatless diet full of nutrients. *Physician and Sportsmedicine* 19:31–34.

Dohm, G., et al. 1985. Protein metabolism during endurance exercise. *Federation Proceedings* 44:348–52.

Evans, W. 1991. Muscle damage: Nutritional considerations. *International Journal of Sports Nutrition* 1: 214–22.

Evans, W., et al. 1983. Protein metabolism and endurance exercise. *Physician and Sportsmedicine* 11:63–71.

Felig, P. 1977. Amino acid metabolism in exercise. *Annals of the New York Academy of Sciences* 301:56–63.

Fitts, R., and Metzger, J. 1988. Mechanisms of muscular fatigue. In: *Principles of Exercise Biochemistry,* ed. J. Poortmans. Basel: Karger.

Harper, A., et al. 1984. Branched-chain amino acid metabolism. *Annual Review of Nutrition* 4:409–54.

Hickson, J., and Wolinsky, I. 1989. Human protein intake and metabolism in exercise and sport. In: *Nutrition in Exercise and Sport,* eds. J. Hickson and I. Wolinsky. Boca Raton, FL: CRC Press.

Hood, D., and Terjung, R. 1990. Amino acid metabolism during exercise and following endurance training. *Sports Medicine* 9:23–35.

Jacobson, B. 1990. Effect of amino acids on growth hormone release. *Physician and Sportsmedicine* 18:63–70.

Kopple, J. 1988. Nutrition, diet, and the kidney. In: *Modern Nutrition in Health and Disease,* ed. M. Shils and V. Young. Philadelphia: Lea & Febiger.

Lemon, P. 1991. Protein and amino acid needs of the strength athlete. *International Journal of Sports Nutrition* 1:127–45.

Lemon, P. 1987. Protein and exercise: Update 1987. *Medicine and Science in Sports and Exercise* 19:S179–S190.

Lemon, P., et al. 1984. The importance of protein for athletes. *Sports Medicine* 1:474–84.

Macintyre, J. 1987. Growth hormone and athletes. *Sports Medicine* 4:129–42.

McCarthy, P. 1989. How much protein do athletes really need? *Physician and Sportsmedicine* 17:170–75.

Munro, H., and Crim, M. 1988. The proteins and amino acids. In: *Modern Nutrition in Health and Disease,* ed. R. Goodhart and M. Shils. Philadelphia: Lea & Febiger.

Newsholme, E. 1990. Effects of exercise on aspects of carbohydrate, fat, and amino acid metabolism. In: *Exercise, Fitness and Health,* eds. Bouchard, C., et al. Champaign, IL: Human Kinetics.

Newsholme, E. 1988. Application of knowledge of metabolic integration to the problem of metabolic limitations in sprints, middle distance and marathon running. In: *Principles of Exercise Biochemistry,* ed. J. Poortmans. Basel: Karger.

Parkhouse, W. 1988. Regulation of skeletal muscle myofibrillar protein degradation: Relationships to fatigue and exercise. *International Journal of Biochemistry* 20:769–75.

Paul, G. 1989. Dietary protein requirements of physically active individuals. *Sports Medicine* 8:154–76.

Poortmans, J. 1988. Protein metabolism. In: *Principles of Exercise Biochemistry,* ed. J. Poortmans. Basel: Karger.

Poortmans, J. 1985. Post-exercise proteinuria in humans: Facts and mechanisms. *Journal of the American Medical Association* 253:236–40.

Sahlin, K., and Katz, A. 1988. Purine nucleotide metabolism. In: *Principles of Exercise Biochemistry,* ed. J. Poortmans. Basel: Karger.

Sherman, W., and Lamb, D. 1988. Nutrition and prolonged exercise. In: *Prolonged Exercise,* eds. D. Lamb and R. Murray, Indianapolis, IN: Benchmark.

Slavin, J., et al. 1988. Amino acid supplements: Beneficial or risky. *Physician and Sportsmedicine* 16:221–24.

Spencer, H., et al. 1989. Do protein and phosphorus cause calcium loss? *Nutrition Today* 24:33–35, January/February.

Teman, A., and Hainline, B. 1991. Eosinophilia–myalgia Syndrome. *Physician and Sportsmedicine* 19:80–86.

Wolfe, R. 1987. Does exercise stimulate protein breakdown in humans? Isotope approaches to the problem. *Medicine and Science in Sports and Exercise* 19:S172–S178.

Young, V. 1986. Protein and amino acid metabolism in relation to physical exercise. *Current Concepts in Nutrition* 15:9–32.

Young, V., et al. 1989. A theoretical basis for increasing current estimates of the amino acid requirements in adult man, with experimental support. *American Journal of Clinical Nutrition* 50:80–92.

Yoshimura, H. 1970. Anemia during physical training (sports anemia). *Nutrition Review* 28:251–53.

Specific Studies

Anderson, D., and Sharp, R. 1990. Effects of muscle glycogen depletion on protein catabolism during exercise. *Medicine and Science in Sports and Exercise* 22:S59.

Beckett, K., and Slagle, R. 1985. Amino acids. *Muscle & Fitness* 47:72, 178–80, September.

Bergstrom, J., et al. 1985. Free amino acids in muscle tissue and plasma during exercise in man. *Clinical Physiology* 5:155–60.

Blomstrand, E., et al. 1988. Changes in plasma concentrations of aromatic and branched-chain amino acids during sustained exercise in man and their possible role in fatigue. *Acta Physiologica Scandinavica* 133:115–21.

Brouns, F., et al. 1990. Ammonia accumulation during highly intensive long-lasting cycling: individual observations. *International Journal of Sports Medicine* 11: Supplement 2P, 578–84.

Bucci, L., et al. 1990. Growth hormone release in bodybuilders after oral ornithine administration. *The FASEB Journal,* 4:A397.

Conlay, L., et al. 1989. Effects of running the Boston marathon on plasma concentrations of large neutral amino acids. *Journal of Neural Transmission* 76:65–71.

Consolazio, C., et al. 1975. Protein metabolism during intensive physical training in the young adult. *American Journal of Clinical Nutrition* 28:29–35.

deHaan, A., et al. 1985. Effects of potassium + magnesium aspartate on muscle metabolism and force development during short intensive static exercise. *International Journal of Sports Medicine* 6:44–49.

Dragan, G., et al. 1985. Researches concerning the effects of Refit on elite weightlifters. *Journal of Sports Medicine and Physical Fitness* 25:246–50.

Einspahr, K., and Tharp, G. 1989. Influence of endurance training on plasma amino acid concentrations in humans at rest and after intense exercise. *International Journal of Sports Medicine* 10:233–36.

Elam, R. 1988. Morphological changes in adult males from resistance exercise and amino acid supplementation. *Journal of Sports Medicine and Physical Fitness* 28:35–39.

Elam, R. 1989. Effects of arginine and ornithine on strength, lean body mass and urinary hydroxyproline in adult males. *Journal of Sports Medicine and Physical Fitness* 29:52–56.

Friedman, J., and Lemon, P. 1989. Effect of chronic endurance exercise on retention of dietary protein. *International Journal of Sports Medicine* 10:118–23.

Galiano, F., et al. 1991. Physiological, endocrine, and performance effects of adding branched chain amino acids to a 6% carbohydrate-electrolyte beverage during prolonged cycling. *Medicine and Science in Sports and Exercise* 23:S14.

Gissal, F., and Hall, L. 1983. Analysis of urinary hydroxyproline levels and delayed muscle soreness resulting from high and low intensity step testing under gelatin-free and gelatin-load dietery regimens. *Medicine and Science in Sports and Exercise* 15:165.

Hackney, A., et al. 1990. Hormonal changes with exercise training: Effects of a dietary protein supplement. *The FASEB Journal* 4:A863.

Hawkins, C., et al. 1991. Oral arginine does not affect body composition or muscle function in male weight lifters. *Medicine and Science in Sports and Exercise* 23:S15.

Hilsendager, D., and Karpovich, P. 1964. Ergogenic effect of glycine and niacin separately and in combination. *Research Quarterly* 35:389–92.

Kreider, R., et al. 1990. Protein gluconeogenesis in repeated ultraendurance cycling. *The FASEB Journal* 4:A282.

Kreider, R., et al. 1991. Effects of amino acid supplementation on substrate usage during ultra endurance triathlon performance. *Medicine and Science in Sports and Exercise* 23:S16.

Krowchuk, D., et al. 1989. High school athletes and the use of ergogenic aids. *American Journal of Diseases in Children* 143:486–89.

Lament, L., et al. 1988. Leucine metabolism in trained humans during rest. *Medicine and Science in Sports and Exercise* 20:S14.

Liappis, N., et al. 1979. Quantitative study of free amino acids in human eccrine sweat excreted from the forearms of healthy trained and untrained men during exercise. *European Journal of Applied Physiology* 42:227–34.

MacLean, D., et al. 1989. Carbohydrate supply and amino acid and ammonia metabolism during prolonged exercise. *Medicine and Science in Sports and Exercise* 21:S106.

Marable, N., et al. 1979. Urinary nitrogen excretion as influenced by a muscle-building exercise program and protein intake variation. *Nutrition Reports International* 19:795–805.

Maughan R., and Sadler, D. 1983. The effects of oral administration of salts of aspartic acid on the metabolic response to prolonged exhausting exercise in man. *International Journal of Sports Medicine* 4:119–23.

Meredith, C., et al. 1989. Dietary protein requirements and body protein metabolism in endurance-trained men. *Journal of Applied Physiology* 66:2850–56.

Mitchell, M., et al. 1991. Effects of amino acid supplementation on metabolic responses to ultraendurance triathlon performance. *Medicine and Science in Sports and Exercise.* 23:S15.

Morin, C., and Clarkson, P. 1990. Increased protein ingestion during recovery from high force eccentric contraction. *Medicine and Science in Sports and Exercise* 22:S37.

Pivarnik, J., et al. 1989. Urinary 3-methylhistidine excretion increases with repeated weight training exercise. *Medicine and Science in Sports and Exercise* 21:283–87.

Poortmans, J., and Labilloy, D. 1988. The influence of work intensity on postexercise proteinuria. *European Journal of Applied Physiology* 57:260–63.

Rasch, P., et al. 1969. Protein dietary supplementation and physical performance. *Medicine and Science in Sports and Exercise* 1:195–99.

Rudman, J., et al. 1990. Effects of human growth hormone in men over 60 years old. *New England Journal of Medicine* 323:1–5.

Segura, R., and Ventura, J. 1988. Effect of L-tryptophan supplementation on exercise performance. *International Journal of Sports Medicine* 9:301–5.

Sharp, R., et al. 1988. Effect of a protein supplement on adaptations to combined aerobic and anaerobic training. *Medicine and Science in Sports and Exercise* 20:S3.

Stein, T., et al. 1989. Protein and energy metabolism during prolonged exercise in trained athletes. *International Journal of Sports Medicine* 10:311–16.

Tarnopolsky, M., et al. 1991. Whole body leucine metabolism during and after resistance exercise in fed humans. *Medicine and Science in Sports and Exercise* 23:326–33.

Tarnopolsky, M., et al. 1988. Influence of protein intake and training status on nitrogen balance and lean body mass. *Journal of Applied Physiology* 64:187–93.

Vandewalle, L., et al. 1991. Effect of branched-chain amino acid supplements on exercise performance in glycogen depleted subjects. *Medicine and Science in Sports and Exercise* 23:S116.

Warren, B., et al. 1991. The effect of amino acid supplementation on physiological responses of elite junior weightlifters. *Medicine and Science in Sports and Exercise* 23:S15.

Weideman, C., et al. 1990. Effects of increased protein intake on muscle hypertrophy and strength following 13 weeks of resistance training. *Medicine and Science in Sports and Exercise* 22:S37.

Wesson, M., et al. 1988. Effects of oral administration of aspartic acid salts on the endurance capacity of trained athletes. *Research Quarterly for Exercise and Sport* 59:234–39.

Williams, M., et al. 1990. Effect of oral inosine supplementation on 3-mile treadmill run performance and VO_2 peak. *Medicine and Science in Sports and Exercise* 22:517–22.

Yarasheski, K., et al. 1990. Effect of strength training and growth hormone administration on whole body and skeletal muscle leucine metabolism. *Medicine and Science in Sports and Exercise* 22:S85.

Key Terms

alpha-tocopherol equivalent

bee pollen

beta-carotene

bioavailability

biotin

coenzyme

CoQ10

enzymes

folic acid (folate)

free oxygen radicals

hypervitaminosis

megadose

niacin

niacin equivalent

osteomalacia

pantothenic acid

retinol

retinol equivalent (RE)

riboflavin (vitamin B_2)

subclinical malnutrition

thiamin (vitamin B_1)

vitamin A

vitamin B_6 (pyridoxine)

vitamin B_{12} (cyanocobalamin)

vitamin B_{15}

vitamin C (ascorbic acid)

vitamin D_3 (cholecalciferol)

vitamin E (alpha-tocopherol)

vitamin K

xerophthalmia

Key Concepts

Vitamins are complex organic compounds that function in the body in a variety of ways. Some act as coenzymes to help regulate metabolic processes, others are antioxidants that protect cell membranes, and one is even classified as a hormone.

Vitamins do not contain energy per se, such as Calories, but they do help regulate energy processes in the body.

The water-soluble vitamins consist of those in the B complex and vitamin C, while the fat-soluble vitamins are A, D, E, and K.

Although most vitamins must be obtained from the food we eat, several may be manufactured in the body.

There may be four stages in a vitamin deficiency, the preliminary stage, the biochemical deficiency stage, the physiologic deficiency stage, and the clinically manifest deficiency stage.

Although several national surveys have reported that some Americans are receiving less than the RDA for several vitamins, actual vitamin deficiencies resulting in disease are rare.

A vitamin deficiency may impair physical performance, usually by interfering with some phase of the energy-producing process. In some cases, impairment may be seen in 3–4 weeks on a deficient diet.

Vitamin supplements are not necessary for the individual on a balanced diet, but they may be recommended for those on a very low-Calorie diet, including athletes who are attempting weight reduction, and others with special dietary needs.

Controlled research, in general, supports the conclusion that vitamin supplements will not improve athletic performance in individuals on a balanced diet. However, additional research is needed to help resolve some conflicting data with several vitamins.

Megadoses of some vitamins may be potentially harmful.

Vitamins: The Organic Regulators
6

Introduction

Vitamins are a diverse class of 13 known specific nutrients which are involved in almost every metabolic process in the human body. Although we need only minute amounts of vitamins in our daily diet, they are one of our most critical nutrients. Noticeable symptoms of a deficiency may appear in 3–4 weeks for several of the vitamins, and major debilitating diseases may occur with prolonged deficiencies. Although vitamin deficiencies appear to be widespread in many developing countries, they are very rare in most industrialized societies. Several of the major nutrition surveys conducted in the United States have indicated that the vast majority of the population are receiving the RDA for all vitamins in their daily diet, which may be attributed to our high caloric intake and to vitamin fortification of processed foods. However, certain segments of the population may not be receiving the RDA for several vitamins and thus may have marginal vitamin deficiencies.

In general, most studies reveal that athletes, like the general population, are receiving the RDA for vitamins in their daily diet. However, certain athletic groups, particularly those who are on weight reduction programs to qualify for competition or to enhance performance, may not receive adequate vitamin nutrition. Furthermore, individual athletes in generally well nourished athletic groups may have a suboptimal vitamin intake.

As noted throughout this chapter, adequate vitamin nutrition is essential for both optimal health and athletic performance. But, if you do not obtain the RDA for a specific vitamin or vitamins, will your health or physical performance suffer? Will vitamin supplements above and beyond the RDA improve your health or performance? A major purpose of this chapter is to provide you with factual data, based upon the available research, to help answer these two very general questions.

A slightly different approach is used in this chapter and in Chapter 7. The first section provides some basic facts about the general role of vitamins in the human body. The next two sections cover the fat soluble and water soluble vitamins, respectively, with each individual vitamin discussed in terms of its RDA, food sources that provide ample amounts, metabolic functions in the body with particular reference to health and the physically active individual, and the findings of research relative to the impact of deficiencies and supplementation. The fourth section focuses on ergogenic aspects of special vitamin preparations, while the final section highlights some health implications of vitamin supplementation.

Basic Facts

What are vitamins and how do they work?

Vitamins are a class of complex organic compounds that are found in small amounts in most foods. They are essential for the optimal functioning of many different physiological processes in the human body. The activity levels of many of these physiological processes are increased greatly during exercise, and an adequate bodily supply of vitamins must be present for these processes to function best.

For the fundamental physiological processes of the body to proceed in an orderly, controlled fashion, a number of complex chemicals known as enzymes are necessary to regulate the diverse reactions involved. Hundreds of enzymes have been identified in the human body. Enzymes are necessary to digest our foods, to make our muscles contract, to release the energy stores in our bodies, to help us transport body gases such as carbon dioxide, to help us grow, to help clot our blood, and so on. Enzymes serve as catalysts; that is, they are capable of inducing changes in other substances without changing themselves.

Enzymes are chemicals that generally consist of two parts (Figure 6.1). One part is a protein molecule and to it is attached the second part, a **coenzyme.** For the enzyme to function properly, both parts must be present. The coenzyme often contains a vitamin or some related compound. The enzyme is not used up in the chemical process that it initiates or in which it participates, but enzymes may deteriorate with time. The coenzymes also may be degraded through body metabolism. It is now known that the B complex vitamins are essential in human nutrition because of their role in the formation of enzymes, and thus a fresh supply of these water soluble vitamins is constantly needed.

Figure 6.1.

Role of vitamin as coenzyme. (1) Substrates, such as pyruvate, need enzymes to be converted into more usable compounds. However, many enzymes need to be activated before a reaction may occur. Note that the enzyme is in a closed position. (2) An enzyme and a vitamin coenzyme (B₁) combine to form an activated complex, in essence opening up the enzyme. (3) The open, activated enzyme accepts the substrate and (4) splits it into two compounds while releasing the enzyme and coenzyme.

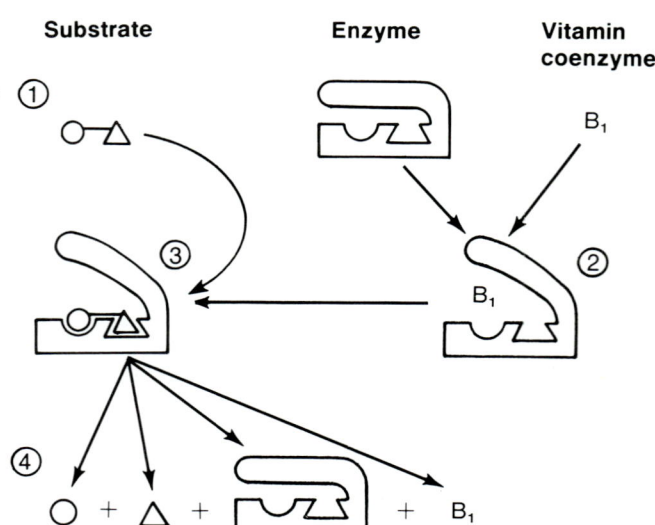

Vitamins may operate in other ways as well. For example, as depicted in Figure 6.2, vitamins C and E may serve as antioxidants, preventing undesired oxidative processes in the body. Vitamin D even functions as a hormone in its active form.

Although vitamins are indispensable for regulating many body functions and for the maintenance of optimal health, they are not a source of energy. They do not have any caloric value. Moreover, they make no significant contribution to the structure of the body, as do protein and some minerals.

What vitamins are essential to human nutrition?

The existence of vitamins was deduced from their physiological actions before their chemical structures had been identified. In assigning names to vitamins, the alphabet was used in order of their time of discovery. In some cases, a large time gap existed between the discovery of the vitamin and determination of its chemical structure. In others, the chemical nature was discovered rapidly, and the chemical name came into early use.

At present the human body is known to need an adequate supply of 13 different vitamins. A well balanced diet will satisfy all the vitamin requirements of most individuals. Four of these vitamins are soluble in fat and are obtained primarily from the fat in our diet, while the other nine water soluble vitamins are distributed rather widely in a variety of foods. Although most vitamins must be obtained in the food we eat, several of them may be formed in the body from other ingested nutrients, by the action of ultraviolet rays from sunlight on our skin, and by the activity of some intestinal bacteria.

A number of other substances mistakenly have been classified as vitamins. Included in this group are inositol, choline, para-amino benzoic acid (PABA), vitamin B₁₅ or pangamic acid, and vitamin B₁₇ or laetrile. Although these substances have been suggested to have vitamin activity, their essentiality in the diet has not been established.

Table 6.1 presents an overview of the 13 essential vitamins with commonly used interchangeable synonyms, the RDA, major food sources, major functions in the body, and symptoms associated with deficiencies or excessive consumption.

In general, how do deficiencies or excesses of vitamins influence health or physical performance?

Whether or not a vitamin deficiency affects one's health or physical performance may depend on the magnitude of the deficiency. Hornig and his associates have describe four stages of vitamin deficiency associated with the duration of undernourishment and inadequate vitamin intake.

1. *A preliminary stage* is associated with inadequate amount or availability of the vitamin in the diet. For example, a drastic change in the diet may influence vitamin **bioavailability** (the amount of a nutrient that the body absorbs), whereas pregnancy may increase the need for several vitamins.

2. *Biochemical deficiency.* In this stage, the body's pool of the vitamin is decreased. For a number of vitamins, biochemical deficiency can be identified by blood or tissue tests. For example, deficiencies of riboflavin may be detected by the activity of an enzyme in the red blood cells.

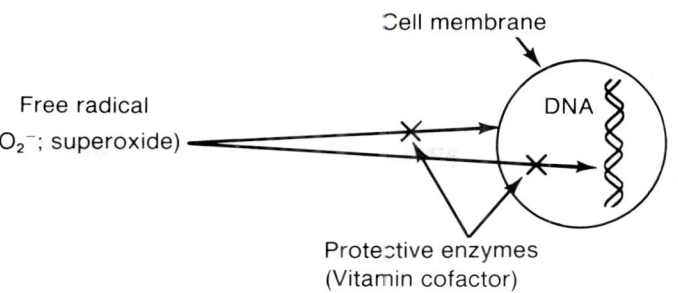

Figure 6.2.
Antioxidant role of vitamins. Some vitamins may serve as antioxidants, preventing free radicals such as superoxide from attacking cell membranes or the genetic material within the cell. Such vitamins are theorized to be protective against cancer and other diseases.

3. *Physiologic* deficiency is associated with the appearance of unspecific symptoms such as loss of appetite, weakness, or physical fatigue.

These first three stages are known as latent or marginal vitamin deficiency, or **subclinical malnutrition.** Whether or not these stages impair physical performance may depend upon the nature of the sport, but weakness or physical fatigue would certainly be counterproductive to optimal performance.

4. A *clinically manifest vitamin deficiency.* In this final stage, specific clinical symptoms are observed. For example, anemia is a clinical symptom associated with a deficiency of several vitamins, such as folic acid and vitamin B_6. Both health and performance would be adversely affected with a clinically manifest vitamin deficiency.

Except for consumption of large amounts of certain foods, such as cod liver oil, it is very difficult to obtain excessive amounts of vitamins through the diet to the point that health or performance is impaired. Even when supplements are taken, the body may rapidly excrete several vitamins, keeping body functions normal. However, certain other vitamins may not be excreted effectively and may accumulate in the tissues, beginning to function as a drug instead of a nutrient. Toxic reactions specific to the vitamin overdose may occur.

Fat-Soluble Vitamins

The four fat-soluble vitamins are A, D, E, and K. Because they are soluble in fat but not in water, dietary sources include foods that have some fat content. The body may contain appreciable stores of each, and several of them may be manufactured by the body, so deficiencies are relatively rare. On the other hand, excessive intakes may be toxic. With the exception of vitamin E, very little research has been conducted relative to deficiency or supplementation effects upon physical performance.

Vitamin A (retinol)

Vitamin A is a fat-soluble, unsaturated alcohol. The physiologically active form of vitamin A is known as **retinol.** The human body is capable of forming retinol from provitamins known as carotenoids, primarily **beta-carotene.** Both preformed vitamin A, or retinol, and beta-carotene are found in the foods we eat.

The RDA for vitamin A may be obtained by consuming retinol, beta-carotene, or a combination of the two. The RDA may be expressed in several ways, usually as **retinol equivalents (RE)** or as international units (IU). The RDA is 1,000 retinol equivalents, or 5,000 IU, for adult males and 800 retinol equivalents, or 4,000 IU, for adult females. The adult male RDA value is the equivalent of one milligram of retinol or six milligrams of beta-carotene. Slightly lesser amounts are needed by children. The RDA for specific ages may be found in Appendix A. The USRDA is 5,000 IU, or 1,000 RE.

Preformed vitamin A is found in substantial amounts in some animal foods, such as liver, butter, cheese, egg yolks, fish liver oils, and fortified milk. Provitamin A, as beta-carotene, is found in dark-green leafy and yellow-orange vegetables as well as in some fruits such as oranges, limes, pineapples, prunes, and cantaloupes. Fortified margarine also contains beta-carotene. One glass of milk provides 10 percent of the RDA, while one medium carrot will supply nearly 200 percent and a serving of liver a whopping 900 percent of RDA.

Vitamin A is essential for maintenance of the epithelial cells, those cells covering the outside of the body and lining the body cavities. It is also essential for proper visual function, such as night vision and peripheral vision. Vitamin A also has a variety of other physiological roles in the body that are not well understood. Beta-carotene may function as an antioxidant and has been theorized to confer some health benefits.

Vitamin A is stored in the body in relatively large amounts, and thus deficiencies are rare. However, an inadequate intake of vitamin A, which has

Table 6.1 Essential vitamins

Vitamin name (Other terms)	RDA or ESADDI for adults*	Major sources
Fat-soluble vitamins		
Vitamin A (retinol; provitamin carotenoids)	1000 RE♂ 800 RE♀	Retinol in animal foods; liver, whole milk, fortified milk, cheese. Carotenoids in plant foods; carrots, green leafy vegetables, sweet potatoes, fortified margarine from vegetable oils.
Vitamin D (cholecalciferol)	400 IU or 10 micrograms	Vitamin D fortified foods like dairy products and margarine, fish oils. Action of sunlight on the skin.
Vitamin E (tocopherol)	10 mg♂ 8 mg♀ alpha-TE	Vegetable oils, margarine, green leafy vegetables, wheat germ, whole grain products, egg yolks.
Vitamin K (antihemorrhagic vitamin)	80 micrograms ♂ 65 micrograms♀	Pork and beef liver, eggs, spinach, cauliflower. Formation in the human intestines by bacteria.
Water-soluble vitamins		
Thiamin (vitamin B₁)	1.5 mg♂ 1.1 mg♀	Ham, pork, lean meat, liver, whole grain products, fortified breads and cereals, legumes.
Riboflavin (vitamin B₂)	1.7 mg♂ 1.3mg♀	Milk and dairy products, meat, fortified grain products, green leafy vegetables, beans.
Niacin (nicotinamide, nicotinic acid)	19 mg♂ 15 mg♀	Lean meats, fish, poultry, whole grain products, beans. May be formed in the body from tryptophan, an essential amino acid.
Vitamin B₆ (pyridoxal, pyridoxine, pyridoxamine)	2 mg♂ 1.6 mg♀	Protein foods, liver, lean meats, fish, poultry, legumes, green leafy vegetables.
Vitamin B₁₂ (cobalamin; cyanocobalamin)	2 micrograms	Animal foods only, meat, fish, poultry, milk, eggs.
Folic acid (folate)	200 micrograms♂ 180 micrograms ♀	Liver, green leafy vegetables, legumes, nuts.
Biotin	30–100 micrograms	Meats, legumes, milk, egg yolk, whole grain products, most vegetables.
Pantothenic acid	4–7 mg	Beef and pork liver, lean meats, milk, eggs, legumes, whole grain products, most vegetables.
Vitamin C (ascorbic acid)	60 mg	Citrus fruits, green leafy vegetables, broccoli, peppers, strawberries, potatoes.

Major functions in the body	Deficiency symptoms	Symptoms of excessive consumption
Fat-soluble vitamins		
Maintains epithelial tissue in skin and mucous membranes, forms visual purple for night vision; promotes bone development.	Night blindness, intestinal infections, impaired growth, xerophthalmia.	Nausea, headache, fatigue, liver and spleen damage, skin peeling, pain in the joints.
Acts as a hormone to increase intestinal absorption of calcium and promote bone and tooth formation.	Rare. Rickets in children and osteomalacia in adults.	Loss of appetite, nausea, irritability, joint pains, calcium deposits in soft tissues such as the kidney.
Functions as an antioxidant to protect cell membranes from destruction by oxidation.	Extremely rare. Disruption of red blood cell membranes, anemia.	General lack of toxicity with doses up to 400 mg.
Essential for blood coagulation processes.	Increased bleeding and hemorrhage.	Possible clot formation (thrombosis), vomiting.
Water-soluble vitamins		
Serves as a coenzyme for energy production from carbohydrate, essential for normal functioning of the central nervous system.	Poor appetite, apathy, mental depression, pain in calf muscles, beriberi.	General lack of toxicity.
Functions as a coenzyme involved in energy production from carbohydrates, and fats, maintenance of healthy skin.	Dermatitis, cracks at the corners of the mouth, sores on the tongue, damage to the cornea.	General lack of toxicity.
Functions as a coenzyme for the aerobic and anaerobic production of energy from carbohydrate, helps synthesize fat and blocks release of FFA, needed for healthy skin.	Loss of appetite, weakness, skin lesions, gastrointestinal problems, pellagra.	Nicotinic acid causes headache, nausea, burning and itching skin, flushing of face.
Functions as a coenzyme in protein metabolism, necessary for formation of hemoglobin and red blood cells, needed for glycogenolysis and gluconeogenesis.	Nervous irritability, convulsions, dermatitis, sores on tongue, anemia.	Loss of nerve sensation; impaired gait.
Functions as coenzyme for formation of DNA, RBC development, and maintenance of nerve tissue.	Pernicious anemia, nerve damage resulting in paralysis.	General lack of toxicity.
Functions as coenzyme for DNA formation and RBC development.	Fatigue, gastrointestinal disorders, diarrhea, anemia.	May prevent detection of pernicious anemia caused by B_{12} deficiency.
Functions as coenzyme in the metabolism of carbohydrates, fats, and protein.	Rare. May be caused by excessive intake of raw egg whites. Fatigue, nausea, skin rashes.	General lack of toxicity.
Functions as part of coenzyme A in energy metabolism.	Rare. Only produced clinically Fatigue, nausea, loss of appetite, mental depression.	General lack of toxicity.
Forms collagen essential for connective tissue development, aids in absorption of iron, helps form epinephrine, serves as antioxidant.	Weakness, rough skin, slows wound healing, bleeding gums, scurvy.	Diarrhea, possible kidney stones, rebound scurvy.

*RDA values for other age groups are found in Appendix A.

been reported in a major national survey, could have serious health implications if prolonged. The gradual loss of night vision is one of the first symptoms of vitamin A deficiency. Other symptoms of mild deficiencies include increased susceptibility to infection and skin lesions. Epidemiological research also has suggested that a deficient intake of beta-carotene could predispose the individual to the development of cancer in the epithelial tissues, such as the skin, lungs, and intestinal lining. Although severe deficiencies are not common in industrialized nations, they do occur in parts of the world and lead to blindness through destruction of the lens of the eye, a condition known as **xerophthalmia.**

Theoretically, vitamin A deficiency could affect physical performance. Some investigators have suggested that a deficiency may impair the process of gluconeogenesis in the liver, which may be an important consideration for the endurance athlete in the latter stages of competition. Others have implied a reduction in the synthesis of muscle protein, or impaired vision, which could negatively affect strength athletes or those involved in sports requiring eye alterness. Very little research is available to support these theoretical views. Beta-carotene has been combined with other antioxidants in an attempt to prevent muscle damage during exercise. This research is discussed later in this chapter.

In general, supplements of vitamin A are not recommended. Excessive amounts of vitamin A, generally caused by self-medication with megadoses, can cause a condition known as **hypervitaminosis A.** Symptoms may include weakness, headache, loss of appetite, nausea, pain in the joints, peeling of skin and liver damage. Similar symptoms were reported in a young soccer player who took about 100,000 IU daily for two months in an attempt to improve performance. The symptoms were relieved when he stopped taking the supplements. Extremely large doses of vitamin A may be fatal. Excessive vitamin A during pregnancy may be teratogenic, causing deformities in the developing embryo or fetus.

In summary, vitamin A supplementation to the diet of the active individual does not have a sound theoretical basis. Moreover, the research conducted with vitamin A and physical performance has shown no beneficial effect. Hence, there appears to be no advantage for the active individual to supplement the diet with vitamin A, particularly not with megadoses that may have undesirable effects.

Vitamin D (cholecalciferol)

Vitamin D, a term representing a number of compounds, has been classified as both a fat-soluble vitamin and as a hormone. The physiologically active form is calcitriol, which is the hormone of this vitamin. In brief, the ultraviolet rays from sunshine convert a compound found in the skin into **cholecalciferol** (vitamin D_3), which is released into the blood and is eventually converted by the liver and kidneys into the active hormone, calcitriol.

The RDA for vitamin D is given in micrograms of cholecalciferol or as IU. One microgram of cholecalciferol is the equivalent of 40 IU. The RDA for vitamin D is higher during bone growth periods, up to age 25, being 10 micrograms, or 400 IU, daily. Recommended amounts are lower for older adults. See Appendix A for particulars. The USRDA is 400 IU.

The RDA for vitamin D may be obtained by exposing the hands, arms, and face to 15–20 minutes of summer sunshine about 2–3 times per week. Longer periods may be necessary in the winter, and it may be difficult to obtain adequate vitamin D by sunlight in northern latitudes, even in northern portions of the United States. Vitamin D does not occur naturally in very many foods. Fish liver oils are good sources, and smaller amounts are found in eggs, tuna, and salmon. Several foods are also fortified with vitamin D, such as milk and margarine. One glass of milk will provide 25 percent of the RDA for a child.

Vitamin D plays a central role in bone metabolism through its effect on calcium and phosphorus. It works in conjunction with several other hormones and helps absorb calcium and phosphorus from the intestinal tract, deposit these minerals in the bone, maintain normal serum calcium levels, and excrete excess amounts through the kidneys.

Deficiencies of vitamin D are unusual in most temperate climates, because the body possesses adequate stores in the liver and can manufacture it through exposure to the sun. However, deficiencies may occur in individuals who have little exposure to sunshine, such as elderly people who are homebound. Deficiencies may lead to inadequate calcium metabolism and bone deformities known as rickets, especially in children. This was a major concern years ago but has nearly been eradicated through the use of vitamin D-fortified foods. Loss of bone tissue may occur in adults, leading to **osteomalacia,** or a softening of the bones, accompanied by muscular weakness. The muscle weakness has been theoretically linked with an impairment of calcium metabolism in the muscle.

In general, vitamin D supplements are not recommended, especially in amounts greater than the RDA. Because vitamin D is fat soluble, megadoses may lead to increased storage in the body, and pathological results have been reported, even in doses five times the RDA. Hypervitaminosis D may lead to vomiting, diarrhea, loss of weight, loss of muscle tone, and possible damage to soft tissues such as the kidney, heart, and blood vessels due to deposits of calcium. As with vitamin A, there appear to be sound medical reasons for healthy individuals not to use vitamin D supplements.

There is very little theoretical basis for athletes to take vitamin D supplements. For this reason, only a few studies have been conducted with vitamin D supplementation and physical performance, and they revealed no beneficial effect, either through single megadoses or supplementation over a two-year period. Some recent research has revealed that weight training increases the serum concentration of vitamin D, and the investigators theorized this could be related to the increased bone mass which is developed through exercise. However, this study does not suggest that vitamin D supplementation would be ergogenic.

Vitamin E (alpha-tocopherol)

Vitamin E is a fat-soluble vitamin. Its physiological activity is derived from a number of different tocopherols and tocotrienols found in the diet, **alphatocopherol** being the most active.

The RDA for vitamin E is given in **alphatocopherol equivalents,** or alpha-TE, although you may also see it expressed in IU. One alpha-TE is the equivalent of 1 mg of alpha-tocopherol or about 1.5 IU. The current RDA is 10 alpha-TE (10 mg or 15 IU) for adult males and 8 alpha-TE (8 mg or 12 IU) for females. The amount is slightly less for children. See Appendix A for specific values. The USRDA, however, is 30 IU, which is generally regarded to be too high.

Vitamin E is one of the most widely distributed vitamins in foods. The best dietary sources are polyunsaturated vegetable oils such as corn, soybean, and safflower oils, and margarines made from these oils. The RDA for vitamin E actually increases as the amount of polyunsaturated oils in the diet increases. Fish oil supplements may be contraindicated in this regard since they are high in polyunsaturated fatty acids, but low in vitamin E unless supplemented. Other good sources of vitamin E include whole-grain products, wheat germ oil, and eggs. Moderate to small amounts are found in meats,

dairy products, fruits, and vegetables. One tablespoon of margarine provides 74 percent of the RDA.

Although the total function of vitamin E in human nutrition is unclear, its principal role is to serve as an antioxidant. Vitamin E helps prevent the oxidation of unsaturated fatty acids in cell membranes and thereby protects the cell from damage. Other claims, extrapolated from research with animals, have suggested that vitamin E may also play a key role in the synthesis of hemoglobin or serve a pro-oxidant effect by activating enzymes in the mitochondria to improve cellular oxygen utilization, but these claims are not well documented in humans.

Because vitamin E is rather widely distributed in foods, and because it is also stored in the body, a true vitamin E deficiency in humans is rare. In one experiment prisoners were fed a vitamin E–deficient diet for 13 months and evidenced no symptoms of a deficiency. However, certain individuals with genetic diseases, such as the inability to absorb fat, do experience a deficiency. In such cases, anemia may occur because the membranes of the red blood cells (RBC) are oxidized and release their hemoglobin. Deficiency symptoms noted in animals include nutritional muscular dystrophy and damage to the heart and blood vessels. Because of its role in preventing cellular damage, a deficiency of vitamin E has been theorized to contribute to the development of heart disease and cancer in humans. Others have suggested that a deficiency will lead to premature aging and decreased fertility.

Although vitamin E deficiency is rare in humans, several authors have used the data from animals and those humans with genetic defects to support the need for supplementation to athletes. They suggest that a vitamin E deficiency may lead to impaired oxygen transport due to RBC damage and to reduced oxidative capacity within the muscle cell. These effects would reduce VO_2 max and lead to a decrease in aerobic endurance capacity.

Vitamin E is one of the most popular nutrient supplements among both sedentary and physically active individuals. There are many health claims for supplementation with this vitamin because of its antioxidant properties, such as a slowing of the aging process or an improvement in sexual potency. Unfortunately, these claims are not substantiated by reputable research involving vitamin E supplements with normal subjects. Some epidemiological research has suggested a relationship between low levels of vitamin E in the body and the development of coronary artery disease or certain forms of cancer, possibly by preventing the oxidation of LDL-cholesterol or the nuclear membrane of the cell.

However, epidemiological research does not substantiate a cause–effect relationship, so we still await support through properly controlled experimental research. In *Diet and Health*, the National Research Council noted that the available evidence does not support claims that vitamin E supplementation above the RDA will delay the development of cancer or cardiovascular disease, although the issue continues to be investigated. There may be some benefits to individuals who have bona fide deficiencies, such as those with certain genetic disorders.

Over a dozen studies have been conducted to investigate the effect of vitamin E supplementation upon physical performance, especially VO_2 max and aerobic endurance capacity. Some of the early studies showed a beneficial effect, particularly at higher altitudes, but the experiments were poorly designed. However, one very well planned experiment by Kobayashi, using a double-blind, placebo protocol, found that 1,200 IU of vitamin E supplements daily for six weeks would improve VO_2 max, reduce blood lactic acid during submaximal exercise, and increase aerobic endurance at altitudes of 5,000 and 15,000 feet. The vitamin E was theorized to prevent the increased rate of oxidation of the RBC membrane that might occur while exercising at altitude. Although this was a well designed study, the subjects were sedentary and were not in a state of training, so it may not be applicable to athletes. More recent research by Simon-Schnass and Pabst has supported these earlier findings. The researchers reported that 400 milligrams of vitamin E given to high-altitude mountain climbers over a 10-week period improved the anaerobic (lactate) threshold. Additional research would appear to be warranted with athletes at altitude. Moreover, one investigator has noted a similar situation may exist with athletes exercising in high-smog areas, where some of the pollutants in the air could damage the RBC. Given the magnitude of sports conducted in cities such as Los Angeles, this topic also might benefit from such research.

On the other hand, the majority of the recent well designed studies, using doses from 400–1,200 IU and using athletes in training as subjects, revealed no significant effect upon physiological functions such as VO_2 max or tests of aerobic endurance when performed at sea level. One possible reason for this finding is that the plasma level of vitamin E appears to rise significantly during intense exercise, as reported by Pincemail and others. The general conclusion is that vitamin E supplementation, even with megadoses, will not improve physical performance of individuals at sea level.

Like beta-carotene, vitamin E has been theorized to prevent muscle damage during exercise, and this topic is covered later in this chapter.

Although the general consensus suggests megadoses of vitamin E ranging from 200–600 IU are relatively nontoxic, large megadoses are not recommended, because the vitamin is fat-soluble and may possibly interfere with normal body functioning as do excessive dosages of vitamins A and D. Reported effects of vitamin E megadoses include headaches, fatigue, and gastrointestinal symptoms such as diarrhea.

Vitamin K (phylloquinone)

Vitamin K is a fat-soluble vitamin. It is often called the blood coagulation vitamin or anti-hemorrhage vitamin. An RDA was established for vitamin K in 1989; for adults it is 65 and 80 micrograms per day for women and men, respectively.

Although vitamin K is found in a variety of plant and animal foods, it is also formed in the intestines by bacterial action. The typical American diet contains about 200–300 micrograms per day, so a deficiency is unlikely.

Vitamin K is needed for the formation of several compounds that are essential in two steps of the blood-clotting process. A deficiency impairs blood clotting and leads to hemorrhage. Although deficiency states are rare, they may occur in some individuals when antibiotic medications kill the intestinal bacteria that produce the vitamin. Vitamin K deficiency has not been related to physical performance. The National Research Council has noted that unlike vitamins A and D, vitamin K is not very toxic when consumed in large doses. However, some synthetic forms may be toxic in large doses.

There is no evidence available that supports vitamin K supplementation as a means to improve health status of the average individual or to improve performance in athletes.

Water-Soluble Vitamins

There are nine water-soluble vitamins, including the eight in the vitamin B complex and vitamin C (ascorbic acid). The B complex vitamins include thiamin, riboflavin, niacin, B_6, B_{12}, folic acid, biotin, and pantothenic acid. Being water soluble they are not, with a few exceptions, stored to any significant extent in the body. The effects of a deficiency may be noted in 2–4 weeks for some of these vitamins, often reducing physical performance capacity.

Excess supplements of these vitamins are usually excreted in the urine and are generally considered to be relatively harmless. However, there are some exceptions.

Because several of the B vitamins work closely together in energy metabolism, many studies have investigated the effect of a deficiency or supplementation of multiple vitamins from the B complex. A summary of this research follows a discussion of each individual vitamin.

Thiamin (vitamin B₁)

Thiamin, also known as **vitamin B₁,** is a water-soluble vitamin and is also known as the anti-beriberi or anti-neuritic vitamin. It was one of the first vitamins discovered.

The RDA for thiamin varies according to the intake of Calories, being approximately 0.5 mg per 1,000 Calories. The average adult male needs approximately 1.5 mg/day, while the adult female needs about 1.1 mg/day. See Appendix A for other age groups. The USRDA is 1.5 mg.

Thiamin is widely distributed in both plant and animal tissues. Good sources include whole-grain cereals, beans, seeds, nuts, pork, milk, cheese, and many fruits and vegetables. There also is some limited synthesis of thiamin by bacteria in the intestinal tract. One lean pork chop contains 30 percent of the RDA.

Thiamin has a central role in the metabolism of glucose. It is part of a coenzyme known as thiamin pyrophosphate, which is needed to covert pyruvate to acetyl CoA for entrance into the Krebs cycle. Thiamin is essential for the normal functioning of the nervous system and energy derivation from glycogen in the muscles.

Deficiency symptoms may occur in several weeks, including loss of appetite, mental confusion, muscular weakness, and pain in the calf muscles. Prolonged deficiencies lead to beriberi, a serious disease involving damage to the nervous system and the heart. Fortunately, thiamin deficiency is not very common, although may be rather prevalent among the homeless, alcoholics and other special groups.

Of importance to the athlete, two factors that increase the need for thiamin are exercise and high carbohydrate intake. A deficiency of thiamin could prove to be detrimental to the active individual who might rely on high levels of carbohydrate metabolism for aerobic energy production during exercise, such as endurance athletes. Indeed, some well controlled research conducted during World War II noted decreased endurance capacity after several weeks of a thiamin-deficient diet. More contemporary research has also investigated the role of thiamin deficiency upon exercise performance, but in conjunction with riboflavin and niacin deficiencies. These reports are discussed below under vitamin B complex.

Unfortunately, no contemporary research appears to exist relative to the effect of thiamin supplementation upon physical performance, although results from a number of studies conducted more than forty years ago are available. Following a careful review of these studies, many with problems in establishing a proper experimental design, there appears to be no conclusive evidence to support the contention that vitamin B₁ intake above and beyond the normal RDA will enhance performance.

As noted above, physical activity, particularly high-level, endurance-type activity, increases the need for thiamin in the diet; this exercise also increases the need for caloric intake. With proper selection of foods, the increased thiamin need may be met by the content in the additional foods eaten. An adequate thiamin intake is one of the reasons physically active individuals need to select foods that are dense in nutrients, and in general to avoid those foods that provide Calories but few nutrients.

Although thiamin supplements are not needed by the individual who is consuming an adequate diet, megadoses of thiamin up to 1,000 mg appear to have no detrimental effect. The excess will be excreted in the urine.

Riboflavin (vitamin B₂)

Riboflavin is also known as **vitamin B₂.** It is a water-soluble vitamin and is a component of the B complex.

The RDA for riboflavin is similar to that of thiamin, only slightly higher, being about 0.6 mg per 1,000 Calories. It averages about 1.7 mg for the adult male and 1.3 mg for the adult female. Appendix A contains the RDA for other age groups. The USRDA is 1.7 mg.

Riboflavin is distributed widely in foods. A major source is milk and other dairy products; one glass of milk contains 20 percent of the RDA. Other good sources include liver; eggs; dark-green, leafy vegetables; wheat germ; yeast; whole-grain products; and enriched breads and cereals.

Riboflavin is important for the formation of several oxidative enzymes known as flavoproteins, involved in energy production from carbohydrate and fats in the body cells. It is also involved in protein metabolism and maintenance of healthy skin tissue.

Deficiencies are very rare but have been seen in alcoholics and those adhering to various food-fad diets. Early signs of deficiency may include cracks at the corners of the mouth and dry, scaly skin at the corners of the nose.

Although the effect of a riboflavin deficiency upon physical performance has not been studied directly, research from Cornell University suggests that physically untrained women who initiate an aerobic training program may need a higher intake of riboflavin to synthesize more flavoproteins in the muscles. Using a blood test, the investigators determined that the RDA did not maintain proper riboflavin status in the early stages of training, but they suggested a value of about 1.1 mg per 1,000 Calories would be sufficient. It should be noted that no data were reported relative to the effect of this deficiency upon performance. Haralambie also reported a possible deficiency in trained athletes but did not relate it to performance.

A review by Keith reveals only one reputable study of the effects of riboflavin supplementation on physical performance. Tremblay and others, studying elite swimmers, reported that 60 mg of riboflavin daily for 16–20 days did not improve VO_2 max, anaerobic (lactate) threshold, or swim performance. Thus, considering the available research data and the absence of riboflavin deficiency in most individuals, one must conclude that riboflavin supplementation to the diet will not enhance physical performance.

No adverse effects of riboflavin megadoses have been reported. Excess riboflavin is apparently excreted.

Niacin

Niacin is also known as nicotinic acid, nicotinamide, or the antipellagra vitamin. It is a water-soluble vitamin in the B complex and is sometimes erroneously referred to as vitamin B_3.

Niacin is found naturally in many foods, but it also may be formed in the body from excess amounts of dietary tryptophan, an essential amino acid. Therefore, the RDA is expressed in **niacin equivalents,** or NE. One NE equals 1 mg of niacin or 60 mg of tryptophan, because 1 mg niacin can be produced from that amount of tryptophan. The RDA for niacin is based upon energy intake, approximating 6.6 mg per 1,000 Calories, which totals about 16–19 NE for adult males and 13–14 NE for adult females. The requirement is different for other age groups, and specific values may be obtained from Appendix A. The USRDA is 20 mg.

Niacin is found in foods that have a high protein content. It is most abundant in lean meats, organ meats, fish, poultry, whole-grain cereal products, legumes such as beans and peanuts, and enriched foods. Milk and eggs contain almost no niacin, but they contain moderate amounts of tryptophan. One-half of a chicken breast contains over 60 percent of the RDA of niacin.

The major function of niacin is to serve as a component of two coenzymes concerned with energy processes within the cell. One of these coenzymes is important in the process of glycolysis, which is the means by which muscle glycogen produces energy both aerobically and anaerobically. The other coenzyme is involved in fat metabolism by promoting fat synthesis in the body.

Although niacin deficiency was prevalent in the past, the enrichment of foods with niacin has nearly eliminated this problem. Deficiency symptoms include loss of appetite, skin rashes, mental confusion, lack of energy, and muscular weakness. Serious deficiencies lead to pellagra, a disease characterized by severe dermatitis, diarrhea, and symptoms of mental illness.

In theory, physical performance would be impaired by a niacin deficiency because the production of energy from carbohydrate could be impaired. Both aerobic- and anaerobic-type performances could be affected. However, no research has been uncovered that has directly studied the effects of such a deficiency on exercise performance.

Because of the role of niacin in energy metabolism, a number of experiments have been conducted relative to niacin supplementation and physical performance capacity. The results of these studies have failed to substantiate any beneficial effect of niacin on physical performance. As a matter of fact, its use is not suggested as a supplement, particularly in long endurance-type exercise such as marathon running, because one of the effects of excessive niacin (3–9 grams/day) is to block the release of FFA from the adipose tissues. This will decrease the supply of FFA to the muscle, which may lead to an increase in the rate of muscle glycogen utilization and a more rapid depletion of this important energy source. As noted by Bulow, niacin supplements may reduce endurance capacity.

Niacin supplements may also increase blood flow to the skin. In a recent experiment, Kolka and Stephenson found that such an effect could lower the sweat rate and decrease body heat storage during exercise. These effects could possibly be ergogenic to athletes exercising in the heat, but further investigation is needed.

Megadoses of niacin have been used in attempts to treat several health problems, being relatively ineffective in the treatment of mental disease and somewhat successful in reducing high serum-lipid levels. Niacin may not only lower total and LDL cholesterol but may also lower triglycerides and raise HDL cholesterol.

Although niacin is generally considered to be nontoxic, large doses in the form of nicotinic acid may cause flushing, with burning and tingling sensations around the face, neck, and hands occurring within 15–20 minutes after ingestion. Taken over long periods, niacin may contribute to liver problems such as hepatitis and peptic ulcers. In particular, timed-release niacin preparations have been implicated as a cause of hepatitis. The Center for Science in the Public Interest recommends that no one take niacin to lower blood cholesterol without guidance from a physician.

In summary, niacin supplements are not recommended for a physically active individual on a balanced diet. Excessive intake may actually impair certain types of athletic performance.

Vitamin B₆ (pyridoxine)

Vitamin B₆ is a collective term for three naturally occurring substances that are all metabolically and functionally related. They are pyridoxine, pyridoxal, and pyridoxamine. **Pyridoxine** is most often used as a synonym. Vitamin B_6 is water-soluble.

The adult RDA for vitamin B_6 is 2 mg/day. Slightly different amounts are needed at different age levels. Consult Appendix A for specific RDA. Actually, the RDA for vitamin B_6 is based on protein intake, so requirements may increase with high-protein diets. The USRDA is 2 mg.

Vitamin B_6 is widely distributed in foods. The best sources are protein foods such as meats, poultry, fish, wheat germ, whole-grain products, brown rice, and eggs. One-half of a chicken breast contains over 25 percent of the RDA.

In its coenzyme form (primarily pyridoxal phosphate), vitamin B_6 is critically involved in the metabolism of protein, but it is also involved in carbohydrate and fat metabolism. It functions with more than 60 enzymes in such processes as the synthesis of dispensable amino acids, the conversion of tryptophan to niacin, the formation of neurotransmitters in the nervous system, and the incorporation of amino acids into body proteins such as hemoglobin, myoglobin, and oxidative enzymes. It is also involved in the breakdown of muscle glycogen as well as gluconeogenesis in the liver.

Vitamin B_6 deficiency is not considered to be a major health problem. The average American diet appears to provide an adequate amount of the vitamin, but poor diets do not. The use of diuretics and oral contraceptives has been associated with deficiencies. Several surveys also have reported inadequate intakes in athletes. Deficiency symptoms include nausea, skin disorders, mouth sores, weakness, mental depression, anemia and epileptic-like convulsions.

Theoretically, a B_6 deficiency could adversely affect endurance activities dependent upon oxygen, for it is involved in the formation of protein compounds such as hemoglobin that are essential to oxidative processes. Its role in carbohydrate metabolism, particularly muscle glycogen utilization, is also important to the endurance athlete. Its role in the formation of neurotransmitters could be important to athletes engaged in fine motor control sports, such as archery and riflery. In addition, the requirement for B_6 increases with protein intake, which may have some implications for those athletes who may be on high-protein diets. However, since B_6 is found in protein products, it should be easily obtainable in such a diet.

No research has been uncovered that has directly studied the effect of a B_6 deficiency upon physical performance. One report did suggest that runners who covered 5–10 miles per day appear to use more B_6 than their sedentary counterparts, but these investigators also noted that exercise may actually promote storage of the vitamin in the athlete, thus helping to prevent a deficiency state. Serum levels of B_6 actually increase during exercise. Hoffman and others noted the source remains to be identified, but it may be derived from the B_6-dependent enzyme phosphorylase, which breaks down muscle glycogen. Although the muscle may store B_6, Coburn and others recently noted that B_6 supplementation did not markedly increase muscle stores.

Several reports relative to the effect of B_6 supplementation upon physical performance are available. In general, the results reveal no significant effect upon metabolic functions during exercise or the capacity to do more work. One investigator suggested B_6 may actually be detrimental to endurance athletes because it may facilitate the use of muscle glycogen and lead to an earlier depletion in prolonged events. Although this theory has not been tested, in one of the more recent studies from this laboratory at Oregon State University, Manore and Leklem recommend that athletes not supplement their high-carbohydrate diets with B_6 above the RDA.

Vitamin B_6 supplementation has been used to treat the nausea of pregnancy, mental depression associated with the use of oral contraceptives, and the premenstrual syndrome (PMS), but its effectiveness for these purposes has received mixed reviews. There appears to be little or no toxicity associated with moderate doses, but several recent case studies of individuals using 2–6 grams daily revealed such problems as loss of natural sensation from the limbs and an impaired gait. The National Research Council noted neurological symptoms with smaller dosages, averaging 117 mg per day for six months to five years.

In summary, B_6 supplementation does not appear to be warranted for the physically active individual.

Vitamin B_{12} (cyanocobalamin)

Vitamin B_{12} (cyanocobalamin) is a water-soluble vitamin. It is part of the B complex and is the latest vitamin to be discovered.

The adult RDA for B_{12} is 2 micrograms per day. The average diet contains about 5–15 micrograms. Slightly different allowances are made for other age groups; see Appendix A. The USRDA is 6 micrograms.

Vitamin B_{12} is found in good supply only in animal foods such as meat, fish, poultry, cheese, eggs, and milk. One glass of milk contains nearly 30 percent of the RDA. It is not found in plant foods such as fruits, vegetables, beans, and grains. However, it is present in microorganisms such as bacteria and yeast, which may be found in some plant foods. Although B_{12} may be produced by microorganisms in the human bowel, the site of production is below the point of absorption.

Vitamin B_{12} is a part of coenzymes present in all body cells and is essential in the synthesis of DNA. It works closely with folic acid, and both have important roles in the development of red blood cells. Vitamin B_{12} is also essential for the formation of the protective sheath around nerve fibers (the myelin sheath).

Deficiency of vitamin B_{12} in humans due to inadequate dietary intake is rare. Even strict vegetarians appear to receive enough in their diet, either through the consumption of microorganisms or the use of fortified products. The body also stores a considerable amount in the liver, which may last for years. A deficiency is caused by the lack of an intrinsic factor in the gastrointestinal tract that is needed for the B_{12} to be absorbed into the body. The major symptoms are a severe form of anemia, known as pernicious anemia, and nerve damage that may cause paralysis.

Because of its role in the formation of RBC, a deficiency of B_{12} resulting in pernicious anemia would be theorized to decrease aerobic endurance capacity. No research is available relative to the effect of a vitamin B_{12} deficiency upon performance, but other types of anemia have been shown to impair exercise performance.

Relative to supplementation, vitamin B_{12} is one of the most abused vitamins in the athletic world, with some reports of athletes receiving large amounts by injection just prior to competition. The belief probably exists that if a little vitamin B_{12} can prevent anemia, then a lot of it will do something magical to increase performance capacity. However, several well controlled studies have been conducted with B_{12} supplementation with the general conclusion that it will not help to increase metabolic functions, such as VO_2 max, or endurance performance.

A coenzyme form of B_{12}, known as Dibencobal, has been advertised for body builders to increase muscle growth and strength. However, in a review for the National Strength and Conditioning Association, Williams noted the claims were based upon fallacious data and no data were available to support an ergogenic effect of Dibencobal.

Megadoses of vitamin B_{12} are considered to be relatively harmless. It may be an effective medical treatment for a particular type of anemia, but it does not appear to benefit the active individual on a balanced diet.

Folic acid (folate)

Folic acid, or **folate,** is a water-soluble vitamin. It is part of the B complex.

The RDA for folic acid is 0.2 mg/day, or 200 micrograms, for adults. Slightly different amounts are set for children and for women during pregnancy and lactation; see Appendix A. The USRDA is 400 micrograms.

Folic acid derives it name from foliage because it is found in green leafy vegetables like spinach. Other good sources include organ meats such as liver and kidney, dry beans, whole-grain products, and some fruits like oranges and bananas. One banana provides almost 10 percent of the RDA.

Folic acid serves as part of a coenzyme that plays a critical role in the formation of DNA, the genetic material that regulates cell division. It is essential for maintaining normal production of RBC, one of the most rapidly dividing cells in the body.

One national survey has reported folate intakes below the RDA for some Americans. Individuals who consume large quantities of alcohol and women who take oral contraceptives may experience deficiencies in folic acid, as these drugs may impair absorption of the vitamin. The major effect of folic-acid deficiency is anemia. Individuals suffering from folate deficiency would benefit from supplementation as reported by Tsui and Nordstrom. Supplements of 400 micrograms per day for two months increased hemoglobin levels in adolescent girls who were folate-deficient.

One advocate of vitamin supplementation to athletes has reported that runners need additional folic acid to replace RBC that may be destroyed in heavy training programs. Unfortunately, no evidence is available to support this theory, nor are there any data that folic acid supplements will benefit physical performance. Only one study has been uncovered related to folate supplementation to athletes. Matter and her colleagues provided folate therapy (5 mg/day for 11 weeks) to female marathon runners who were diagnosed as being folate deficient. Although the folate therapy restored serum folate levels to normal, no improvements were noted in VO_2 max, maximum treadmill running time, peak lactate levels, or running speed at the lactate anaerobic threshold.

Megadoses are usually considered harmless, although it is remotely possible that they could mask a vitamin B_{12} deficiency by preventing the development of anemia that would otherwise be discovered by a blood test. Unfortunately, folic acid does not prevent nerve damage, so the B_{12} deficiency may lead to paralysis if not detected early. The National Research Council does not recommend folate supplementation.

To be sure, anemia resulting from a folic-acid deficiency could have serious consequences for endurance performance, but a balanced diet should prevent this condition from developing.

Pantothenic acid

Pantothenic acid is a water-soluble vitamin. It is a factor in the B complex. Pantothenate is a salt of pantothenic acid.

The Food and Nutrition Board does not list the RDA of pantothenic acid in the main table, but the recommended ESADDI is 4–7 mg. The USRDA is 10 mg.

Pantothenic acid is distributed widely in foods. It is found in all natural animal and plant products, but best sources include organ meat, eggs, legumes, yeasts, and whole grains. It should also be noted that highly refined, processed foods have lost most of the pantothenate content.

Pantothenic acid is an essential component of coenzyme A (CoA), which plays a central role in energy metabolism. You may recall acetyl CoA, which may be derived from carbohydrate, fat, and protein metabolism, is the principal substrate for the Krebs cycle. Pantothenic acid is also involved in gluconeogenesis, in the synthesis and breakdown of fatty acids, and in the synthesis of acetylcholine, a chemical released by a motor neuron to initiate muscle contraction.

Except under experimentally induced conditions, deficiencies are not seen in humans. In such cases deficiencies have been reported to cause a variety of symptoms, including fatigue, muscle cramping, and impairment of motor coordination.

On a theoretical basis, pantothenic acid appears crucial to the active individual because it has an important function at the center of energy pathways. Several investigators have suggested that a deficiency would decrease the availability of acetyl CoA for the Krebs cycle and thus shift energy production to anaerobic glycolysis, which is less efficient. Because deficiencies have not been observed, such effects upon physical performance have not been studied.

However, data for one well designed study with supplements of pantothenic acid, 2 grams per day for 14 days, suggested a beneficial effect by reducing oxygen consumption and lactate production during a submaximal exercise task at 75 percent VO_2 max for 40 minutes. This would suggest that pantothenic acid increased the efficiency of the exercise task. No data on maximal performance was provided. Unfortunately this report was available only as a brief abstract and very few details were presented. Conversely, another well designed study revealed that 1 gram of pantothenic acid given daily for two weeks had no effect upon various blood measures or maximal performance in highly trained distance runners. In his review, Keith analyzed six animal and human studies and suggested a possible relationship between exercise and pantothenic acid metabolism. However, only two studies involved humans, and the results were equivocal as noted above. Thus, more research is desirable.

Supplements of pantothenic acid appear to be relatively nontoxic. However, large doses of 10–20 grams have been known to cause diarrhea.

Biotin

Biotin is a water-soluble vitamin in the B complex. No RDA has been established for biotin, but the recommended ESADDI is 30–100 micrograms. The USRDA is 300 micrograms.

Good dietary sources of biotin include organ meats such as liver, egg yolk, legumes such as peas and beans, and dark-green, leafy vegetables. It is also synthesized in significant amounts in the intestines by bacteria.

Biotin acts as coenzyme for a variety of enzymes involved in amino acid metabolism and the synthesis of fatty acids and glycogen. It could have important implications for carbohydrate-loading programs.

Deficiency states are rare but may occur when the diet contains large amounts of raw egg whites; a protein in the raw egg white binds biotin and prevents its absorption into the body. In such cases symptoms include loss of appetite, mental depression, dermatitis and muscle pains. For athletes who consume eggs for their protein content it may be important to know that cooking the egg white eliminates this problem while providing the same amount of high-quality protein. It should also be mentioned in passing that raw eggs pose a risk of Salmonella, a type of bacteria associated with food poisoning.

Supplements of biotin are considered to be harmless. No research into the effects of biotin supplementation and physical performance has been uncovered. It would appear that supplements are unnecessary for the physically active individual.

There is no evidence that biotin supplementation increases physical performance capacity.

Vitamin B complex

Because several of the vitamins in the B complex work together in energy metabolism, a number of studies have investigated the effect of either a deficiency or supplement of more than one vitamin upon physical performance. Several of these studies were well controlled experiments during World War II, but contemporary evidence is also available.

As might be expected from evidence presented on deficiencies of individual vitamins, a deficiency of several B vitamins together would negatively affect physical performance. This theory has been borne out by those studies in which daily intake was reduced to less than 50 percent of the RDA. Several studies by van der Beek from the Netherlands have shown that a daily intake of less than one-third of the Dutch RDA for several of the B vitamins (B_1, B_2, B_6) and vitamin C would lead to a dramatic decrease of VO_2 max and the anaerobic threshold in less than four weeks. The reduction in performance occurred even when other vitamins in the diet were supplemented at twice the RDA. In the most recent study VO_2 max decreased by 10 percent and the onset of blood lactate accumulation (anaerobic threshold) decreased approximately 20 percent after eight weeks of a deficient diet. The findings support earlier research showing a significant decrease in endurance capacity with a B complex deficiency. A number of studies, several with children, have also shown that when a deficiency state is corrected by vitamin supplements, physical performance is restored to normal.

In general, research supports the idea that individuals who obtain adequate vitamins through a balanced diet will not improve endurance performance through the use of B complex supplements. However, some research with large dosages of B_1, B_6 and B_{12} (about 60–200 times the RDA) has shown increases in fine motor control and performance in pistol shooting. Bonke suggested the beneficial effect was related to the role of these vitamins in promoting the development of neurotransmitters. Additional research is needed to confirm this finding.

Several of the principal Dutch investigators in this area, such as van Erp-Baart and Saris, suggest that B complex supplementation may be useful in sports with a high energy expenditure if these athletes consume large amounts of foods with empty calories—high-sugar and high-fat foods. This again stresses the importance of eating foods that are high in nutrient value.

Vitamin C (ascorbic acid)

Vitamin C, or **ascorbic acid,** is a water-soluble vitamin. Its alleged effects upon health and physical performance have been the subject of much controversy.

The adult RDA and USRDA for vitamin C is 60 mg/day. Slightly lower amounts are recommended for children. See Appendix A for specific recommendations.

The best food sources of vitamin C are fruits and vegetables, primarily the citrus fruits and the leafy parts of green vegetables. Excellent sources include oranges, grapefruit, broccoli, and salad greens. Other good sources are green peppers, potatoes, strawberries, and tomatoes. One orange contains the RDA. Milk, meats, and grain products are low in vitamin C.

Although vitamin C does not directly participate in enzyme-catalyzed conversions of substrate to product, Padh suggests it modifies mineral ions in the enzymes to make them active. Vitamin C has a number of different functions in the body, some of which have important implications for the active individual. Its principal role is in the synthesis of collagen, which is necessary for the formation and maintenance of the connective tissues of the body such as cartilage, tendon, and bone. Vitamin C is also involved in the formation of certain hormones and neurotransmitters, such as epinephrine (adrenaline), which are secreted during stressful situations like exercise. It helps absorb non-heme iron from the intestinal tract and is involved in the synthesis of RBC. Vitamin C helps regulate the metabolism of cholesterol and amino acids. It is also important in the healing of wounds through the development of scar tissue. Finally, vitamin C is a powerful antioxidant.

Serious deficiencies of vitamin C are rare in industrialized societies because fresh or frozen fruits and vegetables are abundant. Also, the human body has a pool of vitamin C ranging from 1.5–3.0 grams. However, smoking, aspirin, oral contraceptives, and stress may increase the need for this vitamin. The major deficiency disease is scurvy, a disintegration of the connective tissue in the gums, skin, tendons, and cartilage. Typical symptoms include bleeding gums, rupture of blood vessels in the skin, impaired wound healing, muscle cramps, and weakness. Anemia also may develop.

It is obvious that many of these symptoms of a vitamin C deficiency would impair physical performance. Sensations of weakness could adversely affect all types of performance, whereas anemia would hamper aerobic endurance. Data available from several studies with vitamin C–deficient subjects do suggest such an effect, particularly the widely known Minnesota starvation experiments during World War II, directed by Ancel Keys.

The effect of vitamin C supplementation upon physical performance has received considerable attention, mainly because it is one of the vitamins that athletes consume in rather substantial quantities. Both early and contemporary research has shown that vitamin C supplementation improves physical performance in subjects who were vitamin C–deficient, but a thorough analysis of these studies supports the general conclusion that vitamin C supplementation does not increase physical performance capacity in subjects who are not vitamin deficient. No solid experimental evidence supports the use of megadoses of 5–10 grams that some athletes take. The interested reader may consult the review by Gerster.

On the other hand, because exercise is a stressor, some investigators have recommended that the active individual may need slightly more vitamin C than the RDA, for example, 200–300 milligrams per day. Some research with runners doing 5–10 miles a day does not support this viewpoint; in any case, this amount could easily be obtained by wise selection of foods high in vitamin C content. Keith also suggests vitamin C supplementation may be beneficial to heat acclimation, a topic that merits additional research with trained athletes.

Megadoses of vitamin C also have been claimed to have significant health benefits, such as the prevention of colds, the reduction of serum cholesterol, and the prevention of cancer. Unfortunately, these health claims generally have not been substantiated in well controlled experiments.

There is some debate regarding the safety of megadoses of vitamin C. Several investigators have found that excessive amounts of vitamin C, such as 5–10 grams daily, may produce some undesirable side effects such as diarrhea, destruction of vitamin B_{12} in the diet, excessive excretion of vitamin B_6, decreased copper bioavailability, predisposition to gout creating pain in the joints, and formation of kidney stones from oxalate salts, one of the breakdown products of vitamin C. Excessive amounts also may interfere with the correct interpretation of certain blood and urine tests. Finally, several case studies revealed the development of a condition known as rebound scurvy when the individual stopped taking the supplements. The researchers suggested a mechanism whereby the increased activity of an enzyme in the body that destroys excess vitamin C during the supplement stages continued after the supplements were stopped, leading to a deficiency and symptoms of scurvy. Conversely, others have reported megadoses to be relatively harmless because excessive amounts are excreted by the kidneys. They criticize the research upon which claims of adverse effects are based, noting that some of the conclusions rest on isolated case studies. Others support a middle viewpoint, noting that larger doses may be harmless to many, but certain individuals may be prone to problems, such as those who have a family history of kidney stones. The National Research Council recommends against the routine use of large supplements.

For the athlete or physically active individual, the general recommendation is to avoid supplements but increase the consumption of more fresh or frozen fruits and vegetables to obtain adequate amounts of vitamin C.

Vitamin Supplements: Health Aspects

Vitamins continue to be one of the most used and abused supplements in the United States today. Certain segments of the population may have a vitamin intake below the RDA, but no disease states are usually associated with these lower intakes, probably because of the safety factor incorporated in the RDA. Moreover, the vast majority of Americans receive the RDA for all vitamins in their daily diets. Nevertheless, certain vitamin pill manufacturers and advertisers have perpetuated the myth that the average U.S. diet contains insufficient amounts of vitamins, a potential cause of many health problems. We now have vitamin supplements on the market that have been designed, or so the manufacturers imply, to combat the stress of everyday life, prevent the common cold, reduce blood cholesterol, and prevent baldness, aging, arthritis, and a host of other diseases, including cancer. These are enticing claims. It is no wonder that approximately 35–40 percent of the U.S. population spends billions of dollars yearly on vitamin supplements. Vitamins are big business. They are marketed for all segments of the population, from infant formulas to the geriatric supplement.

In the preceding sections we have already covered each individual vitamin and the possible effects of deficiencies and supplementation upon health (review Table 6.1 for a broad overview). This section summarizes prudent dietary recommendations for optimal vitamin nutrition, including the possible use of supplements, relative to health.

Can I obtain the vitamins I need through my diet?

If you read the advertisements of vitamin supplement manufacturers, you are left with the impression that it is difficult, if not impossible, to obtain adequate vitamin nutrition through the typical American diet. In contrast, the American Medical Association (AMA) supports the view that a balanced diet will satisfy all nutrient needs of the healthy individual. There is some truth to both positions, for the typical diet of some individuals may not be a balanced diet.

Vitamin intake may be inadequate for several reasons. First, the refining process of many foods removes vitamins. For example, the preparation of flour for white bread removes many of the vitamins found in the outer parts of the grain. Although some of these vitamins are returned by an enrichment process, not all are restored. Thus, many processed foods may be lower in total vitamin content than their natural counterparts. In some cases, however, processing actually increases the vitamin content of foods. Examples include the fortification of milk with vitamin A and D and the use of vitamin C as an antioxidant preservative in some foods. Second, improper storage of foods may lead to vitamin losses. Once fruits and vegetables are harvested, the vitamin content begins to diminish. In general, such foods should be refrigerated or frozen as applicable and stored in dark places to minimize vitamin losses

caused by exposure to heat and light. Third, improper preparation may also lead to significant vitamin losses from foods. Prolonged cooking, excessive heat, and cooking vegetables in water should be avoided. Steaming, microwave cooking, and the use of boiling bags and waterless cookware will help retain the natural vitamin content of foods. Thus, the individual who consumes a diet high in processed foods with empty calories and does not prepare foods properly may receive less than the RDA for several vitamins.

The key to adequate vitamin nutrition is to consume a balanced diet of natural foods that have a high nutrient density. Buy foods in their natural state and store them properly as soon as possible. Prepare them to eat so as to minimize vitamin losses.

In general, healthy sedentary and physically active individuals should obtain the necessary vitamins from the diet. In this way, other nutrients, particularly minerals, will be obtained at the same time, as they also are natural constituents of the food we eat. Vitamins often work in conjunction with minerals, such as vitamin D and calcium, vitamin B_6 and magnesium, and vitamin E and selenium. By obtaining vitamins through the selection of a balanced diet, we may be assured of receiving sufficient amounts of other nutrients necessary for optimal physiological functioning. However, it is recommended that the active individual be selective in choosing foods. The stress of exercise can increase the utilization of some water-soluble vitamins, but these can be replaced easily if the extra Calories expended during exercise are replaced by foods with high nutrient density. Table 6.2 presents a quick overview of foods containing substantial amounts of the major vitamins, while Table 6.3 presents a list of ten foods, totaling approximately 1,200 Calories, that will provide at least 100 percent of the RDA for every vitamin, assuming adequate sunlight for vitamin D and intestinal synthesis of biotin and vitamin K.

Why are vitamin supplements often recommended?

There are many bona fide reasons for vitamin supplementation. For example, pregnancy and lactation increase the RDA for all vitamins, so many physicians recommend a general vitamin supplement. In addition, certain diseases or disorders will increase the need for a specific vitamin. An impaired ability to absorb fat will decrease the availability of the fat-soluble vitamins, while a lack of the intrinsic factor necessitates injections of vitamin B_{12}. An intolerance to certain foods, such as milk, may limit the

Table 6.2   High vitamin content foods

Vitamin A	Beef liver, fish liver oils, egg yolks		**Pantothenic acid**	Meats, poultry, fish
	Milk, butter, cheese, fortified margarine			Milk, cheese
	Yellow vegetables (carrots, sweet potatoes)			Legumes
	Green vegetables (spinach, collards)			Whole grain products
			Folacin	Meats, liver, eggs
Vitamin B₁ (thiamin)	Pork, legumes (dried peas and beans)			Milk
	Milk			Legumes
	Nuts, peanuts			Whole wheat products
	Whole grain and enriched cereal products (bread)			Green leafy vegetables
	All vegetables		**Vitamin B₁₂ (cyanocobalamin)**	Meats, poultry, fish, eggs
	Fruits			Milk, cheese, butter
Vitamin B₂ (riboflavin)	Meats, liver, kidneys, eggs			(not found in plant foods)
	Milk, cheese		**Biotin**	Meats, liver, egg yolk
	Whole gain and enriched cereal products			Legumes, nuts
	Wheat germ			Vegetables
	Green leafy vegetables		**Vitamin C**	Citrus fruits, oranges, grapefruit, melons, berries, tomatoes
Niacin	Lean meats, organ meats (liver), poultry			Broccoli, brussels sprouts, cabbage, salad greens, green peppers, cauliflower
	Legumes, peanuts, peanut butter		**Vitamin D**	Liver, tuna, salmon, cod liver oil, eggs
	Whole grain and enriched cereal products			Fortified milk and margarine
Vitamin B₆ (pyridoxine)	Meat, poultry, fish		**Vitamin E**	Legumes, nuts, seeds
	Whole grain cereals, seeds			Margarine, salad oils, wheat germ oil
	Vegetables			Green leafy vegetables
			Vitamin K	Pork, liver, meats
				Green leafy vegetables, cauliflower, spinach, cabbage

intake of several important vitamins, such as ribo-flavin and vitamin D. Drugs taken to treat or prevent illnesses may lead to problems, such as antibiotics that kill intestinal bacteria and decrease the production of vitamin K. In such cases, specific vitamins will be prescribed by physicians.

Vitamin supplements also have been recommended for other individuals who may be at risk for a deficiency because of their particular life-style. Individuals who are on low-Calorie diets, particularly when less than 1,200 Calories, may need a vitamin supplement in order to obtain the RDA. Even if adequate in Calories, a poor diet in itself will also contain an insufficient amount of some vitamins. Other practices, such as smoking, alcohol consumption, and the use of drugs such as aspirin and oral contraceptives, will increase the need for certain vitamins. In such cases, if an individual feels he or she is not receiving a balanced diet for some reason, most medical authorities agree that a simple, balanced vitamin

Table 6.3   1,200 Calorie diet containing at least 100% of the RDA for each vitamin

Food	Amount
Milk, skim, fortified with vitamins A and D	2 cups
Carrot	1 medium
Orange	1 average
Bread, whole wheat	4 slices
Chicken breast, roasted	3 ounces
Broccoli	1 stalk
Margarine	1 tablespoon
Cereal, Grape-nuts	2 ounces
Tuna fish, in water	3 ounces
Cauliflower	1/2 cup

supplement containing 50–150 percent of the RDA will not do any harm. There are a number of preparations on the market that contain the daily RDA of most vitamins. However, the American Medical Association suggests that use of larger amounts be under medical supervision. Nevertheless millions of Americans consume vitamin megadoses without such supervision.

Why do individuals take vitamin megadoses?
We have all heard of the adage "if a little bit is good, more is better." As already noted, vitamin nutrition for optimal health may be obtained from a proper diet. The RDA for all thirteen vitamins totals approximately 100 milligrams, yet some individuals are consuming prodigious amounts—thousands of milligrams—via supplements, for a variety of health reasons. Vitamin C and E are the two most popular supplements, but beta-carotene is also becoming increasingly popular, probably because all three possess antioxidant properties.

Free oxygen radicals are chemical substances that have a lone, unpaired electron in the outer orbit. As such, they are unstable compounds that possess an unbalanced magnetic field which affects molecular structure and chemical reactions in the body. Free radicals are theorized to contribute to the aging process and to the development of more than sixty diseases, including rheumatoid arthritis, Alzheimer's disease, and cancer.

Free radicals such as superoxide and hydrogen peroxide are produced naturally in the body from several chemical reactions involving oxidation, including oxidative processes in the mitochondria. In pathological amounts, free radicals could damage cellular structure and function, thereby possibly contributing to aging and disease. Fortunately, the human body possesses a variety of enzymes such as superoxide dismutase and glutathione peroxidase, whose main function is to neutralize these free radicals. To function, these enzymes, often referred to as free radical–scavenging enzymes, must contain certain nutrients, such as copper, zinc, and selenium. But other nutrients in foods, particularly the antioxidant vitamins, may also help stabilize the outer ring of the free radical and reduce its reactivity with body cells. Thus, millions of Americans are consuming megadoses of these three vitamins (C, E, and beta-carotene) in attempts to slow aging, prevent disease, or both.

Unfortunately, there is no evidence that large doses of these vitamins, taken individually or in combination, prevent the aging process or diseases such as cancer. Mainly on the basis of epidemiological data reviewed in *Diet and Health,* the National Research Council has concluded that a diet containing foods high in beta-carotene and vitamin C may provide some protection against the development of certain forms of cancer, although the protective effect may be related to other compounds in these foods. Another thorough review is provided by Willet. The evidence for a protective effect of vitamin E is weaker, but the NRC has stated that low levels of vitamin E and selenium may increase risk for certain cancers. Adequate intake of other vitamins, such as folacin, as well as dietary fiber may also be associated with a decreased risk for certain cancers, but again the prudent recommendation is to shift to the Healthy American Diet and not consume supplements. In five words, eat more fruits and vegetables.

Are vitamin megadoses harmful?
A **megadose** generally is defined as an amount ten times the RDA but may be lower for vitamin A (only 5 times) and vitamin D (only 2 times). If the vitamin content of the body is adequate, excessive vitamin intake serves no useful purpose and may even be harmful in certain situations. As noted previously, vitamins function primarily as coenzymes. When a vitamin enters the body, it travels through the bloodstream to a particular body cell and then forms part of the enzyme complex within that cell. The cell has a limited capacity to produce these enzymes, and when that capacity is reached, the vitamin cannot be used for its basic purpose. It may now have other fates. It may be excreted from the body if in excess, particularly if it is a water-soluble vitamin; it may be stored in some body tissue, particularly if it is a fat-soluble vitamin; or it may begin to function in uncharacteristic ways, as a drug instead of a nutrient.

As noted throughout this chapter, megadoses of several vitamins may be pathological, particularly A, D, niacin, and B_6. There are more than 4,000 cases of vitamin/mineral overdose in the United States each year, resulting in about thirty fatalities. Although most of these cases occur in children, the literature contains some case reports of serious health problems with adults, including athletes taking vitamin megadoses in attempts to improve athletic performance.

Vitamin Supplements: Ergogenic Aspects

Like the general population, the vast majority of athletes receive the RDA for vitamins in their daily diet. It is true that some studies report that certain groups of athletes received less than the RDA for some vitamins or even had indicators of a biochemical deficiency, but Sarah Short of Syracuse University, in her exhaustive review of dietary surveys with athletes, found that vitamin deficiency symptoms rarely are reported. Nevertheless, the majority of both high school and college athletes believe vitamins are essential for success, and it is a matter of fact that many do consume vitamin supplements either as nutritional insurance or in the hope of improving performance.

In recent years some vitamin manufacturers have turned their attention to the physically active individual, suggesting through advertisements that their special product enhances athletic performance. In her review, Priscilla Clarkson of the University of Massachusetts suggested such advertisements were a major reason for the use of vitamin supplements by athletes.

Should physically active individuals take vitamin supplements?

There may be some good reasons for physically active individuals to take vitamin supplements. For example, in certain types of athletic activity such as wrestling, gymnastics, and ballet, participants may undertake prolonged semistarvation or starvation diets. As discussed in Chapter 9, this is not a recommended procedure, but some athletes may do it to obtain or maintain an optimal body weight for competition. In such cases, when the energy intake may be well below 1,200 Calories per day, many surveys have shown that the athlete may not be receiving enough vitamins. Research suggests that vitamin depletion, mainly the water-soluble vitamins, can occur rapidly in humans on low-Calorie diets and that these vitamins should be replaced daily. Athletes may also need vitamin supplementation for some of the reasons cited in the previous section, particularly if they are subsisting on poor diets.

However, as is obvious from the evidence presented in this chapter, the athlete who is on a balanced diet has no need for vitamin supplementation to improve performance. Nevertheless, some interesting new research suggests certain vitamin supplements may help prevent muscle tissue damage during training.

Can the antioxidant vitamins prevent muscle damage during training?

It has been known for years that certain forms of physical training for sports, particularly intense training, can induce muscle damage and soreness. Lovlin and others have reported that exhaustive maximal exercise induces free radical generation. Excessive production of free radicals may damage the integrity of cellular and subcellular membranes in the muscles and lead to muscle soreness. It is possible, however, that ongoing physical training itself increases the activity of the free radical–scavenging enzymes to help minimize recurrent damage and thus provides a protective effect.

The adverse effects of free radicals are attributed to the peroxidation of the lipid component of cell membranes. For this reason, several antioxidants serve a theoretical protective role, especially vitamin E but also vitamin C and beta-carotene. For a more detailed coverage of mechanisms, the interested reader is referred to the reviews led by Kagan and by Demopoulous. Several research teams have investigated the effect of antioxidant supplementation on various metabolic markers of exercise-induced muscle trauma. Vitamin E has been studied individually, but "antioxidant cocktails" consisting of approximately 800 IU of vitamin E, 1,000 milligrams of vitamin C, and 10–30 micrograms of beta-carotene have also been used. In general, the studies headed by Goldfarb, Kanter, and Viguie have shown the supplements to have been of some benefit either by enhancing the status of the scavenging enzymes or by reducing indices of lipid peroxidation or muscle damage.

How effective are the special vitamin supplements marketed for athletes?

Special athletic vitamin packs have been appearing on the market, even in single packets at your local convenience store, which have been advertised as a means for the athlete to reach peak performance. Many of these have simply been multivitamin–mineral supplements, while others have been special concoctions like bee pollen. Four such products will be highlighted.

Multivitamin–mineral supplements Because in human metabolism vitamins often work together, and often in conjunction with minerals, the ergogenic potential of multivitamin–mineral compounds has been studied for half a century. In a 1989 review of the older research, Williams reported that although results of a number of studies suggested ergogenic

Figure 6.3.

Roles of vitamins important to sports performance. A number of B vitamins, including thiamin, riboflavin, niacin, B$_6$, and pantothenic acid are essential for the conversion of carbohydrate into energy for muscular contraction. Vitamin B$_{12}$ and folacin are essential for the development of the red blood cells (RBC), which deliver oxygen to the muscle cell, whereas vitamin E helps protect the RBC membrane from destruction by free radicals such as oxides. Vitamin C is needed for the formation of epinephrine (adrenaline), a key hormone during strenuous exercise. Niacin may actually block the release of free fatty acids from the adipose tissue, which could be a disadvantage for ultraendurance athletes. Finally, several of the B vitamins are also involved in the formation of neurotransmitters in the brain which may induce a relaxation effect.

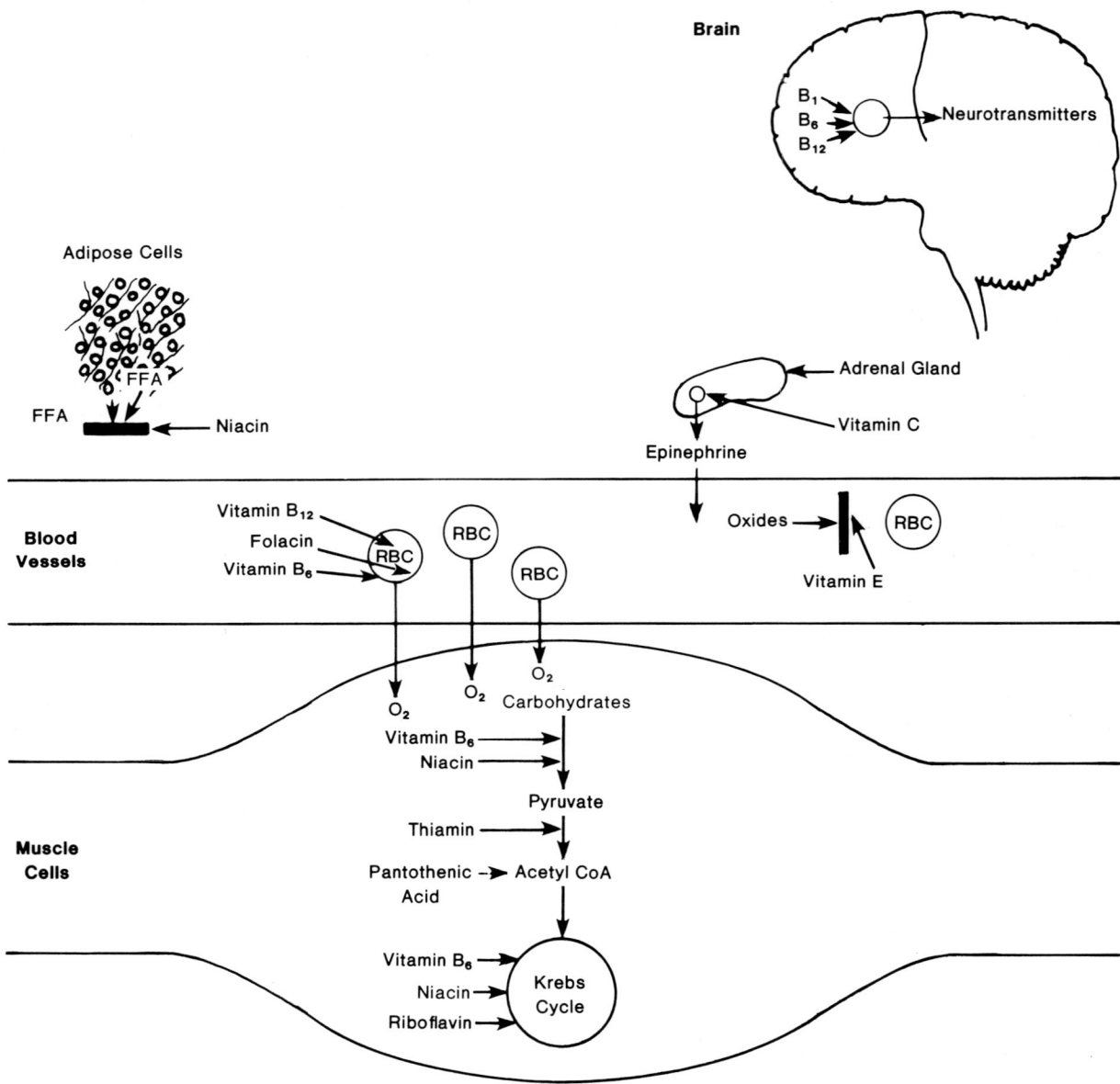

effects, the experimental designs were usually poorly controlled. In contrast, contemporary research indicates that such supplements, consumed for substantial periods, are not ergogenic for the athlete on a balanced diet. Barnett and Conlee found that four weeks of supplementation with a multivitamin–mineral compound (including additional amino acids) had no influence on maximal oxygen uptake. Weight, from Timothy Noakes' laboratory in South Africa, conducted a thorough nine-month double-blind placebo crossover study. Although the supplements did raise blood levels of some vitamins, the authors reported that three months of supplementation did not improve maximal oxygen uptake, the anaerobic (lactate) threshold, treadmill run time to exhaustion, or running performance in a 15-kilometer time trial. Similar results have been reported by Labadarios, also from Noakes' laboratory. A recent well designed double-blind placebo study conducted by Schrijver and others, using a supplement containing ten times the RDA for iron and all vitamins except K for four months, revealed no beneficial effect upon physical performance capacity as measured by heart rate, VO_2 max, or running performance in the Cooper test (1.5 miles). Finally, Richard Telford, the Chief exercise physiologist and nutritionist at the Australian Institute of Sport, supplemented the diet of 43 elite Australian athletes with twelve vitamins substantially above the RDA and nine minerals somewhat below the RDA; an equal number of athletes received a placebo. Following six months, Telford and his associates reported that the supplements had no effect on sport-specific tests of anaerobic or aerobic capacity or strength when compared with athletes whose vitamin and mineral RDA were met by dietary intake.

Thus, all of the current reputable research refutes an ergogenic effect of multivitamin–mineral supplements in adequately nourished athletes.

Bee pollen. **Bee pollen** has been marketed almost specifically for athletes, primarily runners, as a means to improve performance. Chemical analysis of bee pollen reveals it is a mixture of vitamins, minerals, amino acids, and other nutrients. Although no specific physiological effects of bee pollen have been documented, theoretical ergogenic effects are based on some of the roles that vitamins have in the body. Advertising claims for bee pollen cite questionable research: a field study showing faster recovery rates in athletes who took pollen supplements. However, six, well designed studies using double-blind placebo protocols revealed that supplementation with bee pollen has no significant effect upon VO_2 max,

other physiological responses to exercise, endurance capacity, or rate of recovery from exhausting exercise. Moreover, caution is necessary as some individuals may experience an allergic reaction.

Vitamin B₁₅ Another product advertised to improve athletic performance is **vitamin B₁₅**. It should be noted, however, that B_{15} is not considered to be a vitamin because no specific disease state is associated with a deficiency. Indeed, vitamin B_{15} or products marketed with vitamin B_{15} qualities do not appear to have any definite chemical identity, but may be composed of a number of different substances. Pangamic acid is a term often used in conjunction with B_{15}; one patented form is calcium pangamate, a mixture of calcium gluconate and dimethylglycine (DMG), an amino acid. These substances have been labeled as the active ingredients in vitamin B_{15}.

The increasing popularity and use of vitamin B_{15} as an ergogenic aid in the 1980s was based upon Soviet research with rats, suggesting an improvement in aerobic oxidative processes during exercise. Claims of its effectiveness by a world-champion boxer and a professional football team helped bolster its sales to athletes. However, these claims are not supported by reputable research. Four studies revealed that B_{15} supplementation does not improve cardiovascular or metabolic responses during exercise, VO_2 max, or endurance capacity. Thus, contemporary research supports the viewpoint that B_{15} is not an effective ergogenic aid. Moreover, analysis of several vitamin B_{15} compounds revealed the presence of several compounds that could be hazardous to one's health.

CoQ10 The compound **CoQ10,** also known as ubiquinone, is actually a lipid but has characteristics common to vitamins; its chemical structure is similar to vitamin K. CoQ10 is found in the mitochondria of all mammalian tissues but concentrations are relatively high in the heart and other organs in humans. It plays important roles in oxidative metabolism within the mitochondria, and it may have important antioxidant properties as well. It has been used therapeutically for treatment of cardiovascular disease since 1965 because it may protect heart tissue from damage associated with inadequate oxygen.

Because CoQ10 has been shown to increase heart function, maximal oxygen uptake, and exercise performance in cardiac patients, it has been theorized to be ergogenic for athletes. Unfortunately the available research with trained individuals is scant. Bucci cites dated research indicating increases in submaximal and maximal exercise performance in sedentary men after four to eight weeks of supplementation of 60 milligrams CoQ10 daily. Zuliani and others have reported that 100 milligrams of CoQ10 daily for one month exerted little effect on metabolic responses such as serum glucose and lactate levels in untrained men at submaximal and maximal exercise workloads. Free fatty acid levels and glycerol were reduced, however. No performance data were presented. Using college-age males and females, Roberts reported that 100 milligrams of CoQ10 for four weeks did significantly increase CoQ10 levels in the blood but had no effect upon cardiac function or VO_2 max, while Braun and others reported no effect of 100 milligrams daily for eight weeks on VO_2 max or time to exhaustion on a bicycle ergometer.

The available evidence is not sufficient to support an ergogenic effect to trained individuals. On the contrary, Demopoulous and others suggested CoQ10 might actually be the opposite of an ergogenic aid; taken orally it may actually autooxidize, producing free radicals and damaging the mitochondria. The effect of CoQ10 supplementation on physical performance merits additional research efforts, for it is one of the ingredients in a supplement widely advertised for endurance athletes.

In summary, none of the claims of performance enhancement by advertisers of these special (and usually expensive) supplements has been substantiated by scientific research. For athletes who feel they need to take a vitamin–mineral supplement, the typical one-a-day supplement containing 50–150 percent of the RDA for all vitamins and minerals may be recommended.

References

Books

Goodhart, R., and Shils, M., eds. 1988. *Modern Nutrition in Health and Disease.* Philadelphia: Lea & Febiger.

Hickson J., and Wolinksy, I., eds. 1989. *Nutrition in Exercise and Sport.* Boca Raton, FL: CRC Press.

Hunt, S., and Groff, J. 1990. *Advanced Nutrition and Human Metabolism.* St. Paul, MN: West.

Keys, A. 1950. *Human Starvation.* Minneapolis, MN: University of Minnesota Press.

Kutsky, R. 1981. *Handbook of Vitamins, Minerals, and Hormones.* New York: Van Nostrand Reinhold.

National Research Council. 1989. *Recommended Dietary Allowances.* Washington, DC: National Academy Press.

National Research Council. 1989. *Diet and Health: Implications for Reducing Chronic Disease Risk.* Washington, DC: National Academy Press.

Williams, M. H. 1989. *Beyond Training: How Athletes Enhance Performance Legally and Illegally.* Champaign, IL: Leisure Press.

Williams, M. H. 1985. Nutritional aspects of human physical and athletic performance. Springfield, IL: C C Thomas.

Reviews

American Medical Association, Council on Scientific Affairs. 1987. Vitamin preparations as dietary supplements and as therapeutic agents. *Journal of the American Medical Association* 257:1929–36.

Belko, A. 1987. Vitamins and exercise—An update. *Medicine and Science in Sports and Exercise* 19:S191–96.

Block, G. 1991. Vitamin C and cancer prevention: The epidemiologic evidence. *American Journal of Clinical Nutrition* 53:270S–82S.

Boland, R. 1986. Role of vitamin D in skeletal muscle metabolism. *Endocrine Reviews* 7:434–38.

Bucci, L. 1989. Nutritional ergogenic aids. In: *Nutrition in Exercise and Sport,* J. Hickson and I. Wolinsky, eds. Boca Raton, FL: CRC Press.

Bulow, J. 1988. Lipid mobilization and utilization. In: *Principles of Exercise Biochemistry,* ed. J. Poortmans. Basel: Karger.

Clarkson, P. 1991. Vitamins, iron and trace minerals. In: *Ergogenics: Enhancement of Performance in Exercise and Sport,* eds. D. Lamb and M. Williams. Indianapolis, IN: Benchmark.

Demopoulous, H., et al. 1986. Free radical pathology: Rationale and toxicology of antioxidants and other supplements in sports medicine and exercise science. In: *Sport, Health and Nutrition,* ed. F. Katch. Champaign, IL: Human Kinetics.

Gentry, M. 1990. Free radicals: What are they, and how do they affect your health? *American Institute for Cancer Research Newsletter* 28:7.

Gerster, H. 1989. Review: The role of vitamin C in athletic performance. *Journal of the American College of Nutrition* 8:636–43.

Gray, M., and Titlow, L. 1982. B_{15}: Myth or miracle? *Physician and Sportsmedicine* 10:107–12, January.

Greenberg, S., and Frishman, W. 1988. Coenzyme Q10: A new drug for myocardial ischemia? *Medical Clinics of North America* 72:243–55.

Hornig, D., et al. 1988. Vitamin C. In: *Modern Nutrition in Health and Diseases,* eds. M. Shils and V. Young. Philadelphia: Lea & Febiger.

Horwitt, M. 1991. Data supporting supplementation of humans with vitamin E. *Journal of Nutrition* 121:424–29.

Kagan, V., et al. 1989. Vitamin E, physical exercise, and sport. In: *Nutrition in Exercise and Sport,* eds. J. Hickson and I. Wolinsky. Boca Raton, FL: CRC Press.

Keith, R. 1989. Vitamins in sport and exercise. In: *Nutrition in Exercise and Sport,* eds. J. Hickson and I. Wolinsky. Boca Raton, FL: CRC Press.

Krinsky, N. 1988. Membrane antioxidants. *Annals of the New York Academy of Sciences,* 551P: 17–32.

Liebman, B. 1990. Please adopt this vitamin (drug). *Nutrition Action Health Letter* 17:8–9.

Mansfield, L., and Goldstein, G. 1981. Anaphylactic reaction after ingestion of local bee pollen. *Annals of Allergy* 47:154–56.

McCormick, D. 1988. Vitamin B_6. In: *Modern Nutrition in Health and Disease,* ed. M. Shils and V. Young. Philadelphia: Lea & Febiger.

National Strength and Conditioning Association. 1989. Popularized ergogenic aids. *National Strength and Conditioning Association Journal* 11:10–14.

Padh, H. 1991. Vitamin C: Newer insights into its biochemical functions. *Nutrition Reviews* 49:65–70.

Painter, P., et al. 1990. Megavitamin abuse: Vitamin toxicity in an athlete. *Diagnostics and Clinical Testing* 28:24–29.

Rudman, D., and Williams, P. 1983. Megadose vitamins: Use and misuse. *New England Journal of Medicine* 309:488–89.

Schaumburg, H., et al. 1983. Sensory neuropathy from pyridoxine abuse. *New England Journal of Medicine* 309:445–48.

Shephard, R. 1984. Athletic performance and urban air pollution. *Canadian Medical Association Journal* 131:105–9.

Short, S. 1989. Dietary surveys and nutrition knowledge. In: *Nutrition in Exercise and Sport,* eds. J. Hickson and I. Wolinsky. Boca Raton, FL: CRC Press.

Van der Beek, E. 1985. Vitamins and endurance training. Food for running and faddish claims. *Sports Medicine* 2:175–97.

Walter, P., et al. (ed.) 1989. Elevated dosages of vitamins: Benefits and hazards. *International Journal for Vitamin and Nutrition Research,* Supplement 30.

Willet, W. 1990. Vitamin A and lung cancer. *Nutrition Reviews.* 48:201–11.

Williams, M. 1989. Vitamin supplementation and athletic performance. 1989. *International Journal for Vitamin and Nutrition Research,* Supplement 30:161–91.

Yamanaka, W. 1987. Vitamins and cancer prevention. How much do we know? *Postgraduate Medicine* 82:149–51.

Specific Studies

Barnett, D., and Conlee, R. 1984. The effects of a commercial dietary supplement on human performance. *American Journal of Clinical Nutrition* 40:586–90.

Bonke, D. 1986. Influence of vitamin B_1, B_6 and B_{12} on the control of fine motoric movements. *Bibliotheca Nutritio et Dieta,* 38:104–9.

Braur, B., et al. 1991. The effect of coenzyme Q10 supplementation on exercise performance, VO_2 max, and lipid peroxidation in trained cyclists. *International Journal of Sport Nutrition 1:* in press.

Buzina, R., and Suboticanec, K. 1985. Vitamin C and physical working capacity. *International Zeitschrift für Vitämishe Ernährungsforsch* 27:157–66.

Case, H., and Kennedy, J. 1986. The effects of Pollitabs Sport on selected physiological and performance variables in male runners. *Medicine and Science in Sports and Exercise* 18:S6.

Chandler, J., and Hawkins, J. 1984. The effect of bee pollen on physiological performance. *International Journal of Biosocial Research,* 6:107–14.

Coburn, S., et al. 1990. Effect of vitamin B_6 intake on the vitamin content of human muscle. *FASEB Journal* 4:A365.

Coburn, S., et al. 1988. Human vitamin B-6 pools estimated through muscle biopsies. *American Journal of Clinical Nutrition* 48:291–94.

Connett, J., et al. 1989. Relationship between carotenoids and cancer. *Cancer* 64:126–34.

Dreon, D., and Butterfield, G. 1986. Vitamin B_6 utilization in active and inactive young men. *American Journal of Clinical Nutrition* 43:816–24.

Godsen, R., and Bell, N. 1987. The effect of weight training on vitamin D and mineral metabolism. *Medicine and Science in Sports and Exercise* 21:S21.

Goldfarb, A., et al. 1989. Effect of vitamin E on lipid peroxidation at 80% VO_2 max. *Medicine and Science in Sports and Exercise* 21:S16.

Guilland, J., et al. 1989. Vitamin status of young athletes including the effects of supplementation. *Medicine and Science in Sports and Exercise* 21:441–49.

Haralambie, G. 1976. Vitamin B_2 status in athletes and the influence of riboflavin administration on neuromuscular irritability. *Nutrition and Metabolism* 20:1.

Heath, E., et al. 1991. Effect of three weeks of nicotinic acid ingestion on respiratory exchange ratio during exercise. *Medicine and Science in Sports and Exercise* 23:S101.

Hoffman, A., et al. 1989. Plasma pyridoxal phosphate concentrations in response to ingesting water or glucose polymer during a two hour run. *Medicine and Science in Sports and Exercise* 21:S59.

Kanter, M., et al. 1990. Effects of antioxidant supplement on expired pentane production following low and high intensity exercise. *Medicine and Science in Sports and Exercise* 22:S86.

Knekt, P., et al. 1991. Vitamin E and cancer prevention. *American Journal of Clinical Nutrition* 53:2835–65.

Kobayashi, Y. 1974. Effect of vitamin E on aerobic work performance in man during acute exposure to hypoxic hypoxia. Unpublished doctoral dissertation. University of New Mexico.

Kolka, M., and Stephenson, L. 1990. Skin blood flow during exercise after niacin ingestion. *FASEB Journal* 4:A279.

Krowchuk, D., et al. 1989. High school athletes and the use of ergogenic aids. *American Journal of Diseases in Children* 143:486–89.

Labadarios, D., et al. 1989. The effects of vitamin and mineral supplementation on running performance in trained athletes. *American Journal of Clinical Nutrition* 49:1133.

Lovlin, R., et al. 1987. Are indices of free radical damage related to exercise intensity? *European Journal of Applied Physiology* 56:313–16.

Manore, M., and Leklem, J. 1988. Effect of carbohydrate and vitamin B_6 on fuel substrates during exercise in women. *Medicine and Science in Sports and Exercise* 20:233–41.

Matter, M., et al. 1987. The effect of iron and folate therapy on maximal exercise performance in female marathon runners with iron and folate deficiency. *Clinical Science* 72:415–22.

Medeiros, D., et al. 1989. Vitamin and mineral supplementation practices of adults in seven western states. *Journal of the American Dietetic Association* 89:383–86.

Nice, C., et al. 1984. The effects of pantothenic acid on human exercise capacity. *Journal of Sports Medicine and Physical Fitness* 24:26–29.

Ohno, H., et al. 1988. Physical training and fasting erythrocyte activities for free radical scavenging enzyme systems in sedentary men. *European Journal of Applied Physiology* 57:173–76.

Pincemail, J., et al. 1988. Tocopherol mobilization during intensive exercise. *European Journal of Applied Physiology* 57:188–91.

Powers, H., et al. 1985. Effects of a multivitamin and iron supplement on running performance in Gambian children. *Human Nutrition: Clinical Nutrition,* 39: 427–37.

Roberts, J. 1990. The effect of coenzyme Q10 on exercise performance. *Medicine and Science in Sports and Exercise* 22:S87.

Russell, M., et al. 1988. A prospective study of the relationship between serum vitamins A and E and risk of breast cancer. *British Journal of Cancer* 57:213–15.

Schrijver, J., et al. 1987. Effect of vitamin and iron supplementation on physical performance. Presented at International Symposium on Elevated Dosages of Vitamin: Benefits and Hazards. Interlaken, Switzerland. September 1987.

Simon-Schnass, I., and Pabst, H. 1988. Influence of vitamin E on physical performance. *International Journal for Vitamin and Nutrition Research* 58:49–54.

Suboticanec, K., et al. 1990. Effects of pyridoxine and riboflavin supplementation on physical fitness in young adolescents. *International Journal of Vitamin and Nutrition Research* 60:81–88.

Telford, R., et al. 1989. Vitamin / mineral supplementation in athletes. *Proceedings First IOC World Congress on Sport Sciences.* Colorado Springs, CO: United States Olympic Committee.

Tremblay, A., et al. 1984. The effects of a riboflavin supplementation on the nutritional status and performance of elite swimmers. *Nutrition Research* 4:201.

Tsui, J., and Nordstrom, J. 1990. Folate status of adolescents: effects of folic acid supplementation. *Journal of the American Dietetic Association* 90:1551–56.

Van der beek, E., et al. 1988. Thiamin, riboflavin, and vitamins B_6 and C: Impact of combined restricted intake on functional performance in man. *American Journal of Clinical Nutrition* 48:1451–62.

Van der Beek, et al. 1984. Effect of marginal vitamin intake on physical performance of man. *International Journal of Sports Medicine* 5 (Suppl): 28–31.

van Erp-Baart, A., et al. 1989. Nationwide survey on nutritional habits in elite athletes. *International Journal of Sports Medicine* 10: (Suppl 1): S11–S16.

Viguie, C., et al. 1989. Antioxidant supplementation affects indices of muscle trauma and oxidant stress in human blood during exercise. *Medicine and Science in Sports and Exercise* 21:S16.

Weight, L., et al. 1988. Vitamin and mineral supplementation: Effect on the running performance of trained athletes. *American Journal of Clinical Nutrition* 47:192–95.

Weight, L., et al. 1988. Vitamin and mineral status of trained athletes including the effects of supplements. *American Journal of Clinical Nutrition* 47:186–91.

Woodhouse, M., et al. 1987. The effects of varying doses of orally ingested bee pollen extract upon selected performance variables. *Athletic Training* 22:26–28.

Zuliani, U., et al. 1989. The influence of ubiquinone (CoQ10) on the metabolic response to work. *Journal of Sports Medicine and Physical Fitness* 29:57–61.

Key Terms

electrolytes

ferritins

hematuria

heme iron

hemochromatosis

hemolysis

ions

iron deficiency without anemia

iron deficiency anemia

macrominerals

metalloenzymes

mineral

osteoporosis

peak bone mass

secondary amenorrhea

trabecular bone

trace minerals

Key Concepts

Minerals perform two of the three major functions of food, including the formation of several body tissues and the regulation of numerous physiological processes.

Calcium is most prevalent in the milk food group, and although calcium supplements are not necessary for the average individual, they may be recommended for some females, including athletes.

Two keys to the prevention of osteoporosis are weight-bearing exercise and adequate calcium in the diet; hormone-replacement therapy may be recommended for some women.

Phosphate salts have been used for more than 60 years in attempts to improve athletic performance, but the research is equivocal.

A deficiency of magnesium may be associated with muscle cramps.

Iron deficiency, particularly among women and young children, is a major nutritional health concern, so iron-rich foods such as lean meats and beans should be stressed in the diet.

Iron supplementation may be recommended for certain individuals, particularly female endurance athletes and those on low-Calorie diets.

Zinc deficiency has been shown to impair the growth process in children, so it may be a problem for young athletes who incur heavy sweat losses and are on low-Calorie diets, such as wrestlers, dancers, or gymnasts.

There does not appear to be much valid scientific evidence to support an ergogenic effect of trace mineral supplementation. Megadoses of minerals are not recommended.

A diet that provides the RDA for iron, calcium, and Calories from a balanced selection of foods throughout the different food groups will provide adequate amounts of both the major and trace minerals.

Minerals: The Inorganic Regulators
7

Introduction

You may recall the periodic table of the elements hanging on the wall in your high school or college chemistry class. At latest count there were 103 known elements, seventy-eight of them occurring naturally and the remainder being synthetic. Many of the natural elements, including a wide variety of minerals, are essential to human bodily structure and function.

Much research attention is currently being devoted to the role of mineral nutrition in health and disease, including both epidemiological and laboratory research. For example, using the RDA as a basis for comparison, national surveys among the general population have revealed that either an inadequate dietary intake of some minerals or the excessive dietary intake of others in certain segments of the population may be contributing to several health problems. Laboratory studies using either animals or humans as subjects have explored the role of either deficiencies or supplementation of these minerals and others on human health and disease processes.

An increasing number of research studies have been conducted with athletes to evaluate the effect of mineral nutrition on physical performance and the converse—the effect of exercise on mineral metabolism. Because some minerals function similarly to vitamins, a deficiency state could adversely affect performance. Moreover, exercise in itself may be a contributing factor to mineral deficiencies or impaired mineral metabolism in some types of athletes. Additionally, several mineral supplements are being marketed specifically for physically active individuals.

The major purpose of this chapter is to analyze the available data relative to the effect of mineral nutrition on physical performance and health. The first section discusses some basic facts about the general role of those minerals that are essential to human nutrition. The second and third sections cover, respectively, the major minerals and the trace minerals. In these two sections, each of the minerals is discussed in terms of its RDA, good dietary sources, metabolic functions in the body with particular reference to the physically active individual, and an evaluation of the research pertaining to the effects of deficiencies or supplementation. The last section deals with dietary recommendations for those who exercise for health or sport.

Basic Facts

What are minerals and what is their importance to humans?

A **mineral** is an inorganic element found in nature, and the term is usually reserved for those elements that are solid. Hence, a mineral is an element, but an element is not necessarily a mineral. For example, oxygen is an element, but it is not classified as a mineral. In nutrition, the term mineral is usually used to classify those elements essential to life processes.

Minerals serve two of the three basic functions of nutrients. First, many are used as the building blocks for body tissues such as bones, teeth, muscles, and other organic structures. Second, a number of minerals are components of enzymes known as **metalloenzymes,** which are involved in the regulation of metabolism. Several other minerals exist as **ions,** or **electrolytes,** which are small particles carrying electrical charges. They are important components or activators of several enzymes and hormones. Some of the physiological processes regulated or maintained by minerals include muscle contraction, oxygen transport, nerve impulse conduction, acid–base balance of the blood, maintenance of body water supplies, blood clotting, and normal heart rhythm. Minerals do not provide a source of caloric energy, which is the third function of nutrients.

Minerals are found in the soil and are eventually incorporated in growing plants. Animals get their mineral nutrition from the plants they eat, whereas humans obtain their supply from both plant and animal food. Drinking water also may be a good source of several minerals. As minerals are excreted daily from the body in sweat, urine, or feces, they must be replaced. Inadequate mineral nutrition has been associated with a variety of human diseases, including anemia, high blood pressure, diabetes, cancer, tooth decay, and osteoporosis. Thus, proper dietary intake of essential minerals is necessary for optimal health and physical performance.

Table 7.1   Minerals essential to humans, with RDA or estimated safe and adequate daily dietary intakes (ESADDI) for adults*

Mineral	Symbol	RDA or ESADDI (mg)		Amount in adult body (g)
Calcium	Ca	800♂	800♀	1,500
Phosphorus	P	800♂	800♀	850
Potassium	K	2000♂	2000♀	180
Chloride	Cl	750♂	750♀	75
Sodium	Na	500♂	500♀	65
Magnesium	Mg	350♂	280♀	25
Iron	Fe	10♂	15♀	5
Fluoride	F	1.5–4.0♂	1.5–4.0♀	2.5
Zinc	Zn	15♂	12♀	2
Copper	Cu	1.5–3.0♂	1.5–3.0♀	0.1
Selenium	Se	0.070♂	0.055♀	0.013
Manganese	Mn	2.0–5.0♂	2.0–5.0♀	0.012
Iodine	I	0.15♂	0.15♀	0.011
Molybdenum	Mo	0.075–0.25♂	0.075–0.25♀	0.009
Chromium	Cr	0.05–0.2♂	0.05–0.2♀	0.006

The values for sodium and potassium are estimated minimum requirements.
*See Appendix A for extended table values.

What minerals are essential to human nutrition?

Of the 103 elements in the periodic table, twenty-five are currently known to be, or presumed to be, essential in humans. Five of these elements constitute over 96 percent of the body weight. In varying combinations, hydrogen, oxygen, carbon, sulfur, and nitrogen are the components of the body water, protein, fat, and carbohydrate stores. The remaining twenty minerals compose less than 4 percent of the body weight but are equally important.

Table 7.1 lists those minerals considered to be essential to humans. The RDA has been established for seven minerals, and the estimated safe and adequate daily dietary intakes (ESADDI) are available for five others, while an estimated minimal requirement has been established for sodium, chloride, and potassium.

Other minerals such as boron, nickel, silicon, and vanadium, among others, are found in animal tissues and also may be important to human nutrition, but their roles have not yet been completely elucidated.

In general, how do deficiencies or excesses of minerals influence health or physical performance?

Similarly to vitamin deficiencies, mineral deficiencies may occur in several stages. The first three stages (preliminary, biochemical deficiency, and physiological deficiency) may be termed subclinical malnutrition and may or may not have significant effects on health or physical performance. In the clinically manifest deficiency stage, however, health and performance most likely will suffer.

The interaction of exercise and mineral nutrition may pose some special health problems, as we shall see in later sections of this chapter. In regard to the preliminary stage, some athletes may reduce their mineral intake as they shift toward a low-Calorie diet. Changes in food selection may also be important, for the bioavailability of many minerals is markedly influenced by the form in which they are consumed. In general, most minerals are poorly absorbed from the intestine. For example, the RDA for iron is ten times the amount actually needed by the body, because only about 10 percent of the dietary iron is absorbed from the average American diet. Moreover, mineral absorption may be inhibited by certain compounds in foods. In athletes, factors that lower intake and absorption may be compounded because athletic activity may raise some mineral requirements. Additional minerals may be needed for the synthesis of new tissues associated with physical training, or to replace losses in the sweat, urine, and feces often observed during and following intense exercise training.

Sports nutritionists are becoming concerned that the presence of these factors during the preliminary stage of a mineral deficiency could lead to the subsequent stages of subclinical malnutrition or even to a clinically manifest deficiency. Indeed, a number of studies have reported athletes with biochemical deficiencies of several minerals. Experts disagree about the potential adverse effects of such biochemical deficiencies, but certain physiologic and clinically manifest mineral deficiencies are known to have impaired physical performance.

The human body possesses a very effective control system for some minerals. When a deficiency occurs, the body absorbs more of the mineral from the food in the intestine and excretes less via routes such as the urine. When an excess is consumed the opposite is true; less is absorbed and more is excreted. On the other hand, the body has a limited ability to excrete certain other minerals, so excessive consumption may cause a number of health problems, even in relatively small dosages. Additionally, a few minerals not important to human nutrition, such as lead, mercury, cadmium, arsenic, and some industrial forms of chromium may be extremely toxic to the human body.

Macrominerals

The seven **macrominerals** (major minerals) are calcium, phosphorus, magnesium, potassium, sodium, chloride, and sulfur. Minerals are classified as macrominerals if the RDA or ESADDI is greater than 100 mg per day or the body contains more than 5 grams. In general, the human body maintains a proper balance of these minerals through precise hormonal control mechanisms, but deficiencies or excesses may occur and disturb normal physiological functions, thus impairing health or physical performance. Because potassium, sodium, and chloride are the major electrolytes in sweat, they are covered in the following chapter dealing with water and temperature regulation.

Calcium (Ca)
Calcium, a silver-white metallic element, is the most abundant mineral in the body, representing almost 2 percent of the body weight.

The RDA for calcium is 800 mg/day for young children and adults, but 1,200 mg/day between the ages of 11 and 25, the major period of bone growth and development. Pregnancy and lactation also increase the RDA. The National Institute of Health has recommended that the RDA for postmenopausal women be raised to 1,000–1,500 mg/day. The USRDA is 1,000 mg.

Calcium content is highest in dairy products. One glass of skim milk, which contains about 300 mg of calcium, supplies about one-third of the RDA for an adult and one-fourth for an adolescent. It is used as the basis of comparison for other foods. Other equivalent dairy foods are one and one-half ounces of cheese, one cup of yogurt, and one and three-quarters cups of ice cream. Other good sources are fish with small bones such as sardines and canned salmon, dark green leafy vegetables (particularly broccoli, kale, and turnip greens), tofu, legumes, and nuts. Incorporation of milk or cheese into foods such as soups, pasta dishes, and pizza is an excellent way to obtain dietary calcium. For individuals with lactose intolerance, the use of yogurt, lactase enzymes, or smaller portions of milk may be helpful. Calcium is also used as a preservative in some foods, such as breads, which may provide small amounts. Additionally, some food products such as orange juice and sodas are now being fortified with calcium. Foods high in calcium are listed in Table 7.2.

Some nutrients in food, such as vitamin D, lactose, and adequate amounts of protein, may help absorb calcium from the intestines. On the other hand, excessive amounts of dietary fat, caffeine, phosphorus, and fiber may decrease the amount absorbed. Phytates (phytic acid compounds) found in grains and oxalates in green leafy vegetables may diminish the absorption slightly, but the effect does not appear to be as great as once believed. In general, the amounts of protein, phosphorus, fiber, phytates, and oxalates found in the average American diet do not appear to pose a problem for calcium absorption from the diet. Research has also revealed that vegetarian diets provide adequate calcium nutrition as measured by body stores.

The vast majority of body calcium, 98 percent, is found in the skeleton, where it gives strength by the formation of salts such as calcium phosphate. One percent is used for tooth formation. The remainder, which exists in an ionic state or in combination with certain proteins, exerts considerable influence over human metabolism. Calcium ions (Ca^{2+}) are involved in all types of muscle contraction, including that of the heart, skeletal muscle, and smooth muscle found in blood vessels such as the arteries. Calcium activates a number of enzymes; in this capacity it plays a central role in both the synthesis and breakdown of muscle glycogen and liver glycogen. Calcium also helps regulate nerve impulse transmission, blood clotting, and secretion of hormones. It should be noted that the skeletal content

Table 7.2 Foods rich in calcium, phosphorus, and magnesium

Mineral	Food source
Calcium	All dairy products: milk, cheese, ice cream, yogurt; egg yolk; dried beans and peas; dark green vegetables; cauliflower
Phosphorus	All protein products: meat, poultry, fish, eggs, milk, cheese, dried beans and peas; whole-grain products
Magnesium	Milk and yogurt; dried beans; nuts; whole-grain products; fruits and vegetables, especially green leafy vegetables

of calcium is not inert. The physiological functions of calcium, such as nerve cell transmission, take precedence over formation of bone tissue. If the diet is low in calcium for a short time, the body can mobilize some from the skeleton through the action of hormones, such as parathormone and D_3, to maintain an adequate amount in ionic form.

Calcium balance in the human body is rather complex. Figure 7.1 depicts the fate of an RDA of 800 mg. Only 300 mg (about 40 percent) is absorbed while the remaining 500 mg is excreted in the feces. The calcium that is absorbed into the blood interacts with the current body stores, the net result being the excretion of 300 mg through the intestines, kidneys, and sweat to balance the amount originally absorbed. Calcium deficiency may develop from inadequate dietary intake or increased excretion.

Problems do occur in individuals from certain population groups, but calcium balance is usually well regulated in the average individual. The body can adapt to low dietary intake by increasing the rate of absorption from the intestines and decreasing the rate of excretion by the kidneys. Because the skeleton is a large reservoir of body calcium, low serum levels are rare. When they do occur, it usually is because of hormonal imbalances rather than dietary deficiencies.

Nevertheless, owing to the diverse physiological roles of calcium, a low serum level could be expected to cause a number of problems. One of the symptoms may be muscular cramping due to an imbalance of calcium in the muscle and in the surrounding fluids. One theory also suggests that calcium deficiency is involved in the development of high blood pressure through the mechanism of contraction of the smooth muscles in the arterioles. Regarding dietary sources of calcium, some evidence indicates that low levels may contribute to the development of cancer of the colon. Calcium is believed to combine with bile salts, helping to excrete them in the feces and thereby reducing the potential carcinogenic effect of the bile salts on the walls of the colon. However, the National Research Council

reports that the relationship of dietary calcium to both high blood pressure and cancer is weak and the data are inconclusive.

The major health problems associated with impaired calcium metabolism involve diseases of the bones. A number of factors are involved in the formation, or mineralization, of bone tissue, including mechanical stresses such as exercise; hormones such as parathormone, calcitonin, vitamin D_3, and estrogen; and dietary calcium. An imbalance in any one of these factors could lead to bone demineralization, resulting in the development of rickets in children and osteoporosis in adults. **Osteoporosis** (thinning and weakening of the bones related to loss of calcium stores) is prevalent primarily in older women, afflicting more than 60 percent of those between the ages of 55 and 64 and even higher percentages with older age groups. Although there are a number of possible causes, including heredity and life-style, the major cause of osteoporosis in older women is the diminished production of estrogen, a hormone essential for optimal calcium balance in women. Reduced levels of estrogen lead to negative calcium balance and a rapid onset of bone demineralization. This softening of the bones predisposes to fractures, particularly in the spine, the end of the radius, and the neck of the femur at the hip joint. These latter two fractures can be completely debilitating to the older individual. See Figure 7.2. The spine fracture is more common, since the vertebrae are composed of **trabecular bone,** a spongy type of bone more susceptible to calcium loss than the more dense compact bone.

For the physically active individual, a low level of serum calcium could be serious because of the effects on muscular contraction. Fortunately, serious deficiencies of serum calcium are rare. Concern about disturbed calcium metabolism in female athletes, particularly endurance athletes, is growing, however. Some of these athletes develop **secondary amenorrhea;** that is, their menses stops for prolonged periods. There are several theories about the development of this condition, including a low percentage of body fat and a reduced production of estrone, a form of estrogen. Sophisticated techniques

Figure 7.1.

Calcium balance in an adult. On an RDA of 800 mg, only about 300 mg are absorbed into the body, the remaining 500 mg being excreted in the feces. To maintain calcium balance, 300 mg are excreted including an additional 150 mg in the feces, 130 mg through the kidneys to the urine and 20 mg in sweat. See text for further discussion.

Source: Calcium: A Summary of Current Research for the Health Professiona , Courtesy of the National Dairy Council.

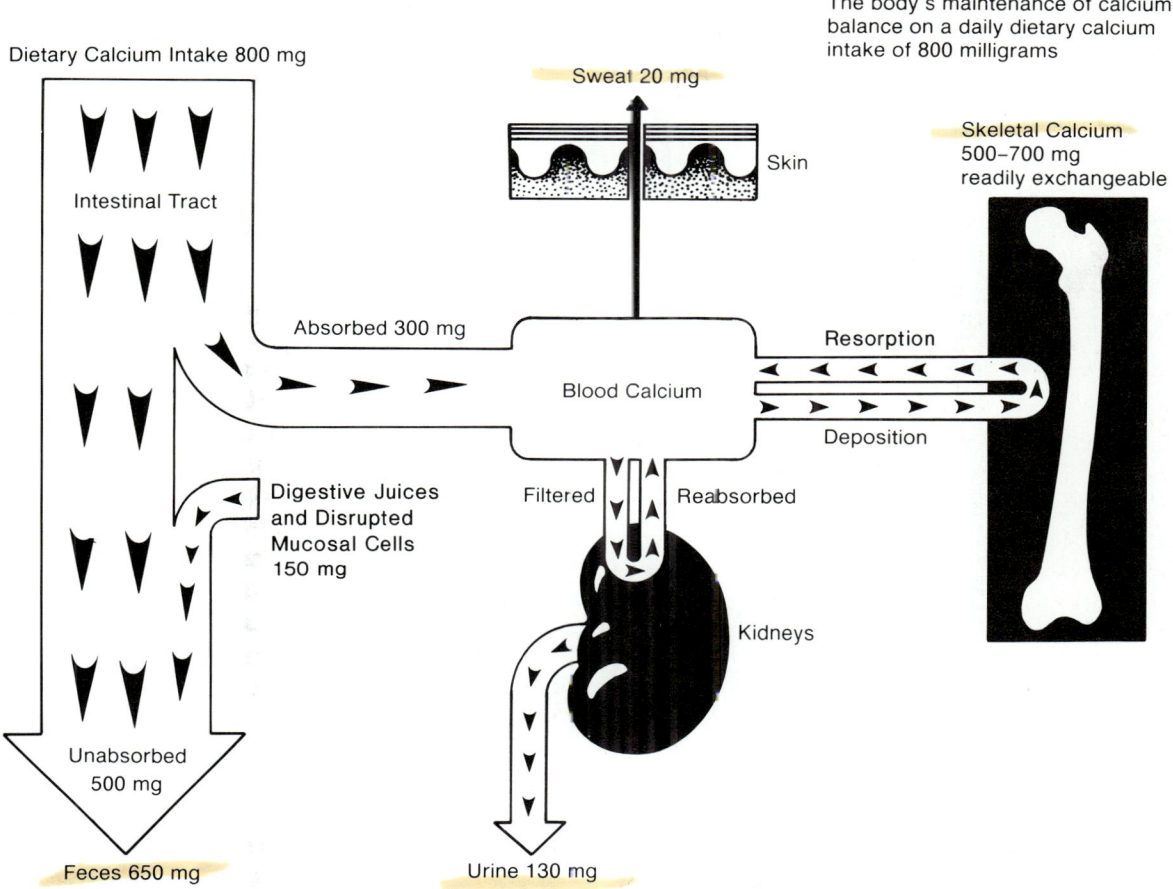

have been used to assess bone density, or bone mineral content. In a number of these studies, amenorrheic distance runners were found to have significantly less bone mineral content in the spine than sedentary women and distance runners who were menstruating normally. Moreover, these amenorrheic athletes had a higher incidence of stress fractures. As with postmenopausal women, the decreased estrogen is believed to be the causative factor in loss of bone density. Some evidence suggests that when amenorrheic runners resume normal menstruation, bone mineral content increases. On the other hand, Barbara Drinkwater, an acknowledged authority in this area, has cited several reports that bone loss in amenorrheic athletes is irreversible.

Interestingly, several studies by Bilanin and Ormerod report decreased spinal bone mass in male

long distance runners. Bilanin and associates suggest that decreased levels of testosterone or increased levels of cortisol often seen in endurance runners could be the cause.

Because of these health problems, some health groups have recommended that the RDA for calcium be increased. Indeed, national surveys of the general population revealed inadequate dietary intakes for children, most women, and elderly men. The average daily intake is only about 450–550 mg. One nutritionist strongly suggests that athletes also need calcium supplements. However, surveys with athletic groups reveal divergent results. Some athletes are getting well above the RDA, particularly males. On the other hand, athletes trying to control their weight, such as female gymnasts, cross-country runners, and ballerinas, have substandard intakes.

Figure 7.2.
Three principal sites of
osteoporosis fractures.

Source: Calcium: A Summary of
Current Research for the Health
Professional, Courtesy of the
National Dairy Council.

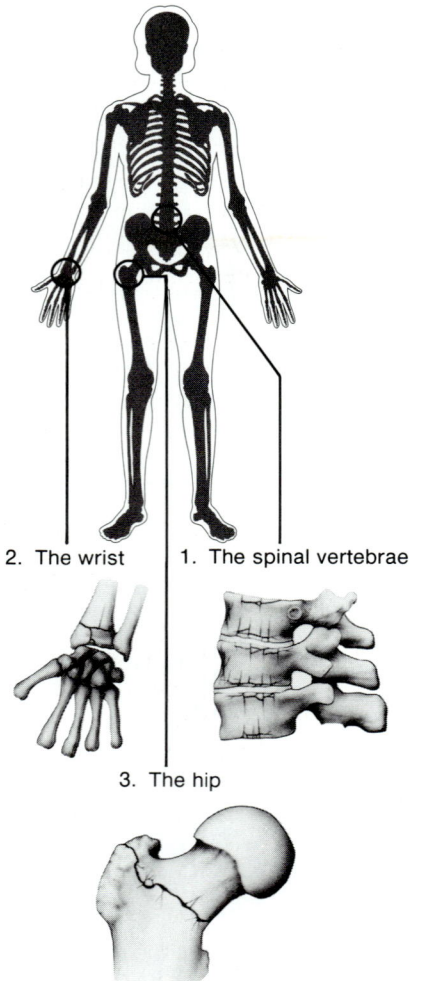

2. The wrist   1. The spinal vertebrae

3. The hip

Contemporary treatment for osteoporosis usually involves three components—hormone replacement therapy, calcium supplements, and exercise. In postmenopausal women, estrogen therapy may be necessary, but estrogen compounds may increase certain health risks in females. Calcitonin, a hormone that helps deposit calcium in the bone, has been useful. Additionally, several recently developed drugs can prevent the slow loss of bone in the spine yet do not have the potential health risks of estrogen. For premenopausal athletes who become amenorrheic and estrogen depleted, oral contraceptive pills have been suggested as practical means of getting additional estrogen. However, the medical treatment suggested for this condition depends on the point of view of the individual endocrinologist, and may include estrogen or progesterone therapy. An appropriate physician should be consulted.

Whether calcium supplements alone are useful in the treatment of osteoporosis has been the subject of debate, for studies have produced conflicting data concerning the prevention of bone loss with dosages ranging from 1,000–1,200 mg per day. Avioli has noted that until more data are available, we must acknowledge that calcium supplements may retard the rate of bone loss in women just prior to or after menopause. Exercise may potentiate the protective role of calcium supplements. Several studies have shown that exercise training combined with a calcium intake of about 1,200 mg per day helps to increase bone mineral content in postmenopausal women. Additional research by Everett Smith has also indicated that exercise alone may retard the loss of bone mass in postmenopausal women. However, although calcium supplements and weight bearing and resistance exercise may be beneficial in the treatment of osteoporosis, most researchers in this area suggest they should not be regarded as replacements for estrogen therapy.

For younger, premenopausal women, the non-pharmacological approach is recommended. The key with younger women is prevention. They need to develop **peak bone mass,** the optimal amount within genetic limitations, prior to age 25, and attempt to keep the bone mass high in the advancing years. Thus, it would appear prudent for young women to develop a lifetime exercise program and obtain the RDA for calcium in the diet. The earlier the better. Weight-bearing exercises, such as walking or jogging, promote bone mineralization by stressing the hips and spine, while modified push-ups are also excellent for the spine and for the radial bone at the wrist joint. Four glasses of skim milk provide 1,200 mg of calcium. In addition, the milk (or its equivalent) would provide 32 grams of protein, which is about 80 percent of the protein RDA for the average woman, and a variety of other vitamins and minerals in less than 400 Calories. Because alcohol and tobacco use are secondary risk factors associated with the development of osteoporosis, moderation or abstinence is advocated.

Calcium supplements come in a variety of forms, such as calcium carbonate, calcium lactate, and calcium gluconate, and are found in certain antacids, such as Tums. The bioavailability may vary considerably according to the brand, and there is speculation that antacids may actually interfere with calcium absorption. Be sure to check the label for the calcium content per tablet, which may range from 50–600 mg depending on the brand. For those who desire to take a calcium supplement, it may be wise to take a tablet with about 200 mg at meals three times a day, rather than one tablet with 600 mg, for it appears more calcium is absorbed when the intake is spread throughout the day. Moreover, when the supplement is combined with meals, gastric acidity and slower transit time in the gut promote calcium absorption. A supplement of 600 mg calcium, combined with a dietary intake of 500–600 mg, should provide adequate calcium nutrition for most individuals. However, the point should be stressed that careful selection of foods will provide the calcium you need from the daily diet, thus eliminating the need for supplements.

Although supplements up to 600 mg per day do not appear to pose much danger, excessive amounts may contribute to abnormal heart contractions, constipation, and the development of kidney stones in susceptible individuals, particularly those with a family history of kidney problems. Moreover, excessive dietary calcium may interfere with the absorption of other key minerals, notably iron and zinc. The National Research Council recommends against supplementation to a total much above the RDA.

Research relating to calcium supplementation and physical performance is almost nonexistent. With the possible exception of the amenorrheic athlete, calcium supplements appear to be unwarranted for the physically active individual. A balanced diet with dairy products and other high-calcium foods will help maintain an adequate body supply. The reserves of calcium in the skeleton are more than adequate to compensate for short-term daily dietary deficiencies.

Phosphorus (P)

Phosphorus is a nonmetallic element and is the second most abundant mineral in the body after calcium. With the exception of the first year of life, the RDA is the same as for calcium. The adult RDA is 800 mg for both men and women. Higher amounts are needed between ages 11 and 25. Specific values for different age groups may be found in Appendix A. The USRDA is 1,000 mg.

As noted earlier in Table 7.2, phosphorus is distributed widely in foods, mainly in conjunction with animal protein. Excellent sources include seafood, meat, eggs, milk, cheese, nuts, dried beans and peas, grain products, and a wide variety of vegetables. Soft drinks have a relatively high phosphorus content. In some foods, phosphorus is also a part of phytate which may diminish the absorption of minerals like calcium, iron, zinc, and copper by forming insoluble phosphate salts in the intestine. However, as noted previously, this is not a major problem with the typical American diet.

In the human body, phosphorus occurs only as the salt phosphate, which exists as inorganic phosphate or is coupled with other minerals or organic compounds. Phosphates are extremely important in human metabolism. About 80–90 percent of the phosphorus in the body combines to form calcium phosphate, which is used for the development of bones and teeth. As with calcium, the bones represent a sizable store of phosphate salts. Other phosphate salts, such as sodium phosphate, are involved in acid–base balance. The remainder of the body phosphates are found in a variety of organic forms, including the phospholipids, which help form cell membranes, and DNA, which is part of the genetic material. Several other organic phosphates are of prime importance to the active individual. For example, organic phosphates are essential to the normal function of most of the B vitamins involved in the energy processes within the cell. They are also part of the high-energy compounds found in the muscle cell, such as ATP and PC which are needed for muscle contraction. Glucose also needs to be phosphorylated in order to proceed through glycolysis. Organic phosphates also are a part of a compound in the RBC known as 2,3–DPG (2,3–diphosphoglycerate), which facilitates the release of oxygen to the muscle tissues.

Because phosphorus is distributed so widely in foods and because hormonal control is very effective, deficiency states are rare. They have been known to occur in individuals with certain diseases and in those who use antacid compounds for long periods, as the antacid decreases the absorption of phosphorus. Symptoms parallel those of calcium deficiency, such as loss of bone material resulting in rickets or osteomalacia. Other symptoms include muscular weakness. Extreme muscular exercise may increase phosphorus excretion in the urine but has not been reported to cause a deficiency state. Phosphorus deficiency could theoretically impair physical performance, but it has not been the subject of study because such deficiencies are rare.

Phosphate salt supplements, such as sodium phosphate and potassium phosphate, were reported to relieve fatigue in German soldiers during World War I. Other research in Germany during the 1930s suggested phosphate salts could improve physical performance. Fifty years ago one reviewer discredited much of this early research, but he did note that phosphates probably could increase human work output when consumed in quantities exceeding the amounts found in the normal diet. Indeed, they still are advertised today in some European sportsmedicine journals and continue to be a favorite among European athletes. They have also been marketed as an ergogenic aid in the United States, most recently as the main ingredient in Phos Fuel, advertised to be the ultimate lactic acid buffer. Leibovitz, in a popular muscle magazine, has called phosphate the power mineral.

The results of more contemporary research relative to the ergogenic effect of phosphate supplementation are somewhat equivocal. A number of studies, using appropriate experimental methods and the recommended phosphate dosages, have shown no effects of phosphate supplementation on a variety of performance variables. Researchers at Brigham Young University reported that Stim-O-Stam, a commercial phosphate salt supplement containing other nutrients, exerted no effect upon measures of strength or anaerobic endurance tests, such as a 2- to 3-minute run to exhaustion on a treadmill. Robert Otto and his research group at Adelphi University also noted no effect of phosphate salt supplementation on maximal oxygen uptake, lactic acid

production, or performance in an 8-kilometer (5-mile) bike race. Mannix and others recently reported that although phosphate supplementation did increase 2,3–DPG levels, it did not improve cardiovascular function or oxygen efficiency in subjects exercising at 60 percent of VO_2 max. Thompson and her associates from the University of Southern Mississippi reported no effect of phosphate salt supplementation on 2,3–DPG, hemoglobin, or VO_2 max. However, there was a nonsignificant 6 percent increase of VO_2 max in the phosphate trial compared to the placebo. These investigators generally concluded that phosphate salts were not ergogenic in nature, at least in relation to the type of performance tested in their studies.

In contrast, the results of other contemporary, well designed studies suggest that phosphate salts may enhance exercise performance. One of the first studies reported was conducted by Robert Cade and his associates at the University of Florida. In a double-blind placebo crossover study, highly trained runners took one gram of sodium phosphate four times a day during the experimental phase. The phosphate salts increased the 2,3–DPG in the RBC, which related very closely to an increase in the VO_2 max. The amount of lactate produced at a standard exercise workload decreased, suggesting more efficient oxygen delivery to the muscles. Although no performance data were presented, the authors did report that the subjects ran longer on the treadmill during the phosphate trials. This University of Florida research group also noted a reduced sensation of psychological stress while exercising at a standard workload.

Other investigators, using a protocol similar to that of Cade and his associates, have also revealed ergogenic effects. Richard Kreider and his colleagues, using highly trained cross-country runners as subjects, found that four grams of trisodium phosphate for six days produced a significant increase in VO_2 max, approximately 10 percent, very similar to the improvement noted in Cade's study. Changes in 2,3–DPG were not the mechanism for this increase, however, since these values did not increase. Moreover, performance in a 5-mile competitive run on a treadmill did not improve, although there was a mean speed increase of approximately 12 seconds during the phosphate trial in these highly trained runners. Ian Stewart and his associates from Australia, using trained cyclists, reported that 3.6 grams of sodium phosphate for three days did significantly increase 2,3–DPG levels and also increased VO_2 max by 11 percent and time to exhaustion on a progressive workload test on a bicycle ergometer by nearly 16 percent. In a follow-up to his previous study, Kreider looked at the effect of 4 grams of trisodium phosphate, one gram 4 times daily for 3–4 days, on physiological and performance factors during a maximal test and a 40 kilometer bike race on a Velodyme. The study followed a double-blind, placebo, crossover protocol. In three separate reports of this study, Cortes and others noted a significant 9 percent increase in VO_2 max, Schenck and others noted a significantly faster 40 km time, improving from 45.75 to 42.25 minutes, and Kreider reported enhanced myocardial efficiency as monitored by echocardiographic techniques. These investigators suggested that phosphate salt supplementation could possess ergogenic qualities but that additional research is needed to confirm these findings and the underlying mechanisms.

Adenosine triphosphate (ATP), as you may recall, is the immediate source of energy for muscle contraction. Although some entrepreneurs have marketed ATP supplements for athletes, there is no available evidence that they enhance physical performance. Most likely, enzymes in the digestive tract would catabolize the ATP before it could get into the muscle.

Excesses of phosphorus in the body are excreted by the kidneys. Phosphorus excess per se does not appear to pose any problems, with the exception of individuals with limited kidney function. Subjects consuming phosphate supplements may experience gastrointestinal distress, which may be alleviated by mixing the salts in a liquid and consuming with a meal. Excessive amounts of phosphate over time may impair calcium metabolism and balance.

Magnesium (Mg)

Magnesium is the fourth most abundant element found in the body; it is a positive ion and is related to calcium and phosphorus. The adult RDA for magnesium is 350 mg for men and 280 mg for women. Slightly different amounts, found in Appendix A, are required by children and adolescents. The USRDA is 400 mg.

Magnesium is widely distributed in foods, particularly nuts, seafood, green leafy vegetables, other fruits and vegetables, and whole-grain products. One-half cup of shrimp contains about 20 percent of the RDA, and a glass of skim milk has 10 percent. Many other foods contain about 2–10 percent of the RDA per serving. About 25–60 percent of dietary magnesium is absorbed. See Table 7.2.

The body stores about 50–60 percent of its magnesium in the skeletal system, which may serve as a reserve during short periods of dietary deficiency. A small percentage is in the serum, but the remainder is found in the soft tissues such as muscle, where it is a component of over 300 enzymes. As such, magnesium plays a key role in a variety of physiological processes, many of which are important to the physically active individual. For example, as a part of ATPase it is involved in muscle contraction and all body functions involving ATP as an energy source. Magnesium helps regulate the synthesis of protein and other compounds, such as 2,3-DPG, which may be essential for optimal oxygen metabolism. It is a part of an enzyme that facilitates the metabolism of glucose in the muscle. Magnesium also helps block some of the actions of calcium in the body, such as contraction in both the skeletal and smooth muscles.

Although Elin has reported that a large segment of the United States population may have an inadequate magnesium intake, the National Research Council has reported that magnesium deficiency is rare. No purely dietary magnesium deficiency has been reported in people consuming normal diets, probably because of its wide availability in a variety of foods, an effective system of conservation by the kidneys and intestines, and a substantial storage in the bone tissue. However, certain health conditions such as kidney malfunction and prolonged diarrhea, as well as the use of diuretics and excessive alcohol, may contribute to a deficiency state. Deficiency symptoms include apathy, muscle weakness, muscle twitching and tremor, muscle cramps (particularly in the feet), and cardiac arrhythmias. The muscular symptoms may occur because the low levels of magnesium are not able to block the stimulating effect of calcium on muscle contraction. In this sense, magnesium deficiency may be related to high blood pressure because excessive calcium may cause the muscles in the arterioles to constrict.

Exercise appears to influence magnesium metabolism but in an unknown way. Deuster has noted that one of the most common research observations is a decrease in plasma levels of magnesium following exercise. It is thought that the magnesium enters the tissues in response to exercise-related requirements, for example, of the muscle tissue for energy metabolism and the adipose tissue for lipolysis. Some investigators also suggested that prolonged exercise increases magnesium losses from the body via urine and sweat. However, the reported sweat losses of 4–15 mg per liter are relatively small in comparison to body stores and daily intake. Casoni and others reported significantly lower serum magnesium levels in Italian endurance athletes as compared with sedentary individuals, but the serum values were well within the normal range. One study reported a correlation between plasma levels of magnesium and VO_2 max in trained individuals, but this finding has not been replicated. On the basis of some of these findings, several reports have recommended that individuals undergoing prolonged, intensive physical training should increase their daily intake of magnesium, but these recommendations are within range of the United States RDA. The extra Calories consumed when energy expenditure increases during exercise should provide the additional magnesium.

In their review, McDonald and Keen indicate they are not aware of any data showing a positive effect of magnesium supplementation on exercise performance in individuals who are in adequate magnesium status. Additionally, there is also little evidence showing a magnesium deficiency in humans severe enough to impair physical performance. However, in a single case report, muscle cramps in the foot of a tennis player who had subnormal magnesium levels in the blood were resolved completely with magnesium supplements that raised the blood levels to normal. This report suggests that a magnesium deficiency may contribute to muscle cramps. As Deuster suggests, we need carefully controlled studies to determine whether current dietary recommendations for magnesium for athletes in training or others who exercise for well-being are adequate, but magnesium supplements are not currently recommended as ergogenic aids.

In general, excessive intake of magnesium does not appear to cause major health problems, except for those with kidney disorders who cannot excrete the excess. Excessive intake may cause nausea, vomiting, and diarrhea, however. The usual cause is the ingestion of magnesium salts, such as found in milk of magnesia.

Trace Minerals

The **trace minerals** (trace elements) are those needed in quantities less than 100 mg per day. These minerals are often known as microminerals. For several the body only needs extremely minute amounts, such as a few micrograms (millionth of a gram) per day; the term ultratrace is applied to these minerals.

Iron (Fe)

Iron is a metallic element that exists in two general forms: ferrous (Fe^{2+}) and ferric (Fe^{3+}). Depending upon age and sex, the average individual needs to replace about 1.0–1.5 mg of iron that is lost from the body daily. However, because the bioavailability of iron is very low, with only about 10 percent of food iron being absorbed, the RDA is ten times the need. Currently the RDA is 10 mg for men and 15 mg for women and teenagers of both sexes. Slightly different amounts are needed by other age groups and may be found in Appendix A. The USRDA is 15 mg. It should be noted that the 1989 RDA for women and adolescents was lowered by 3 mg, from 18 to 15 mg, compared to the 1980 RDA.

Dietary iron comes in two forms. **Heme iron** is associated with hemoglobin and myoglobin and thus is found only in animal foods, such as meat, chicken, and fish. Nonheme iron is found in plant foods. About 60 percent of the iron in animal foods and 100 percent in plant foods is in the nonheme form. Heme iron has greater bioavailability, for about 10–30 percent of it is absorbed from the intestines compared to only 2–10 percent for nonheme iron.

Excellent animal sources of dietary iron include liver, heart, lean meats, oysters, clams, and dark poultry meat. One ounce of lean meat provides about 1 mg of heme iron. Good sources of nonheme iron include dried fruits such as apricots, prunes, and raisins; beans; and whole-grain products. Six dried apricot halves or one-half cup of beans provides about 3 mg of nonheme iron, and some breakfast cereals are fortified to provide 100 percent of the RDA. Cooking in iron pots or skillets also contributes iron to the diet. On a balanced diet, about 6 mg iron is provided in every 1,000 C ingested. See Table 7.3 for foods high in iron.

Certain factors in food may affect the amount of iron absorbed into the body. The MFP factor (meat, fish, poultry) is an unknown agent probably related to heme iron that facilitates the absorption of nonheme iron. The existence of such a factor is suggested by the fact that small amounts of meat added to vegetable or grain products enhance nonheme absorption. Vitamin C prevents the oxidation of ferrous iron to the ferric form and thus facilitates nonheme iron absorption, but it has no effect on absorption of heme iron. Thus, for breakfast, drinking orange juice improves the bioavailability of iron in toast. On the other hand, substances found naturally in some foods, such as tannins, phosphates, phytates, oxalates, and excessive fiber may decrease the bioavailability of nonheme iron by forming insoluble salts or by promoting rapid transport through

Figure 7.3.
Simplified diagram of iron metabolism in humans. After digestion, iron is used in the formation of hemoglobin, myoglobin, and certain cellular enzymes, all of which are essential for transportation of oxygen in the body.

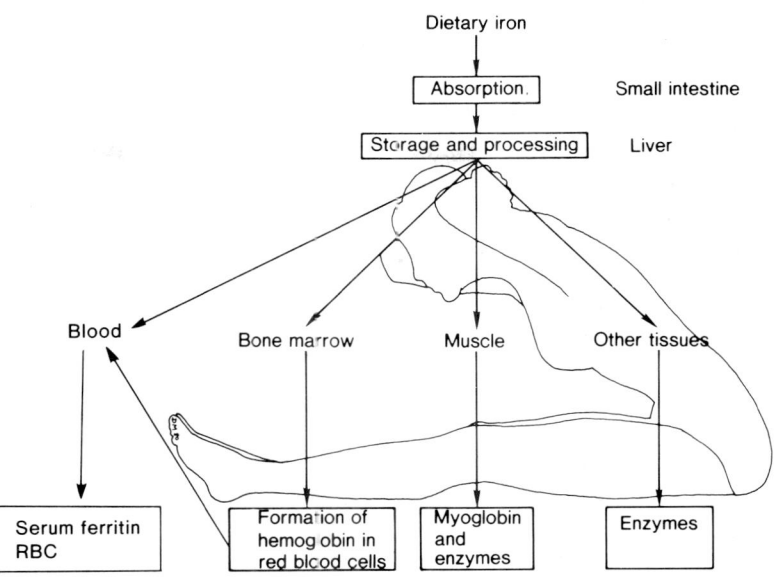

the intestines. Tea, for example, which is high in tannins, decreases iron absorption by 60 percent. However, if the diet is balanced these factors should not pose a major problem for adequate iron nutrition. Certain mineral supplements, particularly calcium, and even the calcium in milk, when taken with a meal, may impair absorption of nonheme iron. This effect may be lessened by ingestion of vitamin C with the meal.

The major function of iron in the body is the formation of compounds essential to the transportation and utilization of oxygen. The vast majority is used to form hemoglobin, a protein–iron compound in the RBC that transports oxygen from the lungs to the body tissues. Other iron compounds include myoglobin, the cytochromes, and Krebs-cycle enzymes, which help use oxygen at the cellular level. The remainder of the body iron is stored in the tissues, principally as compounds called **ferritins.** Hemosiderin is another storage form of iron. The iron in the blood, serum ferritin, is used as an index of the body iron stores, as are a number of other markers such as transferrin, protoporphyrin, and hemoglobin. Other major storage sites include the liver, spleen, and bone marrow. Approximately 30 percent of the body iron is in storage form, the remaining 70 percent being involved in oxygen metabolism. Because iron is so critical to oxygen use in humans, it is essential that those individuals engaged in aerobic endurance-type exercises have an adequate dietary intake. Figure 7.3 represents a brief outline of iron metabolism in humans.

Iron is one of the few nutrients commonly found to be slightly deficient in the diet of many Americans, particularly women and teenagers. The body normally loses very little iron through such routes as the skin, gastrointestinal tract, hair, and sweat. About 10 mg of dietary iron daily will replace these losses. Females also lose some additional iron in the blood flow during menstruation. They need about 15 mg of dietary iron per day to replace their total losses. Adolescent boys need the same amount, as they are increasing muscle tissue and blood volume during this rapid period of growth. With 6 mg of iron per 1,000 C, the adult male has no problem meeting his requirement of 10 mg per day. With a normal intake of 2,900 C, he will receive 17.4 mg. With 2,200 Calories, the average intake for females, only 13.2 mg iron would be provided. This is somewhat short of the 15 mg needed.

National surveys before 1989 revealed that over 90 percent of women were receiving less than the RDA of iron, and many of these women would still have intakes lower than the 1989 RDA. Most have normal hemoglobin and serum-ferritin status. Because the normal loss of iron from the body is relatively low, and because excessive amounts in the body may be harmful, the intestine limits the amount absorbed from the diet. On the other hand, when an individual becomes iron deficient, the intestines may increase the amount of dietary iron absorbed to above 50 percent. The National Research Council has reported that the frequency of iron deficiency without anemia is much greater than that of iron deficiency

Table 7.3 Sources rich in iron, copper, zinc, chromium, and selenium

Mineral	Source
Iron	Organ meats such as liver
	Meat, fish, and poultry
	Shellfish, especially oysters
	Dried beans and peas
	Whole-grain products, breads, cereals
	Green leafy vegetables, broccoli, asparagus
	Dried apricots, dates, figs, raisins
	Iron cookware
Copper	Organ meats, liver
	Shellfish, oysters
	Lamb and pork
	Fish, salmon
	Turkey
	Nuts, peanuts
	Eggs
	Bran cereals
	Avocado, broccoli
	Bananas
Zinc	Organ meats
	Meat, fish, poultry
	Shellfish, especially oysters
	Dairy products, milk, cheese
	Nuts
	Whole-grain products, breads, cereals
	Vegetables such as asparagus and spinach
Chromium	Organ meats such as liver
	Meats
	Oysters
	Cheese
	Whole-grain products
	Asparagus
	Stainless steel cookware
Selenium	Meat, fish, poultry
	Organ meats such as kidney, liver
	Seafood
	Whole grains from selenium-rich soil

anemia. Nevertheless, about 6 percent of the female population has iron deficiency anemia, the most common nutrient-deficiency disorder in the United States.

Iron deficiency occurs in stages. The first stage involves depletion of the bone marrow stores and a decrease in serum ferritin. The second stage involves a further decrease in serum ferritin and less iron in the hemoglobin. Other markers are used to evaluate iron stores in this stage, including free erythrocyte protoporphyrin (FEP), which is used to form hemoglobin. FEP in the blood increases when adequate iron is not available. Serum transferrin, a protein that carries iron in the blood, also increases. In these first two stages the hemoglobin concentration in the blood is still normal. These stages may be characterized as iron depletion and **iron deficiency without anemia.** The third stage consists of a very low level of serum ferritin and decreased he-

moglobin concentration, or **iron deficiency anemia.** Symptoms of iron deficiency anemia include paleness, tiredness, and low vitality, and impaired ability to regulate body temperature in a cold environment.

Because iron is so critical to the oxygen energy system, it is essential for endurance athletes to have adequate iron in the diet to maintain optimal body supplies. There are some differences of opinion about the magnitude of iron deficiency in athletes. A substantial number of studies, using serum ferritin levels as a basis of iron status, revealed that 50–80 percent of female athletes, particularly endurance runners, were at risk of iron deficiency. However, the National Research Council has stated that there is currently no single biochemical indicator available to reliably assess iron adequacy, so several markers should be used. But then, Newhouse and Clement report wide variations in these markers. In a study using serum ferritin and transferrin saturation, Risser and his associates reported no significant differences in iron status between female athletes and nonathletes, possibly owing to a wide variation in individual values, but 31 percent of the athletes and 45 percent of the nonathletes were iron deficient. Although iron deficiency appears not to be a problem in most male athletes, several studies have reported poor iron status in about 15–30 percent of male distance runners. One of these studies used a bone biopsy to determine marrow stores.

After reviewing the literature, Priscilla Clarkson reported that iron deficiency to the point of decreased RBC and hemoglobin production does not appear to be prevalent in the athletic population. Some studies have reported iron deficiency anemia occurs in female athletes at the same rate as in the general U.S. female population, or at a higher rate. The normal hemoglobin level is 14–16 grams per deciliter (100 ml) of blood for males and 12–14 grams for females. Males have been classified as anemic with less than 13 grams, whereas values less than 11 grams, and in some cases 12 grams, have been used as the criterion for anemia in females. Randy Eichner, a hematologist involved in sports medicine, poses the interesting question of whether an athlete whose usual hemoglobin is 16 grams per deciliter is anemic if his level decreases to 14 grams.

Although there may be some debate about the magnitude of the problem of iron deficiency in athletes, most investigators concede that it may be important to monitor the diet and iron status of certain athletes, particularly if performance begins to suffer without any obvious explanation. One report noted that Greg Lemond was struggling in the first stages of the Tour of Italy until his trainer suggested iron therapy. Following several injections, Lemond finished strong in the Tour, winning the last trial race. A month later he won the Tour de France in a remarkable finish.

There may be a number of causes for the low iron or hemoglobin levels found in some athletes. Although adult male athletes appear to obtain sufficient dietary iron, numerous studies have revealed that dietary intake of iron may be inadequate in female and adolescent male athletes. The type of dietary iron may also be important. Ann Snyder and her colleagues noted that although female athletes on a normal mixed diet or a modified vegetarian diet had the same iron intake (14 mg/day), the modified vegetarian diet was associated with significantly lower iron stores in the body, suggestive of a beneficial effect of heme iron.

Exercise, particularly running, may contribute to iron loss in both sexes for a variety of reasons. A condition often seen in distance runners is **hematuria,** the presence of hemoglobin or myoglobin in the urine. This may be caused by repeated foot contact with the ground, rupturing some RBC and releasing hemoglobin (a process called **hemolysis**), some of which may be excreted by the kidney. Hemolysis has also been observed in weightlifters, attributed to the mechanical stress generated in the muscles. Prolonged running may also lead to ruptured muscle cells, releasing myoglobin, which may have the same fate. An irritation of the inner lining of the urinary bladder may also be a source of RBC loss. Even nonimpact athletes like rowers have experienced hemolysis. Several studies also have revealed increased loss of blood in the feces of endurance runners and endurance cyclists, which may be due to loss of cells in the intestinal wall or bleeding caused by the use of aspirin or other antiinflammatory drugs to control pain. Athletes who detect blood loss in the urine or feces should see a physician, for there may be other causes that may need medical treatment.

An additional source of iron loss is the sweat. Although one study has shown that sweat losses of iron are relatively low when induced by sauna (0.02 mg per liter), exercise appears to increase the amount of iron in the sweat; this may be related to the fact that serum iron may actually increase during an exercise session and may be partially excreted in the sweat. The results of several studies, for example Arouma and others, suggest that approximately 0.3–0.4 mg of iron is lost per liter of sweat during exercise. At a 10 percent rate of absorption, it would take 3–4 mg of dietary iron to replace the iron lost in one liter of sweat.

As would be expected, the problem of concern to the endurance athlete is the development of iron deficiency anemia. A number of studies have shown that anemia causes a significant reduction in the ability to perform prolonged high-level exercise. The donation of blood causes a drop in hemoglobin, which may also decrease performance capacity. This is, of course, related to the decreased ability to transport and use oxygen in the body.

One form of anemia associated with endurance training is sports anemia, mentioned previously in the chapter on protein. Sports anemia is not a true anemia. Although the hemoglobin concentration is toward the lower end of the normal range, the other indices of iron status are normal. Whether sports anemia is a beneficial physiological response to endurance exercise or a condition that will hinder performance is not known. A short-term sports anemia appears to develop in some individuals during the early phases of training or when the magnitude of training increases drastically. One of the effects of endurance training is to increase both the plasma volume and the number of RBC. However, the plasma expansion appears to be greater, so there is a dilution of the RBC and a lowering of the hemoglobin concentration. This effect is believed to be beneficial to the athlete, however, because it reduces the viscosity, or thickness, of the blood and allows it to flow more easily. In many athletes the hemoglobin concentration returns to normal after the first month or so of training. A long-term sports anemia is often seen in highly trained endurance athletes. One theory proposes that the production of RBC by the bone marrow is decreased in endurance athletes because the RBC become so efficient in releasing oxygen to the tissues. The authors of this theory suggest that sports anemia is not due to poor iron status.

The effect on physical performance of iron deficiency without anemia is controversial and still under study. Lukaski and others had eleven females live in a metabolic ward for 80–100 days to induce iron deficiency without anemia. They observed a decreased rate of oxygen uptake and reduced energy production during exercise. Other research with iron-deficient, nonanemic human subjects revealed an increased lactate production during maximal exercise, indicative of reduced oxygen utilization in the muscle cells. On the other hand, research has shown that it is possible to maintain VO_2 max, endurance capacity, and maximal functioning of the muscle oxidative enzymes even when the body iron stores are severely diminished or depleted. Swedish investigators Ekblom and Celsing withdrew blood over a four-week period to create an iron deficiency. They then infused the blood back into the subjects so that they were in a condition of iron deficiency without anemia. Even though the iron status was poor, physiological functioning and endurance performance were not impaired. These investigators noted that low serum ferritin levels may not reflect low iron levels in the muscles. One might speculate that differences between these studies, i.e., poor iron status due to diet versus blood withdrawal, could influence the results. But, one of the studies reporting impaired lactate metabolism with diet-induced iron deficiency also reported no effect upon VO_2 max or endurance performance.

The importance of iron to oxygen transport and endurance capacity and the possibility that many athletes, particularly females, may be iron deficient have led a number of investigators in the area of sports nutrition to recommend that more athletes take dietary iron or supplements. Others suggest that the indiscriminate use of iron supplements by athletes be discouraged.

Does iron supplementation improve physical performance? Many studies have been conducted in attempts to answer this question, and the answer appears to be dependent upon the iron status of the individual.

First, if the individual suffers from iron deficiency anemia, iron therapy could help correct this condition and concomitantly increase performance capacity.

Second, most research with iron deficient, nonanemic subjects has shown that iron supplementation improves iron status, by increasing serum ferritin, for example, but appears to have little effect upon maximal physiological functioning as measured by VO_2 max. The effect of supplementation on actual physical performance is controversial, however. A recent well controlled double-blind placebo study did note an improvement in running performance when iron deficient, yet nonanemic, female high school distance runners were treated with iron supplements for one month. Additional beneficial effects have also been observed in several well designed studies with iron deficient, nonanemic subjects. Hudgins and others found that 65 milligrams of iron per day improved the 5-kilometer performance of twelve female cross-country runners. Rowland and associates reported significant improvements in treadmill endurance time in competitive runners following four weeks of ferrous sulfate supplementation, while Lamanca and Haymes revealed a 38 percent improvement in an endurance task following iron supplementation as compared

with a 1 percent decrease in the control group; although this difference is impressive, it was not statistically significant.

Conversely, other researchers have observed no beneficial effect of iron supplementation on physical performance in subjects who had iron deficiency without anemia. Risser and others found no improvement in performance of female college athletes, at least as reported by the athletes or their coaches; no objective measurement of physical performance was documented. Matter and her associates found no improvement in the treadmill endurance performance of female marathon runners following either one or ten weeks of iron supplementation, which was also combined with a folate supplement. Also, Newhouse and others reported no improvement in performance on a variety of exercise tests, both aerobic and anaerobic, in physically active females following eight weeks of oral iron supplementation. Thus, the research relative to the beneficial effects of iron supplementation to those athletes who are iron deficient, yet nonanemic, is contradictory. The subject merits further investigation.

Third, if the individual has normal hemoglobin levels, iron supplementation offers no additional benefits. Some well controlled research has shown that iron supplementation to highly active females in physical training did not raise their hemoglobin levels or the percentage of hemoglobin saturated with iron. It is interesting to note that iron supplementation, up to 36 mg per day, did not prevent the development of sports anemia in female athletes in the early stages of training or in male runners who doubled their mileage for a three-week period.

Some danger may be associated with iron supplements if they lead to excessive iron in the body. Although most adults probably will have no problem with 25 mg of iron per day, this amount may decrease absorption of zinc. Prolonged consumption of large amounts can cause a disturbance in iron metabolism in susceptible individuals. Iron then tends to accumulate in the liver as hemosiderin, which in excess can cause **hemochromatosis** in those genetically predisposed. This condition causes cirrhosis and may lead to the ultimate destruction of the liver. Of every 1,000 Americans, approximately two to three have a genetic predisposition to hemochromatosis. Other health problems associated with excessive iron intake have been detailed by Emery. Excessive iron may be fatal to young children; more than 30 deaths occur each year from overdoses of iron obtained by eating large amounts of candy-flavored vitamin tablets with iron.

In summary, it would be wise for the developing adolescent male and the female of all ages to be aware of the iron content in their diet. This concern is especially important to endurance athletes, although it would appear that the extra Calories they eat to meet the additional energy requirements of training would provide the necessary iron. All active males and females should be aware of heme iron-rich foods, such as lean red meat, and be sure to include them in the daily diet, or at least two to three times a week. Eating foods rich in vitamin C and using iron cookware also will increase iron bioavailability. Moreover, iron supplementation by commercial preparations may be recommended for certain individuals, including female distance runners, those who experience heavy menstrual blood flow, and athletes who are on restricted caloric intake. The usual vitamin pill with iron should contain about 15 mg iron, which is 100 percent of the RDA for females and adolescent boys. One tablet a day may be advisable for these individuals. The individual with iron deficiency anemia should consult a physician for iron therapy, which may consist of 100–200 mg of elemental iron per day until the condition is corrected. Large doses of iron should not be consumed indiscriminately.

Copper (Cu)

Copper is an essential mineral closely associated with the function of iron. There is no RDA for copper, but the ESADDI is 1.5–3.0 mg for adults. The USRDA is 2 mg.

Copper is widely distributed in foods and is high in seafoods, meats, nuts, beans, and grain products. One slice of whole wheat bread contains about 6 percent of the ESADDI. Copper also may be found in drinking water, particularly soft water, which leaches it from copper pipes. Some good food sources are listed in Table 7.3.

Copper functions in the body as a metalloenzyme and works closely with iron in oxygen metabolism. It is needed for the absorption of iron from the intestinal tract, helps in the formation of hemoglobin, and is involved in the activity of a specific cytochrome, an oxidative enzyme in the mitochondria. Copper is also a component of ceruloplasmin, a glycoprotein in the plasma, and in superoxide dismutase (SOD), an enzyme that functions as an antioxidant to quench free radicals.

Copper deficiency due to inadequate dietary intake is not known to exist in humans, although deficiency has occurred in some patients receiving prolonged intravenous feeding of a copper-free solution. The major deficiency symptom is anemia.

The effects of exercise or exercise training on serum copper levels are variable, with studies showing increases, decreases, or no changes. Several studies have reported decreases in serum copper in athletes involved in prolonged training or after an endurance exercise task. The authors theorized that the decreased levels were due to sweat or fecal losses. However, no deficiency symptoms were noted.

No research is available relative to copper supplementation and physical performance. Supplements are not recommended because excessive copper intake, even 5–10 milligrams, may cause nausea and vomiting. However, the National Research Council reports that toxicity from dietary sources is rare.

Zinc (Zn)

Zinc is a blue-white metal that is an essential nutrient for humans. The RDA is 15 mg per day for males and 12 mg per day for adult females. The USRDA is 15 mg per day.

Good sources of zinc are found in animal protein, such as meat, milk, and seafood, particularly oysters. Three ounces of meat contain approximately 33 percent of the RDA, whereas only one oyster will provide over 70 percent. Whole-grain products also contain significant amounts of zinc, but the phytate and fiber content will slightly decrease its bioavailability. In general, if you receive enough protein in the diet you will obtain the RDA for zinc. The MFP factor enhances zinc absorption. About 20–50 percent of the dietary zinc is absorbed. Table 7.3 presents foods high in zinc.

Zinc is found in virtually all tissues in the body as a component of over 100 metalloenzymes. Several of these enzymes are involved in the major pathways of energy metabolism, including lactic acid dehydrogenase (LDH), which is important for the lactic acid energy system. Zinc also is involved in a wide variety of other body functions such as protein synthesis, the growth process, and wound healing.

Helen Lane has noted that zinc nutritional status appears to be well maintained in the average U.S. population, even with marginal intakes. However, several zinc researchers have indicated that a mild dietary zinc deficiency is not uncommon in the United States, particularly in areas where animal protein is relatively low and consumption of grain products is high. Deficiency states have been observed in young children with symptoms of impaired wound healing, depressed appetite, and failure to grow properly.

Zinc deficiency could be a problem for certain athletes, particularly young athletes in sports that stress weight loss for optimal performance or competition. Very low-Calorie or starvation-type diets may induce significant zinc losses. In addition, sweat also may contain substantial amounts of zinc, estimated to be approximately 1 mg per liter. Although few experimental data are available, young wrestlers who use both dieting and sweating techniques to induce weight loss may be at risk for zinc deficiency and possible impairment of optimal growth. Several studies also have reported a low serum zinc level in endurance runners and triathletes, and the cause was attributed to high sweat losses, increased urinary excretion, or low-Calorie diets. However, no zinc deficiency symptoms were noted in these athletes, the authors suggesting that low levels in the serum do not necessarily reflect low levels of zinc in the muscles. Following her review of the available literature, which is limited, Lane noted that, in general, there is no evidence that exercise causes a poor zinc status or that a marginal deficiency impairs performance.

Given the potential ergogenic importance of zinc, it is unusual that only one study has been uncovered that has investigated the effect of zinc supplementation upon physical performance. The subjects were untrained women with an average age of 35 years. In a series of tests for both isometric and isokinetic strength and endurance, zinc supplements improved performance in isometric endurance and in isokinetic strength at one speed. However, performance was not affected in isokinetic endurance or in isokinetic strength at two other speeds of muscle contraction. Although the authors reported a beneficial effect of zinc supplementation and theorized it helped optimize the function of LDH in the muscle during fast contractions, it would appear additional research is needed to confirm this finding. The use of trained subjects would also be an important consideration.

Small amounts of zinc supplements do not appear to pose any major problems to the healthy individual, but larger doses may. Research has shown that zinc supplements, even 25–50 mg per day, may impair the absorption of other essential minerals, such as copper and iron. Supplements over 100 mg/day may increase the amount of LDL-cholesterol and decrease the HDL-cholesterol level, increasing the risk of coronary artery disease. Anemia may also result from such doses. Higher doses may impair the immune system and cause nausea and vomiting; they may even be fatal.

On the basis of available evidence, zinc supplementation is not warranted for most athletes. Foods rich in zinc, similar to the animal protein rich in iron, should be selected to replace the increased Calories expended through exercise. However, those athletes such as wrestlers and others incurring weight losses should be exceptionally aware of high zinc foods. If a supplement for these athletes is recommended, it should not exceed the RDA.

Chromium

Chromium is a very hard metal essential in human nutrition. The ESADDI is 50–200 micrograms per day.

Good sources of chromium include brewers yeast, whole grains, nuts, molasses, cheese, mushrooms, and asparagus. Beer also contains some chromium. One slice of whole wheat bread provides approximately 15 percent of the daily requirement of chromium. Chromium is poorly absorbed from the intestinal tract, less than 1 percent being absorbed with intakes in the ESADDI range. At lower dietary intakes, absorption is somewhat increased.

Chromium is considered to be an essential component of the glucose-tolerance factor associated with insulin in the proper metabolism of blood glucose. In essence, chromium potentiates the activity of insulin and thus may also influence lipid and protein metabolism. In addition to maintenance of blood glucose levels, it may be involved in the formation of glycogen in muscle tissue and may facilitate the transport of amino acids into the muscles. Chromium may also affect cholesterol metabolism.

Clinically manifest deficiencies of chromium are rare, but abnormally high blood-glucose levels have been reported in hospital patients receiving prolonged intravenous nutrition containing no chromium. Richard Anderson, one of the principal investigators in chromium metabolism, observed that the average American intake of chromium is at the lower range of the ESADDI and suggested this may not be optimal. For example, in one study nearly one-half of subjects with impaired glucose tolerance improved on chromium supplementation. The role of chromium in the development of diabetes is currently being studied.

Chromium deficiency could be a problem with both endurance- and strength-type athletes. Impairment in carbohydrate metabolism would not be conducive to optimal performance in endurance events, whereas decreased amino acid transport into the muscle could limit the benefits from a weight training program. On the basis of animal experiments, Anderson has linked chromium to carbohydrate and protein metabolism during exercise, noting for example that chromium-deficient rats use muscle glycogen at a faster rate. Anderson believes that strenuous exercise may increase the need for chromium in humans. He noted that chromium losses are associated with stress, such as exercise, and reported increased excretion of chromium in the urine following a strenuous run.

Very little research has been uncovered relative to the ergogenic potential of chromium, but Gary Evans, a chemistry professor at Bemidji State University in Minnesota, used chromium picolinate as an adjunct to a weight training program to investigate its effect upon body composition. Picolinate is a natural derivative of tryptophan, an amino acid, and apparently facilitates the absorption of chromium into the body. In a recent review article, Evans described two of his studies. In the first study, ten male volunteers from a weight training class were assigned to either a placebo or a chromium supplement group. The chromium dosage was the upper level of the ESADDI, 200 micrograms. Body fat and lean body mass were determined by skinfold and girth measurements. The subjects trained with weights for 40 days, and at the conclusion Evans found that the chromium group had increased their body weight by 2.2 kilograms, 73 percent of which was lean body mass. The placebo group had also increased their body weight by 1.25 kilograms, but Evans noted this increase was due almost totally to body fat. The second study was similar to the first, but 32 football players at Bemidji State University served as subjects. After the 42-day training period, the chromium group actually lost 1.2 kilograms of body weight, but most of it was fat so their proportion of lean body mass increased from 84.2 to 87.8 percent. The placebo group also lost body weight, but their lean body mass only increased from 84.6 to 85.8 percent. In both studies, Evans noted that the results were statistically significant, suggesting that chromium picolinate supplementation enhanced body composition by decreasing body fat and increasing lean body mass.

The findings of this report are certainly interesting, but several points should be noted. First, the studies were reported in a review article on the health benefits of chromium and do not appear to have been published previously in a refereed scientific journal. Second, skinfolds and girth measurements were used to assess body composition, but although these types of measurements may be helpful in weight control

programs, they are not considered to be sufficiently accurate for research purposes. Third, the dietary intake apparently was not controlled, nor were other physical activities that could affect body weight. Finally, no physical performance measures were reported. Additional research, using more elaborate controls, is necessary to verify these preliminary findings.

Following the publicity associated with this study, chromium picolinate was billed in certain muscle magazines as the alternative to anabolic steroids, the advertisers suggesting that its insulin-like effects may be the prime anabolic hormone effects in the body.

Chromium supplements may also possess some health benefits. As already noted, they may help improve glucose metabolism in those with glucose intolerance. Other research has suggested that chromium may help lower total cholesterol and LDL-cholesterol while raising HDL-cholesterol in individuals with unhealthy serum cholesterol levels. However, Anderson has noted that chromium supplements can correct only that part of a health problem which is associated with a deficiency. In other words, individuals who have a health problem in which chromium deficiency plays a part will benefit if the deficiency is corrected, just like any nutrient-deficiency related health problem. Anderson noted that chromium acts as a nutrient, not a therapeutic agent.

The National Research Council indicates that dietary chromium does not appear to be toxic. Amounts of 200 micrograms per day have been used safely.

Selenium

Selenium is a chemical element resembling sulfur. RDA were established for selenium in 1989, being 70 and 55 micrograms per day for males and females, respectively.

Foods rich in selenium include seafoods, organ meats like kidney and liver, other meats, and grains grown in soil abundant in selenium. According to the National Research Council, deficiencies are rare.

Selenium is a component of glutathione peroxidase, an enzyme that helps catabolize free radicals and prevent damage to cellular structures, such as the membranes of RBC. As mentioned in the last chapter, selenium works with vitamin E as an antioxidant and has been theorized to be important in the prevention of cancer.

In theory, selenium may help protect cell membranes from peroxidation during exercise. In studies of lipid peroxidation using animals such as

Table 7.4 Brief summary of essential trace minerals

Mineral	RDA or ESADDI*	Food source	Major body functions
Cobalt (Co)	**	Meat, liver, milk	Component of vitamin B$_{12}$; promotes development of red blood cells
Fluoride (F)	1.5–4.0 mg	Milk, egg yolk, drinking water, seafood	Helps form bones and teeth
Iodine (I)	150 micrograms	Iodized salt, seafood, vegetables	Helps in formation of thyroid hormones
Manganese (Mn)	2.0–5.0 mg	Whole-grain products, dried peas and beans, leafy vegetables, bananas	Many enzymes involved in energy metabolism; bone formation; fat synthesis
Molybdenum (Mo)	75–250 micrograms	Liver, organ meats, whole-grain products, dried beans and peas	Works with riboflavin in enzymes involved in carbohydrate and fat metabolism

*For adults. RDA or ESADDI for other age groups may be found in Appendix A.
**Essential as part of vitamin B$_{12}$.

rats and horses, selenium was administered alone; results were contradictory. In studies using human subjects, selenium was given as part of an "antioxidant cocktail" that also contained vitamins C, E, or beta-carotene. This research is discussed on page 153.

Excessive intake of selenium, in the range of 1 milligram per day, may induce changes in the appearance of the fingernails. Accidental intakes of large amounts, over 25 milligrams per day, have been associated with nausea, vomiting, abdominal pain, hair loss, and unusual fatigue. Although supplements of amounts up to the RDA appear safe, the safety of larger doses has not been confirmed, and they may be potentially harmful.

Other trace minerals
A number of other trace minerals have physiological roles that may have important implications for health or physical performance.

Food sources, RDA or ESADDI, major physiological functions, and the effects of deficiencies or excesses are summarized in Table 7.4. Only trace minerals for which an RDA or ESADDI have been developed are included. Other elements, such as nickel, tin, vanadium, silicon, boron, and arsenic may prove to be essential. It should be noted that deficiencies and excesses due to dietary sources for most of these nutrients are extremely rare. However, to help prevent a deficiency it is important to consume unprocessed foods, because many of the trace elements that are removed during processing are not returned. For example, as already noted, one slice of whole wheat bread provides about 15 percent of the daily requirement of chromium, whereas a slice of white bread contains only 1 percent. Excesses may occur with use of supplements or through industrial exposure.

Two of these trace elements deserve mention for they have been shown to prevent health problems in humans. Fluoride has been shown to prevent dental caries, but excesses in children may cause mottling, or varying shades of whiteness in the outer enamel. Iodine is used in the formation of thyroxine and triiodothyronine, two hormones produced in the thyroid gland. Decreased production of these hormones would lower the body's metabolism, a possible contributing factor to the development of obesity. The use of iodized salt has nearly eliminated iodine deficiency in the United States and has thereby greatly reduced the incidence of goiter, a serious iodine deficiency disease.

Research literature relative to the effect of exercise on the metabolic fate of these trace nutrients is almost nonexistent, nor are there any studies available regarding the effects of supplements on performance. This may be understandable, since deficiencies are rare.

Deficiency effects	Excess effects	Recommended as diet supplement
Not found in humans	Nausea, vomiting, death	No
Higher incidence of dental cavities	Discolored teeth	No
Goiter, an enlarged thyroid gland	Depress thyroid gland activity	No
Poor growth	Weakness; nervous system problems; mental confusion	No
Not found in humans	Rare	No

Mineral Supplements: Exercise and Health

Following her extensive review of dietary surveys, Sarah Short noted that both athletes and health professionals are becoming more concerned with mineral deficiencies. Perusal of athletic and health magazines marketed for the general public reveals a variety of articles and advertisements suggesting that supplementation with certain minerals will enhance athletic performance or health. As the foregoing discussion indicates, individuals who have a mineral deficiency may experience improved health or physical performance if that deficiency is corrected. In general, however, supplementation has little effect on the individual whose mineral status is adequate. This last section summarizes some key points relative to mineral nutrition, focusing on the need for supplementation.

Does exercise increase my need for minerals?

Exercise may induce mineral losses from the body by several mechanisms. Many minerals appear to be mobilized into the circulation during exercise, probably being released from body stores in the muscles or elsewhere. As they circulate, some may be removed by the kidneys and excreted in the urine, whereas others may appear in the sweat, particularly in a warm environment. Losses from the gastrointestinal tract may also occur during exercise, although the mechanism is not totally understood.

The female athlete who develops secondary amenorrhea may need additional calcium, as might the male endurance athlete in whom trabecular bone mass is decreased. On the other hand, the need for iron in the female athlete may decrease somewhat with the cessation of menses in secondary amenorrhea.

Because of these potential mineral losses, at least one investigator in sports nutrition has suggested that mineral supplementation should be considered for athletes. This may be so, but the first concern should be to educate the athlete about obtaining adequate mineral nutrition through dietary means.

Can I obtain the minerals I need through my diet?

As many dietary surveys have shown, many Americans are not obtaining the RDA or ESADDI for a variety of minerals, including iron, zinc, calcium, and chromium. Similar dietary deficiencies have been noted in surveys with athletes, but mainly with athletes who participate in activities such as wrestling, distance running, ballet, and gymnastics, where weight control is a concern. Let us briefly highlight the dietary recommendations that will help ensure adequate amounts of nutrients in the diet.

In general, as with all other nutrients, a balanced diet is essential. Select a wide variety of foods from all the food groups and within each group. Table 7.5 presents the percentage of the USRDA provided by servings of different foods from several

Table 7.5   Percentages of the USRDA in various foods for selected minerals

Food	Serving	Calories	Ca	P	Mg	Fe	Cu	Zn
Milk, skim	1 glass	90	35	28	10	1	2	7
Cheese, cheddar	1 ounce	114	21	15	2	1	0	6
Oyster	1 average	10	1	2	1	6	28	75
Liver, beef	3 ounces	150	1	41	4	50	157	29
Beef, lean sirloin	3 ounces	176	1	22	6	21	3	33
Lamb chop, lean portion	1 medium	95	1	11	3	6	22	14
Beans, lima	1/2 cup	131	3	15	8	19	8	6
Broccoli	1 stalk	25	8	6	3	4	63	1
Bread, whole wheat	1 slice	70	2	5	4	3	6	3
Bread, enriched white	1 slice	70	2	2	4	2	1	1

food groups. Note that the percentage values for the minerals differ not only between food groups but also for some minerals in foods within the same group. For example, note that calcium is high in dairy foods but low in meats. On the other hand, iron is high in meats but low in dairy products. Also, in the meat group, copper is high in pork but low in beef. It is also important to eat foods in their natural state as much as possible. The milling of flour removes many minerals, but only iron is replaced in the enrichment process. Note the differences between whole wheat and enriched white bread in Table 7.5.

A basic principle of mineral nutrition is to eat natural foods that are rich in calcium and iron. If you select a diet to provide your RDA for these two minerals, you will receive adequate amounts of the other major and trace minerals at the same time. Dairy products and meats are excellent sources of these minerals, but other foods such as legumes and dark green leafy vegetables, also may provide significant amounts if selected wisely. Note the foods rich in calcium and iron in Tables 7.2 and 7.3, and compare the similarity to the foods listed for the other minerals in these two tables and Table 7.4.

Should physically active individuals take mineral supplements?

In general, the answer to this question for most athletes is *no* for several reasons. First, contrary to advertising claims of mineral-supplement manufacturers, you can obtain adequate mineral nutrition from the diet if you adhere to some of the guidelines presented in the previous question and throughout this chapter. Second, although some athletes may not be obtaining the RDA of several minerals, such as zinc and calcium, mineral deficiencies to the point of impairing physical performance are rare. Very few data are available on this topic, but the evidence that is available with most minerals suggests that though the serum levels may be low, physical performance is not affected. An exception may be low levels of serum iron for, as noted previously, supplementation, although controversial, has been helpful to some athletes. Third, many minerals may be harmful when taken in excess. As noted throughout this chapter, the absorption rate for most minerals is relatively low. Only 40 percent of calcium is absorbed from the intestinal tract, while the percentages for iron and chromium are, respectively, 10 and 1–2 percent. The reason for this low absorption rate is to prevent the accumulation of excess amounts of minerals in the body, which may interfere with normal metabolism. Large supplemental doses may overload the body and cause numerous health problems, and as noted for several minerals, may be fatal.

However, it is recognized that certain athletes may not be obtaining adequate mineral nutrition from their diets and may possibly benefit from supplementation. As noted previously, athletes who are attempting to lose weight for performance are at most risk for developing a mineral deficiency. Because many of the dietary surveys of these athletes have reported intakes lower than the RDA for iron and calcium, it may be assumed that their diets are also low in other trace minerals.

If there is concern for the nutritional status of the athlete, the ideal situation would be to consult a sports nutritionist or nutritionally oriented physician for advice. Unfortunately, this approach does not appear to be common among athletes who may be in need of nutritional counseling, although the situation is improving. Some elite athletes take iron supplements which are medically prescribed, and dieticians with specialties in exercise physiology and sports nutrition are becoming increasingly available.

For athletes who cannot or will not seek professional advice, it may be prudent to recommend a one-a-day vitamin–mineral supplement to those who are known to have poor nutritional habits. The tablet should contain no more than 50–100 percent of the RDA for any mineral. Additionally, the point should be made to the athlete that the supplement is being recommended to help prevent a deficiency, not for any ergogenic purposes. In the meantime, efforts should be undertaken to educate the athlete concerning sound nutritional practices.

Are mineral megadoses harmful?

One of the generally accepted facts relative to mineral nutrition in the healthy individual is that the levels associated with toxicity can normally be obtained only through the use of supplements, not through dietary sources. Because they hope to improve health or physical performance, many individuals do purchase supplements containing minerals. However, surveys indicate the most common preparations purchased contain the RDA or less, which should pose no health problems to the healthy individual. Unfortunately, as indicated in the last chapter, many individuals self-prescribe, and may consume more than the recommended daily dosage. Although the toxicity and possible health problems associated with excessive intake of several minerals, such as calcium, iron, zinc, and copper, are fairly well documented, the level of safety for intake of a variety of other minerals, particularly some of the trace minerals suggested to be therapeutic in nature, has been more difficult to document. Nevertheless, the National Research Council has noted that all trace minerals are toxic if consumed at high doses for a long enough time.

According to Yetiv, who reviewed the literature on the relationship of minerals to health, individuals who consume mineral supplements should take only amounts similar to the RDA, or less. There are no indications for megasupplements of minerals, except for treatment of specific disease states.

References

Books

Aito, A., et al. (Eds.) 1991. *Trace Elements in Health and Disease.* Boca Raton, FL: CRC Press.

Celsing, F. 1987. *Influence of Iron Deficiency and Changes in Haemoglobin Concentration on Exercise Capacity in Man.* Stockholm: Repro Print.

Emery, T. 1991. *Iron and your health.* Boca Raton, FL: CRC Press.

Fisher, J. 1990. *The Chromium Program.* New York: Harper & Row.

Frieden, E. 1984. *Biochemistry of the Essential Ultratrace Elements.* New York: Plenum Press.

Hickson, J., and Wolinsky, I. 1989. *Nutrition in Exercise and Sport.* Boca Raton, FL: CRC Press.

Hunt, S., and Groff, J. 1990. *Advanced Nutrition and Human Metabolism.* St. Paul, MN: West.

National Research Council. 1989. *Recommended Dietary Allowances.* Washington, DC: National Academy Press.

National Research Council. 1989. *Diet and Health: Implications for Reducing Chronic Disease Risk.* Washington, DC: National Academy Press.

Shils, M., and Young, V. 1988. *Modern Nutrition in Health and Disease.* Philadelphia: Lea & Febiger.

Williams, M. H. 1985. *Nutritional Aspects of Human Physical and Athletic Performance.* Springfield, IL: C C Thomas.

Yetiv, J. 1986. *Popular Nutritional Practices: A Scientific Appraisal.* Toledo, OH: Popular Medicine Press.

Reviews

Anderson, R. 1988. Selenium, chromium, and manganese. (B) Chromium. In: *Modern Nutrition in Health and Disease.* M. Shils and V. Young, eds. Philadelphia: Lea & Febiger.

Avioli, L. 1988. Calcium and phosphorus. In: *Modern Nutrition in Health and Disease,* eds. R. Goodhart and M. Shils. Philadelphia: Lea & Febiger.

Clarkson, P. 1991. Vitamins, iron, and trace minerals. *Ergogenics: Enhancement of Performance in Exercise and Sport,* eds. D. Lamb and M. Williams. Indianapolis, IN: Benchmark.

Clysdale, F. 1989. The relevance of mineral chemistry to bioavailability. *Nutrition Today* 24:23–30, March/April.

Dalsky, G. 1990. Effect of exercise on bone: Permissive influence of estrogen and calcium. *Medicine and Science in Sport and Exercise* 22:281–85.

Deuster, P. 1989. Magnesium in sports medicine. *Journal of the American College of Nutrition* 8:462.

Drinkwater, B. 1989. Amenorrheic athletes: At risk for premature osteoporosis. *Proceedings of the First IOC World Congress on Sport Sciences.* Colorado Springs, CO: United States Olympic Committee.

Eichner, E. R. 1989. Gastrointestinal bleeding in athletes. *Physician and Sportsmedicine* 17:128–40, May.

Eichner, E. R. 1988. Other medical considerations in prolonged exercise. In: *Prolonged Exercise,* eds. D. Lamb and R. Murray. Indianapolis, IN: Benchmark.

Ekblom, B. 1989. Effects of iron deficiency, variations in hemoglobin concentration, and erythropoietin injections on physical performance and relevant physiological parameters. *Proceedings of the First IOC World Congress on Sport Sciences.* Colorado Springs, CO: United States Olympic Committee.

Elin, R. 1988. Magnesium metabolism in health and disease. *Disease-A-Month* 34:161–218.

Evans, G. 1989. The effect of chromium picolinate on insulin controlled parameters in humans. *International Journal of Biosocial and Medical Research* 11:163–80.

Fairbanks, V., and Beutler, E. 1988. Iron. In: *Modern Nutrition in Health and Disease.* R. Goodhart and M. Shils, eds. Philadelphia: Lea & Febiger.

Fosmire, G. 1990. Zinc toxicity. *American Journal of Clinical Nutrition* 51:225–27.

Hallberg, L., and Magnusson, B. 1984. The etiology of sports anemia. *Acta Medica Scandinavica* 216:145–48.

Keen, C., and Hackman, R. 1986. Trace elements in athletic performance. In: *Sport, Health and Nutrition,* ed. F. Katch. Champaign, IL: Human Kinetics.

Lane, H. 1989. Some trace elements related to physical activity: Zinc, copper, selenium, chromium, and iodine. In: *Nutrition in Exercise and Sport,* eds. J. Hickson and I. Wolinsky. Boca Raton, FL: CRC Press.

Levander, O. 1988. Selenium, chromium, and manganese. (A) Selenium. In: *Modern Nutrition in Health and Disease.* M. Shils and V. Young, eds. Philadelphia: Lea & Febiger.

Liebovitz, B. 1990. Nutrition and performance. *Muscular Development* 27:37, July.

Lindsay, R. 1989. Osteoporosis: An updated approach to prevention and management. *Geriatrics* 44:45–46.

Marcus, R. 1989. Understanding and preventing osteoporosis. *Hospital Practice* 24:188–204.

McDonald, R., and Keen, C. 1988. Iron, zinc and magnesium nutrition and athletic performance. *Sports Medicine* 5:171–84.

Mickelsen, O., and Marsh, A. 1989. Calcium requirement and diet. *Nutrition Today* 24:28–32.

Monson, E. 1989. Iron nutrition and absorption: dietary factors which impact iron bioavailability. *Journal of the American Dietetic Association,* 88:786–90.

Newhouse, I., and Clement, D. 1988. Iron status in athletes: An update. *Sports Medicine* 5:337–52.

Pate, R. 1983. Sports anemia: A review of the current research literature. *Physician and Sportsmedicine* 11:115–26.

Risser, W., and Risser, J. 1990. Iron deficiency in adolescents and young adults. *The Physician and Sportsmedicine* 18:December, 86–101.

Rowland, T. 1990. Iron deficiency in the young athlete. *Pediatric Clinics of North America* 37:1153–62.

Scrimshaw, N., and Murray, E. 1988. Lactose intolerance and milk consumption. *American Journal of Clinical Nutrition* 48:1083–1159.

Selby, G. 1991. When does an athlete need iron. *The Physician and Sportsmedicine* 19:April 96–102.

Sharman, I. 1984. Need for micro-nutrient supplementation with regard to physical performance. *International Journal of Sports Medicine* 5 (Suppl):22–24.

Short, S. 1989. Dietary surveys and nutrition knowledge. In: *Nutrition in Exercise and Sport,* eds. J. Hickson and I. Wolinsky. Boca Raton, FL: CRC Press.

Shils, M. Magnesium. 1988. In: *Modern Nutrition in Health and Disease.* eds. R. Goodhart and M. Shils. Philadelphia: Lea & Febiger.

Smith, E., and Gilligan, C. 1989. Osteoporosis, bone mineral and exercise. *American Academy of Physical Education Papers* 22:107–19.

Snow-Harter, C., and Marcus, R. 1991. Exercise, bone mineral density, and osteoporosis. *Exercise and Sport Sciences Reviews* 19:351–88.

Solomons, N. 1988. Zinc and copper. In: *Modern Nutrition in Health and Disease.* eds. R. Goodhart and M. Shils. Philadelphia: Lea & Febiger.

Spencer, H., et al. 1989. Do protein and phosphorus cause calcium loss? *Nutrition Today,* 24:33–35, January/February.

Williams, M. 1986. Minerals and physical performance. In: *Predicting Decrements in Military Performance Due to Inadequate Nutrition.* Washington, DC: National Academy Press.

Specific Studies

Ahlberg, K., et al. 1986. Effect of phosphate loading on cycle ergometer performance. *Medicine and Science in Sports and Exercise* 18:S11.

Anderson, R., et al. 1990. Carbohydrate loading and exercise effects on chromium and zinc losses and serum cortisol and insulin. *FASEB Journal* 4:A777.

Anderson, R., et al. 1986. Strenuous exercise may increase dietary needs for chromium and zinc. In: *Sport, Health and Nutrition,* ed. F. Katch. Champaign, IL: Human Kinetics.

Aruoma, O., et al. 1988. Iron, copper and zinc concentrations in human sweat and plasma: The effect of exercise. *Clinical Chimica Acta,* 177:81–87.

Balaban, E., et al. 1989. The frequency of anemia and iron deficiency in the runner. *Medicine and Science in Sports and Exercise* 21:643–48.

Bilanin, J., et al. 1989. Lower vertebral bone density in male long distance runners. *Medicine and Science in Sports and Exercise* 21:66–70.

Brune, M., et al. 1986. Iron losses in sweat. *American Journal of Clinical Nutrition* 43:438–43.

Cade, R., et al. 1984. Effects of phosphate loading on 2, 3-diphosphoglycerate and maximal oxygen uptake. *Medicine and Science in Sports and Exercise* 16:263–68.

Casoni, I., et al. 1990. Changes in magnesium concentrations in endurance athletes. *International Journal of Sports Medicine* 11:234–37.

Colletti, L., et al. 1989. The effects of muscle-building exercise on bone mineral density of the radius, spine, and hip in young men. *Calcified Tissue International* 45:12–14.

Cortes, C., et al. 1991. Effects of phosphate loading on maximal cycling performance. *Medicine and Science in Sports and Exercise* 23:S76.

Cook, J., et al. 1991. Calcium supplementation: effect on iron absorption. *American Journal of Clinical Nutrition* 53:106–11.

Couzy, F., et al. 1990. Zinc metabolism in the athlete: Influence of training, nutrition, and other factors. *International Journal of Sports Medicine* 11:263–66.

Davies, K., et al. 1982. Muscle mitochondrial bioenergetics, oxygen supply, and work capacity during dietary iron deficiency and repletion. *American Journal of Physiology* 242:E418–27.

Deehr, M., et al. 1990. Effects of different calcium sources on iron absorption in postmenopausal women. *American Journal of Clinical Nutrition* 51:95–99.

Deuster, P., et al. 1989. Zinc status of highly trained women runners and untrained women. *American Journal of Clinical Nutrition* 49:1295–1301.

Dowdy, R., and Burt, J. 1980. Effect of intensive, long-term training on copper and iron nutriture in man. *Federation Proceedings* 39:786.

Drinkwater, B., et al. 1986. Bone mineral density after resumption of menses in amenorrheic athletes. *Journal of American Medical Association* 256:380–82.

Duffy, D., and Conlee, R. 1986. Effects of phosphate loading on leg power and high intensity treadmill exercise. *Medicine and Science in Sports and Exercise* 18:674–77.

Eichner, R., et al. 1989. Intravascular hemolysis in elite college rowers. *Medicine and Science in Sports and Exercise* 21:S78.

Evans, G., and Press, R. 1989. Cholesterol and glucose lowering effect of chromium picolinate. *FASEB Journal* 4:A761.

Gimenez, M., et al. 1988. Serum iron and transferrin during an exhaustive session of interval training. *European Journal of Applied Physiology* 57:154–58.

Hudgins, P., et al. 1990. Effects of iron supplementation on hematologic profile and performance in female endurance athletes. *FASEB Journal* 4:A1197.

Hunt, I., et al. 1989. Bone mineral content in postmenopausal women: Comparison of omnivores and vegetarians. *American Journal of Clinical Nutrition* 50:517–23.

Kreider, R., et al. 1990. Effects of phosphate loading on oxygen uptake, ventilatory anaerobic threshold, and run performance. *Medicine and Science in Sports and Exercise* 22:250–56.

Kreider R., et al. 1991. Effects of phosphate loading on myocardial adaptations to endurance exercise. *FASEB Journal* 5:A1655.

Krotkiewski, M., et al. 1982. Zinc and muscle strength and endurance. *Acta Physiologica Scandinavica* 116:309–11.

Lamanca, J., and Haymes, E. 1989. Effects of dietary iron supplements on endurance. *Medicine and Science in Sports and Exercise* 21:S77.

Lamanca, J., et al. 1988. Sweat iron loss of male and female runners during exercise. *International Journal of Sports Medicine* 9:52–55.

Lindberg, J., et al. 1987. Increased vertebral bone mineral in response to reduced exercise in amenorrheic runners. *Western Journal of Medicine* 146:39–42.

Liu, I., et al. 1983. Hypomagnesemia in a tennis player. *Physician and Sportsmedicine* 11:79–80, May.

Lloyd, T., et al. 1986. Women athletes with menstrual irregularity have increased musculoskeletal injuries. *Medicine and Science in Sports and Exercise* 18:374–79.

Lukaski, H., et al. 1990. Thermogenesis and thermoregulatory function of iron-deficient women without anemia. *Aviation, Space and Environmental Medicine* 61:913–20.

Lukaski, H., et al. 1990. Physical training and copper, iron, and zinc status of swimmers. *American Journal of Clinical Nutrition* 51:1093–99.

Lukaski, H., et al. 1989. Altered energy utilization during exercise in iron deficient women. *Medicine and Science in Sports and Exercise* 21:S43.

Lyle, R., et al. 1991. Effect of oral iron therapy vs increased consumption of muscle foods on hemoglobin in exercising women. *Medicine and Science in Sports and Exercise* 23:S77.

Mannix, E., et al. 1990. Oxygen delivery and cardiac output during exercise following oral phosphate-glucose. *Medicine and Science in Sports and Exercise* 22:341–47.

Matter, M., et al. 1987. The effect of iron and folate therapy on maximal exercise performance in female marathon runners with iron and folate deficiency. *Clinical Science* 72:415–22.

Medeiros, D., et al. 1989. Vitamin and mineral supplementation practices of adults in seven western states. *Journal of the American Dietetic Association* 89:383–86.

Myburgh, K., et al. 1990. Higher bone density and fewer stress fractures in athletes using oral contraceptives. *Medicine and Science in Sports and Exercise* 22:S77.

Newhouse, I., et al. 1989. The effects of prelatent/latent iron deficiency on physical work capacity. *Medicine and Science in Sports and Exercise* 21:263–68.

Ohno, H., et al. 1990. Training effects on blood zinc levels in humans. *Journal of Sports Medicine and Physical Fitness* 30:247–52.

Ormerod, S., et al. 1990. The relationship between weekly mileage and bone density in male runners. *Medicine and Science in Sports and Exercise* 22:S62.

Risser, W., et al. 1988. Iron deficiency in female athletes: its prevalence and impact on performance. *Medicine and Science in Sports and Exercise* 20:116–21.

Rowland, T., et al. 1988. The effect of iron therapy on the exercise capacity of nonanemic iron-deficient adolescent runners. *American Journal of Diseases in Children* 142:165–69.

Schenck, D., et al. 1991. Effects of phosphate loading on 40 km cycling performance. *Medicine and Science in Sports and Exercise* 23:S76.

Schobersberger, W., et al. 1990. Consequences of 6 weeks strength training on red cell O_2 transport and iron status. *European Journal of Applied Physiology* 60:163–68.

Schoene, R., et al. 1983. Iron repletion decreases maximal exercise lactate concentrations in female athletes with minimal iron deficiency anemia. *Journal of Laboratory and Clinical Medicine* 102:306–12.

Schwarzkopf, R., et al. 1986. The effects of iron supplementation on female endurance athletes. *Medicine and Science in Sports and Exercise* 18:S55.

Seiler, D., et al. 1989. Effects of long-distance running on iron metabolism and hematological parameters. *International Journal of Sports Medicine* 10:357–62.

Singh, A., et al. 1990. Zinc and copper status of women by physical activity and menstrual status. *Journal of Sports Medicine and Physical Fitness* 30:29–36.

Smith, E., et al. 1989. Deterring bone loss by exercise intervention in premenopausal and postmenopausal women. *Calcified Tissue International* 44:312–21.

Smith, E., et al. 1989. Calcium supplementation and bone loss in middle-aged women. *American Journal of Clinical Nutrition* 50:833–42.

Snyder, A., et al. 1989. Influence of dietary iron source on measures of iron status among female runners. *Medicine and Science in Sports and Exercise* 21:7–10.

Stewart, I., et al. 1990. Phosphate loading and the effects on VO_2 max in trained cyclists. *Research Quarterly for Exercise and Sport* 61:80–84.

Thompson, D., et al. 1990. Effects of phosphate loading on erythrocyte 2,3-diphosphoglycerate (2,3-DPG), adenosine 5′-triphosphate (ATP), hemoglobin (Hb), and maximal oxygen consumption (VO_2 max). *Medicine and Science in Sports and Exercise* 22:S36.

van Erp-Baart, A., et al. 1989. Nationwide survey on nutritional habits in elite athletes. *International Journal of Sports Medicine* 10 (Suppl 1): S11–S16.

Verde, T., et al. 1982. Sweat composition in exercise and in heat. *Journal of Applied Physiology* 53:1540–45.

Weatherwax, R., et al. 1986. Effects of phosphate loading on bicycle time trial performance. *Medicine and Science in Sports and Exercise* 18:S11–12.

Weight, L., et al. 1988. Vitamin and mineral supplementation: Effect on running performance of trained athletes. *American Journal of Clinical Nutrition* 47:192–95.

Weight, L., et al. 1988. Vitamin and mineral status of trained athletes including the effects of supplementation. *American Journal of Clinical Nutrition* 47:186–91.

Wilhite, J., and Mellion, M. 1990. Occult gastrointestinal bleeding in endurance cyclists. *Physician and Sportsmedicine* 18:75–78.

Key Terms

acclimatization

aldosterone

anhidrotic heat exhaustion

antidiuretic hormone (ADH)

conduction

convection

core temperature

evaporation

exertional heat stroke

extracellular water

glucose–electrolyte solutions (GES)

glucose–polymer solutions (GPS)

heat-balance equation

heat cramps

heat stroke

heat syncope

high blood pressure

homeostasis

hyperhydration

hyperkalemia

hypertension

hyperthermia

hypohydration

hypokalemia

hyponatremia (water intoxication)

hypothermia

insensible perspiration

intercellular water

metabolic water

normohydration

osmolality

radiation

salt-depletion heat exhaustion

shell temperature

sodium bicarbonate

specific heat

tonicity

vascular water

water-depletion heat exhaustion

WBGT Index

Key Concepts

The average adult, who needs 2–3 quarts of water per day, maintains fluid balance primarily by drinking liquids, but substantial amounts of water also are obtained from solid foods in the diet.

Normal water levels in the various body fluid compartments are maintained by a feedback mechanism involving specific receptors for osmotic pressure, the antidiuretic hormone (ADH), and the kidneys.

Water has a number of functions in the body, but its most important benefit for people who exercise is the control of body temperature.

Sodium, chloride, and potassium have vital functions such as generating electrical impulses for contraction of muscles, including the heart. Their concentrations in the body are precisely regulated, and deficiencies or excesses are rare even in cases of heavy sweating.

Humans are heat producers, and their body temperature, regulated by the brain's hypothalamus, is dependent upon the amount of heat they produce and how much they gain from or lose to the environment.

High environmental temperatures, high relative humidity, or radiant heat from the sun can impose a severe heat stress to those who exercise under such conditions.

Exercise can produce significant amounts of heat, but the body temperature usually can be regulated quite effectively by activation of its heat-loss mechanisms, particularly sweating. However, both hyperthermia and dehydration may impair endurance capacity.

Sweat is mainly water with some minerals, primarily sodium and chloride. It is hypotonic compared to the body fluids.

Rehydration with cold water is effective in moderating body temperature during exercise in the heat, but carbohydrate solutions may be equally effective.

Electrolyte replacement generally is not needed during exercise but may be helpful in some situations. Water alone, in combination with a balanced diet, will adequately restore normal electrolyte levels in the body on a day-to-day basis.

Current research suggests that a 5–10 percent solution of glucose, fructose, glucose polymers, or combinations of these different carbohydrates may be effective in athletes who need carbohydrate replacement.

Sodium bicarbonate may be an effective ergogenic aid in exercise tasks that depend primarily upon the lactic acid energy system.

Heat injuries, of which heat stroke is the most potentially dangerous, may be due to increased body core temperature, loss of body fluids, or loss of electrolytes. Some individuals, such as the obese, are more susceptible to heat injury.

The general treatment for heat-stress illnesses is to rest, drink cool liquids, and cool the body. Rapid body cooling is essential in suspected cases of heat stroke.

If you exercise in the heat, you should be aware of signs of impending heat injury. You should also be aware of methods to reduce heat gain to the body and methods to facilitate heat loss.

Acclimatization to exercise in the heat takes about two weeks, but endurance capacity in the heat is still limited somewhat even when one is fully acclimatized.

Excessive sodium chloride intake has been associated with elevated blood pressure in susceptible individuals so current prudent medical advice is to restrict sodium chloride intake to less than 6 grams per day.

Water, Electrolytes, and Temperature Regulation

8

Introduction

Water is a clear, tasteless, odorless fluid. It is a rather simple compound composed of two parts hydrogen and one part oxygen (H_2O). Of all the nutrients essential in the chemistry and functioning of living forms, it is the most important. Although humans may survive about seven days without water under optimal conditions, rapid losses of body water through dehydration may prove fatal in a relatively short time.

Water provides no food energy, but most of the other nutrients essential to life can be used by the human body only because of their reaction with water. Water constitutes the majority of the body weight and provides the medium within which the other nutrients may function. Although water has a number of diverse functions in human metabolism, one of the most important, particularly for the athletic individual, is the regulation of body temperature.

Of the factors that may influence physical performance on any given day, one of the major concerns is the environmental temperature. Anyone who is physically active for prolonged periods is probably aware of the effect that temperature changes have on performance ability. In particular, as the temperature increases, the combination of the environmental heat and the increased body heat from exercise metabolism may disturb body-water supplies and temperature regulation, which at the least may prove detrimental to endurance capacity and at the extreme may have fatal consequences.

Given the seriousness of this topic, the primary focus of this chapter will be upon those problems that may confront you when exercising in the heat and how you may prevent or correct them. Topics covered include the role of water and selected electrolytes in human metabolism, the regulation of body temperature, the effect of fluid and electrolyte losses upon performance, methods of fluid and electrolyte replacement, ergogenic aids, and health-related problems such as heat illnesses and high blood pressure (hypertension).

Water

How much water do you need per day?

The requirement for body water depends on the body weight of the individual. The requirement will vary in different stages of the life cycle. Under normal environmental temperatures and activity levels, the average adult needs about one milliliter of water per Calorie of energy intake. For the average adult female and male, this approximates 2,000 and 2,800 ml, respectively, or about 2 and 3 quarts. This amount will help maintain adequate water balance in the body.

Body-water balance is maintained when the output of body fluids is matched by the input of water. A small amount of water is lost in the feces and through the exhaled air in breathing. **Insensible perspiration** on the skin, which is not visible, is almost pure water and accounts for about 30 percent of body-water losses. Perspiration, or sweat, losses may be increased considerably during exercise and/or hot environmental conditions. Urinary output is the main avenue for water loss. It may increase through the use of diuretics, including alcohol and caffeine, or the use of a high-protein diet that produces urea, which needs to be excreted by the kidney.

Fluid intake by beverages, such as water, soda, milk, coffee, and tea, is the main source of water to replenish losses. However, solid foods also contribute as a water source, and in two different ways. First, food contains water in varying amounts; certain foods such as lettuce, celery, melons, and most fruits contain about 90 percent water, and many others contain more than 60 percent; even bread, an apparently dry food, contains 36 percent water. Second, the metabolism of foods for energy also produces water. Fat, carbohydrate, and protein all produce water when broken down for energy. You may recall the reaction when glucose is metabolized to produce energy, with one of the byproducts being **metabolic water:**

$$C_6H_{12}O_6 + 6O_2 \rightarrow Energy + 6CO_2 + 6H_2O.$$

Table 8.1 summarizes the daily water loss and intake for the maintenance of water balance for an adult female. As shall be seen later, however, these amounts may change drastically under certain conditions.

Where is water stored in the body?

Water is stored in several body compartments but moves constantly between compartments. About 65 percent of the body water is stored inside the body cells as **intracellular water.** The remaining 35 percent is outside the cells and is termed **extracellular water;** the extracellular water is further subdivided into the **intercellular** (interstitial) **water** between or surrounding the cells, the **vascular water** within the blood vessels, and miscellaneous water compartments such as the cerebrospinal fluid. Figure 8.1 represents the distribution of water in the body.

Water is held in the body in conjunction with protein, carbohydrate, and electrolytes. The protein content in the muscles, blood, and other tissues helps bind water to those tissues. Muscle glycogen has considerable amounts of water bound to it (about 3 grams of water per gram of glycogen), which may prove to be an advantage as discussed in Chapter 3. In essence, the metabolism of 350 grams of carbohydrate during exercise will provide nearly one liter of water for body functions. The sodium in the extracellular fluid, including sodium in the circulatory system, attracts water.

Proper water and electrolyte balance within these compartments is of extreme importance to the athletic individual. Fluid shifts such as decreases in blood volume and cellular dehydration, both of which may develop during exercise in the heat, could contribute to the onset of fatigue or heat illness.

Water comprises about 60 percent of the body weight in the average adult male and 50 percent in the adult female, but this percentage may be as low as 40 percent in obese individuals and as high as 70 percent or more in muscular ones. The reason is that fat tissue is low and muscle tissue is high in water content.

How is body water regulated?

Body water is maintained at a normal level through kidney function. Normal body water level is called **normohyration,** or euhydration. Loss of body water results in a state of **hypohydration,** and **hyperhydration** represents a condition in which the body retains excess body fluids. Normal kidneys function very effectively to eliminate excess water during hyperhydration and conserve water during hypohydration.

Because water is so essential to life, it is indeed fortunate that the body possesses an efficient mechanism to maintain proper water balance. **Homeostasis** is the term used to describe the maintenance of a normal internal environment so that the body has the proper distribution and use of water, electrolytes, hormones, and other substances essential

Table 8.1 Daily water loss and intake for water balance in an adult female (60 kg)

Water loss

Urine output	1,100 ml
Water in feces	100 ml
Lungs—exhaled air	200 ml
Skin—insensible perspiration	600 ml
Total	2,000 ml

Water intake

Fluids	1,000 ml
Water in food	700 ml
Metabolic water	300 ml
Total	2,000 ml

for life processes. These homeostatic mechanisms are extremely complex, and a full discussion is beyond the scope of this book. However, in essence, all homeostatic mechanisms work by a series of feedback devices. If these feedback devices are functioning properly, the body usually has no problem in maintaining the normal physical and chemical composition of its fluid compartments.

The main feedback device for the control of body water is the osmolality of the various body fluids. **Osmolality** refers to the amount, or concentration, of dissolved substances, known as solute, in a solution. In the body a number of different substances affect osmolality, including glucose, protein, and several electrolytes, most notably sodium. These substances are dissolved in the body water. One mole of a nonionic substance such as glucose, dissolved in a liter of water is one osmole. However, a mole of a substance that can dissociate into two ions, such as sodium chloride, is equivalent to two osmoles. One millimole of sodium chloride would be two milliosmoles (mOsm).

A term often used in conjunction with osmolality is **tonicity,** which means tension or pressure. When two solutions have the same osmotic pressure they are said to be isosmotic or, more commonly, isotonic. Iso means "same." When two solutions with different solute concentrations are compared, the one with the higher osmotic pressure is called hypertonic and the other is hypotonic.

When two solutions with different solute concentrations are separated by permeable membrane, as in the human body between the fluid compartments, a potential pressure difference may develop between the two that will allow for water movement. This pressure is known as osmotic pressure,

Figure 8.1.
Body-water compartments.
There is a constant
interchange among the
different body-water
compartments. The water
inside the body cells, the
intracellular water, is
important for cell functions.
The other three
compartments are known
collectively as the
extracellular water.
Decreases in blood volume
may adversely affect
endurance capacity.

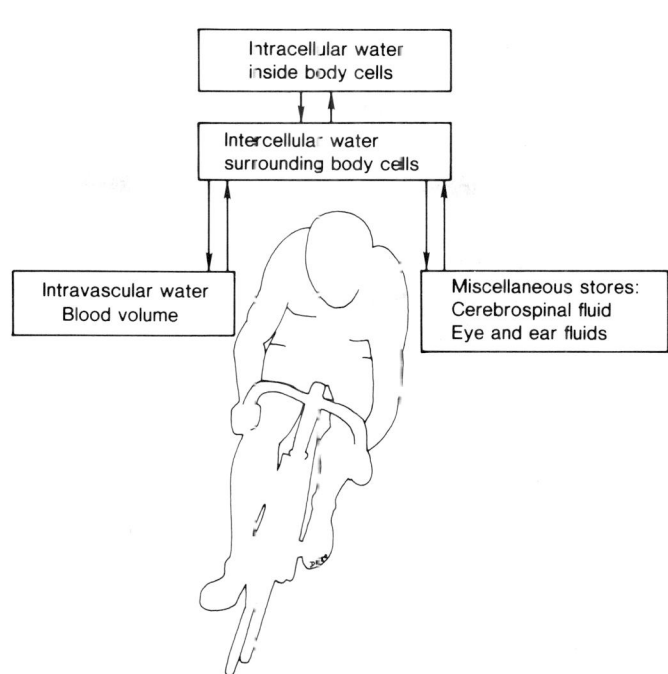

and the water moves across the membrane from the hypotonic solution (low solute concentration and high water content) to the hypertonic solution (high solute concentration and low water content). In essence, high solute concentrations create high osmotic pressures and tend to draw water into their compartments. Figure 8.2 depicts this mechanism between the blood and the body cells.

To briefly illustrate the feedback mechanism for control of body water, let us look at what happens when you become dehydrated owing to excessive body-water losses or lowered water intake. The blood then becomes more concentrated, or hypertonic. Because maintenance of a normal blood volume is of prime importance, the blood tends to draw water from the body cells. Certain cells in the hypothalamus, called osmoreceptors, are sensitive to changes in osmotic pressure. These cells react to the more concentrated body fluids by stimulating the release of a hormone from the pituitary gland, the so-called master gland of the body. This hormone is called the **antidiuretic hormone** (*ADH*). The ADH travels by the blood to the kidneys and directs them to reabsorb more water. Hence, urinary output of water is diminished considerably. During hyperhydration, which would produce a hypotonic condition in the body fluids, a reverse process would occur leading to increased water excretion. As we shall see below, other hormones that influence sodium balance in the body also help regulate water balance.

The osmoreceptors and other mechanisms also may stimulate the sensation of thirst, which is usually a good guide to body water needs and is effective in restoring body water to normal on a day-to-day basis. However, thirst may not be an accurate indicator of the need for water replacement during exercise in a hot environment.

What are the major functions of water in the body?

Water is essential if the other nutrients are to function properly within the human body; it is the solvent for life. It has a number of diverse functions that may be summarized as follows:

1. Water provides the essential building material for cell protoplasm, the fundamental component of all living matter.
2. Because water cannot be compressed, it serves to protect key body tissues such as the spinal cord and brain.
3. Water is essential in the control of the osmotic pressure in the body, or the maintenance of a proper balance between water and the electrolytes. Any major changes in the electrolyte concentration may adversely affect cellular function. A serious departure from normal osmotic pressure cannot be tolerated by the body for long.
4. Water is the main constituent of blood, the major transportation mechanism in the body

Figure 8.2.
Osmosis and tonicity.
A. When the extracellular fluid contains more electrolytes or other osmotic substances, it is hypertonic to the intracellular fluid. In this case water will flow from the interior of the cell to the outside, or to an area of greater osmotic pressure.
B. When the intracellular fluid contains more electrolytes or greater osmotic pressure, water will flow into the cell from the extracellular fluid.

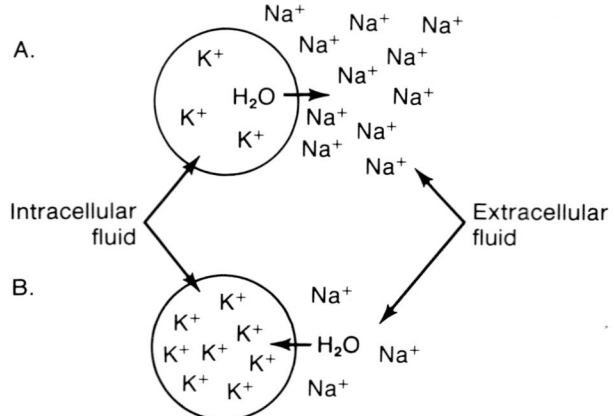

for conveying oxygen, nutrients, hormones, and other compounds to the cells for their use, and waste products of metabolism away from the cells to organs such as the lungs and kidneys for excretion from the body.

5. Water is essential for the proper functioning of our senses. Hearing waves are transmitted by fluid in the inner ear. Fluid in the eye is involved in the reflection of light for proper vision. For the taste and smelling senses to function, the foods and odors need to be dissolved in water.

6. Of primary importance to the active individual is the role that water plays in the regulation of body temperature. Water is the major constituent of sweat, and through its evaporation from the surface of the skin, it can help dissipate excess body heat.

Of all the nutrients, water is the most important to the physically active person and is one of the few that may have beneficial effects on performance when used in supplemental amounts before or during exercise. Hence, the athletic individual should know what is necessary to help maintain proper fluid balance, a topic covered in detail later in this chapter.

Electrolytes

What is an electrolyte?

An **electrolyte** is defined as a substance which, in solution, conducts an electric current. The solution itself may be referred to as an electrolyte solution. Acids, bases, and salts are common electrolytes, and they usually dissociate into ions, particles carrying either a positive (cation) or a negative (anion) electric charge. The major electrolytes in the body fluids are sodium, potassium, chloride, bicarbonate, sulfate, magnesium, and calcium. Electrolytes can act at the cell membrane and generate electrical current, such as in a nerve impulse. Electrolytes can also function in other ways, activating enzymes to control a variety of metabolic activities in the cell. In the last chapter we covered some of the important metabolic functions of calcium, phosphorus, and magnesium; in this chapter the focus is on sodium, chloride, and potassium.

In later sections we shall look at the interaction of these electrolytes with exercise in warm environmental conditions, a possible ergogenic effect of certain sodium salts (comparable to sodium phosphate discussed in the last chapter), and their role in the etiology of high blood pressure. But first, let us briefly cover the function of each of these electrolytes in the human body.

Sodium (Na)

Sodium is a mineral element also known as natrium, from which the symbol *Na* is derived. It is one of the principal positive ions, or electrolytes, in the body fluids. The estimated minimum requirement for sodium in adults is 500 milligrams. Common table salt (sodium chloride) is about 40 percent sodium, so only about 1,250 milligrams (1.25 grams) is needed to supply the minimum requirement. In the National Research Council book *Diet and Health*, the upper recommended intake is 2.4 grams of sodium per day, which amounts to 6 grams of table salt. There is no USRDA for sodium.

Sodium is distributed widely in nature but is found in rather small amounts in most natural foods. However, significant amounts of salt, and hence sodium, are usually added from the salt shaker for flavor. One teaspoon of salt contains about 2,000 milligrams of sodium. Moreover, processing techniques add significant amounts of salt to the foods we buy. For example, a serving of fresh or frozen green peas contains only 2 milligrams of sodium, but increases to 240 milligrams in the canning process. In general, natural foods are low in sodium whereas processed foods are relatively high. Because of health concerns for some individuals with high-sodium diets, food manufacturers have been reducing the salt content in some of their products. Nevertheless, researchers have reported that the average American consumes about 10–12 (4–4.8 grams of sodium) grams of salt per day, approximately 3 grams from natural foods, 3–5 grams from processed foods, and 4 grams from the salt shaker. Table 8.2 highlights the sodium content in several foods within the major food groups. Note the difference in salt content between fresh and processed foods.

Sodium is an important element in a number of body functions. As the principal electrolyte in the extracellular fluids, it serves primarily to help maintain normal body-fluid balance and osmotic pressure. In this regard it is essential in the control of normal blood pressure through its effect on the blood volume. The role of sodium in the etiology of high blood pressure is discussed in a later section.

In conjunction with several other electrolytes, sodium is critical for nerve impulse transmission and muscle contraction. It is also a component of several compounds, such as sodium bicarbonate, that help maintain normal acid-base balance and, as noted in a later section, may be an effective ergogenic aid.

Because the maintenance of normal blood pressure is critical to life, the body has an effective regulatory feedback mechanism allowing for a wide range of dietary sodium intake. If the sodium concentration decreases in the blood, a series of complex reactions leads to the secretion of **aldosterone,** a hormone produced in the adrenal gland, which stimulates the kidney to retain more sodium. On the other hand, excesses of serum sodium will lead to decreased aldosterone production and increased excretion of sodium by the kidney in the urine. Other hormones, notably ADH, help maintain normal sodium equilibrium in the body fluids.

Because this regulatory mechanism is so effective, deficiency states due to inadequate dietary intake are not common. Indeed, humans even have a natural appetite for salt, assuring adequate sodium intake and sodium balance over time. On the other hand, excessive losses of sodium from the body, usually induced by prolonged sweating while exercising in the heat, may lead to short-term deficiencies that may be debilitating to the athletic individual. These problems are discussed below under the headings *fluid and electrolyte replacement* and *health aspects.*

Table 8.2   Sodium content of common foods

Food exchange item	Amount	Sodium (mg)
Milk		
Low fat milk	1 c	120
Cottage cheese		
Creamed	½ c	320
Unsalted	½ c	30
Cheese, American	1 oz	445
Vegetables		
Beans, cooked fresh	1 oz	5
Beans, canned	1 oz	150
Pickles, dill	1 medium	900
Potato, baked	1 medium	6
Fruits		
Banana	1 medium	1
Orange	1 medium	1
Bread/starch		
Bread, whole wheat	1 slice	130
Bran flakes	¾ c	340
Oatmeal, cooked	1 c	175
Pretzels	1 oz	890
Meat		
Luncheon meats	1 oz	450
Frankfurter	1 medium	495
Chicken	3 oz	40
Beef, steak	3 oz	70
Pork sausage	1 medium link	170
Tuna, in oil	3 oz	800
Fish (cod, flounder)	3 oz	100
Deviled crab, frozen	1 c	2085
Fats		
Butter, salted	1 tsp	50
Margarine, salted	1 tsp	50
Canned foods and prepared entrees		
Chop suey, canned	1 c	1050
Spaghetti, canned	1 c	1220
Turkey dinner, frozen	1	1735
Chicken noodle soup	5 oz	655
Condiments		
Mustard	1 tbsp	195
Tomato catsup	1 tbsp	155
Soy sauce	1 tbsp	1320

As you can see in this table, the sodium content of foods can vary greatly. In general, canned and processed foods have a much higher sodium content than do fresh foods. Eat fresh meats, fruits, vegetables, and bread products whenever possible, and prepare them with little or no salt. Avoid highly salted foods like pickles, pretzels, soy sauce, and others. Look for low-sodium labels when shopping for canned foods.

Source: U.S. Department of Agriculture.

Foods with high salt (sodium) content should be reduced in the diet. Be aware of foods that have large amounts of hidden sodium.

(David Corona)

Chloride (Cl)

Chloride is the major negative ion in the extracellular fluids. The estimated daily adult minimum requirement for chloride is 750 milligrams. There is no USRDA for chloride.

Chloride is distributed in a variety of foods. Its dietary intake is closely associated with that of sodium, notably in the form of common table salt, which is 60 percent chloride.

Chloride ions have a variety of functions in the human body. They work with sodium in the regulation of body-water balance and electrical potentials across cell membranes. They also are involved in the formation of hydrochloric acid in the stomach, which is necessary for certain digestive processes.

Under normal circumstances chloride deficiency is rather rare. However, because the losses of sodium and chloride in sweat are directly proportional, the symptoms of chloride loss during excessive dehydration through sweating parallel those of sodium loss. The effects of electrolyte losses and replacement, including chloride, on physical performance and health are covered in later sections of this chapter.

Potassium (K)

Potassium is a mineral element also known as kalium, from which the symbol K is derived. It is a positive ion. The estimated daily adult minimum requirement for potassium is 2,000 milligrams. In *Diet and Health,* an increase in potassium intake to about 3,500 mg per day is recommended. There is no USRDA for potassium.

Potassium is found in most foods and is especially abundant in bananas, citrus fruits, fresh vegetables, milk, meat, and fish. Table 8.3 provides some data on the potassium content of several common foods in the major food groups.

As the major electrolyte inside the body cells, potassium works in close association with sodium and chloride in the maintenance of body fluids and in the generation of electrical impulses in the nerves and the muscles, including the heart muscle. Potassium also plays an important role in the energy processes in the muscle, for it helps in the transport of glucose into the muscle cells, the storage of glycogen, and the production of high-energy compounds.

Potassium balance, like sodium balance is also regulated by aldosterone. A high serum potassium level stimulates the release of aldosterone from the adrenal cortex, leading to an increased excretion of potassium by the kidneys into the urine. A decrease in serum potassium levels elicits a drop in aldosterone secretion and hence a greater conservation of potassium by the kidney. Because a potassium imbalance in the body may have serious health consequences, potassium regulation is quite precise. Deficiencies or excessive accumulation are extremely rare under normal circumstances.

Although potassium deficiencies are rare, they may occur under certain conditions such as during fasting, diarrhea, and the use of diuretics. In such cases **hypokalemia,** or low serum potassium levels, could lead to muscular weakness and even cardiac arrest due to a decreased ability to generate nerve

Table 8.3 Potassium content in some common foods in the major food exchanges

Food	Amount	Milligrams of potassium
Milk		
Skim milk	8 ounce glass	410
Yogurt, lowfat	1 cup	530
Cheese, cheddar	1 ounce	28
Meat		
Chicken breast	1 ounce	70
Beef, lean	1 ounce	100
Fish, flounder	1 ounce	160
Bread/starch		
Bread, whole wheat	1 slice	65
Cereal, Cheerios	1 ounce	110
Fruit		
Banana	1 medium	460
Orange	1 average	260
Apple	1 average	35
Vegetables		
Potato, baked	1 average	780
Broccoli	1 stalk	270
Carrot	1 medium	275

impulses. Several deaths of individuals on unbalanced liquid-protein fasting diets several years ago were associated with potassium deficiencies.

Excessive body potassium stores also are not very common, occurring mainly in conjunction with several disease states or in individuals who overdose on potassium supplements. **Hyperkalemia,** or excessive potassium in the blood, may disturb electrical impulses, causing cardiac arrhythmias and possible death. For this reason, individuals should never take potassium supplements in large doses without the consent of a physician.

In theory, a potassium deficiency could adversely affect physical performance capacity. The effect of exercise on potassium losses and the need for potassium supplementation in athletic individuals have therefore been studied by several investigators. The role of potassium in the etiology of high blood pressure has also been studied. The results of this research are presented in later sections of this chapter.

Regulation of Body Temperature

What is the normal body temperature?

The temperature of different body parts may vary considerably. The skin may be very cold, but the body internally is much warmer. When we speak of body temperature, we mean the internal, or **core temperature,** and not the external shell temperature. **Shell temperature,** which represents the temperature of the skin and the tissues directly under it, varies considerably depending upon the surrounding environmental temperature.

In humans, normal body temperature is approximately 98.6°F (37°C). This core temperature may be measured in a variety of ways, but the two most common methods are orally and rectally. Normal body temperature at rest is relatively constant and may range from 97–99°F (36.1–37.2°C). At rest the rectal temperature is normally about 0.5–1.0°F higher than the oral temperature; however, following a road race one study reported that the rectal temperature was 5.5°F higher than the oral temperature, suggesting that an oral reading may not be an accurate reflection of the true body temperature in an assessment of heat injury.

Humans can survive a range of core temperatures for a short time, but optimal physiological functioning usually occurs within a range of 97–104°F (36.1–40.0°C). A variety of factors may affect the body temperature, but here we are concerned with the effect exercise has on the core temperature and how our body adjusts to help maintain heat balance.

What are the major factors that influence body temperature?

Humans are warm-blooded animals and are able to maintain a constant body temperature under varying environmental temperatures. To do this, the body must constantly make adjustments to either gain or lose heat.

Humans are heat-producing machines. The basal metabolic heat production is provided through normal burning (oxidation) of the three basic foodstuffs in the body—carbohydrate, fat, and protein. A higher basal metabolic rate, infectious diseases, shivering, and exercise are several factors that might increase heat production.

The human body also has a variety of means to lose heat. Heat loss is governed by four physical means—conduction, convection, radiation, and evaporation:

Conduction——Heat is transferred from the body by direct physical contact, as when you sit on a cold seat.

Convection——Heat is transferred by movement of air or water over the body.

Radiation——Heat energy radiates from the body into space.

Evaporation——Heat is lost from the body when it is used to convert sweat to a vapor, known as the heat of vaporization.

Under normal environmental temperatures, the body heat is transported from the core to the shell by way of conduction and convection, the blood being the main carrier of the heat. The vast majority of the heat escapes from the body by radiation and convection, with a smaller amount being carried away by the evaporation of insensible perspiration. A cooler environment, increased air movement such as a cool wind, increased blood circulation to the skin, or an increased radiation surface would facilitate heat loss.

On the other hand, under certain environmental conditions, such as exercising in the sunlight on a hot day, some of these processes may be reversed with the body gaining heat instead of losing it. For example, radiant energy from the sun could add heat to the body.

The well-known **heat balance equation** may be used to illustrate these interrelationships:

$$H = M \pm W \pm C \pm R - E$$

where H = heat balance, M = resting metabolic rate, W = work done (exercise), C = conduction and convection, R = radiation, E = evaporation.

If any of these factors governing heat production or heat loss are not balanced by an opposite reaction, heat balance will be lost and the body will deviate from its normal value. During exercise, W increases heat production. Hence, compensating adjustments in C, R, and E must be made. (See Figure 8.3.)

How does the body regulate its own temperature?

The hypothalamus is an important structure in the brain that is involved in the control of a wide variety of physiological functions, including body temperature. The hypothalamus is thought to function pretty much like a thermostat in your house. If your house gets too cold, the heat comes on; if it gets too warm the air conditioning system starts. The human body makes similar adjustments.

The temperature regulating center in your hypothalamus receives input from several sources. First, receptors in the skin can detect temperature changes and send impulses to the hypothalamus. Second, the temperature of the blood can directly affect the hypothalamus as it flows through that structure.

In general, if the skin receptors detect a warmer temperature or the blood temperature rises, the body will make adjustments in an attempt to lose heat. Two major adjustments may occur. First, the blood will be channeled closer to the skin so that the heat from within may get closer to the outside and radiate away more easily. Second, sweating will begin and evaporation of the sweat will carry away heat from the body.

If the skin receptors detect a colder temperature or the blood temperature is lowered, then the body will react to conserve heat or increase heat production. First, the blood will be shunted away from the skin to the central core part of the body. This decreases heat loss by radiation and helps keep the vital organs at the proper temperature. Second, shivering may begin. Shivering is nothing more than the contraction of muscles, which produces extra heat by increasing the metabolic rate. Figure 8.4 is a simplified schematic of temperature control.

The hypothalamus is usually very effective in controlling the body temperature. However, certain conditions may threaten temperature control. For example, an individual who falls into cold water will lose body heat rapidly, for water is an excellent conductor for heat. Such a situation may lead to **hypothermia** (low body temperature) and a rapid loss of temperature control. Hypothermia may also develop in slower runners during the latter part of a road race under cold, wet, and windy environmental conditions when heat is lost more rapidly than it is produced through exercise. Muscular incoordination and mental confusion are early signs of hypothermia.

On the other hand, the most prevalent threat to the athletic individual is **hyperthermia,** or the increased body temperature that occurs with exercise in a warm or hot environment. Hyperthermia is one of the major factors limiting physical performance and one of the most dangerous.

Figure 8.3.
Sources of heat gain and heat loss to the body during exercise. See text for details.

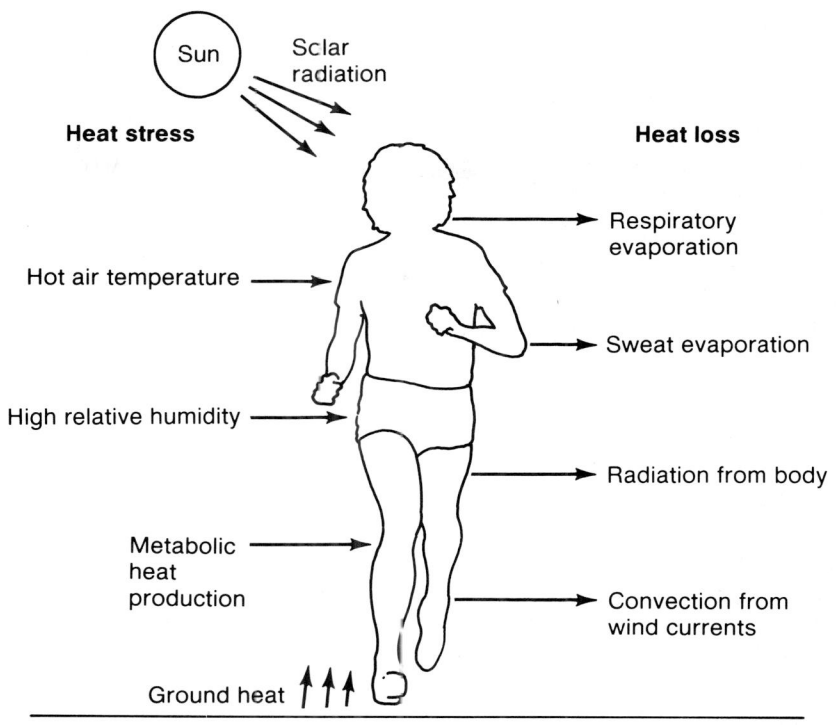

Figure 8.4.
Simplified schematic of body temperature control. The temperature of the blood returning from the muscles and the skin stimulates the temperature regulation center in the hypothalamus, as do nerve impulses from the warmth and cold receptors in the skin. An overall cold effect will elicit a constriction of the blood vessels near the body surface and muscular shivering, thus helping to conserve body heat. An overall warmth effect will elicit a dilation of blood vessels near the skin and sweating, thus increasing the loss of body heat.

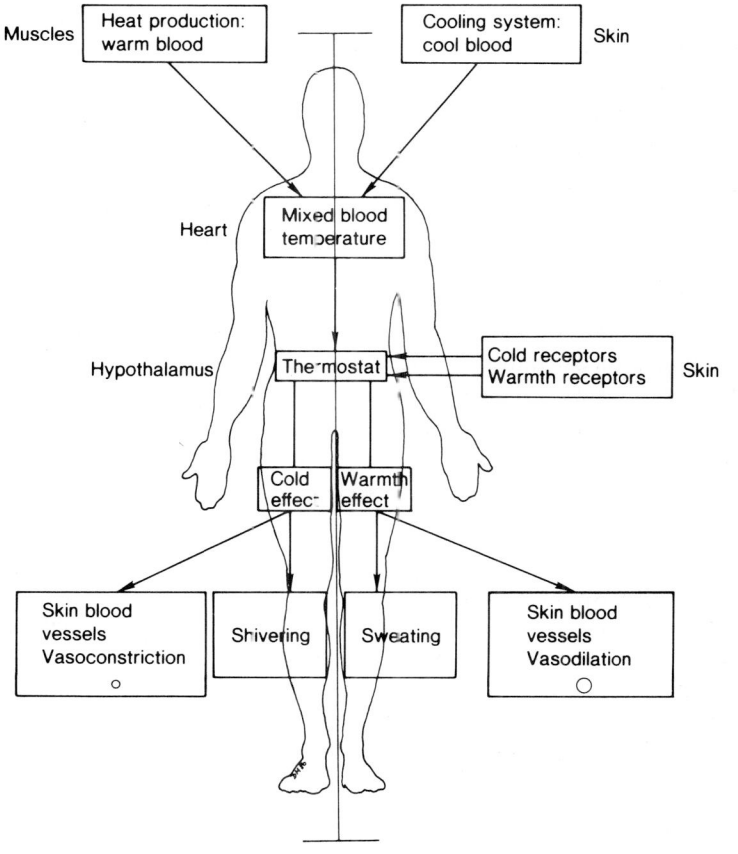

Figure 8.5.
A typical setup for measurement of the wet-bulb globe temperature index (WBGT). The dry bulb measures air temperature, the wet bulb indirectly measures humidity, and the black bulb measures the radiant heat from the sun.

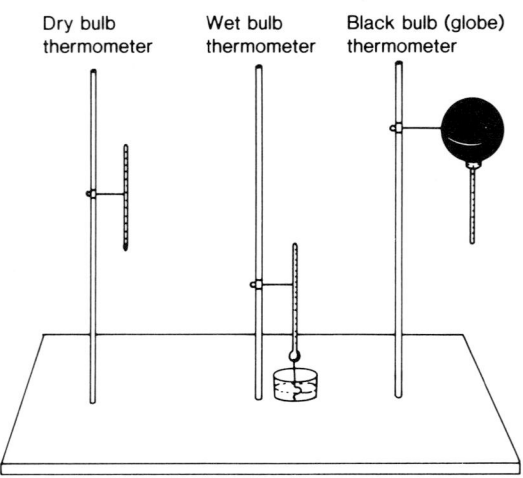

Dry bulb thermometer Wet bulb thermometer Black bulb (globe) thermometer

What environmental conditions may predispose an athletic individual to hyperthermia?

The interaction of four environmental factors are important determinants of the heat stress imposed on an active individual:

1. Air temperature. Caution should be advised when the air temperature is 80°F (27°C) or above. However, if the relative humidity is high, lower air temperatures, even 60°F, may pose a heat stress during exercise.
2. Relative humidity. As the water content in the air increases, the relative humidity rises. The increased humidity impairs the ability of the body sweat to evaporate and thus may restrict the effectiveness of the body's main cooling system when exercising. Caution should be used when the relative humidity exceeds 50–60 percent, especially with warmer temperatures.
3. Air movement. Still air limits heat carried away by convection. Even a small breeze may help keep body temperature near normal by helping to evaporate sweat.
4. Radiation. Radiant heat from the sun may create an additional heat load.

Some useful guidelines have been developed taking these four factors into consideration. The wet-bulb globe temperature (WBGT) thermometer, illustrated in Figure 8.5, measures all four. Small hand-held WBGT thermometers are available. The dry-bulb thermometer (DB) measures air temperature, the globe thermometer (G) measures radiant heat, and the wet-bulb thermometer (WB) evaluates relative humidity and air movement as they influence air temperature. The **WBGT Index** is computed as follows:

WBGT Index = 0.7 WB + 0.2 G + 0.1 DB.

For example, if the WB reads 70, the G is 100, and the DB is 80, then the WBGT = (0.7 × 70) + (0.2 × 100) + (0.1 × 80) = 77°F.

An alternative procedure to calculate the WBGT Index is this formula:

WBGT Index = 0.576 DB + 0.393 environmental water-vapor pressure + 3.94.

The environmental water-vapor pressure may be obtained from a meteorologist at a local airport, radio station or television station.

The American College of Sports Medicine (ACSM) has published a position statement with guidelines for the prevention of heat illnesses during distance running. These guidelines, which also are applicable to other athletes exercising in the heat, are incorporated in the last section of this chapter. A modified version of the ACSM warnings based on the WBGT is presented in Table 8.4.

How does exercise affect body temperature?

As noted in Chapter 2, exercise increases the metabolic rate and the production of energy. Under a normal mechanical efficiency ratio of 20–25 percent, the remaining 80–75 percent of energy is released as heat. The total amount of heat produced in the body depends on the intensity and duration of the exercise. A more intense exercise will produce heat faster, while the longer the exercise lasts the more total heat is produced.

For illustrative purposes only, let us look at a hypothetical example of the body temperature changes that might occur in an exercising individual who was unable to dissipate heat. A physically conditioned person may be able to perform in a steady

Table 8.4   Guidelines for preventing heat illness in runners and other athletes

Flag color/WBGT	Risk	Warnings*
Green/64°F (18°C)	Low	Although the risk is low, heat injury still can occur; caution still needed.
Yellow/64–72°F (18–22°C)	Moderate	Runners should closely monitor for signs of impending heat injury and slow pace if necessary; in long races, heat stress may increase during the course of the race if run in morning to early afternoon.
Red/73–82°F (23–28°C)	High	Runner must slow running pace and be very aware of warning signs of heat injury. Do not run if unfit, ill, unacclimatized, or sensitive to heat and humidity.
Black/above 82°F (28°C)	Extremely high	Even with considerable slowing of pace, great discomfort will be experienced. Races should not start under these conditions.

WBGT = Wet bulb globe temperature
These precautions should be noted not only by the active individual for safety, but also by those who conduct physical training sessions or athletic competition for others. Commercial devices are available to quickly and accurately measure the WBGT and should be used to help assess environmental heat stress and modify training or competition as recommended. For those who wish to construct an inexpensive WBGT device, consult the reference cited for Spickard at the end of this chapter.

*Although these warnings are expressed in regard to running, they are also relevant to other sports involving prolonged exercise in the heat, such as soccer, field hockey, and football.

state for prolonged periods. If a normal-sized male, 154 lbs or 70 kg, were to jog for about an hour he could expend approximately 900 C. Assuming a mechanical efficiency rate of 20 percent, 80 percent, or 720 C, would be released in the body as heat. **Specific heat** is defined as the heat in Calories required to raise the temperature of 1 kilogram of a substance by 1 degree C. Because the specific heat of the body is 0.83, that is, 0.83 C will raise 1 kg of the body 1°C, then 58 C (70 kg × 0.83) would raise the body temperature 1°C in this person. Thus, if this excess heat were not dissipated, his body temperature would increase over 12.4°C (720 / 58), or over 22°F, resulting in a body temperature of 120°F, a fatal condition. Although the core temperature does rise during exercise, it rarely hits these extreme levels. The average core temperature during exercise, even during moderately warm temperatures, may reach about only 102.2–104.9°F (39–40°C). This is because of the body's cooling system.

How is body heat dissipated during exercise?
During exercise in a cold or cool environment, body heat is lost mainly through radiation and convection via the air movement around the body. Some evaporation of sweat may also contribute to maintenance of heat balance.

However, when the environmental temperature rises, the evaporation of sweat becomes the main means of controlling an excessive rise in the core temperature. Only sweat that evaporates has a cooling effect. One liter of sweat, if perfectly evaporated, will dissipate about 580 C. In our example

above, the evaporation of 1.24 liter of sweat (720 / 580) would prevent a rise in the core temperature. However, the evaporation of sweat from the body is not perfect, as sweat can drip off the body and not carry away body heat, so more than 1.24 liter may be lost. If we assume that 2.0 liter were lost, then this individual would have lost 4.4 lbs of body fluids during the one-hour run; 1 liter of sweat weighs 1 kg or 2.2 lbs. It should be noted that sweat rates may vary considerably between individuals. Ron Maughan, an environmental physiologist from Scotland, studied two marathoners who completed the race in the same time and had the same fluid intake; one lost only 1 percent of his body weight while the other lost 6 percent.

Under most warm environmental circumstances, the evaporative mechanisms and the body's natural warning signals are able to keep the core temperature during exercise below 105°F (40.5°C) and prevent heat injuries. However, an excessive rise in the core temperature, above 105°F, or excessive fluid and electrolyte losses, may lead to diminished performance or serious thermal injury.

Fluid and Electrolyte Losses

How does environmental heat affect physical performance?
Although performance in strength, power, or speed events that last less than a minute does not appear to be affected adversely by warm environmental conditions, performance in more prolonged aerobic

endurance activities is normally worse when compared to performance in cooler temperatures. A sprinter may not see any change in speed; a runner in a 5-kilometer race (3.1 miles) will have to slow his or her normal pace somewhat, while a marathoner will suffer a considerable impairment in performance.

In the 5-kilometer race the runner will be performing at a rather high metabolic rate and thus will be producing heat rapidly. To control an excessive rise in body temperature, the skin blood flow will increase so as to dissipate heat to the environment. This shifting of blood to the skin will result in a lesser proportion of blood, and hence oxygen, being delivered to the active musculature. Both Nadel and Young found that under these conditions cellular metabolism changes somewhat, with greater reliance on muscle glycogen as a fuel and a greater production of lactic acid if the runner attempts to maintain the pace normally done in a cool environment. This may result in the runner performing above the steady-state threshold with a greater sensation of stress. In some individuals, the circulatory adjustments may not be adequate and the body temperature will rise rapidly, leading to hyperthermia and symptoms of weakness. Because of these changes, and possibly others not yet identified, the runner normally must slow the pace.

Although the 5-kilometer runner will sweat heavily, the duration of the event is usually short, so an excessive loss of body fluids does not occur. However, in more prolonged events, athletes may suffer the problems noted above plus the adverse effects of dehydration. Marathoners may lose 5 percent or more of their body weight (mostly water) during a race, which may not only deteriorate performance but have serious health consequences as well.

How do dehydration and hypohydration affect physical performance?

The effect of dehydration on physical performance has been studied from two different viewpoints. Voluntary dehydration is often used by athletes such as wrestlers and boxers to qualify for lower weight classes prior to competition. In other athletes, dehydration occurs involuntarily during training or competition as the body attempts to maintain temperature homeostasis.

Dehydration, leading to hypohydration, may be induced in a variety of ways. Voluntary dehydration techniques used by wrestlers have included exercise-induced sweating, thermal-induced sweating such as the use of saunas, diuretics to increase urine losses, and decreased intake of fluids and food. Involuntary dehydration usually occurs via heavy sweat losses during prolonged exercise in the heat.

Much of the research with voluntary dehydration has been conducted with wrestlers. Evaluation criteria have emphasized factors such as strength, power, local muscular endurance, and performance of anaerobic exercise tasks designed to mimic wrestling. Not all studies are in agreement. Many studies conducted in this area suggest that hypohydration, even up to levels of 8 percent of the body weight, will not affect these physical performance factors in events involving brief, intense muscular effort. On the other hand, many other studies have reported significant impairments in such tasks, with body weight losses of 4 percent or higher. The adverse effects on strength are not consistent, but anaerobic muscular endurance tasks lasting longer than 20–30 seconds have been impaired when subjects were hypohydrated. Suggested mechanisms of impairment include loss of potassium from the muscle and higher muscle temperatures during exercise. It should also be noted that there is no evidence that hypohydration improves performance in these exercise tasks.

The adverse effects of dehydration are most severe in aerobic endurance performance. Hypohydration of more than 2 percent of the body weight usually will lead to decrements in performance. The decrease in performance also appears to be proportional to the degree of hypohydration, with greater fluid losses leading to greater impairment. Michael Sawka and Kent Pandolf have suggested that the deterioration in aerobic endurance performance appears related to adverse effects on cardiovascular functions and temperature regulation. They noted that hypohydration would significantly decrease maximal aerobic power by 4–8 percent with a 3 percent weight loss during exercise in a neutral environment, but the impairment would be even greater in a hot environment. Also, a reduction in the plasma volume may reduce cardiac output and blood flow to the skin and the muscles. Reductions in skin blood flow have been shown to lower the sweat rate and raise the core temperature.

Other factors may also contribute to suboptimal performance, including disturbed fluid and electrolyte balance in the muscle cells, affecting energy processes, or adverse effects of hyperthermia upon mental processes.

Because the maximal sweat rate for a trained athlete is about 2–3 liters per hour, it will not take long to incur a 2–3 percent decrease in body weight. Two liters is the equivalent of 4.4 pounds (1 liter = 1 kg = 2.2 pounds), so a 150-pound runner could

Body-water loss can be very rapid during exercise in warm or hot weather.

(Michael DiSpezio)

experience a loss of 3 percent body weight in one hour (4.4/150 = .03; .03 × 100 = 3%). Some athletes, like football players, may lose 5–6 kg (11–13 pounds) over a day with multiple daily workouts. As discussed below, excessive dehydration may not only impair one's physical performance, but possibly also one's health.

What is the composition of sweat?

The human body contains two different types of sweat glands. The apocrine sweat glands are located in hairy areas of the body, such as the armpits, and secrete an oily mixture to decrease friction. We are all aware of the odor that may be generated from these sweat glands under certain conditions. Our concern here is with the eccrine sweat glands, about

2–3 million over the surface of the body, which are primarily involved in temperature regulation.

Sweat is mostly water, about 99 percent, but a number of major electrolytes and other nutrients may be found in varying amounts. Sweat is hypotonic in comparison to the fluids in the body. This means that the concentration of electrolytes is lower in sweat than in the body fluids.

The composition of sweat may vary somewhat from individual to individual and will even be different in the same individual when acclimatized to the heat, as contrasted to the unacclimatized state. The major differences are the concentrations of the solid matter in the sweat, the electrolytes or salts.

The major electrolytes found in sweat are sodium and chloride, because sweat is derived from the extracellular fluids, such as the plasma and intercellular fluids, which are high in these electrolytes. You may actually note the formation of dried salt on your skin or clothing after prolonged sweating. Carl Gisolfi has reported that the concentration of salt in sweat is variable but averages 2.6 grams (45 mEq) per liter of sweat during exercise with sweat losses of about 1–1.5 liters per hour. Other minerals lost in small amounts include potassium, magnesium, calcium, iron, copper, and zinc. Small quantities of nitrogen (N), amino acids, and some of the water-soluble vitamins also are present.

Is excessive sweating likely to create an electrolyte deficiency?

There are two ways to look at this question. What happens to electrolyte balance during exercise? And, what happens during the recovery period on a day-to-day basis?

The concentration of electrolytes in the blood during exercise with excessive sweating has been studied under laboratory conditions as well as immediately after endurance events such as the Ironman Triathlon and a marathon run. In general, exercise raises the concentration of several electrolytes in the blood. Sodium and potassium concentrations are elevated; the sodium increase may be due to greater body-water loss than sodium loss, so a concentration effect occurs. The potassium may leak from the muscle tissue to the blood, thereby increasing the blood concentration of this ion. Chloride and calcium ion concentrations remain relatively unchanged during exercise. Magnesium levels usually fall, possibly because the active muscle cells and other tissues need this ion during exercise and it passes from the blood into the tissues. During acute, prolonged bouts of exercise then, even in marathon running, it appears that an electrolyte deficiency will not occur.

This is not to say that electrolyte replacement is not important. As we shall see in the next section, an electrolyte imbalance may occur in the body during extremely prolonged endurance events, such as ultramarathoning and Ironman–type triathlons, if proper fluid replacement techniques are not used. Moreover, what happens during the recovery period after excessive sweating may contribute to an electrolyte deficiency. Prolonged sweating has been shown to decrease the body content of sodium and chloride by 5–7 percent, while potassium levels dropped about 1 percent. If these electrolytes are not replaced daily, an electrolyte deficiency may occur over time.

As noted in Chapter 7, certain athletes, especially those who lose large amounts of sweat, may need to increase their dietary intake of certain trace minerals, such as iron and zinc, to replace losses during exercise. The next section deals with the need for water and electrolyte replacement.

Fluid and Electrolyte Replacement

Which is most important to replace during exercise—water, electrolytes, or carbohydrate?

In the 1960s Robert Cade, a scientist working at the University of Florida, developed a fluid replacement for athletes that was designed to restore some of the nutrients lost in sweat. This product was eventually marketed as Gatorade (Gator is the nickname for University of Florida athletes) and was the first of many **glucose–electrolyte solutions (GES)**. More recently a number of **glucose–polymer solutions (GPS)**, introduced in Chapter 3, have appeared in the athletic marketplace. Although the composition of these so-called sports drinks may vary with the brand name, most are basically water with different concentrations of electrolytes and carbohydrates, mainly glucose or glucose polymers. Sweat, which consists mostly of water with some electrolytes, contains no glucose, but glucose has been added to the GES and GPS for taste or to help replace energy sources lost during exercise.

Each of the components of GES and GPS may be important to the athlete, depending on the circumstances. When dehydration or hyperthermia is the major threat to performance, water replacement is the primary consideration. In prolonged endurance events, where muscle glycogen is the primary energy source, carbohydrate replacement, as noted in Chapter 3, may help improve performance. In very prolonged exercise in the heat with heavy sweat losses, such as ultramarathons, electrolyte replacement may be essential to prevent heat injury.

The following questions focus on the importance of water, electrolytes, and carbohydrate to the individual exercising under warm environmental conditions and experiencing heavy sweat losses, and on the mechanisms of replacement. Although the effect of carbohydrate intake during exercise was covered in Chapter 3, its role as a component of the GES and GPS is stressed here.

What are some sound guidelines for maintaining water balance during exercise?

As noted previously, excessive loss of body water by dehydration will decrease endurance capacity. In such cases, techniques that help minimize body-water losses may help prevent this decline in performance. Three techniques that have been used for this purpose are rehydration, hyperhydration and skin wetting.

Of the three techniques, research has shown that rehydration is the most effective. Several different approaches have been used to research the effects of rehydration upon physical performance. One approach is related to the sport of wrestling. Athletes who had undergone voluntary dehydration to prepare for competition were rehydrated before the event in an attempt to restore physical performance to its predehydration level. The results of such research are mixed. Some studies reported a partial improvement in endurance performance after rehydration, but usually not all the way back to normal. Others have reported no effect. This is probably because, as some studies have shown, dehydration may not impair strength, power, or local muscular endurance. Thus, rehydration would not improve performance as measured by these criteria beyond that usually seen. However, because rehydration may bring about performance improvements beyond the dehydrated level, it is therefore recommended for wrestlers.

A second approach in studying rehydration is to have subjects ingest fluids during prolonged endurance exercise, particularly in warm environments. Rehydration has been shown to minimize the rise in core temperature, to reduce stress on the cardiovascular system by minimizing the decrease in blood volume, and to help maintain an optimal race pace for a longer period. This beneficial effect is usually attributed to decreased dehydration and the maintenance of a better water balance in the blood and other fluid compartments.

If fluid replacement is to be effective, water has to be absorbed into the circulating blood so that the reduction in blood volume and sweat production that occurs during prolonged endurance exercise will be minimized. Research in which water was labeled with radionuclides showed that water ingested during exercise may appear in plasma and sweat within 10–20 minutes. However, the amount of the ingested fluid that enters the circulation to benefit the athlete depends on two factors: gastric emptying and intestinal absorption.

A number of factors may influence the gastric emptying rate, including drink temperature, exercise intensity, mode of exercise, osmolality, volume, and caloric density. In general, cold fluids empty rapidly and may also help cool the body core. Moderate exercise intensity facilitates emptying, whereas intense exercise greater than 70–75 percent VO_2 max has been reported to exert an inhibitory effect. Little difference is noted in gastric emptying between cycling and running during the first hour even at an exercise intensity of 75 percent VO_2 max, but some research suggests that more fluids appear to be emptied during the latter stages of prolonged cycling. Fluids with a higher osmolality generally inhibit emptying. Adding electrolytes and carbohydrates to fluids increases their osmolality, although glucose polymers have a lesser effect on osmolality than glucose. Some investigators have observed little difference in gastric emptying of fluids that had marked differences in osmotic pressure created by adding glucose or glucose polymers. However, Bennett and Dotson, in a review employing meta-analysis, demonstrated that a glucose polymer–fructose solution inhibited gastric emptying least.

The two factors that appear to exert the most influences are volume and caloric density of the fluid. Gastric emptying increases in proportion to the volume of fluid. Absorption of fluid may be rapid at first, about 20–30 milliliters per minute, but then slows to 3–5 milliliters per minute. Intakes greater than 500–600 milliliters may actually retard emptying. Moreover, large volumes may cause discomfort to the athlete because of abdominal distention. Increases in caloric density, primarily as carbohydrate content in amounts greater than a 10 percent solution, decrease gastric emptying. On the other hand, a number of studies have shown that concentrations up to 10 percent may not adversely affect gastric emptying of fluids.

Factors affecting intestinal absorption of ingested fluids have not been studied as extensively as gastric emptying. Research suggests, however, that the addition of carbohydrate and small amounts of electrolytes may facilitate the absorption of water into the circulation from the intestines when subjects are at rest. Glucose and sodium interact in the intestinal wall; glucose stimulates sodium absorption and sodium is necessary for glucose absorption. When glucose and sodium are absorbed, these solutes tend to pull fluid with them, thus facilitating absorption of water. Additional research is needed to study the effect with different carbohydrate solutions. Research by Ron Maughan has revealed that strenuous exercise, about 80 percent VO₂ max, will inhibit fluid absorption more than lower levels of exercise (about 40 and 60 percent VO_2 max), and these lower levels of exercise inhibit absorption more than at rest.

It should be noted that individual differences in both gastric emptying and intestinal absorption may be significant. In reviewing studies of gastric emptying, Costill noted some subjects could empty 80–90 percent of the ingested solution in 15–20 minutes, whereas others emptied only 10 percent. Some subjects may also develop diarrhea caused by ineffective intestinal absorption of fluids.

Hyperhydration, also known as superhydration, is simply an increase in body fluids by the voluntary ingestion of water or other beverages. It is an attempt to assure that the body-water level is high before exercising in a hot environment. This extra water supply can delay the effects of dehydration and help prolong endurance capacity. Research conducted with hyperhydration before exercise has revealed that it is less effective than rehydration during exercise but may effectively reduce the effects of heat stress on the core temperature and the cardiovascular system. The American College of Sports Medicine recommends that hyperhydration be used prior to exercise in heat stress environments. If you plan to compete or do any prolonged exercise in the heat, it may be wise for you to hyperhydrate. All you need to do is consume about a pint (16 ounces) of cold water about 15–30 minutes before exercising. With experience, you may be able to tolerate larger amounts, although the diuretic effects should be kept in mind if you are to be involved in competition.

Skin wetting techniques, such as sponging the head and torso with cold water or using a water spray have been shown to decrease sweat loss. This could be an important consideration in a long run, as body-water supplies may be depleted less rapidly. These techniques also cool the skin and offer an immediate sense of psychological relief from the heat stress, which may help to improve performance. On the other hand, skin wetting techniques as they may be used in athletic competition have not been shown to cause any major reductions in core temperature or cardiovascular responses. Moreover, some researchers have theorized that skin wetting techniques may be potentially harmful: The psychological sense of relief may encourage athletes to accelerate their pace increasing heat production without providing for control of the body temperature. If the core temperature increases, heat illness may occur. Although some scientists suggest that skin wetting is not beneficial, many endurance athletes claim that it helps. Additional research appears to be warranted.

The following guidelines for maintaining body-fluid balance and improving performance in the heat are based on the evidence currently available:

1. Cold water, about 40–50°F (4.4–10°C) is effective when carbohydrate intake is of no concern, for example, in endurance events less than 60 minutes.

2. If carbohydrate is desired in the drink, the concentration should not be excessive. As discussed below, a 5–10 percent solution appears to be effective in maintaining fluid balance while supplying carbohydrates. Concentrations greater than 10–12 percent may retard gastric emptying.

3. The fluid should contain little, if any, electrolytes. According to the research group at the University of Limburg in the Netherlands, a range of about 400–1100 milligrams of sodium and 120–225 milligrams of potassium per quart would be adequate for those endurance events that could lead to excessive electrolyte losses. Additionally, the sodium might benefit fluid and carbohydrate absorption.

4. The fluid should be palatable, for research has shown that the voluntary intake of fluids increases when they are tasty. Carbonated beverages do not appear to inhibit gastric emptying, nor does the use of aspartame (an artificial sweetener), but Zachwieja and others noted that certain flavorings, such as citric acid, may impair gastric emptying by as much as 25 percent. Other research from Costill's laboratory has shown no difference between carbonated and noncarbonated beverages on temperature regulation while exercising submaximally in the heat.

5. The athlete should hyperhydrate with 16 ounces of cold fluid about 30 minutes before exercising. Adding glycerol to the water may be helpful. A recent study by Lyons and others found that a glycerol-induced hyperhydration was more effective than a water-induced hyperhydration to reduce the thermal stress of moderate exercise in the heat. The dosage was 1 gram of glycerol per kg body weight along with 21.4 ml of water per kg.

6. Rehydrate with 6–8 ounces of cold fluid during exercise at 10- to 15-minute intervals. Such amounts can total to about

one liter per hour, which could be enough to maintain fluid balance with mild to moderate sweating. It is important to start rehydrating early in endurance events because thirst does not develop until about 1–2 percent of body weight has been dehydrated, by which time performance may have begun to deteriorate. Moreover, research by Nancy Rehrer and her colleagues at the University of Limburg has shown that dehydration may also impair gastric emptying and may be related to a higher rate of gastrointestinal distress.

7. Beverages containing caffeine should be avoided because they may cause a diuretic effect, possibly leading to dehydration.

It is important to realize that during periods of heavy sweating, it is very difficult to consume enough fluids to replace all of those lost. Costill has noted that, per minute, 50 milliliters of fluid may be lost through sweating, but only 20–30 milliliters per minute may be absorbed from the intestines. The sweating rate is simply greater than the ability of the stomach to empty the fluid into the small intestine for absorption to occur. Although some dehydration will occur, these techniques will help maintain circulatory stability and heat balance thereby preventing a marked deterioration in endurance capacity.

How should electrolytes be replaced during or following exercise?
Because the major solid component of sweat consists of electrolytes, considerable research has been conducted relative to the need for replacement of these lost nutrients, primarily sodium and potassium. We shall look at this question from two points of view, one dealing with the need for replacement during exercise and the other involving daily replacement.

Because sweat is hypotonic to the body fluids, the concentration of electrolytes in the blood and other body fluids actually increases during exercise and makes the body fluids hypertonic. Thus, electrolyte replacement during exercise is not necessary. Several studies have reported that even during strenuous prolonged exercise like marathon running with high levels of sweat losses, water alone is the recommended fluid replacement to help maintain electrolyte balance. Excessive intake of salts may actually aggravate electrolyte imbalance and impair performance capacity. On the other hand, small amounts of electrolytes have not been shown to be detrimental and may beneficially influence water and carbohydrate absorption.

Moreover, in very prolonged bouts of physical activity, such as marathons, ultramarathons, Ironman-type triathlons, or tennis tournaments where one might play off and on all day, electrolyte replacement during performance may be necessary. Several medical case studies have reported complications resulting from a condition known as **hyponatremia** which may result from excessive sodium losses or water intake (water intoxication). Hyponatremia may develop during exercise bouts lasting longer than 4 hours when an individual loses large amounts of sweat, and thus sodium, and replaces the losses with too much water. In essence, the body fluids become diluted and the sodium level in the blood reaches very low levels. This condition disturbs water balance in the brain, which may lead to epileptic-type seizures and even death. In one Ironman triathlon, 27 percent of the competitors were diagnosed as hyponatremic after the event. To prevent the development of hyponatremia in such prolonged events, a solution with small amounts of salt may be recommended for some athletes. Twenty milliequivalents of sodium and chloride may be found in some commercial sports drinks, but research by Barr and others suggests this amount may be inadequate to prevent a decrease in plasma sodium in prolonged exercise in the heat. Even higher amounts approaching the salt content of sweat (about 40–50 mEq) have been suggested. This would be approximately 2.5 grams of salt per hour.

In general, heavy daily sweat losses do not lead to an electrolyte deficiency. If body levels of sodium and potassium begin to decrease, the kidneys begin to reabsorb more of these minerals and less are excreted in the urine. Research has shown that water alone, in combination with a balanced diet, will adequately maintain proper body electrolyte levels from day to day, even when an individual is exercising and is losing large amounts of sweat.

However, if electrolytes are not adequately replaced, a deficit may occur over 4–7 days of very hard training, especially in hot environmental conditions where fluid losses will tend to be high.

Are salt tablets or potassium supplements necessary?
In general, the use of salt tablets to replace lost electrolytes is not necessary. As noted above, an adequate diet will replace electrolytes lost in sweat.

The concentrations of sodium in sweat may vary; some common figures used are 1.8 grams of sodium per quart of sweat in the unacclimatized person and 0.7 grams in the acclimatized individual.

If an athlete would lose 8 pounds of body fluids during an exercise period, a total of 4 quarts of fluid would be lost, because a quart weighs 2 pounds. Four quarts of sweat would contain, at the most, 7.2 grams of sodium in the unacclimatized individual, but less than 3 grams in one who was acclimatized. Because the average meal contains about 2–3 grams of sodium if well salted, three meals a day would offer 6–9 grams, about enough to just cover the losses in the sweat. However, sodium is lost through other means, primarily in the urine; thus a slight increase may be reasonable for the unacclimatized athlete. Doug Hiller, a physician who has worked extensively with endurance athletes, suggests that during the week or two of acclimatization, athletes should consume about 10–25 grams of salt daily. A more liberal salting of the food should provide an adequate amount; one teaspoon of salt contains about 5 grams of sodium.

Common salt tablets contain only sodium and chloride. They are not necessary to replace lost sodium but may be recommended for unacclimatized athletes who do not replace sodium through normal dietary means in the early stages of an acclimatization program, usually about 7–14 days. They should be taken only if the athlete needs to drink more than 4 quarts of fluid per day to replace that lost during sweating; that is, an 8-pound weight loss. So checking the body weight before and after exercise will offer a fairly exact measure of body-water losses. The general rule is to take one gram of salt with each additional quart of fluid beyond the 4 quarts. This would be two normal salt tablets (the average tablet has one-half gram of sodium). Another way to look at it is to take one pint of water with every salt tablet. The use of salt tablets should be discontinued after the athlete is acclimatized.

Potassium supplements are not recommended for several reasons. First, research by David Costill and his associates has revealed that a deficiency of potassium is rare, even with large sweat losses and a diet low in potassium. Second, excessive potassium may be lethal as it can disturb the electrical rhythm of the heart. The moderate use of substitutes such as potassium chloride, for common table salt, may be helpful in assuring potassium replacement, but investigators recommended particular attention to the diet, citing citrus fruits and bananas as two of the many foods high in potassium. For example, a large glass of orange juice will replace the potassium lost in 2 liters of sweat.

How should carbohydrate be replaced during exercise in the heat?

The value of carbohydrate intake during exercise as a means to improve performance was detailed in Chapter 3, primarily in relationship to performance in a cool environment. Keep in mind that carbohydrate intake may be useful primarily in prolonged exercise, under conditions where one is exercising at a high level of intensity for an hour or more. Carbohydrate is the primary fuel during such exercise tasks, and warm environmental conditions accelerate the use of muscle glycogen. Thus, carbohydrate intake may also improve performance during exercise in the heat, but if temperature regulation is of prime importance, water replacement should receive top priority. Hence, one of the goals of researchers has been to develop a fluid that will help replace carbohydrate during exercise in the heat without affecting water absorption.

The glucose–electrolyte solutions (GES) were the first commercial fluid-replacement preparations designed to replace both fluid and carbohydrate. Common brands today include Gatorade, Squincher, USA Wet, 10–K, and Quickick. Other than water, the major ingredients in these solutions are carbohydrates in the form of fructose, glucose or sucrose, and some of the major electrolytes. The sugar content ranges from 4.7–7.2 percent depending on the brand. The caloric values range from about 5–8 C per ounce. The major electrolytes include sodium chloride, potassium, and phosphorus. These ions also are found in varying amounts in different brands. Some brands also include some of the following: magnesium, calcium, citric acid, vitamin C, and artificial coloring and flavoring.

Glucose polymer solutions (GPS) are designed to provide carbohydrate while decreasing the osmotic concentration of the solution, thus helping to minimize the effect upon gastric emptying. Commercially available brands include Exceed, Gatorlode, and Carboplus. The concentration of the glucose polymers in commercial brands ranges from 5 to 20 percent although weaker or stronger concentrations may be made from the powder form. Guidelines are presented in Chapter 3. Fructose and electrolytes are found in some brands. The contents of selected ingredients for several GES and GPS are presented in Table 8.5.

These solutions may be an effective means to ingest carbohydrate during exercise, and usually the higher the concentration of glucose in the solution,

Table 8.5   Approximate content of several nutrients in eight ounces of selected sports drinks

Brand type	Carbohydrate (grams)	Percent	Calories	Sodium (mg)	Potassium (mg)
Gatorade GES	14	6	56	110	25
Gatorlode GPS	47	20	188	63	0
Exceed GPS	17	7	68	50	45
Exceed high carbohydrate source GPS	59	25	236	117	0

GES = glucose – electrolyte solution

GPS = glucose–polymer solution

the greater the amount that is absorbed from the intestines. Early research with these solutions revealed that the higher osmolality created by the sugar, polymer and electrolyte content would delay gastric emptying and possibly retard water absorption during rest. Thus, solutions with concentrations of carbohydrate greater than 2.5 percent were not recommended during exercise in a warm environment.

A number of earlier investigations compared GES and GPS with water and other such compounds to see whether they offer any particular benefit relative to exercise under heat stress conditions. In general, these investigations revealed that although some of these solutions do offer a scientifically sound means of replenishing body fluids lost through exercise in the heat, they do not appear to be more effective than water alone in controlling body temperature. Thus, water alone has been the recommended method for fluid replenishment when exercising in the heat.

More recent research suggests that an appropriate amount of carbohydrate in solution may also effectively maintain body temperature and possibly help improve performance during prolonged exercise in the heat. It appears that the early research looked at the effect of carbohydrates upon gastric emptying for relatively short periods (15 minutes), usually at rest, and did not measure gastric emptying over prolonged periods in the heat.

Scores of studies have compared the effectiveness of different carbohydrate combinations and concentrations in enhancing physical performance during prolonged endurance tasks. Most of this research is discussed in Chapter 3. This chapter summarizes only the pertinent general findings relative to GES and GPS intake during prolonged exercise under warm environmental conditions.

In general, GES and GPS solutions between 5 to 10 percent seem to empty from the stomach as effectively as water during prolonged exercise in a hot environment. They may possibly also be absorbed more readily from the intestinal tract. No significant adverse effects of these solutions upon plasma volume, sweat rate, or temperature regulation, when compared to water ingestion, have been observed. Actually, they may help maintain plasma volume, liver glycogen, and blood glucose levels during prolonged exercise, and most investigators report that carbohydrate intake during exercise enhances endurance capacity in a variety of prolonged tasks in the heat. Coggan and Coyle recommend about one gram of carbohydrate per minute. Additionally, there appears to be no difference between the forms of carbohydrate relative to these effects. GES and GPS seem to be equally effective.

Although higher concentrations of carbohydrates deliver more glucose to the intestine, solutions higher than 10–12 percent may significantly delay gastric emptying and possibly cause gastrointestinal distress. High concentrations of fructose may be particularly debilitating. However, ultraendurance athletes may experiment with higher concentrations of carbohydrate in training and may adapt to such concentrated solutions for use during competition In a recent case study, Alice Lindeman noted that one cyclist involved in the Race Across America (RAAM) consumed a 23 percent carbohydrate solution.

In summary, water is the essential nutrient that needs to be replenished during prolonged exercise in the heat, for it will help deter some of the adverse responses to dehydration. If carbohydrate replenishment is desired, the current evidence suggests that a 5–10 percent solution of a GES, glucose polymer,

Table 8.6   Fluid consumption (milliliters) at a given percent carbohydrate concentration to obtain desired grams of carbohydrate

Percent concentration	Grams of carbohydrate delivered							
	30	40	50	60	70	80	90	100
2%	1500	2000	2500	3000	3500	4000	4500	5000
4%	750	1000	1250	1500	1750	2000	2250	2500
6%	500	666	833	1000	1166	1333	1500	1666
8%	375	500	625	750	875	1000	1125	1250
10%	300	400	500	600	700	800	900	1000
12%	250	333	417	500	583	667	750	833
15%	225	300	375	450	525	600	675	750
20%	150	200	250	300	350	400	450	500

or glucose polymer/fructose would be recommended. Cola-type drinks or fruit juices may be diluted by adding equal parts of water to achieve a concentration of about 5–10 percent.

Table 8.6 calculates the amount of fluid you must consume, for a given concentration, in order to obtain 30–100 grams of carbohydrate. For example, if you wanted to get 60 grams of carbohydrate per hour, you would need to drink one liter (1,000 ml) of a 6 percent solution, but only one-half liter (500 ml) of a 12 percent solution.

Ergogenic Aspects

If preventing or correcting a nutrient deficiency is seen as an ergogenic technique, then certainly water could be construed to be such an aid. Compared to taking in no fluid before or during exercise, both hyperhydration and rehydration have been shown to enhance exercise performance. On the other hand, some athletes have attempted to lose body water for ergogenic purposes. Although we have seen that hypohydration generally does not improve performance, and indeed may actually impair performance in endurance-type events, certain athletes such as high jumpers may use drugs like diuretics to lose weight rapidly without losses in power. Research has shown that diuretic-induced weight losses may improve vertical jumping ability, because the athlete can develop the same power to move a lower body weight. Detailed coverage of these drugs is beyond the scope of this text. Moreover, the use of diuretics is banned by most athletic governing bodies, such as the United States Olympic Committee and the National Collegiate Athletic Association.

An electrolyte deficiency could impair physical performance, but supplements above and beyond normal electrolyte nutrition have not been shown to enhance performance, with one possible exception.

Does sodium bicarbonate, or soda loading, enhance physical performance?

Sodium bicarbonate is an alkaline salt found naturally in the human body. Its major function is to help control excess acidity by buffering acids. Thus, it is also known as a buffer salt. Its action is comparable to that of medications you may take to control an upset stomach caused by gastric acidity. The baking soda you can purchase in a supermarket is actually sodium bicarbonate.

During high-intensity anaerobic exercise, sodium bicarbonate helps buffer the lactic acid that is produced when the lactic acid energy system is utilized. You may recall from Chapter 2 that the accumulation of excess lactic acid in the muscle cell may interfere with the optimal functioning of various enzymes and thus lead to fatigue. The natural supply of sodium bicarbonate that you have in your blood can help delay the onset of fatigue during anaerobic exercise. It may facilitate the removal of the hydrogen ions associated with lactic acid from the muscle cell, thereby mitigating the adverse effects of the increased acidity. However, fatigue is inevitable if the rate of lactic acid production exceeds the capacity of your sodium bicarbonate supply to buffer it. Theoretically, an increase in the sodium bicarbonate level in the body could delay the onset of fatigue.

A half-century ago, German scientists reported that the ingestion of sodium bicarbonate and other alkaline salts could help improve anaerobic work capacity. Since then, many studies have failed to support this finding, but now a substantial number of well controlled experiments by highly respected investigators in sports nutrition research have provided supportive data.

The usual experimental protocol has been to have subjects about 1–3 hours before the exercise task ingest a dosage of 0.15–0.30 grams of sodium bicarbonate per kilogram body weight. This amount totals less than one ounce for the average adult. Most studies have used a double-blind placebo design in which all subjects took all treatments. The exercise task selected was normally one that stressed the lactic acid energy system, or about 1–3 minutes of maximal exercise. Often these exercise tasks were classified as supramaximal, because they used workloads greater than 100 percent VO_2 max. Repeated bouts of intense exercise interspersed with short rest periods have also been used, such as five 100-yard swims with a two-minute rest between each.

Although the available evidence is not conclusive, the results of about half of these well-controlled studies suggest that the ingestion of sodium bicarbonate will increase the blood pH, reduce acidosis in the muscle cell, decrease the psychological sensation of fatigue at a standardized level of exercise, and increase performance in high-intensity anaerobic exercise tasks to exhaustion. Several field studies even reported a significant improvement in the time to run 400 or 800 meters in highly trained track athletes and 100 meter swims in experienced swimmers.

Although individual studies suggest that sodium bicarbonate may be an effective ergogenic aid, not all reviewers reach that conclusion because approximately half the studies revealed no beneficial ergogenic effect. However, it should be noted that no studies have demonstrated any detrimental performance effects. Other reviewers conclude that sodium bicarbonate ingestion may help some athletes who utilize the lactic acid energy system in their events but will not help athletes in events that stress the ATP–PC or oxygen energy systems. The dosage used in most of these studies, about 300 milligrams per kilogram body weight, appears to be effective yet medically safe. Studies in which lower dosages were used generally have not demonstrated ergogenic effects.

Relative to possible disadvantages, the ingestion of sodium bicarbonate has been suggested to depress aerobic metabolism; however, there is little evidence to support this suggestion. Several studies used exercise tests to exhaustion that lasted 9–10 minutes; such tests would stress both the lactic acid and oxygen energy systems. The results were inconclusive as to any beneficial effect of bicarbonate supplementation, but no adverse effects were noted. On the other hand, several of the investigators noted that some subjects would develop gastrointestinal distress, including nausea and diarrhea. Excessive doses

could lead to alkalosis, with symptoms of apathy, irritability and possible muscle spasms.

The use of sodium bicarbonate (baking soda) by athletes has been dubbed "soda loading," possibly to liken it to carbohydrate loading. As you may recall, the purpose of carbohydrate loading is to increase the storage of muscle and liver glycogen as a means to prevent fatigue in prolonged endurance events. Soda loading is viewed by some in a similar context, an attempt to increase the supply of a natural body ingredient helpful as a means to delay fatigue. However, because sodium bicarbonate may be regarded as a drug, it remains to be seen whether this technique will be deemed illegal and banned by athletic governing bodies such as the International Olympic Committee. Currently there is no test to detect its use, except for urinary pH, which can also be affected by some antacids, and at present it is considered to be legal for use in sports.

Health Aspects: Heat Injuries and High Blood Pressure

For athletes or people who exercise primarily to improve their health, there are two major health considerations related to water and electrolyte balance. We have already noted some of the potential adverse effects of hypohydration and electrolyte losses on physical performance and certain health conditions, such as hyponatremia. This section concentrates on heat injuries, or heat illnesses, that may confront the physically active individual in a warm or hot environment. We shall also discuss high blood pressure, a health problem that may be aggravated by salt ingestion but ameliorated by proper exercise training.

What are the potential health hazards of excessive heat stress imposed on the body?

One of the most serious threats to the performance and health of the physically active individual is heat injury, or heat illness. Any athlete who exercises in a warm environment is susceptible to heat injury, but the increasing popularity of road racing has generated concern for runners who are not prepared for strenuous exercise in the heat, or who participate in races that are poorly organized in regard to preventing and treating heat injuries.

The individual who exercises unwisely under conditions of environmental heat stress may experience one or several of a variety of heat injuries. Three factors may contribute to these injuries: increased core temperature, loss of body fluids, and loss of electrolytes.

Figure 8.6.
Basic flowchart for heat illnesses. The combination of environmental heat and exercise may cause an excessive vasodilation or pooling of blood. These conditions may decrease blood return to the heart and brain, causing dizziness and fainting. Excessive loss of sweat may cause significant losses of body water and electrolytes, leading to various heat illnesses. See text for details.

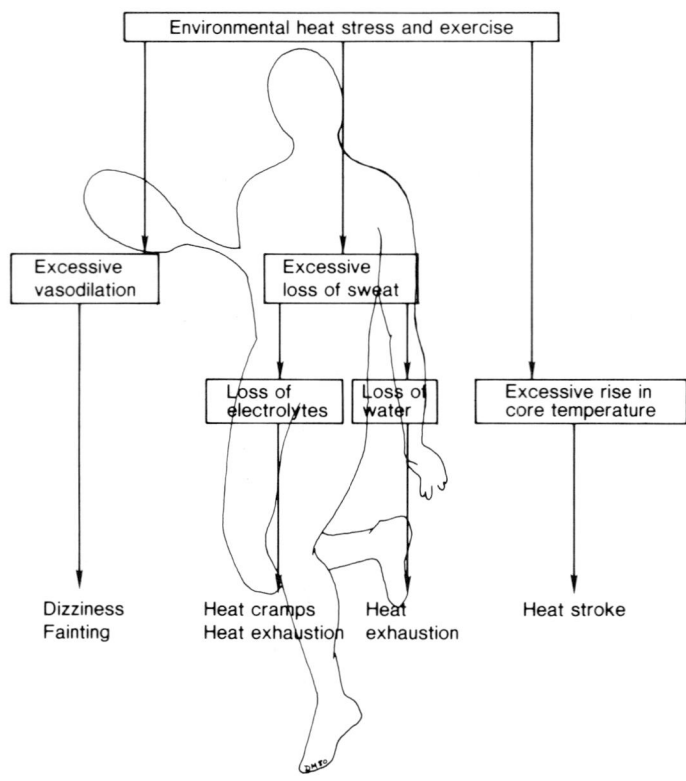

Environmental heat stress and exercise

Excessive vasodilation

Excessive loss of sweat

Loss of electrolytes

Loss of water

Excessive rise in core temperature

Dizziness Fainting

Heat cramps Heat exhaustion

Heat exhaustion

Heat stroke

Figure 8.6 represents a simple flow chart of heat disorders. When a combination of exercise and environmental heat stress is imposed on the body, vasodilation and sweating increase as the body tries to cool itself. When these two adjustments begin to falter, problems develop. In addition, if the exercise metabolic load is very great, heat injuries may develop independent of circulatory and sweating inadequacies.

Excessive vasodilation may contribute to circulatory instability. The blood vessels expand and have a much greater capacity. Owing to a decreased relative blood volume, dizziness, and fainting may occur. This condition is called **heat syncope.**

Although no conclusive evidence is available, **heat cramps** may be caused by excessive loss of sodium, potassium, or magnesium through profuse sweating. Cramps usually appear late in the day following ingestion of large amounts of plain water and usually involve the muscles in the calf of the leg or the abdomen.

Water-depletion heat exhaustion is a common heat injury. It resembles fainting and is caused by inadequate circulation to the brain. Fatigue and nausea are common symptoms, and the individual is usually lying down but conscious. The skin is usually pale, cool, and covered with sweat. The rectal temperature is usually below 104° (40°C). Heat exhaustion may incapacitate the individual for a few hours but is usually responsive to body-cooling treatments.

Anhidrotic heat exhaustion resembles water-depletion heat exhaustion, except that sweating has ceased. The skin is dry. Otherwise, the symptoms and treatment are comparable to those for water-depletion heat exhaustion. If the individual continues to exercise when sweating stops, the core temperature may rise rapidly, leading to heat stroke.

Salt-depletion heat exhaustion occurs most frequently in individuals who are not acclimatized to work in the heat and do not replace the salt they have lost over a period of several days. Symptoms are similar to water-depletion heat exhaustion, although there may be a decrease in the sweat rate. Fatigue is common, and cramps may develop.

Heat stroke is the most dangerous heat injury, as it may be fatal. Heat stroke occurs primarily in the elderly and very young but may also occur in healthy, physically fit athletes. In such cases, it is classified as **exertional heat stroke,** which may be caused by too great an exercise work load under heat-stress conditions without dehydration. It can also occur after excessive loss of body water. It usually is preceded by mental changes ranging from disorientation to unconsciousness. The skin is usually

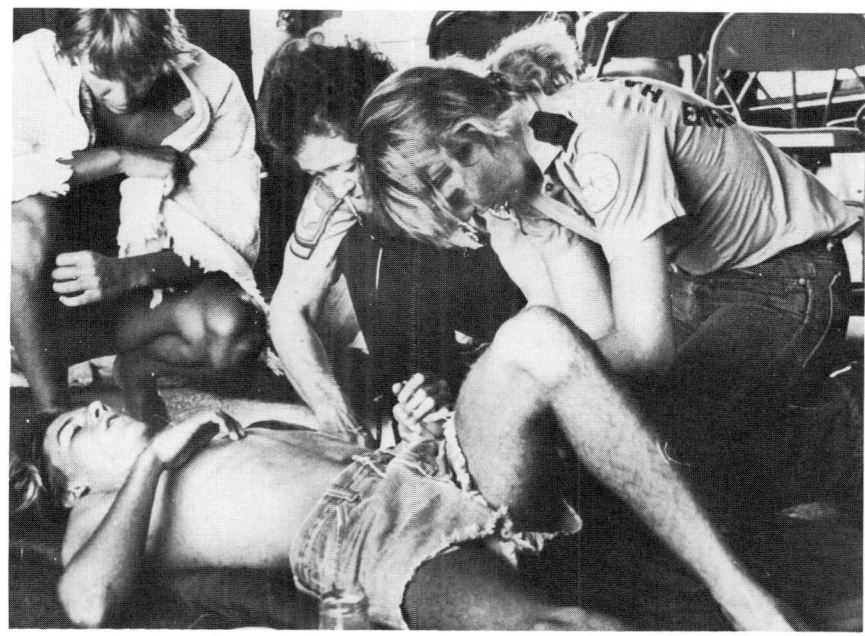

Heat stroke may be caused by exercising in the heat without taking proper precautions. (Wide World Photos, Inc.)

warm and red, and sweating may or may not be present. A rectal temperature over 105.8° (41°C) is a characteristic sign.

What are the symptoms and treatment of heat injuries?

The symptoms of impending heat injury are variable. Among those reported are weakness, feeling of chills, piloerection (goose pimples) on the chest and upper arms, nausea, headache, faintness, disorientation, muscle cramping, and cessation of sweating. Continuing to exercise in a warm environment when experiencing any of these symptoms may lead to heat injury. Table 8.7 presents the major heat injuries along with principal causes, clinical findings, and treatment.

Do some individuals have problems tolerating exercise in the heat?

A number of predisposing factors have been associated with heat injury, including sex, level of physical fitness, age, body composition, previous history of heat injury, and degree of acclimatization.

In earlier studies, investigators found that female subjects tolerated exercise in the heat less well than males. These findings may have been related to the generally lower level of physical fitness of women at that time. More recent studies using subjects with comparable levels of physical fitness found that female responses to heat stress are similar to those found in males. The key point appears to be the physical fitness level of the individual. The

better the fitness level, the better tolerance to a given heat stress. On the other hand, some research by Pivarnik and his associates suggested that thermoregulation may be more impaired during the luteal phase of the menstrual cycle, possibly because of the elevated body temperature associated with increased progesterone levels.

Individuals at both ends of the age spectrum may have problems exercising in the heat. The American Academy of Pediatrics noted that when compared to adults, young children may produce more metabolic heat during exercise in comparison to their body size, do not have as great a sweating capacity, and have a reduced capacity to convey heat from the core to the skin. These factors would increase the chances of heat injury. At high levels of heat stress, tolerance to the heat is decreased in older individuals, possibly because they sweat less. Reduced heat tolerance in the elderly may also be related to fitness levels. As more and more people become and remain physically active throughout middle age and advanced years, we may see the older person tolerating exercise in the heat as well as younger adults.

Obese individuals not only have high amounts of body fat to deter heat losses, but also generate more heat during exercise because of a low level of fitness; thus they are more susceptible to heat injuries.

Individuals who have experienced previous heat injury may be less tolerant to exercise in the heat. Many individuals do regain heat tolerance 8–

Table 8.7   Heat injuries: causes, clinical findings, and treatment

Heat injuries	Causes	Clinical findings	Treatment*
Heat syncope	Excessive vasodilation; pooling of blood in the skin	Fainting Weakness Fatigue	Place on back in cool environment, give cool fluids
Heat cramps	Excessive loss of electrolytes in sweat; inadequate salt intake	Cramps	Rest in cool environment; oral ingestion of salt drinks; salt foods daily; medical treatment in severe cases
Salt-depletion heat exhaustion	Excessive loss of electrolytes in sweat; inadequate salt intake	Nausea Fatigue Fainting Cramps	Rest in cool environment; replace fluids and salt by mouth; medical treatment in severe cases
Water-depletion heat exhaustion	Excessive loss of sweat; inadequate fluid intake	Fatigue Nausea Cool pale skin Active sweating Rectal temperature lower than 104°	Rest in cool environment; drink cool fluids; cool body with water; medical treatment if serious
Anhidrotic heat exhaustion	Same as water-depletion heat exhaustion	Nausea Sweating stopped Dry skin Rectal temperature lower than 104°	Same as water-depletion heat exhaustion
Heat stroke	Excessive body temperature	Headache Vomiting Disorientation Unconsciousness Rectal temperature greater than 105.8 F	Cool body immensely to 102°F (38.9°C) with ice packs, ice or cold water; give cool drinks with glucose if conscious; get medical help immediately

*Begin treatment as soon as possible. In cases of suspected heat stroke, begin immediately.

12 weeks after heat injury. Others lose some of the ability for the circulatory system to adjust to the heat stress, possibly because temperature-regulating centers in the brain are irreversibly damaged. The transfer of heat from the core to the skin becomes impaired and the body temperature rises faster.

One of the more important factors determining an individual's response to exercise in the heat is degree of acclimatization, which is discussed on the following pages.

How can I reduce the hazards associated with exercise in a hot environment?

The following list represents a number of guidelines, which if followed, will reduce considerably your chances of suffering heat injury.

1. Check the temperature and humidity conditions before exercising. Even if the dry temperature is only 65–75°F, a high humidity will increase the heat stress. Warm, humid conditions cause fatigue sooner, so slow your pace or shorten your exercise session.

2. Exercise in the cool of the morning or evening to avoid the heat of the day.

3. Exercise in the shade, if possible, to avoid radiation from the sun.

4. Wear minimal clothing that is loose to allow air circulation, white or a light color to reflect radiant heat, and porous to permit evaporation.

5. If you are running and there is a breeze, plan your route so that you are running into the wind during the last part of your run. The breeze will help cool you more effectively at the time you need it most.

6. Drink cold fluids periodically. For a long training run, plan your route so that it passes some watering holes, such as gas

stations or other sources of water. Take frequent water breaks, consuming about 6–8 ounces of water every 15 minutes or so. During exercise, thirst is not an adequate stimulus to replace water losses, so you should drink before you get thirsty.

7. Replenish your water daily. Keep a record of your body weight. For each pound you lose, drink one pint (16 ounces) of fluid. Your body weight should be back to normal before your next exercise workout.

8. Hyperhydrate if you plan to perform prolonged, strenuous exercise in the heat. In essence, drink about 16–32 ounces of fluid 30–60 minutes prior to exercising.

9. Replenish lost electrolytes (salt) if you have sweated excessively. Put a little extra salt on your meals and eat foods high in potassium, such as bananas and citrus fruits.

10. Avoid excessive intake of protein, as extra heat is produced in the body when protein is metabolized. This may contribute slightly to the heat stress.

11. Avoid beverages with caffeine several hours before exercising. Caffeine may increase the stress in two ways. First, it is a diuretic and may increase body-water losses. Second, caffeine will increase metabolic heat production at rest, which will raise the body temperature prior to exercise.

12. Because alcohol is a diuretic, excess amounts should be avoided the night before competition or prolonged exercise in the heat.

13. If you are sedentary, overweight, or aged, you are less likely to tolerate exercise in the heat and should therefore use extra caution.

14. Be aware of the signs and symptoms of heat exhaustion and heat stroke, as well as the treatment for each. Chills, goose pimples, dizziness, weakness, fatigue, mental disorientation, nausea, and headaches are some symptoms that may signify the onset of heat illness. Stop activity, get to a cool place, and consume some cool fluids.

15. Do not exercise if you have been ill or have had a fever within the last few days.

16. If you are going to compete in a sport held under hot environmental conditions, you must become acclimatized to exercise in the heat.

How can I become acclimatized to exercise in the heat?

It is a well-established fact that **acclimatization** to the heat will help increase performance in warm environments as compared with an unacclimatized state. Simply living in a hot environment confers a small amount of acclimatization. Physical training, in and by itself, provides a significant amount of acclimatization, possibly up to 50 percent of that which can be expected. However, neither of these two adjustments, either singly or together, can prevent the deterioration of exercise performance in the heat by an unacclimatized individual. Thus, a period of active acclimatization is necessary to optimize performance when exercising in the heat.

The technique of acclimatization is relatively simple. Simply cut back on the intensity or duration of your normal activity. When the hot weather begins, moderate your activity. Do not avoid exercise in the heat completely, but after an initial reduction in your activity level, increase it gradually. For example, if you were running five miles a day, cut your distance back to two to three miles in the heat; if you need to do five a day, do the remaining miles in the evening. Eventually build up to three, four and five miles. The acclimatization process usually takes about two weeks to complete. However, even when acclimatized, an athlete's endurance capacity in the heat, particularly with high humidity, still will be less than under cooler conditions.

If you live in a cool climate, like New England, and want to compete in a marathon in Florida in January, how do you become acclimatized? Exercising indoors at a warmer temperature will help. Extra layers of clothes can help prevent evaporation and build a hot, humid microclimate around your body. Research has shown that this technique can provide a degree of acclimatization. However, this is advisable only in cool weather and should not be attempted under hot conditions. Wearing a sweat suit or rubberized suit while exercising in the heat may precipitate heat illness. Moreover, even in a cool environment this technique may cause heat injury. Again, be wary of the symptoms of impending heat illness.

The body makes the following important adjustment during acclimatization to the heat over 7–14 days.

1. The plasma volume expands considerably to increase the total blood volume. This occurs because the blood vessels conserve more protein and sodium, which tend to hold water.

Figure 8.7.
Changes with acclimatization. Acclimatization to the heat for seven to fourteen days will lead to an increase in the blood volume and the ability to sweat. For a standardized exercise task in the heat, these changes will lead to a lower heart rate, less sodium loss, and a lower core temperature. These changes will lead to improved exercise performance in the heat.

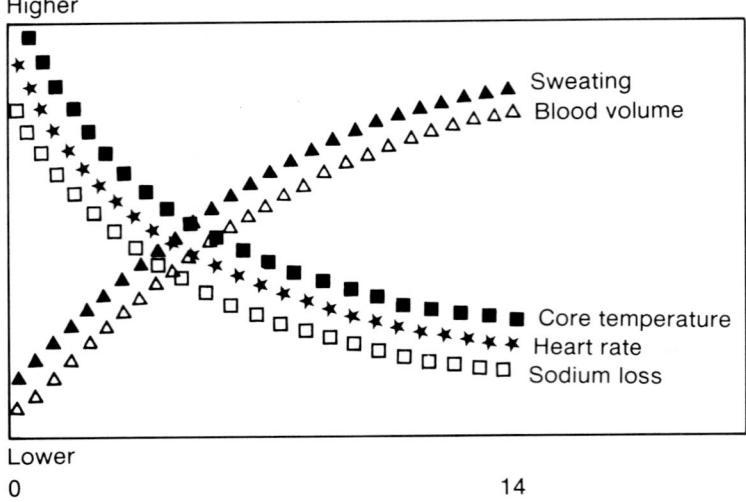

2. The increased blood volume allows the heart to pump more blood per beat, so the stress on the heart is reduced.

3. When volume increases, more blood flows to the muscles and skin. The muscles receive more oxygen and skin cooling increases, improving endurance performance.

4. Less muscle glycogen is used as an energy source at a given rate of exercise, sparing this energy source in endurance events.

5. The sweat glands hypertrophy and secrete about 30 percent more sweat, allowing for greater evaporative heat loss.

6. The amount of salt in the sweat decreases by about 60 percent; evaporation becomes more efficient and electrolytes are conserved.

7. Sweating starts at a lower core temperature, leading to earlier cooling.

8. The core temperature will not rise as high or as rapidly as in the unacclimatized state.

9. The psychological feeling of stress is reduced at a given exercise rate.

In essence, these changes increase the ability of the body to dissipate heat with less stress on the cardiovascular system. The end result is a more effective body-temperature control and improved performance when exercising in the heat. These adaptations may be maintained by exercising in the heat several days per week but are lost in about 7–10 days in a cool environment.

What is high blood pressure, or hypertension?

Everybody has blood pressure, for without it we would not be able to sustain body metabolism. Simply speaking, blood pressure is the force that the blood exerts against the blood vessel walls. Although pressure is present in all types of blood vessels, the arterial blood pressure is the one most commonly measured and most important to our health. Blood pressure is usually measured by a sphygmomanometer, which records the pressure in millimeters of mercury (mmHg). Blood pressure readings are given in two numbers, for example 120/80mmHg. The higher number represents the *systolic* phase, when the heart is pumping blood through the arteries. The lower number represents the *diastolic* phase, when the heart is resting between beats and blood is flowing back into it. Two important determinants of blood pressure are the volume of blood in the circulation and the resistance to blood flow, known as peripheral vascular resistance.

High blood pressure, also known as **hypertension** (hyper = high; tension = pressure), is known as a silent disease. The American Heart Association indicates that nearly 60 million Americans have high blood pressure. However, millions do not know they have it because it has no outstanding symptoms. Some general symptoms include headaches, dizziness, and fatigue, but since they can be caused by a multitude of other factors, they may not be recognized as symptoms of high blood pressure. Although a great deal of research has and is being conducted about the cause of high blood pressure, the exact cause is unknown in about 90 percent of all cases. In these cases, the condition is known as essential hypertension, which cannot be cured, although lifestyle changes or medications can lower the pressure by reducing the blood volume or decreasing the peripheral vascular resistance.

High blood pressure is dangerous for several reasons. The heart must work much harder to pump the extra blood volume or to overcome the peripheral vascular resistance. This normally leads to an enlarged heart, but over time the increase in heart size becomes excessive and the efficiency of the heart actually decreases, making it more prone to a heart attack. Second, high blood pressure may directly damage the arterial walls. It is thought to be a major contributing factor in the development of atherosclerosis and a predisposing factor to coronary disease and stroke. High blood pressure is itself a disease, but it is also involved in the etiology of other diseases.

The National Research Council has noted that any definition of high blood pressure is arbitrary. Traditionally, physicians have used elevations in diastolic blood pressure as the basis for their diagnosis, but the Joint National Committee on Detection, Evaluation and Treatment of High Blood Pressure (JNCDET) included measures of systolic blood pressure when diastolic levels were below 90 mmHg. Table 8.8 provides classification criteria for adults.

How is high blood pressure treated?

Many individuals with essential hypertension need to take medications to control their blood pressure. Diuretics are often used to reduce body water levels, and hence blood volume, and thus reduce blood pressure. Beta-blockers are also used to block the pressure-raising effect of epinephrine and norepinephrine upon the blood vessels and heart. Unfortunately, such drugs may exert other adverse effects, so a nonpharmacologic approach is often a first choice of treatment in cases of mild to moderate hypertension.

A variety of life-style changes may be important in the nonpharmacological treatment of hypertension, including avoidance of tobacco, restriction of alcohol intake, reduction of psychological stress, reduction of body weight, modification of the diet, and exercise. Modification of alcohol intake and reduction of body weight are covered in other chapters, so the next two questions will focus upon other dietary factors and exercise.

Table 8.8 JNCDET classification of blood pressure in adults 18 years or older

Range (mmHg)	Category
Diastolic	
< 85	Normal blood pressure
85–89	High normal blood pressure
90–104	Mild hypertension
105–114	Moderate hypertension
> 115	Severe hypertension
Systolic, when diastolic < 90	
< 140	Normal blood pressure
140–159	Borderline isolated systolic hypertension
> 160	Isolated systolic hypertension

What dietary modifications may help reduce or prevent hypertension?

Reducing body weight may help in reducing high blood pressure, so dietary restriction of Calories may be necessary. There is some evidence to suggest that potassium, calcium, and magnesium are involved in the etiology of high blood pressure, for reduced serum levels or low dietary intake of these minerals have been associated with hypertension. However, the JNCDET has not recommended the use of these mineral supplements but rather an increase in dietary intake from natural foods.

The recommendation of most health organizations is to reduce the dietary intake of sodium chloride. Until the late 1980s, most dietary recommendations for the treatment of hypertension focused upon the reduction of dietary sodium, although whether or not reduction of dietary sodium would reduce blood pressure was controversial. However, Einhorn and Landsberg have noted that most of the sodium controversy actually concerns sodium chloride because chloride may also have important effects on blood pressure. The National Research Council, in *Diet and Health,* suggests that while both sodium and chloride may be necessary to produce hypertension, the matter still remains unresolved.

Despite the ongoing controversy about the etiological role of sodium chloride in hypertension, it may be prudent to restrict consumption. It is true that most individuals possess physiological control systems that effectively maintain a proper balance of sodium in the body. It is also true that current medical and scientific evidence does not support the concept that a normal intake of salt in amounts common to the U.S. diet causes hypertension in persons with normal blood pressure. However, many individuals are sodium-sensitive, or salt-sensitive, in that their blood pressure may increase with excessive consumption of salt. Possibly because of a defect in excretion, sodium accumulates in the body and holds fluids, particularly blood, thereby raising the blood pressure. In the United States, approximately 20 percent of the adult population, or one in every five individuals, is predisposed to high blood pressure. Of this 20 percent, about one-third to one-half, or 6–10 percent of the entire adult population, appears to be sensitive to salt. Since many individuals do not know their blood pressure, millions of Americans may benefit from a reduced salt diet.

The current prudent medical recommendation for dietary prevention or treatment of hypertension is to decrease sodium consumption simply by eating a wide variety of foods in their natural state. Avoid highly salted foods, restrict intake of processed foods, and hide your salt shakers. The recommended upper limit is about six grams of salt per day, just a little over one teaspoon. The Healthy American Diet meets these recommendations, and will also provide adequate amounts of potassium, magnesium, and calcium.

Can exercise help prevent or treat hypertension?

Regular mild- to moderate-intensity aerobic exercise such as jogging, brisk walking, swimming, cycling, and aerobic dancing, has also been recommended to reduce high blood pressure. Since exercise may be an effective means to lose excess body fat, it may exert a beneficial effect through this avenue. However, the exact role or mechanism of exercise as an independent factor in lowering blood pressure has not been totally resolved. Although a number of studies have shown that exercise training helps decrease resting systolic blood pressure in those who are hypertensive (about 5–25 mmHg) and may even elicit a slight decrease in those with normal blood pressure, not all studies are in agreement. Not all individuals will experience a decrease in blood pressure from an exercise program; they may be exercise-insensitive, or nonresponders, just as some individuals are salt-sensitive. Nevertheless, most investigators find the available information sufficient to justify an aerobic exercise program as a useful adjunct for the treatment of high blood pressure. The interested student is referred to the excellent review by Charles Tipton.

Individuals who have high blood pressure should consult with their physicians about mode and intensity of exercise. Although aerobic exercise may help reduce blood pressure at rest and may evoke a lessened blood pressure rise during exercise, a protective effect, other exercises may be harmful. For example, high-intensity aerobic exercise and activities that require intense straining, lifting, or hanging, such as isometric exercises, weight lifting, or pull-ups, should be avoided. The use of hand-held weights in aerobic exercises may also be a concern. These activities create a physiological response that rapidly raises the blood pressure to rather high levels. This increase may be hazardous to someone whose resting blood pressure is already at an elevated level.

References

Books

Gisolfi, C., and Lamb, D. (Eds.). 1990. *Fluid Homeostasis during Exercise.* Indianapolis, IN: Benchmark.

Haymes, E., and Wells, C. 1986. *Environment and Human Performance.* Champaign, IL: Human Kinetics.

Hickson, J., and Wolinsky, I. (Eds.). 1989. *Nutrition in Exercise and Sport.* Boca Raton, FL: CRC Press.

Hunt, S., and Groff, J. 1990. *Advanced Nutrition and Human Metabolism.* St. Paul, MN: West.

Laird, R., and Wheeler, K. (Eds.). 1988. *Medical Coverage of Endurance Athletic Events.* Columbus, OH: Ross Laboratories.

National Research Council 1989. *Recommended Dietary Allowances.* Washington, DC: National Academy Press.

————. 1989. *Diet and Health: Implications for Reducing Chronic Disease Risk.* Washington, DC: National Academy Press.

Shils, M., and Young, V. 1988. *Modern Nutrition in Health and Disease.* Philadelphia: Lea & Febiger.

U.S. Department of Health and Human Services. 1988. *The 1988 Report of the Joint Committee on Detection, Evaluation, and Treatment of High Blood Pressure.* Bethesda, MD: NIH Publication No. 88–1088.

Wadler, G., and Hainline, B. 1989. *Drugs and the Athlete.* Philadelphia: F. A. Davis.

Williams, M. H. 1985. Water and electrolytes in physical activity. Nutritional aspects of human physical and athletic performance. Springfield, IL: C C Thomas.

Reviews

American Academy of Pediatrics. 1982. Climatic heat stress and the exercising child. *Pediatrics* 69: 808–09.

Applegate, E. 1991. Nutritional considerations for ultraendurance performance. *International Journal of Sports Nutrition* 1:118-26.

Armstrong, L., DeLuca, J., and Hubbard, R. 1990. Time course of recovery and heat acclimation ability of prior exertional heatstroke patients. *Medicine and Science in Sports and Exercise,* 22:36-48.

Barr, S., and Costill, D. 1989. Water: Can the endurance athlete get too much of a good thing? *Journal of the American Dietetic Association* 89:1629-32.

Bennett, B., and Dotson, C. 1990. Effects of carbohydrate solutions on gastric emptying: A meta-analysis. *Medicine and Science in Sports and Exercise* 22:S121.

Buskirk, E., and Puhl, S. 1989. Nutritional beverages: Exercise and sport. In: *Nutrition in Exercise and Sport,* eds. J. Hickson and I. Wolinsky. Boca Raton, FL: CRC Press.

Coggan, A., and Coyle, E. 1991. Carbohydrate ingestion during prolonged exercise: effects on metabolism and performance. *Exercise and Sport Sciences Reviews* 19:1-40.

Coleman, E. 1988. Sports drink update. *Sports Science Exchange* 1:1-4, August.

Costill, D. 1990. Gastric emptying of fluids during exercise. In: *Fluid Homeostasis during Exercise,* eds. C. Gisolfi and D. Lamb. Indianapolis, IN: Benchmark.

Costill, D. 1977. Sweating: Its composition and effects on body fluids. *Annals of the New York Academy of Sciences* 301:160-74.

Costrini, A. 1990. Emergency treatment of exertional heatstroke and comparison of whole body cooling techniques. *Medicine and Science in Sports and Exercise* 22:15-18.

Coyle, E., and Hamilton, M. 1990. Fluid replacement during exercise: Effects on physiological homeostasis and performance. In: *Fluid Homeostasis during Exercise,* eds. C. Gisolfi and D. Lamb, Indianapolis, IN: Benchmark.

Einhorn, D., and Landsberg, L. 1988. Nutrition and diet in hypertension. In: *Modern Nutrition in Health and Disease,* eds. M. Shils and V. Young. Philadelphia: Lea & Febiger.

Epstein, Y. 1990. Heat intolerance: Predisposing factor or residual injury? *Medicine and Science in Sports and Exercise* 22:29-35.

Fortney, S., and Vroman, N. 1985. Exercise, performance and temperature control: Temperature regulation during exercise and implications for sports performance and training. *Sports Medicine* 2:8-20.

Friedman, G. 1988. Precursors of essential hypertension: Body weight, alcohol and salt use, and parental history of hypertension. *Preventive Medicine* 17:387-402.

Gisolfi, C., et al. 1989. Electrolyte supplementation. In: *The Theory and Practice of Athletic Nutrition: Bridging the Gap,* eds. A. Grandjean and J. Storlie. Columbus, OH: Ross Laboratories.

Gisolfi, C., et al. 1990. Intestinal absorption of fluids during rest and exercise. In: *Fluid Homeostasis during Exercise,* eds. C. Gisolfi and D. Lamb. Indianapolis, IN: Benchmark.

Gledhill, N. 1984. Bicarbonate ingestion and anaerobic performance. *Sports Medicine* 1:177-80.

Hagberg, J. 1990. Exercise, fitness and hypertension. In: *Exercise, Fitness and Health,* ed. C. Bouchard, et al. Champaign, IL: Human Kinetics.

Harrison, M. 1985. Effects of thermal stress and exercise on blood volume in humans. *Physiological Reviews* 65:149-209.

Feigenhauser, G., and Jones, N. 1991. Bicarbonate loading. In: *Ergogenics: Enhancement of Performance in Exercise and Sport,* eds. D. Lamb and M. Williams. Indianapolis, IN: Benchmark.

Herbert, W. 1983. Water and electrolytes. In: *Ergogenic Aids in Sport,* ed. M. Williams. Champaign, IL: Human Kinetics.

Hiller, D. 1989. Dehydration and hyponatremia during triathlons. *Medicine and Science in Sports and Exercise* 21:S219-S221.

Hubbard, R., and Armstrong, L. 1990. Clinical symposium: Exertional heatstroke: An international perspective. *Medicine and Science in Sports and Exercise* 22:2-48.

————. 1989. Hyperthermia: New thoughts on an old problem. *Physician and Sportsmedicine* 17:97-113, June.

Hubbard, R., et al. 1990. Influence of thirst and fluid palatability on fluid ingestion during exercise. In: *Fluid Homeostasis during Exercise,* eds. C. Gisolfi and D. Lamb. Indianapolis, IN: Benchmark.

Hultman, E., et al. 1988. Work and exercise. In: *Modern Nutrition in Health and Disease,* eds. M. Shils and V. Young. Philadelphia: Lea & Febiger.

Knochel, J. 1989. Heat stroke and related heat stress disorders. *Disease-a-Month* 35:301-77.

Lamb, D., and Brodowicz, G. 1986. Optimal use of fluids of varying formulations to minimize exercise-induced disturbances in homeostasis. *Sports Medicine* 3:247-74.

Linas, S. 1988. Potassium: Weighing the evidence for supplementation. *Hospital Practice* 23:73-79, December.

Luft, F. 1989. Salt and hypertension: recent advances and perspectives. *Journal of Laboratory and Clinical Medicine* 114:215-21.

Maughan, R. 1991. Carbohydrate-electrolyte solutions during prolonged exercise. In: *Ergogenics: Enhancement of Performance in Exercise and Sport,* eds. D. Lamb and M. Williams. Indianapolis, IN: Benchmark.

Murray, R. 1987. The effects of consuming carbohydrate-electrolyte beverages on gastric emptying and fluid absorption during and following exercise. *Sports Medicine* 4:322-51.

Mustafa, M., and Khogali, M. 1989. Pathophysiology of heat induced disorders. *Proceedings of the International Union of Physiological Sciences* 17:251.

Nadel, E. 1988. Temperature regulation and prolonged exercise. In: *Prolonged Exercise,* eds. D. Lamb and R. Murray. Indianapolis, IN: Benchmark.

Randall, H. 1988. Water, electrolytes, and acid-base balance. In: *Modern Nutrition in Health and Disease.* eds. M. Shils and V. Young. Philadelphia: Lea & Febiger.

Sawka, M., and Pandolf, K. 1990. Effects of body water loss on physiological function and exercise performance. In: *Fluid Homeostasis during Exercise,* eds. C. Gisolfi and D. Lamb. Indianapolis, IN: Benchmark.

Schneider, H., et al. 1991. A rationale for electrolyte replacement during endurance exercise. *Medicine and Science in Sports and Exercise* 23:S128.

Senay, L., and Pivarnik, J. 1985. Fluid shifts during exercise. *Exercise and Sport Science Reviews* 13:335–87.

Spickard, A. 1968. Heat stroke in college football and suggestions for prevention. *Southern Medical Journal* 61:791–96.

Taylor, N. 1986. Eccrine sweat glands: Adaptations to physical training and heat acclimation. *Sports Medicine* 3:387–97.

Tipton, C. 1991. Exercise training and hypertension: an update. *Exercise and Sport Sciences Reviews* 19:447–506.

Wheeler, K. 1988. Effect of hypohydration on performance—Fluid and electrolyte requirements. *National Strength and Conditioning Journal* 10:46–48.

Young, A. 1990. Energy substrate utilization during exercise in extreme environments. *Exercise and Sport Sciences Reviews* 18:65–118.

Specific Studies

Anda, R. 1989. Dietary and weight control practices among persons with hypertension: Findings from the 1986 Behavioral Risk Factor Survey. *Journal of the American Dietetic Association* 89:1265–68.

Armstrong, L., et al. 1985. Effects of dietary sodium on body and muscle potassium content during heat acclimation. *European Journal of Applied Physiology* 54:391–97.

————. 1987. Appearance of ingested H_2O_{18} in plasma and sweat during exercise-heat exposure. *Medicine and Science in Sports and Exercise* 19:S56.

Barclay, G., and Turnberg, L. 1988. Effect of moderate exercise on salt and water transport in the human jejunum. *Gut* 29:816–20.

Barr, S., et al. 1991. Fluid replacement during prolonged exercise: Effects of water, saline, and no fluid. *Medicine and Science in Sport and Exercise* 23:811–17.

Bosch, A., et al. 1991. Carbohydrate ingestion during prolonged exercise: a liver glycogen sparing effect in glycogen loaded subjects. *Medicine and Science in Sports and Exercise* 23:S152.

Bouissou, P., et al. 1988. Metabolic and blood catecholamine responses to exercise during alkalosis. *Medicine and Science in Sports and Exercise* 20:228–32.

Brandenberger, G., et al. 1989. The influence of the initial state of hydration on endocrine responses to exercise in the heat. *European Journal of Applied Physiology* 58:674–79.

Brian, D., and McKenzie, D. 1989. The effect of induced alkalosis and acidosis on plasma lactate and work output in elite oarsmen. *European Journal of Applied Physiology* 58:797–802.

Caldwell, J., et al. 1984. Differential effects of sauna- diuretic- and exercise-induced hypohydration. *Journal of Applied Physiology* 57:1018–23.

Carter, J., and Gisolfi, C. 1989. Fluid replacement during and after exercise in the heat. *Medicine and Science in Sports and Exercise* 21:532–39.

Costill, D., et al. 1982. Dietary potassium and heavy exercises: Effects on muscle water and electrolytes. *American Journal of Clinical Nutrition* 36:266–75.

Davis, J., et al. 1988. Effects of ingesting 6% and 12% glucose/electrolyte beverages during prolonged intermittent cycling in the heat. *European Journal of Applied Physiology* 57:553–59.

Davis, J., et al. 1988. Carbohydrate–electrolyte drinks: Effects on endurance cycling in the heat. *American Journal of Clinical Nutrition* 48: 1023–30.

Davis, J., et al. 1990. Effects of isocaloric glucose, sucrose, and maltodextrin drinks in the physiologic and hormone response to exercise in the heat. *Medicine and Science in Sports and Exercise* 22:S120.

Dawson, B., et al. 1989. Improvements in heat tolerance induced by interval running training in the heat and in sweat clothing in cool conditions. *Journal of Sports Sciences* 7:189–203.

Flynn, M., et al. 1987. Influence of selected carbohydrate drinks on cycling performance and glycogen use. *Medicine and Science in Sports and Exercise* 19:37–40.

Gao, J., et al. 1988. Sodium bicarbonate ingestion improves performance in interval swimming. *European Journal of Applied Physiology* 58:171–74.

Goldfinch, J., et al. 1988. Induced metabolic alkalosis and its effects on 400-m racing time. *European Journal of Applied Physiology* 57:45–48.

Gonzalez, J., et al. 1990. Effects of dehydration and fluid replacement on cardiovascular hemodynamics during exercise. *Medicine and Science in Sports and Exercise* 22:S26.

Gopinathan, P., et al. 1988. Role of dehydration in heat stress–induced variations in mental performance. *Archives of Environmental Health* 43:15–17.

Grucza, R., et al. 1987. Thermoregulation in hyperhydrated men during physical exercise. *European Journal of Applied Physiology* 56:603–7.

Hiller, W. D., et al. 1987. Medical and physiological considerations in triathlons. *American Journal of Sports Medicine* 15:164–67.

Horswill, C., et al. 1988. Influence of sodium bicarbonate on sprint performance: relationship to dosage. *Medicine and Science in Sports and Exercise* 20:566–69.

Houmard, J., et al. 1990. Gastric emptying during 1 hr. of cycling and running at 75% VO_2 max. *Medicine and Science in Sports and Exercise* 23:320–25.

Knowles, R., et al. 1989. The effect of sodium bicarbonate ingestion on sprint performance of adolescent swimmers. *Medicine and Science in Sports and Exercise* 21:S48.

Kozlowski, S., et al. 1985. Exercise hyperthermia as a factor limiting physical performance: Temperature effect on muscle metabolism. *Journal of Applied Physiology* 59:766–73.

Lambert, C., et al. 1991. Fluid replacement: Influence of beverage carbonation and carbohydrate content. *Medicine and Science in Sports and Exercise* 23:S129.

Lavender, G., and Bird, S. 1989. Effects of sodium bicarbonate ingestion upon repeated sprints. *British Journal of Sports Medicine* 23:42–44.

Lindeman, A. 1991. Nutrient intake of an ultraendurance cyclist. *International Journal of Sport Nutrition* 1:79–85.

Lyons, T., et al. 1990. Effects of glycerol-induced hyperhydration prior to exercise in the heat on sweating and core temperature. *Medicine and Science in Sports and Exercise* 22:477–83.

Maughan, R., et al. 1990. Effects of exercise intensity on absorption of ingested fluids in man. *Experimental Physiology* 75:419–21.

Maughan, R., Fenn, C., et al. 1989. Effects of fluid, electrolytes and substrate ingestion on endurance capacity. *European Journal of Applied Physiology* 58:481–86.

Millard-Stafford, M., et al. Carbohydrate–electrolyte replacement during a simulated triathlon in the heat. *Medicine and Science in Sports and Exercise* 22:621–28.

Mitchell, J., and Voss, K. 1991. The influence of volume on gastric emptying and fluid balance during prolonged exercise. *Medicine and Science in Sports and Exercise* 23:314–19.

Mitchell, J., et al. 1988. Effects of carbohydrate ingestion on gastric emptying and exercise performance. *Medicine and Science in Sports and Exercise* 20:110–15.

———. 1989. Gastric emptying: Influence of prolonged exercise and carbohydrate concentration. *Medicine and Science in Sports and Exercise* 21:269–74.

Murray, R., et al. 1989. The effects of glucose, fructose, and sucrose ingestion during exercise. *Medicine and Science in Sports and Exercise* 21:275–82.

Murray, R., et al. 1989. Carbohydrate feeding and exercise: Effect of beverage carbohydrate content. *European Journal of Applied Physiology* 58:152–58.

Nelson, P., et al. 1988. Hyponatremia in a marathoner. *Physician and Sportsmedicine* 16:78–87, October.

Neufer, P., et al. 1989. Gastric emptying during walking and running: Effects of varied exercise intensity. *European Journal of Applied Physiology* 58:440–45.

Nielsen, B., et al. 1986. Fluid balance in exercise dehydration and rehydration with different glucose–electrolyte drinks. *European Journal of Applied Physiology* 55:318–25.

Noakes, T., et al. 1990. The incidence of hyponatremia during prolonged ultraendurance exercise. *Medicine and Science in Sports and Exercise* 22:165–70.

Noakes, T., et al. 1991. Metabolic rate, not percent dehydration, predicts rectal temperature in marathon runners. *Medicine and Science in Sports and Exercise* 23:443–49.

Parry-Billings, M., and MacLaren, D. 1986. The effect of sodium bicarbonate and sodium citrate ingestion on anaerobic power during intermittent exercise. *European Journal of Applied Physiology* 55:524–29.

Pivarnik, J., et al. 1990. Menstrual cycle phase affects temperature regulation during endurance exercise. *Medicine and Science in Sports and Exercise* 22:S119.

Poehlman, E., et al. 1989. The effect of prior exercise and caffeine ingestion on metabolic rate and hormones in young adult males. *Canadian Journal of Physiological Pharmacology* 67:10–16.

Rehrer, N., et al. 1989. Exercise and training effects on gastric emptying of carbohydrate beverages. *Medicine and Science in Sports and Exercise* 21:540–49.

Rehrer, N., et al. 1990. Effects of dehydration on gastric emptying and gastrointestinal distress while running. *Medicine and Science in Sports and Exercise* 22:790–95.

Robertson, D., and Siconolfi, S. 1990. Soda loading in female recreational runners. *Medicine and Science in Sports and Exercise* 22:S48.

Robertson, R., et al. 1987. Effect of induced alkalosis on physical work capacity during arm and leg exercise. *Ergonomics* 30:19–31.

Rocker, L., et al. 1989. Influence of prolonged physical exercise on plasma volume, plasma proteins, electrolytes, and fluid-regulating hormones. *International Journal of Sports Medicine* 10:270–74.

Rozycki, T. 1984. Oral and rectal temperatures in runners. *Physician and Sportsmedicine* 12:105–8.

Ryan, A., et al. 1989. Gastric emptying during prolonged cycling exercise in the heat. *Medicine and Science in Sports and Exercise* 21:51–58.

Sahlin, K., and Broberg, S. 1989. Release of K^+ from muscle during prolonged dynamic exercise. *Acta Physiologica Scandinavica* 136:293–94.

Schmidt, W., et al. 1990. The effects of chronic and acute dehydration on high power exercise performance. *Medicine and Science on Sports and Exercise* 22:S89.

Schmieder, R., et al. 1988. Dietary salt intake. A determinant of cardiac involvement in essential hypertension. *Circulation* 78:951–56.

Seidman, D., et al. 1991. The effects of glucose polymer ingestion during prolonged outdoor exercise in the heat. *Medicine and Science in Sports and Exercise* 23:458–62.

Sole, C., and Noakes, T. 1989. Faster gastric emptying for glucose-polymer and fructose solutions than for glucose in humans. *European Journal of Applied Physiology* 58:605–12.

Szlyk, P., et al. 1989. Effects of water temperature and flavoring on voluntary dehydration in men. *Physiology and Behavior* 45:639–47.

Verde, T., et al. 1982. Sweat composition in exercise and in heat. *Journal of Applied Physiology* 53:1540–45.

Webster, S., et al. 1990. Physiological effects of a weight loss regimen practiced by college wrestlers. *Medicine and Science in Sports and Exercise* 22:229–34.

Zachwieja, J., et al. 1991. Effects of drink carbonation on the gastric emptying characteristics of water and flavored water. *International Journal of Sport Nutrition* 1:45–51.

Key Terms

aminostatic theory

android type obesity

anorexia athletica

anorexia nervosa

athletic amenorrhea

bioelectrical impedance (BIA)

body image

Body Mass Index (BMI)

brown fat

bulimia nervosa

cellulite

eating disorder

essential fat

fat free mass

glucostatic theory

gynoid type obesity

hunger center

hyperplasia

hypertrophy

lean body mass

lipostatic theory

morbidly obese

obesity

regional fat distribution

relative-weight method

satiety center

set-point theory

skinfold technique

storage fat

underwater weighing

waist:hip ratio (WHR)

weight cycling

Key Concepts

Height-weight charts do not measure body composition but may be useful as a screening device to determine whether one is overweight or obese.

For practical purposes, body composition may be classified as consisting of two components: fat-free weight, which is about 70 percent water, and body fat.

The body needs a certain amount of fat content, the so-called essential fat, but excessive body fat may contribute to several major health problems and may also impair athletic performance.

All techniques that currently are used to measure body composition are prone to error; even the underwater weighing technique, the gold standard, may be in error by 2–2.5 percent.

Our present level of knowledge does not provide us with the ability to predict precisely what the optimal body composition should be for health or physical performance.

The brain's hypothalamus appears to be the central control mechanism in appetite regulation, which involves a complex interaction of physiological and psychological factors.

Although the ultimate cause of obesity is a positive energy balance, the underlying cause is not known but probably involves the interaction of many genetic and environmental factors.

Excessive body fat is associated with a variety of chronic diseases and impaired health conditions, including coronary heart disease, diabetes, high blood pressure, and arthritis.

For children and adolescents, the major adverse health effects of excessive body fat appear to be social and psychological.

Excessive weight losses, usually associated with behaviors characteristic of eating disorders, may result in health problems ranging from mild to severe and may also have a negative impact upon physical performance.

Although the average body-fat percentages for young men and women are, respectively, 15–18 percent and 22–25 percent, those involved in athletic competition may be advised to reduce these levels.

Body Weight and Composition
9

Introduction

The human body is a remarkable machine. In most cases it may consume nearly a ton of food over a year and not change its weight by a single pound. Individuals are constantly harnessing and expending energy through the intricacies of their bodily metabolism in order to remain in energy balance. To maintain a given body weight, energy input must balance energy output. However, sometimes the energy-balance equation becomes unbalanced, and the normal body weight will either increase or decrease.

The term **body image** refers to the mental image we have of our own physical appearance, and it can be influenced by a variety of factors, including how much we weigh or how that weight is distributed. Body weight appears to be a major concern of many Americans. Research has revealed that about 40 percent of adult men and 55 percent of adult women are dissatisfied with their current body weight. Similar findings have also been reported at the high school and even the elementary school level, primarily with female students. A study by Drewnowski and Yee has found that 85 percent of both male and female first-year college students desired to change their body weight. The primary cause of this concern is the value that American society, in general, assigns to physical appearance. Thinness is currently an attribute that females desire highly. Males generally desire muscularity, which also is becoming increasingly popular among women. Most individuals who are dissatisfied with their physical appearance feel that they are overweight.

Being overweight also may have a significant effect upon health and physical performance. Excessive body weight, particularly in the form of body fat, has been associated with a wide variety of health problems. Obesity is one of the most prominent medical concerns in industrialized societies today. For some athletes, simply being a little overweight may prove to be detrimental to physical performance because it costs energy to move the extra body mass. On the other hand, increased body weight, provided it is of the right composition, may be advantageous to other athletes.

At the other end of the body weight continuum, weight losses leading to excessive thinness also may have an impact upon one's health and physical performance. Anorexia nervosa and bulimia are two serious health disorders associated with obsessive concern about body weight. Excessive weight losses also may have a negative impact upon athletic performance.

The major focus of this chapter is on the basic nature of body composition and its effect on health and physical performance. The following two chapters deal with weight control methods used to modify body composition.

Body Weight and Composition

What is the ideal body weight?

We all have heard at one time or another that there is an ideal body weight for our particular height. But ideal in terms of what? Health? Appearance? Physical performance? There appears to be no sound evidence to suggest a specific ideal weight for a given individual. However, data collected during the past century, mainly by life insurance companies, have been compiled into normal or desirable ranges of body weight for a given height and age. These height-weight charts represent those weights at which Americans can expect to live the longest.

Tables 9.1 and 9.2 represent two of the more popular desirable height-weight charts developed for adults by the Metropolitan Life Insurance Company. The height is measured without shoes and with light clothing. Body weight ranges are given for three body frames—small, medium, and large. Table 9.3 provides a procedure for estimating your body frame size.

Although the Metropolitan Life Insurance Company released new height-weight tables for Americans in 1983, the data in tables 9.1 through 9.3 represent figures generated in 1959. Unfortunately the 1983 report has been challenged by several major health groups, including the American Heart Association, because the average body weights are generally higher than the 1959 figures. In general, other health factors that have changed in American society may have biased the new tables. For example, there is an increasing death rate among heavy smokers, who are usually underweight, which would increase the average weights in the 1983 tables because they are based on mortality.

Table 9.1 Desirable weights for females age 25 and over

Height (ft/in.)	(cm)	Small frame (lb)	(kg)	Medium frame (lb)	(kg)	Large frame (lb)	(kg)
5'10''	177.8	134–144	60.8–65.3	140–155	63.5–70.3	149–169	67.6–76.6
5'9''	175.3	130–140	59.0–63.5	136–151	61.7–68.5	145–164	65.8–74.4
5'8''	172.7	126–136	57.2–61.7	132–147	59.9–66.7	141–159	64.0–72.1
5'7''	170.2	122–131	55.3–59.4	128–143	58.1–64.9	137–154	62.1–69.9
5'6''	167.6	118–127	53.5–57.6	124–139	56.2–63.1	133–150	60.3–68.1
5'5''	165.1	114–123	51.7–55.8	120–135	54.4–61.2	129–146	58.5–66.2
5'4''	162.6	110–119	49.9–54.0	116–131	52.6–59.4	125–142	56.7–64.4
⮕5'3''	160.0	107–115	48.5–52.2	112–126	50.8–57.2	121–138	54.9–62.6
5'2''	157.5	104–112	47.2–50.8	109–122	49.4–55.3	117–134	53.1–60.8
5'1''	154.9	101–109	45.8–49.4	106–118	48.1–53.5	114–130	51.7–59.0
5'0''	152.4	98–106	44.4–48.1	103–115	46.7–52.2	111–127	50.3–57.6
4'11''	149.8	95–103	43.1–46.7	100–112	45.4–50.8	108–124	49.0–56.2
4'10''	147.3	92–100	41.7–45.4	97–109	44.0–49.4	105–121	47.6–54.9
4'9''	144.7	90–97	40.8–44.0	94–106	42.6–48.1	102–118	46.3–53.5

For women between eighteen and twenty-five, subtract one pound for each year under 25. Height measured without shoes.
Source: Used with permission of the Metropolitan Life Insurance Company.

Table 9.2 Desirable weights for males age 25 and over

Height (ft/in.)	(cm)	Small frame (lb)	(kg)	Medium frame (lb)	(kg)	Large frame (lb)	(kg)
6'3''	190.5	157–168	71.2–76.2	165–183	74.9–83.0	175–197	79.4–89.3
6'2''	188.0	153–164	69.4–74.4	160–178	72.6–80.8	171–192	77.6–87.1
6'1''	185.4	149–160	67.6–72.6	155–173	70.3–78.5	166–187	75.3–84.8
6'0''	182.9	145–155	65.8–70.3	151–168	68.5–76.2	161–182	73.0–82.6
5'11''	180.3	141–151	64.0–68.5	147–163	66.7–74.0	157–177	71.2–80.3
5'10''	177.8	137–147	62.1–66.7	143–158	64.9–71.7	152–172	69.0–78.0
5'9''	175.3	133–143	60.3–64.9	139–153	63.1–69.4	148–167	67.1–75.3
5'8''	172.7	129–138	58.5–62.6	135–149	61.2–67.6	144–163	65.3–74.0
5'7''	170.2	125–134	56.7–60.8	131–145	59.4–65.8	140–159	63.5–72.1
5'6''	167.6	121–130	54.9–59.0	127–140	57.6–63.5	135–154	61.2–69.9
5'5''	165.1	117–126	53.1–57.2	123–136	55.8–61.7	131–149	59.4–67.6
5'4''	162.6	114–122	51.7–55.3	120–132	54.4–59.9	128–145	58.1–65.8
5'3''	160.0	111–119	50.3–54.0	117–129	53.1–58.5	125–141	56.7–64.0
5'2''	157.5	108–116	49.0–52.6	114–126	51.7–57.2	122–137	55.3–62.1
5'1''	154.9	105–113	47.6–51.3	111–122	50.3–55.3	119–134	54.0–60.8

Height measured without shoes
Source: Used with permission of the Metropolitan Life Insurance Company.

Table 9.3   Approximation of body frame size

Extend your arm and bend the forearm upward at a 90 degree angle. Keep fingers straight and turn the inside of your wrist toward your body. If you have a caliper, use it to measure the space between the two prominent bones on either side of your elbow. Without a caliper, place thumb and index finger of your other hand on these two bones. Measure the space between your fingers against a ruler or tape measure. For your height, compare it with figures in the right hand column in the accompanying tables that list elbow measurements for medium-framed men and women. Measurements lower than those listed indicate that you have a small frame. Higher measurements indicate a large frame.

Height (ft/in.)	Elbow breadth (in.)
Men (1″ heels)	
5′2″–5′3″	2½″–2⅞″
5′4″–5′7″	2⅝″–2⅞″
5′8″–5′11″	2¾″–3″
6′0″–6′3″	2¾″–3⅛″
6′4″	2⅞″–3¼″
Women (1″ heels)	
4′10″–5′3″	2¼″–2½″
5′4″–5′11″	2⅜″–2⅝″
6′0″	2½″–2¾″

Source: Used with permission of the Metropolitan Life Insurance Company

Tables 9.1 and 9.2 have been developed for females and males 25 years of age and over. For women under the ages of 18 and 25, one pound should be subtracted for each year under 25. As an example, a 5-foot 8-inch, 20-year-old woman with a medium frame would have a weight range of 127–142, or 5 pounds below the desirable level at age 25. Although different age levels are not built into this scale, the range of values for each height and body frame helps account for this. In general, as we get older our body weight should decrease slightly, although it usually increases. This may be more relevant to the sedentary individual, who may be developing more body fat and less muscle tissue, than to the active individual who may be maintaining good body composition through training.

What are the values and limitations of height-and-weight charts?

Height-and-weight charts are based on measurements obtained from large populations of people. The data obtained are then treated statistically, and the values that tend to cluster toward the midpoint (the median) are considered to be normal, average, or desirable, at least as related to a lower rate of mortality. The Metropolitan Life Insurance Company tables have been criticized because they are based upon a selective population, insurance policy holders, which may not represent the average American population. Non-caucasians are underrepresented in these tables. Moreover, data from the National Institute of Aging (NIA) suggest that age was not taken into account. Although the tables reflect data for the ages 25–59, the NIA report suggests that the recorded desirable weights are too high for the younger age groups, just right for the 40s, and too low for older age groups.

Nevertheless, in relation to determining whether an individual possesses normal body weight for a given age and sex, these tables may have some value as a screening device. If you are more than 10 percent below the average you may be considered to be underweight. Ten percent over the normal value may be classified as overweight, and 20 percent above normal is often used as a criterion for obesity.

As an example, suppose you are a young male and your desirable weight for your height (5′10″) is 143–158. If you weigh 176 pounds, and if we use the upper limit of the weight range, then you are about 112 percent of your desirable weight (176/158 × 100). Thus, you are 12 percent above the desirable weight and could be considered to be overweight.

However, these tables reveal nothing to us about our body composition. Two individuals may be exactly the same height and weight; however, the distribution of their body weight might be so different that one individual could possibly be considered obese while the other might be considered very muscular. For the example cited above, the 12 percent additional weight could represent muscle mass developed through a strength training program or it could be body fat resulting from a sedentary lifestyle.

What is the composition of the body?

The human body contains many of the elements of the earth, twenty-five of which appear to be essential for normal physiological functioning. About 4 percent of our body is composed of minerals, primarily calcium and phosphorus in the bones, but also including others such as iron, potassium, sodium, chloride, and magnesium. The vast majority of our body consists of four elements—carbon, hydrogen, oxygen, and nitrogen. These elements are the structural basis for body protein, carbohydrate, fat, and water.

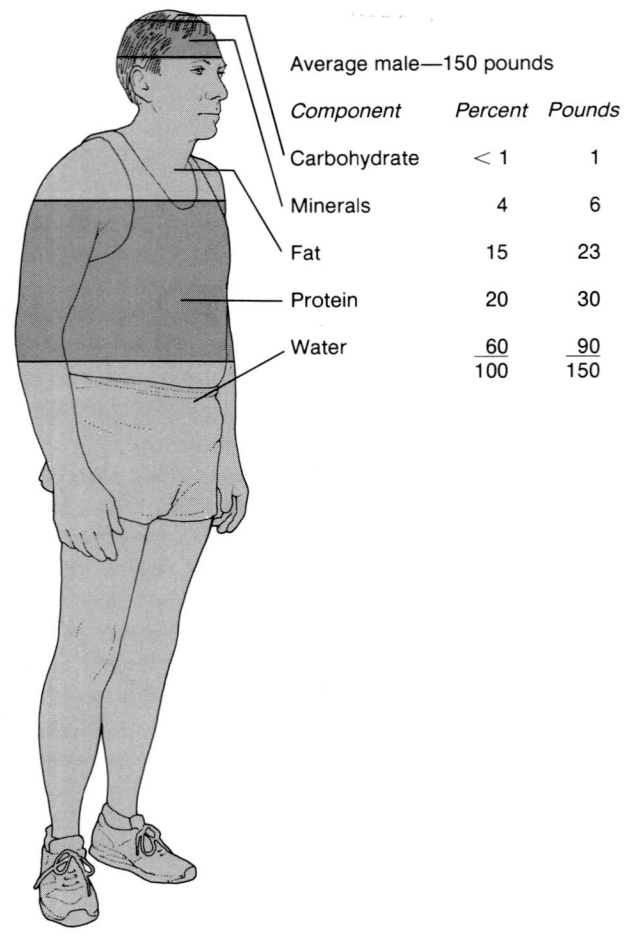

Figure 9.1.
The majority of body weight is water, while varying amounts of fat, protein, and carbohydrate make up the solid tissues. Body weight losses or gains may be related to changes in any of these components.

Average male—150 pounds

Component	Percent	Pounds
Carbohydrate	< 1	1
Minerals	4	6
Fat	15	23
Protein	20	30
Water	60	90
	100	150

When doing exacting research, scientists use sophisticated techniques to analyze the composition of the body. In essence, they divide the body into four components: water, bone tissue, protein tissues, and fat. Each of these components has a different density. Density represents mass divided by volume, and in body composition analysis is usually expressed as grams per milliliter (g/ml) or grams per cubic centimeter (g/cc³). The standard for comparison is water, which has a density of 1.0, or 1 g/ml. Corresponding densities for the other components are approximately 1.3–1.4 for bone, 1.1 for fat-free protein tissue, and 0.9 for fat. The density of the human body as a whole may have a wide range, approximately 1.020 to 1.100. The body-density value may be used to determine the body-fat percentage; a higher density represents a greater amount of fat-free mass and a lower amount of body fat.

For our purposes, we may condense body composition into two components—total body fat and fat-free mass. The total amount of fat in the body consists of both essential fat and storage fat. **Essential**

fat is necessary in certain body structures such as the brain, nerve tissue, bone marrow, heart tissue, and cell membranes. Essential fat in adult males represents about 3 percent of the body weight. Adult females also have additional essential fat associated with their reproductive processes. This additional 9–12 percent of sex-specific fat gives them a total of 12–15 percent essential fat. **Storage fat** is simply a depot for excess energy, and the quantity of body fat in this form may vary considerably.

Some storage fat is found around body organs for protection, but over 50 percent of total body fat is found just under the skin and is known as subcutaneous fat. When this latter type of fat is separated by connective tissue into small compartments, it gives a dimpled look to the skin and is popularly known as **cellulite.** Cellulite is primarily fat, but may contain high concentrations of glycoproteins, particles that can attract water and possibly give cellulite skin that waffle-like appearance.

Fat-free mass primarily consists of protein and water, with smaller amounts of minerals and glycogen. The tissue of skeletal muscles is the main component of fat-free mass, but the heart, liver, kidneys, and other organs are included also. Another term that is often used interchangeably with fat-free mass is **lean body mass;** technically however, lean body mass includes essential fat.

The average adult body weight is approximately 60 percent water, the remaining 40 percent consisting of dry weight materials that exist in this internal water environment. Some tissues, like the blood, have a high water content, whereas others, like bone tissue, are relatively dry. The fat-free mass is about 70 percent water, while adipose fat tissue is less than 10 percent. Under normal conditions the water concentration of a given tissue is regulated quite nicely relative to its needs. When we look at the percentage of the body weight that may be attributed to a given body tissue, the weight of that tissue includes its normal water content. For the average adult male and female then, the following values represent approximate percentages of the body weight derived from a specific tissue:

	Adult Male	Adult Female
Muscle	43	36
Bone	15	12
Total fat	15	26
Essential fat	3	15
Storage fat	12	11
Other tissues	27	26
Total	100%	100%

Body composition may be influenced by a number of factors such as age, sex, diet, and level of physical activity. Age effects are significant during the developmental years as muscle and other body tissues are being formed. Also, during adulthood, muscle mass may decrease, probably because the level of physical activity declines. There are some minor differences in body composition between boys and girls up to the age of puberty, but at this age the differences become fairly great. In general, girls deposit more fat beginning with puberty, while boys develop more muscle tissue. Diet can affect body composition over the short haul, such as during acute water restriction and starvation, but the main effects are seen over the long haul. For example, chronic overeating may lead to increased body-fat stores. Physical activity may also be very influential, with a sound exercise program helping to build muscle and lose fat.

What techniques are available to measure my body composition and how accurate are they?

The measurement of body fat has become very popular in recent years. Many high school and university athletic departments routinely analyze the body composition of their athletes in attempts to predict an optimal weight for competition. Fitness and wellness centers also usually include a body-fat analysis as one of their services. Unfortunately, few of the individuals who analyze body composition in these situations are aware of the limitations of the tests they employ.

The only direct method to analyze body composition is by chemical extraction of all fat from body tissues, obviously not appropriate with living humans. Thus a variety of indirect methods have been developed to assess body composition, some relatively simple, such as visual observation by an experienced judge, and others rather complex, such as nuclear magnetic resonance imaging, using million-dollar machines. Theoretically, all techniques are designed to measure the amount of body fat in comparison to fat-free mass. The simpler techniques may give you a general approximation of body fatness, while the more sophisticated procedures may give you a more accurate body-fat percentage.

Before continuing this discussion, it must be emphasized that all techniques currently used to measure body density or percentage of body fat are only estimates and are prone to error, particularly when used to determine the body fat of a given individual. Such errors usually are expressed statistically as standard errors of measurement or estimate, which can be used to show the accuracy of the body-fat measurement. Without going into the statistics of standard errors, look at the following example. Let us suppose that a formula using skinfold techniques predicts your body fat at 17 percent, yet the formula has a standard error of 3 percent. What this means is that your true body fat percentage is probably somewhere between one standard error of the predicted value, or somewhere between 14–20 percent. It may even be lower than 14 and higher than 20 percent, but less likely so. Thus, you should not think of body-fat determinations as precise measures, but consider them as a possible range associated with the error of measurement.

One of the most common research techniques for determining body density is **underwater weighing.** The technique is based on Archimedes' principle that

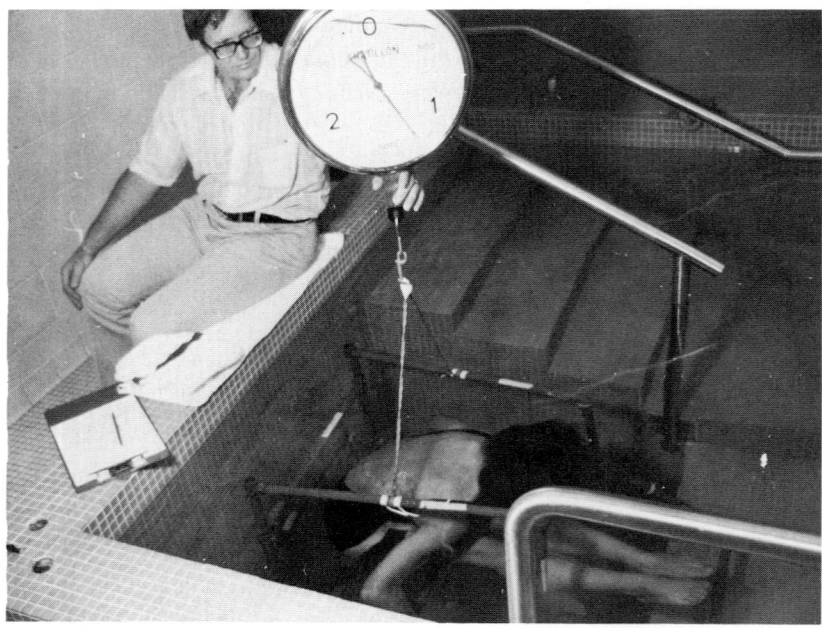

Underwater weighing is one of the more accurate means for determining body composition.

(The Center for Fitness and Sport Research. The University of Michigan)

a body immersed in a fluid is acted upon by a buoyancy force in relation to the amount of fluid the body displaces. Since fat is less dense and bone and muscle tissue more dense than water, a given weight of fat will displace a larger volume of water and exhibit a greater buoyant effect than the corresponding weight of bone and muscle tissue. Different formulas are recommended for determination of body density, depending upon the age and sex of the individual. Although this technique is often referred to as the "gold standard" in body-composition analysis, the standard error is still about 2 to 2.5 percent. Because the underwater weighing technique is rather time consuming and difficult for some individuals, other techniques have been developed either for research purposes or practical applications.

The newer, more sophisticated techniques for measuring body composition usually are reserved for research or medical applications when a highly accurate analysis is needed. These techniques, which can accurately measure total body water, bone mass, or protein tissue, include magnetic resonance imaging (MRI), computed tomography (CT), total body electrical conductivity (TOBEC), photon and dual energy x-ray absorptiometry, neutron activation analysis, whole-body potassium counting, and a variety of others. However, such methods are expensive.

Most of the less expensive, more practical methods involve anthropometry, or measures of body parts. Examples include body girths such as the neck and abdomen; bone diameters such as the hip, shoulders, elbow, and wrist; and a wide variety of skinfold sites. Girth measurements of the abdomen, hips, buttocks, thigh, and other body parts, may be important indicators of **regional fat distribution** which is a concept representing the anatomical distribution of fat over the body. As noted below, regional fat distribution may be associated with several major health problems. A measure of regional fat distribution is the **waist/hip ratio (WHR),** which is the abdominal or waist circumference (measured by a flexible tape at the narrowest section of the waist as seen from the front) divided by the gluteal or hip circumference (measured at the largest circumference including the buttocks).

The **skinfold technique** is designed to measure the subcutaneous fat (see Figure 9.2). It appears to be the most common procedure for nonresearch purposes. The values obtained are inserted into an appropriate formula to calculate the body fat percentage. To improve the accuracy of this technique, skinfold measures should be obtained from a variety of body sites, because using a single skinfold site may be unrepresentative of total storage fat. The test also should be administered with an acceptable pair of skinfold calipers by an experienced tester. Ultrasound techniques are also available to assess skinfold thicknesses, but these are more expensive than calipers. The formula chosen should be specific to the sex and age of the individual. Some formulas also have been developed for specific athletic groups.

Figure 9.2.

A schematic drawing showing the skinfold of fat that is pinched up away from the underlying muscle tissue.

Source: Reprinted by permission of the American Alliance for Health, Physical Education, Recreation and Dance, 1900 Association Drive, Reston, VA 22091.

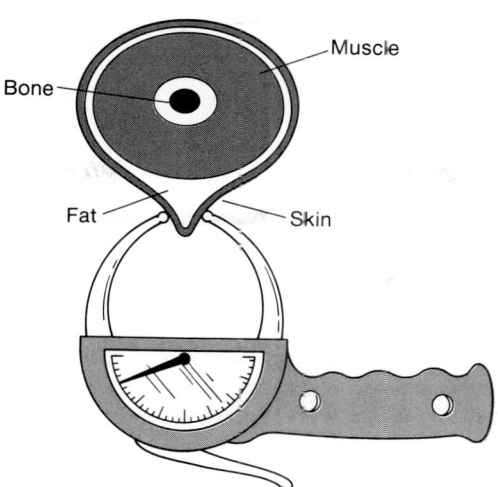

Because this method involves some measurement error, and because the formulas usually are based upon the underwater weighing technique, the standard error for the skinfold technique is about 3 to 3.5 percent, which should be kept in mind when using this method to estimate body fat. For those who have access to a good skinfold caliper, generalized equations for the calculation of body fat may be found in Appendix F for males and females of several ages.

A recent, but more expensive, practical technique which has spread rapidly is **bioelectrical impedance analysis (BIA)**. BIA is based on the principle of resistance to an electrical current that is applied to the body. The less the recorded resistance, the greater is the water content and hence the greater the body density. Early research with BIA revealed large standard errors in predicting lean body mass, so it was not considered to be very valid. However, body composition researchers, including Richard Boileau, Larry Golding, Tim Lohman, Karen Segal, Wayne Sinning, and Jack Wilmore have developed newer techniques and formulae with lower standard errors, approximately 3–4 percent. Nevertheless, several problems still appear to exist, including the application to the very obese, the lean athlete, and the elderly. The BIA may not accurately predict lean body mass in those with abnormal body water supplies; it may underestimate lean body mass in athletes and overestimate it in the obese.

Another device recently marketed commercially is based upon near infrared interactance (NIR). However, two recent studies by Davis and Israel, in conjunction with their associates, have shown NIR to be relatively ineffective.

Gilbert Forbes, probably the leading expert in body composition analysis over several decades, has noted that the goal of developing a highly precise method for estimating body composition may never be achieved. In any case, most of us do not need a highly accurate assessment of body composition. The critical question probably should be, "How can I tell if I am too fat?" Jean Mayer, an internationally renowned nutritionist, has suggested the use of the mirror test to answer this question. He suggests you look at yourself, nude, from the front and from the side in a full-length mirror. This is usually all the evidence we need if we study ourselves objectively. We probably have a pretty good idea of how we would like our bodies to look, and this test offers us a guide to our desirable physical appearance, at least as far as body weight distribution is concerned. Exceptions to this suggestion are individuals who are obsessed with thinness and believe they are always too fat, no matter how thin they get. This topic is covered later in this chapter.

How much fat should I have?

That is a complex question, and the response depends on whether you are concerned primarily about appearance, health, or physical performance. From the perspective of physical appearance, you are the best judge of how you wish to look. However, a distorted image may lead to serious health problems or impairment in physical performance.

For health purposes, the body has a need for the essential fat described previously. At a minimum this value approximates 3 percent for males and 12–15 percent for females. Several authorities have included additional levels of storage fat and suggested that minimal levels of total body fat for health range from 5–10 percent for males and 15–18 percent for females. The average percentage of body fat for U.S. males and females are, respectively, approximately 15–18 and 22–25 percent.

Lower levels of body fat may be required for optimal performance in certain types of athletic events. Certain male athletes such as wrestlers and gymnasts may function effectively at 5–7 percent body fat. Recommendations have been made for females who compete in distance running to have no more than 10 percent body fat. However, some athletes have performed very successfully even though their body fat percentage was higher than the recommended values.

Unfortunately, our present level of knowledge does not provide us with the ability to predict precisely what the optimal weight or percent body fat should be for health or physical performance. However, some general guidelines are available, and these are covered in the following two sections.

Body Composition and Health

What is obesity?

By medical definition, **obesity** is simply an accumulation of an excessive amount of fat in the adipose tissues. Obesity is also referred to as a disease or disorder, the most common nutritional health problem in the United States. The actual measurement and determination of clinical obesity is a controversial issue. Several approaches have been used to define the point at which a person is classified as clinically obese.

The **relative-weight method** (weight to height ratio) is based upon the height-weight tables. An example was presented in an earlier section. Although various investigators have used values ranging from 115–130 percent of the desirable weight as the determining point of obesity, the National Institute of Health uses a value of 120 percent, which is 20 percent above the desirable weight. Thus, an individual who has a desirable weight of 150 would be classified as obese at a weight of 180 (150 × 1.20).

Another approach is the **Body Mass Index (BMI)**. The BMI is a weight:height ratio using the metric system. The formula is:

$$\frac{\text{Body weight in kilograms}}{(\text{Height in meters})^2}$$

An individual who weighed 70 kg (154 pounds) and was 1.78 meters (70 inches) in height would have a BMI of 22.1 [70 ÷ (1.78)^2] In general, a BMI range of 20–25 is considered to be desirable but a suggested desirable range for females is 21.3–22.1 and for males, 21.9–22.4. The National Research Council notes that BMI values above 27.3 for women and 27.8 for men are indicators of excessive weight

Table 9.4   Ratings of body-fat percentage levels for males and females age 18–30

Rating	Males	Females
Excellent	6–10	10–15
Good	11–14	16–19
Acceptable	15–18	20–25
Too fat	19–24	26–29
Obese	25 or over	30 or over

Note: Keep in mind that these are approximate values. The excellent category may apply particularly to athletes who compete in events where excess body fat may be a disadvantage.

and have been associated with increased incidence rates for several health problems, including high blood pressure and diabetes. A BMI of 30 is classified as obese. Although weight:height ratios may be useful for screening procedures, they have inherent limitations because they do not directly assess body composition. Remember, obesity and overweight are not synonymous terms. As noted previously, an individual may be overweight but not classified as obese if the weight is primarily muscle tissue.

A third approach is to measure body-fat percentages. This may be the desired procedure when the preceding two methods produce questionable results. Although different levels of body-fat percentages have been cited as the criterion for clinical obesity, the American Dietetic Association and the National Research Council set the value at 25 percent for males and 30 percent for females. A proposed rating scale is presented in Table 9.4.

How does the human body normally control its own weight?

As noted previously, you may eat over a ton of food a year and yet not gain one pound of body weight. For this to occur, your body must possess an intricate regulatory system that helps to balance energy intake and output. The regulation of human energy balance is complex. At the present time we do not appear to know the exact physiological mechanisms whereby body weight is maintained relatively constant over long periods, but some information is available relative to both energy intake and energy expenditure.

Appetite regulation in relation to energy needs involves a complex interaction of numerous physiological factors including the appetite centers in the brain, feedback from peripheral centers outside the

Figure 9.3.
Basic control mechanisms for body weight. The control of food intake (energy intake) and resting metabolism (energy output) is governed primarily by the hypothalamus in the brain. The numerous control centers in the hypothalamus are influenced by feedback from the body, such as the blood concentrations of glucose and other nutrients. In turn, food intake and energy expenditure may influence the hypothalamus. For example, exercise will stimulate the hypothalamus, leading to the secretion of several hormones by the endocrine glands in the body. The effects of exercise will also influence the temperature control center and the blood levels of several nutrients, which will in turn influence the hypothalamus. See the text for an expanded discussion.

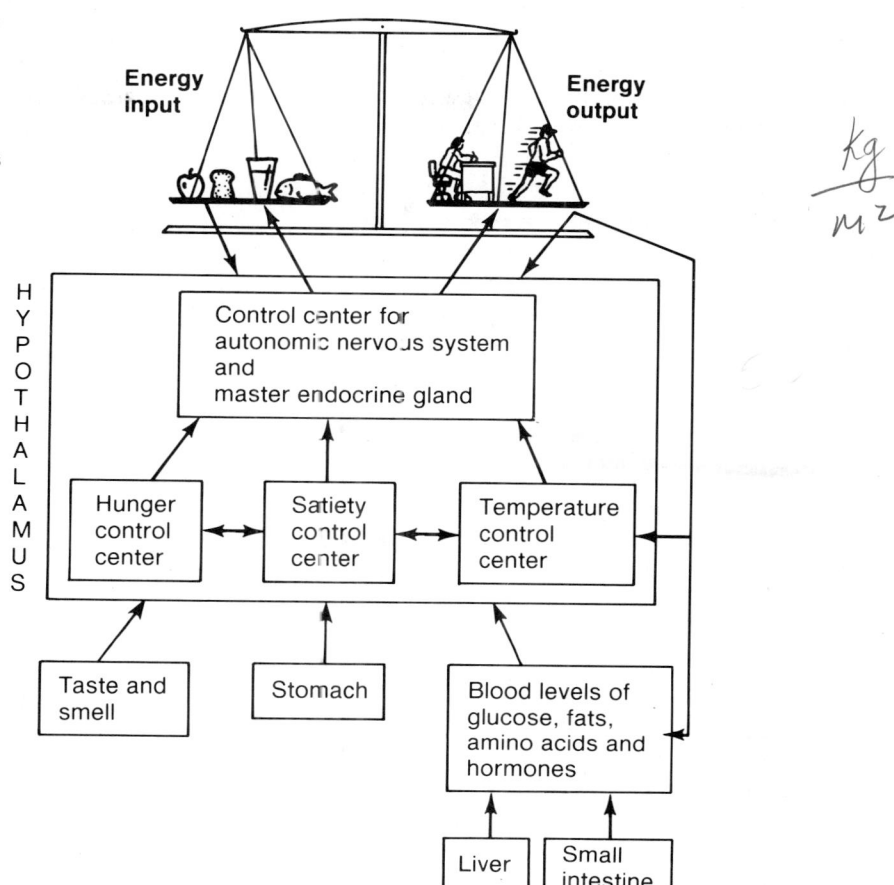

brain such as the liver and intestines, metabolism of ingested foods, and hormone actions. Environmental conditions, such as the home environment, also influence food intake. These factors may interact to regulate the appetite on a short-term basis (daily basis), or on a long-term basis as in keeping the body weight constant for a year.

The control of the appetite appears to be centered in the hypothalamus. A **hunger center** may stimulate eating behavior. A **satiety center,** when stimulated will inhibit the hunger center. No single specific biochemical mechanism has been identified, but a number of factors have been theorized to influence the function of these centers to control food intake. The following may be involved in one way or another.

Stimulation of several senses like sight, taste and smell. We are all aware of how these factors may stimulate or depress our appetites.

An empty or full stomach. An empty stomach may stimulate the hunger center by various neural pathways, whereas a full stomach may stimulate the satiety center.

Receptors in the hypothalamus, liver, or elsewhere that may be able to monitor blood levels of various nutrients. In regard to this, three theories center on the three energy nutrients. The **glucostatic theory** suggests that food intake is related to changes in the levels of blood glucose. A fall will stimulate appetite whereas an increased blood-glucose level would decrease appetite. The **lipostatic theory** suggests a similar mechanism for fats as does the **aminostatic theory** for amino acids, or protein.

Changes in body temperature. A thermostat in the hypothalamus may respond to an increase in body temperature and inhibit the feeding center.

Secretions of hormones. A number of different hormones in the body have been shown to affect feeding behavior, including insulin, thyroxine, and several others, particularly a number of peptides produced in the intestines that can function as hormones or neurotransmitters.

Although all of the above may be involved in the physiological regulation of food intake, the other side of the energy-balance equation is energy expenditure, or metabolism. Although exercise is one way to increase energy expenditure, the vast majority of the energy that is expended by the body on a daily basis is accounted for by the basal metabolic rate (BMR), as was detailed in Chapter 2. Changes in the BMR may be involved in the regulation of body weight. Several mechanisms have been proposed.

Brown fat. **Brown fat,** which is distinct from the white fat that comprises most fat tissue in the body, is found in small amounts around the neck, back, and chest areas. It has a high rate of metabolism and releases energy in the form of heat. Activity of the brown fat tissue may be increased or decreased under certain conditions, such as after a meal or exposure to the cold. This activity is referred to as nonshivering thermogenesis. The amount of brown fat in humans appears to be small, about 1 percent of body fat or less, but Stock indicates that as little as 50 grams (about 2 ounces) could make a contribution of 10–15 percent energy turnover in humans. Its role in the etiology of obesity is being researched.

Hormones. Levels of hormones from the thyroid and adrenal glands may rise or fall and affect energy metabolism accordingly. Triiodothyronine and thyroxine, hormones from the thyroid gland, may be involved in the stimulation of brown adipose tissue. Hormones, such as epinephrine, also may increase the activity of certain enzymes resulting in increased energy expenditure. Decreases in hormonal activity may depress energy metabolism.

As noted in an earlier chapter, the human body has developed a number of physiological systems, called feedback systems, to regulate most body processes. Temperature control is a good example. The **set-point theory** of weight control is a proposed feedback mechanism. This theory proposes that your body is programmed to be a certain weight or a set point. If you begin to deviate from that set point, your body will make physiological adjustments to return you to normal. This is often referred to as adaptive thermogenesis. Although developed primarily with rats and still only a theory, the set-point concept does involve the interaction of those factors cited above, such as a glucostat and lipostat, which

may influence energy intake and expenditure in humans. For example, when individuals go on a starvation-type diet, the resting metabolic rate decreases in an attempt to conserve body energy stores. The body recognizes that it is being deprived of energy intake and this slows down the rate of energy output. When subjects are overfed in experiments, the BMR does increase but usually in relation to the (DIT) effect. However, there is usually a significant decrease in voluntary food intake, an indication that some metabolic change has depressed the appetite. Thus, the set-point theory may explain why most people maintain a normal body weight throughout life.

What is the cause of obesity?

Energy processes in the human body, like those of other machines, are governed by the laws of thermodynamics. If the human body consumes less energy in the form of food Calories than it expends in metabolic processes, then a negative energy balance will occur and the individual will lose body weight. Conversely, a greater caloric intake in comparison to energy expenditure will result in a positive energy balance and a gain in body weight. In simple terms, obesity is caused by this latter condition of energy imbalance.

For the vast majority of individuals who have had a normal body weight during childhood and adolescence, but begin to put on weight gradually in young adulthood (ages 20–40) the basic cause of this creeping obesity is usually an increased consumption of Calories and a decreased level of physical activity, or a combination of the two. Several recent studies have shown that the risk of developing obesity is directly related to the amount of time spent watching television, a sedentary activity usually accompanied by consumption of high Calorie snack foods.

On the other hand, the underlying cause of most severe cases of obesity has not been determined. At the present time a multicausal theory has been proposed involving the interaction of a number of genetic and environmental factors.

Heredity appears to be a very important factor. For example, several genetic diseases result in clinical obesity. Also, studies of children who have been adopted, including both fraternal and identical twins who have been separated and adopted by different families, have shown a greater relationship of the body composition between the children and their biological parents as compared to the adoptive parents. Thus, heredity may determine those internal factors in the body that may predispose one to gain

Figure 9.4.

Adult-onset obesity is often referred to as creeping obesity, for it creeps up on adults slowly. As little as 200 additional Calories per day above normal requirements would result in a gain of approximately 20 pounds of body fat in one year.

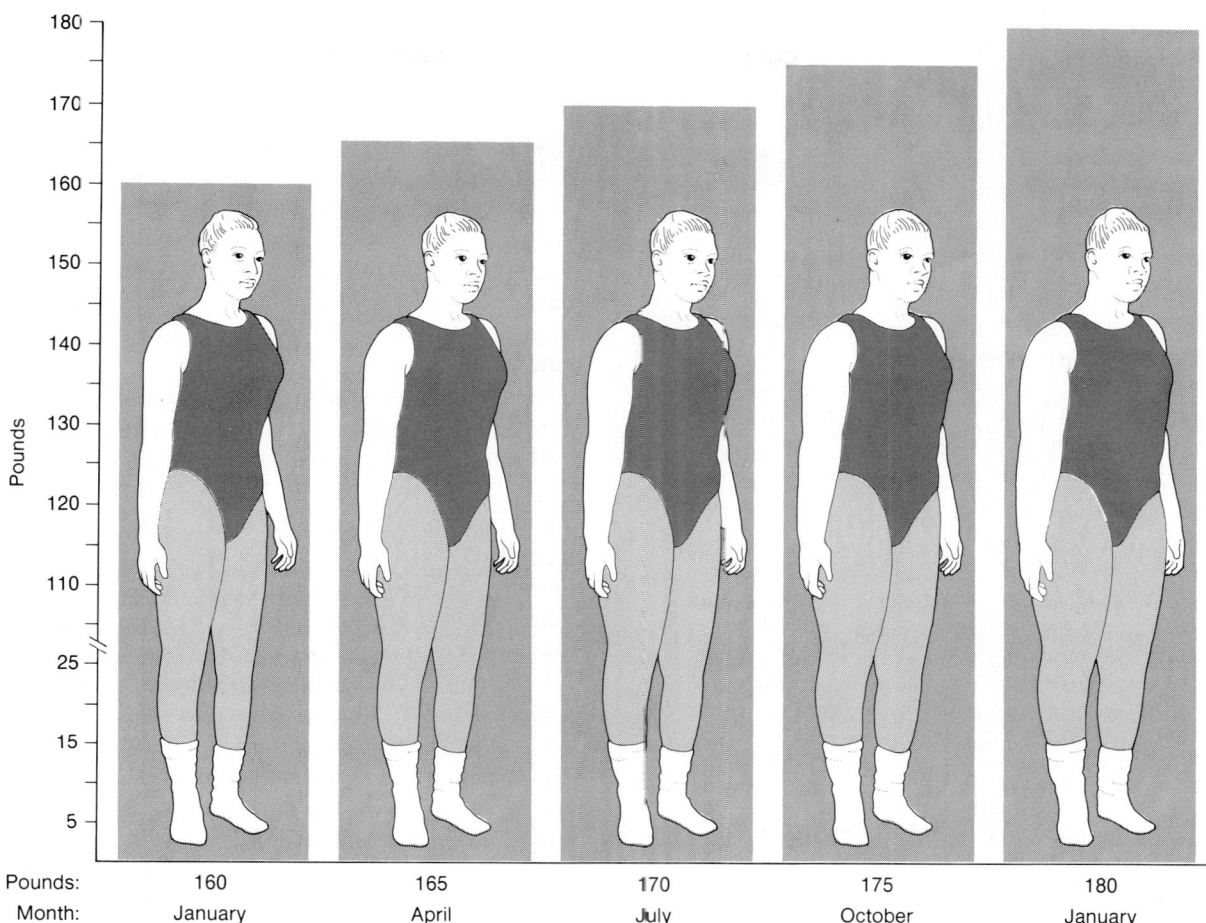

Pounds:	160	165	170	175	180
Month:	January	April	July	October	January

weight. Although no specific obesity gene has yet been identified, several genetic factors that have been implicated include a lower BMR, a decreased DIT, an enhanced metabolic efficiency in storing fat, a greater number of fat cells, a smaller percentage of slow-twitch muscle fibers, lower levels of spontaneous physical activity during the day, and lower levels of energy expenditure during light exercise. For a review of two meticulous studies of the genetic role in obesity, the interested reader is referred to the recent reports by Bouchard and others on long-term overfeeding of identical twins, and by Stunkard and others on the Body Mass Index of twins who had been raised apart.

Although heredity may predispose one to obesity, environmental factors also are highly involved. The two key environmental factors that contribute to the development of obesity are excessive intake of Calories, particularly as dietary fat, and physical inactivity. As noted above, an increase in food intake and a decrease in physical activity are the major factors involved in the development of creeping obesity during adulthood. However, the role of these two factors in the development of obesity during childhood, when the most severe cases of obesity begin to develop, is not totally clear. Of the two, an improper diet appears to be the major problem. There also may be a familial factor involved here, as the child may be raised in a family where large meals and overeating are common. Also, the supermarket diet of today makes it easy to consume large amounts of Calories. Sugar and fat are found in a wide variety of foods that we eat and constitute three out of every five Calories, or 60 percent, of the average American diet. Although some studies have shown that obese children do not consume more Calories than their nonobese peers, the data were

Figure 9.5.
Sugar and fat in the typical American diet. Refined sugar and fat comprise about 60 percent of the daily Calories in the typical American diet, or three out of every five Calories.

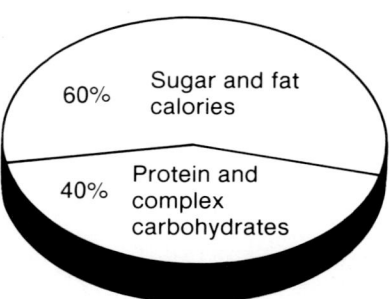

not collected during the period when the obese children were gaining weight. Studies in which the investigators actually lived with the children suggest that the obese child does eat more, and also eats faster. The role of physical inactivity in the etiology of childhood obesity does not appear to be as important as the diet. In general, studies show that obese children are just as physically active as the nonobese. This may not be surprising in that typical nonobese American children are not very physically active either.

These comments should not be construed as suggesting that exercise is unimportant in the prevention and treatment of obesity. It is important, as will be documented in the next chapter.

Although genetics plays an important role in the etiology of obesity, a desirable body weight may be achieved and maintained in those individuals so predisposed. It may be more difficult and may involve a lifetime of vigilance, but it can be done with an appropriate program of diet and exercise.

How is fat deposited in the body?
The actual deposition of fat in the human body may occur in two ways: **hyperplasia** (an increase in the number of fat cells), or **hypertrophy** (an increase in the amount of fat in each cell). Earlier research appeared to support the theory that hyperplasia is a major cause in the development of childhood obesity whereas hypertrophy is the primary cause in adulthood. However, Widdowson has criticized the research upon which these theories are based, and recently noted that the assumptions and limitations in calculating the number of adipocytes (fat cells) in an individual are so great that the concepts of a hyperplastic or hypertrophic obesity have largely been abandoned. Moreover, Forbes noted that there are not two types of obesity but rather a gradual increase in both size and number of adipocytes. Existing fat cells apparently have a maximal size potential, which when exceeded stimulates the formation of new fat cells or the accumulation of fat in

preadipocytes, small cells in the adipose tissue that have the potential to become adipocytes. Thus, although a genetic predisposition to inherit a greater number of fat cells, thereby facilitating the development of obesity, may exist, individuals without this genetic predisposition may still become obese with a positive energy balance stored as fat.

What health problems are associated with obesity?
Obesity shortens life, possibly by as much as four years. Even in ancient Greece, the physician Hippocrates recognized that persons who are naturally fat are apt to die sooner than slender individuals. Reports from the National Institute of Health conclude that being overweight contributes to serious health consequences and that obesity is a killer disease. One report has noted that obesity is associated with 26 known health conditions and accounts for 15–20 percent of deaths annually. Some health problems associated with obesity are kidney disease, cirrhosis of the liver, arthritis, and cancer of the colon and rectum.

The primary health condition associated with excess body fat is coronary heart disease (CHD). Excess body fat increases the risk of developing high blood pressure, hypercholesterolemia, and diabetes, all of which are risk factors leading to the development of CHD. Data from the renowned Framingham Heart Study also suggest that obesity is an independent risk factor associated with CHD. The National Center for Health Statistics has reported that susceptibility to CHD increases substantially when the BMI exceeds 27.8 for males and 27.3 for females. The detrimental effects of obesity relative to the development of chronic disease occur when it persists for ten years or more.

Although overall obesity does increase the risk of developing chronic diseases, the location of the body fat appears to be even more important. Classifications of different types of obesity based upon regional fat distribution have been proposed, the most popular differentiation being the android versus the gynoid types. **Android** (male) **type obesity** is characterized by accumulation in the abdominal region—particularly the intraabdominal region—of deep, visceral fat, but also of subcutaneous fat. Android type obesity is also known by other terms, such as central, upper body, or lower trunk obesity, and is sometimes referred to as the apple-shape obesity. **Gynoid** (female) **type obesity** is characterized by fat accumulation in the gluteal-femoral region—the hips, buttocks, and thighs. It is also known as lower body obesity, and is often referred to as pear-shape obesity. Both types of obesity have a strong genetic component. The waist:hip ratio (WHR) is also known as the abdominal:gluteal ratio, or android:gynoid ratio. As a measure of regional fat distribution, an increased risk of coronary heart disease in males is associated with a WHR greater than 0.90, while women are at increased risk with a WHR of 0.80.

The android type obesity is increasingly being recognized as causing a greater health risk than obesity itself. It appears that android type and gynoid type fat cells possess dissimilar biochemical functions because of differences in the activity of lipoprotein lipase, an enzyme that regulates fat metabolism. For example, recent data from animal studies have provided the first direct evidence that the interaction of insulin and fat cell metabolism varies in different fat regions. This finding may be related to humans, for epidemiological data have shown that android type obesity is associated with hyperinsulinemia, insulin resistance, hypercholesteremia, hypertriglyceridemia, diabetes, and hypertension, all risk factors for coronary heart disease. Fat cells in the deep visceral depots are large and highly metabolically active. They readily release free fatty acids into the blood when stimulated by epinephrine, and thus may contribute to abnormalities in glucose and lipid metabolism, particularly in individuals under psychological stress. On the other hand, exercise, which also increases epinephrine levels comparable to psychological stress, will mobilize fatty acids from these cells for use as an energy source by the active muscles, and may actually help reduce android type obesity and its related adverse health effects.

Gynoid type fat cells appear to store fat more readily and tend to lose it less readily, and thus the health risks do not appear to be as great compared with those associated with android type obesity. Although gynoid type fat cells are the primary type found in females, a recent study by Judith Rodin and her associates at Yale University found that women who repeatedly lose and gain body weight, known as **weight cycling,** are more prone to deposit fat in the abdominal area, thereby developing an android type obesity and increased health risks. Although a combined diet-exercise program may help to reduce gynoid type obesity, the pear-shape figure appears to be more resistant to change compared with the apple shape.

It should be noted that although android type obesity may be related to the development of various chronic diseases, other factors may also be involved. For example, Seidell and others noted that males who were less physically active or who smoked heavily had higher waist:hip ratios. Both of these factors may contribute to the development of cardiovascular disease, and thus may confound the true relationship between regional fat distribution and chronic disease. Additional research certainly will be forthcoming on the topic of regional fat distribution and risk of chronic diseases, but it would appear to be a prudent health behavior to prevent the development of obesity, particularly android type obesity, or to reduce obesity if present.

Although obesity also increases the risk factors associated with CHD in children and adolescents, the major adverse health effects of excess body fat appear to be social and psychological rather than medical. Because personality development occurs primarily during childhood and adolescence, excessive body fat may contribute more greatly to social-emotional problems at this time than during adult-onset obesity. The Nutrition Committee of the Canadian Paediatric Society noted that obesity interferes with the development of a satisfying self-image and social status, thereby impairing psychological development. Obese children often are rejected by their peers, superiors, and even parents, resulting in a negative self-image, low self-esteem, and even serious psychological illness. A contributing factor to the development of psychological problems may be the adverse effect of excessive body fat on physical fitness and athletic performance. A child who is unsuccessful in play activities probably will not participate, and thus will miss the socializing aspects of play. It should also be noted that adults are not immune to the adverse psychological consequences of obesity.

Approximately 30 percent of the adult population and 25 percent of adolescents and children in the United States are carrying too much body fat for optimal health. Not all who are overweight or obese develop medical or psychosocial problems, just as not all cigarette smokers contract lung cancer.

However, excessive body fat, particularly abdominal fat, increases the risk of developing such problems and should be corrected as early as possible. Individuals who are **morbidly obese,** defined as being at least 100 pounds over the ideal body weight or having a BMI greater than 40, are in dire need of prompt medical attention.

Researchers are looking for clues that can predict which children will become obese, such as genetic, metabolic, or anthropometric markers. In the meantime, some successful programs for the prevention and treatment of obesity have been developed, and appropriate guidelines are presented in the next chapter.

What health problems are associated with excessive weight losses?

Losing excess body fat and attaining a desirable body weight may confer some significant health benefits by counteracting the adverse effects of obesity. However, many individuals attempt to lose weight for other reasons. Slimness is currently very fashionable, particularly among females of all ages. It is desired not only for attractiveness but also for psychological undertones of independence, achievement, and self-control. Also, both male and female athletes, such as distance runners, gymnasts, wrestlers, jockeys, and dancers, practice weight control to improve their performance. Losing body weight for improved performance may also provide some health benefits, for Paul Williams theorized that the elevated HDL-cholesterol concentrations of long-distance runners are primarily a result of reduced adiposity. However, excessive weight loss may actually lead to deterioration of health if done to excess.

As shall be noted in the next chapter, a well-designed diet and proper exercise are the cornerstones of a sound weight control program. However, some individuals may establish unrealistically low body-weight goals, which may lead to pathogenic weight-control behaviors. Such techniques as complete starvation, self-induced vomiting, or the use of diet pills, laxatives, and diuretics may initially be employed to achieve rapid weight losses but may evolve into serious medical disorders if prolonged. The general effects of excessive rapid and long-term weight losses on health are highlighted below.

Rapid weight losses over a week or two usually are achieved by starvation-type diets and dehydration. Apparently little or no harm is caused by a one- or two-day fast, and some authorities have reported that a healthy man or woman can fast completely for two weeks and suffer no permanent ill effects. However, certain physiological changes occur during fasting that may be harmful to individuals with certain preexisting medical conditions. Low blood sugar, increased ketones in the blood, electrolyte disorders, decreased HDL cholesterol, impaired phagocytic function of the white blood cells, inflammation of the intestines and pancreas, kidney problems, decreases in heart muscle tissue, decreases in blood volume, and low blood pressure are some of the observed changes. Fatigue and weakness develop in most individuals.

Dehydration may be induced by exercise, exposure to the heat (as with a sauna), or the use of diuretics and laxatives. The effect of dehydration upon one's health, particularly in relation to heat illnesses, was detailed in the previous chapter. The use of diuretics and laxatives may increase potassium losses from the body, which may lead to electrolyte imbalances and disturbed neurological function, including heart function. Disturbed kidney function has also been observed following severe dehydration.

The medical problems associated with rapid weight losses are, in general, believed to be temporary. The body generally returns to normal after several days of balanced food and fluid intake. However, as noted above, weight cycling that involves rapid losses and gains of body weight may increase one's health risks. This point will be discussed further in Chapter 10 in relation to very-low-Calorie diets.

One of the major medical concerns is the effect that severe weight restriction over a longer period may have upon children who are still in the growth and development stages of life. For example, young athletes are at a critical age as far as nutritional needs are concerned, yet the importance of making weight for certain sports often outweighs consideration of a balanced diet, adequate fluid intake, and a minimum caloric requirement. Hence they may go for months without adequate intake of essential nutrients like protein, iron, zinc, and calcium. Although numerous studies have revealed nutrient deficiencies and pathogenic weight-control behaviors in young athletes such as wrestlers and ballet dancers, unfortunately we have very few data on the long-range effects of such practices. A recent study by Benardot and Czerwinski, comparing the height: age and weight: age percentiles for female gymnasts between the ages of 7 and 10 versus 11 and 14, suggested that the decreased percentiles in the older gymnasts could be attributed to nutritional deficits, sport-specific selection factors favoring retention of small muscular gymnasts, or a combination of the two.

One health problem that has emerged is associated with the cessation of menstruation in athletes, a condition known as **athletic amenorrhea,** Although the precise cause of this form of secondary amenorrhea has not been identified, a number of theories have been proposed, including: a vegetarian diet; decreased intake of Calories, protein and fat; increased exercise intensity; increased levels of psychological stress; and excessive losses of body weight. The focus of research is upon how these factors may affect hormonal activity that governs menstruation. The hypothalamus may be influenced by all of these factors, possibly modifying the production of a number of important regulatory hormones relative to menstruation and metabolism, including epinephrine, corticoids, and estrogen.

Although no specific body fat percentage has been associated with the development of athletic amenorrhea, the available evidence suggests that decreased fat levels may lead to a decreased production of one form of estrogen. As noted in Chapter 7, one of the functions of estrogen is to regulate the activity of another hormone, calcitonin, which is involved in bone metabolism. In essence, decreased estrogen levels will impair bone tissue formation, leading to loss of bone mass and the development of osteoporosis. Although exercise is generally advocated as a means to prevent osteoporosis, it does not appear to counteract the adverse effects associated with decreased estrogen levels in athletic amenorrhea. A number of studies have shown that amenorrheic athletes have lower bone-density levels in non-weight-bearing bones such as the spine, and are more prone to musculoskeletal injuries than athletes who have normal menstruation. Other hormonal changes in athletic amenorrhea may reduce the resting metabolic rate. These problems are currently the focus of some extensive research, but unfortunately studies with humans are difficult to control since the cause of athletic amenorrhea itself is not known.

For highly active athletes, often a decrease in the intensity and duration of exercise will restore normal menstruation. However, the suggested medical treatment for this condition varies according to the viewpoint of several leading endocrinologists and may involve estrogen or progesterone therapy. Mona Shangold, a leading sports gynecologist, has suggested that any athlete who becomes amenorrheic should consult a physician for a diagnosis, for there may be causes that are not associated with exercise.

An obsession with having a low body weight may lead to a number of different **eating disorders,** which may become serious health problems. **An-**orexia nervosa is a complex disorder that is not completely understood but is thought to be a sign of other psychological problems. It is characterized by a fear of fatness and a resultant self-induced starvation. The diagnostic criteria for anorexia nervosa, as developed by the American Psychiatric Association, are summarized below:

1. An intense fear of becoming obese, which does not diminish as weight loss progresses.
2. A disturbed body image, believing to be fat even when emaciated.
3. A weight loss of at least 25 percent of the original body weight or, for those under 18, a weight loss from the original body weight of 9.25 percent plus the weight gain expected from normal growth curves.
4. Refusal to maintain the body weight over a minimal normal weight for age and height.
5. No known medical or psychiatric illness that would account for the weight loss.

The prevalence of anorexia nervosa is relatively low, less than 1 percent in the general population, but reported to be as high as 2 percent in college underclassmen. It appears that the person with the highest probability of developing anorexia nervosa is a perfectionistic and self-critical individual who comes from an upper-middle socioeconomic status. Anorexia nervosa is generally found in adolescent women, and about 85–95 percent of those affected are young females, usually under the age of 25. Medical consequences can be very serious, including anemia, a decreased heart muscle mass, heart beat arrhythmias, and even death. The treatment is generally prolonged for several years and primarily involves psychological therapy.

The term **bulimia nervosa** means *morbid hunger,* and the disorder involves a loss of control over the impulse to binge. The individual repeatedly ingests large quantities of food, but follows this by self-induced vomiting and other measures to avoid weight gain; this is the binge-purge syndrome. The American Psychiatric Association and other criteria for bulimia nervosa include:

1. Recurrent episodes of binge eating, at least two per week for three months.
2. Lack of control over eating during the binge.
3. Regular use of self-induced vomiting, laxatives, diuretics, fasting, or excessive exercise to control body weight.
4. Frequent fluctuations of body weight by 10 pounds because of binges and fasts.
5. Persistent concern with body weight and body shape.

Bulimia is more prevalent than anorexia nervosa, some studies reporting prevalence of bulimic symptoms in college students of approximately 20 percent, although the prevalence in the general population is only about 2–3 percent. Adverse health effects include erosion of tooth enamel, tears in the esophagus, aspiration pneumonia, and heart failure, all of which may be vomiting-induced.

In recent years the term **anorexia athletica** has been applied to those athletes who become overly concerned with their weight and exhibit some of the diagnostic criteria associated with anorexia nervosa or bulimia nervosa. Studies have revealed that approximately 20–40 percent of female athletes may exhibit such criteria, and rates from 50–74 percent have been reported for certain sports, such as gymnastics, distance running, and competitive body building. In general, this condition improves when the athletic season is completed and the athlete resumes normal dietary habits. However, what begins as a means to control weight for athletic competition on a short-term basis may develop into a long-term medical problem. Several investigators have suggested that special attention should be devoted to young female athletes, particularly those involved in such sports as gymnastics and ballet, because they may meet the age, sex, and socioeconomic-status criteria that may predispose to anorexia nervosa. Coaches and others should look for unexplained weight losses, obsession with exercise, excessive concern with body weight and appearance, and evidence of bizarre eating practices.

A detailed guide on how to identify pathogenic weight-control behavior is presented in Appendix G. Local dieticians and psychologists are excellent contacts if assistance is needed in dealing with this problem, and many hospitals have eating disorder programs. They may be able to provide questionnaires to help detect an eating disorder. The National Collegiate Athletic Association also offers brochures and videotapes to help develop awareness among athletes of the potential health risks associated with these disorders.

Body Composition and Physical Performance

What effect does excess body weight have on physical performance?

In some sports, extra body weight might prove to be an advantage, especially in football, ice hockey, sumo wrestling, and other sports in which body contact may occur or in which maintaining body stability is important. The effect of the extra weight may be neutralized, however, if the individual loses a corresponding amount of speed. Hence, increases in body weight for sports competition should maximize muscle mass and minimize body-fat gains. In rare instances, such as long-distance swimming in cold water, extra body fat may be helpful for its insulation and buoyancy effects.

On the other hand, there are a variety of sports where excess body weight may be disadvantageous. Whenever the body has to be moved rapidly or efficiently, excess weight in the form of body fat only serves as a burden. Take a good look at high jumpers, long jumpers, ballet dancers, gymnasts, sprinters, and long-distance runners. The amount of musculature may vary in each, but the body-fat percentage is extremely low. Research has also shown that even professional football players have relatively low percentages of body fat.

According to basic principles of physics, body fat in excess of the amount necessary for optimal functioning will impair physical performance. Body fat increases the mass, or inertia, of the individual but does not contribute directly to energy production, so excess fat will detract from performance in events in which the body must be moved. For example, a high jumper can develop only so much power through muscular force when taking off. Basic laws of physics tell us that an extra five pounds of body fat would decrease the height to which the body center of gravity could be raised, thus decreasing the height that could probably be cleared. Extra poundage on a marathoner over a 26.2-mile course could add a considerable energy cost. A 160-pound runner who loses about 5 percent of body fat, or about 8 pounds, could expect to improve the running time for the marathon by about 6 minutes. Adding body fat would slow the running pace. In essence, the body becomes a less efficient machine when it must transport extra weight that has no useful purpose. That extra weight is usually excess body fat.

For a number of reasons it is difficult to predict with certainty a precise percentage of body fat for a given athlete that will result in optimal performance. Nevertheless, studies with elite athletes have given us some general guidelines. Male sprinters, long-distance runners, wrestlers, gymnasts, basketball players, soccer players, swimmers, body builders, and football backs have functioned effectively with 5–10 percent body fat. Other male athletes such as baseball players, football linemen, tennis players, weight lifters, and weight men in track and field may average 11–15 percent, or just below the average for the nonathletic individual.

Several authorities have suggested that female athletes should carry no more than 20 percent fat while others note it should be below 15 percent. Female gymnasts and distance runners have been recorded well below 15 percent; some gymnasts were even below 10 percent. Most other female athletes range between 15 and 20 percent, with some of the strength-type athletes, such as discus throwers, recording values of 25 percent or greater. Although these are some general guidelines, it should be noted that body fat percentage is only one of many factors that may influence physical performance, and athletes may perform well even though their body fat is above these levels. However, everything else being equal, excess body fat is a disadvantage.

Care should be taken in advising athletes to lose body weight to achieve an arbitrary predetermined goal, i.e., 5 percent body fat. First, recall that the measurement techniques for body composition have a 2–4 percent error rate or higher for estimating body fat. Second, the nature of the athlete's body composition may make it impossible to achieve that low level. And third, excessive weight losses may actually lead to a decrease in physical performance, just the opposite of the desired goal.

Does excessive weight loss impair physical performance?

Weight-reduction programs used by wrestlers and other athletes have been condemned by sports medicine groups, not only for health reasons but also because these practices may impair physical performance. Reports by the American College of Sports Medicine and the Committee on Medical Aspects of Sports of the American Medical Association noted that food restriction, fluid deprivation, and dehydration could produce a reduction in muscular strength and a decrease in work performance. This impairment in performance may be attributed to a decreased blood volume, impaired cardiovascular function, a decreased ability to regulate body temperature, hypoglycemia, or a depletion of muscle and liver glycogen stores. However, the ultimate effect upon performance may be dependent upon the technique used—dehydration or starvation—and the time over which the weight is lost.

The effect of rapid weight loss by dehydration upon physical performance was covered in Chapter 8. In general, events characterized by power, strength, and speed may not be adversely affected by short-term dehydration, whereas aerobic and anaerobic endurance events are likely to deteriorate, particularly if done under warm environmental conditions.

Starvation and semistarvation studies have been conducted over periods ranging from one day to a year. Short-term starvation may impair physical performance if blood-glucose and muscle-glycogen levels are lowered substantially. Although strength and VO_2 max generally are not affected by acute starvation, recent studies using a 24-hour fast have shown that anaerobic and aerobic endurance performance will suffer if dependent upon muscle glycogen or normal blood-glucose levels. Long term semistarvation may lead to significant losses of lean muscle tissue and decreased performance in almost all fitness components.

It was interesting to note that in some semistarvation studies in which fewer than 1,000 Calories were consumed daily, vigorous exercise programs were maintained even though the subjects were losing substantial amounts of body weight. In general, the authors noted that the key point was to prevent hypoglycemia, dehydration, and excessive loss of lean muscle mass. If these goals could be achieved, physical performance need not deteriorate on weight-loss programs. Nevertheless, Horswill and others recently found that performance on a high-intensity arm exercise task decreased significantly after subjects lost 6 percent of their body weight by either a hypocaloric low-carbohydrate diet or a hypocaloric high-carbohydrate diet. However, the impairment was less with the high-carbohydrate diet, suggesting that athletes undergoing weight loss for competition should increase the carbohydrate proportion of the hypocaloric diet.

It is difficult to predict the specific body weight at which physical performance will begin to deteriorate for a given individual. For those athletes who are on a weight-loss program, it may be wise to monitor performance through certain standardized tests appropriate for their sport. Some examples include basic fitness tests with measures of strength, local muscular endurance, and cardiovascular endurance. A decrease in performance may be indicative that the weight loss is excessive. Personality changes, excessive tiredness, weakness, and lack of enthusiasm may also be telltale clues.

As suggested by the two questions in this section, weight losses may either improve or diminish performance. The key is to lose weight properly, primarily body fat. The basic guidelines for the development of such a program to improve physical performance, or health, are presented in the next chapter.

References

Books

American Psychiatric Association, 1987. *Diagnostic and Statistical Manual of Mental Disorders.* Third edition, revised-DSM-III-R Washington, DC:. American Psychiatric Association.

Bouchard, C., and Johnston, F. (Eds.). 1988. *Fat Distribution During Growth and Later Outcomes.* New York: Alan R. Liss.

Hunt, S., and Groff, J. 1990. *Advanced Nutrition and Human Metabolism.* St. Paul: West Publishing.

National Research Council. 1989. *Recommended Dietary Allowances.* Washington, DC: National Academy Press.

National Research Council. 1989. *Diet and Health: Implications for Reducing Chronic Disease Risk.* Washington, DC: National Academy Press.

Roche, A. (Ed.) 1985. *Body Composition Assessments in Youth and Adults.* Columbus, OH: Ross Laboratories.

Shils, M., and Young, V. 1988. *Modern Nutrition in Health and Disease.* Philadelphia: Lea & Febiger.

Williams, M. H. 1985. *Nutritional Aspects of Human Physical and Athletic Performance.* Springfield, IL: C C Thomas.

Reviews

American College of Sports Medicine. 1976. Position stand on weight loss in wrestlers. *Medicine and Science in Sports* 8:xi–xiii.

American College of Sports Medicine. 1983. Proper and improper weight loss programs. *Medicine and Science in Sports and Exercise* 15:ix–xiii.

American Dietetic Association. 1989. Position of the American Dietetic Association: Optimal weight as a health promotion strategy. *Journal of the American Dietetic Association,* 89:1814–17.

Anderson, G. 1988. Metabolic regulation of food intake. In: *Modern Nutrition in Health and Disease,* eds. M. Shils and V. Young. Philadelphia: Lea & Febiger.

Baumgartner, R., et al. 1990. Bioelectric impedance for body composition. *Exercise and Sport Sciences Reviews,* 18:193–224.

Bishop, P., and Smith, J. 1988. Body composition—practical considerations for coaches and athletes. *National Strength and Conditioning Association Journal* 10:27–31.

Blumenthal, A., et al. 1985. Anorexia and exercise: Implications from recent findings. *Sports Medicine* 2:237–47.

Bouchard, C. 1989. Genetic factors in obesity. *Medical Clinics of North America,* 73:67–82.

Bouchard, C., and Despres, J. 1989. Variation in fat distribution with age and health implications. *American Academy of Physical Education Papers,* 22:78–106.

Bray, G. 1989. Nutrient balance and obesity: An approach to control of food intake in humans. *Medical Clinics of North America,* 73:29–46.

Bray, G. 1989. Classification and evaluation of the obesities. *Medical Clinics of North America* 73:161–84.

Bray, G. 1991. Treatment for obesity: A nutrient balance/nutrient partition approach. *Nutrition Reviews* 49:33–45.

Campaigne, B. 1990. Body fat distribution in females: Metabolic consequences and implications for weight loss. *Medicine and Science in Sports and Exercise* 22:291–97.

Cash, T., et al. 1986. The great American shape-up. *Psychology Today* 20: 30–37.

Czajka-Narins, D., and Parham, E. 1990. Fear of fat: Attitudes towards obesity. *Nutrition Today* 25: 26–32.

Dalsky, G. 1990. Effect of exercise on bone: Permissive influence of estrogen and calcium. *Medicine and Science in Sports and Exercise* 22:281–85.

Despres, J., et al. 1990. Regional distribution of body fat, plasma lipoproteins, and cardiovascular disease. *Arteriosclerosis* 10:497–511.

Drinkwater, B. 1989. Amenorrheic athletes: At risk for premature osteoporosis? *Proceedings First IOC World Congress on Sport Sciences.* Colorado Springs, CO: United States Olympic Committee.

Flatt, J. 1989. The difference in the storage capacities for carbohydrate and for fat, and its implications in the regulation of body weight. *Annals of the New York Academy of Science* 499P:104–23.

Gray, D. 1989. Diagnosis and prevalence of obesity. *Medical Clinics of North America* 73: 1–14.

Griffin, J. 1989. Dying to win—eating disorders in sport. *Proceedings First IOC World Congress on Sport Sciences.* Colorado Springs, CO: United States Olympic Committee.

Heymsfield, S., and Williams, P. 1988. Nutritional assessment by clinical and biochemical methods. In: ed. M. Shils and V. Young. *Modern Nutrition in Health and Disease,* Philadelphia: Lea & Febiger.

Hirsch, J., et al., 1989. The fat cell. *Medical Clinics of North America* 73: 83–96.

Jackson, A., and Pollock, M. 1985. Practical assessment of body composition. *Physician and Sportsmedicine* 13: 76–90.

Keesey, R. 1989. Physiological regulation of body weight and the issue of obesity. *Medical Clinics of North America* 73: 15–28.

Kemnitz, J. 1985. Body weight set point theory. *Contemporary Nutrition* 10: 1–2.

Kissebah, A., et al. 1989. Health risks of obesity. *Medical Clinics of North America* 73: 111–38.

Kloss, S. 1989. A coach's guide to eating disorders. *National Strength and Coaching Association Journal* 11: 68–72.

Loucks, A. 1990. Effects of exercise training on the menstrual cycle: Existence and mechanisms. *Medicine and Science in Sports and Exercise,* 22: 275–80.

Lucas, A., and Huse, D. 1988. Behavioral disorders affecting food intake: Anorexia nervosa and bulimia. In: eds. M. Shils and V. Young. *Modern Nutrition in Health and Disease,* Philadelphia: Lea & Febiger.

Miller, W. 1991. Clinical symposium: Obesity: Diet composition, energy expenditure, and treatment of the obese patient. *Medicine and Science in Sports and Exercise* 23:273–97.

Moore, M. 1983. New height–weight tables gain pounds, lose status. *Physician and Sportsmedicine* 11: 25.

National Institute of Nutrition. 1989. An overview of the eating disorders anorexia nervosa and bulimia nervosa. *Nutrition Today* 24: 27–29.

Pi-Sunyer, F. 1990. Effect of the composition of the diet on energy intake. *Nutrition Reviews* 48: 94–105.

Prior, J. 1990. Reproduction: exercise-related adaptations and the health of women and men. In: *Exercise, Fitness and Health,* eds. C. Bouchard et al. Champaign, IL: Human Kinetics.

Raithel, K. 1988. Are American children really unfit? *Physician and Sportsmedicine* 16: 146–53.

Rodin, J., et al. 1989. Psychological features of obesity. *Medical Clinics of North America* 73: 47–66.

Schocken, D., et al. 1989. Weight loss and the heart. *Archives of Internal Medicine* 149: 877–80.

Schulz, L. 1987. Brown adipose tissue: regulation of thermogenesis and implications for obesity. *Journal of the American Dietetic Association* 87: 761–64.

Shangold, M. 1985. Athletic amenorrhea. *Clinical Obstetrics and Gynecology* 28: 664–69.

Shangold, M. 1986. How I manage exercise-related menstrual disturbances. *Physician and Sportsmedicine* 14: 113–20.

Stamford, B. 1986. What is cellulite? *Physician and Sportsmedicine* 14: 226.

Stamford, B. 1991. Apples and pears. *Physician and Sportsmedicine* 19: 123–24.

Stock, M. 1989. Thermogenesis and brown fat: Relevance to human obesity. *Infusiontherapie* 16:282–84.

Stricker, E., and Verbalis, J. 1990. Control of Appetite and satiety: Insights from biologic and behavioral studies. *Nutrition Reviews* 48: 49–56.

Thornton, J. 1990. Feast or famine: Eating disorders in athletes. *Physician and Sportsmedicine* 18: 116–22.

Thornton, J. 1990. How can you tell when an athlete is too thin. *Physician and Sportsmedicine* 18: 124–33.

Widdowson, E. 1988. Nutrition and cell and organ growth. In: *Modern Nutrition in Health and Disease,* eds. M. Shils and V. Young, Philadelphia: Lea & Febiger.

Williams, M. 1986. Weight control through exercise and diet for children and young athletes. *American Academy of Physical Education Papers* 19: 88–113.

Wilmore, J. 1991. Eating and weight disorders in the female athlete. *International Journal of Sport Nutrition* 1: 104–17.

York, D. 1990. Metabolic regulation of food intake. *Nutrition Reviews* 48: 64–70.

Specific Studies

Barrow, G., and Saha, S. 1988. Menstrual irregularity and stress fractures in collegiate female distance runners. *American Journal of Sports Medicine,* 16: 209–16.

Benardot, D., and Czerwinski, C. 1991. Selected body composition and growth measures of junior elite gymnasts. *Journal of the American Dietetic Association* 91: 29–33.

Bennett, S., et al. 1989. Bulimia nervosa and resting metabolic rate. *International Journal of Eating Disorders,* 8: 417–24.

Bergh, V., et al. 1991. The relationship between body mass and oxygen uptake during running in humans. *Medicine and Science in Sports and Exercise* 23: 205–11.

Black, D., and Burckes-Miller, M. 1988. Male and female college athletes: Use of anorexia nervosa and bulimia nervosa weight loss methods. *Research Quarterly for Exercise and Sport* 59: 252–56.

Bouchard, C., et al. 1989. Genetic effect in resting and exercise metabolic rates. *Metabolism* 38: 364–70.

Bouchard, C., et al. 1990. The response to long-term overfeeding in identical twins. *New England Journal of Medicine* 322: 1477–82.

Brown, T., et al. 1989. Body-image disturbances in adolescent female binge-purgers: A brief report of the results of a national survey in the U.S.A. *Journal of Child Psychology and Psychiatry,* 30: 605–13.

Davis, P., et al. 1989. Near infrared interactance vs. hydrostatic weighing to measure body composition in lean, normal and obese women. *Medicine and Science in Sports and Exercise* 21 S100.

Deurenberg, P., et al. 1990. Assessment of body composition by bioelectrical impedance in a population aged > 60 y. *American Journal of Clinical Nutrition* 51: 3–6.

Drewnowski, A., et al. 1988. The prevalence of bulimia nervosa in the US college student population. *American Journal of Public Health* 78: 1322–25.

Drewnowski, A., and Yee, D. 1987. Men and body image: Are males satisfied with their body weight. *Psychosomatic Medicine* 49: 626–34.

Fleck, S. 1983. Body composition of elite American athletes. *American Journal of Sports Medicine* 11: 398–403.

Frisch, R., et al. 1989. Lower prevalence of nonreproductive system cancers among female former college athletes. *Medicine and Science in Sports and Exercise* 21: 250–53.

Gleeson, M., et al. 1988. Influence of a 24 h fast on high intensity cycle exercise performance in man. *European Journal of Applied Physiology* 57: 553–59.

Hassager, C., et al. 1989. Body composition measurement by dual photon absorptiometry: Comparison with body density and total body potassium measurement. *Clinical Physiology* 9: 353–60.

Horswill, C., et al. 1990. Changes in the protein nutritional status of adolescent wrestlers. *Medicine and Science in Sports and Exercise* 22: 599–604.

Horswill, C., et al. 1990. Weight loss, dietary carbohydrate modifications, and high intensity, physical performance. *Medicine and Science in Sports and Exercise*. 22: 470–76.

Israel, R., et al. 1989. Validity of NIR for estimating human body composition. *Medicine and Science in Sports and Exercise,* 21: S103.

Jackson, A., and Pollock, M. 1978. Generalized equations for predicting body density in men. *British Journal of Nutrition* 40: 497–504.

Jackson, A., et al. 1980. Generalized equations for predicting body fat in women. *Medicine and Science of Sports* 12: 175–81.

Kaiserauer, S., et al. 1989. Nutritional, physiological, and menstrual status of distance runners. *Medicine and Science in Sports and Exercise* 21: 120–25.

Kirkwood, S., et al. 1990. Spontaneous physical activity is a major determinant of 24-hour sedentary energy expenditure. *Medicine and Science in Sports and Exercise* 22: S49.

Klinging, J., and Karpowicz, W. 1986. The effects of rapid weight loss and rehydration on a wrestling performance test. *Journal of Sports Medicine* 26: 149–52.

Kono, I., et al. 1988. Weight reduction in athletes may adversely affect the phagocytic function of monocytes. *Physician and Sports Medicine* 16: 56–65.

Lloyd, T., et al. 1986. Women athletes with menstrual irregularity have increased musculoskeletal injuries. *Medicine and Science in Sports and Exercise* 18: 374–79.

Loosli, A., et al. 1986. Nutrition habits and knowledge in competitive adolescent female gymnasts. *Physician and Sportsmedicine,* 14: 119–30, August.

Lotti, T., et al. 1990. Proteoglycans in so-called cellulite. *International Journal of Dermatology* 29: 272–74.

Mansfield, M., and Emans, S. 1989. Anorexia nervosa, athletics, and amenorrhea. *Pediatric Clinics of North America* 36: 533–49.

McLeod, W., et al. 1983. Performance measurement and percent body fat in the high school athlete. *American Journal of Sports Medicine* 11: 390–97.

Myerson, M., et al. 1991. Resting metabolic rate and energy balance in amenorrheic and eumenorrheic runners. *Medicine and Science in Sports and Exercise* 23: 15–22.

Newman, B., et al. 1990. Nongenetic influences of obesity on other cardiovascular disease risk factors: an analysis of identical twins. *American Journal of Public Health* 80: 675–78.

Pate, R., et al. 1989. Relationship between skinfold thickness and performance of health related fitness test items. *Research Quarterly for Exercise and Sport* 60: 183–88.

Peiris, A., et al. 1989. Adiposity, fat distribution and cardiovascular risk. *Annals of Internal Medicine,* 110: 867–72.

Roberts, S., et al. 1990. Body weight regulation in young men. Contributions of adaptive variations in nutrient intakes and energy expenditure. *FASEB Journal* 4: A783.

Roberts, W., and Elliot, D. 1991. Malnutrition in a compulsive runner. *Medicine and Science in Sports and Exercise* 23: 513–16.

Rodin, J., et al. 1990. Weight cycling and fat distribution. *International Journal of Obesity* 14: 303–10.

Schutz, Y., et al. 1989. Failure of dietary fat intake to promote fat oxidation: A factor favoring the development of obesity. *American Journal of Clinical Nutrition* 50: 307–14.

Segal, K., et al. 1988. Lean body mass estimation by bioelectrical impedance analysis: A four-site cross-validation study. *American Journal of Clinical Nutrition* 47: 7–14.

Seidell, J., et al. 1991. Body fat distribution in relation to physical activity and smoking habits in 38-year-old European men. *American Journal of Epidemiology* 133: 257–65.

Steen, S. N., and Brownell, K. 1990. Patterns of weight loss and regain in wrestlers: Has the pattern changed? *Medicine and Science in Sports and Exercise* 22: 762–68.

Stunkard, A., et al. 1986. A twin study of obesity. *Journal of the American Medical Association* 256: 51–54.

Stunkard, A., et al. 1990. The body-mass index of twins who have been reared apart. *New England Journal of Medicine* 322: 1483–87.

Sztalryd, C., et al. 1990. Insulin regulation of adipocyte metabolism vary as a function of anatomical region. *FASEB Journal* 4: A917.

Tran, Z., and Weltman, A. 1989. Generalized equation for predicting body density of women from girth measurements. *Medicine and Science in Sports and Exercise* 21: 101–4.

Tremblay, A., et al. 1989. Impact of dietary fat content and fat oxidation on energy intake in humans. *American Journal of Clinical Nutrition* 49: 799–805.

Tremblay, A., et al. 1991. Nutritional determinants of the increase in energy intake associated with a high fat diet. *American Journal of Clinical Nutrition* 53: 1134–37.

Tucker, L., and Friedman, G. 1989. Television viewing and obesity in adult males. *American Journal of Public Health* 79: 516–18.

Wade, A., et al. 1990. Muscle fibre type and aetiology of obesity. *Lancet* 335: 805–8.

Walberg, J., and Johnson, C. 1991. Menstrual function and eating behavior in female recreational weight lifters and competitive body builders. *Medicine and Science in Sports and Exercise* 23: 30–36.

Webster, S., et al. 1990. Physiological effects of a weight loss regimen practiced by college wrestlers. *Medicine and Science in Sports and Exercise* 22: 229–34.

Williams, P. 1990. Weight set-point theory and the high-density lipoprotein concentrations of long-distance runners. *Metabolism* 39: 460–67.

Key Terms

aerobic walking

behavior modification

duration concept

exercise frequency

exercise intensity

Food Exchange System

interval training

long-haul concept

maximal heart rate (HR max)

maximal heart rate reserve

quality Calories

rating of perceived exertion (RPE)

spot reducing

target range/target HR

very-low-Calorie diets (VLCD)

warm-down

warm-up

Key Concepts

The caloric deficit, which represents caloric intake minus caloric expenditure, may be useful as a means to predict body-weight losses on a long-term basis, because 3,500 Calories equals approximately one pound of body fat.

The average adult female should be able to maintain her body weight with a daily average of approximately 14–17 Calories per pound of body weight, while males need about 15–18 Calories per pound of body weight. Slightly higher amounts of Calories are needed by children, adolescents, and physically active individuals.

For the overweight individual who desires to lose weight without the guidance of a physician, the recommended maximal value is two pounds per week.

Keeping a record of your daily eating habits will help you identify behavioral patterns relative to overeating and may be used as a basis for the elimination of cues that trigger eating.

Rapid loss of body weight, which may occur during the early stages of dieting, is due primarily to body-water changes, but the rate at which weight loss occurs will slow down as your body weight decreases, for then body-fat stores are the prime source of weight loss.

The key principle to dieting is to select low-Calorie high-nutrient foods from among the six food exchanges that appeal to your taste and are easily incorporated into your daily life-style.

Counting Calories may be a useful technique to develop during the early stages of a diet, for the more knowledge you have about the caloric and nutrient content of foods, the better equipped you are to make a wise selection.

Very low-Calorie diets may be effective for weight loss under strict medical supervision but are not recommended for the average individual trying to lose excess pounds.

Exercise can increase energy expenditure considerably, but in order to lose body fat through exercise one should think in terms of months, not days.

Weight-reduction exercises need to involve large muscle masses, such as the legs in jogging or bicycling or the arms and legs in swimming.

The general design of the weight-reduction exercise program involves three phases: warm-up, exercise stimulus, and warm-down.

An effective means of monitoring exercise intensity is the exercise heart rate (HR), but the exercise target HR varies depending upon age and level of conditioning.

A slow, steady progression in exercise intensity is important in preventing excess stress and injuries.

The minimum exercise goals for losing weight are an intensity of 50–85 percent maximal HR reserve, a duration of 20–60 minutes, and a frequency of 3 or 4 times per week; however, duration and frequency of exercise are more important than intensity for losing weight.

For several reasons weight loss may not occur in the early stages of an exercise program; however, the body composition changes are favorable, i.e., a decrease in body fat and increase in fat-free mass.

The rapid weight loss observed after a single bout of exercise is due to water loss through sweating.

Although diet and exercise may each be effective in losing body weight, a combination of the two would be even more beneficial. A comprehensive weight-control program involves a balanced low-Calorie diet, an aerobic exercise program, and appropriate behavior modification.

Prevention of obesity is more effective than treatment, and appropriate programs should be developed early for children and adolescents.

Weight Maintenance and Loss Through Proper Nutrition and Exercise

10

Introduction

Given the obsession we have with slimness in the United States and the fact that millions of Americans are overweight, it is no wonder that a multibillion-dollar weight-control industry has developed. Weight-loss centers and health and fitness spas cater to this obsession and promise us a new body just in time for the swimsuit season. Pharmaceutical companies produce drugs, both prescription and over-the-counter types, to help us lose fat the easy way. Food manufacturers market convenient, low-Calorie, prepackaged—but expensive—meals. Each year at least one diet book on the best-seller list is advertised as the last diet we will ever need.

A variety of techniques are used to stimulate weight loss. Drugs are used to depress the appetite or increase metabolism. Surgical techniques include intestinal bypasses, removal or stapling part of the stomach, excising or suction removal of subcutaneous fat tissue, and wiring the jaw shut. Weight-loss diets involve almost every possible manipulation, including the high-fat diet, the high-protein diet, grapefruit diet, the starvation diet, and even the "no diet" diet. Exercising programs in specially designed clothing are advertised as helping you lose inches of fat in hours. Psychological techniques such as hypnosis or behavior modification are designed to change your eating habits.

In severe cases of clinical obesity, treatment usually is administered under medical supervision and may involve a combination of many of these techniques, including surgery, hormone therapy, drugs, and starvation-type diets. An individualized, medically supervised weight-control program is very important for the clinically obese because so many health risks are related to obesity. Unfortunately, clinical obesity is very resistant to treatment and the vast majority, 95–99 percent, of those individuals who lose weight regain it within a year or two, and may do this repeatedly. In a recent review, Kelly Brownell noted that these fluctuations in body weight, known as weight cycling, may exert deleterious effects on metabolism and health.

Weight-control programs have greater chances for success in individuals who have accumulated excess body fat through environmental conditions, such as excessive eating and decreased physical activity, and who do not have a strong genetic predisposition to obesity.

Such a treatment program may be beneficial to the typical adult, for substantial amounts of body fat appear to accumulate between the ages of 25 and 35. It is interesting to note that the average American male, age 25–50, increased his BMI from 22 to 25 between the 1980 and 1989 RDA; the average female went from about 21 to 24. Moreover, prevention of excess weight gain is more effective than treatment. Prevention of excess weight gain should be a lifelong life-style, beginning in childhood and continuing through adulthood, as suggested by the data presented above. Maintenance of a healthy body weight through prevention techniques may be especially helpful during the first two years of college when young females typically gain 10–15 pounds. Additionally, prevention may also help curtail the weight gain in those genetically predisposed, as supported by the recent twin study of Newman and others.

This chapter centers on some basic questions relative to the construction, implementation, and maintenance of a sound weight-control program. The principles and suggestions advanced here apply to the overweight individual who wants to lose excess body fat, and also to the person with normal body weight who may want to maintain that weight level or even lose additional poundage in order to improve physical performance.

A comprehensive weight-control program involves three components: (1) a dietary regimen stressing balanced nutrition but with reduced caloric intake; (2) an aerobic exercise program to increase caloric expenditure; and (3) a behavior modification program to facilitate the implementation of the first two components. These components are emphasized in this chapter.

Basics of Weight Control

How many Calories are in a pound of body fat?

One pound is equivalent to 454 grams. Because we know that 1 gram of fat is equal to 9 Calories, it would appear that a pound of fat would equal about 4,086 Calories (9 × 454). However, the fat stored in adipose tissue contains small amounts of protein, minerals, and water, which reduces the caloric content of one pound of body fat to approximately 3,500 Calories.

Is the caloric concept of weight control valid?

The caloric concept of weight control is relatively simple. If you take in more Calories than you expend, you will gain weight. If you expend more than you take in, you lose weight. To maintain your body weight, caloric input and output must be equal. As far as we know, human energy systems are governed by the same laws of physics that rule all energy transformations. The First Law of Thermodynamics is as pertinent to us in the conservation and expenditure of our energy sources as it is to any other machine. Because a Calorie is a unit of energy, and because energy can neither be created nor destroyed, those Calories that we eat must either be expended in some way or conserved in the body. No substantial evidence is available to disprove the caloric theory. It is still the physical basis for body-weight control.

Keep in mind, however, that the total body weight is made up of different components, those notable in weight-control programs being body water, protein in the fat-free mass, small amounts of carbohydrate, and fat stores. Changes in these components may bring about body weight fluctuations that would appear to be contrary to the caloric concept since protein and carbohydrate contain only 4 Calories per gram and water contains no Calories. You may lose five pounds in an hour, but it will be mostly water weight. Starvation techniques may lead to rapid weight losses, but some of the weight loss will be in glycogen stores and body-protein stores such as muscle mass. In programs to lose body weight, we usually desire to lose excess body fat, and certain dietary and exercise techniques may help to maximize fat losses while minimizing protein losses.

The metabolism of human energy sources is complex, and although the caloric theory is valid relative to body-weight control, one must be aware that weight changes will not always be exactly in line with caloric input and output, and that weight losses may not be due to body fat loss alone. Also keep in mind one of the concepts advanced in the last chapter relative to individual variability in metabolic rates; two individuals may consume the same amount of Calories, yet one may gain while the other may maintain or even lose weight. These concepts are explored further in this chapter.

How many Calories do I need per day to maintain my body weight?

This depends on a number of factors, notably age, body weight, sex, basal metabolic rate (BMR), dietary induced thermogenesis (DIT), and physical activity levels.

The caloric requirement per kilogram of body weight is very high during the early years of life when a child is developing and adding large amounts of body tissue. The Calorie/kilogram requirement decreases throughout the years from birth to old age, with exceptions during pregnancy and lactation.

Body weight influences the total amount of daily Calories you need, but not the Calorie/kilogram level. The large individual simply needs more total Calories to maintain body weight. Body weight is the most significant factor determining daily caloric intake necessary to maintain weight, although body composition also may be important.

Up to the age of 11 or 12, the caloric needs of boys and girls are similar in terms of Calories/kilogram body weight. After puberty, however, males need more Calories/kilogram, probably because of their greater percentage of muscle tissue in comparison to females.

Individual variations in BMR may either increase or decrease daily caloric needs, depending on whether the BMR is above or below normal. Individual variations may vary 10–20 percent from normal. An extended discussion of the BMR was presented in Chapter 2.

The DIT effect may also vary among individuals. The DIT is also covered in more detail in Chapter 2.

Physical activity levels above resting may have a very significant impact upon caloric needs. Some sports, like bowling, may increase energy needs only slightly, while other high-energy sports may add 1,000–1,500 or more Calories to the daily energy requirement. You may wish to review Chapter 2 regarding the caloric cost of exercise.

All of these factors make it difficult to make an exact recommendation relative to daily caloric needs. The Food and Nutrition Board of the National Research Council, for example, notes a 20 percent variation in daily caloric needs for those who engage in light to moderate physical activity. Using the data presented in Appendix A, the calculated range of caloric needs for the average adult male and female, aged 19–24, would be, respectively, 2,320–3,480 and 1,760–2,640 Calories per day. Additional ranges for other age levels may be calculated from Appendix A.

For children involved in normal activities and for adults involved in light work, Table 10.1 presents caloric needs based on body weight, expressed in both kilograms and pounds. These data are derived from the National Research Council recommendations in Appendix A, and they represent the average daily caloric intake. To calculate your average caloric needs, simply multiply your body weight by the appropriate figure in the table. For example, a 25-year-old woman who weighs 55 kg or 121 lbs would need approximately 1,980 Calories/day (55 × 36).

Table 10.2 represents some figures from the American Heart Association. It may be a more appropriate guide for those who want to lose some extra body fat since it provides information relative to activity level. The Calories allocated per pound are somewhat less than those advocated by the National Research Council. For example, a sedentary individual who weighs 170 pounds needs approximately 2,380 Calories per day (170 × 14) simply to maintain body weight. To lose or gain weight, the caloric intake must be adjusted downward or upward. Keep in mind that the figures in both tables are approximations, and actual daily caloric needs may vary somewhat. However, these tables do offer an estimate of daily caloric needs and may be useful in starting a weight-control program.

How much weight may I lose safely per week?

If you decide to lose weight without medical supervision, the recommended maximal value is 2 pounds per week. Because there are 3,500 Calories in a pound of body fat, this would necessitate a deficit of 7,000 Calories for the week, or 1,000 Calories per day. For growing children who carry excess fat, the general recommendation is only about 1 pound per week, or a daily 500-Calorie deficit.

As we shall see later in this chapter, weight losses may not parallel the caloric deficit we incur during early stages of a weight-reduction program, and the 2-pound limit may be adjusted during this time period. In addition, as mentioned previously, we want our weight loss to be body-fat tissue, not lean body mass. A loss of 10 pounds of body weight may help improve physical performance, but if 5 pounds is muscle tissue, then performance could possibly deteriorate. Thus, you should monitor your weight loss not only with a scale but also with skinfolds and girth measures to help ensure that you are losing body fat, hopefully in the right places.

Table 10.1 Recommended dietary allowances for energy

Age	Males		Females	
	C/lb	C/kg	C/lb	C/kg
11–14	25	55	21	47
15–18	20	45	18	40
19–24	18	40	17	38
25–50	17	37	16	36
51 and over	14	30	14	30

Keep in mind that the values in this table are approximations. They are based on National Research Council data and represent caloric needs for children involved in normal activities and adults in light, sedentary occupations. These values may be increased significantly in those individuals who are physically active.

Table 10.2 Approximate daily caloric intake needed to maintain desirable body weight

Activity level	Calories per pound
1. Very sedentary (movement restricted such as patient confined to house)	13
2. Sedentary (most Americans, office job, light work)	14
3. Moderate activity (weekend recreation)	15
4. Very active (meet ACSM standards for vigorous exercise three times/week)	16
5. Competitive athlete (daily vigorous activity in high-energy sport)	17 +

Behavior Modification

What is behavior modification?

One of the key components of a successful weight-control program is the need to identify and modify those behaviors that contribute to the weight problem. The subject of human behavior development and change is very complex, but psychologists note that three factors are generally involved—the physical environment, the social environment, and the personal environment. For the person with a weight problem, a refrigerator brimming with food (physical environment), a family that consumes high-Calorie snack food around the house (social environment), and an acquired taste for sweet foods (personal environment) may trigger behaviors that make it very difficult to maintain a proper body weight.

A model often used to explain the development or modification of health behaviors, such as a proper diet and exercise program for weight control, involves three steps—knowledge, values and behavior. First, proper knowledge is essential. There exists a considerable amount of misinformation relative to the roles of nutrition and exercise in weight control, so you need to possess accurate information. Second, the health implications of this knowledge may help you develop a set of personal values, or attitudes, toward a specific health behavior. If you perceive excess body fat as a threat to your personal physical or psychological health, you are more likely to initiate behavioral changes. Third, your health behavior should then reflect the knowledge you acquired and the values you developed.

Behavior modification is a technique often used in psychological therapy to elicit desirable behavioral changes. The rationale underlying behavior modification is that many behavioral patterns are learned via stimulus–response conditioning; for example, a stimulus in your environment such as a commercial break in a television program elicits a response of a mad dash to the refrigerator. Because such responses are learned, they also may be unlearned. For a discussion of a comprehensive program conducted by a behavioral psychologist, the reader is referred to the review by Brownell and Kramer. Relative to a self-designed program of weight control, behavior modification is used primarily to reduce or eliminate physical or social stimuli that may lead to excessive caloric intake or decreased physical activity. George Bray, an international authority on obesity treatment, recently noted that the most important component of any weight-control program is the associated behavior modification through which the individual learns new ways to deal with old problems.

How do I apply behavior modification techniques in my weight-control program?

When breaking any well-established habit, self-discipline, or will power, is the key. The most important component of a weight-control program is

you. You must want to lose weight and you must take the major responsibility for achieving your goals. You must be convinced that reduced body weight will enhance your life and you must establish this goal as a high priority.

Both long-range and short-range realistic goals need to be established. A long-range goal may be to lose 40 pounds over six-months, whereas a short-range goal would be to lose about 1–2 pounds per week. A long-range goal may also include a large number of behavioral changes to achieve the 40-pound weight loss, but the number of changes would be phased in gradually on a short-term basis. Do not expect to make all recommended behavioral changes overnight. (See Figure 10.1.)

One of the first steps in a behavior modification program is to identify those physical and social environmental factors that may lead to problem behaviors. Keeping a diary of your daily activities for a week or two may help you identify some behavioral patterns that may contribute to overeating and extra body weight. The following are some of the factors that might be recorded each time you eat, along with a brief explanation of their possible importance. You should also record your daily physical activity.

Type of food and amount This may be related to the other factors. For example, do you eat a high-Calorie food during your snacks?

Meal or snack You may find yourself snacking four or five times a day.

Time of day Do you eat at regular hours or have a full meal just before retiring at night?

Degree of hunger How hungry were you when you ate—very hungry or not hungry at all? You may be snacking when not hungry.

Activity What were you doing while eating? You may find TV watching and eating snack foods are related.

Location Where do you eat? The office or school cafeteria may be the place you eat a high-Calorie meal.

Persons involved Whom do you eat with? Do you eat more when alone or with others? Being with certain people may trigger overeating.

Emotional feelings How do you feel when eating? You might eat more when depressed than when happy, or vice versa.

Exercise How much walking, stair climbing, or regular exercise do you get? Do you ride when you could possibly walk? How much time do you just sit?

Figure 10.1.
Goal setting is an important factor in an exercise program.

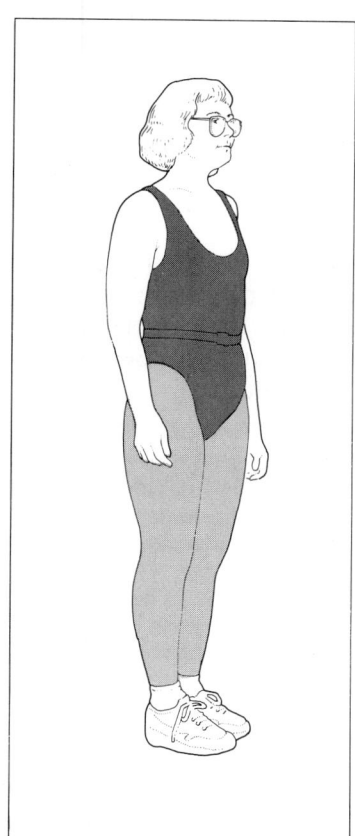  

	Short-term goals	Long-term goals
Time	1 month	6 months
Running	1 mile nonstop	5 miles nonstop
Weight	Lose 6 pounds	Lose 30 pounds

Recording this information may make you aware of the physical and social circumstances under which you tend to overeat or be physically inactive. This awareness may be useful to help implement behavioral changes that may make weight control easier. The following suggestions are often helpful:

Foods to eat:

1. Use low-Calorie foods for snacks.
2. Plan low-Calorie, high-nutrient meals.
3. Plan your food intake for the entire day.
4. Eat only foods that have had minimal or no processing.
5. Allow yourself very small amounts of high-Calorie foods that you like, but stay within daily caloric limitations.
6. Know the Food Exchange System.

Food purchasing:

1. Do not shop when hungry.
2. Prepare a shopping list and do not deviate from it.
3. Buy only foods that are low in Calories and high in nutrient value.
4. Buy only natural foods as much as possible.

Food storage:

1. Keep high-Calorie food out of sight and in sealed containers or cupboards.
2. Have low-Calorie snacks like carrots and radishes readily available.

Food preparation and serving:

1. Only buy foods that need preparation of some type.
2. Do not add fats or sugar in preparation, if possible.
3. Prepare only small amounts.
4. Do not use serving bowls on the table.
5. Put the food on the plate, preferably a small one.

Location:

1. Eat only in one place, such as the kitchen or dining area.
2. Avoid food areas such as the kitchen or snack table at a party.
3. Avoid restaurants where you are most likely to buy high-Calorie items.

Restaurant eating:

1. When eating out, select the low-Calorie items.
2. Request they be prepared without fat.
3. Have condiments like butter, mayonnaise, and salad dressing served on the side.

Methods of eating:

1. Eat slowly; chew food thoroughly or drink water between bites.
2. Eat with someone, for conversation can slow down the eating process.
3. Cut food up into small pieces.
4. Do not do anything else while eating, such as watching TV.
5. Relax and enjoy the meal.
6. Eat only at specified times.
7. Eat only until pleasantly satisfied, not stuffed.
8. Spread your Calories over the day, eating small amounts more often.

Activity:

1. Walk more. Park the car or get off the bus some distance from work.
2. Use the stairs instead of the elevator when possible.
3. Take a brisk walk instead of a coffee-donut break.
4. Get involved in activities with other people, preferably physical activities that will burn Calories.
5. Avoid sedentary night routines.
6. Start a regular aerobic exercise program.

Mental attitude:

1. Recognize that you are not perfect and lapses may occur.
2. Deal positively with your lapse; put it behind you and get back on your program.
3. Put reminders on the refrigerator door at home or on your telephone at work.
4. Reward yourself for sticking to your plans.

Self-discipline and self-control:

1. Establish weight loss as a high priority.
2. Think about this priority before eating.

For the interested reader, the books by Dusek and the Mahoneys provide an in-depth coverage of behavior modification for weight-control purposes. Many of the commercial, medically oriented weight-loss centers as well as organizations such as Weight Watchers International also may be sources of information.

Individuals with clinical obesity may need professional assistance from health counselors to implement a behavior modification program for weight control. However, others with less severe weight problems may be able to initiate their own program if they have adequate accurate information. The remainder of this chapter focuses on the development of a proper diet and exercise program for losing weight safely.

Dietary Modifications

How can I determine the number of Calories in a diet to lose weight?

To determine the number of Calories you may consume daily on your diet, you need to estimate your daily energy expenditure, which includes your basal metabolic rate and your normal daily activities. To estimate your daily energy expenditure refer to Table 10.2 on page 245 to determine the approximate number of Calories per day you need to maintain your body weight.

For our purposes, we will use the value of 3,500 Calories to represent one pound of body-fat, or bodyweight, loss. To lose one pound of body fat, you must create a 3,500 Calorie deficit. To lose one pound per week your daily caloric deficit should be 500 (3,500/7). To lose two pounds per week, the recommended maximum unless under medical supervision, the daily caloric deficit should be 1,000 (7,000/7).

Once you calculate your daily energy expenditure, simply subtract your daily caloric deficit from it; the result will be your recommended daily caloric intake. An example is presented below:

Example: 35-year-old sedentary woman who weighs 140 pounds desires to lose 1 pound per week.

1. From Table 10.2, Calories/lb needed to maintain body weight:
   14

2. Predicted total number of Calories to maintain body weight:

   $14 \times 140 = 1,960$ Calories/day

3. Recommended daily caloric deficit = 500 Calories/day

4. Recommended daily caloric intake = 1,460 Calories

   $(1,960 - 500 = 1,460$ Calories/day$)$

Table 10.3   Approximate number of days required to lose weight for a given caloric deficit

Daily caloric deficit	To lose 5 pounds	To lose 10 pounds	To lose 15 pounds	To lose 20 pounds	To lose 25 pounds
100	175	350	525	700	875
200	87	175	262	350	438
300	58	116	175	232	292
400	44	88	131	176	219
500	35	70	105	140	175
600	29	58	87	116	146
700	25	50	75	100	125
800	22	44	66	88	109
900	19	39	58	78	97
1,000	17	35	52	70	88
1,250	14	28	42	56	70
1,500	12	23	35	46	58

See text for explanation.

Another technique that has been recommended simply multiplies the body weight in pounds by 10 Calories. This technique is based upon the premise that the body weight may not be maintained at this level of caloric intake. For our example above, the recommended daily caloric intake would be 1,400 (10 × 140).

How can I predict my body-weight loss through dieting?

As mentioned in the last chapter, the human body is composed of different components, most commonly compartmentalized into body fat and lean body mass; lean body mass is about 70 percent water. On a dietary program, weight loss may reflect decreases in body fat, body water, or muscle mass, all of which present different caloric values. For example, one pound of body fat equals about 3,500 Calories, while an equivalent weight of water contains no Calories. Because of this fact, it is difficult to predict exactly how much body weight one will lose on any given diet, but an approximate value of the time it will take to lose excess body fat may be obtained.

The key point is the caloric deficit. The number of days it takes for this daily deficit to reach 3,500 is how long it will take you to lose one pound.

Table 10.3 illustrates the importance of the caloric deficit in determining the rapidity of weight loss by dieting. The higher the deficit, the faster you lose weight. However, rapid weight-loss programs are not usually desirable, and the dieter should realize that a moderate caloric deficit, say 500

Calories/day, may effectively reduce weight in time and yet provide a satisfying diet.

This table is based upon the value of 3,500 Calories for a pound of body fat. There is one precaution, however. Once you lose five pounds and every succeeding five pounds thereafter, you must adjust the number of Calories it takes to maintain your body weight, for now you are five pounds lighter. In our example above, for every 5-pound loss the woman would need to reduce about 70 Calories (5 × 14 = 70 Calories) from her diet to keep the caloric deficit at 500 Calories/day.

Although these prediction methods are good for the long run, daily body-weight changes may not coincide with daily caloric deficits.

Why does a person usually lose the most weight during the first week on a reducing diet?

If you start a diet with a significant caloric deficit, say 1,000 Calories/day, it would normally take you about 3.5 days to lose one pound of body fat. However, body-weight loss would be more rapid than this during the first several days, possibly totaling as much as 3–4 pounds. A large percentage of this weight loss would be due to a decrease in body carbohydrate and associated water stores. When you restrict your food intake, the body would then draw on its reserves to meet its energy needs. These reserves consist of both fat and carbohydrate stores, but much of the carbohydrate, stored as liver and muscle glycogen, could be used up in several days. Because 1 gram of glycogen is stored with about 3 grams of water, a significant weight loss could occur. For example, 300 grams of glycogen, along with 900 grams of water stored with it, would account for a loss of 1,200 grams, or 1.2 kilograms; this would equal over 2.5 pounds alone. About 70 percent of the weight loss during the first few days of a reduced Caloric diet is due to body-water losses. About 25 percent comes from body fat stores and 5 percent from protein tissue. It should be noted that loss of body protein is also accompanied by body-water losses, about 4–5 grams of water per gram of protein. Also, as noted later, very-low-Calorie diets may lead to greater protein losses.

If you desired to lose a maximal amount of weight during a two- to three-day period, water restriction would cause an even greater weight loss. However, this practice is not recommended, as you would only be decreasing body water levels. They would return to normal when you returned to normal water intake. There is one additional point relative to body water. At the conclusion of your diet, if you return to a normal caloric diet to maintain your new body weight, you may experience a rapid weight gain of two or three pounds. This may represent a replenishment of your body glycogen stores with the accompanying water weight. It is important to keep in mind that rather large fluctuations in daily body weight, say in the order of two to three pounds, are not due to rapid changes in body fat or lean body mass; these fluctuations are due primarily to body-water changes accompanying carbohydrate and protein losses.

Why does it become more difficult to lose weight after several weeks or months on a diet program?

Weight loss is rapid during the first few days on a diet, primarily because of water loss. Because water contains no Calories, our caloric loss does not need to total 3,500 in order to lose one pound of weight. We may lose one pound of body weight with a deficit of only about 1,200 Calories, because 70 percent of the weight loss is water. The 1,200 Calories is mostly from fat with a small amount of protein. However, by the end of the second week of dieting, water loss may account for only about 20 percent of body-weight loss; one pound of weight loss will now cost us approximately 2,800 Calories. At the end of the third week, water losses are minimal. The energy deficit to lose one pound of body weight now approximates 3,500 Calories. In essence, as you continue your diet, weight losses cost you more Calories because less body water is being lost. At the end of three weeks, you still can be losing weight, but at a much slower rate than during the early stages.

Another factor also slows down the rate of weight loss. As you lose weight, you need fewer Calories to maintain your new body weight. Let's take an example. Suppose you are an athlete who weighs 200 pounds and from Table 10.2 you see that you need 17 Calories/pound body weight to maintain your weight. At 200 pounds this would represent 3,400 Calories/day (200 × 17). However, if your weight drops to 180 pounds after dieting for ten weeks, you now need only 3,060 Calories, a difference of 340 Calories per day. If you want to continue to have a standard caloric deficit, then you will have to adjust your caloric intake as you lose weight. Suppose our 200-pounder wanted to have a daily caloric deficit of 1,000 Calories. His initial diet should then contain about 2,400 Calories/day (3,400–1,000). However, once he is down to 180 pounds, his diet should now include only 2,060 Calories/day (3,060 − 1,000). If he did not adjust his diet from 2,400 Calories, then the daily deficit would only be 660 Calories/day (3,060–2,400), not the standard 1,000 he wanted. Weight loss would continue, but at a slower rate.

You should realize that the rate of weight loss will slow as a natural consequence of your diet, but the weight you are losing at that point is primarily body fat. To keep a standard caloric deficit may also require an additional reduction in caloric intake as you progress on your diet. Knowledge of these factors may help you through the latter stages of a diet designed to attain a set weight goal. Other factors associated with very-low-Calorie diets and exercise, discussed later, may also influence the magnitude of the caloric intake necessary to sustain a given rate of weight loss.

What are the major characteristics of a sound diet for weight control?

As you probably are aware, literally hundreds of different diet plans are available to help you lose weight. Hardly a month goes by without a new miracle diet being revealed in a leading magazine or Sunday newspaper supplement. Some of these plans may be highly recommended, for they satisfy the criteria for a safe and effective weight-reduction diet. On the other hand, many of these diets may be nutritionally deficient or even potentially hazardous to your health. For example, an analysis of eleven popular diets revealed deficiencies in one or more of several key nutrients, containing less than 70 percent of the USRDA for several of the B vitamins, calcium, iron, or zinc. Moreover, one of the diets contained 70 percent of the Calories as fat, and such a high content of fat and/or cholesterol may contribute to cardiovascular disease problems in certain individuals.

Certain types of diets should be avoided, including one-food diets such as the rice diet or the bananas-and-milk diet, for they may be deficient in certain key nutrients. Avoid diets that are advertised to contain a special weight-reducing formula or fat-burning enzymes, for such compounds simply do not exist or are not effective. In general, you should avoid diets that promise fast and easy weight losses. There is no fast and easy dietary method to lose excess body fat.

Highly recommended diets are based upon sound nutritional principles and also are designed to satisfy the individual's personal food tastes. Research with dieters has shown that any weight reduction diet, to be safe, effective, and realistic, should adhere to the following principles:

1. It should be low in Calories and yet supply all nutrients essential to normal body functions.
2. It should contain a wide variety of foods that appeal to your taste and help prevent hunger sensations between meals.
3. It should be suited to your current life-style, being easily obtainable whether you eat most of your meals at home or you dine out frequently.
4. It should provide for a slow rate of weight loss, about 1–2 pounds per week.
5. It should be a life-long diet, one that will satisfy the first three principles once you attain your desired weight.

In addition, foods should be selected that adhere to the principles of healthful eating. This information will be summarized in Chapter 12, but for now the major concern is with Calories.

Is it a good idea to count Calories when attempting to lose body weight?

There are both pros and cons to counting Calories. On the con side, counting Calories may not be practical for many who are too busy to plan a daily menu designed around a caloric limit. How many Calories are in the lunch or dinner you eat out daily? And how about serving sizes? Can you picture three ounces of roast beef or an ounce of cheese? Also, it may be difficult to calculate the exact amount of Calories consumed, as the caloric content in foods may vary somewhat. For example, certain slices of bread are larger than others and may have a correspondingly higher caloric content. Although these problems are not difficult to solve, it does take some effort.

On the pro side, counting Calories may be very helpful during the early stages of a diet. Knowledge of the food exchange lists will enable you to substitute one low-Calorie food for another in your daily menu. As you become familiar with the caloric content of various foods it becomes easier to select those that are low in Calories, but high in nutrient value, and to avoid those foods just the opposite, high in Calories and low in nutrients. It will require a little effort in the beginning phases of a diet to learn the Calories in a given quantity of a certain food, but once learned and incorporated into your life-style this knowledge is a valuable asset to possess not only when trying to lose weight, but also when maintaining a healthy weight over a lifetime. As you incorporate low-Caloric, high-nutrient foods into your diet, it will eventually become second nature to you, and you may eliminate the need to count Calories.

Once you have attained your desired weight, a good set of scales would be most helpful. Keeping track of your weight on a day-to-day basis will enable you to decrease your caloric intake for several days once you notice your weight beginning to increase again. Short-term prevention is more effective than long-term treatment. The dietary habits you acquire during the Calorie-counting phase of your diet will help you during these short-term prevention periods.

What is the Food Exchange System?

At this time it is important to expand our discussion of the Food Exchange System, which was introduced in Chapter 1. The **Food Exchange System** was developed by a group of health organizations, including the American Dietetic Association, as a means to advise patients about healthy eating. In essence, six food groups were established and foods were assigned to these groups on the basis of similar caloric content and nutritional value. For our purposes at this time, we will concentrate upon the caloric value.

The six food exchange lists may be found in Appendix H. You should study these lists and get an idea of the types and amounts of foods in each that constitute one exchange. Memorizing the caloric value of each food exchange is instrumental in determining the number of Calories you consume daily and also in planning a healthful, low-Calorie diet. The caloric content of one serving from each of the six exchanges is listed below and expressed in Figure 10.2.

1 vegetable exchange	=	25 Calories
1 fruit exchange	=	60 Calories
1 fat exchange	=	45 Calories
1 starch/bread exchange	=	80 Calories

Figure 10.2.
Knowledge of the various food exchanges and their caloric values can be very helpful in planning a diet. With a little effort, you can learn to estimate the caloric value of most basic foods.

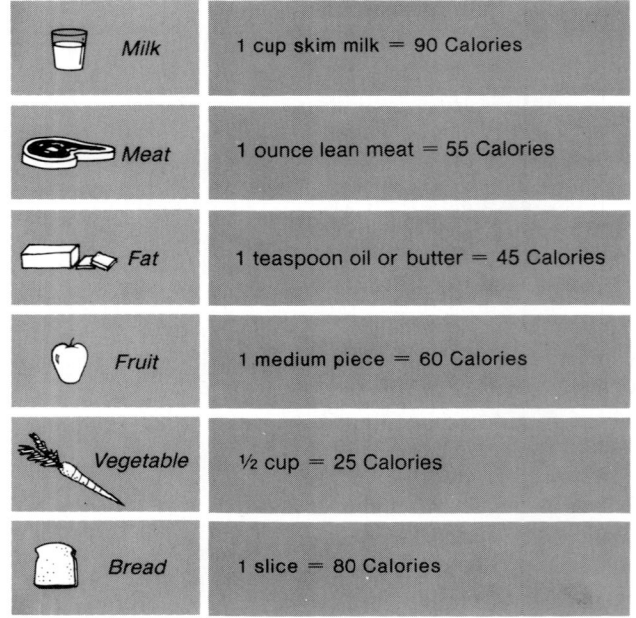

	Milk	1 cup skim milk = 90 Calories
	Meat	1 ounce lean meat = 55 Calories
	Fat	1 teaspoon oil or butter = 45 Calories
	Fruit	1 medium piece = 60 Calories
	Vegetable	½ cup = 25 Calories
	Bread	1 slice = 80 Calories

1 meat exchange	=	55–100 Calories
Lean	=	55 Calories
Medium fat	=	75 Calories
High fat	=	100 Calories
1 milk exchange	=	90–150 Calories
Skim	=	90 Calories
Lowfat	=	120 Calories
Whole	=	150 Calories

Table 10.4 presents a breakdown of the carbohydrate, fat, protein, and Calorie content of each food exchange.

How can I determine the number of calories I eat daily?

Simply keep an accurate daily record of what you eat and then determine the caloric value from Appendix H. Food intake should be recorded over a 3–7 day period, as one single day may give a biased value. Experiments have shown that this method may provide relatively accurate accounts of caloric intake if the amounts of food ingested are measured accurately. The main problem for most people is determining what and how much has been eaten. An eight-ounce glass of skim milk is easy to record, and the caloric value in Appendix H is rather precise. However, how many Calories are in a slice of pizza at your favorite Italian restaurant? How big was the piece? What is the caloric content of the cheese, green peppers, pepperoni, and mushrooms? When we deal with complex food combinations such as this, our estimates of caloric content are not as precise. However, some estimates are presented in Appendix

H. For example, one-quarter of a 10-inch pizza with thin crust contains two starch/bread, one medium-fat meat, and one fat exchange, or the equivalent of 280 Calories. See the section on combination foods.

Although you may wish to use a ruler, a small measuring scale, and a measuring cup at home to accurately record the amount of food you eat, they are not practical for many dining situations. The following may serve as guidelines for you to record the type and amount of food you eat:

1. Keep a small notepad with you. Record the foods you have eaten as soon as possible, noting the kind of food and the amount.
2. Check the labels of the foods you eat. Most commercial products today have nutritional information listed, including the number of Calories per serving. Record these data when available.
3. Calories for most fluids are given in relationship to ounces. For fluids, remember that one cup or regular glass is about eight ounces. Most regular canned drinks contain twelve ounces, although smaller and larger sizes are available.
4. Calories for meat, poultry, fish, and other related products are usually given by ounces. To get an idea of how many ounces are in these products, you could purchase a set weight of meat, say sixteen ounces, and cut it into four equal pieces. Each would weigh approximately four ounces. Get a mental picture of this size and use it as a guide to portion sizes.

Table 10.4   Carbohydrate, fat, protein, and Calories in the six food exchanges

Food exchange	Carbohydrate	Fat	Protein	Calories	Average Serving Size*
Vegetables	5	0	2	25	½ cup cooked; 1 cup raw
Fruits	15	0	0	60	½ cup fresh fruit or juice
Fat	0	5	0	45	1 teaspoon (5 grams)
Meat					1 ounce
Lean	—	3	7	55	
Medium fat	—	5	7	75	
High fat	—	8	7	100	
Starch/bread	15	trace	3	80	⅓–½ cup cereal, pasta / 1 slice
Milk					1 cup (8 fluid ounces)
Skim	12	trace	8	90	
Lowfat	12	5	8	120	
Whole	12	8	8	150	

*See Appendix H for specific foods.
Carbohydrate, fat, and protein in grams.

1 g carbohydrate = 4 Calories
1 g fat = 9 Calories
1 g protein = 4 Calories

Source: Exchange Lists for Meal Planning. American Diabetes Association and American Dietetic Association. Chicago: ADA, 1986.

5. For fruits and vegetables the caloric values are usually expressed relative to one-half cup or a small-sized piece. At home, measure one-half cup of vegetables or fruit and place it in a bowl or on a plate. Again, make a mental picture of this serving size and use it as a reference. Compare the sizes of different fruits and notice the difference between a small, medium, and large piece.

6. For starch/bread products, the Calories are most often expressed per serving, such as an average-size slice of bread or a dinner roll. In these cases it is relatively easy to determine quantity. Depending on the type of cereal, pasta, grain, or starchy vegetable, the measure for one exchange is usually 1/3 or 1/2 cup. Use the mental picture concept again to estimate quantities.

7. For substances such as sugar, jams, jellies, nondairy creamers, and related products, make a mental picture of a teaspoon and tablespoon. These are common means whereby Calories are given. One level teaspoon of sugar is about 20 Calories; jams and jellies contain similar amounts. Caloric values of other products may be obtained from nutrition labels.

8. Some combination foods, such as a homemade casserole, are included in Appendix H. However, for combination foods not listed, you will need to list the ingredients separately to calculate the caloric content. Labels on most food products list caloric content per serving.

9. Caloric values for many fast-food restaurant items may be found in Appendix 1.

Through experience you should be able to readily identify, within a small error range, the quantities of food you eat. This is not only helpful for determining your caloric intake but may also serve as a motivational device to restrict portion sizes when you are on a weight-loss diet.

The following represents an example of how you might record one meal and calculate the caloric intake from Appendix H.

Breakfast

Food	Quantity	Calories
Milk, skim	1 glass, 8 ounces	90
Eggs	2, poached	150
Toast, whole wheat	2 slices	160
with butter	2 pats	90
with jelly	1 tablespoon	50
Orange juice frozen diluted with water	1 glass, 8 ounces	120
Coffee	1 cup, 8 ounces	0
with sugar	1 teaspoon	20
TOTAL		680

A key dietary principle is to select foods high in nutrients but low in Calories.

(David Corona)

Computer programs are available to calculate caloric intake as well as nutrient content. Local hospitals or universities should be able to direct you to a source. Moreover, nutritional analysis software programs are available for personal home computers.

Knowledge, however, is not the total answer; your behavior should reflect your knowledge. For example, you may know that regular milk contains about 60 more Calories per glass than skim milk, but if you cannot develop a taste for skim milk then the advantage of your knowledge is lost in this instance.

What are some general guidelines I can use in the selection and preparation of foods to reduce caloric intake?

As for the diet itself, there are a variety of helpful suggestions in the battle against Calories.

1. The key principle is to select foods with **quality Calories**—low-Calorie, high-nutrient foods from across the six food exchanges. Avoid refined, processed foods as much as possible and include more natural, unrefined products in your diet. If you do buy convenience meals, select those that are low in Calories and fat. Check the percentage of Calories derived from fat. Review the technique presented in Chapter 4.

2. Reduce the amount of fat in the diet. Dietary fat appears to play several roles in the development of obesity. First, it appears to stimulate the appetite, thereby leading to an increase in caloric intake. Second, dietary fat appears to be stored as fat more efficiently than either carbohydrate or protein, even if the caloric intake is similar; this is especially true in individuals who have lost weight and may be one of the most important reasons why they regain weight so readily. Third, dietary fat may also be stored preferentially in the abdominal region, which may increase health risks. In a recent study, Wayne Miller and his colleagues found that lean subjects obtained a lower percentage of their dietary Calories from fat compared with obese subjects. Suggestions for reducing dietary fat are included in the following guidelines, but you may wish to review Chapter 4 for additional information.

3. Reduce the amount of simple, refined sugars in the diet. This may be accomplished by restricting the amount of sugar added

directly to foods and limiting the consumption of highly processed foods that may add substantial amounts of sweeteners. Artificial sweeteners may be helpful. In a recent review, F. Xavier Pi-Sunyer noted that substitution of artificial sweeteners, such as aspartame, for sugar has been shown to reduce caloric intake without leading to an increased consumption of other foods. In many cases simply reducing the fat and sugar content of the diet will save substantial amounts of Calories and may be all that is needed. Did you know that fat and sugar together account for nearly 60 percent of the Calories in the average American diet? That represents three out of every five Calories.

4. Milk exchange products are excellent sources of protein but may contain excessive Calories unless the fat is removed. Use skim milk, low-fat cottage cheese, low-fat yogurt, and nonfat dried milk instead of their high-fat counterparts like whole milk, sour cream, and powdered creamers.

5. The meat exchange products are sources of high-quality protein and many other nutrients but also may contain excessive fat Calories. Use leaner cuts of meat. Fish, chicken, and egg whites are excellent low-Calorie meat exchanges, although egg yolks are very high in cholesterol. Trim away excess fat; broil or bake your meats to let the fat drip away. If you eat in fast food restaurants, select foods that are low in fat, such as grilled chicken, lean meats, and salads. Avoid the high-fat foods, which normally contain 40–60 percent fat Calories.

6. The starch-bread exchanges are high in vitamins, minerals, and fiber. Use whole grain breads, cereals, brown rice, oatmeal, beans, bran products, and starchy vegetables for dietary fiber. Limit the use of processed grain products that add fat and sugar. Substitute products low in fat, such as bagels, for those high in fat, like croissants.

7. Foods in the fruit exchange are high in vitamins and fiber. Select fresh fruits or those canned or frozen in their own juices. Avoid those in heavy sugar syrups. Limit the intake of dried fruits, which are high in Calories. Eat at least one citrus fruit daily.

8. The vegetable exchange foods are low in Calories yet high in vitamins, minerals, and fiber. Select dark green leafy and yellow-orange vegetables daily. Low-Calorie items like carrots, radishes, and celery are highly nutritious snacks for munching. Many of these vegetables are listed as free exchanges in Appendix H because they contain fewer than 20 Calories per serving. Fruits and vegetables may provide bulk to the diet and a sensation of fullness without excessive amounts of Calories.

9. Avoid high-Calorie fat exchanges like salad dressings, butter, margarine, and cooking oil. Do not prepare foods in fats, such as with frying. Use nonstick cooking utensils. If necessary, substitute low-Calories dietary versions instead.

10. Beverages other than milk and juices should have no Calories. Fluid intake should remain high, for it helps create a sensation of satiety during a meal. Water is the recommended fluid, although diet drinks and unsweetened coffee and tea may be used. Consult the free food list in Appendix H.

11. Limit your intake of alcohol. It is high in Calories and zero in nutrient value. One gram of alcohol is equal to seven Calories, almost twice the value of protein and carbohydrate. For 100 Calories in a shot of gin you receive zero nutrient value, but for the same amount of Calories in approximately two ounces of chicken breast you get nearly one-third of your RDA in protein plus substantial amounts of iron, zinc, niacin, and other vitamins. If you desire alcohol, select the light varieties of wine and beer available. Substitution of a light beer for a regular beer will save about 50 Calories. You may wish to try the nonalcoholic beers, which contain even fewer Calories.

12. Salt intake should be limited to that which occurs naturally in our foods. Try to use dry herbs, spices, and other nonsalt seasonings as substitutes to flavor your food.

13. Instead of two or three large meals a day, eat five or six smaller ones. Use low-Calorie, nutrient-dense foods for snacks. Research has shown that this may help control sensations of hunger between meals and may help in other ways, possibly by minimizing the release of insulin, which assists in the storage of fat in the body.

14. Only cook and serve small portions of food for meals. The temptation to overeat may be removed.

15. Learn what foods are low in Calories in each of the six food exchanges and incorporate those palatable to you in your diet. Learn to substitute low-Calorie foods for high-Calorie ones. The key to a lifelong weight-maintenance diet is your knowledge of sound nutritional principles and the application of this knowledge to the design of your personal diet.

How can I plan a nutritionally balanced, low-Calorie diet?

The key to a sound diet for weight loss is nutrient density, or the selection of low-Calorie, high-nutrient foods. The fifteen points addressed in the previous question represent important guidelines to implement such a diet. Table 10.5 presents a suggested meal pattern based upon the Food Exchange System. The foods should be selected from the food exchange lists found in Appendix H.

The total caloric values are close approximations for a three-meal pattern. If you decide to include snacks in your diet, such as a fruit or vegetable, then remove each snack from one of the main meals. The beverages, other than milk and fruit juice, should contain no Calories. The salads should contain vegetables with negligible Calories, such as lettuce and radishes. Note that under the exchange system, starchy vegetables such as potatoes are included in the starch/bread group because their caloric content is similar.

Although only seven levels of caloric intake are presented in Table 10.5, you may adjust it according to your needs by simply adding or subtracting appropriate food exchanges. For example, if you wanted a 1,700-Calorie diet, you could subtract two lean meat exchanges (110 Calories) from the 1,800-Calorie diet.

After you have determined the number of Calories you need daily, select the appropriate diet plan from Table 10.5. To help implement your diet plan and to keep day-to-day track of the food exchanges you eat, you should design a 3″ × 5″ card similar to the model below for the number of food exchanges in your daily diet. As you consume an exchange at each meal, simply cross it off on the card. Make a new card for each day. The model shown is for 1,500 Calories. The total exchanges are summed from Table 10.5.

Daily meal plan		1,500 Calories
Milk exchange, skim	(2)	1 2
Meat exchange, lean	(7)	1 2 3 4 5 6 7
Starch/bread exchange	(6)	1 2 3 4 5 6
Vegetable exchange	(3)	1 2 3
Salads	(2)	1 2
Fruit exchange	(4)	1 2 3 4
Fat exchange	(2)	1 2
Beverages	(3)	1 2 3

Keep in mind that this is not a rigid diet plan. At a minimum you should have 2 skim milk exchanges, 5 lean meat exchanges, 4 starch/bread exchanges, 2 vegetable exchanges and 2 fruit exchanges. Once you have guaranteed these minimum requirements, you may do some substitution between the various exchanges so long as you keep the total caloric content within range of your goals. For example, you may delete 2 starch/bread exchanges (160 Calories) in the model and substitute 1 skim milk and 1 lean meat (145 Calories). You may also shift a limited number of the exchanges from one meal to another. If you prefer a more substantial breakfast and a lighter lunch, simply shift some of the exchanges from lunch to breakfast.

It may be a good idea to take a little time and construct a diet for yourself, using the following guidelines for your calculations.

Personal diet

1. Calculate the number of Calories you want per day. See pages 248–49 for guidelines.
2. Use Table 10.5 to determine how many servings you need from each group.
3. Multiply the number of servings by the Calories per serving to get the total Calories. Add the total Calories column to get total daily intake.
4. Select appropriate foods from the exchange list in Appendix H.

Table 10.5 Suggested daily meal pattern based on the Food Exchange System

	Approximate Daily Caloric Intake						
	1,000	1,200	1,500	1,800	2,000	2,200	2,500
Breakfast							
Milk, skim	1	1	1	1	1	1	1
Meat, lean	1	1	2	2	2	3	3
Starch/bread	1	1	2	3	3	3	3
Fruit	1	1	1	1	2	2	2
Fat	0	0	1/2	1	1	2	2
Beverage	1	1	1	1	1	1	1
Lunch							
Milk, skim	1	1	1	1	1	1	2
Meat, lean	2	2	2	3	3	3	4
Starch/bread	2	2	2	2	2	3	3
Vegetable	1	1	1	2	2	2	2
Salad	1	1	1	1	1	1	1
Fruit	1	2	2	2	2	2	2
Fat	1/2	1/2	1/2	2	2	2	2
Beverage	1	1	1	1	1	1	1
Dinner							
Milk, skim	0	0	0	0	1	1	1
Meat, lean	2	2	3	3	3	3	4
Starch/bread	1	2	2	3	3	4	4
Vegetable	1	2	2	2	2	2	2
Salad	1	1	1	1	1	1	1
Fruit	0	0	1	1	2	2	2
Fat	1/2	1	1	1	1	1	2
Beverage	1	1	1	1	1	1	1
Totals							
Milk, skim	2	2	2	2	3	3	4
Meat, lean	5	5	7	8	8	9	11
Starch/bread	4	5	6	8	8	10	10
Vegetable	2	3	3	4	4	4	4
Salad	2	2	2	2	2	2	2
Fruit	2	3	4	4	6	6	6
Fat	1	2	2	4	4	5	6
Beverage	3	3	3	3	3	3	3

Key points.

1. Caloric values:

        Milk exchange, skim = 90
        Meat exchange, lean = 55
            Fruit exchange = 60
        Vegetable exchange = 25
    Starch/Bread exchange = 80
            Fat exchange = 45
            Beverage = 0
            Salad = 20

2. See Appendix H for a listing of foods in each exchange. Note the following:
   a. Foods other than milk, such as yogurt, are included in the milk exchange.
   b. The meat list includes foods such as eggs, cheese, fish, and poultry; low-fat legumes, like beans and peas, may be considered as meat substitutes.
   c. Some starchy vegetables are included in the bread list.
3. Foods should not be fried or prepared in fat unless you count the added fat as a fat exchange. Broil or bake foods instead.
4. Low-Calorie vegetables like lettuce and radishes should be used in the salads. Use only small amounts of very low-Calorie salad dressing.
5. Beverages should contain no Calories.

Calories: _____

Food Group	Number of servings	Calories per serving	Total Calories	Foods selected
Breakfast				
Milk, skim		90		
Meat, lean		55		
Fruit		60		
Vegetable		25		
Starch/bread		80		
Fat		45		
Beverage		0		
Lunch				
Milk, skim		90		
Meat, lean		55		
Fruit		60		
Vegetable		25		
Salad		20		
Starch/bread		80		
Fat		45		
Beverage		0		
Dinner				
Milk, skim		90		
Meat, lean		55		
Fruit		60		
Vegetable		25		
Salad		20		
Starch/bread		80		
Fat		45		
Beverage		0		

One final point: If your diet contains less than 1,600 Calories, it would be wise to take a daily vitamin/mineral supplement with the RDA for all essential vitamins and key minerals such as iron and zinc.

Table 10.6 presents an example of a 1,500-Calorie diet based on the Food Exchange System.

Are very low-Calorie diets effective and desirable means to lose body weight?

Very low-Calorie diets (VLCD) are defined technically as containing less than 800 Calories and are often referred to as modified fasts. In some medical institutions, total fasting programs are used. Under proper medical supervision, such diets are generally regarded as being safe and have been effective in inducing rapid weight loss in very obese patients. Atkinson notes, however, that there may be some contraindications to their use and they should be used only after a thorough medical examination. A variety of complications may also arise with the use of VLCD, including headaches, nausea, constipation, loss of libido, kidney stones, gallbladder disease, fatigue, loss of stamina, cardiac arrhythmias, and even death.

VLCD are not recommended for the individual who wants to lose 10–15 pounds or for the individual who is not under medical supervision, not only because of the possible adverse health consequences noted above but also because they may be counterproductive to the ultimate goal of long-term weight loss. For one, these diets do not conform to the general principles of a sound diet mentioned earlier in this section. Moreover, research has revealed that VLCD may lead to a decreased dietary-induced thermogenesis, a significant loss of lean body mass, a decreased resting metabolic rate (RMR), and an enhanced food efficiency (less energy wasted in processing dietary Calories). In essence, your body is recognizing that it is being starved and will attempt to conserve body stores of energy by reducing energy output. When you resume normal eating, these energy-conservation mechanisms may continue to function for some time, so you may actually gain more weight. Also, a good proportion of the weight lost during the fasting stage is protein, primarily from muscle tissue, which is used to produce glucose for the central nervous system. When you resume eating, the protein tissue is not readily replaced, so the extra Calories are likely to be converted to fat. A vicious cycle may develop, with repeated bouts of weight loss followed by weight gain, leading to increased amounts of body fat at the same body weight. An individual who engages in this weight cycling, also known as the yo-yo syndrome, may start out at 200 pounds with 30 percent body fat and, after several cycles, eventually return to the same weight, but at 35 percent fat. Research has suggested that obese subjects who repeatedly lose and gain weight are at an increased risk for cardiovascular disease compared to those obese subjects whose weight remains stable, which may be related to the prevalence of android-type obesity seen with weight cycling as noted in Chapter 9. Weight cycling also increases the risk of other health problems, such as gallstones.

It is recommended that any individual contemplating the use of VLCD should consult a physician and a dietician.

Table 10.6   A 1,500-Calorie diet based on the Food Exchange System

Exchange	Number of servings	Calories per exchange	Total calories	Foods selected
Breakfast				
Meat, lean	2	55	110	1 ounce lean ham and
Fat	1/2	45	25	1 ounce diet cheese melted on
Starch/ bread	2	80	160	2 pieces whole grain toasted bread
Fruit	1	60	60	4 ounces orange juice
Beverage	1	0	0	1 cup coffee with noncaloric sweetener
Lunch				
Milk, lowfat	1	120	120	8 ounces plain lowfat yogurt
Fruit	1	60	60	with cut-up fresh fruit added
Meat	2	55	110	turkey sandwich with
Starch/ bread	2	80	160	2 ounces turkey breast on whole grain bun
Vegetable	1	25	25	1 carrot
Salad	1	20	20	lettuce with
Fat	1/2	45	25	low-Calorie dressing
Beverage	1	0	0	diet cola
Dinner				
Milk, skim	1	90	90	1/2 cup ice milk
Meat	3	55	165	3 ounces broiled fish
Starch/ bread	2	80	160	1 baked potato
Vegetable	2	25	50	1 cup steamed broccoli
Salad	1	20	20	cucumbers
Fat	1	45	45	small amount of margarine for potato and low-Calorie dressing for salad
Fruit	2	60	120	1 banana cut up on ice milk
Beverage	1	0	0	iced tea
Total			1,525	

Exercise Programs

What role does exercise play in weight reduction and weight maintenance?

Humans are meticulously designed for physical activity, and yet our modern mechanical age has eliminated many of the opportunities our ancient ancestors once had to incorporate moderate physical activity as a natural part of daily living. The regulation of our food intake has not adapted to the highly mechanized conditions in today's society. As discussed in Chapter 9, whether or not physical inactivity is a cause of obesity is debatable. However, experts in obesity note that in reality inactivity may be a consequence of obesity and can maintain it. For example, a sedentary life-style, principally TV watching, has been significantly associated with obesity in adolescents and adults. Indeed, Dr. Jean Mayer, an international authority on weight control, has reported that no single factor is more frequently responsible for obesity than lack of physical exercise.

A considerable amount of knowledge substantiates the point that exercise can help reduce and control body weight. In addition to the physiological effects upon energy expenditure, exercise may also confer significant psychological and medical benefits.

Exercise burns Calories. The primary function of exercise in a weight-control program is simply to increase the level of energy expenditure and help unbalance the caloric equation so that energy output is greater than energy input. As mentioned in Chapter 2, the metabolic rate may be increased tremendously during exercise. For example, while the average person may expend only about 60–70 Calories per hour during rest, this value may approach 1,000 Calories per hour during a sustained high-level activity such as rapid walking, running, swimming, or bicycling. Athletes involved in endurance events

Exercise can be an effective means of increasing energy expenditure and losing excess Calories.

(John Maker / EKM-Nepenthe)

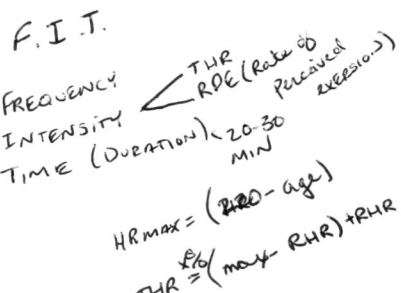

F.I.T.

FREQUENCY

INTENSITY ⟨ THR
RPE (Rate of Perceived Exertion.)

TIME (DURATION) ⟨ 20-30 MIN

HR MAX = (220 - age)

THR = ⁿ/ₒ (max - RHR) + RHR

such as the Tour de France and ultradistance runners, such as Yannis Kouros, have been reported to consume between 6,000 and 13,000 Calories per day.

If you are overweight, the same amount of exercise will cost you more Calories than your leaner counterpart. Because you have more weight to move, you will expend more energy and lose more body fat in the long run. For example, the energy cost of jogging one mile would be 70 Calories for the 100-pound individual and 140 for someone twice that weight. Figure 10.3 depicts this concept graphically for one type of exercise—walking.

One major misconception may deter many individuals from initiating an exercise program for weight control. They believe that exercise is a poor means to lose body weight because it expends so few Calories. For example, they have heard that you have to jog about thirty-five miles to lose a pound of body fat. Because the average-sized male uses approximately 100 Calories per mile, and because one pound of body fat contains about 3,500 Calories, there is some truth to that statement. However, you must look at the **long-haul concept** of weight control (Figure 10.4). Jogging about two miles a day will expend about 6,000 Calories in a month, accounting for almost two pounds of body fat. Over six to eight months or longer, the weight loss may be substantial.

In addition to the direct effect of increased energy output during exercise, exercise has been theorized to facilitate weight loss by other means. As noted in Chapter 2, exercise may increase the RMR during the period immediately following the

exercise bout and may also increase dietary-induced thermogenesis (DIT). Unfortunately, the magnitude of this increased energy expenditure is relatively minor and not considered to be of any practical importance in a weight loss program. Thus, it does not matter if you exercise before or after a light meal, although as noted below, exercise before a meal may help curb the appetite.

However, exercise may have a beneficial effect on the RMR in other ways. As noted previously, very-low-Calorie diets (VLCD) may reduce the RMR, and this effect may be counterproductive in a weight loss program. Less severe caloric restriction also may reduce the RMR. Although exercise will not totally prevent this decrease in the RMR normally seen with weight loss, the available research suggests that it may help minimize the decrease, thereby helping maintain energy expenditure near normal levels during rest.

Moreover, during exercise, the body mobilizes its fat cells to supply energy to the muscle cells. Hence, body fat stores are reduced. Exercise may also stimulate the development of muscle tissue and thus increase lean body mass. Recall that in dieting alone, some lean muscle mass may be lost. In the long run, this change in body composition may actually favor an increase in the RMR because muscle tissue is more active metabolically than fat tissue.

It should be noted that some research suggests exercise may decrease the RMR in individuals who are already lean, suggesting that the body is attempting to preserve its energy reserves. Although

Figure 10.3.

Effect of speed (mph) and gross body weight (lbs) on energy expenditure (Calories/minute) of walking. The heavier the individual, the greater the expenditure of Calories for any given speed of walking. The same would be true for running and other physical activities in which the body must be moved by foot.

(From *Textbook of Work Psychology* by P. O. Astrand and K. Rodahl. Copyright © 1977, by McGraw-Hill, Inc. Used with permission of McGraw-Hill Book Company.)

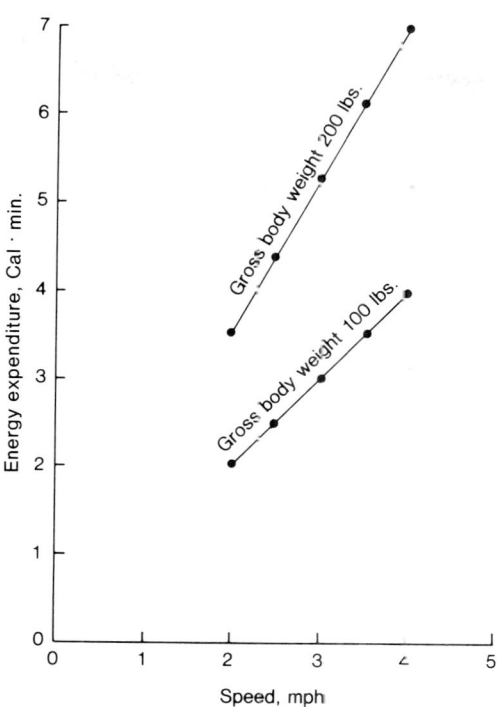

Figure 10.4.

To lose body fat by exercising, you must look at the long-haul concept of weight control. The average-weight individual needs to jog about 35 miles to burn off one pound of body fat. This would be nearly impossible for most of us to do in one day. At 2 miles per day, however, it could be done in about 2½ weeks—and at 5 miles per day, in only one week. Even though it takes time, an exercise program is a very effective approach to reducing excess body fat.

35 miles

2 miles

this does not appear to be of any concern to overweight individuals who desire to lose weight, it may pose a problem to the lean athlete attempting to shed a few additional pounds for competition.

Other than the physiological effects noted above, exercise also may confer some significant psychological benefits to the overweight individual. As the fitness level and body composition improve, the individual may experience improvements in mood, energy levels, body image, and self-esteem. Exercise may also be the psychological catalyst that helps individuals to improve their nutritional habits and other health-related behaviors.

Exercise also may render significant health benefits. For example, the American Heart Association has noted that exercise may help protect against coronary heart disease and may improve the likelihood of survival from a heart attack. Many of the health benefits of exercise are related to the reduction of excess body weight and were covered in the preceding chapter, although independent effects of exercise training such as changes in serum-cholesterol levels reported in Chapter 4 are also important. Exercise appears to be particularly effective in reducing abdominal fat stores, those most related to increased chronic disease risk.

For individuals with normal body weight, exercise is highly recommended for its preventive role. It is generally recognized that prevention of obesity or excess body weight is more effective than treatment. Prevention is especially important for our children; the National Research Council recently noted that the long-term well-being of our children may depend on increased physical activity. Most people do not become overweight overnight, but rather accumulate an extra 75–150 Calories per day, which over time will lead to excessive fat tissue. A daily exercise program could easily counteract the effect of these additional Calories. For those who like to eat but yet not gain weight, exercise is the intelligent alternative.

Does exercise affect the appetite?

On a long-term basis, in general, increased energy expenditure through physical activity is counterbalanced by an increased food intake. This is one of the major mechanisms whereby normal body weight is controlled in the average individual. However, this may not be universally true for sedentary individuals with excess body fat. Research has shown that overweight individuals who begin an exercise program do not increase food consumption above normal, the caloric intake actually decreasing in some cases.

An important concern for the athletic individual is the fact that the appetite may not normally decrease with a decreased activity level. If you are physically active, but then must curtail your activity because of an injury or some other reason, the appetite may remain elevated above what you need to maintain body weight at your reduced energy levels. Body fat will increase. Hence, you must reduce your food intake to balance the caloric equation or suffer the consequences.

As will be discussed later, a combined diet and exercise program would be most effective as a means to body weight control. In this regard, exercise, particularly intense exercise, may be used to curb the appetite on a short-term basis at an appropriate time. Thompson and others found that low-intensity exercise did not suppress hunger, but high intensity exercise (68 percent VO_2 max) did. Research has related the appetite-suppressing effect of exercise to increased body temperature. The close anatomical relationship of the temperature and hunger centers in the hypothalamus may provide a rationale for the inhibition of the hunger center. Both exercise and the DIT effect of food intake will increase the core temperature of the body, so the body simply may be attempting to protect itself against an excessive rise in core temperature by suppressing the appetite to avoid the DIT effect. Exercise also will stimulate the secretion of several hormones in the body, notably adrenaline, which may also depress the appetite.

If you exercise before a meal, your food intake may be reduced considerably. Try it and see if it works for you. If you have the facilities available, a good half-hour of intense exercise may be an effective substitute for a large lunch. You may lose Calories two ways, expending them through exercise and replacing the large lunch with a low-Calorie, nutritious snack. Although intense exercise may be an effective means to suppress the appetite on a short-term basis, it may not be as effective on a long-term basis. Thus, it may help to curb your appetite at lunch, but unless you are cautious you may increase your caloric intake above normal at dinner.

What types of exercise programs are most effective for losing body fat?

As you are probably well aware, a number of different exercise programs designed to reduce body weight are available. Perusal of the daily newspaper reveals numerous advertisements for weight reduction programs sponsored by various commercial fitness centers. Weight training with sophisticated equipment, Slimnastics exercises, aerobic dancing,

and special exercise apparatus are a few of the approaches often advertised as the best means to lose body fat fast. The truth is that you do not need any special apparatus or any specially designed program. You can design your own program once you know a few basic principles about exercise and energy expenditure.

The best type of exercise program for losing body fat involves aerobic exercises, those that utilize the oxygen energy system (Figure 10.5). This type of exercise program is also the one that conveys the most significant health benefits. The key points of an aerobic exercise program are as follows:

1. The mode of exercise must involve large muscle groups. The muscles of the legs comprise a good portion of the total body mass, as do the muscles of the arms. Many people do not realize that the major muscles in the chest and back are attached to the upper arm and are actively involved in almost all arm movements. Walking, jogging, hiking, stair climbing, running, and bicycling primarily involve the legs while swimming and rowing primarily stress the arms. The use of hand-held weights in walking incorporates arm action with the legs. Cross-country skiing and rope jumping

use both the arms and legs, as does a good aerobic dance routine. These are good large-muscle activities, although there are a host of others.

2. The second factor is the intensity level. The higher the **exercise intensity,** the more Calories you expend. Per unit of time, normal walking uses fewer Calories than easy jogging, which uses fewer Calories than fast running. Simply put, it costs you more energy to move your body weight at a faster pace. However, there is an optimal intensity level for each person depending on how long the exercise will last. You can run at a very high intensity for fifty yards, but you certainly could not maintain that same fast pace for two miles. Intensity and duration are interrelated.

To get an idea of exercises with high intensity, check Appendix C for Calorie cost per minute relative to your body weight. It is a composite table of a wide variety of individual reports in the literature. When using this appendix, keep these points in mind.

A. The figures are approximate and include the resting metabolic rate. Thus, the total cost of the exercise includes not only the energy expended by the exercise itself, but also the amount you would have used anyway during the same period. Suppose you ran for 1 hour and the calculated energy cost was 800 Calories. During that same time at rest you may have expended 75 Calories, so the net cost of the exercise is 725 Calories.

B. The figures in the table are only for the time you are performing the activity. For example, in an hour of basketball, you may exercise strenuously only for 35 to 40 minutes, as you may take time-outs and may rest during foul shots. In general, record only the amount of time that you are actually moving during the activity.

C. The figures may give you some guidelines to total energy expenditure, but actual caloric costs might vary somewhat according to such factors as skill level, environmental factors (running against the wind or up hills), and so forth.

D. Not all body weights could be listed, but you can approximate by going to the closest weight listed.

E. There may be small differences between men and women, but not enough to make a marked difference in the total caloric value for most exercises.

Appendix C or Table 2.5 on page 38 may be a useful means to determine which types of activities may be of the appropriate intensity for your weight-control program. Listing those activities with higher caloric expenditure per minute may suggest several that you could blend into your life-style.

3. Probably the most important factor in energy expenditure is the duration of the exercise. In swimming, bicycling, running, or walking, distance is the key. For example, running a mile will cost the average-sized individual about 100 Calories. Five miles would approximate 500 Calories. An individual running one mile a day would take over one month to lose one pound of fat, whereas running five miles a day would shorten the time span to about one week. Thus, if the purpose of the exercise program is to lose weight, the individual should stress the **duration concept.**

One of the key points about the duration concept is the notion of distance traveled rather than time. For example, tennis and running are both good exercises. However, the runner will expend considerably more Calories in an hour than the tennis player because the activity involved in running is continuous. The tennis player has a number of rest periods in which the energy expenditure is lower. Consequently, at the end of an hour's activity, the runner may have expended two to three times as many Calories as the tennis player.

A major reason many adults do not use exercise as a weight-loss mechanism is that their level of physical fitness is so low they cannot sustain a moderate level of exercise intensity for very long. However, keep in mind that, as you continue to train, your body will begin to adapt so that in time you will be able to exercise for longer and longer periods.

Additionally, intensity and duration are interrelated, and if balanced, will result in equal weight losses. Douglas Ballor and his associates found that high-intensity exercise for 25 minutes and low-intensity exercise (half the intensity of the high-intensity exercise) for 50 minutes resulted in equal weight losses over an 8-week period.

4. **Exercise frequency** complements duration and intensity. Frequency of exercise refers to how often each week you participate. As would appear obvious, the more often you exercise, the greater the total weekly caloric expenditure. In general, three to four times per week would be satisfactory, provided duration and intensity were adequate, but six to seven times would just about double your caloric output. A daily exercise program is recommended if weight control is the primary goal.

5. An important factor is enjoyment of the exercise. For an activity to be effective in the long run, it should be one that you enjoy, yet one that will help expend Calories because it has a recommended intensity level, can be performed for a long time, or both. For example, you may not enjoy jogging or running, but other activities may be substituted. Fast walking with a vigorous arm action, golf (pulling a cart), swimming, bicycling, tennis, handball, racquetball, and a variety of other activities may produce a greater feeling of enjoyment and still burn a considerable number of Calories. Even leisure activities and home chores done vigorously such as gardening, yard work, washing the car, and home repairs may be useful in burning Calories and developing fitness. Exercise need not be unpleasant. Enjoy your exercise. Try to make it a lifelong habit by viewing it as play. Next time you vacuum the house or mow the lawn, try to think about it as a good workout rather than work.

6. Practicality is another important factor. You may enjoy swimming, tennis, racquetball, and a variety of other sports, but lack of facilities, poor weather conditions, or high costs may limit your ability to participate. For the active person who travels, this may be a major concern. You probably have noticed by now that an underlying bias toward walking and running exists throughout this book. It is probably because, to me, they satisfy all the previously mentioned criteria necessary for maintaining proper body weight. Moreover, they are very practical activities. All you need is a good pair of shoes and proper clothes for the weather and nothing short of an injury should deter you from your daily exercise routine. Walking, jogging, or running can be very practical substitutes on those days when you cannot participate in your regular physical activity. For those who are physically unfit, overweight, or elderly, walking is probably the best choice of exercise.

Is weight training recommended during a weight loss program?

Weight training programs are detailed in the next chapter in relation to gaining body weight, but such programs may also be very helpful during weight-loss programs. Research by Douglas Ballor and his associates has revealed that weight training may help preserve lean body mass during weight loss. Recall that protein tissue, primarily muscle, may be lost along with body fat during a weight-reduction program. However, weight training may stimulate muscular development and help prevent significant decreases in lean body mass. Such an effect may also help prevent decreases in the RMR. Additionally, as is noted in the next chapter, dynamic weight training programs may also be used to burn additional Calories.

If I am inactive now, what precautions would be advisable before I start an exercise program?

Before initiating any exercise program, you should be aware of any personal medical problems that possibly could be aggravated. If you have any concern about any facet of your health, it would be a good idea to check with your physician before starting an exercise program. This is especially important in weight-reduction exercise programs where the main stress is placed on the heart and blood vessels, the cardiovascular (CV) system.

Your initial level of physical fitness is an important determinant of the intensity of exercise during the early stages of the program. If you are completely unconditioned, you should start at a lower intensity level—walk before you jog for example. Keep in mind that it took time for you to gain weight and become unconditioned, so it will also take time to reverse the process. A gradual progression is the key point. Examples are presented later.

Other general precautions involve safety factors, timing of meals, environmental hazards, and equipment. The individual should adhere to safety principles for the activity selected, particularly swimming, bicycling, and pedestrian safety. Strenuous exercise should not be undertaken within two or three hours of a heavy meal, but may be done earlier with a light meal or just liquids. As noted in

Figure 10.6.
The exercise prescription. The exercise prescription is divided into three phases: warm-up period, stimulus period, and warm-down period. The stimulus period is the key.

	Warm-up	Stimulus	Warm-down
Duration	5–10 minutes	15–60 minutes	5–10 minutes
Intensity	Low	Medium-high	Low

Chapter 8, a hot environment poses the most serious threat to the person in training. Be aware of signs of heat exposure such as dizziness, nausea, and weakness. If these occur, stop exercising and find a means to help cool your body. Proper equipment should be selected for the chosen activity. For example, of critical importance to the jogger or walker is a well-designed pair of shoes. They may help prevent certain medical problems, such as tendinitis and shin splints, which may occur during early stages of training.

What is the general design of exercise programs for weight reduction?

In essence, exercise programs to reduce body fat or to help maintain an optimal weight are based on the same principles that underlie exercise programs to improve the efficiency of the cardiovascular system. The total exercise program is based on a balance of exercise intensity, duration, and frequency. However, each daily exercise bout is usually subdivided into three phases—warm-up, stimulus, and warm-down, in that order (Figure 10.6). A proper warm-up and warm-down are important components of the aerobic exercise prescription. Both may help prevent excessive strain on the heart and may also be helpful in the prevention of muscular soreness or injuries.

The **warm-up** precedes the stimulus period and may be done in several ways. It may be general in nature, such as calisthenics, or specific to the type of exercise you plan to do, such as initially exercising at a lower level of intensity of the actual mode of exercise. Some gentle stretching exercises are also helpful in the warm-up period.

For most aerobic-type exercise, it is probably better to warm up the specific muscles to be used. For example, if you plan to use jogging as your mode of aerobic exercise, you should stretch your leg muscles gently at first and then jog at a slower than normal pace for several minutes. Breaking into a sweat is a good external sign that you have sufficiently elevated your body temperature; by using a specific type of warm-up, the temperature of your exercising muscles will also be increased.

The **warm-down** phase follows the stimulus period and is designed primarily to help restore the CV system to normal. If one stops exercising abruptly, blood may possibly pool in the exercised body parts, thereby decreasing return of blood to the heart. With less blood to the heart, less will be pumped to the brain and hence dizziness may result. When the warm-down occurs gradually after strenuous exercise—by walking or jogging after a strenuous run, for example—the muscles help massage the blood through the veins back to the heart. Research indicating that abrupt cessation of exercise may increase certain blood hormone levels, which may cause abnormal rhythm of the heart, emphasizes the importance of a gradual warm-down. Complete your warm-down by stretching. Since the muscles are now warm from the exercise they are easier to stretch, which may help prevent muscle stiffness.

The most important phase is the stimulus period. By modifying the intensity of the exercise, the individual achieves the level of stimulus necessary to elicit a conditioning effect. For the average individual, the heart rate is the most practical gauge of stimulus intensity.

What is an appropriate level of exercise intensity?

The heart rate (HR) is the number of heartbeats per minute. It is easily obtained, and since it parallels increases in oxygen uptake, it is a practical measure of exercise intensity. The pulse rate is the same as the HR in most individuals. To obtain your pulse rate, press lightly with your index and middle fingers at the carotid artery, which is located just under the jawbone and beside the Adam's apple. Alternatively, you may obtain your radial artery pulse by placing all four fingers on the inside of the wrist on the thumb side. These are the two most common locations for monitoring pulse rate, but other locations such as the temple, inside the upper arm, and the groin may be used (Figure 10.7).

To obtain your heart rate in terms of beats per minute, simply count the pulse rate for ten seconds and multiply by six. Resting and recovery heart rates are easily obtainable because they may be taken while the individual is motionless. It is difficult to monitor the HR manually while exercising. However, research has shown that the exercise HR is correlated very highly with the HR during the early stages of recovery. Hence, to monitor your exercise HR, obtain the pulse immediately upon cessation of exercise and count the beats in ten seconds. This will provide a reliable measure of exercise HR.

There is rather widespread general agreement that, to obtain a conditioning effect, the HR response should be in the range of 50–85 percent of the **maximal heart rate reserve,** which is defined as the difference between the resting HR and the **maximum heart rate (HR max).** A general guide for the prediction of the HR max is 220 minus your age. Thus, a 40-year-old individual would have a predicted HR max of 180. However, if you plan to swim for exercise, the maximal heart rate formula should be 220 minus 13 added to your age. In this case, the predicted HR max for our 40-year-old is 167 [220 − (40 + 13)]. Keep in mind, however, that there is considerable individual variation relative to estimated HR max. For example, a 40-year-old man may have an estimated HR max of 180, yet it actually may be 200 or 160; it may be even much lower if he is a victim of coronary heart disease.

Continuing with our example of the 40-year-old man, we can calculate the HR range needed to elicit a training effect; this is called the **target range,** or **target HR.** To do the calculations, we need to know the age-predicted HR max and the resting HR (RHR), which should be determined under relaxed circumstances. Let us assume an RHR of 70. The following formula is used to calculate the target range:

Target HR = X% (HR max − RHR) + RHR

For the 50 percent level, the target HR would be calculated as follows:

0.5(180 − 70) + 70 = 125

For the 85 percent level, the target HR would be:

0.85(180 − 70) + 70 = 163

Thus, in order to get a training effect, our 40-year-old man needs to train within a target HR range of 125–163. If you wish to bypass the calculations, Table 10.7 provides target HR ranges for different age groups for a range of RHR. The table is based upon a predicted HR max of 220 − age.

Figure 10.7.
Palpation of the heart rate. The pulse rate may be taken at a variety of body locations (*a*), but the two most common locations are (*b*) the neck (carotid artery) and (*c*) the wrist (radial artery).

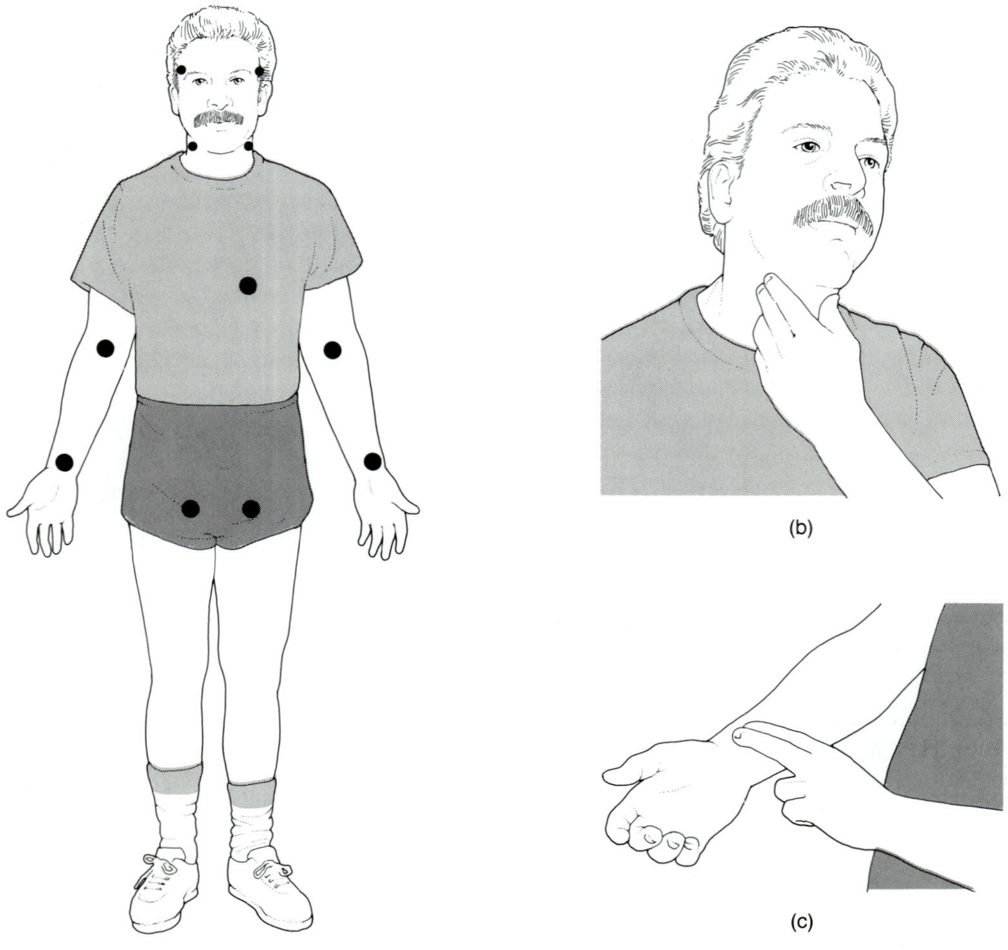

(a)

(b)

(c)

Table 10.7   Target heart rate zones

RHR	Age											
	15–19	20–24	25–29	30–34	35–39	40–44	45–49	50–54	55–59	60–64	65–69	70–74
45–49	125–180	123–175	120–171	118–167	115–163	113–158	110–154	108–150	105–146	103–141	100–137	98–133
50–54	127–181	125–176	122–172	120–168	117–164	115–159	112–155	110–151	107–147	105–142	102–138	100–134
55–59	130–181	128–176	125–172	123–168	120–164	118–159	115–155	113–151	110–147	108–142	105–138	103–134
60–64	132–182	130–177	127–173	125–169	122–165	120–160	117–156	115–152	112–148	110–143	107–139	105–135
65–69	135–183	133–178	130–174	128–170	125–166	123–161	124–157	118–153	115–149	113–144	110–140	100–136
70–74	137–184	135–179	132–175	130–171	127–167	125–162	122–158	120–154	117–150	115–145	112–141	110–137
75–79	140–184	138–180	135–176	133–172	130–168	128–163	125–159	123–155	120–151	118–146	115–142	113–138
80–84	142–185	140–181	137–177	135–173	132–169	130–164	127–160	125–156	122–152	120–147	117–143	115–139
85–89	145–186	143–181	140–177	138–173	135–169	133–164	130–160	128–156	125–152	123–147	120–143	118–139

The target zone (50–85 percent threshold) is based upon the median figure for each age range and resting heart rate range.

An associated measure of stimulus intensity is the **rating of perceived exertion (RPE)**. The individual simply rates the perceived strenuousness of the exercise according to the following scale:

6
7 very, very light
8
9 very light
10
11 fairly light
12
13 somewhat hard
14
15 hard
16
17 very hard
18
19 very, very hard
20

This scale was designed originally to reflect HR response; adding a zero to the rating should approximate the HR response. As noted below, the RPE may be used as a guide to appropriate exercise intensity.

Although the target HR approach is a sound means to monitor your exercise intensity, you may also wish to use the RPE scale. As you exercise and monitor your HR, also assess the difficulty of the exercise by the RPE scale. You may possibly learn to estimate your HR response by your RPE score.

How can I determine the exercise intensity to achieve my target HR range?

To determine the exercise intensity necessary to reach your target HR range, all you need is a stopwatch. Where distances are involved such as with running, swimming, or cycling, an accurate measure is needed. An ideal situation for walking or running would be a one-quarter-mile high school or college track.

A steady-state HR response may be obtained in three to five minutes of evenly paced activity. A sound method for walking, jogging, or running follows, but this system may be adapted easily to other activities such as swimming, cycling, calisthenics, and aerobic dance.

Mark a one-half mile course. Two laps on a quarter-mile track would be ideal, but you can pace out a quarter-mile on the sidewalks near your home. Measure your resting HR. Walk until you have an even pace and then time yourself for the one-half mile. Immediately record your HR at the conclusion of the exercise. During your walk, mentally record the RPE. Did you reach the target HR? Was your

RPE related to your HR? If the HR response is in the target range or the RPE was not too strenuous, you are at a level to begin your training program. If the HR response is not in the target range, rest until your HR returns close to normal and then take the test at a faster pace. Repeat this procedure until you have a plot of the HR, RPE, and time for the one-half mile. Keep a record of this as it will be useful in evaluating the effects of your conditioning program.

For example, suppose you recorded the following data on the one-half mile test on four trials (Figure 10.8).

Test	Time	RPE	HR	Minutes/Mile
1	8:00	11	108	16:00
2	7:10	13	132	14:20
3	6:30	15	156	13:00
4	6:00	18	180	12:00

As your speed increases, both RPE and HR naturally increase. If your predicted HR max is 200, and your resting HR is 70, the 50–85 percent target range approximates 135–180. Test 1 does not provide adequate stimulus intensity, Test 2 is just below the minimum target HR, Test 3 is in the middle of the range, while Test 4 is at your upper limit. Thus, your training intensity should be between 12 and 14 minutes per mile. The RPE may offer a means of judging the intensity of the exercise when you do not have a set distance and watch.

To determine your speed for these tests, simply double the time for the 1/2 mile and you have the time per mile. The last trial was 12 minutes per mile. The caloric expenditure could be obtained from Appendix C.

How may I design my own exercise program?

The exercise program that you design should not only be safe and effective, but it should be one to which you will adhere for a lifetime. Unfortunately, over 50 percent of the individuals who begin an exercise program to lose excess body weight drop out within a short time. Research with successful exercisers has revealed several clues that increase the likelihood of staying with an exercise program. First, do not exceed your abilities during the early stages of the program. Start slowly and progress gradually. Second, set both short-term and long-term goals. A short-term goal may be to walk a mile in 15 minutes, while a long-term goal may be the completion of a local 10-kilometer (6.2-mile) road race. Third, keep a record of your exercise. This will allow you to evaluate your progress toward your goals. Fourth, you

Figure 10.8.
Plot of heart rate and RPE following a ½-mile walk in determination of the threshold heart rate.

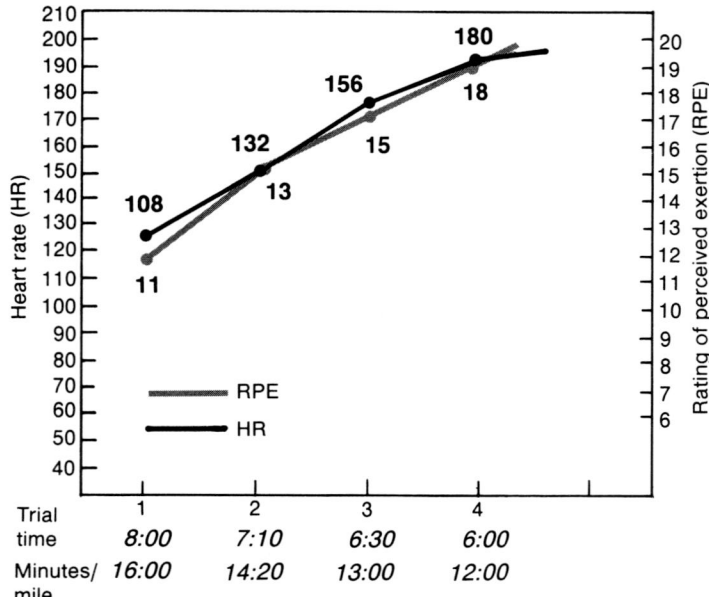

Trial	1	2	3	4
time	*8:00*	*7:10*	*6:30*	*6:00*
Minutes/mile	*16:00*	*14:20*	*13:00*	*12:00*

must have the available time to exercise. Most of us are busy with work, school, family, and friends, so finding the time to exercise is often difficult. You need to incorporate exercise into your daily schedule just as you do for other activities. Fifth, a place to exercise must be convenient. You are more likely to find an excuse not to exercise if you have to travel five miles in heavy traffic to a health spa. Find a convenient location. Finally, self-motivation is probably the most important determinant of adherence to an exercise program. Enjoying your exercise program, being capable at the exercise task, and knowing that it will help you attain your goals will improve your motivation and hopefully make daily exercise a lifetime habit.

Although diverse modes of aerobic exercise may be used to lose body weight and to help condition the cardiovascular system, the major focus here will be on walk–jog–run programs. This is because they satisfy many of the criteria that may encourage adherence to an exercise program.

Walking may be the ideal exercise program for many individuals. Compared to jogging and running there is less stress on the legs due to impact because one foot is always on the ground supporting the body weight. However, leisurely walking usually will not provide an adequate stimulus to achieve the target HR, so the walking pace must be brisk. Walking at a faster-than-normal pace is often called **aerobic walking,** and if done properly can expend Calories at about the same rate as jogging or running. Vigorous arm action is needed, and the length of the stride as well as the step rate must be increased. Also,

using the popular hand weights will increase the energy expenditure by about 5–10 percent and also will help tone the arm muscles if used vigorously. Adding three pounds to each wrist will increase energy output about one Calorie per minute. Carrying the weights in the hands tends to increase the blood pressure more, so it may be helpful to use the types of weights that strap around the wrist. However, you may use similar amounts of Calories by simply walking faster or longer without hand weights.

A wide variety of methods may be used to initiate an aerobic exercise program of walking, jogging or running. The key is to begin slowly, gradually increasing the exercise intensity as you become better conditioned. Once you determine the intensity of exercise necessary to achieve the target HR, it becomes a relatively simple matter to individualize the exercise program. The two tables presented below include exercise programs for individuals who have been sedentary and have low levels of physical fitness. Use your target HR guidelines throughout the 12- to 15-week program.

In the early weeks you should only attempt to exercise at the 50–60 percent target HR range. However, if you find that the exercise intensity needed to achieve this level is too strenuous, reduce it to 40 percent of your calculated heart-rate reserve. As you become better fit, gradually increase your target HR to the 50–85 percent level.

Table 10.8 presents a sample aerobic walking program. It is designed to progress you gradually

Table 10.8   Sample aerobic walking program

	Warm-up	Target zone exercising	Warm-down	Total time
Week 1*	Walk slowly 5 minutes	Walk briskly 5 minutes	Walk slowly 5 minutes	15 minutes
Week 2	Walk slowly 5 minutes	Walk briskly 7 minutes	Walk slowly 5 minutes	17 minutes
Week 3	Walk slowly 5 minutes	Walk briskly 9 minutes	Walk slowly 5 minutes	19 minutes
Week 4	Walk slowly 5 minutes	Walk briskly 11 minutes	Walk slowly 5 minutes	21 minutes
Week 5	Walk slowly 5 minutes	Walk briskly 13 minutes	Walk slowly 5 minutes	23 minutes
Week 6	Walk slowly 5 minutes	Walk briskly 15 minutes	Walk slowly 5 minutes	25 minutes
Week 7	Walk slowly 5 minutes	Walk briskly 18 minutes	Walk slowly 5 minutes	28 minutes
Week 8	Walk slowly 5 minutes	Walk briskly 20 minutes	Walk slowly 5 minutes	30 minutes
Week 9	Walk slowly 5 minutes	Walk briskly 23 minutes	Walk slowly 5 minutes	33 minutes
Week 10	Walk slowly 5 minutes	Walk briskly 26 minutes	Walk slowly 5 minutes	36 minutes
Week 11	Walk slowly 5 minutes	Walk briskly 28 minutes	Walk slowly 5 minutes	38 minutes
Week 12	Walk slowly 5 minutes	Walk briskly 30 minutes	Walk slowly 5 minutes	40 minutes

From week 13 on, check your pulse periodically to see if you are exercising within your target heart rate range. As you become more fit, walk faster to increase your heart rate toward the upper levels of your target range. Follow the principle of progression.

Note: If you find a particular week's pattern tiring, repeat it before going on to the next pattern. *You do not have to complete the walking program in 12 weeks.* Remember that your goal is to continue getting the benefits you are seeking and enjoying your activity. Listen to your body and progress less rapidly, if necessary.

*Program should include at *least* three exercise sessions per week.

Source: U.S. Department of Health and Human Services.

through 12 weeks to a point where the exercise intensity and duration may make a significant contribution to weight loss over time. If you feel fit you may progress more rapidly than the table indicates, but stay within your target HR range and do not become unduly fatigued.

Table 10.9 presents an exercise program with a rapid progression to jogging, using an interval-training approach. **Interval training** alternates periods of rest and exercise. Again, the target HR method should be used during this exercise program.

Whatever mode of exercise you select, the duration of the stimulus period should be fifteen to thirty minutes. The target HR should be maintained for twenty to thirty minutes. This may be continuous or intermittent. If twenty minutes is the allotted time, the target R should be achieved for twenty continuous minutes or four five-minute intervals of exercise with several minutes of rest in between.

The frequency of exercise should be daily or at least three to four times per week. The American College of Sports Medicine has documented a number of studies that support a frequency level of at least three times per week as being necessary to develop and maintain cardiovascular health. During the early stages, however, it may be advisable to exercise daily in order to form sound habits. The exercise intensity at this time may not be too severe, such as walking, and hence daily exercise bouts may be undertaken without serious muscle soreness or related injury patterns. If you switch to jogging or running, decrease the frequency to 3 or 4 times per week to avoid overuse injuries. The frequency per week may be increased as you become better physically conditioned.

For weight-control purposes, duration and frequency of exercise are key elements. The longer and more often you exercise, the greater will be the total amount of energy expended. Aerobic walking for five miles on a daily basis is the equivalent of approximately one pound of body fat per week.

There are a number of other excellent conditioning programs available for the unconditioned individual. Probably the most popular is the aerobics program developed by Dr. Kenneth Cooper. His most recent programs may be found in *The Aerobics Program for Total Well Being,* a highly recommended paperback found in most bookstores. Also, the Rockport Walking Institute has developed a detailed fitness walking test and walking exercise program. You may obtain a copy by sending SASE to the institute at Box 480, Marlboro, MA, 01752.

Table 10.9 Sample aerobic jogging program (interval training)

	Warm-up	Target zone exercising	Warm-down	Total time
Week 1*	Stretch and limber up 5 minutes	Walk (nonstop) 10 minutes	Walk slowly 3 minutes; stretch 2 minutes	20 minutes
Week 2	Stretch and limber up 5 minutes	Walk 5 minutes; jog 1 minute; walk 5 minutes; jog 1 minute	Walk slowly 3 minutes; stretch 2 minutes	22 minutes
Week 3	Stretch and limber up 5 minutes	Walk 5 minutes; jog 3 minutes; walk 5 minutes; jog 3 minutes	Walk slowly 3 minutes; stretch 2 minutes	26 minutes
Week 4	Stretch and limber up 5 minutes	Walk 5 minutes; jog 4 minutes; walk 5 minutes; jog 4 minutes	Walk slowly 3 minutes; stretch 2 minutes	28 minutes
Week 5	Stretch and limber up 5 minutes	Walk 4 minutes; jog 5 minutes; walk 4 minutes; jog 5 minutes	Walk slowly 3 minutes; stretch 2 minutes	28 minutes
Week 6	Stretch and limber up 5 minutes	Walk 4 minutes; jog 6 minutes; walk 4 minutes; jog 6 minutes	Walk slowly 3 minutes; stretch 2 minutes	30 minutes
Week 7	Stretch and limber up 5 minutes	Walk 4 minutes; jog 7 minutes; walk 4 minutes; jog 7 minutes	Walk slowly 3 minutes; stretch 2 minutes	32 minutes
Week 8	Stretch and limber up 5 minutes	Walk 4 minutes; jog 8 minutes; walk 4 minutes; jog 8 minutes	Walk slowly 3 minutes; stretch 2 minutes	34 minutes
Week 9	Stretch and limber up 5 minutes	Walk 4 minutes; jog 9 minutes; walk 4 minutes; jog 9 minutes	Walk slowly 3 minutes; stretch 2 minutes	36 minutes
Week 10	Stretch and limber up 5 minutes	Walk 4 minutes; jog 13 minutes	Walk slowly 3 minutes; stretch 2 minutes	27 minutes
Week 11	Stretch and limber up 5 minutes	Walk 4 minutes; jog 15 minutes	Walk slowly 3 minutes; stretch 2 minutes	29 minutes
Week 12	Stretch and limber up 5 minutes	Walk 4 minutes; jog 17 minutes	Walk slowly 3 minutes; stretch 2 minutes	31 minutes
Week 13	Stretch and limber up 5 minutes	Walk 2 minutes; jog slowly 2 minutes; jog 17 minutes	Walk slowly 3 minutes; stretch 2 minutes	31 minutes
Week 14	Stretch and limber up 5 minutes	Walk 1 minute; jog slowly 3 minutes; jog 17 minutes	Walk slowly 3 minutes; stretch 2 minutes	31 minutes
Week 15	Stretch and limber up 5 minutes	Jog slowly 3 minutes; jog 17 minutes	Walk slowly 3 minutes; stretch 2 minutes	30 minutes

*Program should include at *least* three exercise sessions per week.

From week 16 on, check your pulse periodically to see if you are exercising within your target zone. As you become more fit, try exercising within the upper range of your target zone.

Note: If you find a particular week's pattern tiring, repeat it before going on to the next pattern. *You do not have to complete the jogging program in 15 weeks.* Remember that your goal is to continue getting the benefits you are seeking and enjoying your activity.

Source: U.S. Department of Health and Human Services.

Figure 10.9.

Exercise helps to release fat (free fatty acids) from the adipose tissues. The fat then travels by way of the bloodstream to the muscles where the free fatty acids are oxidized to provide the energy for exercise. Thus, exercise is an effective measure of reducing body fat.

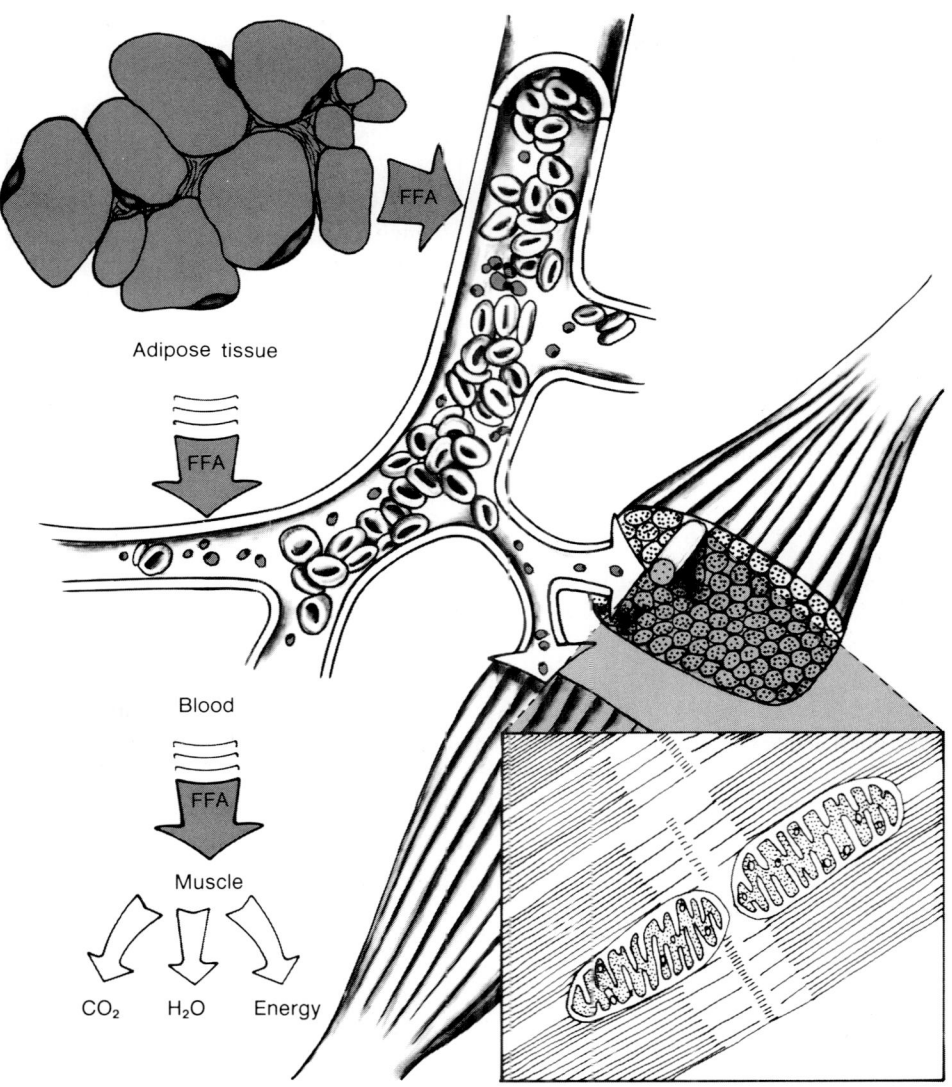

Adipose tissue

FFA

Blood

FFA

Muscle

CO_2 H_2O Energy

From what parts of the body does the weight loss occur during an exercise weight-reduction program?

As mentioned previously, weight loss may come from any one of three body sources—body water, lean tissue such as muscle, and body fat stores. A diet program, especially one very low in Calories, will cause a rapid weight loss due to decreases in body water and lean tissue. Body-fat losses are minimal at first but may increase in later stages of the diet. On the other hand, weight lost through an exercise program alone is lost at a much slower rate. Body water levels remain relatively normal after replacement of water lost through exercise. The lean tissues, particularly muscle, might actually increase in amount from the stimulating effect of exercise on muscle development. Because a good proportion of the energy demands for exercise comes from the oxidation of fat, most of the body-weight reduction comes from the body-fat stores, particularly in the abdominal area (Figure 10.9). As we learned previously, the caloric cost of one pound of fat is much higher than water or lean muscle tissue.

Is spot reducing effective?

Spot reducing uses isolated exercises in an attempt to deplete local fat depots in specific body spots. These techniques do not appear to be effective. In one study the fat tissue was biopsied to determine whether sit-ups would reduce fat in the abdominal area. Subjects did a total of 5,000 sit-ups over a 27-day period, but this localized exercise did not preferentially reduce the adipose cell size in the abdominal area.

The current view suggests that the reduction of fat in body areas is most likely to occur where fat deposits are the most conspicuous, regardless of the exercise format. However, some areas of the body are somewhat resistant to change, particularly the gymoid type fat distribution around the hips and thighs. Although both large-muscle activities and local isolated-muscle exercises may both be beneficial in reducing fat stores, the former are recommended because the total caloric expenditure will be larger.

Is it possible to exercise and still not lose body weight?

Many individuals are disappointed during the early stages of an exercise program because they do not lose weight very rapidly. Unless they understand what is happening in their bodies, the results on the scale may convince them that exercise is not an effective means to reduce weight, and they may quit exercising altogether. There are several reasons why an individual may not lose weight during the early stages of a weight-reduction program, and also why it becomes more difficult after weight loss has occurred.

When a sedentary individual begins a daily exercise program, the body reacts to the exercise stress and changes so it can more easily handle the demands of exercise (Figure 10.10):

1. The muscles may increase in size because of hypertrophy of the muscle cells. The increased protein will hold water.
2. Certain structures within the muscle cell that process oxygen, along with numerous enzymes involved in oxygen use, will increase in quantity.
3. Energy substances in the cell will increase, particularly glycogen, which binds water.
4. The connective tissue will toughen and thicken.
5. The total blood volume may increase. An increase of approximately 500 milliliters, or about a pound, has been recorded in one week.

At the same time, however, body-fat stores will begin to diminish somewhat as fat is used as a source of energy for exercise. Overall, there may be an increase in the lean body mass, particularly the muscle tissues, and a decrease in body fat. These changes may counterbalance each other, and the individual may not lose any weight. However, although little or no weight is lost during those early phases, the body composition changes are favorable. Body fat is being lost.

Once these adaptive changes have occurred, which may take about a month, body weight should decrease in relationship to the number of Calories lost through exercise. Keep in mind that weight loss will be slow on an exercise program, but if you can build up to an exercise energy expenditure of above 300 Calories per day, then about three pounds per month will be exercised away.

After several months you may begin to notice that your body weight has stabilized even though you continue to exercise and have not reached your weight goal. Part of the reason may be your lower body weight. If you look at Appendix C, you can see that the less you weigh, the fewer Calories you burn for any given exercise. If you have been doing the same amount of exercise all along, you may now be at the body weight where your energy output is matched by your energy input in food and your body weight has stabilized. In addition you may become more skilled, and hence more efficient, in your physical activity. Fewer Calories may then be expended for any given amount of time. However, this is usually only true of activities that involve a skill factor. It can be highly significant in swimming, but not as great in jogging.

In summary, your body weight may not change during the early stages of an exercise program; it may then begin to drop during a second stage, and then plateau at the third stage. If you are aware of these possible stages your adherence to an exercise program may be enhanced. Also, during the third stage, if you desire to lose more weight by exercise, then the amount of exercise will need to be increased.

What about the five or six pounds a person may lose during an hour of exercise?

A rapid weight loss may occur during exercise. Some individuals have lost as much as 10–12 pounds in an hour or so. As you probably suspect, this weight loss may be attributed to body-water losses. This is particularly evident while exercising in warm or hot weather. The weight loss is temporary, and under normal food and water intake the body-water content will return to normal. Each pound of weight lost

Figure 10.10.

Body weight may not change much during the beginning phases of an aerobic exercise program. However, body composition may change. The exercise stimulates an increase in muscle tissue, blood volume, and muscle glycogen stores, which tend to increase weight. Body fat is reduced, but the increases in the other components can balance out the fat losses with no net loss of body weight. Eventually, body weight begins to drop as the exercise program is continued.

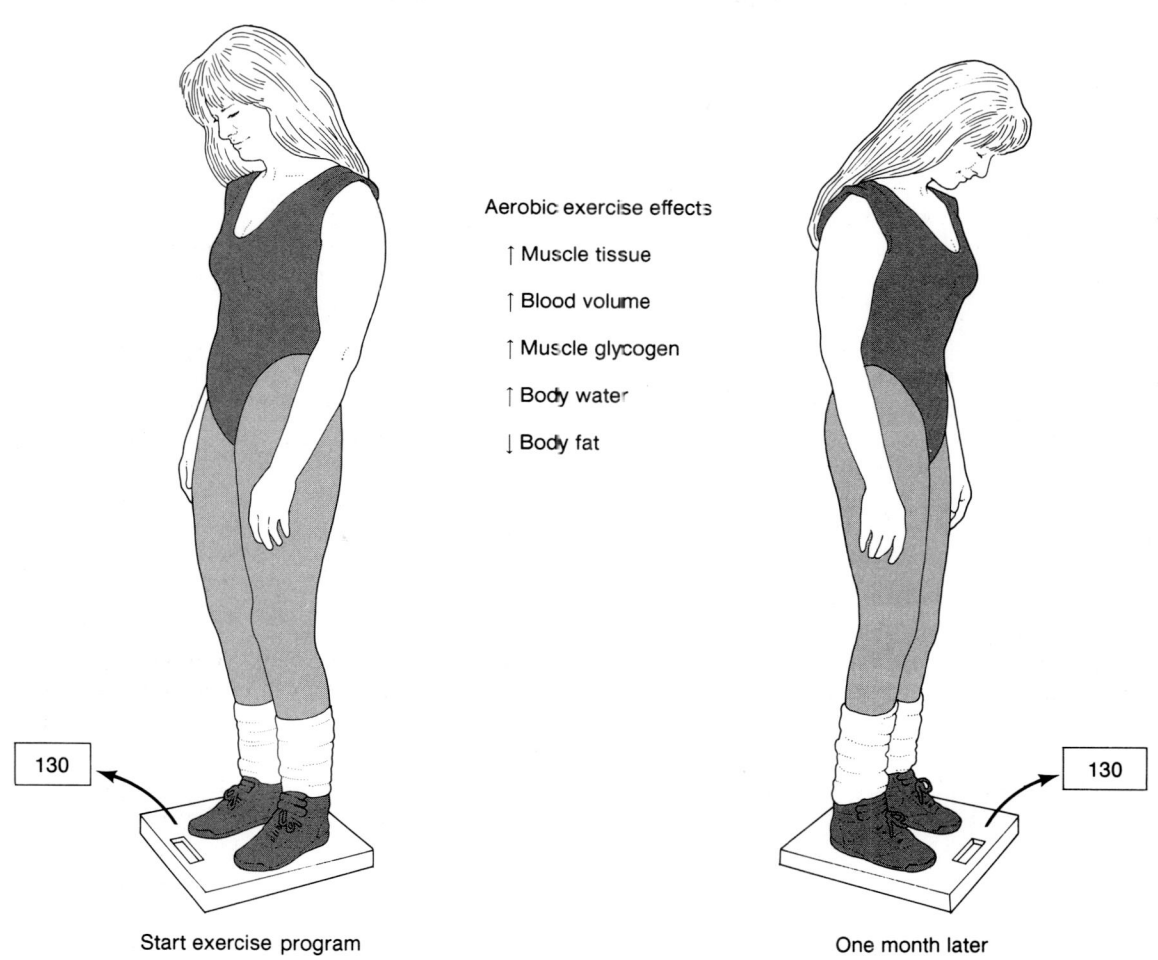

Aerobic exercise effects

↑ Muscle tissue

↑ Blood volume

↑ Muscle glycogen

↑ Body water

↓ Body fat

130

Start exercise program

130

One month later

this way is one pint of fluid, or 16 ounces. A 2.2-pound weight loss would be the equivalent of one liter.

In the heat of summer, you may occasionally see an individual training with heavy sweat clothes or a rubberized suit. The reason often given is to lose more body weight. The individual will lose more body weight, but again it will be body water which will be regained as soon as he or she drinks fluids. In this regard, the technique is worthless. Moreover, it may predispose the individual to an unusually high heat stress, causing severe medical problems. Remember, only sweat that actually evaporates will help reduce the heat stress on the body.

Any water lost through dehydration should be replaced before the next exercise session, especially

when exercising in warm environments. The importance of rehydration and problems associated with exercise in the heat were covered in Chapter 8.

Comprehensive Weight-Control Programs

Which is more effective for weight control—dieting or exercise?

Dieting alone or exercise alone may be effective means to reduce body fat, but both techniques have certain advantages and disadvantages. However, it appears that the advantages of one technique help counterbalance the disadvantages of the other. Dieting will contribute to a negative caloric balance

Figure 10.11.
The most effective-weight reduction program involves both dieting and exercise. Mild caloric restriction and an aerobic exercise program can be combined effectively to lose two pounds per week.

Wholesome low-Calorie foods

Energy in

Daily aerobic exercise

Energy out

and may help bring about a rapid weight reduction early in the program, but may lead to decreases in lean body mass and the RMR. Exercise usually results in a slower rate of weight loss but may help develop and maintain the lean body mass and prevent the decrease in the RMR. Garfinkel and Coscina recently noted that weight lost by dieting is about 75 percent fat and 25 percent protein, but combining exercise and dieting reduces the protein loss to only 5 percent. Weight training (covered in the next chapter) added to a weight-reduction program may also be very effective in helping to maintain lean body mass.

Hence, a comprehensive weight-reduction program involving both a dietary and an exercise regimen, along with supportive behavioral modification techniques, is highly recommended by major health-related organizations such as the American Dietetic Association and the American College of Sports Medicine. The principles of developing such a program have been presented in the preceding three sections of this chapter. A number of research studies with men, women, and children have supported the value of this type of program. In almost all cases, a combined diet and exercise program was more effective for weight reduction than either diet or exercise alone.

Research also has been conducted with individuals who have successfully lost weight and maintained their desired level. In essence, they assumed responsibility for their need to lose weight and planned their own program. They did not necessarily diet per se, but simply decreased the amount of fat and sugar in their diet, ate less between meals, and often skipped meals. They also initiated a reasonable exercise program.

Consider the following. A dietary reduction of 500 Calories per day, along with an exercise energy expenditure of 500 Calories per day, could lead to approximately two pounds of weight loss per week, about the maximal amount recommended unless under medical supervision. The removal of 500 Calories from the diet could be done immediately by simply reducing the amount of sugar and fat in the daily diet and using some of the behavioral modification techniques cited earlier. You should review those suggestions given earlier relative to the substitution of nutrient-dense foods for high-Caloric ones. Relative to exercise it may take a month or more before you may be able to use 500 Calories daily, but by following the progressive plan outlined earlier in this chapter you should be able to reach that level safely. In the meantime, change your usual behavior by climbing stairs and walking more to add to your caloric expenditure (Figure 10.11).

What type of weight-reduction program is advisable for young athletes?

In sports in which athletes compete in weight classes, such as wrestling, or in those where excess body fat may hinder performance, such as gymnastics, most competitors and their coaches believe that it is best to attain the lowest weight possible to increase chances of success. Although most of the concern in the past was devoted to the sport of wrestling, there is increasing concern about this practice in a variety of other sports.

As noted in the preceding chapter, potentially acute health problems may arise when the youngster sets an unrealistically low body-weight goal and uses nonrecommended techniques, such as starvation, diuretics, laxatives, appetite-suppressing drugs, and dehydration. Suzanne Steen and her associates at the University of Pennsylvania have found that athletes, such as wrestlers, who lose and gain weight repeatedly throughout the season may find it more difficult to lose weight because their metabolism may slow down to conserve energy. However, studies by Schmidt, Loprinzi, and Melby recently noted that the decrease in the RMR is transient or returns to normal preseason values following completion of the competitive wrestling season. There is also some concern by medical personnel that weight loss during the growth and development years may have adverse long-term effects. On the other hand, many coaches and athletes still remain unconvinced that current weight-control practices pose any immediate or future health hazard. Unfortunately, the available scientific data are very limited, and this general area is in dire need of long-term research.

Nevertheless, on the basis of the data that are available, organizations such as the American Medical Association and the American College of Sports Medicine have made some general recommendations to help alleviate potential problems and make weight control practices in sports as safe as possible.

1. Weight should be lost gradually. The comprehensive program involving a balanced diet of 1,500–2,400 Calories and exercise should be used in the preseason to lose most of the body weight. With appropriate carbohydrate, protein, minerals, and vitamins in the diet, a limited number of Calories possibly may enable a wrestler or other athlete to lose body weight effectively and yet still maintain high levels of aerobic and anaerobic activity in training.
2. Dehydration techniques such as saunas, steam baths, and diuretics should be prohibited.
3. In the sport of wrestling, having the weigh-in immediately prior to performance may discourage rapid dehydration and weight gain techniques. Also, suggestions have been made to allow more intermediate weight classes, because there are more boys at these weight levels.
4. Attempts have been made to predict a minimum body-fat percentage or body weight and although used in several states, these methods generally have not been applied extensively. Suggestions have been made to have a physician certify a minimum weight for each wrestler, but again this has not been used extensively.

What is the importance of prevention in a weight-control program?

Health practices designed to prevent the development of chronic diseases currently are being promoted heavily by several major health organizations. Changing your diet by reducing caloric intake, saturated fats, and cholesterol, and eating more nutritious foods (quality Calories), and concurrently initiating and continuing a good endurance-type exercise program are considered to be two steps toward positive health and the possible prevention of certain health problems. These two steps are also the key elements of a sound weight control program (Figure 10.12).

Although most of this chapter has focused on treatment programs for the reduction of excess body fat, the same guidelines may be applied to a prevention program. Obesity in our society is a serious medical problem of epidemic proportions. Although treatment programs for the clinically obese may be successful on a short-term basis, unfortunately much of the weight loss is regained by the vast majority of those treated. We need to have strong prevention programs in our schools and communities, particularly for children and adolescents, for this appears to be the time of life when chronic cases of obesity develop. It is incumbent upon those involved with the food habits and physical activity of our youth, notably parents and health and physical educators, to instruct and motivate them toward sound health habits. According to the American Medical Association, prevention is the treatment of choice in dealing with obesity.

References

Books

American Diabetes Association and American Dietetic Association. 1986. Exchange lists for meal planning. Chicago: American Dietetic Association and American Diabetes Association.

Dusek, D. 1989. *Weight management: The Fitness Way*. Boston: Jones and Bartlett.

Katch, F., and McArdle, W. 1988. *Nutrition, Weight Control, and Exercise*. Boston: Houghton Mifflin.

Logue, A. 1986. *The Psychology of Eating and Drinking*. New York: W. H. Freeman.

Mahoney, M., and Mahoney, K. 1970. *Permanent Weight Control: The Total Solution to the Dieter's Dilemma*. New York: Norton.

Mayer, J. 1968. *Overweight: Causes, cost and control*. Englewood Cliffs, NJ: Prentice-Hall.

Figure 10.12.
It is very easy to consume 200 additional Calories per day, which can lead to an increase of about 2 pounds of body fat per month. However, increased physical activity may help to expend these Calories.

200 Calorie milkshake =

| 3 mile leisurely walk at 3 MPH | or | 30 minutes of easy tennis | or | 5 miles of leisurely bicycling at 5 MPH |

National Research Council. 1989. *Diet and Health: Implications for Reducing Chronic Disease Risk.* Washington, DC: National Academy Press.

National Research Council. 1989. *Recommended Dietary Allowances.* Washington, DC: National Academy Press.

Shils, M., and Young, V. 1988. *Modern Nutrition in Health and Disease.* Philadelphia: Lea & Febiger.

Stamford, B., and Shimer, P. 1990. *Fitness without Exercise.* New York: Warner Books.

Weight Watchers International. 1981. *Weight Watchers 365-day Menu Cookbook.* New York: New American Library.

Williams, M. 1985. *Nutritional Aspects of Human Physical and Athletic Performance.* Springfield, IL: C C Thomas.

Williams, M. 1990. *Lifetime Fitness and Wellness: A Personal Choice.* Dubuque, IA: Wm. C. Brown.

Reviews

American College of Sports Medicine. 1976. Position stand on weight loss in wrestlers. *Medicine and Science in Sports* 8: xi–xiii.

American College of Sports Medicine. 1983. Proper and improper weight loss programs. *Medicine and Science in Sports and Exercise* 15: ix–xiii.

American College of Sports Medicine. 1990. The recommended quantity and quality of exercise for developing and maintaining cardiorespiratory and muscular fitness in healthy adults. *Medicine and Science in Sports and Exercise* 22: 265–74.

American Dietetic Association. 1990. Position of the American Dietetic Association: Very-low-Calorie weight loss diets. *Journal of the American Dietetic Association* 90:722–26.

American Heart Association, Council on Scientific Affairs. 1988. Treatment of obesity in adults. *Journal of the American Medical Association* 260:2547–51.

Atkinson, R. 1989. Low and very low calorie diets. *Medical Clinics of North America* 73: 203–16.

Birk, T., and Birk, C. 1987. Use of ratings of perceived exertion for exercise prescription. *Sports Medicine* 4:1–8.

Bjorntop, P. 1990. Adipose tissue adaptation to exercise. In: *Exercise, Fitness and Health,* eds. C. Bouchard et al. Champaign, IL: Human Kinetics.

Blair, S. 1990. Fitness levels inversely related to early all-cause mortality. *Obesity '90 Update,* March / April:3.

Bouchard, C., and Despres, J. 1989. Variation in fat distribution with age and health implications. *American Academy of Physical Education Papers* 22: 78–106.

Bray, G. 1990. Exercise and obesity. In: *Exercise, Fitness and Health,* eds. C. Bouchard et al. Champaign, IL: Human Kinetics.

Brownell, K. 1989. Weight cycling. *American Journal of Clinical Nutrition* 49: 937.

Brownell, K., and Kramer, F. 1989. Behavioral management of obesity. *Medical Clinics of North America* 73: 185–202.

Brownell, K., and Steen, S. 1987. Modern methods of weight control. *Physician and Sportsmedicine* 15: 122–37.

Brownell, K., et al. 1987. Weight regulation practices in athletes: Analysis of metabolic and health effects. *Medicine and Science in Sports and Exercise* 19: 546–56.

Dennison, D. 1982. How many calories should you eat per day? *Health Education* 13: 53.

Dietz, W. 1983. Childhood obesity: Susceptibility, cause and management. *Journal of Pediatrics* 103: 676–86.

Dishman, R. 1986. Exercise compliance: A new view for public health. *Physician and Sportsmedicine* 14: 127–45.

Fisher, M., and Lachance, P. 1985. Nutrition evaluation of published weight-reducing diets. *Journal of the American Dietetic Association* 85: 450–54.

Garfinkel, P., and Coscina, D. 1990. Discussion: Exercise and obesity. In: *Exercise, Fitness and Health,* eds. C. Bouchard, et al. Champaign, IL: Human Kinetics.

Goldstein, D. 1989. Clinical applications for exercise. *Physician and Sportsmedicine* 17: 82–93.

Hoffer, L. 1988. Starvation. In: *Modern Nutrition in Health and Disease,* eds. M. Shils and V. Young. Philadelphia: Lea & Febiger.

Hoffman, C., and Coleman, E. 1991. An eating plan and update on recommended dietary practices for the endurance athlete. *Journal of the American Dietetic Association* 91: 325–30.

Horton, E. 1986. Metabolic aspects of exercise and weight reduction. *Medicine and Science in Sports and Exercise* 18: 10–18.

King, A., and Tribble, D. 1991. The role of exercise in weight regulation in nonathletes. *Sports Medicine* 11: 331–49.

Miller, W. 1991. Diet composition, energy intake, and nutritional status in relation to obesity in men and women. *Medicine and Science in Sports and Exercise* 23: 280–84.

Farker, D., et al. 1991. Juvenile obesity: The importance of exercise and getting children to do it. *Physician and Sportsmedicine* 19: June 113–25.

Pi-Sunyer, F. X. 1990. Effect of the composition of the diet on energy intake. *Nutrition Reviews* 48: 94–105.

Pi-Sunyer, F. X. 1988. Obesity. In: *Modern Nutrition in Health and Disease,* eds. M. Shils and V. Young. Philadelphia: Lea & Febiger.

Poehlman, E. 1989. A review: Exercise and its influence on resting energy metabolism in man. *Medicine and Science in Sports and Exercise* 21: 515–25.

Rippe, J., et al. 1988. Walking for health and fitness. *Journal of the American Medical Association* 259: 2720–24.

Rolls, B. 1991. Effects of intense sweeteners on hunger, food intake, and body weight: A review. *American Journal of Clinical Nutrition* 53: 872–78.

Schelkun, P. 1991. The risks of riding the weight-loss roller coaster. *Physician and Sportsmedicine* 19: 149–56.

Segel, K. and Pi-Sunyer, F. 1989. Exercise and obesity. *Medical Clinics of North America* 73: 217–37.

Stamford B. 1989. Meals and timing of exercise. *Physician and Sportsmedicine* 17: 151.

Thompson, J., et al. 1982. Exercise and obesity: Etiology, physiology and intervention. *Psychological Bulletin* 91: 55–79.

Tipton, C. 1980. Physiologic problems associated with the making of weight. *American Journal of Sports Medicine* 8: 449–50.

Tremblay A., et al. 1989. Impact of dietary fat content and fat oxidation on energy intake in humans. *American Journal of Clinical Nutrition* 49: 799–805.

Williams, M. 1986. Weight control through exercise and diet for children and young athletes. *American Academy of Physical Education Papers* 19: 88–113.

Wilmore J. 1983. Appetite and body composition consequent to physical activity. *Research Quarterly for Exercise and Sport* 54: 415–25.

Wooley, S., and Wooley, O. 1984. Should obesity be treated at all? *Research Publications: Association for Research in Nervous and Mental Disease* 62: 185–92.

Young, J., and Ruderman, N. 1988. Exercise and metabolic disorders. In: *Principles of Exercise Biochemistry,* ed. J. Poortmans. Basel: Karger.

Zamula, E. 1985. Extreme treatments for extreme obesity. *FDA Consumer* 19: 9–13.

Specific Studies

Abadie, B. 1990. Physiological responses to grade walking with wrist and hand-held weights. *Research Quarterly for Exercise and Sport* 61: 93–95.

Amatruda, J., et al. 1988. The safety and efficacy of a controlled low-energy (very-low-calorie) diet in the treatment of non-insulin-dependent diabetes and obesity. *Archives of Internal Medicine* 148: 873–77.

Ballor, D., et al. 1988. Resistance weight training during caloric restriction enhances lean body weight maintenance. *American Journal of Clinical Nutrition* 47: 19–25.

Ballor, D., et al. 1990. Exercise intensity does not affect the composition of diet- and exercise-induced body mass loss. *American Journal of Clinical Nutrition* 51: 142–46.

Bernhauer, E., et al. 1989. Exercise reduces depressed metabolic rate produced by severe caloric restriction. *Medicine and Science in Sports and Exercise* 21: 29–33.

Brehm, B., and Gutin, B. 1986. Recovery energy expenditure for steady state exercise in runners and nonexercisers. *Medicine and Science in Sports and Exercise* 18: 205–10.

Bubb, W., and Seay, H. 1990. The effects of various intensities of exercise on post-exercise resting metabolic rate. *Medicine and Science in Sports and Exercise* 22: S49.

Cohen, B., and Sedlock, D. 1990. The effect of exercise intensity on postexercise energy expenditure in women. *Medicine and Science in Sports and Exercise* 22: S50.

Colvin, R., and Olson, S. 1983. A descriptive analysis of men and women who have lost significant weight and are highly successful at maintaining the loss. *Addictive Behaviors* 8: 287–95.

Convertino, V., et al. 1980. Exercise training–induced hypervolemia: Role of plasma albumin, renin and vasopressin. *Journal of Applied Physiology* 48: 665–69.

Despres, J., et al. 1990. Metabolic effects of aerobic exercise training–induced loss of abdominal fat in obese women. *Medicine and Science in Sports and Exercise* 22: S128.

Elliot, D., et al. 1989. Sustained depression of the resting metabolic rate after massive weight loss. *American Journal of Clinical Nutrition* 49: 93–96.

Feder, S., et al. 1990. Effects of supplemented fasting and aerobic dance on cardiovascular functioning and anthropometric measurements in obese females. *Medicine and Science in Sports and Exercise* 22: S129.

Forbes, G., and Brown, M. 1989. Energy need for weight maintenance in human beings: Effect of body size and composition. *Journal of the American Dietetic Association* 89: 499–502.

Frey-Hewitt, B., et al. 1990. The effect of weight loss by dieting or exercise on resting metabolic rate in overweight men. *International Journal of Obesity* 14: 327–34.

Gwinup, G. 1987. Weight loss without dietary restriction: Efficacy of different forms of aerobic exercise. *American Journal of Sports Medicine* 15: 275–79.

Hagan, R., et al. 1986. The effects of aerobic conditioning and/or caloric restriction in overweight men and women. *Medicine and Science in Sports and Exercise* 18: 87–93.

Hendler, R., and Bonde, A. 1988. Very-low-calorie diets with high and low protein content: Impact on triiodothyronine, energy expenditure, and nitrogen balance. *American Journal of Clinical Nutrition* 48: 1239–47.

Holland, G., et al. 1990. Treadmill vs steptreadmill ergometry. *Physician and Sportsmedicine* 18: 79–84.

Jakicec, J., et al. 1989. Metabolic rate and body composition 12 months post very low calorie diet (VLCD). *Medicine and Science in Sports and Exercise* 21: S33.

Jenkins, K., et al. 1989. Nibbling versus gorging: Metabolic advantages of increased meal frequency. *New England Journal of Medicine* 321: 929–34.

Katch, F., et al. 1980. Preferential effects of abdominal exercise training on regional adipose cell size. *Medicine and Science in Sports and Exercise* 12: 96.

Lavery, M., et al. 1989. Long-term follow-up of weight status of subjects in a behavioral weight control program. *Journal of the American Dietetic Association* 89: 1259–64.

Loprinzi, M., et al. 1991. Resting metabolic rate of varsity wrestlers: Effects of repetitive weight loss. *Medicine and Science in Sports and Exercise* 23: S75

McMurray, R., et al. 1985. Responses of endurance-trained subjects to caloric deficits induced by diet or exercise. *Medicine and Science in Sports and Exercise* 17: 574–79.

Makalous, S., et al. 1988. Energy expenditure during walking with hand weights. *Physician and Sportsmedicine* 16: 139–48.

Maxwell, B., et al. 1986. Effects of exercise intensity and duration on hunger. *Medicine and Science in Sports and Exercise* 18: S19.

Melby, C., et al. 1990. Resting metabolic rate in weight cycling collegiate wrestlers compared to physically active non-cycling controls. *FASEB Journal* 4: A397.

Miller, W., et al. 1990. Diet composition, energy intake, and exercise in relation to body fat in men and women. *American Journal of Clinical Nutrition* 52: 426–30.

Mole, P., et al. 1989. Exercise reverses depressed metabolic rate produced by severe caloric restriction. *Medicine and Science in Sports and Exercise* 21: 29–33.

Newman, B., et al. 1990. Nongenetic influences of obesity on other cardiovascular disease risk factors: An analysis of identical twins. *American Journal of Public Health* 80: 675–78.

Parker, S., et al. 1989. Failure of target heart rate to accurately monitor intensity during aerobic dance. *Medicine and Science in Sports and Exercise* 21: 230–34.

Pavlou, K., et al. 1988. Physical activity as a supplement to a weight-loss dietary regimen. *American Journal of Clinical Nutrition* 49: 1110–14.

Phinney, S., et al. 1988. Effects of aerobic exercise on energy expenditure and nitrogen balance during very low calorie dieting. *Metabolism* 37: 758–65.

Poehlman, E., et al. 1988. Resting metabolic rate and postprandial thermogenesis in highly trained and untrained males. *American Journal of Clinical Nutrition* 47: 793–98.

Rolls, B., et al. 1990. Effects of sucrose and aspartame on hunger. *FASEB Journal* 4: A787.

Romieu, I., et al. 1988. Energy intake and other determinants of relative weight. *American Journal of Clinical Nutrition* 47: 406–12.

Rontoyannis, G., et al. 1989. Energy balance in ultramarathon running. *American Journal of Clinical Nutrition* 49: 976–79.

Saris, W., et al. 1989. Study on food intake and energy expenditure during extreme sustained exercise. The Tour de France. *International Journal of Sports Medicine* 10: S26–S31.

Schmidt, W., et al. 1991. Two competitive seasons of weight cycling does not lower resting metabolic rate in college wrestlers. *Medicine and Science in Sports and Exercise* 23: S53.

Schutz, Y., et al. 1989. Failure of dietary fat intake to promote fat oxidation: A factor favoring the development of obesity. *American Journal of Clinical Nutrition* 50: 307–14.

Sedlock, D., et al. 1989. Effect of exercise intensity and duration on postexercise energy expenditure. *Medicine and Science in Sports and Exercise* 21: 662–66.

Staten, M. 1991. The effect of exercise on food intake in men and women. *American Journal of Clinical Nutrition* 53: 27–31.

Steen, S., et al. 1988. Metabolic effects of repeated weight loss and regain in adolescent wrestlers. *Journal of the American Medical Association* 260: 47–50.

Thompson, D., et al. 1988. Acute effects of exercise intensity on appetite in young men. *Medicine and Science in Sports and Exercise* 20: 222–27.

Thompson, J., et al. 1990. Resting metabolic rate and thermic effect of a meal in low-calorie intake endurance athletes. *Medicine and Science in Sports and Exercise* 22: S550.

Tremblay, A., et al. 1990. Effect of intensity of physical activity on body fatness and fat distribution. *American Journal of Clinical Nutrition* 51: 153–57.

Tremblay, A., et al. 1990. Long-term exercise training with constant energy intake. 2: Effect on glucose metabolism and resting energy expenditure. *International Journal of Obesity* 14: 75–84.

van Dale, D., and Saris, W. 1989. Repetitive weight loss and weight regain: Effects on weight reduction, resting metabolic rate, and lipolytic activity before and after exercise and/or diet treatment. *American Journal of Clinical Nutrition* 49: 409–16.

Webb, P. 1985. Direct calorimetry and the energetics of exercise and weight loss. *Medicine and Science in Sports and Exercise* 18: 3–5.

Widerman, P., and Hagan, R. 1982. Body weight loss in a wrestler preparing for competition. A case report. *Medicine and Science in Sports and Exercise* 14: 413–18.

Woo, R., and Pi-Sunyer, F. 1985. Effect of increased physical activity on voluntary intake in lean women. *Metabolism* 34: 836–41.

Yost, T., and Eckel, R. 1988. Fat calories may be preferentially stored in reduced-obese women: A permissive pathway for resumption of the obese state. *Journal of Clinical and Endocrinological Metabolism* 67: 259–63.

Key Terms

anabolic steroids

bulk-up method

circuit aerobics

circuit weight training

concentric method

eccentric method

isokinetic method

isometric method

isotonic method

muscle hypertrophy

overload principle

principle of exercise-sequence

principle of progressive-
resistance exercise

principle of recuperation

principle of specificity

repetition maximum (RM)

strength-endurance continuum

Valsalva phenomenon

Key Concepts

There may be a variety of reasons why an individual is underweight, and the cause should be determined before a treatment is prescribed.

For those who want to gain weight, a weekly increase of one pound is a sound approach, but the weight gain should be primarily muscle tissue and not body fat.

In essence, adequate rest and sleep, increased caloric intake, and a proper weight training program should be effective in helping to increase lean body mass.

The use of drugs or hormones to increase body weight may lead to a variety of health problems.

A basic principle underlying all weight training programs is the overload principle, which simply means the muscles should be stressed beyond normal daily levels.

Progressive resistance is also a basic principle of weight training, for as you get stronger through use of the overload principle, you must progressively increase the resistance.

To increase muscle mass and body weight, you should exercise near the strength end of the strength–endurance continuum.

Your weight training program should exercise all major muscle groups in the body.

A variety of methods and apparatus are available for weight training, but research suggests that they are equally effective as a means to gain strength and muscle mass if the basic principles of weight training are followed.

Although weight training programs are recommended for gaining body weight, it is also highly recommended that one add an aerobics exercise program to help condition the cardiovascular system.

The Food Exchange System can serve as the basis for increasing caloric intake to gain body weight, if the aspirant eats greater quantities of nutritious foods from each of the six lists in three balanced meals plus several high-Calorie, high-nutrient snacks.

The individual attempting to gain body weight should obtain the necessary protein for muscle synthesis through a well-balanced diet, rather than by consuming expensive protein supplements.

Weight Gaining Through Proper Nutrition and Exercise
11

Introduction

As noted in the previous chapter, there are basically three reasons why individuals attempt to lose excess body weight: to improve appearance, health, or athletic performance. Some individuals may also wish to gain weight for the same three reasons. This may be a typical feeling for the male teenage athlete undergoing a significant growth spurt during puberty without the necessary weight gain to fill out his body. He may desire to gain weight to improve his general physical appearance and athletic ability, both of which may make positive contributions to his psychological health. Increasing numbers of females are also lifting weights for sport or an improved body image.

No matter what the reason for gaining body weight, you should be concerned about where the extra pounds will be stored. The energy-balance equation works equally as well for gaining weight as it does for losing weight, but excess body fat in general will not improve physical appearance, health, or athletic performance. On the contrary, it may detract from all three. To put on body weight you have to concentrate on means to increase the fat-free mass, particularly muscle tissue, with little or no increase in body-fat stores.

Numerous approaches are employed in attempts to increase muscle mass. Specialized exercise equipment or exercise techniques are advertised as the most effective methods available to build muscles. Protein supplements have been a favorite among weight lifters for years, but today athletes can buy specific amino acid products or mineral compounds that are advertised to produce an anabolic, or muscle-building, effect. Some athletes and nonathletes even use drugs to gain weight for enhanced performance or appearance.

Like weight-loss programs, weight-gaining programs may be safe and effective or they can be potentially harmful to your health. Although gaining weight is difficult for some individuals, the purpose of this chapter is to present basic information on the type of exercise and diet program that is most likely to be effective as a means to put on weight without compromising your health.

Basic Considerations

Why are some individuals underweight?

Being significantly under a healthy body weight may be due to several factors. Heredity may be an important factor, as your parents' genetic material may have predisposed their children toward leanness. For example, a high basal metabolic rate may have been acquired through your parents. Medical problems could adversely affect food intake and digestion, so a physician should be consulted to rule out nutritional problems caused by organic disease, hormonal imbalance, or inadequate absorption of nutrients. Social pressures, such as the strong desire of a teenage girl to have a slender body, could lead to undernutrition; an extreme example is anorexia nervosa, discussed in Chapter 9. Emotional problems also may affect food intake. In many cases, food intake is increased during periods of emotional crisis, but the appetite may also be depressed in some individuals for long periods.

Being considerably underweight, such as 10 percent below the standard height–weight tables or a Body Mass Index below 19, may be considered a symptom of malnutrition or undernutrition. It is important to determine the cause before prescribing a treatment. Our concern is with the individual who does not have any of these medical or psychological problems, but who simply is expending more Calories than are being consumed. Caloric input has to be increased, and the output has to be modified somewhat.

What steps should I take if I want to gain weight?

The following guidelines may help you develop an effective program to maximize your gains in muscle mass and keep body-fat increases relatively low.

1. Have an acceptable purpose for the weight gain. The desire for an improved physical appearance and body image may be reason enough. For athletics, increased muscle mass may be important for a variety of sports, particularly if strength and power are improved. However, you do not want to gain weight at the expense of speed.

2. Calculate your average energy needs daily. Use Table 10.1 on page 245 to determine how many Calories you need just to maintain body weight. These values are slightly higher than those in Table 10.2.

3. Keep a three- to seven-day record of what you normally eat. See pages 252–54 for guidelines to determine your average daily caloric intake. If the obtained value is less than your energy needs calculated under item 2 above, this may be a reason why you are not gaining weight.

4. Check your living habits. Do you get enough rest and sleep? If not, you are burning more energy than the estimate in point 2 above. Smoking increases your metabolic rate almost 10 percent and may account for approximately 200 Calories per day. Caffeine in coffee and soft drinks also increases the metabolic rate for several hours. Getting enough rest and sleep and eliminating smoking and caffeine will help decrease your energy output.

5. Set a reasonable goal within a certain time period. In general, about one pound per week is a sound approach, but weight gaining is difficult for some individuals and may occur at a slower rate. Specific goals may also include muscular hypertrophy in various parts of the body.

6. Increase your caloric intake. A properly designed diet should include adequate Calories and protein and not violate the principles of healthful nutrition.

7. Start a weight training exercise program. This type of exercise program will serve as a stimulus to build muscle tissue.

8. Use a good cloth or steel tape to take body measurements before and during your weight-gaining program. Be sure you measure at the same points about once a week. Those body parts measured should include the neck, upper and lower arm, chest, abdomen, hips, thigh, and calf. This is to ensure that body weight gains are proportionately distributed. You should look for good gains in the chest and limbs; the abdominal and hip girth increase should be kept low because that is where the fat is more likely to be stored.

In summary, adequate rest, increased caloric intake, and a proper weight training program may be very effective as a means to gain the right kind of body weight.

What about the use of drugs or hormones to gain body weight?

Certain drugs and hormones have been taken by some athletes because of their potential to increase muscle mass. Testosterone, the male sex hormone, was one of the first to be used, and more recently human growth hormone (HGH) has become more readily available through genetic engineering. However, the synthetic **anabolic steroids,** patterned after testosterone, have been the drugs of choice for many strength athletes and body builders. Anabolic steroids appear to increase muscle mass and strength effectively if used in conjunction with a weight training program and increased caloric intake.

Unfortunately the use of these agents may have adverse medical implications. Testosterone and HGH are potent hormones with a wide variety of physiological effects in the body. Disturbing the normal hormonal balance may lead to serious disorders as noted for HGH in Chapter 5. Anabolic steroids have been implicated in a number of minor health problems such as acne and loss of hair, but continued use may predispose adults to coronary heart disease by decreasing HDL cholesterol and increasing the blood pressure as documented in both epidemiological and experimental studies. A recent review has also indicated that prolonged steroid use may possibly lead to impaired development of tendons, decreasing their strength and contributing to a potential for rupture. Prolonged use has resulted in severe liver diseases, including cancer. Anabolic steroids may cause premature cessation of bone growth in children and adolescents and may result in the appearance of several male secondary sex characteristics in females, some of which may be irreversible, such as a deepening of the voice. Because of these medical problems, the U.S. Congress has passed legislation to classify anabolic steroids as controlled substances, thus limiting their production and distribution by pharmaceutical companies. Penalties may be severe, up to 5 years in prison and $250,000 in fines for a first offense. Additionally, most individuals obtain these drugs illegally on the black market where quality is not controlled, and chemical analysis has revealed some potentially hazardous constitutents in these "homemade" drugs.

As is obvious, the use of these agents for the purpose of gaining body weight and strength is not recommended. Moreover, their use by athletes is grounds for disqualification for future competition. The American College of Sports Medicine has developed a position statement on the use of anabolic steroids in sports. Although an extensive discussion of anabolic steroids is beyond the scope of this text,

Figure 11.1.
Figure 11.1.
The overload principle in
action with weight training. If
improvement in strength is to
continue, weights must be
increased.

(Melvin H. Williams)

the ACSM report in Appendix J provides a detailed review for the interested reader.

The use of chromium supplements to increase body weight, possibly by enhancing the activity of the hormone insulin, was discussed in Chapter 7. At the present time, chromium supplements do not have adequate scientific support to justify their use in a weight-gaining program, but they appear to be safe and are not considered to be illegal.

Exercise Considerations

In the last chapter we discussed the design of an aerobic exercise program for the loss of excess body fat but also mentioned that a weight training program could also be helpful, for it might help prevent the loss of lean body mass. In this chapter, the focus is upon weight training, sometimes called resistance training, as a means to actually increase lean body mass and body weight. Before we discuss the principles underlying the design of a proper weight training program, let us introduce some basic terminology.

Repetition simply means the number of times you do a specific exercise. *Intensity* is determined by the weight, or resistance, that is lifted. A term used to describe the interrelationship between repetitions and intensity in weight training is **repetition maximum (RM)**. If you perform an exercise such as a bench press and lift 150 pounds once, but you cannot do a second repetition, you have done one repetition maximum, or 1RM. If you bench press a lighter weight, say 120 pounds, for five repetitions but cannot do a sixth, you have done five repetition maximum, or 5RM. A *set* is any particular number of repetitions, such as five or ten. The total volume of work you do in a single workout is the product of sets, repetitions, and resistance. For example, if you bench press three sets of five repetitions with a re-

sistance of 100 pounds, your total volume of work is 1,500 pounds ($3 \times 5 \times 100$). The *recovery period* may represent the rest intervals between sets in a single workout or the rest interval between workouts during the week.

What are the basic principles of weight training?

The following five principles are not restricted to weight training but apply to all forms of training, even aerobic exercise training programs as introduced in Chapter 10. For example, intensity of exercise is simply another way of phrasing the overload principle.

The **overload principle** is the most important principle in all weight training programs. The use of weights places a greater than normal stress on the muscle cell. This overload stress stimulates the muscle to grow—to become stronger—in effect to overcome the increased resistance imposed by the weights. (See Figure 11.1.)

To overload the muscle you must increase the volume of work it must do. There are basically two ways to do this. One is to increase the amount of resistance or weight that you use; the other way is to increase the number of repetitions and sets you do. Although there is no single best combination of sets and repetitions, usually two or three sets with 5 to 10 RM provide an adequate stimulus for muscle growth. If you know your 1RM, you should be able to do 5 to 10 RM if you use 70 to 80 percent of your 1RM value. For example, if your bench press 1RM is 150 pounds, you should be able to do at least 5RM with 80 percent of that value, or 120 pounds (.80 $\times$ 150).

As the muscle continues to get stronger during your training program, you must increase the amount of resistance, the overload, to continue to get the proper stimulus for sustained muscle growth. This is known as **progressive resistance exercise**

Figure 11.2.
The principle of progressive resistance exercise (PRE) states that as you get stronger, you need to progressively increase the resistance in order to continue to gain strength and muscle.

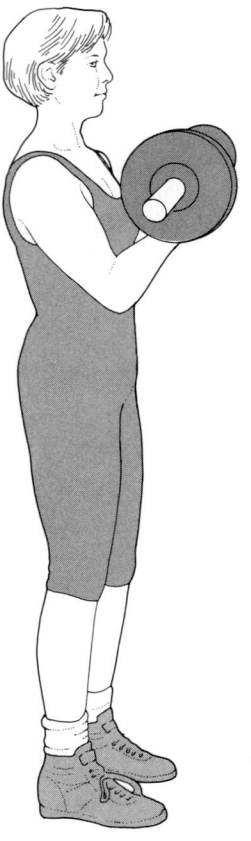

Week:	1	4	7	10	13	16
Weight:	50	50	60	60	70	70
Repetitions:	5	10	5	10	5	10
Sets:	4	4	4	4	4	4

(**PRE**) and is another basic principle of weight training.

Following a learning period, a recommended program for beginners is three to five sets with 5RM in each set. The first step is to determine the maximum amount of weight that you can lift for five repetitions. If you can do more than five repetitions, the weight is too light and you need to add more poundage. As you get stronger during the succeeding weeks, you will be able to lift the original weight more easily. When you can perform ten repetitions, add more weight to force you back down to five repetitions; this is the progressive resistance principle. Over several months' time, the weight will probably need to be increased several times as you continue to get stronger. Such a transition is illustrated in Figure 11.2.

Specificity of training is a broad principle with many implications for weight training, including specificity for various sports movements, strength gains, endurance gains, and body-weight gains. For example, a swimmer who wants to gain strength and endurance for a stroke should attempt to find a weight training program that exercises the specific muscles in a way as close as possible to the form used in that stroke. If you want to gain muscle mass in a certain part of the body, those muscles must be exercised.

Your exercise routine should be based upon the **principle of exercise sequence.** This means that if you have ten exercises in your routine, they should be arranged in a logical order so that fatigue does not limit your lifting ability. For example, the first exercise in a sequence of ten might stress the biceps muscle, the second the abdominals, the third the quadriceps, and so forth. After you perform one full set of each of the ten exercises, you then do a complete second set, followed by the third set. This approach may be best for beginners.

Figure 11.3.
The strength–endurance continuum. To gain strength, you need to train on the strength end of the continuum; to gain endurance, you need to train on the endurance end of the continuum.

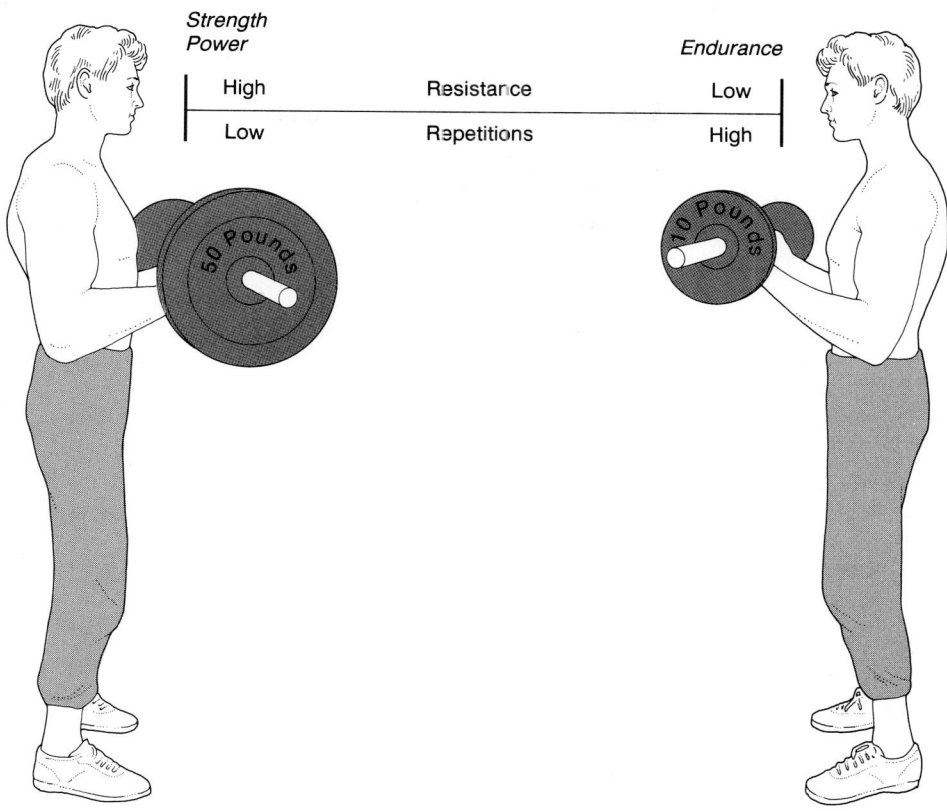

Strength Power		Endurance
High	Resistance	Low
Low	Repetitions	High

Another popular option is to do three sets of the same exercise with a rest between sets; then do three sets of the second exercise, and so on. This approach may be a little more fatiguing since you are using the same muscle group in three successive sets, but it appears to be very effective.

Weight training, if done properly to achieve the greatest gains, imposes a rather severe stress on the muscles, requiring a period of recovery both during the workout and between workouts. Research has shown that exercises of 5 to 10RM can lead to rapid depletion of ATP and PC, the high energy phosphates stored in the muscles; however, most of these high energy compounds may be restored in about 2 to 3 minutes' recovery. This is the **principle of recuperation.** Thus, several minutes should intervene between sets if you are using the same exercise. Additionally, for beginners, weight training should generally be done about three days per week, with a rest or recuperation day in between. This day of rest allows sufficient time for your muscle to repair itself and to synthesize new protein as it continues to grow.

These general principles should serve as guidelines during the beginning phase of your weight training program and should be used to guide your progress during the first three months of the basic weight training program described below.

What is an example of a weight training program that may help me to gain body weight as lean muscle mass?

As is probably obvious to you, there is an inverse relationship between the amount of weight you can lift and the number of repetitions you can do. If your 1RM in the bench press is 150 pounds, you can do more repetitions with 100 pounds than you can with 140. The **strength–endurance continuum** is a training concept that focuses upon the interrelationship between resistance and repetitions. As depicted in Figure 11.3, to train for strength you must combine high resistance with a low number of repetitions. Conversely, to train for endurance, you must combine a low resistance with a high number of repetitions.

Since the ATP–PC energy system predominates in strength and power activities, the lactic acid energy system is primarily involved in anaerobic endurance, and the oxygen system is involved in aerobic endurance activities, weight training programs may be designed to train all three of the human energy systems.

If your goal is to gain significant amounts of muscle mass, you may wish to use the **bulk-up method.** This method involves the use of six to ten different exercises that stress the major muscle groups of the body. About three to five sets of each exercise are done. You should exercise near the strength end of the continuum. The PRE concept is used, starting with a weight you can handle for five repetitions and progressively increasing the repetitions to ten. After you reach ten repetitions, increase the weight until you must come back to five repetitions.

The bulk-up method should be used for several months to increase your weight. You may then wish to shape that bulk, a technique that body builders call razoring or "cutting up." This technique uses a wide variety of exercises done with lighter weights and many repetitions at high speed; you are exercising on the endurance end of the continuum. Once you have achieved your desired weight, you may alternate the bulk-up and razoring techniques to maintain your weight and shape.

The beginner should adhere to the following procedure using the basic weight training program.

1. Learn the proper technique for each exercise with a light weight, possibly only the bar itself, for two weeks. Do ten to twelve repetitions of each exercise to develop form. Do not strain during this initial learning phase.
2. For each exercise, determine the maximum weight that you can lift for five repetitions after the two-week learning phase.
3. Do one set of the eight exercises shown in Figures 11.4 to 11.11.
   The sequence of exercises should be:
   a. Bench press: chest muscles
   b. Lat machine pull down or bent-arm pullover: back muscles
   c. Half squat: thigh muscles
   d. Standing lateral raise: shoulder muscles
   e. Heel raise: calf muscles
   f. Standing curl: front upper arm muscles
   g. Seated overhead press: back upper arm muscles
   h. Curl-up: abdominal muscles
4. A weekly record form, similar to the one in Table 11.1, should be used to keep track of your progress.
5. Since the exercise sequence is designed to stress different muscle groups in order, not much recuperation is necessary between exercises—possibly only 30 seconds or so.
6. Do three to five complete sets. You may wish to rest 2 to 3 minutes between sets.
7. Exercise three days per week; in each succeeding day try to do as many repetitions as possible for each exercise in each set. When you can do ten repetitions each after a month or so, add more weight to the bars so you can do only five repetitions.
8. Repeat step 7 as you progressively increase your strength.

Since barbells and dumbbells appear to be the most common means of doing weight training, this is the method utilized. However, other apparatus such as the Nautilus, Universal Gym, and others can also be used effectively to gain weight and strength (see Fig. 11.12). Most of the exercises described here using barbells or dumbbells have similar counterparts on other apparatus.

Note that muscles seldom operate alone, and that most weight training exercises stress more than one muscle group. Thus, keep in mind that although an exercise may be listed specifically for the chest muscles, it may also stress the arm and shoulder muscles. The exercises described in this section generally stress more than one body area, although their main effect is on the area noted.

These eight exercises stress most of the major muscle groups in the body and thus provide an adequate stimulus for gaining body weight and strength through an increase in muscle mass. Literally hundreds of different weight training exercises and techniques to train are available; if you become interested in diversifying your program (such as using the razoring technique), consult a book specific to weight training. Several may be found in the reference list at the end of this chapter.

Chest
Figure 11.4

Exercise	Bench press
Chest Muscles	Pectoralis major
Other Muscles	Deltoid, triceps
Sets	3–5
Repetitions	5–10, PRE concept
Safety	Have spotter stand behind bar to assist as fatigue sets in.
Equipment	Bench with support for weight, or two spotters to hand weight to you
Description	Lie supine on bench. Use wide grip for chest development. Secure bar and lower *slowly* to chest. Press bar straight up to full extension. Do not arch back.

Figure 11.4.

The bench press. The bench press primarily develops the pectoralis major muscle group in the chest; it also develops the deltoids in the shoulder and the triceps at the back of the arm.

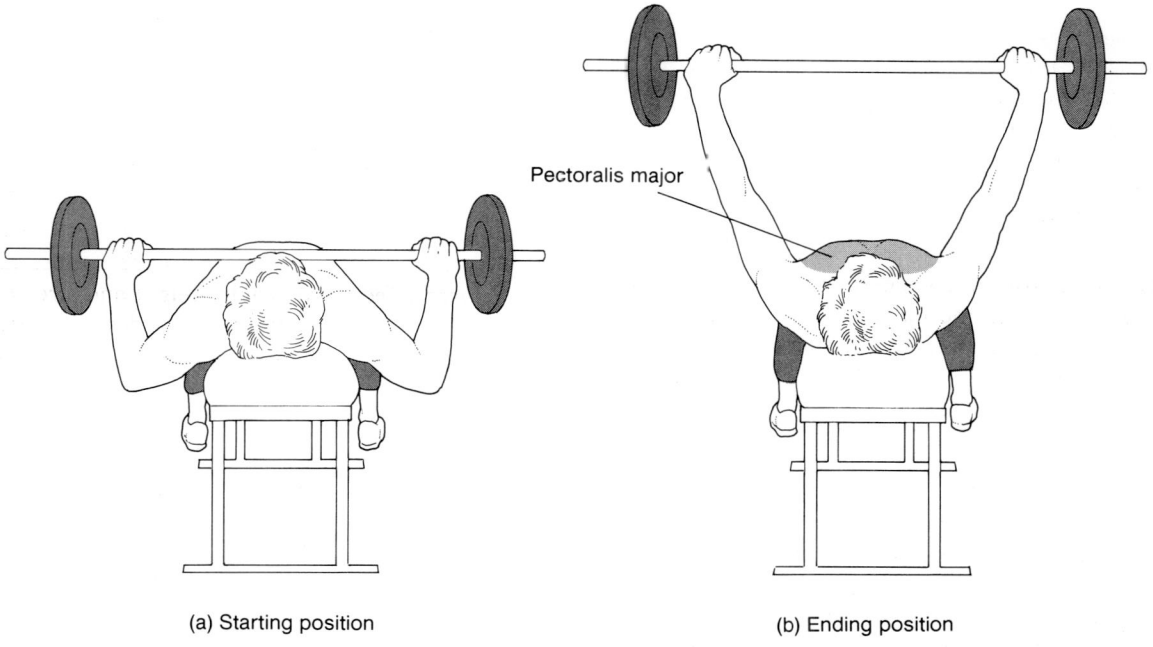

Pectoralis major

(a) Starting position

(b) Ending position

Back
Figure 11.5A and 11.5B

Exercise	Lat machine pull down
Back Muscles	Latissimus dorsi
Other Muscles	Biceps, pectoralis major
Sets	3–5
Repetitions	5–10, PRE concept
Safety	A very safe exercise
Equipment	Lat machine
Description	From seated or kneeing position, take a wide grip at arm's length on the bar overhead. Pull bar down until it reaches back of the neck. Return slowly to starting position.

Note: If a lat machine is not available, the bent arm pullover may be substituted.

Figure 11.5A.
The lat machine pulldown. The lat machine pulldown trains the latissimus dorsi in the back and side of the upper body, but it also develops the biceps on the front of the upper arm and the pectoralis major in the chest.

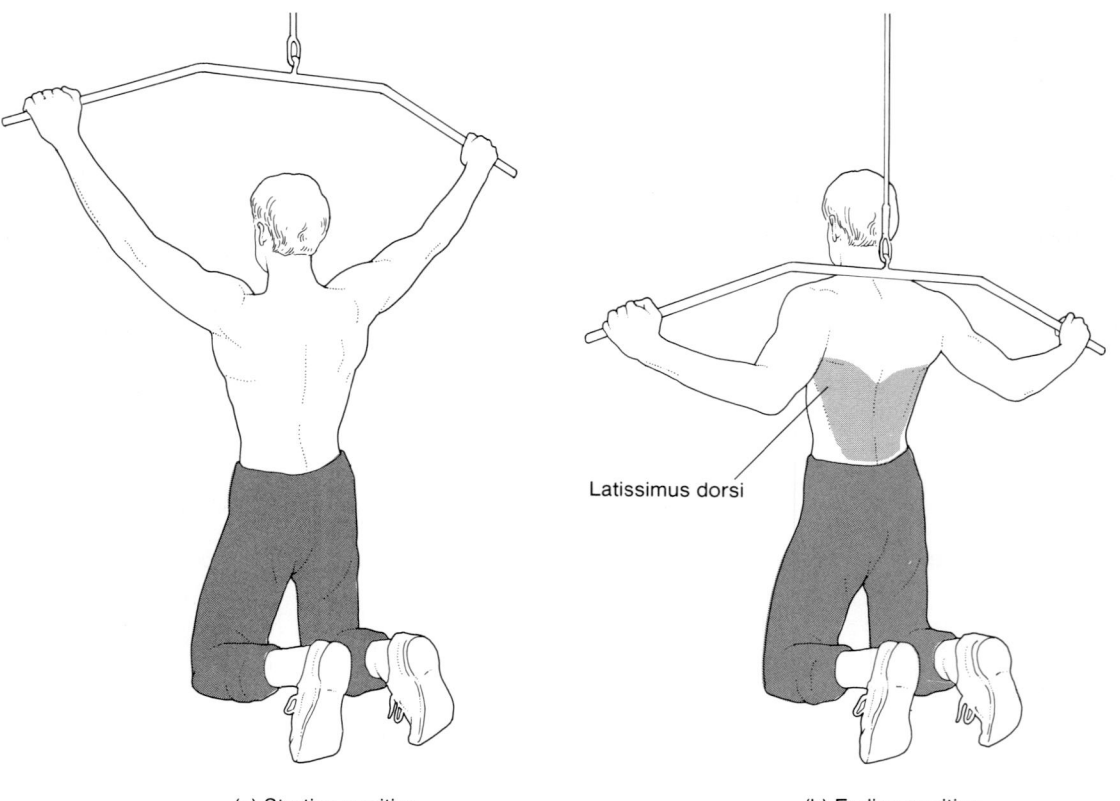

Latissimus dorsi

(a) Starting position   (b) Ending position

Figure 11.5B.

The bent-arm pullover. The bent-arm pullover trains the latissimus dorsi and develops the pectoralis major.

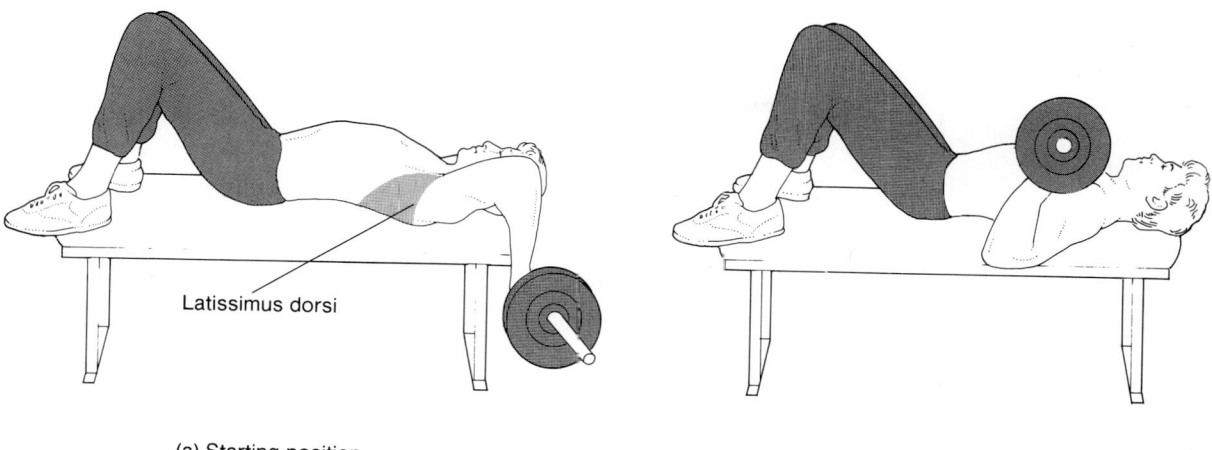

Latissimus dorsi

(a) Starting position

(b) Ending position

Alternate Exercise	Bent-arm pullover
Back Muscles	Latissimus dorsi
Other Muscles	Pectoralis major
Sets	3–5
Repetitions	5–10, PRE concept
Safety	Do not arch back. Start with light weights when learning the technique.
Equipment	Bench
Description	Lie supine on bench, entire back in contact with the bench, feet on the bench, knees bent. Hold weight on chest with elbows bent. Swing weight over head, just brushing hair, and lower as far as possible without taking back off the bench. Keeping elbows in, return the weight to the chest.

Thigh
Figure 11.6

Exercise	Half-squat or parallel squat
Thigh Muscles	Quadriceps (front), hamstrings (back)
Other Muscles	Gluteus maximus
Sets	3–5
Repetitions	5–10, PRE concept
Safety	Have two spotters to assist if using free weights. Keep back straight. Drop weight behind you if you lose balance. Do not squat more than halfway down.
Equipment	Squat rack if available. Pad the bar with towels if necessary.
Description	In standing position, take bar from squat rack or spotters and rest on the shoulders behind the head. Squat until thighs are parallel to ground or until buttocks touch a chair at this parallel positon. Do not squat beyond halfway. Keep back as straight as possible. Return to standing position.

Figure 11.6.
The half-squat or parallel squat. The half-squat develops the quadriceps muscle group on the front of the thigh and the hamstrings on the back of the thigh.

Quadriceps

Hamstrings

(a) Starting position (b) Ending position

Shoulders
Figure 11.7

Exercise	Standing lateral raise
Shoulder Muscles	Deltoid
Other Muscles	Trapezius
Sets	3–5
Repetitions	5–10, PRE concept
Safety	Do not arch back.
Equipment	Dumbbells
Description	Stand with dumbbells in hands at sides. With palms down, raise straight arms sideways to shoulder level. Bend elbows slightly. Return slowly to starting position.

Figure 11.7.
Standing lateral raise. The standing lateral raise primarily develops the deltoid muscles in the shoulder; the trapezius in the upper back and neck area is also trained.

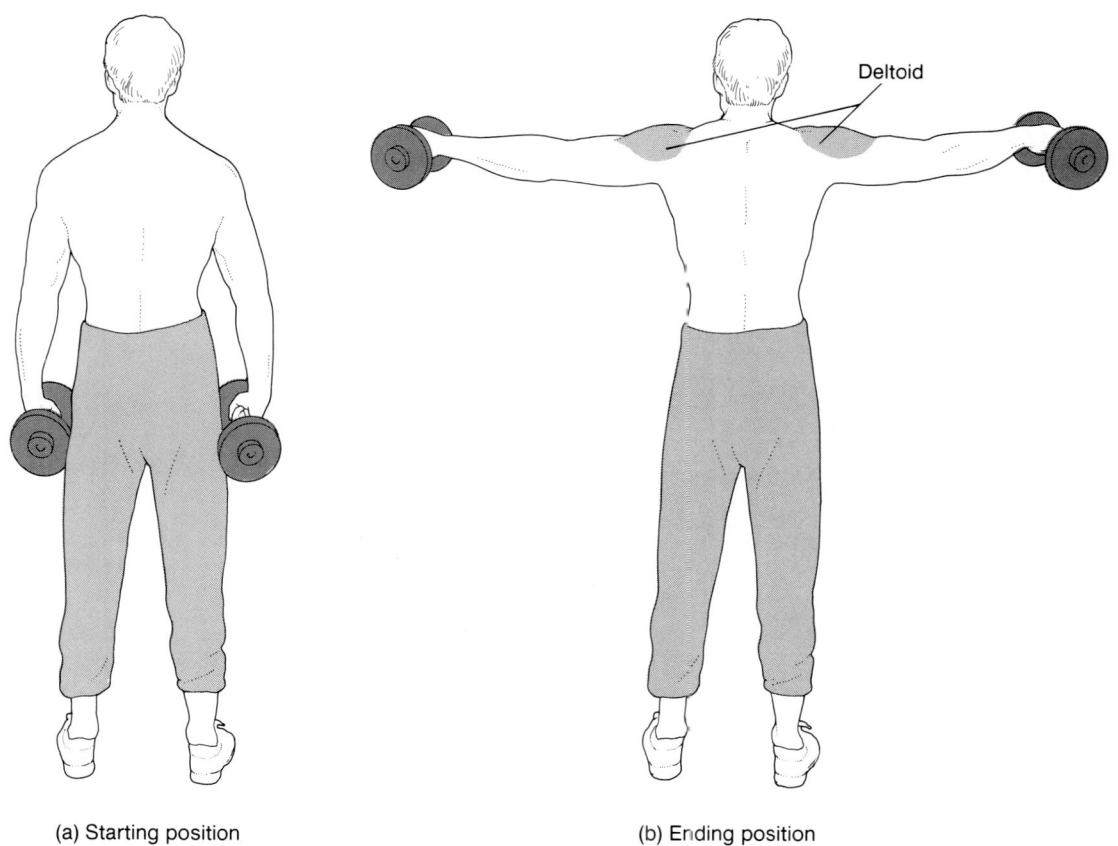

(a) Starting position   (b) Ending position

Calf
Figure 11.8

Exercise	Heel raises
Calf Muscles	Gastrocnemius, soleus
Other Muscles	Deep calf muscles
Sets	3–5
Repetitions	5–10, PRE concept
Safety	Have two spotters if you use free weights.
Equipment	Squat rack, if available. Pad the bar with a towel if necessary.
Description	Place bar on back of shoulders as in squat exercise. Raise up on your toes as high as possible, and then return to standing position. Place the toes on a board so heels can drop down lower than normal. Point toes in, out, and straight ahead during different sets to work the muscles from different angles.

Figure 11.8.
Heel raise. The heel raise develops the two major calf muscles—the gastrocnemius and the soleus.

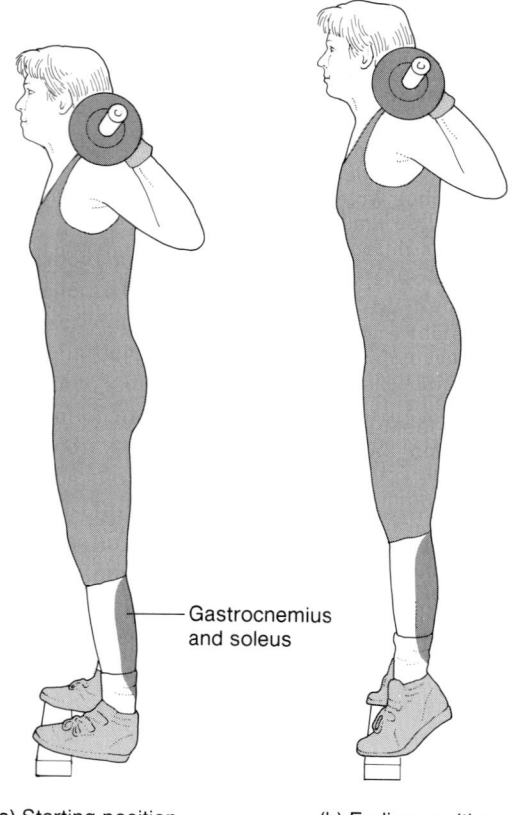

Gastrocnemius and soleus

(a) Starting position   (b) Ending position

Exercise	Standing curl
Arm Muscle	Biceps
Other Muscles	Several elbow flexors
Sets	3–5
Repetitions	5–10, PRE concept
Safety	Do not arch back. Place back against wall to control arching motion.
Equipment	Curl bar if available
Description	Stand with weight held in front of body, palms forward. Place back against wall. Bend the elbows and bring the weight to the chest. Lower it slowly.

Figure 11.9.
The standing curl. The standing curl strengthens the biceps muscle in the front of the upper arm as well as several other muscles in the region that bend the elbow.

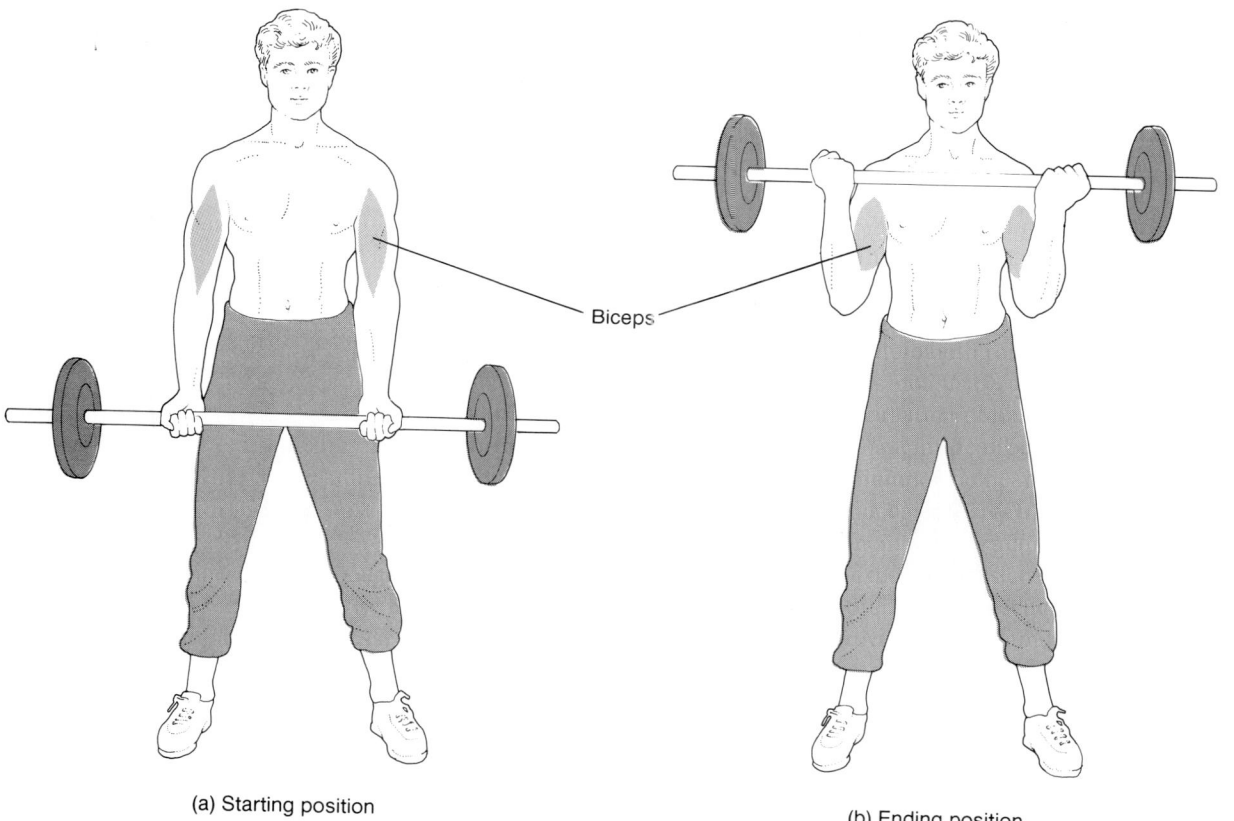

Biceps

(a) Starting position

(b) Ending position

Exercise	Seated overhead press
Arm Muscle	Triceps
Other Muscles	Trapezius
Sets	3–5
Repetitions	5–10, PRE concept
Safety	Do not arch back excessively. Have spotter available as fatigue sets in.
Equipment	Bench or chair
Description	Sit on bench with weight held behind the head near the neck. Hands should be close together, elbows bent. Straighten elbows and press weight over head to arm's length. Lower weight slowly to starting position.

Figure 11.10.
The seated overhead press. The seated overhead press primarily develops the triceps muscle on the back of the upper arm; the exercise also trains the trapezius in the upper back and neck.

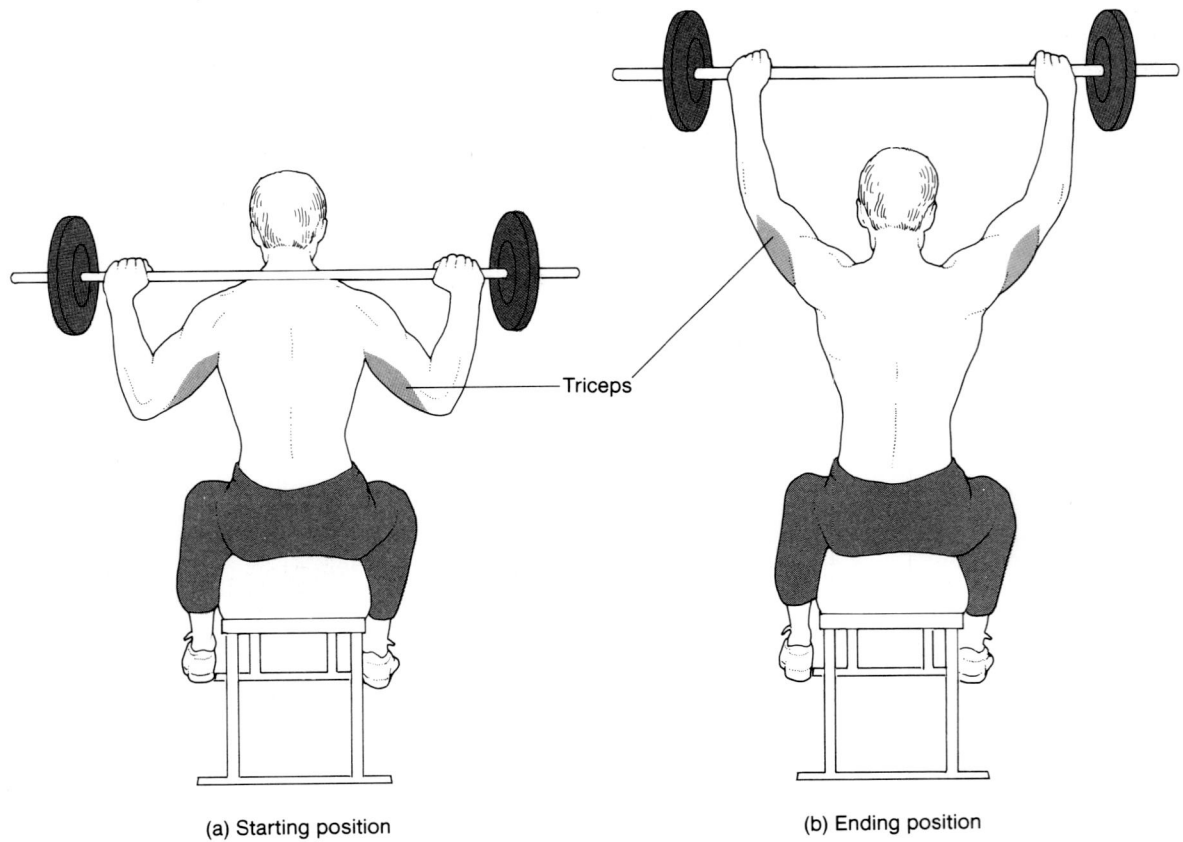

Triceps

(a) Starting position   (b) Ending position

Abdominal area
Figure 11.11

Exercise	Curl-ups
Abdominal Muscles	Rectus abdominis
Other Muscles	Oblique abdominis muscles
Sets	3–5
Repetitions	5–10, PRE concept
Safety	Develop sufficient abdominal strength before using weights with this exercise. Do not arch back when exercising.
Equipment	Free weight plates; incline sit-up bench if available.
Description	Lie on back, knees bent with heels close to buttocks, hands should hold weights on chest. Curl up about a third to half way. Return to starting position slowly.

Note: This exercise may be done without weights, but with an increased number of repetitions.

Figure 11.11.
The curl-up. The curl-up trains the rectus abdominis and the oblique abdominis muscles.

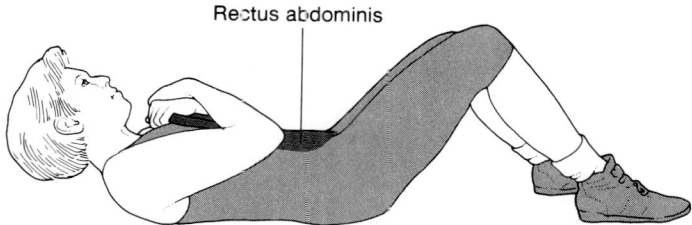

Rectus abdominis

(a) Starting position

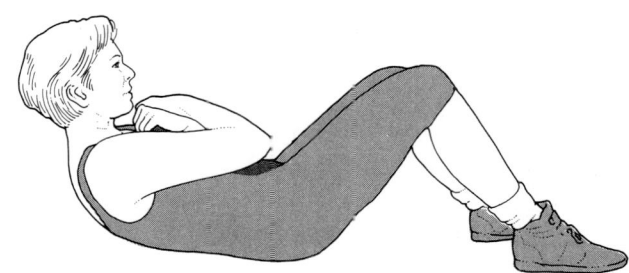

(b) Ending position

Table 11.1 Weekly weight-training record, basic eight exercises

Date _____	Chest (Bench press) Wt / Reps	Back (Lats exercise) Wt / Reps	Thigh (Half squat) Wt / Reps	Shoulder (Lateral raise) Wt / Reps	Calf (Heel raise) Wt / Reps	Front arm (Curls) Wt / Reps	Back arm (Seated press) Wt / Reps	Abdominal area (Curl-ups) Wt / Reps
Set 1								
Set 2								
Set 3								
Set 4								
Set 5								
Date _____ Set 1								
Set 2								
Set 3								
Set 4								
Set 5								
Date _____ Set 1								
Set 2								
Set 3								
Set 4								
Set 5								
Date _____ Set 1								
Set 2								
Set 3								
Set 4								
Set 5								

Figure 11.12.
Machines such as Nautilus provide an alternative to free weights for development of muscular strength and endurance.

How does the body gain weight with a weight training program?

Muscle hypertrophy simply means increased muscle size. Figure 11.13 depicts the microstructure of muscle tissue. Weight training exercises place a heavy overload on the muscle cell; over time the muscle cell tends to adapt to such stress by increasing its size. It may do so in several possible ways. First, the individual muscle cells and myofibrils may simply increase their size by incorporating more protein. Second, the myofibrils in each cell may multiply, which will increase the size of each muscle fiber. Third, the amount of connective tissue around each muscle fiber and around each bundle of muscle may increase and thicken, leading to an overall increase in the size of the total muscle. Fourth, the cell may increase its content of enzymes and energy storage, particularly ATP and glycogen. Fifth, bone mineral content may increase. Finally, the muscle fibers themselves may increase in number, but current evidence suggests this is much less likely to occur compared with muscle hypertrophy.

Weight training may be an effective means to increase muscle size and mass. Such increases help improve muscular strength and endurance and may be important components in weight-control programs. Although females do not normally experience the same amount of hypertrophy that males do, they do experience proportional gains in strength and endurance. Moreover, research revealed a significant increase in muscle cell size when women engaged in an intense, concentrated weight training program. Additionally, research data indicate that weight training exercises will increase bone mineral content, possibly owing to increased muscle tension effects, an important consideration for females in their developing years to help prevent osteoporosis later in life.

Is any one type of weight training program or equipment more effective than others for gaining body weight?

There are a variety of methods for training with weights. **Isometric methods** involve a muscle contraction against an immovable object, such as trying to pull a telephone pole out of the ground. However, if you succeed in moving the object, then you are doing an isotonic exercise. **Isotonic methods** are of two types. The **concentric method** means the muscle is shortening, as the biceps does in the up phase of a pull-up. The **eccentric method** means the muscle is lengthening even though it is trying to shorten. In the down phase of the pull-up the biceps is now contracting eccentrically as it slows your rate of descent. Gravity is attempting to pull you down, but

your biceps is resisting it. Finally, the **isokinetic method** uses machines or other devices to regulate the speed at which you can shorten your muscles. For example, you may try to move your arm as fast as possible, but you will only be able to move as fast as the setting on the isokinetic machine. Isokinetic exercise is also known as accommodating-resistance exercise because the resistance automatically adjusts to the force exerted, thus controlling the speed of movement.

Several different weight training apparatuses are available, such as Nautilus, Universal Gym, Cybex, Hydra-Gym, Soloflex, and other similar machines. Depending upon the model, they are designed to utilize one or more of the training methods cited above.

A number of research studies have been conducted to determine which of these methods or machines is best, particularly in relation to strength and power gains. Research suggests that at the present time it is probably safe to say that isotonic and isokinetic programs are comparable in their ability to produce gains in muscle size and strength. Also, other than possible safety considerations, recent research suggests that the use of specialized machines and weight training devices does not appear to have any advantage over the use of free weights, such as barbells and dumbbells. All methods may be effective in increasing body weight provided the basic principles of weight training, particularly the overload principle, are followed. If you use machines, be sure to exercise all major muscles areas. Free weights are relatively inexpensive and can be used for a wide variety of exercises. They also may be constructed at home, using pipe or solid broomstick handles for the bar and different-sized tin cans filled with cement for the weights.

If exercise burns Calories, won't I lose weight on a weight training program?

Although exercise does cost Calories, the amount expended during weight training is relatively small compared to more active aerobic exercises. Weight training can be a high-intensity exercise, but the time spent actually lifting during a typical workout is usually short, therefore limiting the number of calories used. For example, in an hour workout, only about fifteen minutes may be involved in actual exercise, the remaining time being recovery between each exercise. Based upon metabolic data collected in research studies, the average-sized male would use about 200 Calories in a typical workout, while the average-sized female would use about 150. (See Figure 11.14.)

Figure 11.13.
Muscle structure. The whole muscle is composed of separate bundles of individual muscle fibers. Each fiber is composed of numerous myofibrils, each of which contains thin protein filaments arranged so that they can slide by each other to cause muscle shortening or lengthening. Several layers of connective tissue surround the muscle fibers, bundles, and whole muscles, which eventually band together to form the tendon.

Source: From Hole, John W., Jr., *Human Anatomy and Physiology*, 3d ed. © 1978, 1981, 1984, Wm. C. Brown Publishers, Dubuque, Iowa. All Rights Reserved. Reprinted by Permission.

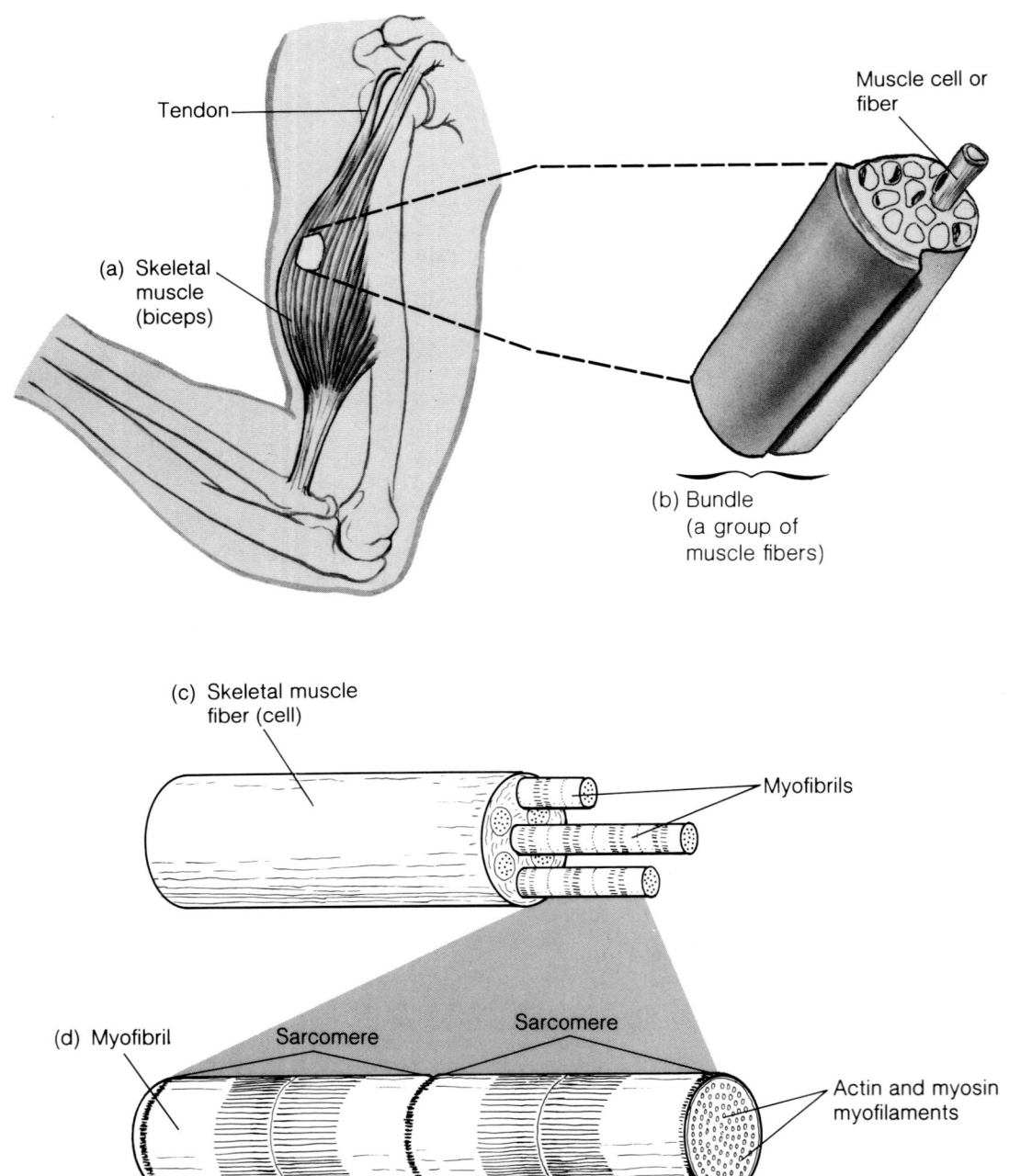

Tendon

Muscle cell or fiber

(a) Skeletal muscle (biceps)

(b) Bundle (a group of muscle fibers)

(c) Skeletal muscle fiber (cell)

Myofibrils

(d) Myofibril

Sarcomere

Sarcomere

Actin and myosin myofilaments

Figure 11.14.
All modes of exercise increase caloric expenditure. However, an hour of regular weight training expends only about one-third to one-fourth as many Calories as vigorous aerobic activity. Combining aerobic exercises with weight training (circuit aerobics) helps burn more Calories than weight training alone; it also provides cardiovascular health benefits while increasing muscular strength and endurance.

1 hour = 600–800 Calories   1 hour = 150–200 Calories

Are there any contraindications to weight training?

There are several health conditions that may be aggravated by weight training, primarily by the increased pressures that occur within the body when you strain to lift heavy weights and hold your breath at the same time. Because the blood pressure can increase rapidly and excessively during weight lifting, to 300 mmHg or higher, individuals with resting blood pressures over 90 mmHg diastolic and 140 mmHg systolic should refrain from heavy lifting, for they may be exposed to an increased risk of blood vessel rupture and a possible stroke. Lifting with the arms and straining exercises also increase the stress on the heart and thus should be avoided by individuals who have heart problems. Individuals with a hernia (a weakness in the musculature of the abdominal wall) also should refrain from strenuous weight lifting because the increased pressure may cause a rupture. Low back problems also may be aggravated by improper weight lifting techniques. Individuals with these types of health problems should

seek medical advice before initiating a weight training program.

There has been some concern about the advisability of prepubescent youth lifting weights. Damage to the growth plate in the bones may occur when children try to lift weights in excess of their ability. However, the American Academy of Pediatrics endorsed the concept of weight training for youngsters, provided proper techniques were taught and the program was supervised. Recent research has suggested that prepubescent boys may obtain significant gains in strength through a well-designed weight lifting program.

Weight training is generally regarded as a relatively safe sport, particularly if appropriate safety precautions are taken.

1. Learn to breathe properly. During the most strenuous part of the exercise you are likely to hold your breath. This is a natural response; it helps to stabilize your chest cavity to provide a more stable base for your

muscles to function. Usually the breath hold is short and no problems occur. However, if prolonged, it may increase the chances of suffering some of the problems noted previously, such as a hernia.

Also associated with prolonged breath holding is a response known as the **Valsalva phenomenon** (Valsalva maneuver), which may lead to a possible blackout. Here is what happens. As you reach a sticking point in your lift and strain to overcome it, you normally hold your breath; this causes your glottis to close over your windpipe and the pressure in your chest and abdominal area to rise rapidly. This pressure creates resistance to blood flow, reducing the return of blood to the heart, and eventually leading to decreased blood flow to the brain and a possible blackout.

A recommended breathing system that will help minimize these adverse effects is to breathe out while lifting the weight and breathe in while lowering it. You should breathe through both your mouth and nose while exercising. Practice proper breathing when you learn new weight training exercises.

2. When using free weights, use spotters when doing exercises that may be potentially dangerous, such as the bench press. If you are doing a bench press alone and reach a sticking point in your lift, the Valsalva phenomenon may lead to serious consequences if you lose control of the weight directly above your head. The use of machines such as Nautilus and Universal Gym helps eliminate the need for spotters.

3. If using free weights, place lock collars on the bar ends so the plates do not fall off and cause injury to the feet. Again, the use of machines eliminates this safety hazard. However, do not attempt to change weight plates on machines while they are being used. Your fingers may get caught between the weights.

4. Warm up with proper stretching exercises.

5. Use light weights to learn the proper technique of a given exercise so that you do not strain yourself if an improper technique is used. When the proper technique is mastered, the weights may be increased.

6. Avoid exercises that may cause or aggravate low back problems. Try to prevent an excessive forward motion or stress in the lower back region. Figure 11.15 illustrates some positions to be avoided.

7. Lower weights slowly. If you lower them rapidly, your muscles have to contract rapidly to slow the weights down as you reach the starting position. This necessitates the development of a large amount of force that may tear some connective tissue and cause muscle soreness.

For health reasons, should I do other exercises besides weight training during a weight gaining program?

Although weight training is recommended mainly as a means of gaining muscle mass, body weight, and strength, it may confer some additional physiological benefits. One possible benefit, particularly for females, is an increase in bone mineral content. Accumulating evidence suggests that weight training programs, particularly those at the endurance end of the strength–endurance continuum, may increase VO_2 max and improve cardiovascular efficiency both at rest and during exercise. Some, but not all, studies also report improvement in several risk factors associated with coronary heart disease, such as increased levels of HDL_2 cholesterol and improved glucose tolerance. These findings are contrary to the belief that weight training does not confer any health benefits comparable to aerobic exercise. It is also notable that many cardiac rehabilitation programs now incorporate weight training exercises.

Nevertheless, it still appears to be prudent health behavior to incorporate some aerobic exercise into your life-style, even when trying to gain body weight. Although the American College of Sports Medicine has recently added weight training to its recommended exercise program for healthy adults, it is designed to complement aerobic exercise, not to substitute for it. (See Appendix N.) To be sure, aerobic exercise programs do consume more Calories, so you would have to balance the expenditure with increased food intake. However, the expenditure does not need to be excessive to provide a beneficial training effect. For example, running two to three miles about four days per week would provide you with an adequate training effect for your heart, but it would cost you only about 200–300 Calories a day. This 200- to 300-Calorie expenditure could be replaced easily by consuming two glasses of orange juice or similar small amounts of food.

Figure 11.15.
Avoid exercises or body positions that place excessive stress on the low back region. Poor form in exercises like (a) the bench press and (b) the curl exaggerates the lumbar curve. Be sure to keep the lower back as flat as possible. Exercises similar to (c) the bentover row place tremendous forces on the lower back because the weight or resistance is so far in front of the body.

(a)   (b)   (c)

Can I combine aerobic and weight training exercises into one program?

Although the principles underlying the development of an aerobic training program and a weight training program are similar, the purposes of each are rather different. An aerobic exercise program is designed to improve the efficiency of the cardiovascular system; the basic purpose of a weight training program is to increase muscle size, strength, and body weight.

One form of weight training that has been used to provide some moderate benefits to the cardiovascular system is **circuit weight training,** a method in which the individual moves rapidly from one exercise to the next. Generally, this type of program has used lighter weights with greater numbers of repetitions, thus increasing the aerobic component of training. Recent research reported energy expenditure of approximately 10 Calories per minute for males and 7 Calories per minute for females.

A newer version of this method is **circuit aerobics.** Circuit aerobics may be done in a variety of ways, but basically it involves an integration of aerobic and weight training exercises. It is actually a form of interval aerobic training, but instead of resting or doing a lower level of aerobic activity during the recovery interval, you do weight training exercises. Circuit aerobics may offer you benefits such as improved cardiovascular fitness, increased caloric expenditure for loss of body fat, improved muscular strength and endurance, and increased muscle tone in body areas not normally stressed by aerobic exercise alone.

However, if the main purpose of your weight training program is to gain body weight as muscle mass, then you need to train near the strength end of the strength–endurance continuum.

Nutritional Considerations

How many Calories are needed for one pound of muscle?

Muscle tissue consists of about 70 percent water, 22 percent protein, and the remainder is fat, carbohydrate, and minerals. Because the vast majority of muscle tissue is water, which has no caloric value, the total caloric value is only about 700–800 per pound. However, extra energy is needed to help synthesize the muscle tissue.

It is not known exactly how many additional Calories are necessary to form one pound of muscle tissue in human beings, nor is it known in what form these Calories have to be consumed. The National Research Council notes that 5 Calories are needed to support the addition of one gram of tissue during growth, while Forbes cites a value of 8 Calories per gram in adults. Since one pound equals 454 grams, a range of 2,300–3,500 additional Calories appears to be a reasonable amount. With a recommended weight gain of one pound per week, about 400–500 Calories above your daily needs would provide an amount in the suggested range, 2,800–3,500 Calories per week. One recent study by Robert Bartels and his associates at The Ohio State University revealed that an additional 500 Calories per day resulted in nearly a one pound increase lean body weight during a weight training program.

How can I determine the amount of Calories I need daily to gain one pound per week?

First, you need to use Table 10.1 to determine the number of Calories needed simply to maintain your current body weight. Then you need to add the Calories that you expend during exercise and the additional amount needed to synthesize the muscle tissue. Table 11.2 presents an example of a 150-pound teenage boy who desires to gain a pound per week. You may modify the figures according to your own needs.

Is protein supplementation necessary during a weight-gaining program?

Gilbert Forbes indicates we need adequate amounts of protein to support increases in lean body mass, otherwise we would gain body fat. One pound of muscle is equal to 454 grams, but only about 22 percent of this tissue, or about 100 grams, is protein. If we divide 100 grams by 7 days, we would need approximately 14 grams of protein per day above our normal protein requirements if we are in protein balance. However, the average American diet already contains extra protein beyond the RDA, so this need probably is satisfied. Incidentally, 14 grams of protein could be obtained in such small amounts of food as 2 glasses of milk, 2 ounces of cheese, two scrambled eggs, or 2 ounces of meat, fish, or poultry. (See Figure 11.16.)

Although the daily RDA for protein is about 1 gram per kilogram body weight, some authorities in sports nutrition have recommended 2.0–2.5 grams per kilogram for the athlete who is training to increase muscle mass. As noted in Chapter 5, a slight

Table 11.2 Caloric intake for a 150-pound teenage boy to gain one pound per week

Source	Daily Calories needed
1. Recommended caloric intake to maintain current weight 19 Calories/pound	2,850
2. Weight training expenditure 200 Calories per session 4 sessions per week 800/7	115
3. Aerobics exercise 300 Calories per session 4 sessions per week 1,200/7	170
4. Muscle tissue synthesis 3,500 Calories per pound 3,500/7	500
Total daily caloric intake	3,635

increase in the protein content of the typical American daily diet would meet even this recommendation. A brief review of the mathematics in Table 5.5 and the related discussion on pages 122–23 will help substantiate this statement.

Supplementation by expensive protein powders or amino acids is not necessary. The average American diet provides sufficient high-quality protein to meet the needs of a weight-gaining program, even more so if a high-Calorie diet is used as recommended below.

What is an example of a balanced diet that will help me gain weight?

As with losing weight, the Food Exchange System may serve as the basis for a sound weight-gaining diet. Foods must be selected for high nutrient value as well as additional Calories to support the weight gain.

The following suggestions may be helpful for those trying to gain weight.

Milk exchange—Drink 1% or 2% milk instead of skim milk, which will add 15–30 Calories per glass. Prepare milk shakes with dry milk powder and supplement with fruit. Add low-fat cheeses to sandwiches or snacks. Eat yogurt supplemented with fruit. The milk exchange is high in protein.

Meat exchange—Increase your intake of lean meats, poultry, and fish. Legumes such as beans and dried peas are high in protein and Calories and low in fat. Use nuts, seeds, and limited amounts of peanut butter for snacks. The meat exchange is also high in protein.

Figure 11.16.
To add a pound of muscle tissue per week, you need to consume approximately 400 additional Calories and 14 grams of additional protein per day. A weight training program is an essential part of a muscle-building program. One glass of skim milk, three slices of whole wheat bread, and two hard-boiled egg whites provide the necessary Calories and about 23 grams of protein.

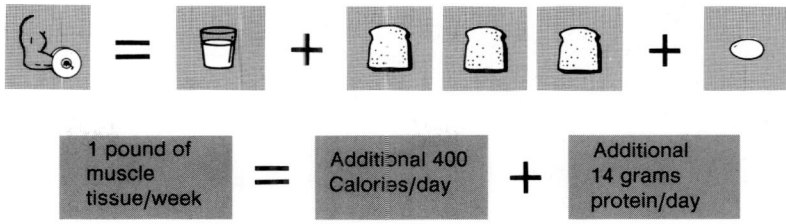

Starch/bread exchange—Increase your consumption of whole grain products. Pasta and rice are nutritious side dishes that provide adequate Calories. Starchy vegetables like potatoes are also nutritious sources of Calories. Breads and muffins can possibly be supplemented with fruits and nuts. Whole grain breakfast cereals can provide substantial Calories and even make a tasty dessert or snack with added fruit. The starch/bread exchange is high in complex carbohydrates but also contains about 15 percent of its calories as protein.

Fruit exchange—Add fruit to other food exchanges. Drink more fruit juices, which are high in both Calories and nutrients. Dried fruits such as apricots, pineapple, dates, and raisins are high in Calories and make excellent snacks.

Vegetable exchange—Use fresh vegetables like broccoli and cauliflower as snacks with melted low-fat cheese or a nutritious dip.

Fat exchange—Try to minimize the intake of saturated fats, using monounsaturated and polyunsaturated fats instead. Salad dressings and margarine added to vegetables can increase their caloric content.

Beverages—Milk and juices are nutritious and high in Calories. Those who drink alcohol should obtain only limited amounts of Calories in this way. Some liquid supplements are available commercially and may contain 300–400 Calories with substantial amounts of protein. However, check the label for fat and sugar content.

Snacks—Eat three balanced meals per day supplemented with two or three snacks. Dried fruits, nuts, and seeds are excellent snacks. Some of the high-Calorie, high-nutrient liquid meals on the market also make good snacks.

Table 11.3 presents an example of a high-Calorie diet plan based upon the Food Exchange System. It consists of three main meals and three snacks and totals about 4,000 Calories with 160 grams of protein, which is 16 percent of the Calories. Alternative foods may be substituted from the food exchange list presented in Appendix H. This suggested diet provides the necessary nutrients, Calories, and protein essential to increased development of muscle mass and yet fewer than 30 percent of the Calories are derived from fat. The total number of Calories can be adjusted to meet individual needs.

Would such a high-Calorie diet be ill advised for some individuals?

As noted in Chapter 4, one of the general recommendations for an improved diet is to reduce the consumption of fats, particularly saturated fats. Unfortunately, many high-Calorie diets are also high in fats. If there is a history of heart disease in the family or if an individual is known to have high blood-lipid levels, then high-fat diets are contraindicated. Individuals with kidney problems also may have difficulty processing high-protein diets because of the increased need to excrete urea. Any person initiating such a weight-gaining program as advised here should be aware of his or her medical history.

Selection of food for a weight-gaining diet, if done wisely, can satisfy the criteria for healthful nutrition. Foods high in complex carbohydrates with moderate amounts of protein and a low-fat content are able to provide substantial amounts of Calories and nutrients and yet minimize health risks that have been associated with the typical American diet. To gain weight wisely, you need to continue to eat healthful foods, but just more of them.

Table 11.3 A high-Calorie diet based on the Food Exchange System

Exchange		Calories
Breakfast		
Milk	8 ounces 2% milk	120
Meat	1 poached egg	80
	2 ounces lean ham	110
Starch/bread	2 slices whole wheat toast	160
Fruit	8 ounces of orange juice	120
Other	1 tablespoon jelly	50
Mid-morning Snack		
Fruit	8 ounces apricot nectar	160
Starch/bread	2 slices whole wheat bread	160
Meat	1 tablespoon peanut butter	100
Lunch		
Milk	8 ounces 2% milk	120
Meat	4 ounces lean sandwich meat	220
Starch/bread	2 slices whole wheat bread	160
	2 granola cookies	100
Fruit	1 banana	120
Vegetable, starchy	1 order french fries	300
Afternoon Snack		
Fruit	1/4 cup raisins	120
Dinner		
Milk	8 ounces 2% milk	120
Meat	5 ounces chicken breast	275
Starch/bread	2 slices whole wheat bread	160
Fruit	1 piece apple pie	350
Vegetable, starchy	1 cup peas	160
	1 sweet potato, candied	300
Evening Snack		
Fruit	1/2 cup dried peaches	210
Milk	8 ounces 2% milk with banana	240
Total		4,015

References

Books

Bouchard, C., et al. 1990. *Exercise, Fitness, and Health*. Champaign, IL: Human Kinetics.

Fleck, S., and Kraemer, W. 1988. *Designing Resistance Training Programs*. Champaign, IL: Life Enhancement Publications.

National Research Council. 1989. *Recommended Dietary Allowances*. Washington, DC: National Academy of Sciences.

Rasch, P. 1982. *Weight Training*. Dubuque, IA: Wm. C. Brown.

Wadler, G., and Hainline, B. 1989. *Drugs and the Athlete*. Philadelphia: F. A. Davis.

Wescott, W. 1982. *Strength Fitness*. Boston: Allyn and Bacon.

Reviews

American Academy of Pediatrics. 1983. Weight training and weight lifting: Information for the pediatrician. *Physician and Sportsmedicine* 11: March, 157–61.

American College of Sports Medicine. 1990. Position stand: The recommended quantity and quality of exercise for developing and maintaining cardiorespiratory and muscular fitness in healthy adults. *Medicine and Science in Sports and Exercise* 22:265–74.

Aronson, V. 1984. A healthy high-calorie diet. *Runner's World* 19 (November): 53–55.

Dreyfuss, I. 1990. Congress considers restricting steroids. *Physician and Sportsmedicine* 18:38, March.

Dudley, G. 1988. Metabolic consequences of resistive-type exercise. *Medicine and Science in Sports and Exercise* 20:S158–S161.

Fleck, S. 1988. Cardiovascular adaptations to resistance training. *Medicine and Science in Sports and Exercise* 20:S146–S151.

Fleck, S., and Kraemer, W. 1988. Resistance training: Basic principles. *Physician and Sportsmedicine*, 16:160–171.

Fleck, S., and Kraemer, W. 1988. Resistance training: Physiological responses and adaptations. *Physician and Sportsmedicine* 16:108–124, April.

Fleck, S., and Kraemer, W. 1988. Resistance training: Physiological responses and adaptations. *Physician and Sportsmedicine*, 16:63–76, May.

Foran, B. 1985. Advantages and disadvantages of isokinetics, variable resistance, and free weights. *National Strength and Conditioning Association Journal* 7:24–25.

Forbes, G. 1988. Body composition: Influence of nutrition, disease, growth and aging. In: *Modern Nutrition in Health and Disease*, eds. M. Shils and V. Young. Philadelphia: Lea & Febiger.

Franklin, B. 1989. Aerobic exercise training programs for the upper body. *Medicine and Science in Sports and Exercise*, 21:S141–S148.

Goldberg, A. 1989. Aerobic and resistive exercise modify risk factors for coronary heart disease. *Medicine and Science in Sports and Exercise*, 21:669–74.

Houtkooper, L. 1986. Nutritional support for muscle weight gain. *National Strength and Conditioning Association Journal* 8:62–63.

Hurley, B. 1989. Effects of resistive training on lipoprotein–lipid profiles: A comparison to aerobic exercise training. *Medicine and Science in Sports and Exercise* 21:689–93.

Kokkinos, P., and Hurley, B. 1990. Strength training and lipoprotein-lipid profiles: A critical analysis and recommendations for further study. *Sports Medicine* 9:266–72.

Kraemer, W. 1988. Endocrine responses to resistance exercise. *Medicine and Science in Sports and Exercise* 20:S152–S157.

Kraemer, W., and Fleck, S. 1988. Resistance training: Exercise prescription. *Physician and Sportsmedicine* 16:69–81, June.

Laseter, J., and Russell, J. 1991. Anabolic steroid-induced tendon pathology: A review of the literature. *Medicine and Science in Sports and Exercise* 23:1–3.

National Strength and Conditioning Association. 1989. Strength training for female athletes: A position paper: Part I. *National Strength and Conditioning Association Journal* 11:43–55.

National Strength and Conditioning Association. 1989. Strength training for female athletes: A position paper. Part II. *National Strength and Conditioning Association Journal* 11:29–36.

National Strength and Conditioning Association. 1987. Breathing during weight training. *National Strength and Conditioning Association Journal* 9:17–24.

Pauletto, B. 1986. Choice and order of exercises. *National Strength and Conditioning Association Journal* 8:71–73.

Pendergast, D. 1989. Cardiovascular, respiratory, and metabolic responses to upper body exercise. *Medicine and Science in Sports and Exercise* 21:S121–S125.

Schafer, J. 1991. Prepubescent and adolescent weight training: Is it safe? Is it beneficial? *National Strength and Conditioning Association Journal* 13:39–46.

Slavin, J. 1986. Calorie supplements for athletes. *Physician and Sportsmedicine* 14 (Nov):201–203.

Stewart, K., and Kelemen, M. 1989. Symposium. Resistive weight training: A new approach to exercise for cardiac and coronary disease prone populations. *Medicine and Science in Sports and Exercise* 21:667–97.

Stone, M. 1988. Implications for connective tissue and bone alterations resulting from resistance exercise training. *Medicine and Science in Sports and Exercise* 20:S162–S168.

Tesch, P. 1988. Skeletal muscle adaptations consequent to long-term heavy resistance exercise. *Medicine and Science in Sports and Exercise* 20:S132–S134.

Vogel, J. 1988. Introduction to the symposium: Physiological responses and adaptations to resistance exercise. *Medicine and Science in Sports and Exercise* 20:S131.

Specific Studies

Ballor, D., et al. 1989. Energy output during hydraulic resistance circuit exercise for males and females. *Journal of Applied Sport Science Research* 3:7–12.

Ballor, D., et al. 1988. Resistance weight training during caloric restriction enhances lean body weight maintenance. *American Journal of Clinical Nutrition* 47:19–25.

Bartels, R., et al. 1989. Effect of chronically increased consumption of energy and carbohydrate on anabolic adaptations to strenuous weight training. In: *Report of the Ross Symposium on the Theory and Practice of Athletic Nutrition, Bridging the Gap,* eds. J. Storlie and A. Grandjean. Columbus, OH: Ross Laboratories.

Colletti, L., et al. 1989. The effects of muscle-building exercise on bone mineral density of the radius, spine, and hip in young men. *Calcified Tissue International* 45:12–14.

Gettman, L., et al. 1982. A comparison of combined running and weight training with circuit weight training. *Medicine and Science in Sports and Exercise* 14:229–34.

Gieck, J., and Haskvitz, E. 1982. The effects of a liquid supplement on weight gain and percent body fat in college football players during a weight training program. *National Strength Coaches Association Journal* 4:45–46.

Heinrich, C., et al. 1990. Bone mineral content of cyclically menstruating female resistance and endurance trained athletes. *Medicine and Science in Sports and Exercise* 22:558–63.

Hofstetter, A., et al. 1986. Increased 24-hour energy expenditure in cigarette smokers. *New England Journal of Medicine* 314:79–82.

Hurley, B., et al. 1988. Resistive training can reduce coronary risk factors without altering VO$_2$max or percent body fat. *Medicine and Science in Sports and Exercise* 20:150–154.

Kokkinos, P., et al. 1988. Effects of low- and high-repetition resistive training on lipoprotein–lipid profiles. *Medicine and Science in Sports and Exercise* 20:50–54.

Konig, M., and Biener, K. 1990. Sport specific injuries in weight lifting. *Schweizerische Zeitschrift für Sport Medizine* 38:25–30.

MacDougall, J., et al. 1985. Arterial blood pressure response to heavy resistance exercise. *Journal of Applied Physiology* 58:785–90.

Marcinik, E., et al. 1989. Strength training improves endurance performance and lactate threshold without altering VO$_2$max. *Medicine and Science in Sports and Exercise* 21:S23.

Maresh, C., et al. 1989. Effects of heavy resistance exercise on hemodynamic, stress hormone and fluid-regulatory factors. *Medicine and Science in Sports and Exercise* 21:S37.

McKillop, G., and Ballantyne, D. 1987. Lipoprotein analysis in bodybuilders. *International Journal of Cardiology* 17:281–88.

Miller, W. et al. 1984. Effect of strength training on glucose tolerance and post-glucose insulin response. *Medicine and Science in Sports and Exercise* 16:539–43.

Peterson, S., et al. 1989. The influence of high-velocity circuit resistance training on VO₂max and cardiac output. *Canadian Journal of Sport Sciences.* 14:158–63.

Poehlman, E., et al. 1985. Influence of caffeine on the resting metabolic rate of exercise-trained and inactive subjects. *Medicine and Science in Sports and Exercise* 17:689–94.

Staron, R., et al. 1990. Muscle hypertrophy and fast fiber type conversions in heavy resistance-trained women. *European Journal of Applied Physiology* 60:71–78.

Tucker, L. 1987. Effect of weight training on body attitudes: Who benefits most. *Journal of Sports Medicine and Physical Fitness* 27:70–78.

Wallace, M., et al. 1991. Acute effects of resistance exercise on parameters of lipid metabolism. *Medicine and Science in Sports and Exercise* 23:199–204.

Wilmore, J. 1974. Alterations in strength, body composition and anthropometric measurements consequent to a 10 week weight training program. *Medicine and Science in Sports* 6:133–138.

Wilmore, J., et al. 1978. Energy cost of circuit weight training. *Medicine and Science in Sports* 10:79.

Windsor, R., and Dumitru, D. 1989. Prevalence of anabolic steroid use by male and female adolescents. *Medicine and Science in Sports and Exercise* 21:494–97.

Key Concepts

Although exercise is not to be considered a panacea for all health problems, the available scientific evidence suggests that it may be an effective adjunct to proper nutrition in the prevention and treatment of several major health problems.

The Food Exchange System—meat, milk, starch/bread, fruit, vegetable, and fat—should be viewed as an educational approach to help individuals obtain proper nutrition. Foods of similar nutrient value are found in each of the six exchanges.

There are eight key nutrients (protein, vitamin A, thiamin, riboflavin, niacin, vitamin C, calcium, and iron) that, if adequate in the diet and obtained from wholesome foods, should provide an ample supply of all nutrients essential to human nutrition.

Some foods contain a greater proportion of these key essential nutrients than other foods and thus have a greater nutrient density or nutritional value.

Vegetarians must be careful in selecting foods in order to obtain a balanced mixture of amino acids and adequate amounts of riboflavin, B_{12}, calcium, iron, and zinc.

Nonvegetarian diets may confer the same health benefits of a vegetarian diet if animal foods are carefully chosen.

Those interested in becoming vegetarians may do so on a gradual basis, but conversion to a total vegetarian diet will require some extensive reading.

Food processing does not necessarily result in a nutritionally inferior product, but wise selection is necessary in order to avoid those processed foods with excessive amounts of highly refined products like sugar, oils, unenriched white flour, and questionable additives.

Information provided through nutritional labeling on most food products may serve as a useful guide to foods that have a high nutrient density.

The precompetition meal should be easily digestible, high in complex carbohydrates, moderate in protein, and low in fat, and it should be consumed about three or four hours prior to competition.

In general, nutritional guidelines for the improvement of health are completely compatible with those for improvement of physical performance.

Twelve general recommendations for healthier nutrition include: (1) maintaining a healthy body weight, (2) consuming a wide variety of natural foods, (3) eating foods rich in calcium and iron, (4) eating adequate amounts of protein from both animal and plant sources, (5) increasing the dietary intake of complex carbohydrates and dietary fiber by choosing a diet with plenty of vegetables, fruits, and grain products, (6) using sugars only in moderation, (7) choosing a diet low in fat, saturated fat, and cholesterol, (8) using salt and sodium in moderation, (9) obtaining enough fluoride, (10) avoiding excess supplements, (11) eating fewer foods containing questionable additives, and (12) moderating alcohol consumption.

Nutrition for Optimal Health and Physical Performance
12

Introduction

At a national level, the health care of Americans has improved tremendously over the past century. Primarily because of the dedicated work of medical researchers, we no longer fear the scourge of acute infectious diseases such as polio, smallpox, or tuberculosis. However, we have become increasingly concerned with the treatment and prevention of chronic diseases. Cardiovascular diseases and cancer, the two major chronic diseases, account for over half of the deaths in the United States each year, and this figure is destined to increase as the U.S. population becomes increasingly older, particularly during the first quarter of the twenty-first century as the baby-boomers of the 1950s and 1960s reach their senior years.

Although the treatment of these major chronic diseases has greatly improved through techniques such as coronary artery bypass surgery and radiation therapy, these treatments are usually prolonged and very expensive. Foreseeing a financial health care crisis for the government in the twenty-first century, most health professionals have advocated prevention as the best approach to address this potential major health problem. In this regard, the Public Health Service of the United States Department of Health and Human Services has published a report entitled *Healthy People 2000: National Health Promotion/Disease Prevention Objectives.* One of the major sections of this report deals with health promotion, which includes a number of life-style factors that are basically under the control of the individual. Those that are relevant to this discussion include physical fitness and exercise, nutrition, and misuse of alcohol, all of which have become major concerns of the wellness movement in the United States.

As noted in Chapter 1, one of the key factors determining success in sport is the ability to exercise and train specific human energy systems to optimize genetic potential, and the major focus of this book has been on how nutrition could complement physical training to enhance athletic performance. Additionally, proper physical training may enhance one's health, and an attempt has been made to incorporate the health-related aspects of exercise, where appropriate, throughout the preceding chapters. Considerable research is available to support the importance of an aerobic exercise program, the design of which was discussed in Chapter 10, as an integral component of a healthy life-style. We have noted that aerobic exercise may reduce excess body fat and help maintain a desirable body weight, may reduce the risk of developing diabetes by improving glucose tolerance, may help prevent osteoporosis by stimulating bone remodeling, and may reduce the risk of atherosclerosis and cardiovascular disease by favorable effects on serum lipids, blood pressure, and psychological stress. In the consensus statement from the voluminous tome *Exercise, Fitness and Health,* Claude Bouchard and his associates noted that the available evidence suggests that physical activity may contribute to positive mental health, reduce the incidence and severity of chronic disease, and perhaps extend the life by a few years, but more importantly, enhance the quality of life in the later years. To many physicians, exercise is a medicine.

Although a proper exercise training program is important to the athlete both for health and physical performance, it is not to be considered a panacea for curing health problems or the only determinant of optimal physical performance. You can be fit, but you may not be healthy. You can be fit, but not perform at your best. Other factors may influence your health and performance, particularly nutrition, and the purpose of this chapter is to summarize earlier chapters and present some general guidelines for a dietary program to maximize chances for optimal health and physical performance. The most interesting finding is that the diet that is optimal for your health is also the optimal diet for your performance.

The Balanced Diet and Nutrient Density

One of the concepts advanced by nutritionists over the years to teach proper nutrition is that of the balanced diet, and to convey this concept to the public a number of different educational approaches have been developed. The most prevalent approaches in the United States have been the Basic Four Food

Figure 12.1.
The key to sound nutrition is a balanced diet that is high in nutrients and low in Calories. Select a wide variety of foods from among and within the Exchange Lists (Appendix H) for balance.

(All photos, Bob Coyle)

Groups, introduced in Chapter 1, and the Food Exchange Lists, introduced in Chapter 1 and detailed in Chapter 10. Although these approaches can be effective, they may also be misused and result in a poorly designed diet that may contribute to the development of several chronic diseases. Hence, the concept of nutrient density has been applied to help facilitate the selection of foods with enhanced health-promoting qualities. Since the Basic Four Food Groups and the Food Exchange Lists are highly interrelated, we shall focus only upon the Food Exchange Lists.

What is a balanced diet?

As noted in Chapter 1, the human body needs more than 50 different nutrients to function properly. The roles of many of these nutrients have been detailed in preceding chapters. The concept of the balanced diet is that by eating a wide variety of foods you will obtain all the nutrients you need to support growth and development of all tissues, regulate metabolic processes, and provide adequate energy for proper weight control. (See Figure 12.1.)

Although everyone's diet requires the essential nutrients, the proportions differ at different stages of the life cycle. The infant has needs differing from his grandfather, and the pregnant or lactating woman has needs differing from her adolescent daughter. There also are differences between the needs of the sexes, particularly in regard to the iron content of the diet. Moreover, individual variations in life-style may impose different nutrient requirements. A long-distance runner in training for a marathon has some distinct nutritional needs compared to a sedentary colleague. The individual trying

to lose weight needs to balance Calorie losses with nutrient adequacy. The diabetic individual needs strict nutritional counseling for a balanced diet. Thus, there are a number of different conditions that may influence nutrient needs and the concept of a balanced diet.

The food supply in the United States is extremely varied, and most individuals who consume a wide variety of foods do receive an adequate supply of nutrients. However, there appears to be some concern that many Americans are not receiving optimal nutrition because they consume excessive amounts of highly processed foods. This may be true, as improper food processing may lead to depletion of key nutrients and the addition of high-Calorie and low-nutrient ingredients, such as fat and sugar. As noted previously, three out of every five Calories that the average American eats are derived from fat and sugar.

An unbalanced diet is due not to the unavailability of proper foods but rather to our choice of foods. To improve our nutritional habits we need to learn to select our foods more wisely.

What is the key nutrient concept for obtaining a balanced diet?

As already noted, humans require many diverse nutrients, including twenty amino acids, thirteen vitamins, and more than twenty-five minerals. To plan our daily diet to include all of these nutrients would be mind-boggling, so simplified approaches to diet planning have been developed.

The nutritional composition of foods varies tremendously. If you examine a food-composition

Figure 12.2.

The key-nutrient concept. Obtaining the RDA for these eight key nutrients from a balanced diet of wholesome, natural foods among the six food exchanges will most likely support your daily needs for all other essential nutrients.

Protein
Vitamin A
Thiamin
Riboflavin
Niacin
Vitamin C
Iron
Calcium

table, you will quickly see that no two foods are exactly alike in nutrient composition. However, certain foods are similar enough in nutrient content to be grouped accordingly. This fact is the basis for approaching nutrition education by way of the Basic Four Food Groups and the Food Exchange Lists. In essence, foods are grouped or listed according to approximate caloric content and nutrients in which they are rich.

Eight nutrients are central to human nutrition: protein, thiamin, riboflavin, niacin, vitamins A and C, iron, and calcium (Figure 12.2). When found naturally in plant and animal sources, these nutrients are usually accompanied by other essential nutrients. The central theme of the **key-nutrient concept** is simply that if these eight key nutrients are adequate in your diet, you will probably receive an ample supply of *all* nutrients essential to humans. It is important to note that in order for the key-nutrient concept to work, you must obtain the nutrients from a wide variety of wholesome natural foods. For example, highly processed foods to which some vitamins have been added will not contain all of the trace elements, such as chromium, that were removed during processing.

Table 12.1 presents the eight key nutrients and some significant plant and animal sources. You can see that the Food Exchange Lists can be a useful guide to securing these eight key nutrients. Keep in mind, however, that there is some variation in the proportion of the nutrients, not only between the food exchanges but also within each food exchange. For example, the starch/bread exchange does contain some protein, but it is not as good a source as the meat or milk exchange. Within the fruit exchange, oranges are an excellent source of vitamin C, but peaches are not, although peaches are high in vitamin A. If you select a wide range of foods within each group, the nutrient intake should be balanced over time. Table 12.2 presents a daily diet based upon the exchange lists. An example of a low-Calorie diet plan based upon the Food Exchange Lists is presented in Chapter 10, together with methods for planning a diet based upon a specific number of Calories.

What is the concept of nutrient density?

As mentioned before, the nutrient content of foods varies considerably, the differences between food groups being more distinct than the differences between foods in the same group. **Nutrient density** is an important concept relative to the proportions of essential nutrients such as protein, vitamins, and minerals, that are found in specific foods. In essence, a food with high nutrient density possesses a significant amount of a specific nutrient or nutrients per serving compared to its caloric content. We refer to these as quality Calories.

Let's look at an extreme example between two different food groups. Consider the nutrient differences between a six-ounce can of tuna fish packed in water and a piece of Boston cream pie. The tuna fish would provide you with over 100 percent of your RDA for two key nutrients (protein and niacin) along with substantial amounts of several other vitamins and minerals, but very little fat. The caloric content would be only 220. For 220 Calories of Boston cream pie, you would receive little protein, few vitamins, and few minerals, with greater amounts of fat and refined carbohydrates. Hence, the tuna fish has greater nutrient density and considerably greater nutritional value. Another example is presented in Figure 12.3.

Let's also look at a comparison of two foods within the same group, the meat group. Consider the following nutritional data for three ounces of tuna fish and three ounces of clams:

	Calories	Protein	Iron
3 oz. Tuna:	110	24 g	1.6 mg
3 oz. Clams:	65	11 g	5.2 mg

The protein density is similar in the two foods, as you get approximately 1 gram of protein for 5 Calories of tuna fish (110/24) and 1 gram of protein for 6 Calories from clams (65/11). However, clams contain more than three times the amount of iron

Table 12.1   Eight key nutrients and significant food sources from plants and animals

Nutrient	USRDA	Plant source	Animal source	Food exchange
Protein	56 g	Dried beans and peas, nuts	Meat, poultry, fish, cheese, milk	Meat, milk
Vitamin A	5000 IU	Dark green leafy vegetables, orange-yellow vegetables, margarine	Butter, fortified milk, liver	Fruit, vegetable, fat
Vitamin C	60 mg	Citrus fruits, broccoli, potatoes, strawberries, tomatoes, cabbage, dark green leafy vegetables	Liver	Fruit, vegetable
Thiamin (vitamin B_1)	1.5 mg	Breads, cereals, pasta, nuts	Pork, ham	Starch/bread, meat
Riboflavin (vitamin B_2)	1.7 mg	Breads, cereals, pasta	Milk, cheese, liver	Starch/bread, milk
Niacin	20 mg	Breads, cereals, pasta, nuts	Meat, fish, poultry	Starch/bread, meat
Iron	15 mg	Dried peas and beans, spinach, asparagus, dried fruits	Meat, liver	Meat, starch/bread
Calcium	1000 mg	Turnip greens, okra, broccoli, spinach, kale	Milk, cheese, sardines, salmon	Milk, vegetable

per serving, and if you consider the fact that the caloric content of the clams is less than that of the tuna fish, the nutrient density of iron is over five times greater in the clams than in the tuna fish. Both foods are excellent sources of protein for the amount of Calories consumed, and although tuna fish is also a good source of iron, clams are a much superior source. This illustrates the need to consume a wide variety of foods within each food group to satisfy your nutrient needs.

Another term related to nutrient density is the **Index of Nutritional Quality (INQ)** of a given food. The INQ is a comparison of the nutrient content of a food to the RDA for that nutrient in relation to the caloric content of the food and the caloric RDA for an average individual. As an example, look at the INQ for vitamin C in a baked potato for an average adult female:

	Baked potato content	**RDA for Adult woman**
Calories	140	2100
Vitamin C	30	60

$$INQ = \frac{30/60}{140/2100} = 7.5$$

An INQ of 1.0 means that the food is supplying you with the same proportion of your daily RDA for both Calories and the nutrient analyzed.

If the INQ is less than 1.0 then the food is not a good source for that nutrient. The higher the INQ, the better. Thus, a baked potato is an exceptionally nutritious food in relationship to vitamin C.

Adopting a healthful diet, as discussed in the next section, will automatically increase nutrient density simply by decreasing the amount of dietary fat and sugar.

Dietary Recommendations for Better Health

As noted in previous chapters, a deficiency or excess of any essential nutrient may lead to acute health problems, but these acute health problems are usually remedied rather promptly by restoration of proper nutrition. Deficiencies or excesses of various nutrients may also lead to the development of several major chronic diseases, which may also be prevented or treated by proper nutrition. (See Figure 12.4.)

Most chronic diseases have a genetic basis; if one of your parents has had coronary heart disease or cancer, you have an increased probability of developing that disease. Such diseases may go through three stages: initiation, promotion, and progression. Your genetic predisposition may lead to the initiation stage of the disease, but factors in your environment promote its development and eventual

Table 12.2 Example of a daily menu based on the food exchanges

Exchange	Food selections	Exchange	Food selections
Breakfast		**Dinner**	
Meat	Canadian bacon	Meat	Baked beans
Starch/bread	English muffin	Starch/bread	Rice or pasta
Milk	Skim milk		Bagel
Fruit	Orange juice	Milk	Yogurt
Fat	Vegetable margarine	Fruit	Sliced peaches (in yogurt)
Lunch		Vegetable	Mixed salad
Meat	Tuna fish (water pack)	Fat	Low-fat salad dressing
Starch/bread	Whole wheat bread	**Snacks**	
Milk	Skim milk	Fruit	Banana
Fruit	Apple		
Vegetable	Lettuce and tomato		
Fat	Low-fat mayonnaise		

Note: This table presents some common examples of foods within each of the six food exchanges. As discussed in the text, however, you should select food wisely among exchanges and within each exchange. For example, to avoid excessive amounts of Calories, cholesterol, and saturated fats, you should select skim milk, lean meats such as skinless turkey and chicken, water-packed tuna fish, low-fat yogurt, and corn-oil margarine.

Figure 12.3.
The concept of nutrient density. The key principle is to select foods that are high in nutrients and low in Calories. Compare the nutrient value of the three beverages in this figure. As you can see, orange juice and milk are significant sources of several key nutrients, whereas cola simply contains Calories in the form of simple carbohydrates.

Amount	8 ounces	8 ounces	8 ounces
Calories	120	150	100
Protein (grams)	0	8*	0
Fat (grams)	0	8	0
Carbohydrates (grams)	30	12	25
Calcium (milligrams)	27	352*	0
Iron (milligrams)	0.5	0.1	0
Vitamin A (IU)	500*	500*	0
Thiamin (milligrams)	0.2*	0.1	0
Riboflavin (milligrams)	0.07	0.5*	0
Niacin (milligrams)	1.0	0.2	0
Vitamin C (milligrams)	152*	2	0
	Orange juice	Milk, whole	Cola

*Significant source of this key nutrient, over 10% of the RDA.

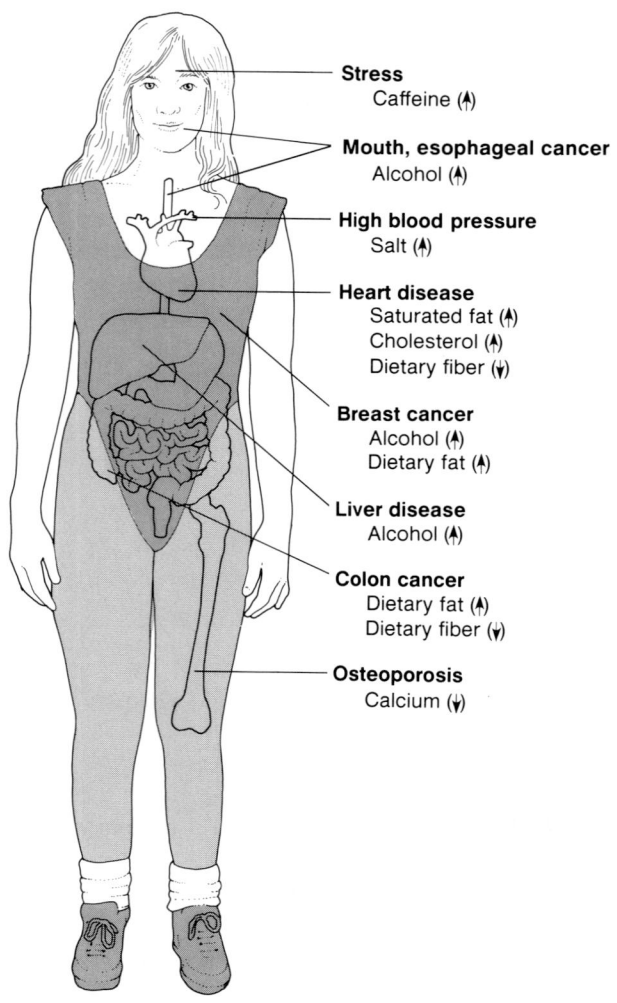

Figure 12.4.
Some possible health problems associated with poor dietary habits. An upward arrow (↑) indicates excessive intake while a downward arrow (↓) indicates low intake or deficiency.

Stress
Caffeine (↑)

Mouth, esophageal cancer
Alcohol (↑)

High blood pressure
Salt (↑)

Heart disease
Saturated fat (↑)
Cholesterol (↑)
Dietary fiber (↓)

Breast cancer
Alcohol (↑)
Dietary fat (↑)

Liver disease
Alcohol (↑)

Colon cancer
Dietary fat (↑)
Dietary fiber (↓)

Osteoporosis
Calcium (↓)

progression. In this regard, some nutrients are believed to be **promoters** that lead to the progression of the disease, whereas other nutrients are believed to be **antipromoters** that deter the initiation process from progressing to a serious health problem. What you eat plays an important role in the development or progress of chronic diseases such as coronary heart disease, diabetes, high blood pressure, osteoporosis, obesity, and a variety of different cancers. For example, the National Cancer Institute estimates that one third of all cancers are linked in some way to diet.

The Healthy American Diet, introduced in Chapter 1, is relatively simple to understand but may be somewhat more difficult to implement in our contemporary, fast-paced society. In this section, we shall look at basic guidelines underlying the Healthy American Diet, and several means to help incorporate it into our life-style.

What are the recommended dietary guidelines for reducing the risk of chronic disease?

Although there is no absolute proof that dietary changes will enhance the health status of every member of the population, the following appear to be prudent recommendations for most individuals and are based upon the available scientific evidence. These recommendations represent a synthesis of a number of reports from both health and government organizations such as the American Heart Association, the National Cancer Institute, the National Research Council, and the U.S. Department of Health and Human Services, including the comprehensive sources, *Diet and Health: Implications for Reducing Chronic Disease Risk* and the *Surgeon General's Report on Nutrition and Health*. Taken together, these recommendations may be helpful in preventing most chronic diseases, including cardiovascular diseases and cancer. Exercise is also a healthful adjunct to several of these dietary recommendations.

1. Maintain a healthy body weight. To avoid becoming overweight, you should consume only as many Calories as you expend daily. Methods of regulating your body weight were presented in detail in chapter 10. An aerobic exercise program and adherence to the concept of nutrient density, which includes a number of the following recommendations, could serve as the basis for a sound weight-control program.

2. Eat a wide variety of natural foods from within and among the Exchange List food groups. Eating a wide variety of natural foods will assure you of obtaining a balanced and adequate intake of all essential nutrients. Select a wide variety of foods from each and within each of the six Exchange Lists. Stress foods that are high in the key nutrients.

3. Eat foods rich in calcium and iron. This is particularly true for women and children. Skim or low-fat milk and other low-fat dairy products are excellent sources of calcium. For example, one glass of skim milk provides nearly one third the RDA for calcium. Certain vegetables, such as broccoli, are also good sources of calcium. Iron is found in good supply in the meat and starch/bread exchanges. Lean meats should be selected so as to limit fat intake, while enriched, whole grain products contain more iron than those made with bleached, unenriched white flour. (See Table 12.3.)

4. Consume moderate amounts of protein. The recommended dietary intake is 0.8 grams of protein per kilogram body weight, which averages out to about 50 to 60 grams per day, or 10–12 percent of the daily Calories. The National Research Council recommends an upper limit of 1.6 grams per kilogram body weight. Since the average daily American intake of protein is about 100 grams, we appear to be staying within the guidelines. However, most of the protein Americans eat is of animal origin. Although animal products are an excellent source of complete protein, they tend to be higher in saturated fats and cholesterol compared with foods high in plant protein. On the other hand, animal protein is usually a better source of dietary iron and other minerals like zinc and copper than plant protein is.

Table 12.3 Foods rich in calcium and iron

Mineral	Food source
Calcium	All dairy products: milk, cheese, ice milk, yogurt; egg yolk; dried peas and beans; dark green, leafy vegetables such as beet greens, spinach, and broccoli; cauliflower
Iron	Organ meats such as liver; meat, fish, and poultry; shellfish, especially oysters; dried beans and peas; whole grain products such as breads and cereals; dark green, leafy vegetables such as spinach and broccoli; dried fruits such as figs, raisins, apricots, and dates

Four ounces of meat, fish, or poultry, together with two glasses of skim milk, will actually provide the average individual with the daily RDA for protein, totaling about 45 grams of high-quality protein. Combining this animal protein intake with plant foods high in protein, such as whole grain products, beans and peas, and vegetables, will substantially increase your protein intake and more than meet your needs.

Seafood is another excellent source of protein which is usually low in fat. In addition, many fish are rich in omega-3 fatty acids.

5. Eat more complex carbohydrates and dietary fiber by including plenty of vegetables, fruits, and grain products in your diet. (See Figure 12.5.) In general, about 60 percent of your daily Calories should come from carbohydrates, about 50 percent from complex carbohydrates and the other 10 percent from simple, natural carbohydrates. To accomplish this, you need to eat more whole grain products (breads and cereals), legumes (beans and peas), and vegetables and fruits. In particular, eat vegetables. Stress vegetables and fruits high in beta-carotene and vitamin C (the antioxidant vitamins), such as carrots, peaches, squash, and sweet potatoes. Deep yellow and orange fruits and vegetables, as well as dark green, leafy vegetables are usually good sources of these vitamins. Also increase your intake of cruciferous vegetables, those from the cabbage family, such as broccoli, cauliflower, brussels sprouts, and all cabbages. These fruits and vegetables appear to protect you against stomach, colon, and rectal cancer.

Figure 12.5.
Include in your diet foods high in plant starch and fiber. Eat more fruits, vegetables, and whole grain products.

(Bob Coyle)

Another benefit of complex carbohydrates is their high fiber content. Whole grain products and numerous vegetables are excellent sources of water-insoluble fiber. Fruits, beans, and products derived from oats, such as oatmeal and oat bran, are rich in the water-soluble type of fiber. The high fiber content of these foods is believed to be important in the prevention of diseases such as cancer of the colon and coronary heart disease.

6. Use sugars only in moderation. The recommended dietary goal is to reduce consumption of refined sugar from the current level of 24 percent of the daily Calories to 10 percent or less. Excessive consumption of refined sugar has been associated with high blood triglyceride levels. Sticky sugars are a major contributing factor to dental cavities. Sugars also significantly increase the caloric content of foods without an increase in nutritional value, so they may contribute to body weight problems.

To meet this goal you should reduce your intake of common table sugar and products high in refined sugar. Sugar is one of the major additives to processed foods, so check the labels. If sugar is listed first, it is the main ingredient. Also look for terms such as corn syrup, dextrose, fructose, and malt sugar, which are also primarily refined sugars (Figure. 12.6).

Use natural sugars to satisfy your sweet tooth.

7. Choose a diet low in total fat, saturated fats, and cholesterol. There is no specific requirement for fat in the diet. However, a need exists for an essential fatty acid (linoleic fatty acid) and vitamins that are components of fat. Since almost all foods contain some fat, sufficient amounts of the essential fatty acid and vitamins are found in the average diet. Even on a vegetarian diet of fruits, vegetables, and grain products, about 5 to 10 percent of the Calories are derived from fat, thus supplying enough of these essential nutrients. Fat, however, currently comprises almost 40 percent of our Calories; the recommended dietary goal is less than 30 percent. In addition, the amount of saturated fat in the diet should be 10 percent or less, and cholesterol intake should be limited to 300 milligrams or less per day.

The following practical suggestions will help you meet the recommended dietary goal.
a. Eat less meat with a high fat content. Avoid hot dogs, luncheon meats, sausage, and bacon. Trim off excess fat

Figure 12.6.
Nutritional labeling as a guide to sugar and fat in processed foods. Refined sugar and fats may appear in processed foods in a variety of forms. Check for these terms on nutrition labels.

Sugars	Fats
Sucrose	Oil
Glucose	Lard
Fructose	Palm oil
Corn syrup	Coconut oil
Honey	Monoglycerides
Molasses	Diglycerides
Sorbitol	Triglycerides
Mannitol	Stearate
Brown sugar	Palmitate
Dextrose	Vegetable shortening
Levulose	Hydrogenated oils
Invert sugar	

before cooking. Eat only lean red meat and more white meat, such as turkey, chicken, and fish, which have less fat. Remove the skin from poultry.

b. Eat only two to three eggs per week. One egg yolk contains about 250 milligrams of cholesterol, close to the limit of 300 milligrams per day. Egg whites have no cholesterol and are an excellent source of high-quality protein. You may use commercially prepared egg substitutes, particularly those which are low in fat.

c. Eat fewer dairy products that are high in fat. Switch from whole milk to skim milk. Eat other dairy products made from skim or nonfat milk, such as yogurt and cottage cheese. If you like cheese, switch from hard cheeses to soft cheeses, although most cheeses, except low-fat cottage cheese, are still high in fat and Calories.

d. Eat less butter, which is high in saturated fats, by substituting soft margarine made from liquid oils that are monounsaturated or polyunsaturated such as corn oil. Avoid margarine made from hydrogenated oils, which basically are saturated fats. Eat butter and margarine sparingly.

e. Eat fewer commercial prepared baked goods made with eggs and saturated or hydrogenated fats.

f. Limit your consumption of fast foods. Although fast-food chains generally serve grade A foods, many of their products are high in fat. The average fast-food sandwich contains

approximately 50 percent of its Calories in fat. Appendix I provides a breakdown of the fat Calories and milligrams of cholesterol in products served by popular fast-food restaurants. Some fast-food restaurants do serve nutrient-dense foods, and the trend is toward lower fat items. Wise choices, such as baked fish, grilled skinless chicken, lean meat, baked potatoes, and salads can provide healthy nutrition.

g. Check food labels for main ingredients that indicate fat. Look for terms such as oil, shortening, lard, coconut or palm oil, monoglycerides, diglycerides, triglycerides, stearate, and palmitate. All of these are other names for fat, particularly saturated fat. (See Figure 12.6.) Incidentally, products labeled as containing vegetable oils only are not necessarily low in saturated fats, since tropical oils (palm and coconut) are very high in saturated fat.

h. Broil, bake, or microwave your foods. Limit frying. If you must use oil in your cooking, try to use monounsaturated oils such as olive or peanut oil.

i. Eat more fish. Many fish, such as sardines, salmon, tuna, and mackerel, are rich in omega-3 fatty acids. White fish, such as flounder, is very low in fat Calories.

In general, decrease your intake of cholesterol, total fat, and saturated fat, substituting monounsaturated, polyunsaturated, and omega-3 fatty acids for saturated or hydrogenated fats.

8. Use salt and sodium only in moderation. Restrict sodium intake to less than 2,400 mg daily, which is the equivalent of 6,000 milligrams, or 6 grams, of table salt. This lower amount will provide sufficient sodium for normal physiological functioning.

    Sodium is found naturally in a wide variety of foods, so it is not difficult to get an adequate supply. Several key suggestions may help you reduce the sodium content in your diet.

    a. Get rid of your salt shaker. One teaspoon of salt is 2,000 mg of sodium; the average well-salted meal contains about 3,000 to 4,000 mg. Put less salt on your food both in your cooking pot and on your table.

    b. Reduce the consumption of obviously high-salt foods such as most pretzels and potato chips, pickles, and other such snacks.

    c. Check food labels for sodium content. If salt or sodium is one of the ingredients listed, you have a high-sodium food. Salt is a major additive in many processed foods, often disguised by terms such as monosodium glutamate and others.

    d. Eat more fresh fruits and vegetables, which are very low in sodium. Fruits, both fresh and canned, have less than 8 mg sodium per serving. Fresh and frozen vegetables may have 35 mg or less, but if canned may contain up to 460 mg.

    e. Use fresh herbs, spices that do not contain sodium, or lite salt as seasoning alternatives.

9. Maintain an adequate intake of fluoride. This is particularly important during childhood when the primary and secondary teeth are developing, for fluoride helps prevent tooth decay by strengthening the tooth enamel. Your water supply may contain sufficient fluoride—naturally or artificially—to provide an adequate amount, but if not, fluoride supplements or use of fluoride toothpaste is recommended.

10. Avoid taking dietary supplements in excess of the daily RDA. As noted in Chapters 6 through 8, dietary supplements of most vitamins and minerals are not necessary for individuals consuming a balanced diet. If you adhere to the recommendations listed here, you are not likely to need any supplementation at all, for the consumption of nutrient-dense foods should guarantee adequate vitamin and mineral nutrition. However, if you feel a supplement is needed, the ingredients should not exceed 100 percent of the daily RDA for any vitamin or mineral. Many one-a-day vitamin–mineral supplements do adhere to this standard. Excessive supplementation, as noted in previous chapters, may elicit some serious adverse health effects.

11. Eat fewer foods with questionable additives. Do you ever read the list of ingredients on the labels of highly processed food products? If not, check one out soon. My guess is you will not know what half the ingredients are or why they are there. A recently purchased pie had the main ingredients of water, sugar, wheat flour, fruit, and margarine—along with the salt, artificial flavors, artificial colors, agar, locust bean gum, microcrystalline cellulose, sodium propionate, potassium sorbate, polysorbate 60, sorbitan monostearate, sodium phosphate, carboxymethylcellulose, and calcium carrageenan. The pie was delicious, but were all these additives necessary?

    The Food and Drug Administration (FDA) classifies a **food additive** as any substance added directly to food. There are more than forty different purposes for the additives in the foods we eat, but the four most common are to add flavor, to enhance color, to improve the texture, and to preserve the food. For example, vanilla flavoring may be added to ice cream to impart a vanilla flavor, vitamin C (ascorbic acid) may be added to fruits and vegetables to prevent discoloration, emulsifiers may be added to help blend oil evenly throughout a product, and sodium propionate may be used to prolong shelf life.

    To earn FDA approval, additives must be **generally recognized as safe (GRAS)**. They may be added only to specific foods for specific purposes, and in general must improve the quality of the food without posing any hazards to humans. Only the minimum amount necessary to achieve the desired purpose may be added.

    Although we may realize that absolute safety does not exist in anything we do, including eating, we do have a right to expect that the food we purchase is generally safe for consumption. The government and food manufacturers must take utmost care to ensure that food additives do not create any appreciable risks to our health. On the other hand, we as consumers also have a responsibility to select foods necessary for good nutrition. Food product labeling has helped us in this regard, for we now can tell what ingredients we are eating, although we may not always know why they are there.

Although the general consensus appears to be that most additives used in processed foods are relatively safe, several health agencies, such as the Center for Science in the Public Interest, recommend caution with some. Read the labels on processed foods and select those products which have the least number of additives. Avoid or reduce the consumption of foods that contain questionable additives, such as artificial colors and dyes, saccharin, BHT, sodium nitrate, sodium nitrite, and sulfites. Eating fresh, natural foods is one of the best approaches to avoiding additives.

12. If you drink alcohol, do so in moderation. The current available scientific evidence does not suggest that light to moderate daily alcohol consumption will cause any health problems to the healthy, nonpregnant adult. Light to moderate drinking is based upon a limit of one drink for every 50 pounds of body weight. A drink is defined as one 12-ounce bottle of beer, one 4-ounce glass of wine, or 1.5 ounces of 80-proof distilled spirits. Thus, for an average-size male of 150 pounds, light to moderate drinking would be three drinks daily. However, excessive alcohol consumption is one of the most serious health problems in our society today, and even small amounts may pose health problems to some individuals. An expanded discussion is presented in Chapter 3.

Your health depends on a variety of factors such as heredity and certain aspects of your environment. Adherence to these twelve simple guidelines will not guarantee you good health; however, the available data indicate that these dietary changes have the potential to keep you healthy or even to improve upon your current health status.

Although it may not appear obvious, the general nature of the Healthy American Diet is a shift towards vegetarianism, so it may be important to address the nature of this dietary regimen.

Is a vegetarian diet more healthful than an omnivorous diet?

The American Dietetic Association, in a position paper devoted to vegetarian diets, noted that such diets are healthful and nutritionally adequate, but deficiencies may occur if the diet is not planned appropriately. As noted in Chapter 5, there are a variety of ways to be a vegetarian. A strict vegetarian, known also as a vegan, eats no animal products at all. Ovovegetarians include eggs in their diet while lactovegetarians include foods in the milk group such as cheese and other dairy products. An ovolacto-vegetarian eats both eggs and milk products. Semivegetarians may also include white meat in their diet but exclude red meats. In practice, then, a vegetarian may range on a continuum from one who eats nothing but fruits and nuts to someone who eats a typical American diet with the exception of red meat. The concern for obtaining a balanced intake of nutrients depends upon where a vegetarian is on that continuum. If foods are not selected carefully, the vegetarian may suffer nutritional deficiencies involving Calories, vitamins, minerals, and protein.

Caloric deficiency is one of the lesser concerns of a vegetarian diet. However, because plant products are generally low in caloric content, a vegetarian may be on a diet with insufficient Calories for proper body maintenance. This may be particularly true for the active individual who may be expending over a thousand Calories per day through exercise. The solution is to eat greater quantities of the foods that constitute the diet, and to include some of the higher-Calorie foods like nuts, beans, corn, green peas, potatoes, sweet potatoes, avocados, orange juice, raisins, dates, figs, whole wheat bread, and pasta products. These foods may be used in main meals and as snacks. On the other hand, the low caloric content of vegetarian diets may be a desirable attribute as it may be useful in weight-reduction programs or helpful in maintenance of proper body weight.

Strict vegetarians may incur a vitamin B_{12} deficiency because this vitamin is not found in plant foods. Vitamin B_{12} is found in many animal products such as meat, eggs, fish, and dairy products, so the addition of these foods to the diet will help prevent a deficiency state. An ovolactovegetarian should have no problem getting required amounts. A vegan will need a source of B_{12}, such as soy milk, or a B_{12} supplement. If not exposed to sunlight, vegans will also need dietary supplements of vitamin D, which is not found in plant foods.

Riboflavin (vitamin B_2) is low in many fruits, vegetables, breads, and cereals. Green leafy vegetables, such as beet greens, broccoli, collards, and turnip greens, are relatively good sources of riboflavin for the vegan. Dairy products, such as milk, yogurt, and cheese, add substantial amounts of riboflavin to the diet.

Mineral deficiencies of iron, calcium, and zinc may occur, particularly if the vegetarian diet contains large amounts of grains, legumes, and green, leafy vegetables. During the digestion process, these foods form compounds called phytates and oxalates that can bind these minerals so that they cannot be absorbed into the body. Avoidance of unleavened bread helps reduce this effect, as does thorough cooking of legumes such as beans. Foods rich in these minerals should also be included in the vegetarian diet. Iron-rich plant foods include nuts, beans, peanuts, split peas, green, leafy vegetables (like spinach), dates, prune juice, raisins, and many iron-enriched grain products. Calcium-rich plant foods include many green vegetables like broccoli, cabbage, mustard greens, and spinach. Research has revealed that a balanced intake of grains, legumes, and vegetables will not significantly impair mineral absorption. Dairy products added to the diet supply very significant amounts of calcium. Zinc-rich plant foods include whole wheat bread, peas, corn, and carrots. Egg yolk and seafood also add substantial zinc to the diet.

The major concern of the vegetarian is to obtain adequate amounts of the right type of protein, particularly in the case of young children. As you may recall in our earlier discussion in Chapter 5, proteins are classified as either complete or incomplete. A protein is complete if it contains all of the essential amino acids that the human body cannot manufacture. Animal products generally contain complete proteins, whereas plant proteins are incomplete. However, certain vegetable products may also provide good sources of protein. Grain products such as wheat, rice, and corn, as well as soybeans, peas, beans, and nuts, have a substantial protein content. However, most vegetable products lack one or more essential amino acids in sufficient quantity. They are incomplete proteins and, eaten individually, are not generally adequate for maintaining proper human nutrition. But, if certain plant foods are eaten together, they may supply all the essential amino acids necessary for human nutrition and may be as good as meat protein. (See Figure 12.7.)

To receive a balanced distribution of essential amino acids, the vegan must eat vegetable foods that possess what is known as protein complementarity, in which a vegetable product low in a particular amino acid is eaten together with a food that is high in that same amino acid. Grains and cereals that are low in lysine need to be complemented by legumes, such as beans, that have adequate amounts of lysine. A detailed discussion is presented in Chapter 5 on pages 128–29.

The vegetarian diet has not been proven to be healthier than a diet that includes foods in the meat and milk groups, but it is based on certain nutritional concepts that may help in the prevention of some degenerative diseases common to industrialized society. First, the total fat and saturated fat content in a vegetarian diet is usually low, since the small amounts of fats found in plant foods are generally polyunsaturated. Second, plants do not contain cholesterol; this compound is found only in animal products. These two factors account for the finding that vegetarians generally have lower blood triglycerides and cholesterol than meat eaters, and these lower levels may be important to the prevention of coronary heart disease. Third, plant foods possess a high content of fiber and other nutrients that have been associated with reduced levels of serum cholesterol and the prevention of certain disorders in the intestinal tract. Fourth, if the proper foods are selected, the vegetarian diet supplies more than an adequate amount of nutrients and is rather low in caloric content. Plant foods can be high nutrient density foods, providing bulk in the diet without the added Calories of fat. Hence, the vegetarian diet can be an effective dietary regimen for losing excess body weight.

As a general guide for vegetarians, Table 12.4 represents the amounts of food that should help meet daily nutrient requirements. The amounts may be increased to provide additional calories. Foods rich in iron, calcium, and riboflavin should be included daily.

The scope of this book does not permit a discussion of food preparation. A number of excellent cookbooks for vegetarian meals are available at local bookstores, the titles of which may be obtained from a local dietitian or local branch of the American Heart Association. They provide the vegetarian with a variety of appetizing recipes that not only incorporate complementary proteins with a balance of vitamins and minerals but also make vegetarianism a gastronomical delight.

Choosing to adopt a vegetarian diet is up to the individual and represents a significant change in dietary habits. Anyone desiring to make an abrupt change to a vegetarian diet should do some serious reading on the matter beforehand. Once you have done some reading on vegetarianism, there may be several ways to gradually phase yourself into a vegetarian diet. You may become a partial vegetarian

Figure 12.7.

It is important for the vegetarian to eat protein foods that complement each other (e.g., nuts and bread, rice and beans) so that all the essential amino acids are obtained in the diet.

(David Corona)

Table 12.4   Daily food guidelines for a vegetarian diet

Starch/bread exchange

Servings: 4 or more daily
Note: Use whole wheat or other whole grains. Products made of oats, rice, rye, corn, and whole wheat are good sources of protein, vitamin B, and iron, more so if they are enriched products.

Food examples:

Barley	Macaroni, enriched
Bran flakes	Oatmeal
Bread, whole wheat	Potatoes
Buckwheat pancakes	Rice, brown
Corn	Rye wafers
Corn muffins	Spaghetti, enriched
Farina, cooked	Wheat, shredded

Legumes (meat exchange substitute)

Servings: 2 or more daily
Note: Good sources of protein, niacin, iron, and Calories.

Food examples:

Great northern beans	Soybeans
Navy beans	Black-eyed peas
Red kidney beans	Split peas
Pinto beans	Chickpeas
Lima beans	Lentils

Nuts and seeds (fat exchange)

Servings: 2 or more daily
Note: Good sources of Calories, protein, niacin, and iron. May be excellent snack foods.

Food examples:

Almonds	Pecans
Brazil nuts	Walnuts
Cashew nuts	Sesame seeds
Peanuts	Sunflower seeds
Peanut butter	Pumpkin seeds

Fruit exchange

Servings: 3 or more daily
Note: Fruits are generally good sources of vitamins and minerals. At least one fruit should come from the citrus group and one from the high-iron group.

Food examples:

Regular	*Citrus*	*High iron*
Apples	Oranges	Dried apricots
Bananas	Orange juice	Dried prunes
Grapes	Grapefruit	Dried dates
Peaches	Grapefruit juice	Dried figs
Pears	Strawberries	Dried peaches
Pineapple	Tomato juice	Raisins
	Lemon juice	Prune juice

Vegetable exchange

Servings: 2 or more daily
Note: Vegetables are good sources of vitamins and minerals. At least one serving should come from the dark green or deep yellow vegetables.

Food examples:

Regular	*Dark green or deep yellow*
Artichokes	Beet greens
Asparagus	Broccoli
Beans, green	Carrots
Cabbage	Collard greens
Cauliflower	Lettuce
Cucumbers	Spinach
Eggplants	Squash
Radishes	Sweet potatoes
Tomatoes	

simply by eating less red meat. You may have several meatless days per week, or one or two meatless meals each day (breakfast and lunch). For example, you may skip the ham or sausage at breakfast, and have a big salad for lunch. You may wish to substitute white meat, with its generally lower fat content, for red meat. Eat more fish, chicken, and turkey. You may wish to become an ovolactovegetarian, eating eggs and dairy products. These excellent sources of complete protein can be blended with many vegetable products or eaten separately. You may use the above methods as forerunners to a strict vegetarian diet, gradually phasing out animal products altogether as you learn to select and prepare vegetable foods with protein complementarity.

It should be emphasized, however, that the nonvegetarian who carefully selects food from the meat and milk group, including lean red meat, may attain the same health benefits as the vegetarian. The major nutritional difference between a vegetarian and a nonvegetarian diet appears to be the higher content of saturated fats and cholesterol in the latter. Selection of animal products with a low fat and low cholesterol content helps avoid this problem and also assures consumption of a very high-quality protein. The National Research Council, in *Diet and Health,* did not recommend against eating meat, but recommended eating leaner meat in smaller and fewer portions than is customary in the United States.

How can I determine the nutritional quality of the food I buy?

One of the major features of the Healthy American Diet is the consumption of wholesome, natural, low-fat foods. But most of us do consume a wide variety of packaged foods, some of which may be highly processed and may be of questionable nutritional value. There has been increasing concern over the years that the nutritional quality of our food has been declining because many of our foods are overprocessed. They contain too much refined sugar, extracted oils, or white flour, all products of a refinement process. Refined sugar is pure carbohydrate with no nutritional value except Calories. The same can be said for extracted oils, which are pure fat. In the bleaching and processing of wheat to white flour, at least twenty-two known essential nutrients are removed, including the B vitamins, vitamin E, calcium, phosphorus, potassium, and magnesium. In addition, many fruits and vegetables are artificially ripened before they have reached maturity and contain smaller quantities of vitamins and minerals than naturally ripened ones do. We also consume many totally synthetic products such as artificial orange juice, nondairy creamers, and imitation ice cream, which do not possess the same nutrient value as their natural counterparts. Concern about the declining nutritional value of our food supply appears to be legitimate. Much of the blame is assigned to the processing of food, but this is not necessarily so.

In the mind of the public, processed foods more and more are thought to be inferior foods as compared with natural sources: for example, frozen peas versus fresh peas. The major purpose of food processing is to prevent waste through deterioration or spoilage. There are a variety of ways to do this, including heat, dehydration, refrigeration, freezing, and the use of chemicals. Food is processed by companies preparing their products for sale, but food processing also occurs at home in the preparation of a meal. You may wash, cut, cook, and freeze a variety of foods at home. Food processing, both at home and by commercial organizations, results in the loss of some nutrients. However, research suggests that commercial preservation techniques in common use today do not cause major nutrient losses in the foods we eat. Commercial food processing may actually cause less nutrient loss than home processing. In addition, food companies may enrich or fortify certain products before marketing. Examples include the addition of some B vitamins and iron to grain products, vitamins A and D to milk, vitamin A to margarine, and iodine to table salt. In some cases not all of the nutrients that were removed in processing are returned, but in some products a greater amount is returned or added.

A few nutrients may be susceptible to loss through processing. Borenstein and Lachance have noted with some reservations that carbohydrates, lipids, protein, niacin, vitamin K, and minerals are relatively stable during food processing and storage. Vitamins A, D, E, B_2, B_6, B_{12}, pantothenic acid, and folacin are a little less stable, while B_1 and vitamin C may be seriously depleted by commercial and home food processing.

The key point is that processing of food will not necessarily lead to a nutritionally inferior product. Even if processing does cause a slight decrease in nutritional quality, it will help provide a greater and more varied food supply with adequate amounts of dietary nutrients. The major problem with food processing is the excessive use of highly refined products like sugar, oils, unenriched white flour, salt, and questionable additives. Wise food selection can help avoid these problems, though this may be somewhat tricky in today's food marketplace. It requires careful reading of labels.

Food manufacturers view labels as a device for persuading you to buy their product instead of a competitor's products. Just walk down the cereal aisle next time you visit the supermarket and notice the bewildering number of choices. As manufactured food products multiplied over the years, and as competition for your food dollar intensified, food companies began to manipulate their labels to enhance sales. Unfortunately many of these practices were deceptive and the consumer had a difficult time determining the nutritional quality of many processed foods. Thus, Congress passed a law designed to establish a set of standards so that most Americans could base their choice of what to eat on sound nutritional information.

This set of standards resulted in **nutritional labeling,** whereby major nutrients found in a food product must be listed on the label. It is not the total solution to the problem of poor food selection existing among many Americans, but combined with an educational program to increase nutritional awareness it may effectively improve the nutritional health of our nation.

Some foods are exempt from the law if they meet certain **standards of identity.** For example, specific proportions of eggs, vegetable oil, and vinegar constitute the ingredients in mayonnaise and if these are present, the product need not specify nutritional information. However, most products do carry nutrition labels, which have to include the following information: serving size, servings per container, Calories, percentages of the eight key nutrients, and sodium content. Additional information such as carbohydrate (simple and complex), fat (saturated and polyunsaturated), cholesterol content, and the content of other vitamins and minerals in addition to the key nutrients, is optional.

Food manufacturers also must list all ingredients in order of the amount contained in the product by weight. A product that lists gravy, turkey, salt, and so forth has more gravy than turkey. What may appear to be a good nutritional buy really is not. Moreover, the label must list any additives.

To be of practical value to the consumer, the nutrient content is listed as a percentage of the United States Recommended Daily Allowance (USRDA). The percentages for most nutrients are based upon the USRDA for the average adult male, but the percentage for iron is based upon the USRDA for the adult female because her need is greater. Remember, because of these reference points, you must interpret the USRDA with care. For example, a USRDA for protein of 50 percent from a given food product may be 70 percent for one person and 30 percent for another if they weigh considerably less or more, respectively, than the average individual upon which the USRDA is based—a 70-kilogram (154-pound) male.

Protein is listed twice on the label, once as the amount in grams and second as a percentage of the USRDA. The percentage amount reflects the fact that not all protein quality is the same. For example, 8 grams of protein from milk, a complete protein, is listed as 20 percent of the USRDA for protein; however, a similar amount of protein in spaghetti, an incomplete protein, represents only 10 percent of the USRDA.

With a little bit of mathematics you also can determine the percentage of Calories that is derived from the energy nutrients in a food. In the example of the skim milk below, fat represents 10 percent of the Calories. One gram of fat equals 9 Calories, which when divided by the total Calories in one serving equals 0.1, or 10 percent ($9/90 \times 100$). Table 12.5 presents an example of a nutrition label for a quart of skim milk.

Skim milk would be an excellent source of protein, vitamin A, riboflavin, calcium, vitamin D, vitamin B_{12}, phosphorus, and magnesium; a fair source of vitamins B_6 and C, zinc, and pantothenic acid; and a poor source of niacin and iron.

You also may calculate a simplified INQ from the label if you know your recommended daily caloric intake. If you needed 3,000 Calories per day, 90 Calories would represent 3 percent of your daily energy needs ($90/3,000 \times 100$). Any nutrient listed with a percentage of the USRDA higher than 3 percent would have an INQ greater than 1.0. The INQ for protein in this case would be 6.6 ($20/3$).

Many individuals consider nutritional labeling, as it exists today, to be too confusing to the average consumer. Thus, because of pressure from a variety of consumer interest groups, a major overhaul of the nutritional labeling program has recently been completed and signed into law as the Nutritional Labeling and Education Act. It requires a listing of the total fat, saturated fat, total carbohydrate, complex carbohydrate, dietary fiber, and total protein found in each serving. Nutrient information for fruits and vegetables also will be posted. Additionally, the Food and Drug Administration (FDA) has proposed even more stringent food labeling requirements that would include meat, poultry, and seafood. Some nutrient data are currently available for these products, such as Meat Nutri-Facts posted in the store, but these voluntary labels would become mandatory under the FDA proposal

Table 12.5 An example of a nutrition label for a quart of skim milk

Nutrition information per serving

Serving size	One 8-ounce glass
Servings per container	4
Calories	90
Protein	8 g
Carbohydrate	12 g
Fat	1 g

Percentage of U.S. recommended daily allowances (USRDA)

Protein	20	Vitamin D	25
Vitamin A	10	Vitamin B_6	4
Vitamin C	4	Vitamin B_{12}	15
Thiamin	8	Phosphorus	25
Riboflavin	30	Magnesium	10
Niacin	*	Zinc	6
Calcium	30	Pantothenic acid	6
Iron	*		

* Contains less than 2% of the USRDA of the nutrients

Table 12.6 Food label terms: What do they really mean?

Caloric content

Reduced Calorie: One-third or more fewer Calories than standard product
Low Calorie: No more than 40 Calories per serving, or 0.4 Calories/gram
Diet or dietetic: Same as low Calorie or reduced Calorie, unless specified otherwise

Fat and cholesterol content

Low fat: Milk products, 2% or less fat; meat products, 10% or less fat
Leaner: Meat, reduction in fat content by 25 percent or more
Lean: Meat, 10% or less of weight by fat
Extra lean: Meat, 5 percent or less of fat by weight
95% fat free: 5% or less fat content by weight, but may actually be 30–50 percent or more fat Calories
Cholesterol reduced: Decreased cholesterol content by 75% or more
Low cholesterol: Less than 20 milligrams per serving
Cholesterol free: Less than 2 milligrams per serving

Sodium or salt content

Reduced sodium: Sodium content decreased by 75% or more
Low sodium: 140 milligrams or less per serving
Very low sodium: 35 milligrams or less per serving
Sodium free: 5 milligrams or less per serving
Salt free: No salt, *but* may be high in sodium

Miscellaneous

Sugar free: No sucrose (table sugar), but may have other sweeteners that contain the same caloric value as sucrose
Wheat: Not necessarily whole wheat unless whole wheat is listed as the first ingredient
Natural: Meat products—no artificial or synthetic flavors, colors, or additives
Enriched: Thiamin, riboflavin, niacin, and iron added after milling process
Fortified: Added nutrients above amounts normally contained in the food
Imitation: Nutritionally inferior to the imitated product
Substitute: Nutritionally equivalent to the substituted product

Meaningless terms—No legal definition*

Lean, except for meat products
Natural, except for meat products
Organic
Light, lite: may mean lighter color, texture, flavor, less sodium, or fewer calories

*Many terms placed on labels or food products for advertising purposes have specific legal restrictions as established by the Food and Drug Administration (FDA), Federal Trade Commission (FTC), or the United States Department of Agriculture (USDA), whereas others are relatively meaningless since no legal definition exists.

A number of other subtle points about nutritional labeling could be made, but in general the nutritional information presented may serve as a practical guide for determining nutrient density and choosing foods wisely. For those trying to lose weight, foods with high concentrations of nutrients but low Calorie content may be chosen. Foods with a high iron content may be chosen for women and children. Nutritional labeling may serve as a useful guide for those who want or need to restrict saturated fats, cholesterol, or sodium in their diets, although terms used in advertising may be confusing. See Table 12.6 for a brief definition of common food label terms.

In addition, nutrition labeling can help you get the most nutrition for your money. Reading labels carefully and comparing brands and prices may reveal significant savings and no loss of nutrient value when a store or generic brand is purchased instead of one that is nationally advertised. In general, you should look for food products providing the greatest percentages of the USRDA for the key nutrients at the lowest price.

Dietary Recommendations for Better Physical Performance

Articles about nutrition for athletes in popular sports magazines, and food supplements advertised therein, give the impression that athletes have special nutritional requirements above those of the nonathlete.

Vitamin and mineral supplements, protein mixtures, and special "athletic nutritional compounds" often are highly recommended as means to improve athletic performance. However, if you have progressed through this text to this point, you are probably aware that such is not the case for the vast majority of athletes. Previous chapters have focused upon specific recommendations relative to the use of various nutrients to enhance physical performance, so the purpose of this final section is to provide some general summarizing comments.

Does the stress of athletic competition or exercise training impose any additional nutritional demands on the body?

Nutrition for the physically active person may be viewed from two aspects: nutrition for competition and nutrition for training. Of the three basic purposes of food—to provide energy, to regulate metabolic processes, and to support growth and development—the first two are of prime importance during athletic competition, while all three need to be considered during the training period in preparation for competition.

In competition an athlete will utilize specific body energy sources and systems, depending upon the intensity and duration of the exercise. Briefly, the high-energy phosphates are utilized during short, high-intensity exercise; muscle glycogen is used in intense exercise lasting about one to three minutes; and the oxidation of glycogen and fats becomes increasingly important in endurance activities lasting longer than five minutes. The release of energy in each one of these systems may require certain vitamins and minerals for optimal efficiency.

If an individual is well nourished, athletic competition will not impose any special demands for any of the six major classes of nutrients. Body energy stores of carbohydrate and fat are adequate to satisfy the energy demands of most activities lasting less than one hour. Protein is not generally considered a significant energy source during exercise. The vitamin and mineral content of the body will be sufficient to help regulate the increased levels of metabolic activity, and body-water supply will be adequate under normal environmental conditions.

On the basis of the available research evidence, only two nutrients have reliably been shown to improve performance if consumed prior to or during competition—and then only in certain athletic endeavors. These two dietary modifications are carbohydrate intake prior to and during exercise bouts of long duration at moderate to high intensity and adequate fluid intake prior to and during similar endurance events conducted in warm or hot environmental conditions. Specific dietary recommendations have been presented in Chapters 3 and 8. Although not all research findings are in agreement, a number of well designed studies with several other nutrients and related compounds have

documented ergogenic effects upon laboratory and field exercise tasks comparable to competitive athletic events. Additional research is especially needed to confirm or refute the potential ergogenic effects of supplementation with magnesium and potassium aspartates, phosphate salts, sodium bicarbonate, and the food drug caffeine. Finally, numerous commercial nutritional products are targeted specifically for the athlete prior to competition, but except for the various carbohydrate products, may have no scientific support. It is incumbent upon sports scientists to adequately research the purported ergogenic effect of these products to provide data that either support or contradict their advertised claims.

Proper nutrition during training is one of the keys to success in competition. Because energy expenditure increases during a training period, the caloric intake needed to maintain body weight may increase considerably—an additional 500–1,000 Calories or more per day in certain activities. By selecting these additional Calories wisely from the Food Exchange lists, you should obtain an adequate amount of all nutrients essential for the formation of new body tissues and proper functioning of the energy systems that work harder during exercise. A balanced intake of carbohydrate, fat, protein, vitamins, minerals, and water is all that is necessary. For endurance athletes, dietary carbohydrates should receive even greater emphasis.

During the early phases of training the body will begin to make adjustments in the energy systems so that they become more efficient. This is the so-called **chronic-training effect,** and many of the body's adjustments incorporate certain specific nutrients. For example, one of the chronic effects of long distance running is an increased hemoglobin content in the blood and increased myoglobin and cytochromes in the muscle cells; all three compounds need iron in order to be formed. Hence, the daily diet would need to contain adequate amounts to make effective body adjustments due to the chronic effects of training.

The need for sound nutrition is especially important for all females and for young males who engage in strenuous physical training. Females need to pay special attention to the iron and calcium content of their diet because of possible problems noted in Chapter 7. During the growth and development years of childhood and adolescence, the need for protein, calcium, and iron, as well as many other nutrients, is relatively high because the muscle, bone, and other body tissues are growing rapidly. Strenuous exercise may increase these needs slightly.

Nutrient supplementation does not appear to be necessary for the well-nourished athlete during training. Research is needed to investigate the advertised claims that amino acids, chromium salts, or other supplements will enhance the training effect. However, nutrient supplements may be warranted in some cases. In activities where excess body weight may serve to handicap performance, a loss of some body fat may be helpful. Recommended procedures for such weight losses were presented in Chapter 10. Although the procedure is not recommended, some athletes still use a very low-Calorie diet to achieve a desirable competitive weight; in such cases, a vitamin-mineral supplement may be recommended.

In general, however, the dietary guidelines that have been advocated earlier in this chapter for better health are the same for better physical performance. The key to sound nutrition for the athletic individual is to eat a wide variety of healthful foods.

Will a vegetarian diet affect physical performance potential?

As noted in the last section, a diet that follows vegetarian principles is considered to be more healthful than the typical American diet today. But will such a diet have any significant impact upon physical performance? Very little experimental research has investigated the value of a vegetarian diet as a means of increasing performance capacity. Moreover, most of the research that has been done was conducted nearly eighty years ago. The research methods employed do not meet today's standards for reliability. In one recent, rather well-designed study by Hanne and others, no differences were found in the aerobic or anaerobic capacities of vegetarian men or women compared with nonvegetarians. Other research has noted that performance in a distance run was neither improved nor impaired significantly after a fourteen-day diet consisting primarily of fruits. Although the available evidence does not support either a beneficial or a detrimental effect of a vegetarian diet upon physical performance capacity, active individuals should have a good understanding of vegetarian dietary principles before attempting an extreme diet such as the fruitarian plan, which relies primarily upon fruits and nuts to supply nutrient needs.

Some world-class athletes have been vegetarians, and on occasion their diet has been cited as a reason for their success. On the other hand, there are a far greater number of world-class athletes who eat a balanced diet including animal products. Both types of diet may supply the nutrients necessary for the physically active individual if foods are selected properly. It is especially important for female endurance athletes who are vegetarians to obtain adequate amounts of iron and calcium. Moreover, vegetarian diets have been associated with athletic amenorrhea in female endurance athletes. However, if adequate amounts of the nutrients are in the diet, the performance of either the world-class athlete or the weekend racer will not be affected one way or the other.

David Nieman notes that the vegetarian diet is usually high in carbohydrate content, which may be of importance to the individual who trains at a high level about an hour or so per day. Long-distance swimmers, runners, and bicyclists fall into this category. The carbohydrate content will help ensure replacement of body glycogen stores. However, meat eaters can also include substantial amounts of high-carbohydrate foods in their daily diets and achieve the same effect.

In the last section we noted that if you wanted to shift toward a vegetarian diet, you would need to do some careful reading beforehand, and then could initiate the process gradually. During the process, you should listen to your body—a common phrase among many athletes today. If you are active, how do you feel during your workouts? Do you have more or less stamina? Are you gaining or losing weight? Is your physical performance getting better or worse? The answers to these questions, together with other body reactions, may offer you some feedback as to whether the dietary change is beneficial.

Remember, there is nothing magical about a vegetarian diet that will increase your physical performance capacity. It can be a healthful way to obtain the nutrients your physically active body needs, but so too is a well-balanced diet containing animal products.

When and what should I eat prior to competition?

From a nutritional point of view, the most important aspect of preparation for an athletic event includes a tapering of exercise intensity for a day or two prior to competition combined with a balanced diet, preferably high in complex carbohydrates. This technique should help rest the athlete and also ensure adequate supplies of muscle glycogen for both aerobic- and anaerobic-type exercise. However, the precompetition meal is also important because all of the training and preparation for competition may be wasted if basic principles relative to timing and composition of the meal are violated.

In Chapter 3 we covered the special pre-event nutrition needs of athletes involved in prolonged exercise tasks, such as the marathon. Most of their dietary practices, such as carbohydrate loading and substantial intake of carbohydrates in the pre-event meal, are designed to maximize their body stores of muscle and liver glycogen. Although most athletic events are not prolonged endurance events, there may be some important points to consider regarding the timing and composition of the meal prior to competition.

It is a well-established fact that the ingestion of food just prior to competition will not benefit physical performance in most athletic events, yet the pregame meal, so to speak, is one of the major topics of discussion among athletes. A number of special meals have been utilized throughout the years because of their alleged benefits to physical performance, and special products have been marketed as pre-event nutritional supplements. Although research has not substantiated the value of any one particular precompetition meal, some general guidelines have been developed from practical experience over the years.

There are several major purposes of the precompetition meal that may be achieved through proper timing and composition. In general, the precompetition meal should:

1. Allow for the stomach to be relatively empty at the start of competition.
2. Help avoid a sensation of hunger.
3. Not adversely affect body energy supplies.
4. Help minimize gastrointestinal distress.
5. Provide for an adequate amount of body water.

In general, a solid meal should be eaten about three to four hours prior to competition. This should allow ample time for digestion to occur so that the stomach is relatively empty, and yet hunger sensations are minimized. However, pre-event emotional tension or anxiety may delay digestive time, as will a meal with a high fat or protein content. Hence, the composition of the meal is critical. It should be high in carbohydrate and low in fat and protein, providing for easy digestibility.

Liquid meals have some advantages over solid meals for precompetition nutrition. The available **liquid meals** are well balanced in nutrition value, have a high carbohydrate content, have no bulk, are easily digested and assimilated, and may be more practical and economical than a solid meal.

A number of different liquid meal products are available commercially, including Nutrament, Ensure, Ensure-Plus, and others associated with weight loss programs, such as Slim Fast. The composition of each may vary somewhat, and checking the label will reveal the exact nutrient content. The energy content is usually about 250–400 Calories. Most liquid meals are high in carbohydrates, moderate in protein and low in fat. Vitamins and minerals may be added in varying amounts.

Because the liquid meal may be assimilated more readily than a solid meal, it may be taken closer to competition, say two to three hours before. Research has shown that there is no difference between a liquid meal and a solid meal relative to subsequent hunger, nausea, diarrhea or weight changes prior to competition. In addition, liquid meals will not affect physical performance any differently than a well-planned solid precompetition meal.

From a practical standpoint, liquid meals may save time and money. The time and expense of stopping for a solid meal prior to an event may be avoided by the proper use of liquid meals. Although they are rather economically priced in comparison to a solid meal, they may be prepared even more economically at home. The following formula will provide one quart of a tasty liquid meal:

½ cup water
½ cup of nonfat dry milk
¼ cup of a glucose polymer
3 cups of skim milk
1 teaspoon of flavoring for palatability (cherry, vanilla or chocolate extract)

Finally, liquid meals should be used primarily as a substitute for precompetition nutrition and should not be used on a long-term basis to replace the balanced diet-concept.

The composition of the precompetition meal should not contribute to any gastrointestinal distress, such as flatulence, increased acidity in the stomach, heartburn, or increased bulk that may stimulate the need for a bowel movement during competition. In general, foods to be avoided include gas formers like beans, spicy foods that may elicit heartburn, and bulk foods like bran products. High sugar compounds may delay gastric emptying or create a reverse osmotic effect, possibly increasing the fluid content of the stomach, which may lead to a feeling of distress, cramps, or nausea. High sugar loads, particularly fructose, may also lead to other forms of gastrointestinal distress, such as diarrhea. Large amounts of concentrated-sugar can cause a reactive hypoglycemia in susceptible individuals. Through experience, you should learn what foods disagree with you during performance, and of course, you should avoid these prior to competition.

Adequate fluid intake should be assured prior to an event, particularly if the event will be of long duration or conducted under hot environmental conditions. Diuretics such as caffeine and alcohol, which increase the excretion of body water, should be avoided. Large amounts of protein increase the water output of the kidneys and thus should be avoided. Fluids may be taken up to fifteen to thirty minutes prior to competition, and doing so will help ensure adequate hydration. Details are provided in Chapter 8.

A wide variety of foods may be selected for the precompetition meal. The meal should consist of foods that are high in complex carbohydrates with moderate to low amounts of protein. Examples of such foods have been presented in previous chapters and also may be found in Appendix H, particularly those in the starch/bread list.

The foods should be agreeable to you. You should eat what you like within the guidelines presented above.

Two examples of precompetition meals, each containing about 500–600 Calories with substantial amounts of carbohydrate, are as follows:

One cup low-fat yogurt	Glass of orange juice
Banana	One bowl of oatmeal
Toasted Bagel	2 Pieces of toast with jelly
One ounce turkey breast	Sliced peaches with skim milk
One-half cup of raisins	

One important last point. Meals other than the precompetition meal eaten on the same day should not be skipped. They should adhere to the basic principles set forth earlier in this chapter.

Breakfast may be especially important. A balanced breakfast may provide a significant amount of Calories and other nutrients in the daily diet of the physically active person. A breakfast of skim milk, a poached egg, whole grain toast, fortified high-fiber cereal, and orange juice will help provide a substantial part of the RDA for protein, calcium, iron, fiber, vitamin C, and other nutrients, and is also relatively high in complex carbohydrates. A balanced breakfast high in fiber with an average amount of protein also will help prevent the onset of midmorning hunger. The fiber and protein may help maintain a feeling of satiety throughout the morning, whereas a breakfast of refined carbohydrates, like doughnuts, may trigger an insulin response and produce hypoglycemia in the middle of the morning. The resultant hunger is typically satisfied by eating other refined carbohydrates, which will satisfy the hunger urge only until about lunch time. A balanced breakfast having a high nutrient density is therefore preferable to a breakfast based on refined carbohydrate products. Nontraditional breakfast foods, such as pizza, may also provide a balanced meal for breakfast.

Skipping breakfast would be comparable to a small fast, as the individual might not eat for twelve to fourteen hours. This could conceivably produce hypoglycemia with resultant symptoms of weakness and possible impairment of training. Although individual preferences should be taken into account, a balanced breakfast could provide a good source of some major nutrients to the individual who is involved in a physical conditioning program. For the individual on a tight time schedule, a bowl of ready-to-eat, fortified high-fiber cereal with skim milk and fruit may be an ideal choice. Nancy Clark notes it is not only quick, easy, and convenient but also rich in carbohydrate, fiber, iron, calcium, and vitamins, and low in fat, cholesterol, and Calories.

What should I eat during competition?

There is no need to consume anything during most types of athletic competition with the possible exception of carbohydrate and water. Carbohydrate may provide additional supplies of the preferred energy source during prolonged exercise, while water intake may be critical for regulation of body temperature when exercising in warm environments. In very rare cases, such as ultradistance competition, a hypotonic salt solution may be recommended. Appropriate details are presented in Chapters 3 and 8.

What should I eat after competition or a hard training session?

In general, a balanced diet is all that is necessary to meet your nutrient needs and restore your nutritional status to normal following competition or daily, hard physical training. Carbohydrate and fat are the main nutrients used during exercise and can be replaced easily from foods among the food exchange lists. The increased caloric intake that is needed to replace your energy expenditure also will help provide you with the additional small amounts of protein, vitamins, minerals, and electrolytes that may be necessary for effective recovery. Thirst will normally help replace water losses on a day-to-day basis; you can check this by recording your body weight each morning to see if it is back to normal.

Those individuals involved in daily physical activity of a prolonged nature, such as long-distance running and swimming or prolonged tennis bouts, should stress complex carbohydrate foods in their daily diet. This will help replenish muscle glycogen, which is necessary for continued daily workouts at high intensity. Complex carbohydrates are also rich in the vitamins and minerals necessary for their metabolism in the body. As noted in Chapter 3, simple sugars eaten immediately after a hard workout may help restore muscle glycogen fairly rapidly.

For those persons who must compete several times daily and eat between competitions, such as in tennis tournaments or swim meets, the principles relative to pregame meals may be relevant.

How can I eat more nutritiously when traveling?

Athletes who must travel to compete are often faced with the problem of obtaining proper pre-event and postevent nutrition. At this point in the book, you should be aware of how to select foods that are high in carbohydrate, low in fat, and moderate in protein. Thus, one possible solution is to pack your own food and fluids in a travel bag or cooler. Foods from each of the exchange lists can be easily packed or kept on ice, such as skim milk; precooked low-fat meats; bagels and cereal; fruits, juices, and vegetables; and high-carbohydrate snacks including whole wheat crackers and pretzels and low-fat cookies such as Fig Newtons and vanilla wafers. Small containers of condiments can also be easily transported in the cooler, along with proper eating utensils. Taking your own food means you can not only eat your pre-event or postevent meal as planned but may save money as well. Such an approach may be very effective for short, one-day trips and may also be used to complement other meals on longer journeys.

Again, on the basis of your knowledge, you should also be able to select a healthful diet whether you buy your food in a convenience store, a supermarket, a fast-food restaurant, or even a gourmet restaurant. The following suggestions may be helpful if you are dining in a fast-food or budget-type restaurant, such as McDonald's, Wendy's, Arby's, Pizza Hut, or Ponderosa. Many supermarkets also have takeout departments or salad bars from which to select lunch or dinner.

Breakfast selections

English muffins, unbuttered, with jelly
English muffins with Canadian bacon
Whole wheat pancakes
French toast
Bran muffins, low-fat
Hot whole grain cereal, oatmeal
Ready-to-eat fortified, high-fiber cereal
Low-fat or skim milk
Orange juice

Lunch or dinner selections

Any low-fat sandwiches, no mayonnaise or high-fat sauces
Grilled chicken breast sandwich (whole grain)
Lean roast beef sandwich (whole grain)
Single, plain hamburger
Baked potato, with toppings on the side (add sparingly)
Pasta dishes, spaghetti, macaroni
Rice dishes
Soups, rice and noodle
All whole grain and other breads
Salads, dressing on the side
Salad bar (focus on vegetables and high-carbohydrate foods, avoid high-fat items)
Pizza, thick crust, vegetable type with minimum cheese topping
Low-fat or skim milk
Orange juice
Frozen yogurt
Sherbet

References

Books

American Heart Association, 1985. *An Eating Plan for Healthy Americans.* Dallas, TX: American Heart Association.

Bouchard, C., et al. (Eds.) 1990. *Exercise, Fitness and Health.* Champaign, IL: Human Kinetics.

National Research Council. 1989. Diet and Health: *Implications for Reducing Chronic Disease Risk.* Washington, DC: National Academy Press.

Public Health Service. United States Department of Health and Human Services. 1990. *Healthy People 2000: National Health Promotion/ Disease Prevention Objectives.* Washington, DC: U.S. Government Printing Office.

Shils, M., and Young, V. 1988. *Modern Nutrition in Health and Disease.* Philadelphia: Lea & Febiger.

Stamforc, B., and Shimer, P. 1990. *Fitness without Exercise.* New York: Warner Books.

Williams, M. 1985. *Nutritional Aspects of Human Physical and Athletic Performance.* Springfield, IL: C. C. Thomas.

Yetiv, J. 1986. *Popular Nutritional Practices: A Scientific Appraisal.* Toledo, OH: Popular Medicine Press.

Reviews

American Dietetic Association. 1988. Position of the American Dietetic Association: Vegetarian diets. *Journal of the American Dietetic Association* 88:351–55.

American Dietetic Association. 1989. Nutrition information on food labels. *Journal of the American Dietetic Association* 89:266–68.

Anderson, J. 1988. Nutrition management of diabetes mellitus. In: *Modern Nutrition in Health and Disease,* eds. M. Shils and V. Young. Philadelphia: Lea and Febiger.

Applegate, L. 1988. Fad diets and supplement use in athletes. *Sports Science Exchange* 1:1–4, December.

Beaton, G. 1988. Criteria of an adequate diet. In: *Modern Nutrition in Health and Disease,* eds. M. Shils and V. Young. Philadelphia: Lea & Febiger.

Berning, J. 1988. Wise food choices for athletes on the road. *Sports Science Exchange* 1:1–4, April.

Bierman, E., and Chait, A. 1988. Nutrition and diet in relation to hyperlipidemia and atherosclerosis. In: *Modern Nutrition in Health and Disease,* eds. M. Shils and V. Young. Philadelphia: Lea & Febiger.

Blair, S. 1988. Exercise, health and longevity. In: *Prolonged Exercise,* eds. D. Lamb and E. Murray. Indianapolis, IN: Benchmark.

Borenstein, B., and Lachance, P. 1988. Effects of processing and preparation on the nutritional value of foods. In: *Modern Nutrition in Health and Disease,* eds. M. Shils and V. Young. Philadelphia: Lea & Febiger.

Byers, T. 1988. Food, additives, and cancer. *Postgraduate Medicine* 84:275–81.

Clark, N. 1987. Breakfast of champions. *Physician and Sportsmedicine* 15 (Jan.):209–12.

Clark, N. 1985. Eating nutritiously on the road. *Physician and Sportsmedicine* 13 (Nov.):133–39.

Costill, D., et al. 1980. Energy metabolism in diabetic distance runners. *Physician and Sportsmedicine* 8:64–71.

Dwyer, J. 1988. Health aspects of vegetarian diets. *American Journal of Clinical Nutrition,* 48:712–38.

Eichner, E. 1985. Alcohol versus exercise for coronary protection. *American Journal of Medicine* 79:231–40.

———. 1987. Exercise, lymphokines, calories and cancer. *Physician and Sportsmedicine* 15 (June):109–18.

Ekoe, J. 1989. Overview of diabetes mellitus and exercise. *Medicine and Science in Sports and Exercise* 21:353–55.

Fiala, E., et al. 1985. Naturally occurring anticarcinogenic substances in foodstuffs. *Annual Review of Nutrition* 5:295–31.

Garn, S., and Leonard, W. 1989. What did our ancestors eat? *Nutrition Reviews* 47:337–44.

Goldstein, D. 1989. Clinical applications of exercise. *Physician and Sportsmedicine* 17 (Aug.):82–93.

Grandjean, A. 1987. The vegetarian athlete. *Physician and Sportsmedicine* 15 (May):191–94.

———. 1981. The pre-game meal. *The Olympian* 8:23–27.

Haskell, W. 1987. Is there an exercise RDA for health? *Western Journal of Medicine* 146:223–24.

Haymes, E. 1987. Nutritional concerns: Need for iron. *Medicine and Science in Sports and Exercise* 19:S197–S200.

Herbert, V. 1987. Health claims in food labeling and advertising. *Nutrition Today* 22:25–30.

Horton, E. 1988. Exercise and diabetes mellitus. *Medical Clinics of North America* 72:1301–21.

Hotchkiss, J. 1989. Assessment and management of food safety risks. *Contemporary Nutrition* 14:1–2.

Jacobs, C., and Dwyer, J. 1988. Vegetarian children: Appropriate and inappropriate diets. *American Journal of Clinical Nutrition* 48:811–18.

Jacobson, M. (Ed.). 1988. Reducing the risk of breast cancer. *Nutrition Action Health Letter* 15 (Mar.):4–6.

Kendler, B. 1984. Vegetarianism: Nutritional aspects and implications for health professionals. *Journal of Holistic Medicine* 6:161–70.

Kessler, D. 1989. The federal regulation of food labeling. *New England Journal of Medicine* 321:717–23.

Larson, D., and Fisher, R. 1987. Management of exercise-induced gastrointestinal problems. *Physician and Sportsmedicine* 15:112–26.

Love, R. 1988. Dietary fat and human breast cancer: Epidemiological evidence. *Food & Nutrition News* 60:13–15.

Mutch, P. 1988. Food guides for the vegetarian. *American Journal of Clinical Nutrition* 48:913–19.

Nieman, D. 1988. Vegetarian dietary principles and endurance performance. *American Journal of Clinical Nutrition* 48:754–61.

Rippe, J. 1987. The health benefits of exercise (Part 1 of 2). *Physician and Sportsmedicine,* 15 (Oct.):115–32.

———. 1987. The health benefits of exercise (Part 2 of 2). *Physician and Sportsmedicine* 15 (Nov.):121–31.

Olson, R. 1986. Eleventh Marabou Symposium: The nutritional reemergence of starchy foods. *Nutrition Reviews* 44:33–91.

Senti, F. 1988. Food additives and contaminants. In: *Modern Nutrition in Health and Disease,* eds. M. Shils and V. Young. Philadelphia: Lea & Febiger.

Sherman, W. M. 1989. Pre-event nutrition. *Sports Science Exchange* 1 (Feb.):1–4.

Sherman, W. M., and Wright, D. 1989. Preevent nutrition for prolonged performance. In: *Report of the Ross Symposium on the theory and principles of Athletic Nutrition: Bridging the Gap,* eds. J. Storlie and A. Grandjean. Columbus, OH: Ross Laboratories.

Smith, M. 1988. Development of a quick reference guide to accommodate vegetarianism in diet therapy for multiple disease conditions. *American Journal of Clinical Nutrition* 48:806–9.

Tran, Z., et al. 1983. The effects of exercise on blood lipids and lipoproteins: A meta-analysis of studies. *Medicine and Science in Sports and Exercise* 15:393–402.

Wood, P., and Stefanik, M. 1990. Exercise, fitness and atherosclerosis. In: *Exercise, Fitness and Health,* eds. C. Bouchard et al. Champaign, IL: Human Kinetics.

Specific Studies

Alberici, J., et al. 1989. Effects of preexercise candy bar ingestion on substrate utilization and performance in trained subjects. *Medicine and Science in Sports and Exercise* 21:S47.

Dougherty, R., et al. 1988. Nutrient content of the diet when the fat is reduced. *American Journal of Clinical Nutrition,* 48:970–79.

Frisch, R., et al. 1985. Lower prevalence of breast cancer and cancers of the reproductive system among former college athletes compared to non-athletes. *British Journal of Cancer* 52:885–91.

Grundy, S. 1986. Comparison of monounsaturated fatty acids and carbohydrates for lowering plasma cholesterol. *New England Journal of Medicine* 314:745–48.

Hanne, N., et al. 1986. Physical fitness, anthropometric and metabolic parameters in vegetarian athletes. *Journal of Sports Medicine* 26:180–85.

Haskell, W., et al. 1984. The effects of cessation and resumption of moderate alcohol intake on serum high-density-lipoprotein subfractions. *New England Journal of Medicine* 310:805–10.

Jennings, G., et al. 1986. The effects of changes in physical activity on major cardiovascular risk factors, hemodynamics, sympathetic function, and glucose utilization in man: A controlled study of four levels of activity. *Circulation* 73:30–40.

Levine, A., et al. 1989. Effect of breakfast cereals on short-term food intake. *American Journal of Clinical Nutrition* 50:1303–07.

Lindhal, O., et al. 1984. A vegan regimen with reduced medication in the treatment of hypertension. *British Journal of Nutrition* 52:11–20.

Lombard, K., et al. 1989. Carnitine status of lactoovovegetarians and strict vegetarian adults and children. *American Journal of Clinical Nutrition* 50:301–306.

Willit, W., et al. 1987. Dietary fats and the risk of breast cancer. *New England Journal of Medicine* 316:22–28.

Appendixes

Appendix A

1989 Recommended Dietary Allowances

Food and Nutrition Board, National Academy of Sciences—National Research Council Recommended Daily Dietary Allowance,[a] Revised 1989.

Designed for the maintenance of good nutrition of practically all healthy people in the United States.

Category	Age (years) or Condition	Weight[b] (kg)	Weight[b] (lb)	Height[b] (cm)	Height[b] (in)	Protein (g)	Fat-soluble vitamins Vitamin A (μg RE)[c]	Vitamin D (μg)[d]	Vitamin E (mg α-TE)[e]	Vitamin K (μg)
Infants	0.0–0.5	6	13	60	24	13	375	7.5	3	5
	0.5–1.0	9	20	71	28	14	375	10	4	10
Children	1–3	13	29	90	35	16	400	10	6	15
	4–6	20	44	112	44	24	500	10	7	20
	7–10	28	62	132	52	28	700	10	7	30
Males	11–14	45	99	157	62	45	1,000	10	10	45
	15–18	66	145	176	69	59	1,000	10	10	65
	19–24	72	160	177	70	58	1,000	10	10	70
	25–50	79	174	176	70	63	1,000	5	10	80
	51+	77	170	173	68	63	1,000	5	10	80
Females	11–14	46	101	157	62	46	800	10	8	45
	15–18	55	120	163	64	44	800	10	8	55
	19–24	58	128	164	65	46	800	10	8	60
	25–50	63	138	163	64	50	800	5	8	65
	51+	65	143	160	63	50	800	5	8	65
Pregnant						60	800	10	10	65
Lactating	1st 6 months					65	1,300	10	12	65
	2nd 6 months					62	1,200	10	11	65

[a]The allowances, expressed as average daily intakes over time, are intended to provide for individual variations among most normal persons as they live in the United States under usual environmental stresses. Diets should be based on a variety of common foods in order to provide other nutrients for which human requirements have been less well defined.

[b]Weights and heights of Reference Adults are actual medians for the U.S. population of the designated age, as reported by NHANES II. The median weights and heights of those under 19 years of age were taken from Hamill et al. (1979). The use of these figures does not imply that the height-to-weight ratios are ideal.

Note: μg = microgram.

Water-soluble vitamins　　　　　Minerals

Vitamin C (mg)	Thiamin (mg)	Riboflavin (mg)	Niacin (mg NE)[f]	Vitamin B$_6$ (mg)	Folate (µg)	Vitamin B$_{12}$ (µg)	Calcium (mg)	Phosphorus (mg)	Magnesium (mg)	Iron (mg)	Zinc (mg)	Iodine (µg)	Selenium (µg)
30	0.3	0.4	5	0.3	25	0.3	400	300	40	6	5	40	10
35	0.4	0.5	6	0.6	35	0.5	600	500	60	10	5	50	15
40	0.7	0.8	9	1.0	50	0.7	800	800	80	10	10	70	20
45	0.9	1.1	12	1.1	75	1.0	800	800	120	10	10	90	20
45	1.0	1.2	13	1.4	100	1.4	800	800	170	10	10	120	30
50	1.3	1.5	17	1.7	150	2.0	1 200	1,200	270	12	15	150	40
60	1.5	1.8	20	2.0	200	2.0	1 200	1,200	400	12	15	150	50
60	1.5	1.7	19	2.0	200	2.0	1 200	1,200	350	10	15	150	70
60	1.5	1.7	19	2.0	200	2.0	800	800	350	10	15	150	70
60	1.2	1.4	15	2.0	200	2.0	800	800	350	10	15	150	70
50	1.1	1.3	15	1.4	150	2.0	1,200	1,200	280	15	12	150	45
60	1.1	1.3	15	1.5	180	2.0	1,200	1,200	300	15	12	150	50
60	1.1	1.3	15	1.6	180	2.0	1,200	1,200	280	15	12	150	55
60	1.1	1.3	15	1.6	180	2.0	800	800	280	15	12	150	55
60	1.0	1.2	13	1.6	180	2.0	800	800	280	10	12	150	55
70	1.5	1.6	17	2.2	400	2.2	1,200	1,200	320	30	15	175	65
95	1.6	1.8	20	2.1	280	2.6	1,200	1.200	355	15	19	200	75
90	1.6	1.7	20	2.1	260	2.6	1,200	1 200	340	15	16	200	75

[c]Retinol equivalents. 1 retinol equivalent = 1 µg retinol or 6 µg β-carotene.
[d]As cholecalciferol. 10 µg cholecalciferol = 400 IU of vitamin D.
[e]α-Tocopherol equivalents. 1 mg d-α tocopherol = 1 α-TE.
[f]1 NE (niacin equivalent) is equal to 1 mg of niacin or 60 mg of dietary tryptophan.

Summary Table   **Estimated Safe and Adequate Daily Dietary Intakes of Selected Vitamins and Minerals**[a]

Category	Age (years)	Vitamins	
		Biotin (μg)	Pantothenic Acid (mg)
Infants	0–0.5	10	2
	0.5–1	15	3
Children and adolescents	1–3	20	3
	4–6	25	3–4
	7–10	30	4–5
	11 +	30–100	4–7
Adults		30–100	4–7

Trace Elements[b]

Category	Age (years)	Copper (mg)	Manganese (mg)	Fluoride (mg)	Chromium (μg)	Molybdenum (μg)
Infants	0–0.5	0.4–0.6	0.3–0.6	0.1–0.5	10–40	15–30
	0.5–1	0.6–0.7	0.6–1.0	0.2–1.0	20–60	20–40
Children and adolescents	1–3	0.7–1.0	1.0–1.5	0.5–1.5	20–80	25–50
	4–6	1.0–1.5	1.5–2.0	1.0–2.5	30–120	30–75
	7–10	1.0–2.0	2.0–3.0	1.5–2.5	50–200	50–150
	11 +	1.5–2.5	2.0–5.0	1.5–2.5	50–200	75–250
Adults		1.5–3.0	2.0–5.0	1.5–4.0	50–200	75–250

[a]Because there is less information on which to base allowances, these figures are not given in the main table of RDA and are provided here in the form of ranges of recommended intakes.

[b]Since the toxic levels for many trace elements may be only several times usual intakes, the upper levels for the trace elements given in this table should not be habitually exceeded.

Median Heights and Weights and Recommended Energy Intake

Category	Age (years) or Condition	Weight (kg)	Weight (lb)	Height (cm)	Height (in)	REE[a] (kcal/day)	Average Energy Allowance (kcal)[b] Multiples of REE	Average Energy Allowance (kcal)[b] Per kg	Average Energy Allowance (kcal)[b] Per day[c]
Infants	0.0–0.5	6	13	60	24	320		108	650
	0.5–1.0	9	20	71	28	500		98	850
Children	1–3	13	29	90	35	740		102	1,300
	4–6	20	44	112	44	950		90	1,800
	7–10	28	62	132	52	1,130		70	2,000
Males	11–14	45	99	157	62	1,440	1.70	55	2,500
	15–18	66	145	176	69	1,760	1.67	45	3,000
	19–24	72	160	177	70	1,780	1.67	40	2,900
	25–50	79	174	176	70	1,800	1.60	37	2,900
	51 +	77	170	173	68	1,530	1.50	30	2,300
Females	11–14	46	101	157	62	1,310	1.67	47	2,200
	15–18	55	120	163	64	1,370	1.60	40	2,200
	19–24	58	128	164	65	1,350	1.60	38	2,200
	25–50	63	138	163	64	1,380	1.55	36	2,200
	51 +	65	143	160	63	1,280	1.50	30	1,900
Pregnant	1st trimester								+ 0
	2nd trimester								+ 300
	3rd trimester								+ 300
Lactating	1st 6 months								+ 500
	2nd 6 months								+ 500

Author Notes

[a]REE is resting energy expenditure; see Chapter 2 for explanation. Calculation is based on Food and Agriculture Organization equations, then rounded.

[b]In the range of light to moderate activity, the coefficient of variation is ± 20%. Thus, for an individual with an average energy allowance of 2,500 Calories per day, the typical range might be 2,000–3,000, which is plus or minus 500 Calories (.20 × 2,500). See Chapter 2 for expanded discussion of energy requirement based upon physical activity levels.

[c]Figure is rounded.

Source: National Research Council. 1989. Recommended Dietary Allowances. 10th Edition. Washington, DC: National Academy Press.

Appendix B

Units of Measurement: English System— Metric System Equivalents

The Metric System and Equivalents

To measure ingredients, a standardized system known as the System Internationale (SI) has been established that is interpreted on an international basis. The SI is based on the metric system. However, in the United States we also employ another set of measure and weight. In the field of dietetics, both systems are employed. The following tables give the quantities of the measures besides stating equivalents. With this information it is possible to calculate in either system of measure and weight.

Household Measures (Approximations)

For easy computing purposes, the cubic centimeter (cc) is considered equivalent to 1 gram:

1 cc = 1 gram = 1 milliliter (ml)

For easy computing purposes, one ounce equals 30 grams or 30 cubic centimeters.

1 quart	=	960 grams
1 pint	=	480 grams
1 cup	=	240 grams
1/2 cup	=	120 grams
1 glass (8 ounces)	=	240 grams
1/2 glass (4 ounces)	=	120 grams
1 orange juice glass	=	100 to 120 grams
1 tablespoon	=	15 grams
1 teaspoon	=	5 grams

Level Measures and Weights

1 teaspoon	=	5 cc or 5 ml 5 grams
3 teaspoons	=	1 tablespoon 15 cc 15 grams
2 tablespoons	=	30 cc 30 grams 1 ounce (fluid)
4 tablespoons	=	1/4 cup 60 cc 60 grams
8 tablespoons	=	1/2 cup 120 cc 120 grams
16 tablespoons	=	1 cup 240 grams 240 ml (fluid) 8 ounces (fluid) 1/2 pound
2 cups	=	1 pint 480 grams 480 ml (fluid) 16 ounces (fluid) 1 pound
4 cups	=	2 pints 1 quart 960 cc 960 ml (fluid) 2 pounds
4 quarts	=	1 gallon

Units of Weight

		Ounce	Pound	Gram	Kilogram
1 ounce	=	1.0	0.06	28.4	0.028
1 pound	=	16.0	1.0	454	0.454
1 gram	=	0.035	.002	1.0	0.001
1 kilogram	=	35.3	2.2	1,000	1.0

Units of Volume

	Ounce	Pint	Quart	Milliliter	Liter
1 ounce	1.0	0.062	0.031	29.57	0.029
1 pint	16.0	1.0	0.5	473	.473
1 quart	32.0	2.0	1.0	946	.946
1 milliliter	0.034	0.002	0.001	1.0	0.001
1 liter	33.8	2.112	1.056	1,000	1.0

Units of Length

	Millimeter	Centimeter	Inch	Foot	Yard	Meter
1 millimeter	1.0	0.1	0.0394	0.0033	0.0011	0.001
1 centimeter	10.0	1.0	0.394	0.033	0.011	0.01
1 inch	25.4	2.54	1.0	0.083	0.028	0.025
1 foot	304.8	30.48	12.0	1.0	0.333	0.305
1 yard	914.4	91.44	36.0	3.0	1.0	0.914
1 meter	1,000	100	39.37	3.28	1.094	1.0

Units of Mechanical, Thermal, and Chemical Energy (Approximate Equivalents)

	Foot-pounds	Kilogram-meters	Kilojoules	Watts*	Kilocalories	Oxygen**
1 foot-pound	1	0.138	0.00136	0.0226	0.00032	0.000064
1 kilogram-meter	7.23	1	0.0098	0.163	0.0023	0.00046
1 kilojoule	737	102	1	16.66	0.239	0.047
1 watt*	44.27	6.12	0.06	1	0.0143	0.0028
1 kilocalorie	3,088	427	4.18	0.00024	1	0.198
1 liter oxygen**	15,585	2,154	21.1	351.9	5.047	1

*Watts are units of power expressed per minute.

**Equivalents are based upon one liter of oxygen metabolizing carbohydrate. Energy equivalents would be slightly less on a mixed diet of carbohydrate, fat, and protein. For example, one liter of oxygen would equal only 4.82 kilocalories.

Note: Read all tables across, such as 1 watt equals 44.27 pounds; one foot-pound equals 0.0226 watt.

Appendix C

Approximate Caloric Expenditure Per Minute for Various Physical Activities*

Body weight												
Kilograms	45	48	50	52	55	57	59	61	64	66	68	70
Pounds	100	105	110	115	120	125	130	135	140	145	150	155
Sedentary activities												
Lying quietly	.99	1.0	1.1	1.1	1.2	1.3	1.3	1.4	1.4	1.5	1.5	1.5
Sitting and writing, card playing, etc.	1.2	1.3	1.4	1.5	1.5	1.6	1.7	1.7	1.8	1.8	1.9	2.0
Standing with light work, cleaning, etc.	2.7	2.9	3.0	3.1	3.3	3.4	3.5	3.7	3.8	3.9	4.1	4.2
Physical activities												
Archery	3.1	3.3	3.5	3.6	3.8	4.0	4.1	4.3	4.5	4.6	4.8	4.9
Badminton												
Recreational singles	3.6	3.8	4.0	4.2	4.4	4.6	4.7	4.9	5.1	5.3	5.4	5.6
Social doubles	2.7	2.9	3.0	3.1	3.3	3.4	3.5	3.7	3.8	3.9	4.1	4.2
Competitive	5.9	6.1	6.4	6.7	7.0	7.3	7.6	7.9	8.2	8.5	8.8	9.1
Baseball												
Player	3.1	3.3	3.4	3.6	3.8	4.0	4.1	4.3	4.4	4.5	4.7	4.8
Pitcher	3.9	4.1	4.3	4.5	4.7	4.9	5.1	5.3	5.5	5.7	5.9	6.0
Basketball												
Half court	3.0	3.1	3.3	3.5	3.6	3.8	3.9	4.1	4.2	4.4	4.5	4.7
Recreational	4.9	5.2	5.5	5.7	6.0	6.2	6.5	6.7	7.0	7.2	7.5	7.7
Vigorous competition	6.5	6.8	7.2	7.5	7.8	8.2	8.5	8.8	9.2	9.5	9.9	10.2
Bicycling, level												
(mph) (min/mile)												
5 12:00	1.9	2.0	2.1	2.2	2.3	2.4	2.5	2.6	2.7	2.8	2.9	3.0
10 6:00	4.2	4.4	4.6	4.8	5.1	5.3	5.5	5.7	5.9	6.1	6.4	6.6
15 4:00	7.3	7.6	8.0	8.4	8.7	9.1	9.5	9.8	10.0	10.5	10.9	11.3
20 3:00	10.7	11.2	11.7	12.3	12.8	13.3	13.9	14.4	14.9	15.5	16.0	16.5
Bowling	2.7	2.8	3.0	3.1	3.3	3.4	3.5	3.7	3.8	3.9	4.1	4.2
Calisthenics												
Light type	3.4	3.6	3.8	4.0	4.1	4.3	4.5	4.7	4.8	5.0	5.2	5.4
Timed vigorous	9.7	10.1	10.6	11.1	11.6	12.1	12.6	13.1	13.6	14.1	14.6	15.1
Canoeing												
(mph) (min/mile)												
2.5 24	1.9	2.0	2.1	2.2	2.3	2.4	2.5	2.6	2.7	2.8	2.9	3.0
4.0 15	4.4	4.6	4.9	5.1	5.3	5.5	5.8	6.0	6.2	6.4	6.7	6.9
5.0 12	5.7	6.0	6.3	6.6	6.9	7.2	7.5	7.8	8.1	8.4	8.7	9.0
Dancing												
Moderately (waltz)	3.1	3.3	3.5	3.6	3.8	4.0	4.1	4.3	4.5	4.6	4.8	4.9
Active (square, disco)	4.5	4.7	5.0	5.2	5.4	5.6	5.9	6.1	6.3	6.6	6.8	7.0
Aerobic (vigorously)	6.0	6.3	6.7	7.0	7.3	7.6	7.9	8.2	8.5	8.8	9.1	9.4

*Note: The energy cost, in Calories, will vary for different physical activities in a given individual depending on several factors. For example, the caloric cost of bicycling will vary depending on the type of bicycle, going uphill or downhill, and wind resistance. Walking with hand weights or ankle weights will increase energy output. Thus, the values expressed here are approximations and may be increased or decreased depending upon factors that influence energy cost.

73	75	77	80	82	84	86	89	91	93	95	98	100
160	165	170	175	180	185	190	195	200	205	210	215	220

73	75	77	80	82	84	86	89	91	93	95	98	100
1.6	1.6	1.7	1.7	1.8	1.8	1.9	1.9	2.0	2.0	2.1	2.1	2.2
2.0	2.1	2.2	2.2	2.3	2.4	2.4	2.5	2.5	2.6	2.7	2.7	2.8
4.4	4.5	4.6	4.8	4.9	5.0	5.2	5.3	5.4	5.6	5.7	5.9	6.0
5.1	5.3	5.4	5.6	5.7	5.9	6.0	6.2	6.4	6.5	6.7	6.9	7.0
5.8	6.0	6.2	6.4	6.6	6.7	6.9	7.1	7.3	7.4	7.6	7.8	8.0
4.4	4.5	4.6	4.8	4.9	5.0	5.2	5.3	5.4	5.6	5.7	5.9	6.0
9.4	9.7	10.0	10.3	10.6	10.9	11.2	11.5	11.8	12.1	12.4	12.7	13.0
5.0	5.2	5.3	5.5	5.6	5.8	5.9	6.1	6.3	6.4	6.6	6.8	6.9
6.3	6.5	6.7	6.9	7.1	7.3	7.4	7.7	7.9	8.0	8.2	8.5	8.6
4.8	5.0	5.1	5.3	5.4	5.6	5.7	5.9	6 0	6.2	6.4	6.5	6.7
8.0	8.2	8.5	8.7	9.0	9.2	9.5	9.7	10 0	10.2	10.5	10.7	11.0
10.5	10.9	11.2	11.5	11.9	12.2	12.5	12.9	13.2	13.5	13.8	14.2	14.5
3.1	3.2	3.3	3.4	3.5	3.6	3.7	3.8	3.9	4.0	4.1	4.2	4.3
6.8	7.0	7.2	7.4	7.6	7.9	8.1	8.3	8.5	8.7	8.9	9.1	9.4
11.6	12.0	12.4	12.7	13.1	13.4	13.8	14.2	14.5	14.9	15.3	15.6	16.0
17.1	17.6	18.1	18.7	19.2	19.7	20.3	20.8	21.3	21.9	22.4	22.9	23.5
4.4	4.5	4.6	4.8	4.9	5.0	5.2	5.3	5.5	5.6	5.7	5.9	6.0
5.5	5.7	5.9	6.1	6.3	6.4	6.6	6.8	7.0	7.1	7.3	7.5	7.7
15.6	16.1	16.6	17.1	17.6	18.1	18.6	19.1	19.6	20.0	20.5	21.0	21.5
3.1	3.2	3.3	3.4	3.5	3.6	3.7	3.8	3.9	4.0	4.1	4.2	4.3
7.1	7.4	7.6	7.8	8.0	8.2	8.5	8.7	8.9	9.1	9.4	9.6	9.8
9.3	9.5	9.8	10.1	10.4	10.7	11.0	11.3	11.6	11.9	12.2	12.5	12.8
5.1	5.3	5.4	5.6	5.7	5.9	6.0	6.2	6.4	6.5	6.7	6.9	7.0
7.3	7.5	7.7	7.9	8.2	8.4	8.6	8.9	9.1	9.3	9.5	9.8	10.0
9.7	10.0	10.3	10.6	10.9	11.2	11.5	11.8	12.1	12.4	12.7	13.0	13.3

Body weight												
Kilograms	45	48	50	52	55	57	59	61	64	66	68	70
Pounds	100	105	110	115	120	125	130	135	140	145	150	155

Fencing												
Moderately	3.3	3.5	3.6	3.8	4.0	4.1	4.3	4.5	4.6	4.8	5.0	5.2
Vigorously	6.6	7.0	7.3	7.7	8.0	8.3	8.7	9.0	9.4	9.7	10.0	10.4
Football												
Moderate	3.3	3.5	3.6	3.8	4.0	4.1	4.3	4.5	4.6	4.8	5.0	5.2
Touch, vigorous	5.5	5.8	6.1	6.4	6.6	6.9	7.2	7.5	7.8	8.0	8.3	8.6
Golf												
Twosome (carry clubs)	3.6	3.8	4.0	4.2	4.4	4.6	4.7	4.9	5.1	5.3	5.4	5.6
Foursome (carry clubs)	2.7	2.9	3.0	3.1	3.3	3.4	3.5	3.7	3.8	3.9	4.1	4.2
Power-cart	1.9	2.0	2.1	2.2	2.3	2.4	2.5	2.6	2.7	2.8	2.9	3.0
Handball												
Moderate	6.5	6.8	7.2	7.5	7.8	8.2	8.5	8.8	9.2	9.5	9.9	10.2
Competitive	7.7	8.0	8.4	8.8	9.2	9.6	10.0	10.4	10.8	11.1	11.5	11.9
Hiking, pack (3 mph)	4.5	4.7	5.0	5.2	5.4	5.6	5.9	6.1	6.3	6.6	6.8	7.0
Hockey, field	5.0	6.3	6.7	7.0	7.3	7.6	7.9	8.2	8.5	8.8	9.1	9.4
Hockey, ice	6.6	7.0	7.3	7.7	8.0	8.3	8.7	9.0	9.4	9.7	10.0	10.4
Horseback riding												
Walk	1.9	2.0	2.1	2.2	2.3	2.4	2.5	2.6	2.7	2.8	2.9	3.0
Sitting to trot	2.7	2.9	3.0	3.1	3.3	3.4	3.5	3.7	3.8	3.9	4.1	4.2
Posting to trot	4.2	4.4	4.6	4.8	5.1	5.3	5.5	5.7	5.9	6.1	6.4	6.6
Gallop	5.7	6.0	6.3	6.6	6.9	7.2	7.5	7.8	8.1	8.4	8.7	9.0
Horseshoes	2.5	2.6	2.8	2.9	3.0	3.1	3.3	3.4	3.5	3.7	3.8	3.9
Jogging (see Running)												
Judo	8.5	8.9	9.3	9.8	10.2	10.6	11.0	11.5	11.9	12.3	12.8	13.2
Karate	8.5	8.9	9.3	9.8	10.2	10.6	11.0	11.5	11.9	12.3	12.8	13.2
Mountain climbing	6.5	6.8	7.2	7.5	7.8	8.2	8.5	8.8	9.2	9.5	9.8	10.2
Paddle ball	5.7	6.0	6.3	6.6	6.9	7.2	7.5	7.8	8.1	8.4	8.7	9.0
Pool (billiards)	1.5	1.6	1.6	1.7	1.8	1.9	1.9	2.0	2.1	2.2	2.2	2.3
Racketball	6.5	6.8	7.1	7.5	7.8	8.1	8.4	8.8	9.1	9.4	9.8	10.1
Roller skating (9 mph)	4.2	4.4	4.6	4.8	5.1	5.3	5.5	5.7	5.9	6.1	6.4	6.6
Running (steady state)												
(mph) (min/mile)												
5.0 12:00	6.0	6.3	6.6	7.0	7.3	7.6	7.9	8.2	8.5	8.8	9.1	9.4
5.5 10:55	6.7	7.0	7.3	7.7	8.0	8.4	8.7	9.0	9.4	9.7	10.0	10.4
6.0 10:00	7.2	7.6	8.0	8.4	8.7	9.1	9.5	9.8	10.2	10.6	10.9	11.3
7.0 8:35	8.5	8.9	9.3	9.8	10.2	10.6	11.0	11.5	11.9	12.3	12.8	13.2
8.0 7:30	9.7	10.2	10.7	11.2	11.6	12.1	12.6	13.1	13.6	14.1	14.6	15.1
9.0 6:40	10.8	11.3	11.9	12.4	12.9	13.5	14.0	14.6	15.1	15.7	16.2	16.8
10.0 6:00	12.1	12.7	13.3	13.9	14.5	15.1	15.7	16.4	17.0	17.6	18.2	18.8
11.0 5:28	13.3	14.0	14.6	15.3	16.0	16.7	17.3	18.0	18.7	19.4	20.0	20.7
12.0 5:00	14.5	15.2	16.0	16.7	17.4	18.2	18.9	19.7	20.4	21.1	21.9	22.6
Sailing, small boat	2.7	2.9	3.0	3.1	3.3	3.4	3.5	3.7	3.8	3.9	4.1	4.2
Skating, ice (9 mph)	4.2	4.4	4.6	4.8	5.1	5.2	5.5	5.7	5.9	6.1	6.4	6.6
Skiing, cross country												
(mph) (min/mile)												
2.5 24:00	5.0	5.2	5.5	5.7	6.0	6.2	6.5	6.7	7.0	7.2	7.5	7.8
4.0 15:00	6.5	6.8	7.2	7.5	7.8	8.2	8.5	8.8	9.2	9.5	9.9	10.2
5.0 12:00	7.7	8.0	8.4	8.8	9.2	9.6	10.0	10.4	10.8	11.1	11.5	11.9
Skiing, downhill	6.5	6.8	7.2	7.5	7.8	8.2	8.5	8.8	9.2	9.5	9.9	10.2
Soccer	5.9	6.2	6.6	6.9	7.2	7.5	7.8	8.1	8.4	8.7	9.0	9.3

73	75	77	80	82	84	86	89	91	93	95	98	100
160	165	170	175	180	185	190	195	200	205	210	215	220
5.3	5.5	5.7	5.8	6.0	6.2	6.3	6.5	6.7	6.8	7.0	7.1	7.3
10.7	11.0	11.4	11.7	12.1	12.4	12.7	13.1	13.4	13.8	14.1	14.4	14.8
5.3	5.5	5.7	5.8	6.0	6.2	6.3	6.5	6.7	6.8	7.0	7.1	7.3
8.9	9.2	9.4	9.7	10.0	10.3	10.6	10.8	11.1	11.4	11.7	12.0	12.2
5.8	6.0	6.2	6.4	6.6	6.7	6.9	7.1	7.3	7.4	7.6	7.8	8.0
4.4	4.5	4.6	4.8	4.9	5.0	5.2	5.3	5.4	5.6	5.7	5.9	6.0
3.1	3.2	3.3	3.4	3.5	3.6	3.7	3.8	3.9	4.0	4.1	4.2	4.3
10.5	10.9	11.2	11.5	11.9	12.2	12.5	12.9	13.2	13.5	13.8	14.2	14.5
12.3	12.7	13.1	13.5	13.9	14.3	14.7	15.0	15.4	15.8	16.2	16.6	17.0
7.3	7.5	7.7	7.9	8.2	8.4	8.6	8.9	9.1	9.3	9.5	9.8	10.0
9.7	10.0	10.3	10.6	10.9	11.2	11.5	11.8	12.1	12.4	12.7	13.0	13.3
10.7	11.0	11.4	11.7	12.1	12.4	12.7	13.1	13.4	13.8	14.1	14.4	14.8
3.1	3.2	3.3	3.4	3.5	3.6	3.7	3.8	3.9	4.0	4.1	4.2	4.3
4.4	4.5	4.6	4.8	4.9	5.0	5.2	5.3	5.4	5.6	5.7	5.9	6.0
6.8	7.0	7.2	7.4	7.6	7.9	8.1	8.3	8.5	8.7	8.9	9.1	9.4
9.3	9.5	9.8	10.1	10.4	10.7	11.0	11.3	11.6	11.9	12.2	12.5	12.8
4.0	4.2	4.3	4.4	4.5	4.7	4.8	4.9	5.2	5.2	5.3	5.4	5.6
13.6	14.1	14.5	14.9	15.4	15.8	16.2	16.6	17.1	17.5	17.9	18.4	18.8
13.6	14.1	14.5	14.9	15.4	15.8	16.2	16.6	17.1	17.5	17.9	18.4	18.8
10.5	10.8	11.2	11.5	11.8	12.1	12.5	12.8	13.1	13.5	13.8	14.1	14.5
9.3	9.5	9.8	10.1	10.4	10.7	11.0	11.2	11.6	11.9	12.2	12.5	12.8
2.4	2.5	2.6	2.6	2.7	2.8	2.9	2.9	3.0	3.1	3.2	3.2	3.3
10.4	10.7	11.1	11.4	11.7	12.0	12.4	12.7	13.0	13.4	13.7	14.0	14.4
6.8	7.0	7.2	7.4	7.6	7.9	8.1	8.3	8.5	8.7	8.9	9.1	9.4
9.7	10.0	10.3	10.6	10.9	11.2	11.6	11.9	12.2	12.5	12.8	13.1	13.4
10.7	11.1	11.4	11.7	12.1	12.4	12.8	13.1	13.4	13.8	14.1	14.5	14.8
11.7	12.0	12.4	12.8	13.1	13.5	13.8	14.3	14.6	15.0	15.4	15.7	16.1
13.6	14.1	14.5	14.9	15.4	15.8	16.2	16.6	17.1	17.5	17.9	18.4	18.8
15.6	16.1	16.6	17.1	17.6	18.1	18.5	19.0	19.5	20.0	20.5	21.0	21.5
17.3	17.9	18.4	19.0	19.5	20.1	20.6	21.2	21.7	22.2	22.8	23.3	23.9
19.4	20.0	20.7	21.3	21.9	22.5	23.1	23.7	24.2	24.8	25.4	26.0	26.7
21.4	22.1	22.7	23.4	24.1	24.8	25.4	26.1	26.8	27.5	28.1	28.8	29.5
23.3	24.1	24.8	25.6	26.3	27.0	27.8	28.5	29.2	30.0	30.7	31.5	32.2
4.4	4.5	4.6	4.8	4.9	5.0	5.2	5.3	5.4	5.6	5.7	5.9	6.0
6.8	7.0	7.2	7.4	7.6	7.9	8.1	8.3	8.5	8.7	8.9	9.1	9.4
8.0	8.3	8.5	8.8	9.0	9.3	9.5	9.8	10.0	10.3	10.6	10.8	11.1
10.5	10.9	11.2	11.5	11.9	12.2	12.5	12.9	13.2	13.5	13.8	14.2	14.5
12.3	12.7	13.1	13.5	13.9	14.3	14.7	15.0	15.4	15.8	16.2	16.6	17.0
10.5	10.9	11.2	11.5	11.9	12.2	12.5	12.9	13.2	13.5	13.8	14.2	14.5
9.6	9.9	10.2	10.5	10.8	11.1	11.4	11.7	12.0	12.3	12.6	12.9	13.2

Body weight												
Kilograms	45	48	50	52	55	57	59	61	64	66	68	70
Pounds	100	105	110	115	120	125	130	135	140	145	150	155

Squash												
Normal	6.7	7.0	7.3	7.7	8.0	8.4	8.7	9.1	9.5	9.8	10.1	10.5
Competition	7.7	8.0	8.4	8.8	9.2	9.6	10.0	10.4	10.8	11.1	11.5	11.9
Swimming (yards/min)												
Backstroke												
25	2.5	2.6	2.8	2.9	3.0	3.1	3.3	3.4	3.5	3.7	3.8	3.9
30	3.5	3.7	3.9	4.1	4.2	4.4	4.6	4.8	4.9	5.1	5.3	5.5
35	4.5	4.7	5.0	5.2	5.4	5.6	5.9	6.1	6.3	6.6	6.8	7.0
40	5.5	5.8	6.1	6.4	6.6	6.9	7.2	7.5	7.8	8.0	8.3	8.6
Breaststroke												
20	3.1	3.3	3.5	3.6	3.8	4.0	4.1	4.3	4.5	4.6	4.8	4.9
30	4.7	5.0	5.2	5.4	5.7	5.9	6.2	6.4	6.7	6.9	7.1	7.4
40	6.3	6.7	7.0	7.3	7.6	8.0	8.3	8.6	8.9	9.3	9.6	9.9
Front crawl												
20	3.1	3.3	3.5	3.6	3.8	4.0	4.1	4.3	4.5	4.6	4.8	4.9
25	4.0	4.2	4.4	4.6	4.8	5.0	5.2	5.4	5.6	5.8	6.0	6.2
35	4.8	5.1	5.4	5.6	5.9	6.1	6.4	6.6	6.8	7.0	7.3	7.5
45	5.7	6.0	6.3	6.6	6.9	7.2	7.5	7.8	8.1	8.4	8.7	9.0
50	7.0	7.4	7.7	8.1	8.5	8.8	9.2	9.5	9.9	10.3	10.6	11.0
Table tennis	3.4	3.6	3.8	4.0	4.1	4.3	4.5	4.7	4.8	5.0	5.2	5.4
Tennis												
Singles, recreational	5.0	5.2	5.5	5.7	6.0	6.2	6.5	6.7	7.0	7.2	7.5	7.8
Doubles, recreational	3.4	3.6	3.8	4.0	4.1	4.3	4.5	4.7	4.8	5.0	5.2	5.4
Competition	6.4	6.7	7.1	7.4	7.7	8.1	8.4	8.7	9.1	9.4	9.8	10.1
Volleyball												
Moderate, recreational	2.9	3.0	3.2	3.3	3.5	3.6	3.8	3.9	4.1	4.2	4.4	4.5
Vigorous, competition	6.5	6.8	7.1	7.5	7.8	8.1	8.4	8.8	9.1	9.4	9.8	10.1

Walking													
(mph)	(min/mile)												
1.0	60:00	1.5	1.6	1.7	1.8	1.8	1.9	2.0	2.1	2.2	2.2	2.3	2.4
2.0	30:00	2.1	2.2	2.3	2.4	2.5	2.6	2.8	2.9	3.0	3.1	3.2	3.3
2.3	26:00	2.3	2.4	2.5	2.7	2.8	2.9	3.0	3.1	3.2	3.4	3.5	3.6
3.0	20.00	2.7	2.9	3.0	3.1	3.3	3.4	3.5	3.7	3.8	3.9	4.1	4.2
3.2	18:45	3.1	3.3	3.4	3.6	3.8	4.0	4.1	4.3	4.4	4.5	4.7	4.8
3.5	17:10	3.3	3.5	3.7	3.9	4.0	4.2	4.4	4.6	4.7	4.9	5.1	5.3
4.0	15:00	4.2	4.4	4.6	4.8	5.1	5.3	5.5	5.7	5.9	6.1	6.4	6.6
4.5	13:20	4.7	5.0	5.2	5.4	5.7	5.9	6.2	6.4	6.7	6.9	7.1	7.4
5.0	12:00	5.4	5.7	6.0	6.3	6.5	6.8	7.1	7.4	7.7	7.9	8.2	8.4
5.4	11:10	6.2	6.6	6.9	7.2	7.5	7.9	8.2	8.5	8.8	9.2	9.5	9.8
5.8	10:20	7.7	8.0	8.4	8.8	9.2	9.6	10.0	10.4	10.8	11.1	11.5	11.9

Water skiing	5.0	5.2	5.5	5.7	6.0	6.2	6.5	6.7	7.0	7.2	7.5	7.8
Weight training	5.2	5.4	5.7	6.0	6.2	6.5	6.8	7.0	7.3	7.6	7.8	8.1
Wrestling	8.5	8.9	9.3	9.8	10.2	10.6	11.0	11.5	11.9	12.3	12.8	13.2

| 73 | 75 | 77 | 80 | 82 | 84 | 86 | 89 | 91 | 93 | 95 | 98 | 100 |
160	165	170	175	180	185	190	195	200	205	210	215	220
10.8	11.2	11.5	11.8	12.2	12.5	12.9	13.2	13.5	13.9	14.2	14.6	14.9
12.3	12.7	13.1	13.5	13.9	14.3	14.7	15.0	15.4	15.8	16.2	16.6	17.0
4.0	4.2	4.3	4.4	4.5	4.7	4.8	4.9	5.1	5.2	5.3	5.4	5.6
5.6	5.8	6.0	6.2	6.4	6.5	6.7	6.9	7.1	7.2	7.4	7.6	7.8
7.3	7.5	7.7	7.9	8.2	8.4	8.6	8.9	9.1	9.3	9.5	9.8	10.0
8.9	9.2	9.4	9.7	10.0	10.3	10.6	10.8	11.1	11.4	11.7	12.0	12.2
5.1	5.3	5.4	5.6	5.7	5.9	6.0	6.2	6.4	6.5	6.7	6.9	7.0
7.6	7.9	8.1	8.3	8.6	8.8	9.1	9.3	9.5	9.8	10.0	10.3	10.5
10.2	10.5	10.9	11.2	11.5	11.9	12.2	12.5	12.8	13.1	13.5	13.8	14.1
5.1	5.3	5.4	5.6	5.7	5.9	6.0	6.2	6.4	6.5	6.7	6.9	7.0
6.4	6.6	6.8	7.0	7.2	7.4	7.6	7.8	8.0	8.2	8.4	8.6	8.8
7.8	8.0	8.3	8.5	8.8	9.0	9.2	9.4	9.7	9.9	10.2	10.4	10.7
9.3	9.5	9.8	10.1	10.4	10.7	11.0	11.3	11.6	11.9	12.2	12.5	12.8
11.3	11.7	12.0	12.4	12.8	13.1	13.5	13.8	14.2	14.5	14.9	15.2	15.6
5.5	5.7	5.9	6.1	6.3	6.4	6.6	6.8	7.0	7.1	7.3	7.5	7.7
8.0	8.3	8.5	8.8	9.0	9.3	9.5	9.8	10.0	10.3	10.6	10.8	11.1
5.5	5.7	5.9	6.1	6.3	6.4	6.6	6.8	7.0	7.1	7.3	7.5	7.7
10.4	10.8	11.1	11.4	11.8	12.1	12.4	12.8	13.1	13.4	13.7	14.1	14.4
4.7	4.8	5.0	5.1	5.3	5.4	5.6	5.7	5.9	6.0	6.1	6.3	6.4
10.4	10.7	11.1	11.4	11.7	12.0	12.4	12.7	13.0	13.4	13.7	14.0	14.4
2.4	2.5	2.6	2.7	2.8	2.9	2.9	3.0	3.1	3.2	3.2	3.3	3.4
3.4	3.5	3.6	3.7	3.9	4.0	4.1	4.2	4.3	4.4	4.5	4.6	4.7
3.7	3.8	4.0	4.1	4.2	4.3	4.4	4.5	4.7	4.8	4.9	5.0	5.1
4.4	4.5	4.6	4.8	4.9	5.0	5.2	5.3	5.4	5.6	5.7	5.9	6.0
5.0	5.2	5.3	5.5	5.6	5.8	5.9	6.1	6.3	6.4	6.6	6.8	6.9
5.4	5.6	5.8	6.0	6.2	6.3	6.5	6.7	6.9	7.0	7.2	7.4	7.6
6.8	7.0	7.2	7.4	7.6	7.9	8.1	8.3	8.5	8.7	8.9	9.1	9.4
7.6	7.9	8.1	8.3	8.6	8.8	9.1	9.3	9.5	9.8	10.0	10.3	10.5
8.7	9.0	9.2	9.5	9.8	10.1	10.4	10.6	10.9	11.2	11.5	11.8	12.0
10.1	10.4	10.8	11.1	11.4	11.8	12.1	12.4	12.7	13.0	13.4	13.7	14.0
12.3	12.7	13.1	13.5	13.9	14.3	14.7	15.0	15.4	15.8	16.2	16.6	17.0
8.0	8.3	8.5	8.8	9.0	9.3	9.5	9.8	10.0	10.3	10.6	10.8	11.1
8.3	8.6	8.9	9.1	9.4	9.7	9.9	10.2	10.5	10.7	11.0	11.2	11.5
13.6	14.1	14.5	14.9	15.4	15.8	16.2	16.6	17.1	17.5	17.9	18.4	18.8

Appendix D

Self-Test on Drinking Habits and Alcoholism

Here is a self-test to help you review the role alcohol plays in your life. These questions incorporate some of the common symptoms of alcoholism. This test is intended to help you determine if you or someone you know needs to find out more about alcoholism; it is not intended to be used to establish the diagnosis of alcoholism.

		Yes	No
1.	Do you drink heavily when you are disappointed, under pressure or have had a quarrel with someone?	___	___
2.	Have you ever been unable to remember part of the previous evening, even though your friends say you didn't pass out?	___	___
3.	When drinking with other people, do you try to have a few extra drinks when others won't know about it?	___	___
4.	Are you in more of a hurry to get your first drink of the day than you used to be?	___	___
5.	Do you sometimes feel a little guilty about your drinking?	___	___
6.	When you're sober, do you sometimes regret things you did or said while drinking?	___	___
7.	Have you tried switching brands or drinks, or following different plans to control your drinking?	___	___
8.	Have you sometimes failed to keep promises you made to yourself about controlling or cutting down on your drinking?	___	___
9.	Have you ever had a DWI (driving while intoxicated) or DUI (driving under the influence of alcohol) violation, or any other legal problem related to your drinking?	___	___
10.	Do you try to avoid family or close friends while you are drinking?	___	___

Any "yes" answer indicates you may be at greater risk for alcoholism. More than one "yes" answer may indicate the presence of an alcohol-related problem or alcoholism, and the need for consultation with an alcoholism professional. To find out more, contact the National Council on Alcoholism and Drug Dependence in your area.

Reprinted courtesy of the National Council on Alcoholism and Drug Dependence. For a brochure that contains these and other questions, please send $0.50 to NCADD, 12 West 21st Street, New York, NY, 10010.

Appendix E

American College of Sports Medicine Position Stand: The Prevention of Thermal Injuries during Distance Running

Purpose of the Position Stand

1. To alert sponsors of distance-running events to potentially serious health hazards during distance running—especially thermal injury.
2. To advise sponsors to consult local weather history and plan events at times when the environmental heat stress would most likely be acceptable.
3. To encourage sponsors to identify the environmental heat stress existing on the day of a race and communicate this to the participants.
4. To educate participants regarding thermal injury susceptibility and prevention.
5. To inform sponsors of preventive actions that may reduce the frequency and severity of this type of injury.

This position stand replaces that of *"Prevention of Heat Injury During Distance Running,"* published by the American College of Sports Medicine in 1975. It has been expanded to consider thermal problems that may affect the general community of joggers, fun runners, and elite athletes who participate in distance-running events. Although hyperthermia is still the most common serious problem encountered in North American fun runs and races, hypothermia can be a problem for slow runners in long races such as the marathon, in cold and/or wet environmental conditions or following races, when blood glucose is low and the body's temperature regulatory mechanism is impaired.

Because the physiological responses to exercise and environmental stress vary among participants, strict compliance with the recommendations, while helpful, will not guarantee complete protection from thermal illness. The general guidelines in this position stand do not constitute definitive medical advice, which should be sought from a physician for specific cases. Nevertheless, adherence to these recommendations should help to minimize the incidence of thermal injury.

Position Stand

It is the position of the American College of Sports Medicine that the following recommendations be employed by directors of distance runs or community fun runs.

1. **Medical Director**

    A medical director knowledgeable in exercise physiology and sports medicine should coordinate the preventive and therapeutic aspects of the running event and work closely with the race director.

2. **Race Organization**

    a. Races should be organized to avoid the hottest summer months and the hottest part of the day. As there are great regional variations in environmental conditions, the local weather history will be most helpful in scheduling an event to avoid times when an unacceptable level of heat stress is likely to prevail. Organizers should be cautious of unseasonably hot days in the early spring, as entrants will almost certainly not be heat acclimatized.

    b. The environmental heat stress prediction for the day should be obtained from the meteorological service. It can be measured as wet-bulb globe temperature (WBGT) (see Appendix I), which is a temperature/humidity/radiation index (1). If WBGT is above 28°C (82°F), consideration should be given to rescheduling or delaying the race until safer conditions prevail. If below 28°C, participants may be alerted to the degree of heat stress by using color-coded flags at the start of the race and at key positions along the course (Appendix II).

    c. All summer events should be scheduled for the early morning, ideally before 8:00 A.M., or in the evening after 6:00 P.M., to minimize solar radiation.

d. An adequate supply of water should be available before the race and every 2–3 km during the race. Runners should be encouraged to consume 100–200 ml at each station.

e. Race officials should be educated as to the warning signs of an impending collapse. Each official should wear an identifiable arm band or badge and should warn runners to stop if they appear to be in difficulty.

f. Adequate traffic and crowd control must be maintained at all times.

g. There should be a ready source of radio communications from various points on the course to a central organizing point to coordinate responses to emergencies.

3. **Medical Support**

a. **Medical Organization and Responsibility:** The Medical Director should alert local hospitals and ambulance services to the event and should make prior arrangements with medical personnel for the care of casualties, especially those suffering from heat injury. The mere fact that an entrant signs a waiver in no way absolves the organizers of moral and/or legal responsibility. Medical personnel supervising races should have the authority to evaluate, examine, and/or stop a runner who displays the symptoms and signs of impending heat injury, or who appears to be mentally and/or physically out of control for any other reason.

b. **Medical Facilities:**

   i. Medical support staff and facilities should be available at the race site.

   ii. The facilities should be staffed with personnel capable of instituting immediate and appropriate resuscitation measures. Apart from the routine resuscitation equipment, ice packs and fans for cooling are required.

   iii. Persons trained in first aid, appropriately identified with an arm band, badge, etc., should be stationed along the course to warn runners to stop if they exhibit signs of impending heat injury.

   iv. Ambulances or vans with accompanying medical personnel should be available along the course.

   v. Although the emphasis in this stand has been on the management of hyperthermia, on cold, wet and windy days, athletes may be chilled and require "space blankets," blankets, and warm drinks at the finish to prevent or treat hypothermia (23, 45).

4. **Competitor Education**

The education of fun runners has increased greatly in recent years, but race organizers must not assume that all participants are well informed or prepared. Distributing guidelines at the pre-registration, publicizing guidelines in the press, and holding clinics/seminars before runs are valuable.

The following persons are particularly prone to heat illness: the obese (3, 17, 43), unfit (13, 29, 39, 43), dehydrated (6, 14, 31, 37, 38, 47), those unacclimatized to the heat (20, 43), those with a previous history of heat stroke (36, 43), and anyone who runs while ill (41). Children perspire less than adults and have a lower heat tolerance (2). Based on the above information, all participants should be advised of the following.

a. Adequate training and fitness are important for full enjoyment of the run and also to prevent heat-related injuries (13, 28, 29, 39).

b. Prior training in the heat will promote heat acclimatization and thereby reduce the risk of heat injury. It is wise to do as much training as possible at the time of day at which the race will be held (20).

c. Fluid consumption before and during the race will reduce the risk of heat injury, particularly in longer runs such as the marathon (6, 14, 47).

d. Illness prior to or at the time of the event should preclude competition (41).

e. Participants should be advised of the early symptoms of heat injury. These include clumsiness, stumbling, excessive sweating (and also cessation of sweating), headache, nausea, dizziness, apathy, and any gradual impairment of consciousness (42).

f. Participants should be advised to choose a comfortable speed and not to run faster than conditions warrant (18, 33).

g. Participants are advised to run with a partner, each being responsible for the other's well-being (33).

Background for Position Stand

There has been an exponential rise in the number of fun runs and races in recent years and, as would be expected, a similar increase in the number of running-related injuries. Minor injuries such as bruises, blisters and musculoskeletal injuries are most common (41,45). Myocardial infarction or cardiac arrest is, fortunately, very rare and occurs almost exclusively in patients with symptomatic heart disease (44). Hypoglycemia may be seen occasionally in normal runners (11) and has been observed following marathons (21) and shorter fun runs (41).

The most serious injuries in fun runs and races are related to problems of thermoregulation. In the shorter races, 10 km (6.2 miles) or less, hyperthermia with the attendant problems of heat exhaustion and heat syncope dominates, even on relatively cool days (4,5,10,15,16,18,27,41). In longer races, heat problems are common on warm or hot days (31), but on moderate to cold days, hypothermia may be a real risk to some participants (23).

Thermoregulation and hyperthermia. Fun runners may experience hyperthermia or hypothermia, depending on the environmental conditions and clothing worn. The adequately clothed runner is capable of withstanding a wide range of environmental temperatures. Hyperthermia is the potential problem in warm and hot weather, when the body's rate of heat production is greater than its ability to dissipate this heat (1). In cold weather, scanty clothing may provide inadequate protection from the environment, and hypothermia may develop, particularly toward the end of a long race when running speed and, therefore, heat production, are reduced.

During intense exercise, heat production in contracting muscles is 15–20 times that of basal metabolism and is sufficient to raise body core temperature in an average-sized individual by 1°C every 5 minutes if no temperature-regulating mechanisms were activated (25). With increased heat production, thermal receptors in the hypothalamus sense the increased body temperature and respond with an increased cutaneous circulation; thus, the excess heat is transferred to the skin surface to be dissipated by physical means, primarily the evaporation of sweat (9). The precise quantitative relationships in heat transfer are beyond the scope of this position stand, but are well reviewed elsewhere (24,25).

When the rate of heat production exceeds that of heat loss for a sufficient period of time, thermal injury will occur. In long races, sweat loss can be significant and result in a total body-water deficit of 6–10% of body weight (47). Such dehydration will subsequently reduce sweating and predispose the runner to hyperthermia, heat stroke, heat exhaustion, and muscle cramps (47). For a given level of dehydration, children have a greater increase in core temperature than do adults (2). Rectal temperatures have been reported above 40.6°C after races and fun runs (7,22,31,35) and as high as 42–43°C in fun run participants who have collapsed (32,34, 41,42).

Fluid ingestion before and during prolonged running will minimize dehydration (and reduce the rate of increase in body core temperature) (7,14). However, in fun runs of less than 10 km, hyperthermia may occur in the absence of significant dehydration (41). Runners should avoid consuming large quantities of highly concentrated sugar solution during runs, as this may result in a decrease in gastric emptying (8,12).

Thermoregulation and hypothermia. Heat can be lost readily from the body when the rate of heat production is exceeded by heat loss (46). Even on moderately cool days, if the pace slows and/or if weather conditions become cooler en route, hypothermia may ensue (23). Several deaths have been reported from hypothermia during fun runs in mountain environments (30,40). Hypothermia is common in inexperienced marathon runners who frequently run the second half of the race much more slowly than the first half. Such runners may be able to maintain core temperature initially, but with the slow pace of the second half, especially on cool, wet or windy days, hypothermia can develop (23).

Early symptoms and signs of hypothermia include shivering, euphoria, and an appearance of intoxication. As core temperature continues to fall, shivering may stop, lethargy and muscular weakness may occur with disorientation, hallucinations, and often a combative nature. If core temperature falls below 30°C, the victim may lose consciousness.

Organizers of distance races and fun runs and their medical support staff should anticipate the medical problems and be capable of responding to significant numbers of hyperthermic and/or hypothermic runners. Thermal injury can be minimized with appropriate education of participants and with adequate facilities, supplies, and support staff.

Appendix I
Measurement of Environmental Heat Stress

Ambient temperature is only one component of environmental heat stress; others are humidity, wind velocity, and radiant heat. Therefore, measurement of ambient temperature, dry bulb alone, is inadequate. The most useful and widely applied approach is wet-bulb globe temperature (WBGT).

$$WBGT = (0.7\ Twb) + (0.2\ Tg) + (0.1\ Tdb),$$

where Twb = temperature (wet-bulb thermometer), Tg = temperature (black-globe thermometer), and Tdb = temperature (dry-bulb thermometer).

The importance of wet-bulb temperature can be readily appreciated, as it accounts for 70% of the index, whereas dry-bulb temperature accounts for only 10%. A simple, portable heat-stress monitor that gives direct WBGT in degrees C or degrees F to monitor conditions during fun runs has proven useful (19).

Alternatively, if a means for readily assessing WBGT is not available from wet-bulb, globe, and dry-bulb temperatures, one can use the following equation (48).

$$WBGT = (0.567\ Tdb) + (0.393\ Pa) + 3.94,$$

where Tdb = temperature (dry-bulb thermometer) and Pa = environmental water vapor pressure. These environmental variables should be readily available from local weather or radio stations.

Instruments to measure WBGT are available commercially. Additional information may be obtained from the American College of Sports Medicine.

Appendix II
Use of Color-Coded Flags to Indicate the Risk of Thermal Stress*

1. A red flag: High risk: when WBGT is 23–28°C (73–82°F).
   This signal would indicate that all runners should be aware that heat injury is possible and any person particularly sensitive to heat or humidity should probably not run.

*This scale is determined for runners clad in running shorts, shoes and a T-shirt. In warmer weather, the less clothing the better. For males, wearing no shirt or a mesh top is better than wearing a T-shirt because the surface for evaporation is increased. However, in areas where radiant heat is excessive, a light top may be helpful.

2. An amber flag: Moderate risk: when WBGT is 18–23°C (65–73°F).
   It should be remembered that the air temperature, probably humidity, and almost certainly the radiant heat at the beginning of the race will increase during the course of the race if conducted in the morning or early afternoon.
3. A green flag: Low risk: when WBGT is below 18°C (65°F).
   This in no way guarantees that heat injury will not occur, but indicates only that the risk is low.
4. A white flag: Low risk for hyperthermia, but possible risk for hypothermia: when WBGT is below 10°C (50°F).
   Hypothermia may occur, especially in slow runners in long races, and in wet and windy conditions.

Appendix III
Road Race Checklist

Medical Personnel
1. Have aid personnel available if the race is 10 km (6.2 miles) or longer and run in warm or cold weather.
2. Recruit back-up personnel from existing emergency medical services (police, fire rescue, emergency medical service).
3. Notify local hospitals of the time and place of the road race.

Aid Stations
1. Provide major aid station at the finish point, which is cordoned off from public access.
2. Equip the major aid station with the following supplies:
   —tent
   —cots
   —bath towels
   —water in large containers
   —ice in bag or ice chest or quick-cold packs
   —hose with spray nozzle
   —tables for medical supplies and equipment
   —stethoscopes
   —blood pressure cuffs
   —rectal thermometers or meters (range up to 43°C)
   —dressings
   —blankets

—aluminum thermal sheets ("space blankets")
—elastic bandages
—splints
—skin disinfectants
—intravenous fluids (supervision by a physician is required).

3. Position aid stations along the route at 4-km (2.5-mile) intervals for races over 10 km and at the halfway point for shorter races.

4. Stock each aid station with enough fluid (cool water is the optimum) for each runner to have 300–360 ml (10–12 ounces) at each aid station. A margin of 25% additional cups should be available to account for spillage and double usage.

Communications/Surveillance

1. Set up communication between the medical personnel and the major aid station.
2. Arrange for a radio-equipped car or van to follow the race course, and provide radio contact with director.

Instructions To Runners

1. Apprise the race participants of potential medical problems in advance of the race so precautions may be followed.
2. Advise the race director to announce the following information by loudspeaker immediately prior to the race:
   —the flag color; the risks for hyperthermia and/or hypothermia
   —location of aid stations and type of fluid available
   —reinforcement of warm-weather or cold-weather self-care.
3. Advise the race participants to print their names, addresses, and any medical problems on the back of the registration number.

Appendix IV
Medical Stations
General Guidelines

Staff for Large Races

1. Physician, podiatrist, nurse or EMT, a team of three per 1,000 runners. Double or triple this number at the finish area.

Table 1. Equipment needed at aid stations and the field hospital (per 1,000 runners).

Aid stations

No.	Item
	ice in small plastic bags or quick-cold packs
5	stretchers (10 at 10 km and beyond)
5	blankets (10 at 10 km and beyond)
6 each	6-inch and 4-inch elastic bandages
½ case	4 × 4-inch gauze pads
½ case	1½-inch tape
½ case	surgical soap small instrument kits adhesive strips moleskin
½ case	petroleum jelly
2 each	inflatable arm and leg splints athletic trainer's kit

Field hospital

No.	Item
10	stretchers
4	sawhorses
10–20	blankets (depending on environmental conditions)
10	intravenous set-ups
2 each	inflatable arm and leg splints
2 cases	1½-inch tape
2 cases each	elastic bandages (2, 4, and 6 inches)
2 cases	sheet wadding underwrap
2 cases	4 × 4-inch gauze pads adhesive strips moleskin
½ case	surgical soap
2	oxygen tanks with regulators and masks
2	ECG monitors with defibrillators ice in small plastic bags small-instrument kits

Adapted from reference 26.
Reprinted with permission of the American College of Sports Medicine. Copyright 1988 American College of Sports Medicine.

2. One ambulance per 3,000 runners at finish area; one cruising vehicle.
3. One physician to act as triage officer at finish.

Water

Estimate 1 liter (0.26 gallon) per runner per 16 km (10 miles), or roughly, per 60–90 minutes running time, and depending on number of stations.

For 10 km, the above rule is still recommended.

Cups = (number of entrants × number of stations) + 25% additional per station.

= (2 × number of entrants) extra at finish area.

Double this total if the course is out and back. In cold weather, an equivalent amount of warm drinks should be available.

REFERENCES

1. Adolph, E. I. *Physiology of Man in the Desert.* New York: Interscience, 1947, pp. 5–43.
2. Bar-Or, O. Climate and the exercising child—a review. *Int. J. Sports Med.* 1:53–65, 1980.
3. Bar-Or, O., H. M. Lundegren, and E. R. Buskirk. Heat tolerance of exercising lean and obese women. *J. Appl. Physiol.* 26:403–409, 1969.
4. Buskirk, E. R., P. F. Iampietro, and D. E. Bass. Work performance after dehydration: effects of physical conditioning and heat acclimatization. *J. Appl. Physiol.* 12:189–194, 1958.
5. Clowes, G. H. A., Jr. and T. F. O'Donnell, Jr. Heat stroke *N. Engl. J. Med.* 291:564–567, 1974.
6. Costill, D. L., R. Cote, E. Miller, T. Miller, and S. Wynder. Water and electrolyte replacement during days of work in the heat. *Aviat. Space Environ. Med.* 46:795–800, 1970.
7. Costill, D. L., W. F. Kammer, and A. Fisher. Fluid ingestion during distance running. *Arch. Environ. Health* 21:520–525, 1970.
8. Costill, D. L. and B. Saltin. Factors limiting gastric emptying during rest and exercise. *J. Appl. Physiol.* 37:679–683, 1974.
9. Ellis, F. P., A. N. Exton-Smith, K. G. Foster, and J. S. Weiner. Eccrine sweating and mortality during heat waves in very young and very old persons. *Isr. J. Med. Sci.* 12:815–817, 1976.
10. England, A. C., III, D. W. Fraser, A. W. Hightower, et al. Preventing severe heat injury in runners: suggestions from the 1979 Peachtree Road Race experience. *Ann. Intern. Med.* 97:196–201, 1982.
11. Felig, P., A. Cherif, A. Minagawa, and J. Wahren. Hypoglycemia during prolonged exercise in normal men. *N. Engl. J. Med.* 306:895–900, 1982.
12. Fordtran, J. A. and B. Saltin. Gastric emptying and intestinal absorption during prolonged severe exercise. *J. Appl. Physiol.* 23:331–335, 1967.
13. Gisolfi, C. V. and J. Cohen. Relationships among training, heat acclimation and heat tolerance in men and women: the controversy revisited. *Med. Sci. Sports* 11:56–59, 1979.
14. Gisolfi, C. V. and J. R. Copping. Thermal effects of prolonged treadmill exercise in the heat. *Med. Sci. Sports* 6:108–113, 1974.
15. Hanson, P. G. and S. W. Zimmerman. Exertional heatstroke in novice runners. *JAMA* 242:154–157, 1979.
16. Hart, L. E., B. P. Egier, A. G. Shimizu, P. J. Tandan, and J. R. Sutton. Exertional heat stroke: the runner's nemesis. *Can. Med. Assoc. J.* 122:1144–1150, 1980.
17. Haymes, E. M., R. J. McCormick, and E. R. Buskirk. Heat tolerance of exercising lean and obese prepubertal boys. *J. Appl. Physiol.* 39:457–461, 1975.
18. Hughson, R. L., H. J. Green, M. E. Houston, J. A. Thomson, D. R. MacLean, and J. R. Sutton. Heat injuries in Canadian mass participation runs. *Can. Med. Assoc. J.* 122:1141–1144, 1980.
19. Hughson, R. L., L. A. Standl, and J. M. Mackie. Monitoring road racing in the heat. *Phys. Sportsmed.* 11(5):94–105, 1983.
20. Knochel, J. P. Environmental heat illness: an eclectic review. *Arch. Intern. Med.* 133:841–864, 1974.
21. Levine, S. A., B. Gordon, and C. L. Derick. Some changes in the chemical constituents of the blood following a marathon race. *JAMA* 82:1778–1779, 1924.
22. Maron, M. B., J. A. Wagner, and S. M. Horvath. Thermoregulatory responses during competitive distance running. *J. Appl. Physiol.* 42:909–914, 1977.
23. Maughan, R. J., I. M. Light, P. H. Whiting, and J. D. B. Miller. Hypothermia, hyperkalemia, and marathon running. *Lancet* 11:1336, 1982.
24. Nadel, E. R. Control of sweating rate while exercising in the heat. *Med. Sci. Sports* 11:31–35, 1979.
25. Nadel, E. R., C. B. Wenger, M. F. Roberts, J. A. J. Stolwijk, and E. Cafarelli. Physiological defenses against hyperthermia of exericse. *Ann. NY Acad. Sci.* 301:98–109, 1977.
26. Noble, H. B. and D. Bachman. Medical aspects of distance race planning. *Phys. Sportsmed.* 7(6):78–84, 1979.
27. O'Donnell, T. J., Jr. Acute heatstroke. Epidemiologic, biochemical, renal and coagulation studies. *JAMA* 234:824–828, 1975.
28. Pandolf, K. B., R. L. Burse, and R. F. Goldman. Role of physical fitness in heat acclimatization, decay and reinduction. *Ergonomics* 20:399–408, 1977.
29. Piwonka, R. W., S. Robinson, V. L. Gay, and R. S. Manalis. Preacclimatization of men to heat by training. *J. Appl. Physiol.* 20:379–384, 1965.
30. Pugh, L. G. C. E. Cold stress and muscular exercise with special reference to accidental hypothermia. *Br. Med. J.* 2:333–337, 1967.
31. Pugh, L. G. C. E., J. L. Corbett, and R. H. Johnson. Rectal temperatures, weight losses and sweat rates in marathon running. *J. Appl. Physiol.* 23:347–352, 1967.
32. Richards, D., R. Richards, P. J. Schofield, V. Ross, and J. R. Sutton. Management of heat exhaustion in Sydney's *The Sun* City-to-Surf fun runners. *Med. J. Aust.* 2:457–461, 1979.

33. Richards, R., D. Richards, P. J. Schofield, V. Ross, and J. R. Sutton. Reducing the hazards in Sydney's *The Sun* City-to-Surf fun runs, 1971 to 1979. *Med. J. Aust.* 2:453–457, 1979.

34. Richards, R., D. Richards, P. J. Schofield, V. Ross, and J. R. Sutton. Organization of *The Sun* City-to-Surf fun run, Sydney, 1979. *Med. J. Aust.* 2:470–474, 1979.

35. Robinson, S., S. L. Wiley, L. G. Boudurant and S. Mamlin, Jr. Temperature regulation of men following heatstroke. *Isr. J. Med. Sci.* 12:786–795, 1976.

36. Shapiro, Y., A. Magazanik, R. Udassin, G. Ben-Baruch, E. Shvartz, and Y. Shoenfeld. Heat tolerance in former heatstroke patients. *Ann. Intern. Med.* 90:913–916, 1979.

37. Shibolet, S., R. Coll, T. Gilat, and E. Sohar. Heatstroke: its clinical picture and mechanism in 36 cases. *Q. J. Med.* 36:525–547, 1967.

38. Shibolet, S., M. C. Lancaster, and Y. Danon. Heat stroke: a review. *Aviat. Space Environ. Med.* 47:280–301, 1976.

39. Shvartz, E., Y. Shapiro, A. Magazanik, et al. Heat acclimation, physical fitness, and responses to exercise in temperate and hot environments. *J. Appl. Physiol.* 43:678–683, 1977.

40. Sutton, J. Community jogging vs. arduous racing. *N. Engl. J. Med.* 286:951, 1972.

41. Sutton, J., M. J. Coleman, A. P. Millar, L. Lazarus, and P. Russo. The medical problems of mass participation in athletic competition. The "City-to-Surf" race. *Med. J. Aust.* 2:127–133, 1972.

42. Sutton, J. R. Heat illness. In: *Sports Medicine*, R. H. Strauss (Ed.). Philadelphia: W. B. Saunders, 1984, pp. 307–322.

43. Sutton, J. R. and O. Bar-Or. Thermal illness in fun running. *Am. Heart J.* 100:778–781, 1980.

44. Thompson, P. D., M. P. Stern, P. Williams, K. Duncan, W. L. Haskell, and P. D. Wood. Death during jogging or running. A study of 18 cases. *JAMA* 242:1265–1267, 1979.

45. Williams, R. S., D. D. Schocken, M. Morey, and F. P. Koisch. Medical aspects of competitive distance running. *Postgrad. Med.* 70:41–51, 1981.

46. Winslow, C. E. A., L. P. Herrington, and A. P. Gagge. Physiological reactions of the human body to various atmospheric humidities. *Am. J. Physiol.* 120:288–299, 1937.

47. Wyndham, C. H. and N. B. Strydom. The danger of inadequate water intake during marathon running. *S. Afr. Med. J.* 43:893–896, 1969.

48. Yaglou, C. P. and D. Minard. Control of heat casualities at military training centers. *AMA Arch. Ind. Health* 16:302–305, 1957.

Appendix F

Generalized Equations for Predicting Body Fat

Women[*]

$BD = 1.0994921 - 0.0009929 (X_1) + 0.0000023 (X_1)^2 - 0.0001392 (X_2)$

BD = Body density

X_1 = Sum of triceps, thigh and suprailium skinfolds

X_2 = Age

Men[**]

$BD = 1.10938 - 0.0008267 (X_1) + 0.0000016 (X_1)^2 - 0.0002574 (X_2)$

BD = Body density

X_1 = Sum of chest, abdomen and thigh skinfolds

X_2 = Age

To calculate percent body fat, plug into Siri's equation $\left(\dfrac{4.95}{BD} - 4.5\right) \times 100$

[*]From Jackson, A., Pollock, M., and Ward, A. 1980. Generalized equations for predicting body density of women. *Medicine and Science in Sports and Exercise,* 12: 175–182.

[**]Jackson, A., and Pollock, M. 1978. Generalized equations for predicting body density of men. *British Journal of Nutrition* 40: 497–504.

Percent fat estimate for men: sum of chest, abdomen, and thigh skinfolds

Sum of skinfolds (mm)	Under 22	23–27	28–32	33–37	Age to last year 38–42	43–47	48–52	53–57	Over 57
8–10	1.3	1.8	2.3	2.9	3.4	3.9	4.5	5.0	5.5
11–13	2.2	2.8	3.3	3.9	4.4	4.9	5.5	6.0	6.5
14–16	3.2	3.8	4.3	4.8	5.4	5.9	6.4	7.0	7.5
17–19	4.2	4.7	5.3	5.8	6.3	6.9	7.4	8.0	8.5
20–22	5.1	5.7	6.2	6.8	7.3	7.9	8.4	8.9	9.5
23–25	6.1	6.6	7.2	7.7	8.3	8.8	9.4	9.9	10.5
26–28	7.0	7.6	8.1	8.7	9.2	9.8	10.3	10.9	11.4
29–31	8.0	8.5	9.1	9.6	10.2	10.7	11.3	11.8	12.4
32–34	8.9	9.4	10.0	10.5	11.1	11.6	12.2	12.8	13.3
35–37	9.8	10.4	10.9	11.5	12.0	12.6	13.1	13.7	14.3
38–40	10.7	11.3	11.8	12.4	12.9	13.5	14.1	14.6	15.2
41–43	11.6	12.2	12.7	13.3	13.8	14.4	15.0	15.5	16.1
44–46	12.5	13.1	13.6	14.2	14.7	15.3	15.9	16.4	17.0
47–49	13.4	13.9	14.5	15.1	15.6	16.2	16.8	17.3	17.9
50–52	14.3	14.8	15.4	15.9	16.5	17.1	17.6	18.2	18.8
53–55	15.1	15.7	16.2	16.8	17.4	17.9	18.5	19.1	19.7
56–58	16.0	16.5	17.1	17.7	18.2	18.8	19.4	20.0	20.5
59–61	16.9	17.4	17.9	18.5	19.1	19.7	20.2	20.8	21.4
62–64	17.6	18.2	18.8	19.4	19.9	20.5	21.1	21.7	22.2
65–67	18.5	19.0	19.6	20.2	20.8	21.3	21.9	22.5	23.1
68–70	19.3	19.9	20.4	21.0	21.6	22.2	22.7	23.3	23.9
71–73	20.1	20.7	21.2	21.8	22.4	23.0	23.6	24.1	24.7
74–76	20.9	21.5	22.0	22.6	23.2	23.8	24.4	25.0	25.5
77–79	21.7	22.2	22.8	23.4	24.0	24.6	25.2	25.8	26.3
80–82	22.4	23.0	23.6	24.2	24.8	25.4	25.9	26.5	27.1
83–85	23.2	23.8	24.4	25.0	25.5	26.1	26.7	27.3	27.9
86–88	24.0	24.5	25.1	25.7	26.3	26.9	27.5	28.1	28.7
89–91	24.7	25.3	25.9	26.5	27.1	27.6	28.2	28.8	29.4
92–94	25.4	26.0	26.6	27.2	27.8	28.4	29.0	29.6	30.2
95–97	26.1	26.7	27.3	27.9	28.5	29.1	29.7	30.3	30.9
98–100	26.9	27.4	28.0	28.6	29.2	29.8	30.4	31.0	31.6
101–103	27.5	28.1	28.7	29.3	29.9	30.5	31.1	31.7	32.3
104–106	28.2	28.8	29.4	30.0	30.6	31.2	31.8	32.4	33.0
107–109	28.9	29.5	30.1	30.7	31.3	31.9	32.5	33.1	33.7
110–112	29.6	30.2	30.8	31.4	32.0	32.6	33.2	33.8	34.4
113–115	30.2	30.8	31.4	32.0	32.6	33.2	33.8	34.5	35.1
116–118	30.9	31.5	32.1	32.7	33.3	33.9	34.5	35.1	35.7
119–121	31.5	32.1	32.7	33.3	33.9	34.5	35.1	35.7	36.4
122–124	32.1	32.7	33.3	33.9	34.5	35.1	35.8	36.4	37.0
125–127	32.7	33.3	33.9	34.5	35.1	35.8	36.4	37.0	37.6

Reprinted by permission of *The Physician and Sportsmedicine*, a McGraw-Hill publication.

Percent fat estimate for women: sum of triceps, suprailium, and thigh skinfolds

Sum of skinfolds (mm)	Under 22	23–27	28–32	33–37	38–42	43–47	48–52	53–57	Over 57
23–25	9.7	9.9	10.2	10.4	10.7	10.9	11.2	11.4	11.7
26–28	11.0	11.2	11.5	11.7	12.0	12.3	12.5	12.7	13.0
29–31	12.3	12.5	12.8	13.0	13.3	13.5	13.8	14.0	14.3
32–34	13.6	13.8	14.0	14.3	14.5	14.8	15.0	15.3	15.5
35–37	14.8	15.0	15.3	15.5	15.8	16.0	16.3	16.5	16.8
38–40	16.0	16.3	16.5	16.7	17.0	17.2	17.5	17.7	18.0
41–43	17.2	17.4	17.7	17.9	18.2	18.4	18.7	18.9	19.2
44–46	18.3	18.6	18.8	19.1	19.3	19.6	19.8	20.1	20.3
47–49	19.5	19.7	20.0	20.2	20.5	20.7	21.0	21.2	21.5
50–52	20.6	20.8	21.1	21.3	21.6	21.8	22.1	22.3	22.6
53–55	21.7	21.9	22.1	22.4	22.6	22.9	23.1	23.4	23.6
56–58	22.7	23.0	23.2	23.4	23.7	23.9	24.2	24.4	24.7
59–61	23.7	24.0	24.2	24.5	24.7	25.0	25.2	25.5	25.7
62–64	24.7	25.0	25.2	25.5	25.7	26.0	26.2	26.4	26.7
65–67	25.7	25.9	26.2	26.4	26.7	26.9	27.2	27.4	27.7
68–70	26.6	26.9	27.1	27.4	27.6	27.9	28.1	28.4	28.6
71–73	27.5	27.8	28.0	28.3	28.5	28.8	29.0	29.3	29.5
74–76	28.4	28.7	28.9	29.2	29.4	29.7	29.9	30.2	30.4
77–79	29.3	29.5	29.8	30.0	30.3	30.5	30.8	31.0	31.3
80–82	30.1	30.4	30.6	30.9	31.1	31.4	31.6	31.9	32.1
83–85	30.9	31.2	31.4	31.7	31.9	32.2	32.4	32.7	32.9
86–88	31.7	32.0	32.2	32.5	32.7	32.9	33.2	33.4	33.7
89–91	32.5	32.7	33.0	33.2	33.5	33.7	33.9	34.2	34.4
92–94	33.2	33.4	33.7	33.9	34.2	34.4	34.7	34.9	35.2
95–97	33.9	34.1	34.4	34.6	34.9	35.1	35.4	35.6	35.9
98–100	34.6	34.8	35.1	35.3	35.5	35.8	36.0	36.3	36.5
101–103	35.3	35.4	35.7	35.9	36.2	36.4	36.7	36.9	37.2
104–106	35.8	36.1	36.3	36.6	36.8	37.1	37.3	37.5	37.8
107–109	36.4	36.7	36.9	37.1	37.4	37.6	37.9	38.1	38.4
110–112	37.0	37.2	37.5	37.7	38.0	38.2	38.5	38.7	38.9
113–115	37.5	37.8	38.0	38.2	38.5	38.7	39.0	39.2	39.5
116–118	38.0	38.3	38.5	38.8	39.0	39.3	39.5	39.7	40.0
119–121	38.5	38.7	39.0	39.2	39.5	39.7	40.0	40.2	40.5
122–124	39.0	39.2	39.4	39.7	39.9	40.2	40.4	40.7	40.9
125–127	39.4	39.6	39.9	40.1	40.4	40.6	40.9	41.1	41.4
128–130	39.8	40.0	40.3	40.5	40.8	41.0	41.3	41.5	41.8

Reprinted by permission of *The Physician and Sportsmedicine*, a McGraw-Hill publication.

Figure F.1.
The chest and abdomen skinfold. Chest—A diagonal fold is taken between the axillary fold and the nipple. Use a midway point for males, but only one-third the distance from the axilla for females. Abdomen—A vertical fold is taken about 2.5 centimeters (1 inch) to the side of the umbilicus.

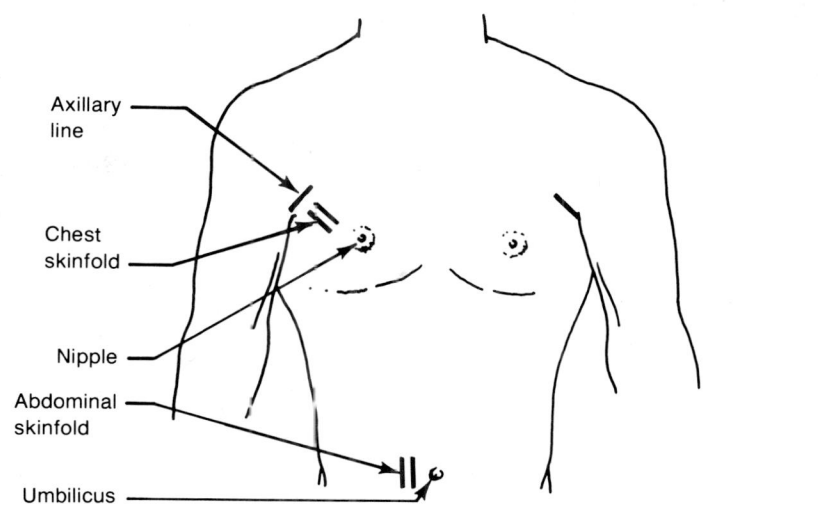

Axillary line

Chest skinfold

Nipple

Abdominal skinfold

Umbilicus

Figure F.2.
The suprailiac skinfold. A diagonal fold is taken at about a 45-degree angle just above the crest of the ilium.

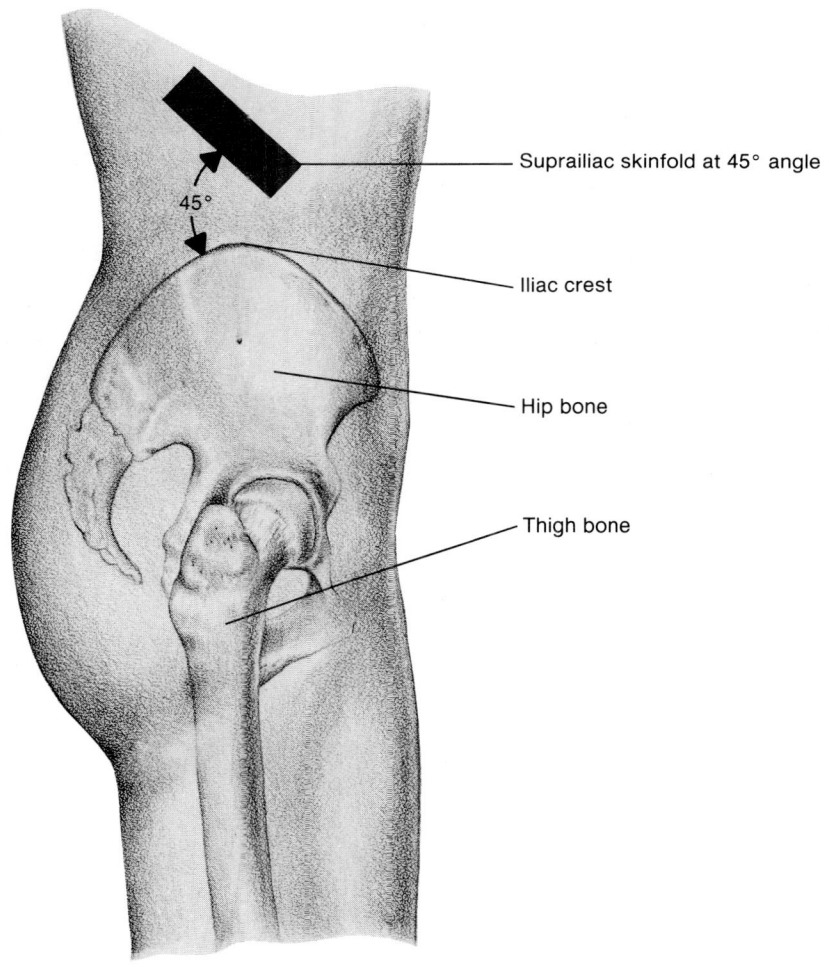

45°

Suprailiac skinfold at 45° angle

Iliac crest

Hip bone

Thigh bone

Figure F.3.
The thigh skinfold. A vertical fold is taken on the front of the thigh midway between the anterior iliac spine and the patella.

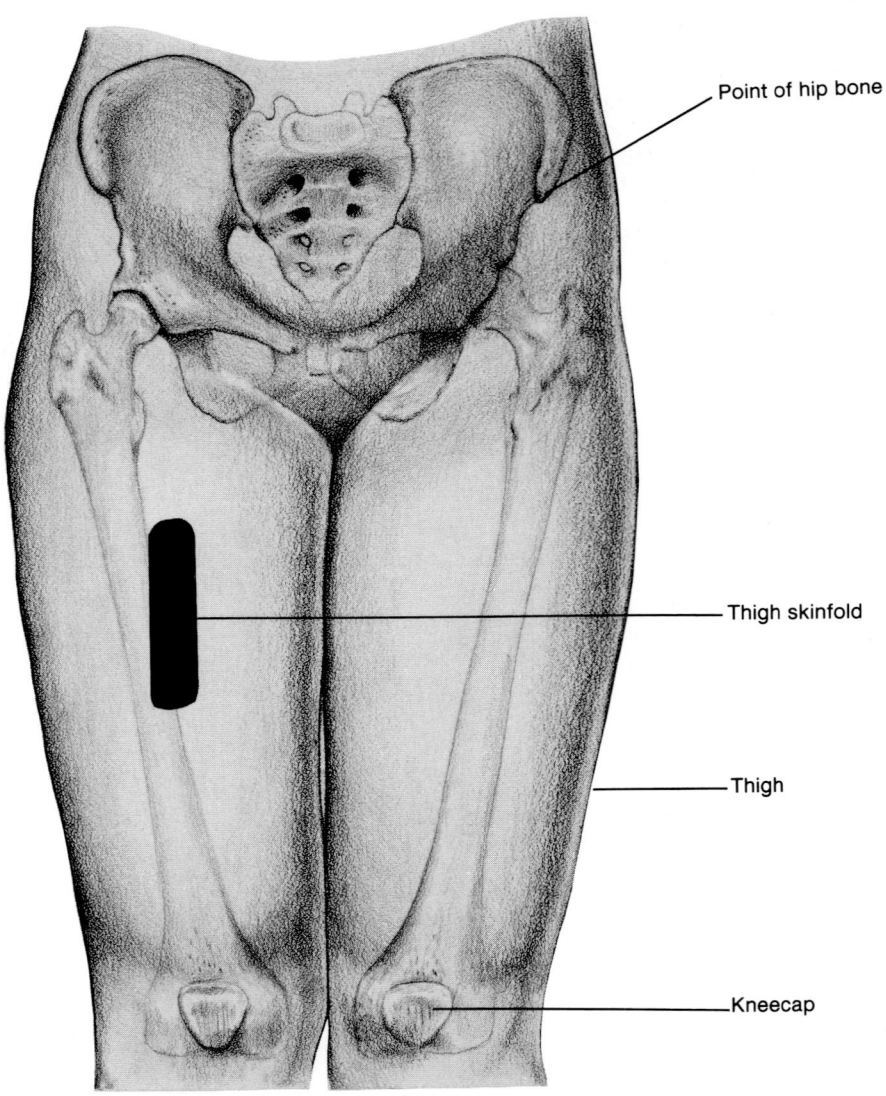

Point of hip bone

Thigh skinfold

Thigh

Kneecap

Figure F.4.
The triceps and subscapular skinfolds. In the triceps skinfold, a vertical fold is taken over the triceps muscle one-half the distance from the acromion process to the olecranon process at the elbow. The subscapular skinfold is taken just below the lower angle of the scapula, at about a 45-degree angle to the spinal column.

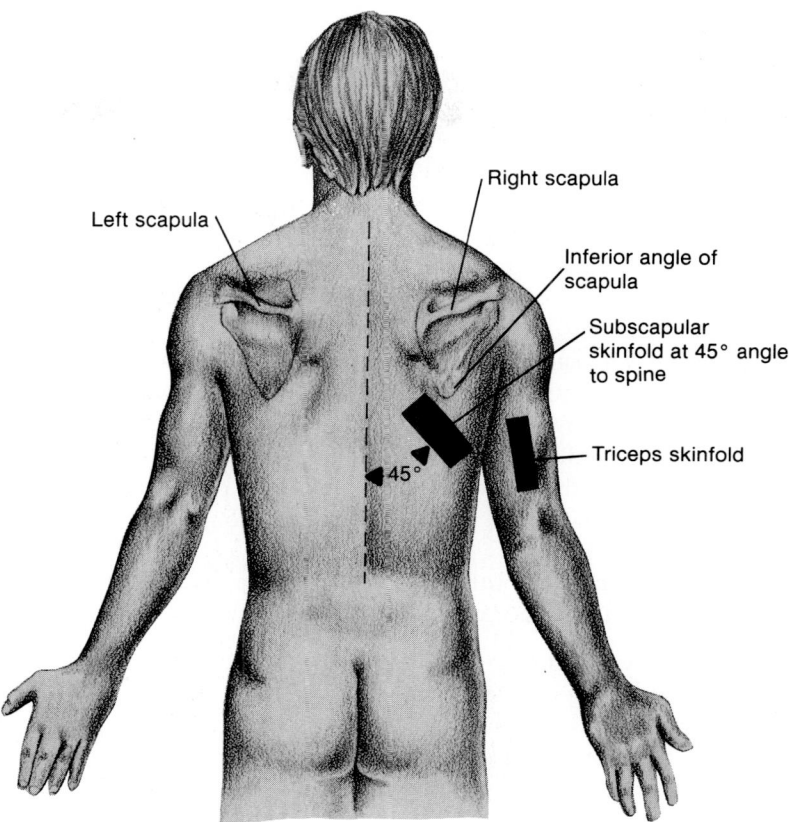

Left scapula

Right scapula

Inferior angle of scapula

Subscapular skinfold at 45° angle to spine

45°

Triceps skinfold

Appendix G

How to Identify Pathogenic Weight Control Behavior

Female athletes have gone to extraordinary lengths to lower their body-fat stores in an effort to improve performance. A pattern of eating disorders has emerged from this desperate, health-threatening situation. The following protocol was developed to advise the athletic training staff how to identify symptoms in athletes who suffer from one or more features of pathogenic weight-control behavior. Many of the items do not by themselves prove the presence of an eating disorder, but identification of one or more may justify further attention to the possible presence of a problem.

Reports or observation of the following signs or behaviors should arouse concern:

1. Repeatedly expressed concerns by an athlete about being or feeling fat even when weight is below average.
2. Expressions of fear of being or becoming obese that do not diminish as weight loss continues.
3. Refusal to maintain even a minimal normal weight consistent with the athlete's sport, age, and height.
4. Consumption of huge amounts of food not consistent with the athlete's weight.
5. Clandestine eating or stealing of food (e.g., many candy wrappers, food containers, etc., found in the athlete's locker, around his or her room); repeated disappearance of food from the training table.
6. A pattern of eating substantial amounts of food followed promptly by trips to the bathroom and resumption of eating shortly thereafter.
7. Bloodshot eyes, especially after trips to the bathroom.
8. Vomitus or odor of vomit in the toilet, sink, shower, or wastebasket.
9. Wide fluctuations in weight over short time spans.
10. Complaints of light-headedness or disequilibrium not accounted for by other medical causes.

11. Evidence of use of diet pills (e.g., irritability fluctuating with lethargy over short periods of time).
12. Complaints or evidence of bloating or water retention that cannot be attributed to other medical causes (e.g., premenstrual edema).
13. Excess laxative use or laxative packages seen in the athlete's area, locker, wastebasket, etc.
14. Periods of severe calorie restriction or repeated days of fasting.
15. Evidence of purposeless, excessive physical activity (especially in a thin athlete) that is not part of the training regimen.
16. Depressed mood and self-deprecating expression of thoughts following eating.
17. Avoiding situations in which the athlete may be observed while eating (e.g., refusing to eat with teammates on road trips, making excuses such as having to eat before or after the team meal).
18. Appearing preoccupied with the eating behavior of other people such as friends, relatives, or teammates.
19. Certain changes in the athlete's physical appearance (e.g., rounding or pouch-like dilation at or just under the angle of the jaw, ulceration or sores at the corners of the mouth or on the tongue, thinning or loss of hair).
20. Known or reported family history of eating disorders or family dysfunction.

If an athlete who seems to have an eating disorder is practicing one or more pathogenic weight-control techniques, the following recommendations are in order:

1. The coaching or training staff person who has the best rapport with the athlete should arrange a private meeting with him or her.
2. The tone of the meeting should be entirely supportive. Express concern for the best interests of the individual and make it clear that this concern transcends the issue of the individual as an athlete.

Reprinted by permission of *The Physician and Sportsmedicine*, a McGraw-Hill publication.

3. In as nonpunitive a manner as possible, indicate to the athlete what specific observations were made that aroused your concern. Let the individual respond.

4. Affirm and reaffirm that the athlete's role on the team will not be jeopardized by an admission that an eating problem exists. Participation on a team should be curtailed only if evidence shows that the eating disorder has compromised the athlete's health in a way that could lead to injury should participation be continued.

5. Try to determine if the athlete feels that he or she is beyond the point of being able to voluntarily abstain from the problem behavior.

6. If the athlete refuses to admit that a problem exists in the face of compelling evidence, or if it seems that the problem either has been long-standing or cannot readily be corrected, consult a clinician with expertise in treating eating disorders. Remember, most individuals with this problem have tried repeatedly to correct it on their own and failed. Failure is especially demoralizing to athletes, who are constantly oriented toward success. Let the individual know that outside help is often required and that this need should not be regarded as a failure or lack of effort.

7. Arrange for regularly scheduled follow-up meetings apart from practice times, or, if the athlete is seeing a specialist, obtain advice as to how you may continue to help.

8. Be aware that most athletes resorting to pathogenic weight-control techniques have been told at various times that they had a weight problem. It is important to know what role, if any, past or present coaches or trainers may have played in the development of this problem. Let the athlete know that you realize that the demands of the sport may well have played a role in the development of this behavior.

What not to do:

1. Question teammates instead of talking directly to the athlete.

2. Immediately discipline the athlete if you find evidence that a problem exists.

3. Indicate to the athlete that you know what's going on, but tell nothing as to how or why you've become suspicious.

4. Tell the athlete to straighten up and that you'll be checking back from time to time.

5. Conclude that if the athlete really wants to be okay, he or she will make it happen, and failure to improve shows a lack of effort.

6. Dissociate yourself and the demands of the sport from any aspect of the development of the problem.

7. Refuse to obtain outside assistance, but rather "keep it in the family."

Appendix H

Food Exchange Lists

The reason for dividing food into six different groups is that foods vary in their carbohydrate, protein, fat, and Calorie content. Each exchange list contains foods that are alike—each choice contains about the same amount of carbohydrate, protein, fat, and Calories.

The following chart shows the amount of these nutrients in one serving from each exchange list. As you read the exchange lists, you will notice that one choice often is a larger amount of food than another choice from the same list. Because foods are so different, each food is measured or weighed so that the amount of carbohydrate, protein, fat, and Calories is the same in each choice.

You will notice symbols on some foods in the exchange groups. Foods that are high in fiber (3 grams or more per normal serving) have a ⚕ symbol. High-fiber foods are good for you. It is important to eat more of these foods.

Foods that are high in sodium (400 milligrams or more of sodium per normal serving) have a ⚕ symbol. It's a good idea to limit your intake of high salt foods, especially if you have high blood pressure.

If you have a favorite food that is not included in any of these groups, ask your dietitian about it. That food can probably be worked into your meal plan, at least now and then.

Exchange list	Carbohydrate (grams)	Protein (grams)	Fat (grams)	Calories
Starch/bread	15	3	trace	80
Meat				
Lean	—	7	3	55
Medium-fat	—	7	5	75
High-fat	—	7	8	100
Vegetable	5	2	—	25
Fruit	15	—	—	60
Milk				
Skim	12	8	trace	90
Lowfat	12	8	5	120
Whole	12	8	8	150
Fat	—	—	5	45

Starch/Bread List

Each item in this list contains approximately 15 grams of carbohydrate, 3 grams of protein, a trace of fat, and 80 Calories. Whole grain products average about 2 grams of fiber per serving. Some foods are higher in fiber. Those foods that contain 3 or more grams of fiber per serving are identified with the fiber symbol 🌾

You can choose your starch exchanges from any of the items on this list. If you want to eat a starch food that is not on this list, the general rule is that:

- ½ cup of cereal, grain, or pasta is one serving
- 1 ounce of a bread product is one serving.

Your dietitian can help you be more exact.

Cereals/Grains/Pasta

🌾 Bran cereals, concentrated (such as Bran Buds,® All Bran®)	⅓ cup
🌾 Bran cereals, flaked	½ cup
Bulgur (cooked)	½ cup
Cooked cereals	½ cup
Cornmeal (dry)	2½ Tbsp.
Grapenuts	3 Tbsp.
Grits (cooked)	½ cup
Other ready-to-eat unsweetened cereals	¾ cup
Pasta (cooked)	½ cup
Puffed cereal	1½ cup
Rice, white or brown (cooked)	⅓ cup
Shredded wheat	½ cup
🌾 Wheat germ	3 Tbsp.

Dried Beans/Peas/Lentils

🌾 Beans and peas (cooked) (such as kidney, white, split, blackeye)	⅓ cup
🌾 Lentils (cooked)	⅓ cup
🌾 Baked beans	¼ cup

Starchy Vegetables

🌾 Corn	½ cup
🌾 Corn on cob, 6 in. long	1
🌾 Lima beans	½ cup
🌾 Peas, green (canned or frozen)	½ cup
🌾 Plantain	½ cup
Potato, baked	1 small (3 oz.)
Potato, mashed	½ cup
Squash, winter (acorn, butternut)	¾ cup
Yam, sweet potato, plain	⅓ cup

Bread

Bagel	½ (1 oz.)
Bread sticks, crisp, 4 in. long × ½ in.	2 (⅔ oz.)
Croutons, low fat	1 cup
English muffin	½
Frankfurter or hamburger bun	½ (1 oz.)
Pita, 6 in. across	½
Plain roll, small	1 (1 oz.)
Raisin, unfrosted	1 slice (1 oz.)
🌾 Rye, pumpernickel	1 slice (1 oz.)
Tortilla, 6 in. across	1
White (including French, Italian)	1 slice (1 oz.)
Whole wheat	1 slice (1 oz.)

Crackers/Snacks

Animal crackers	8
Graham crackers, square 2½ in.	3
Matzoh	¾ oz.
Melba toast	5 slices
Oyster crackers	24
Popcorn (popped, no fat added)	3 cups
Pretzels	¾ oz.
Rye crisp, 2 in. × 3½ in.	4
Saltine-type crackers	6
Whole wheat crackers, no fat added (crisp breads, such as Finn®, Kavli®, Wasa®)	2–4 slices (¾ oz.)

Starch Foods Prepared with Fat

(Count as 1 starch/bread serving, plus 1 fat serving)

Biscuit, 2½ in. across	1
Chow mein noodles	½ cup
Corn bread, 2 in. cube	1 (2 oz.)
Cracker, round butter type	6
French fried potatoes, 2 in. to 3½ in. long	10 (1½ oz.)
Muffin, plain, small	1
Pancake, 4 in. across	2
Stuffing, bread (prepared)	¼ cup
Taco shell, 6 in. across	2
Waffle, 4½ in. square	1
Whole wheat crackers, fat added (such as Triscuits®)	4–6 (1 oz.)

⤺ 3 grams or more of fiber per serving

Meat List

Each serving of meat and substitutes on this list contains about 7 grams of protein. The amount of fat and number of Calories vary, depending on what kind of meat or substitute you choose. The list is divided into three parts based on the amount of fat and Calories: lean meat, medium-fat meat, and high-fat meat. One ounce (one meat exchange) of each of these includes:

	Carbohydrate (grams)	Protein (grams)	Fat (grams)	Calories
Lean	0	7	3	55
Medium-fat	0	7	5	75
High-fat	0	7	8	100

You are encouraged to use more lean and medium-fat meat, poultry, and fish in your meal plan. This will help decrease your fat intake, which may help decrease your risk for heart disease. The items from the high-fat group are high in saturated fat, cholesterol, and Calories. You should limit your choices from the high-fat group to three (3) times per week. Meat and substitutes do not contribute any fiber to your meal plan.

Tips

1. Bake, roast, broil, grill, or boil these foods rather than frying them with added fat.
2. Use a nonstick pan spray or a nonstick pan to brown or fry these foods.
3. Trim off visible fat before and after cooking.
4. Do not add flour, bread crumbs, coating mixes, or fat to these foods when preparing them.
5. Weigh meat after removing bones and fat, and after cooking. Three ounces of cooked meat is about equal to 4 ounces of raw meat. Some examples of meat portions are:

   2 ounces meat (2 meat exchanges) =
   1 small chicken leg or thigh
   ½ cup cottage cheese or tuna

   3 ounces meat (3 meat exchanges) =
   1 medium pork chop
   1 small hamburger
   ½ of a whole chicken breast
   1 unbreaded fish fillet
   cooked meat, about the size of a deck of cards
6. Restaurants usually serve prime cuts of meat, which are high in fat and Calories.

Lean meat and substitutes

(One exchange is equal to any one of the following items.)

Beef:	USDA Good or Choice grades of lean beef, such as round, sirloin, and flank steak; tenderloin; and chipped beef †	1 oz.
Pork:	Lean pork, such as fresh ham; canned, cured or boiled ham † ; Canadian bacon † , tenderloin.	1 oz.
Veal:	All cuts are lean except for veal cutlets (ground or cubed). Examples of lean veal are chops and roasts.	1 oz.
Poultry:	Chicken, turkey, Cornish hen (without skin)	1 oz.
Fish:	All fresh and frozen fish	1 oz.
	Crab, lobster, scallops, shrimp, clams (fresh or canned in water †)	2 oz.
	Oysters †	6 medium
	Tuna † (canned in water)	¼ cup
	Herring (uncreamed or smoked)	1 oz.
	Sardines (canned)	2 medium
Wild game:	Venison, rabbit, squirrel	1 oz.
	Pheasant, duck, goose (without skin)	1 oz.
Cheese:	Any cottage cheese	¼ cup
	Grated parmesan	2 Tbsp.
	Diet cheeses † (with less than 55 calories per ounce)	1 oz.
Other:	95% fat-free luncheon meat	1 oz.
	Egg whites	3 whites
	Egg substitutes with less than 55 calories per ¼ cup	¼ cup

† 400 mg or more of sodium per exchange

Medium-fat meat and substitutes

(One exchange is equal to any one of the following items.)

Beef:	Most beef products fall into this category. Examples are: all ground beef, roast (rib, chuck, rump), steak (cubed, Porterhouse, T-bone), and meatloaf.	1 oz.
Pork:	Most pork products fall into this category. Examples are: chops, loin roast, Boston butt, cutlets.	1 oz.
Lamb:	Most lamb products fall into this category. Examples are: chops, leg, and roast.	1 oz.
Veal:	Cutlet (ground or cubed, unbreaded)	1 oz.
Poultry:	Chicken (with skin), domestic duck or goose (well-drained of fat), ground turkey	1 oz.
Fish:	Tuna † (canned in oil and drained)	¼ cup
	Salmon † (canned)	¼ cup
Cheese:	Skim or part-skim milk cheeses, such as:	
	Ricotta	¼ cup
	Mozzarella	1 oz.
	Diet cheeses † (with 56–80 calories per ounce)	1 oz.
Other:	86% fat-free luncheon meat †	1 oz.
	Egg (high in cholesterol, limit to 3 per week)	1
	Egg substitutes with 56–80 calories per ¼ cup	¼ cup
	Tofu (2½ in. × 2¾ in. × 1 in.)	4 oz
	Liver, heart, kidney, sweetbreads (high in cholesterol)	1 oz.

† 400 mg or more of sodium per exchange

† Meats and meat substitutes that have 400 milligrams or more of sodium per exchange are indicated with this symbol.

High-fat meat and substitutes

Remember, these items are high in saturated fat, cholesterol, and Calories, and should be used only three (3) times per week.

(One exchange is equal to any one of the following items.)

Beef:	Most USDA Prime cuts of beef, such as ribs, corned beef ▲	1 oz.
Pork:	Spareribs, ground pork, pork sausage ▲ (patty or link)	1 oz.
Lamb:	Patties (ground lamb)	1 oz.
Fish:	Any fried fish product	1 oz.
Cheese:	All regular cheeses ▲ , such as American, Blue, Cheddar, Monterey, Swiss	1 oz.
Other:	Luncheon meat ▲ , such as bologna, salami, pimento loaf	1 oz.
	Sausage ▲ , such as Polish, Italian	1 oz.
	Knockwurst, smoked	1 oz.
	Bratwurst ▲	1 oz.
	Frankfurter ▲ (turkey or chicken)	1 frank (10 / lb.)
	Peanut butter (contains unsaturated fat)	1 Tbsp.

Count as one high-fat meat plus one fat exchange:

	Frankfurter ▲ (beef, pork, or combination)	1 frank (10 / lb.)

▲ 400 mg or more of sodium per exchange

Vegetable List

Each vegetable serving on this list contains about 5 grams of carbohydrate, 2 grams of protein, and 25 Calories. Vegetables contain 2–3 grams of dietary fiber. Vegetables which contain 400 mg of sodium per serving are identified with a ▮ symbol.

Vegetables are a good source of vitamins and minerals. Fresh and frozen vegetables have more vitamins and less added salt. Rinsing canned vegetables will remove much of the salt.

Unless otherwise noted, the serving size for vegetables (one vegetable exchange) is:

½ cup of cooked vegetables or vegetable juice
1 cup of raw vegetables

Artichoke (½ medium)
Asparagus
Beans (green, wax, Italian)
Bean sprouts
Beets
Broccoli
Brussels sprouts
Cabbage, cooked
Carrots
Cauliflower
Eggplant
Greens (collard, mustard, turnip)
Kohlrabi
Leeks
Mushrooms, cooked
Okra
Onions
Pea pods
Peppers (green)
Rutabaga
Sauerkraut ▮
Spinach, cooked
Summer squash (crookneck)
Tomato (one large)
Tomato/vegetable juice ▮
Turnips
Water chestnuts
Zucchini, cooked

▮ 400 mg or more of sodium per serving

Starchy vegetables such as corn, peas, and potatoes are found on the Starch/Bread List.

For free vegetables, see Free Food List on page 373.

Fruit List

Each item on this list contains about 15 grams of carbohydrate and 60 Calories. Fresh, frozen, and dry fruits have about 2 grams of fiber per serving. Fruits that have 3 or more grams of fiber per serving have a 🍃 symbol. Fruit juices contain very little dietary fiber.

The carbohydrate and Calorie content for a fruit serving are based on the usual serving of the most commonly eaten fruits. Use fresh fruits or fruits frozen or canned without sugar added. Whole fruit is more filling than fruit juice and may be a better choice for those who are trying to lose weight. Unless otherwise noted, the serving size for one fruit serving is:

½ cup of fresh fruit or fruit juice
¼ cup of dried fruit

Fresh, Frozen, and Unsweetened Canned Fruit

Apple (raw, 2 in. across)	1 apple
Applesauce (unsweetened)	½ cup
Apricots (medium, raw) or	4 apricots
Apricots (canned)	½ cup, or 4 halves
Banana (9 in. long)	½ banana
🍃 Blackberries (raw)	¾ cup
🍃 Blueberries (raw)	¾ cup
Cantaloupe (5 in. across)	⅓ melon
(cubes)	1 cup
Cherries (large, raw)	12 cherries
Cherries (canned)	½ cup
Figs (raw, 2 in. across)	2 figs
Fruit cocktail (canned)	½ cup
Grapefruit (medium)	½ grapefruit
Grapefruit (segments)	¾ cup
Grapes (small)	15 grapes
Honeydew melon (medium)	⅛ melon
(cubes)	1 cup
Kiwi (large)	1 kiwi
Mandarin oranges	¾ cup

Mango (small)	½ mango
🍃 Nectarine (1½ in. across)	1 nectarine
Orange (2½ in. across)	1 orange
Papaya	1 cup
Peach (2¾ in. across)	1 peach, or ¾ cup
Peaches (canned)	½ cup, or 2 halves
Pear	½ large, or 1 small
Pears (canned)	½ cup or 2 halves
Persimmon (medium, native)	2 persimmons
Pineapple (raw)	¾ cup
Pineapple (canned)	⅓ cup
Plum (raw, 2 in. across)	2 plums
🍃 Pomegranate	½ pomegranate
🍃 Raspberries (raw)	1 cup
🍃 Strawberries (raw, whole)	1¼ cup
Tangerine (2½ in. across)	2 tangerines
Watermelon (cubes)	1¼ cup

Dried Fruit

🍃 Apples	4 rings
🍃 Apricots	7 halves
Dates	2½ medium
🍃 Figs	1½
🍃 Prunes	3 medium
Raisins	2 Tbsp.

Fruit Juice

Apple juice/cider	½ cup
Cranberry juice cocktail	⅓ cup
Grapefruit juice	½ cup
Grape juice	⅓ cup
Orange juice	½ cup
Pineapple juice	½ cup
Prune juice	⅓ cup

🍃 3 or more grams of fiber per serving

Milk List

Each serving of milk or milk products on this list contains about 12 grams of carbohydrate and 8 grams of protein. The amount of fat in milk is measured in percent (%) of butterfat. The Calories vary, depending on what kind of milk you choose. The list is divided into three parts based on the amount of fat and Calories: skim/very lowfat milk, lowfat milk, and whole milk. One serving (one milk exchange) of each of these includes:

	Carbohydrate (grams)	Protein (grams)	Fat (grams)	Calories
Skim/very lowfat	12	8	trace	90
Lowfat	12	8	5	120
Whole	12	8	8	150

Milk is the body's main source of calcium, the mineral needed for growth and repair of bones. Yogurt is also a good source of calcium. Yogurt and many dry or powdered milk products have different amounts of fat. If you have questions about a particular item, read the label to find out the fat and calorie content.

Milk is good to drink, but it can also be added to cereal, and to other foods. Many tasty dishes such as sugar-free pudding are made with milk (see the Combination Foods list). Add life to plain yogurt by adding one of your fruit servings to it.

Skim and Very Lowfat Milk

Skim milk	1 cup
½% milk	1 cup
1% milk	1 cup
Lowfat buttermilk	1 cup
Evaporated skim milk	½ cup
Dry nonfat milk	⅓ cup
Plain nonfat yogurt	1 cup

Lowfat Milk

2% milk	1 cup
Plain lowfat yogurt (with added nonfat milk solids)	1 cup

Whole Milk

The whole milk group has much more fat per serving than the skim and lowfat groups. Whole milk has more than 3¼% butterfat. Try to limit your choices from the whole milk group as much as possible.

Whole milk	1 cup
Evaporated whole milk	½ cup
Whole plain yogurt	1 cup

Fat List

Each serving on the fat list contains about 5 grams of fat and 45 Calories.

The foods on the fat list contain mostly fat, although some items may also contain a small amount of protein. All fats are high in Calories and should be carefully measured. Everyone should modify fat intake by eating unsaturated fats instead of saturated fats. The sodium content of these foods varies widely. Check the label for sodium information.

Unsaturated Fats

Avocado	⅛ medium
Margarine	1 tsp.
*Margarine, diet	1 Tbsp.
Mayonnaise	1 tsp.
*Mayonnaise, reduced-Calorie	1 Tbsp.
Nuts and Seeds:	
Almonds, dry roasted	6 whole
Cashews, dry roasted	1 Tbsp.
Other nuts	1 Tbsp.
Peanuts	20 small or 10 large
Pecans	2 whole
Pumpkin seeds	2 tsp.
Seeds, pine nuts, sunflower (without shells)	1 Tbsp.
Walnuts	2 whole
Oil (corn, cottonseed, safflower, soybean, sunflower, olive, peanut)	1 tsp.
*Olives	10 small or 5 large
*Salad dressing (all varieties)	1 Tbsp.
Salad dressing, mayonnaise-type	2 tsp.
Salad dressing, mayonnaise-type, reduced-calorie	1 Tbsp.
▮ Salad dressing, reduced-calorie	2 Tbsp.

(Two tablespoons of low-calorie salad dressing is a free food.)

Saturated Fats

*Bacon	1 slice
Butter	1 tsp.
Chitterlings	½ ounce
Coconut, shredded	2 Tbsp.
Coffee whitener, liquid	2 Tbsp.
Coffee whitener, powder	4 tsp.
Cream, sour	2 Tbsp.
Cream (light, coffee, table)	2 Tbsp.
Cream (heavy, whipping)	1 Tbsp.
Cream cheese	1 Tbsp.
*Salt pork	¼ ounce

*If more than one or two servings are eaten, these foods have 400 mg. or more of sodium.
▮ 400 mg. or more of sodium per serving.

Free Foods

A free food is any food or drink that contains less than 20 calories per serving. You can eat as much as you want of those items that have no serving size specified. You may eat two or three servings per day of those items that have a specific serving size. Be sure to spread them out through the day.

Drinks:
Bouillon, low-sodium
Bouillon ▮ or broth without fat
Carbonated drinks, sugar-free
Carbonated water
Club soda
Cocoa powder, unsweetened (1 Tbsp.)
Coffee/Tea
Drink mixes, sugar-free
Tonic water, sugar-free

Nonstick pan spray

Fruit:
Cranberries, unsweetened (½ cup)
Rhubarb, unsweetened (½ cup)

Vegetables:
(raw, 1 cup)
Cabbage
Celery
Chinese cabbage 🌾
Cucumber
Green onion
Hot peppers
Mushrooms
Radishes
Zucchini 🌾

Salad greens:
Endive
Escarole
Lettuce
Romaine
Spinach

Sweet Substitutes:

Candy, hard, sugar-free

Gelatin, sugar-free

Gum, sugar-free

Jam/Jelly, sugar-free (2 tsp.)

Pancake syrup, sugar-free (1–2 Tbsp.)

Sugar substitutes (saccharin, aspartame)

Whipped topping (2 Tbsp.)

Condiments:

Catsup (1 Tbsp.)

Horseradish

Mustard

Pickles 🛆 , dill, unsweetened

Salad dressing, low-calorie (2 Tbsp.)

Taco sauce (1 Tbsp.)

Vinegar

Seasonings can be very helpful in making food taste better. Be careful of how much sodium you use. Read the label, and choose those seasonings that do not contain sodium or salt.

Basil (fresh)	Lemon pepper
Celery seeds	Lime
Chili powder	Lime juice
Chives	Mint
Cinnamon	Onion powder
Curry	Oregano
Dill	Paprika
Flavoring extracts	Pepper
(vanilla, almond,	Pimento
walnut,	Soy sauce 🛆
peppermint, butter,	Soy sauce, low sodium
lemon, etc.)	("lite")
Garlic	Spices
Garlic powder	Wine, used in cooking
Herbs	(¼ cup)
Hot pepper sauce	Worcestershire sauce
Lemon	
Lemon juice	

〰 3 grams or more of fiber per serving,

🛆 400 mg or more of sodium per serving

Combination Foods

Much of the food we eat is mixed together in various combinations. These combination foods do not fit into only one exchange list. It can be quite hard to tell what is in a certain casserole dish or baked food item. This is a list of average values for some typical combination foods. This list will help you fit these foods into your meal plan. Ask your dietitian for information about any other foods you'd like to eat. The *American Diabetes Association/American Dietetic Association Family Cookbooks* and the *American Diabetes Association Holiday Cookbook* have many recipes and further information about many foods, including combination foods. Check your library or local bookstore.

Food	Amount	Exchanges
Casseroles, homemade	1 cup (8 oz.)	2 starch, 2 medium-fat meat, 1 fat
Cheese pizza 🇦 , thin crust	¼ of 15 oz. or ¼ cf 10″	2 starch, 1 medium-fat meat, 1 fat
Chili with beans 🌾 , 🇦 (commercial)	1 cup (8 oz.)	2 starch, 2 medium-fat meat, 2 fat
Chow mein 🌾 , 🇦 (without noodles or rice)	2 cups (16 oz.)	1 starch, 2 vegetable, 2 lean meat
Macaroni and cheese 🇦	1 cup (8 oz.)	2 starch, 1 medium-fat meat, 2 fat
Soup:		
Bean 🌾 , 🇦	1 cup (8 oz.)	1 starch, 1 vegetable, 1 lean meat
Chunky, all varieties 🇦	10¾ oz. can	1 starch, 1 vegetable, 1 medium-fat meat
Cream 🇦 (made with water)	1 cup (8 oz.)	1 starch, 1 fat
Vegetable 🇦 or broth 🇦	1 cup (8 oz.)	1 starch
Spaghetti and meatballs 🇦 (canned)	1 cup (8 oz.)	2 starch, 1 medium-fat meat, 1 fat
Sugar-free pudding (made with skim milk)	½ cup	1 starch
If beans are used as a meat substitute:		
Dried beans 🌾 , peas 🌾 , lentils 🌾	1 cup (cooked)	2 starch, 1 lean meat

🌾 3 grams or more of fiber per serving, 🇦 400 mg or more of sodium per serving

Foods for Occasional Use

Moderate amounts of some foods can be used in your meal plan, in spite of their sugar or fat content, as long as you can maintain blood-glucose control. The following list includes average exchange values for some of these foods. Because they are concentrated sources of carbohydrate, you will notice that the portion sizes are very small. Check with your dietitian for advice on how often and when you can eat them.

Food	Amount	Exchanges
Angel food cake	1/12 cake	2 starch
Cake, no icing	1/12 cake, or a 3″ square	2 starch, 2 fat
Cookies	2 small (1¾″ across)	1 starch, 1 fat
Frozen fruit yogurt	⅓ cup	1 starch
Gingersnaps	3	1 starch
Granola	¼ cup	1 starch, 1 fat
Granola bars	1 small	1 starch, 1 fat
Ice cream, any flavor	½ cup	1 starch, 2 fat
Ice milk, any flavor	½ cup	1 starch, 1 fat
Sherbet, any flavor	¼ cup	1 starch
Snack chips 🇦 , all varieties	1 oz.	1 starch, 2 fat
Vanilla wafers	6 small	1 starch, 1 fat

🇦 If more than one serving is eaten, these foods have 400 mg. or more of sodium.

Management Tips

Here are some tips that can help you change the way you eat.

Make changes gradually—Don't try to do everything all at once. It may take longer to accomplish your goals, but the changes you make will be permanent!

Set short-term, realistic goals—If weight loss is your goal, try to lose two pounds in two weeks, not 20 pounds in one week. Walk two blocks at first, not two miles. Success will come more easily, and you'll feel good about yourself!

Reward yourself—When you make your short-term goal, do something special for yourself. Go to a movie, buy a new shirt, read a book, visit a friend.

Measure foods—It is important to eat the right serving sizes of food. You will need to learn how to estimate the amount of food you are served. You can do this by measuring all the food you eat for a week or so. Measure liquids with a measuring cup. Some solid foods (tuna, cottage cheese, canned fruits) can be measured with a measuring cup, too. Measuring spoons (teaspoon, tablespoon) are used for measuring smaller amounts such as oil, salad dressing, or peanut butter. A scale can be very useful to measure almost anything, especially meat, poultry, and fish. All food should be measured or weighed after cooking.

Some food you buy uncooked will weigh less after you cook it. This is true of most meats. Starches often swell in cooking, so a small amount of uncooked starch will become a much larger amount of cooked food. The following table shows some of the changes.

Food (starch group)	Uncooked	Cooked
Cream of Wheat	2 level Tbsp.	½ cup
Dried beans	3 Tbsp.	⅓ cup
Dried peas	3 Tbsp.	⅓ cup
Grits	3 level Tbsp.	½ cup
Lentils	2 Tbsp.	⅓ cup
Macaroni	¼ cup	½ cup
Noodles	⅓ cup	½ cup
Oatmeal	3 level Tbsp.	½ cup
Rice	2 level Tbsp.	⅓ cup
Spaghetti	¼ cup	½ cup
Food (meat group)		
Chicken	1 small drumstick	1 ounce
	½ of a whole chicken breast	3 ounces
Hamburger	4 ounces	3 ounces

The Exchange Lists are the basis of a meal planning system designed by a committee of the American Diabetes Association and the American Dietetic Association. While designed primarily for people with diabetes and others who must follow special diets, the Exchange Lists are based on principles of good nutrition that apply to everyone. © 1986 American Diabetes Association, Inc., American Dietetic Association.

Appendix I

Calories, Percent Fat, and Cholesterol in Selected Fast-Food Restaurant Products

	Calories	% Fat Calories	Cholesterol (milligrams)
Arby's			
Regular roast beef	353	38	39
Roast Chicken Deluxe	373	47	20
Potato cakes	204	48	0
Jamocha shake	368	26	35
Burger King			
Apple pie	311	40	4
Double cheeseburger	483	50	100
Double Whopper with cheese	935	59	194
Onion rings	339	50	0
Vanilla milk shake	334	27	33
Croissan'wich with egg/cheese	315	57	222
Bagel	272	20	29
Domino's Pizza			
Cheese, 2 slices	376	24	18
Pepperoni, 2 slices	460	34	28
Veggie, 2 slices	498	33	36
Double cheese/pepperoni, 2 slices	545	42	48
Hardee's			
Steak biscuit	500	52	30
Hamburger, regular	270	33	20
Bacon cheeseburger	610	57	80
Big country breakfast	670	51	345
Chef salad	240	56	115
Turkey club sandwich	390	37	70
All-beef hot dog sandwich	300	51	25
Kentucky Fried Chicken			
Cole slaw	119	50	4
Mashed potatoes with gravy	71	20	1
Side breast (Lite'n crispy)	204	55	53
Side breast (Extra crispy)	379	64	77
Long John Silver's			
Baked fish	120	6	110
Baked shrimp-scampi	120	15	205
Baked chicken	140	26	70
Fish with batter, one piece	202	50	31
Coleslaw	140	39	15
Hush puppies, two pieces	145	43	1
McDonald's			
McLean Deluxe	320	28	60
Big Mac	570	55	83
Chicken McNuggets	270	51	56
Egg McMuffin	290	35	226
Hotcakes with margarine and syrup	410	20	8
French Fries, medium	320	48	0
Sausage biscuit	467	60	48
Apple bran muffin	190	0	0
Chunky chicken salad	140	22	78

	Calories	% Fat Calories	Cholesterol
Continued			
Pizza Hut			
Pan pizza, cheese, 2 slices	492	33	34
Handtossed, cheese, 2 slices	518	35	55
Personal Pan Pizza, Supreme (whole pizza)	647	39	49
Taco Bell			
Bean burrito	343	32	*
Beef tostada	291	47	*
Taco	186	39	*
Wendy's			
Big classic hamburger	570	52	80
Fish fillet sandwich	460	49	50
Grilled chicken fillet	100	27	50
Plain potato	250	1	0
Potato with bacon and cheese	520	31	20

*Data on cholesterol not available. Compare to similar foods offered by other chains for approximate cholesterol content.

Fat content is expressed as percentage of total Calories; cholesterol is expressed in milligrams per serving.

Appendix J

American College of Sports Medicine Position Stand: The Use of Anabolic-Androgenic Steroids in Sports

Based on a comprehensive literature survey and a careful analysis of the claims concerning the ergogenic effects and the adverse effects of anabolic-androgenic steroids, it is the position of the American College of Sports Medicine that:

1. Anabolic-androgenic steroids in the presence of an adequate diet can contribute to increases in body weight, often in the lean mass compartment.

2. The gains in muscular strength achieved through high-intensity exercise and proper diet can be increased by the use of anabolic-androgenic steroids in some individuals.

3. Anabolic-androgenic steroids do not increase aerobic power or capacity for muscular exercise.

4. Anabolic-androgenic steroids have been associated with adverse effects on the liver, cardiovascular system, reproductive system, and psychological status in therapeutic trials and in limited research on athletes. Until further research is completed, the potential hazards of the use of the anabolic-androgenic steroids in athletes must include those found in therapeutic trials.

5. The use of anabolic-androgenic steroids by athletes is contrary to the rules and ethical principles of athletic competition as set forth by many of the sports-governing bodies. The American College of Sports Medicine supports these ethical principles and deplores the use of anabolic-androgenic steroids by athletes.

This document is a revision of the 1977 position stand of the American College of Sports Medicine concerning anabolic-androgenic steroids (4).

Background

In 1935 the long-suspected positive effect of androgens on protein anabolism was documented (56). Subsequently, this effect was confirmed (53,77), and the development of 19-nortestosterone heralded the synthesis of steroids that have greater anabolic

properties than natural testosterone but less of its virilizing effect (39). The use of androgenic steroids by athletes began in the early 1950s (106) and has increased through the years (60,62,83,98,104,106), despite warnings about potential adverse reactions (4,83,106,112) and the banning of these substances by sports governing bodies.

Anabolic-androgenic Steroids, Body Composition and Athletic Performance

Body composition. Animal studies investigating the effect of anabolic-androgenic steroids on body composition have shown increases in lean body mass, nitrogen retention and muscle growth in castrated males (37,57,58) and normal females (26,37,71). The effects of anabolic-androgenic steroids on the body weights of normal, untrained, male animals (37,40,71,105,114), treadmill-trained (43,97) or isometrically-trained rats (82), or strength-trained monkeys (80) have been minimal to absent; however, the effects of steroids on animals undergoing heavy resistance training have not been adequately studied. Human males who are deficient in natural androgens by castration or other causes have shown significant increases in nitrogen retention and muscular development with anabolic-androgenic steroid therapy (23,58,103). Human males and females involved in experimental (38) and therapeutic trials of anabolic steroids (15,16,93) have shown increases in body weight.

The majority of the strength-training studies in which body weight was reported showed greater increases in weight under steroid treatment than under placebo (17,41,42,50,61,74,94,96,107). Other training studies have reported no significant changes in body weight (21,27,31,34,100,108). The weight gained was determined to be lean body mass in three studies that made this determination with hydrostatic weighing techniques (41,42,107). Four other studies found no significant differences in lean body mass between steroid and placebo treatments (17,21,27,34), but in two of those the mean differences favored the steroid treatment (21,27). The extent to which increased water retention accounts for steroid-induced changes in body composition is controversial (17,42) and has yet to be resolved.

In summary, anabolic-androgenic steroids can contribute to an increase in body weight in the lean mass compartment of the body. The amount of weight gained in the training studies has been small but statistically significant.

Muscular strength. Strength is an important factor in many athletic events. The literature concerning the efficacy of anabolic steroids for promoting strength development is controversial. Many factors contribute to the development of strength, including heredity, intensity of training, diet, and the status of the psyche (112). It is very difficult to control all of these factors in an experimental design. The additional variable of dosage is included when drug research is undertaken. Some athletes claim that doses greater than therapeutic are necessary for strength gains (106) even though positive results have been reported using therapeutic (low-dose) regimens (50,74,94,107). Double-blind studies using anabolic-androgenic steroids are also difficult to conduct because of the physical and/or psychological effects of the drug that, for example, allowed 100 percent of the participants in one "double-blind" study to correctly identify the steroid phase of the experiment (32). The placebo effect has been shown to be a factor in studies of anabolic-androgenic steroids as in all drug studies (6).

In animal studies, the combination of anabolic-androgenic steroids and overload training has not produced larger gains in force production than training alone (80,97). However, steroid-induced gains in strength have been reported in experienced (42,74,94,107) and inexperienced weight trainers (50,51,96) with (50,51,74,94) and without dietary control or supplemental protein (42,96). In contrast, no positive effect of steroids on gains in strength over those produced by training alone were reported in other studies involving experienced (21,34,54) and inexperienced weight trainers (17,27,31,41,54, 61,100,108) with (21,34,61,100) and without dietary control or supplemental protein (17,27,31, 41,54,108). The studies that reported no changes in strength with anabolic-androgenic steroids have been criticized (112) for the use of inexperienced weight trainers, lack of dietary control, low-intensity training (17,27,31,61), and nonspecific testing of strength (21). The studies that have shown strength gains with the use of anabolic-androgenic steroids have been criticized (83) for inadequate numbers of subjects (74,94,107), improper statistical designs, inadequate execution, and the unsatisfactory reporting of experimental results.

There have been no studies of the effects of the massive doses of steroids used by some athletes over periods of several years. Similarly, there have been no studies of the use of anabolic-androgenic steroids and training in women or children. Theoretically, anabolic and androgenic effects would be greater in women and children because they have naturally lower levels of androgens than men.

Three proposed mechanisms for the actions of the anabolic-androgenic steroids for increases in muscle strength are:

1. Increase in protein synthesis in the muscle as a direct action of the anabolic-androgenic steroid (81,82,92).
2. Blocking of the catabolic effect of glucocorticoids after exercise by increasing the amount of anabolic-androgenic hormone available (1,92,112).
3. Steroid-induced enhancement of aggressive behavior that promotes a greater quantity and quality of weight training (14).

In spite of controversial and sometimes contradictory results of the studies in this area, it can be concluded that the use of anabolic-androgenic steroids, especially by experienced weight trainers, often can increase strength gains beyond those seen with training and diet alone. This positive effect on strength is usually small and obviously is not exhibited by all individuals. The explanation for this variability in steroid effects is unclear. When small increments in strength occur, they can be important in athletic competition.

Aerobic capacity. The effect of anabolic-androgenic steroids on aerobic capacity also has been questioned. The potential of these drugs to increase total blood volume and hemoglobin (88) might suggest a positive effect of steroids on aerobic capacity. However, only three studies indicated positive effects (3,51,54), and there has been no substantiation of these results in subsequent studies (27,41,50,52). Thus, the majority of evidence shows no positive effect of anabolic-androgenic steroids on aerobic capacity over aerobic training alone.

Adverse Effects

Anabolic-androgenic steroids have been associated with many undesirable or adverse effects in laboratory studies and therapeutic trials. The effects of major concern are those on the liver, the cardiovascular and reproductive systems, and on the psychological status of individuals who are using the anabolic-androgenic steroids.

Adverse effects on the liver. Impaired excretory function of the liver, resulting in jaundice, has been associated with anabolic-androgenic steroids in a number of therapeutic trials (76,84,90). The possible cause-and-effect nature of this association is strengthened by the observation of jaundice remission after discontinuance of the drug (76,84). In studies of athletes using anabolic-androgenic steroids (65 athletes tested) (89,98,104), no evidence of cholestasis has been found.

Structural changes in the liver following anabolic-steroid treatment have been found in animals (95,101) and in humans (73,86). Conclusions concerning the clinical significance of these changes on a short- or long-term basis have not been drawn. Investigations in athletes for these changes have not been performed, but there is no reason to believe that the athlete using anabolic-androgenic steroids is immune from these effects of the drugs.

The most serious liver complications associated with anabolic-androgenic steroids are peliosis hepatitis (blood-filled cysts in the liver of unknown etiology) and liver tumors. Cases of peliosis hepatitis have been reported in individuals treated with anabolic-androgenic steroids for various conditions (7–10,13,35,65,66,70,88,102). Rupture of the cysts or liver failure resulting from the condition was fatal in some individuals (9,70,102). In other case reports the condition was an incidental finding at autopsy (8,10,66). The possible cause-and-effect nature of the association between peliosis hepatitis and the use of anabolic-androgenic steroids is strengthened by the observation of improvement in the condition after discontinuance of drug therapy in some cases (7,35). There are no reported cases of this condition in athletes using anabolic-androgenic steroids, but investigations specific for this disorder have not been performed in athletes.

Liver tumors have been associated with the use of anabolic-androgenic steroids in individuals receiving these drugs as a part of their treatment regimen (28,29,49,67,69,99,115). These tumors are generally benign (29,67,69,115), but there have been malignant lesions associated with individuals using these drugs (28,99,115). The possible cause-and-effect nature of this association between the use of the drug and tumor development is strengthened by a report of tumor regression after cessation of drug treatment (49). The 17-alpha-alkylated compounds are the specific family of anabolic steroids indicted in the development of liver tumors (46,49). There is one reported case of a 26-year-old male body builder who died of liver cancer after having abused a variety of anabolic steroids for at least four years (75).

The testing necessary for discovery of these tumors is not commonly performed, and it is possible that other tumors associated with steroid use by athletes have gone undetected.

Blood tests of liver function have been reported to be unchanged with steroid use in some training studies (31,41,54,94) and abnormal in other training studies (32,51) and in tests performed on athletes known to be using anabolic-androgenic steroids (54,89,104). However, the lesions of peliosis hepatitis and liver tumors do not always result in blood-test abnormalities (8,28,29,49,67,115), and some authors state that liver radioisotope scans, ultrasound, or computed tomography scans are needed for diagnosis (28,29,113).

In summary, liver-function tests have been shown to be adversely affected by anabolic-androgenic steroids, especially the 17-alpha-alkylated compounds. The short- and long-term consequences of these changes, though potentially hazardous, have yet to be reported in athletes using these drugs.

Adverse effects on the cardiovascular system. The steroid-induced changes that may affect the development of cardiovascular disease include hyperinsulinism and altered glucose tolerance (111), decreased high-density lipoprotein cholesterol levels (72,98), and elevated blood pressure (68). These effects are variable for different individuals in various clinical situations. Triglycerides are lowered by anabolic-androgenic steroids in certain individuals (24,72) and are increased in others (18,78). Histological examinations of myofibrils and mitochondria from cardiac tissue obtained from laboratory animals have shown that administration of anabolic steroids leads to pathological alterations in these structures (5,11,12). The cardiovascular effects of the anabolic-androgenic steroids, though potentially hazardous, need further research before any conclusions can be made.

Adverse effects on the male reproductive system.
The effects of the anabolic-androgenic steroids on the male reproductive system are oligospermia (small number of sperm) and azoospermia (lack of sperm in the semen), decreased testicular size, abnormal appearance of testicular biopsy material, and reductions in testosterone and gonadotropic hormones. These effects have been shown in training studies (19,41,100), studies of normal volunteers (38), therapeutic trials (44), and studies of athletes who were using anabolic-androgenic steroids (55,79,104). In view of the changes shown in the pituitary-gonadal axis, the dysfunction accounting for

these abnormalities is believed to be steroid-induced suppression of gonadotrophin production (19,36,38,79). The changes in these hormones are ordinarily reversible after cessation of drug treatment, but the long-term effects of altering the hypothalamic-pituitary-gonadal axis remain unknown. However, there is a report of residual abnormalities in testicular morphology of healthy men six months after discontinuing steroid use (38). It has been reported that the metabolism of androgens to estrogenic compounds may lead to gynecomastia in males (23,58,98,112).

Adverse effects on the female reproductive system. The effect of androgenic steroids on the female reproductive system include reduction in circulating levels of luteinizing hormone, follicle-stimulating hormone, estrogens, and progesterone; inhibition of folliculogenesis and ovulation; and menstrual-cycle changes including prolongation of the follicular phase, shortening of the luteal phase, and amenorrhea (20,63,91).

Adverse effects on psychological status. In both sexes, psychological effects of anabolic-androgenic steroids include increases or decreases in libido, mood swings, and aggressive behavior (38,98), which is related to plasma testosterone levels (25,85). Administration of steroids causes changes in the electroencephalogram similar to those seen with psycho-stimulant drugs (47,48). The possible ramifications of uncontrollably aggressive and possible hostile behavior should be considered prior to the use of anabolic-androgenic steroids.

Other adverse effects. Other side effects associated with the anabolic-androgenic steroids include: ataxia (2); premature epiphysial closure in youths (23,58,64,109,110); virilization in youths and women, including hirsutism (45), clitoromegaly (63,112), and irreversible deepening of the voice (22,23); acne; temporal hair recession; and alopecia (45). These adverse reactions can occur with the use of anabolic-androgenic steroids and are believed to be dependent on the type of steroid, dosage and duration of drug use (58). There is no method for predicting which individuals are more likely to develop these adverse effects, some of which are potentially hazardous.

The Ethical Issue

Equitable competition and fair play are the foundation of athletic competition. If competition is to remain on this foundation, rules are necessary. The International Olympic Committee (IOC) has defined "doping" as "the administration of or the use of a competing athlete of any substance foreign to the body or of any physiological substance taken in abnormal quantity or taken by an abnormal route of entry into the body, with the sole intention of increasing in an artificial and unfair manner his performance in competition." Accordingly, the medically unjustified use of anabolic steroids with the intention of gaining an athletic advantage is clearly unethical. Anabolic-androgenic steroids are listed as banned substances by the IOC in accordance with the rules against doping. The American College of Sports Medicine supports the position that the eradication of anabolic-androgenic steroid use by athletes is in the best interest of sport and endorses the development of effective procedures for drug detection and of policies that exclude from competition those athletes who refuse to abide by the rules.

The "win at all cost" attitude that has pervaded society places the athlete in a precarious situation. Testimonial evidence suggests that some athletes would risk serious harm and even death if they could obtain a drug that would ensure their winning an Olympic gold medal. However, the use of anabolic-androgenic steroids by athletes is contrary to the ethical principles of athletic competition and is deplored.

References

1. Aakvaag, A., O. Bentdol, K. Quigstod, P. Walstod, H. Renningen, and F. Fonnum. Testosterone and testosterone binding globulin (TeBg) in young men during prolonged stress. *Int. J. Androl.* 1:22–31, 1978.

2. Agrawal, B. L. Ataxia caused by fluoxymesterone therapy in breast cancer. *Arch. Intern. Med.* 141:953–959, 1981.

3. Albrecht, H. and E. Albrecht. Ergometric, rheographic, reflexographic and electrographic tests at altitude and effects of drugs on human physical performance. *Fed. Proc.* 28:1262–1267, 1969.

4. American College of Sports Medicine. Position statement on the use and abuse of anabolic-androgenic steroids in sports. *Med. Sci. Sports* 9(4):xi–xiii, 1977.

5. Appell, H. J., B. Heller-Umpfenbach, M. Feraudi, and H. Weicker. Ultrastructural and morphometric investigations on the

effects of training and administration of anabolic steroids on the myocardium of guinea pigs. *Int. J. Sports Med.* 4:268–274, 1983.

6. Ariel, G. and W. Saville. Anabolic steroids: the physiological effects of placebos. *Med. Sci. Sports* 4:124–126, 1972.

7. Arnold, G. L. and M. M. Kaplan. Peliosis hepatitis due to oxymetholone—a clinically benign disorder. *Am. J. Gastroenterol.* 71:213–216, 1979.

8. Asano, A., H. Wakasa, S. Kaise, T. Nishimaki, and R. Kasukawa. Peliosis hepatitis. Report on two autopsy cases with a review of literature. *Acta Pathol. Jpn.* 32:861–877, 1982.

9. Bagheri, S. and J. Boyer. Peliosis hepatitis associated with androgenic-anabolic steroid therapy—a severe form of hepatic injury. *Ann. Intern. Med.* 81:610–618, 1974.

10. Bank, J. I., D. Lykkebo, and I. Hagerstrand. Peliosis hepatitis in a child. *Acta Ped. Scand.* 67:105–107, 1978.

11. Behrendt, H. Effect of anabolic steroid on rat heart muscle cells. I. Intermediate filaments. *Cell Tissue Res.* 180:305–315, 1977.

12. Behrendt, H. and H. Boffin. Myocardial cell lesions caused by anabolic hormone. *Cell Tissue Res.* 181:423–426, 1977.

13. Benjamin, D. C. and B. Shunk. A fatal case of peliosis of the liver and spleen. *Am. J. Dis. Child.* 132:207–208, 1978.

14. Brooks, R. V. Anabolic steroids and athletes. *Phys. Sportsmed.* 8(3):161–163, 1980.

15. Buchwald, D., S. Argyres, R. E. Easterling, et al. Effects of Nandrolone Decanoate on the anemia of chronic hemodialysis patients. *Nephron* 18:232–238, 1977.

16. Carter, C. H. The anabolic steroid, Stanozolol, its evaluation in debilitated children. *Clin. Pediatr.* 4:671–680, 1965.

17. Casner, S. W., R. G. Early, and B. R. Carlson. Anabolic steroid effects on body composition in normal young men. *J. Sports Med. Phys. Fitness* 11:98–103, 1971.

18. Choi, E.S. K., T. Chung, R. S. Morrison, C. Myers, and M. S. Greenberg. Hypertriglyceridemia in hemodialysis patients during oral dromostanolone therapy for anemia. *Am. J. Clin. Nutr.* 27:901–904, 1974.

19. Clerico, A., M. Ferdeghini, C. Palombo, et al. Effects of anabolic treatment on the serum levels of gonadotropins, testosterone, prolactin, thyroid hormones and myoglobin of male athletes under physical training. *J. Nuclear Med. Allied Sci.* 25:79–88, 1981.

20. Cox, D. W., W. L. Heinrichs, C. A. Paulsen, et al. Perturbations of the human menstrual cycle by oxymetholone. *Am. J. Obstet. Gynecol.* 121:121–126, 1975.

21. Crist, D. M., P. J. Stackpole, and G. T. Peake. Effects of androgenic-anabolic steroids on neuromuscular power and body composition. *J. Appl. Physiol.* 54:366–370, 1983.

22. Damste, P. H. Voice change in adult women caused by virilizing agents. *J. Speech Hear. Disord.* 32:126–132, 1967.

23. Dorfman, R. I. and R. A. Shipley. *Androgens; Biochemistry, Physiology and Clinical Significance.* New York: J. Wiley and Sons, 1956.

24. Doyle, A. E., N. B. Pinkus, and J. Green. The use of oxandrolone in hyperlipidaemia. *Med. J. Australia* 1:127–129, 1974.

25. Ehrenkranz, J., E. Bliss, and M. H. Sheard. Plasma testosterone correlation with aggressive behavior and social dominance in man. *Psychosom. Med.* 36:469–475, 1974.

26. Exner, G. U., H. W. Staudte, and D. Pette. Isometric training of rats—effects upon fast and slow muscle and modification by an anabolic hormone (Nandrolone Decanoate) I. Female rats. *Pflugers Arch.* 345:1–14, 1973.

27. Fahey, T. D. and C. H. Brown. The effects of an anabolic steroid on the strength, body composition and endurance of college males when accompanied by a weight training program. *Med. Sci. Sports* 5:272–276, 1973.

28. Falk, H., L. Thomas, H. Popper, and H. G. Ishak. Hepatic angiosarcoma associated with androgenic-anabolic steroids. *Lancet* 2:1120–1123, 1979.

29. Farrell, G. C., D. E. Joshua, R. F. Uren, P. J. Baird, K. W. Perkins, and H. Kronenberg. Androgen-induced hepatoma. *Lancet* 1:430, 1975.

30. Forsyth, B. T. The effect of testosterone propionate at various protein calorie intakes in malnutrition after trauma. *J. Lab. Clin. Med.* 43:732–740, 1954.

31. Fowler, W. M., Jr., G. W. Gardner, and G. H. Egstrom. Effect of an anabolic steroid on physical performance in young men. *J. Appl. Physiol.* 20:1038–1040, 1965.

32. Freed, D. L., A. J. Banks, D. Longson, and D. M. Burley. Anabolic steroids in athletics: crossover double-blind trial on weightlifters. *Br. Med. J.* 2:471–473, 1975.

33. Gelder, L. V. Psychosomatic aspects of endocrine disorders of the voice. *J. Commun. Disord.* 7:257–262, 1974.

34. Golding, L. A., J. E. Freydinger, and S. S. Fishel. The effect of an androgenic-anabolic steroid and a protein supplement on size, strength, weight and body composition in athletics. *Phys. Sportsmed.* 2(6):39–45, 1974.

35. Groos, G., O. H. Arnold, and G. Brittinger. Peliosis hepatitis after long-term administration of oxymetholone. *Lancet* 1:874, 1974.

36. Harkness, R. A., B. H. Kilshaw, and B. M. Hobson. Effects of large doses of anabolic steroids. *Br. J. Sports Med.* 9:70–73, 1975.

37. Heitzman, R. J. The effectiveness of anabolic agents in increasing rate of growth in farm animals; report on experiments in cattle. In: *Anabolic Agents in Animal Production,* F. C. Lu and J. Rendell (Eds.). Stuttgart: Georg Thieme Publishers, 1976, pp. 89–98.

38. Heller, C. G., D. J. Moore, C. A. Paulsen, W. O. Nelson, and W. M. Laidlaw. Effects of progesterone and synthetic progestins on the reproductive physiology of normal men. *Fed. Proc.* 18:1057–1065, 1959.

39. Hershberger, J. G., E. G. Shipley, and R. K. Meyer. Myotrophic activity of 19-nortestosterone and other steroids determined by modified levator ani muscle method. *Proc. Soc. Exper. Biol. Med.* 83:175–180, 1953.

40. Hervey, G. R. and I. Hutchinson. The effects of testosterone on body weight and composition in the rat. *J. Endocrinol.* 57: xxiv–xxv, 1973.

41. Hervey, G. R., I. Hutchinson, A. V. Knibbs, et al. Anabolic effects of methandienone in men undergoing athletic training. *Lancet* 2:699–702, 1976.

42. Hervey, G. R., A. V. Knibbs, L. Burkinshaw, et al. Effects of methandienone on the performance and body composition of men undergoing athletic training. *Clin. Sci.* 60:457–461, 1981.

43. Hickson, R. C., W. W. Heusner, W. D. Van Huss, et al. Effects of Dianabol and high-intensity sprint training on body composition of rats. *Med. Sci. Sports* 8:191–195, 1976.

44. Holma, P. and H. Aldercreutz. Effect on an anabolic steroid (methandienon) on plasma LH, FSH, and testosterone and on the response to intravenous administration of LRH. *Acta Endorcrinol.* 83:856–864, 1976.

45. Houssay, A. B. Effects of anabolic-androgenic steroids on the skin including hair and sebaceous glands. In: *Anabolic-Androgenic Steroids,* C. D. Kochankan (Ed.). New York: Springer-Verlag, 1976, pp. 155–190.

46. Ishak, K. G. Hepatic lesions caused by anabolic and contraceptive steroids. *Sem. Liver Dis.* 1:116–128, 1981.

47. Itil, T. M. Neurophysiological effects of hormones in humans: computer EEG profiles of sex and hypothalamic hormones. In: *Hormones, Behavior and Psychotherapy,* E. J. Sachar (Ed.). New York: Raven Press, 1976, pp. 31–40.

48. Itil, T. M., R. Cora, S. Akpinar, W. M. Herrmann, and C. J. Patterson. Psychotropic action of sex hormones: computerized EEG in establishing the immediate CNS effects of steroid hormones. *Curr. Ther. Res.* 16:1147–1170, 1974.

49. Johnson, F. L., K. G. Lerner, M. Siegel, et al. Association of androgenic-anabolic steroid therapy with development of hepatocellular carcinoma. *Lancet* 2:1273, 1972.

50. Johnson, L. C., G. Fisher, L. J. Silvester, and C. C. Hofheins. Anabolic steroid: effects of strength, body weight, oxygen uptake and spermatogenesis upon mature males. *Med. Sci. Sports* 4:43–45, 1972.

51. Johnson, L. C. and J. P. O'Shea. Anabolic steroid: effects on strength development. *Science* 164:957–959, 1969.

52. Johnson, L. C., E. S. Roundy, P. E. Allsen, A. G. Fisher, and L. J. Silvester. Effect of anabolic steroid treatment on endurance. *Med. Sci. Sports* 7:287–289, 1975.

53. Kenyon, A. T., K. Knowlton, and I. Sandiford. The anabolic effects of the androgens and somatic growth in man. *Ann. Intern. Med.* 20:632–654, 1944.

54. Keul, J., H. Deus, and W. Kinderman. Anabole hormone: Schadigung, Leistungsfahigkeit und Stoffwechses. *Med. Klin.* 71:497–503, 1976.

55. Kilshaw, B. H., R. A. Harkness, B. M. Hobson, and A. W. M. Smith. The effects of large doses of the anabolic steroid, methandrostenolone, on an athlete. *Clin. Endocrinol.* 4:537–541, 1975.

56. Kochakian, C. D. and J. R. Murlin. The effect of male hormones on the protein and energy metabolism of castrated dogs. *J. Nutr.* 10:437–458, 1935.

57. Kochakian, C. D. and B. R. Endahl. Changes in body weight of normal and castrated rats by different doses of testosterone propionate. *Proc. Soc. Exper. Biol. Med.* 100:520–522, 1959.

58. Kruskemper, H. L. *Anabolic Steroids.* New York: Academic Press, 1968, pp. 128–133, 162–164, 182.

59. Landau, R. L. The metabolic effects of anabolic steroids in man. In: *Anabolic-Androgenic Steroids,* C. D. Kochakian (Ed.). New York: Springer-Verlag, 1976, pp. 45–72.

60. Ljungqvist, A. The use of anabolic steroids in top Swedish athletes. *Br. J. Sports Med.* 9:82, 1975.

61. Loughton, S. J. and R. O. Ruhling. Human strength and endurance responses to anabolic steroid and training. *J. Sports Med.* 17:285–296, 1977.

62. MacDougall, J. D., D. G. Sale, G. C. B. Elder, and J. R. Sutton. Muscle ultrastructural characteristics of elite powerlifters and bodybuilders. *Eur. J. Applied Physiol.* 48:117–126, 1982.

63. Maher, J. M., E. L. Squires, J. L. Voss, and R. K. Shideler. Effect of anabolic steroids on reproductive function of young mares. *J. Am. Vet. Med. Assoc.* 183:519–524, 1983.

64. Mason, A. S. Male precocity: the clinician's view. In: *The Endocrine Function of the Human Testis,* V. H. T. James, M. Serra, and L. Martini (Eds.). New York: Academic Press, 1974, pp. 131–143.

65. McDonald, E. C. and C. E. Speicher. Peliosis hepatitis associated with administration of oxymetholone. *JAMA* 240:243–244, 1978.

66. McGiven, A. R. Peliosis hepatitis: case report and review of pathogenesis. *J. Pathol.* 101:283–285, 1970.

67. Meadows, A. T., J. L. Naiman, and M. Valdes-Dapena. Hepatoma associated with androgen therapy for aplastic anemia. *J. Pediatr.* 85: 109–110, 1974.

68. Messerli, F. H. and E. D. Frohlich. High blood pressure: a side effect of drugs, poisons, and food. *Arch. Intern. Med.* 139:682–687, 1979.

69. Mulvihill, J. J., R. L. Ridolfi, F. R. Schultz, M. S. Brozy, and P. B. T. Haughton. Hepatic adenoma in Fanconi anemia treated with oxymetholone. *J. Pediatr.* 87:122–124, 1975.

70. Nadell, J. and J. Kosek. Peliosis hepatitis. *Arch. Pathol. Lab. Med.* 101:405–410, 1977.

71. Nesheim, M. C. Some observations on the effectiveness of anabolic agents in increasing the growth rate of poultry. In: *Anabolic Agents in Animal Production,* F. C. Lu and J. Rendel (Eds.). Stuttgart: Georg Thieme Publishers, 1976, pp. 110–114.

72. Olsson, A. G., L. Oro, and S. Rossner. Effects of oxandrolone on plasma lipoproteins and the intravenous fat tolerance in man. *Atherosclerosis* 19:337–346, 1974.

73. Orlandi, F., A. Jezequel, and A. Melliti. The action of some anabolic steroids on the structure and the function of human liver cell. *Tijdschr. Gastro-Enterol.* 7:109–113, 1964.

74. O'Shea, J. P. The effects of an anabolic steroid on dynamic strength levels of weightlifters. *Nutr. Rep. Int.* 4:363–370, 1971.

75. Overly, W. L., J. A. Dankoff, B. K. Wang, and U. D. Singh. Androgens and hepatocellular carcinoma in an athlete. *Ann. Intern. Med.* 100:158–159, 1984.

76. Palva, I. P. and C. Wasastjerna. Treatment of aplastic anaemia with methenolone. *Acta Haematol.* 47:13–20, 1972.

77. Papanicolaou, G. N. and G. A. Falk. General muscular hypertrophy induced by androgenic hormone. *Science* 87:238–239, 1938.

78. Reeves, R. D., M. D. Morris, and G. L. Barbour. Hyperlipidemia due to oxymetholone therapy. *JAMA* 236:464–472, 1976.

79. Remes, K., P. Vuopio, M. Jarvinen, M. Harkonen, and H. Adlercreutz. Effect of short-term treatment with an anabolic steroid (methandienone) and dehydroepiandrosterone sulphate on plasma hormones, red cell volume and 2,3-diphosphoglycerate in athletes. *Scand. J. Clin. Lab. Invest.* 37:577–586, 1977.

80. Richardson, J. H. A comparison of two drugs on strength increase in monkeys. *J. Sports Med. Phys. Fitness* 17:251–254, 1977.

81. Rogozkin, V. A. The role of low molecular weight compounds in the regulation of skeletal muscle genome activity during exercise. *Med. Sci. Sports* 8:1–4, 1976.

82. Rogozkin, V. A. Anabolic steroid metabolism in skeletal muscle. *J. Steroid Biochem.* 11:923–926, 1979.

83. Ryan, A. J. Anabolic steroids are fool's gold. *Fed. Proc.* 40:2682–2688, 1981.

84. Sacks, P., D. Gale, T. H. Bothwell, K. Stevens. Oxymetholone therapy in aplastic and other refractory anaemias. *S. Afr. Med. J.* 46:1607–1615, 1972.

85. Scaramella, T. J. and W. A. Brown. Serum testosterone and aggressiveness in hockey players. *Psychosom. Med.* 40:262–265, 1978.

86. Schaffner, F., H. Popper, and V. Perez. Changes in bile canaliculi produced by norethandrolone: electron microscopic study of human and rat liver. *J. Lab. Clin. Med.* 56:623–628, 1960.

87. Shahidi, N. T. Androgens and erythropoiesis. *N. Engl. J. Med.* 289:72–80, 1973.

88. Shapiro, P., R. M. Ikedo, B. H. Ruebner, M. H. Conners, C. C. Halsted, and C. F. Abildgaard. Multiple hepatic tumors and peliosis hepatitis in Fanconi's anemia treated with androgens. *Am. J. Dis. Child.* 131: 1104–1106, 1977.

89. Shephard, R. J., D. Killinger, and T. Fried. Responses to sustained use of anabolic steroid. *Br. J. Sports Med.* 11:170–173, 1977.

90. Skarberg, K. O., L. Engstedt, S. Jameson, et al. Oxymetholone treatment in hypoproliferative anaemia. *Acta Haematol.* 49:321–330, 1973.

91. Smith, K. D., L. J. Rodriguez-Rigau, R. K. Tcholakian, and E. Steinberg. The relation between plasma testosterone levels and the lengths of phases of the menstrual cycle. *Fertil. Steril.* 32:403–407, 1979.

92. Snochowski, M., E. Dahlberg, E. Eriksson, and J. A. Gustafsson. Androgen and glucocorticoid receptors in human skeletal muscle cytosol. *J. Steroid Biochem.* 14:765–771, 1981.

93. Spiers, A. S. D., S. F. DeVita, M. J. Allar, S. Richards, and N. Sedransk. Beneficial effects of an anabolic steroid during cytotoxic chemotherapy for metastatic cancer. *J. Med.* 12:433–445, 1981.

94. Stamford, B. A. and R. Moffatt. Anabolic steroid: effectiveness as an ergogenic aid to experienced weight trainers. *J. Sports Med. Phys. Fitness* 14:191–197, 1974.

95. Stang-Voss, C. and H. J. Appel. Structural alterations of liver parenchyma induced by anabolic steroids. *Int. J. Sports Med.* 2:101–105, 1981.

96. Steinbach, M. Uber den Einfluss Anaboler wirkstoffe auf Korpergewicht, Muskelkraft and Muskeltraining. *Sportarzt Sportmed.* 11:485–492, 1968.

97. Stone, M. H., M. E. Rush, and H. Lipner. Responses to intensive training and methandrostenolone administration: II. Hormonal, organ weights, muscle weights and body composition. *Pflugers Arch.* 375:147–151, 1978.

98. Strauss, R. H., H. E. Wright, G. A. M. Finerman, and D. H. Catlin. Side effects of anabolic steroids in weight-trained men. *Phys. Sportsmed.* 11(12):87–96, 1983.

99. Stromeyer, F. W., D. H. Smith, and K. G. Ishak. Anabolic steroid therapy and intrahepatic cholangiocarcinoma. *Cancer* 43:440–443, 1979.

100. Stromme, S. B., H. D. Meen, and A. Aakvaag. Effects of an androgenic-anabolic steroid on strength development and plasma testosterone levels in normal males. *Med. Sci. Sports* 6:203–208, 1974.

101. Taylor, W., S. Snowball, C. M. Dickson, and M. Lesna. Alterations of liver architecture in mice treated with anabolic androgens and diethylnitrosamine. *NATO Adv. Study Inst. Series, Series A.* 52:279–288, 1982.

102. Taxy, J. B. Peliosis: a morphologic curiosity becomes an iatrogenic problem. *Hum. Pathol.* 9:331–340, 1978.

103. Tepperman, J. *Metabolic and Endocrine Physiology.* Chicago: Yearbook Medical Publishers, 1973, p. 70.

104. Thomson, D. P., D. R. Pearson, and D. L. Costill. Use of anabolic steroids by national level athletes. *Med. Sci. Sports Exerc.* 13:111, 1981. (Abstract)

105. VanderWal, P. General aspects of the effectiveness of anabolic agents in increasing protein production in farm animals, in particular in bull calves. In: *Anabolic Agents in Animal Production,* F. C. Lu and J. Rendel (Eds.). Stuttgart: Georg Thieme Publishers, 1976, pp. 60–78.

106. Wade, N. Anabolic steroids: doctors denounce them, but athletes aren't listening. *Science* 176:1399–1403, 1972.

107. Ward, P. The effect of an anabolic steroid on strength and lean body mass. *Med. Sci. Sports* 5:277–282, 1973.

108. Weiss, V. and H. Muller. Aur Frage der Beeinflussung des Krafttrainings durch Anabole Hormone. *Schweiz. Z. Sportmed.* 16:79–89, 1968.

109. Whitelaw, M. J., T. N. Foster, and W. H. Graham. Methandrostenolone (Dianabol): a controlled study of its anabolic and androgenic effect in children. *Pediatric. Pharm. Ther.* 68:291–296, 1966.

110. Wilson, J. D. and J. E. Griffin. The use and misuse of androgens. *Metabolism* 29:1278–1295, 1980.

111. Woodard, T. L., G. A. Burghen, A. E. Kitabchi, and J. A. Wilimas. Glucose intolerance and insulin resistance in aplastic anemia treated with oxymetholone. *J. Clin. Endocrinol. Metab.* 53:905–908, 1981.

112. Wright, J. E. Anabolic steroids and athletes. *Exerc. Sport Sci. Rev.* 8:149–202, 1980.

113. Yamagishi, M., A. Hiraoka, and H. Uchino. Silent hepatic lesions detected with computed tomography in aplastic anemia patients administered androgens for a long period. *Acta Haematol. Jpn.* 45:703–710, 1982.

114. Young, M., H. R. Crookshank, and L. Ponder. Effects of an anabolic steroid on selected parameters in male albino rats. *Res. Q.* 48:653–656, 1977.

115. Zevin, D., H. Turani, A. Cohen, and J. Levi. Androgen-associated hepatoma in a hemodialysis patient. *Nephron* 29:274–276, 1981.

Appendix K

A Cardiac Risk Index

1.	*Age*	10 to 20 1	21 to 30 2	31 to 40 3	41 to 50 4	51 to 60 6	61 to 70 and over 8
2.	*Heredity*	No known history of heart disease 1	1 relative with cardiovascular disease over 60 2	2 relatives with cardiovascular disease over 60 3	1 relative with cardiovascular disease under 60 4	2 relatives with cardiovascular disease under 60 6	3 relatives with cardiovascular disease under 60 8
3.	*Weight*	More than 5 lbs. below standard weight 0	Standard weight 1	5–20 lbs. overweight 2	21–35 lbs. overweight 3	36–50 lbs. overweight 5	51–65 lbs. overweight 7
4.	*Tobacco Smoking*	Nonuser 0	Cigar and/or pipe 1	10 cigarettes or less a day 2	20 cigarettes a day 3	30 cigarettes a day 5	40 cigarettes a day or more 8
5.	*Exercise*	Intensive occupational and recreational exertion 1	Moderate occupational and recreational exertion 2	Sedentary work and intense recreational exertion 3	Sedentary occupational and moderate recreational exertion 5	Sedentary work and light recreational exertion 6	Complete lack of all exercise 8
6.	*Cholesterol or % fat in diet*	Cholesterol below 180 mg. Diet contains no animal or solid fats 1	Cholesterol 181–205 mg. Diet contains 10% animal or solid fats 2	Cholesterol 206–230 mg. Diet contains 20% animal or solid fats 3	Cholesterol 231–255 mg. Diet contains 30% animal or solid fats 4	Cholesterol 256–280 mg. Diet contains 40% animal or solid fats 5	Cholesterol 281–330 mg. Diet contains 50% animal or solid fats 7
7.	*Blood Pressure*	100 upper reading 1	120 upper reading 2	140 upper reading 3	160 upper reading 4	180 upper reading 6	200 or over upper reading 8
8.	*Sex*	Female 1	Female over 45 2	Male 3	Bald Male 4	Bald short male 6	Bald short stocky male 7

Total Score: _____

Reprinted with permission of Dr. John Boyer, San Diego State University. San Diego, California.

To score your cardiac risk index, total the point values from the small boxes as they relate to you for each of the eight factors listed.

Cardiovascular disease risk index scoring table

Group I	6 to 11	= very low risk
Group II	12 to 17	= low risk
Group III	18 to 25	= average risk
Group IV	26 to 32	= high risk
Group V	33 to 42	= dangerous risk
Group VI	42 to 60	= extremely dangerous risk

Appendix L

How Healthful Is Your Diet?

You may analyze your diet in a variety of ways. One of the most effective techniques is to keep a detailed record of what you eat for three to seven days and then analyze it using one of the many dietary analysis computer programs that are available. Computer programs provide you with a detailed breakdown of your nutrient intake and how it compares with your Recommended Dietary Allowance. Hopefully, you have access to such a program.

    This inventory is designed to provide you with a rather broad analysis of your general eating habits as they relate to the guidelines to healthier eating presented in Chapter 12.

    Respond to each of the following twenty-five questions as they relate to your general eating habits and score each question as noted for each of the four different sections.

A.   Score each of the following questions using this scale:

    Almost always = 4
    Frequently or often = 3
    Sometimes or occasionally = 2
    Rarely or never = 1

____   1.   Do you eat a wide variety of foods each day, selecting foods from each of the Basic Four Food Groups or the six Food Exchanges?
____   2.   Do you have pasta as a main meal about two or three times per week?
____   3.   Do you eat legumes (dried beans such as navy or kidney, split peas, or lentils) several times per week?
____   4.   Do you try to eat foods that are high in dietary fiber?

B.   Score each of the following questions using this scale (Note that it is the opposite of the one above):

    Almost always = 1
    Frequently or often = 2
    Sometimes or occasionally = 3
    Rarely or never = 4

____   5.   Do you eat foods that are high in refined sugar, such as common table sugar, candy, cakes, and soda?
____   6.   Do you eat a lot of hard cheeses, such as cheddar cheese?
____   7.   Do you eat a lot of packaged lunch meats, such as salami, bologna, and other processed meats?
____   8.   Do you add salt to your meals?
____   9.   Do you have at least one typical high fat meal per day at a fast-food restaurant?
____   10.   Do you eat a lot of highly processed packaged foods that contain numerous additives?
____   11.   Do you have eggs or foods containing eggs in your diet on a daily basis?
____   12.   Do you eat salty snacks, such as chips or other vending machine products?

C.   Score each of the following questions using this scale:

    More than five days/week = 4
    Three to four days/week = 3
    One or two days/week = 2
    Zero to two days/month = 1

____   13.   How often do you have at least two pieces of fresh fruit?
____   14.   How often do you have dark green leafy vegetables such as spinach, dark orange vegetables such as carrots, or deep yellow vegetables such as squash?

_____ 15. How often do you have cruciferous vegetables or vegetables in the cabbage family, such as broccoli, cauliflower, brussels sprouts, or cabbage?

_____ 16. When you eat animal protein, how often do you keep the serving sizes fairly small, such as 4 to 6 ounces?

_____ 17. How often do you eat whole wheat breads, cereals, or other grain products?

_____ 18. How often do you include oat bran, oatmeal, or other oat products in your diet?

_____ 19. How often do you have at least two glasses of milk per day?

D. Score each of the following questions as indicated:

_____ 20. Which type of milk do you normally drink?
4—skim or non-fat milk
3—1% milk
2—2% milk
1—whole milk

_____ 21. Which of the following protein sources do you normally select?
4—fish or plant protein
3—chicken, turkey, or other poultry
2—red meat, such as beef or pork
1—hard cheeses

_____ 22. What do you normally put on bread?
4—nothing or low-sugar spreads
3—diet margarine
2—regular margarine
1—butter

_____ 23. What do you normally have for sweet snacks or dessert?
4—fresh fruit
3—presweetened yogurt
2—sherbet or ice milk
1—ice cream or candy bar

_____ 24. What do you normally have on a sandwich?
4—tuna fish
3—chicken or turkey
2—roast beef or peanut butter
1—packaged, processed lunch meat

_____ 25. How do you normally cook your foods?
4—bake, broil, steam, or microwave
3—use olive or peanut oil
2—use other vegetable oil
1—use butter, lard, coconut or palm oil

Scoring Table:

Use the following scoring table as a guide to your dietary habits. You should strive to score in the good to excellent category. Check those answers in the one to two point categories for guidelines to improvement.

100–90—Excellent
89–75—Good
74–60—About average
59–45—Below average
44–24—Poor

Appendix M

American College of Sports Medicine Position Stand: Proper and Improper Weight Loss Programs

Millions of individuals are involved in weight reduction programs. With the number of undesirable weight loss programs available and a general misconception by many about weight loss, the need for guidelines for proper weight loss programs is apparent.

Based on the existing evidence concerning the effects of weight loss on health status, physiologic processes, and body composition parameters, the American College of Sports Medicine makes the following statements and recommendations for weight loss programs.

For the purposes of this position stand, body weight will be represented by two components, fat and fat-free (water, electrolytes, minerals, glycogen stores, muscular tissue, bone, etc.):

1. Prolonged fasting and diet programs that severely restrict caloric intake are scientifically undesirable and can be medically dangerous.
2. Fasting and diet programs that severely restrict caloric intake result in the loss of large amounts of water, electrolytes, minerals, glycogen stores, and other fat-free tissue (including proteins within fat-free tissues), with minimal amounts of fat loss.
3. Mild calorie restriction (500–1000 kcal less than the usual daily intake) results in a smaller loss of water, electrolytes, minerals, and other fat-free tissue and is less likely to cause malnutrition.
4. Dynamic exercise of large muscles helps to maintain fat-free tissue, including muscle mass and bone density, and results in losses of body weight. Weight loss resulting from an increase in energy expenditure is primarily in the form of fat weight.
5. A nutritionally sound diet resulting in mild calorie restriction coupled with an endurance exercise program along with behavioral

modification of existing eating habits is recommended for weight reduction. The rate of sustained weight loss should not exceed 1 kg (2 lb) per week.
6. To maintain proper weight control and optimal body fat levels, a lifetime commitment to proper eating habits and regular physical activity is required.

Research Background for the Position Stand

Each year millions of individuals undertake weight loss programs for a variety of reasons. It is well known that obesity is associated with a number of health-related problems. These problems include impairment of cardiac function due to an increase in the work of the heart and to left ventricular dysfunction; hypertension; diabetes; renal disease; gall bladder disease; respiratory dysfunction; joint diseases and gout; endometrial cancer; abnormal plasma lipid and lipoprotein concentrations; problems in the administration of anesthetics during surgery; and impairment of physical working capacity. As a result, weight reduction is frequently advised by physicians for medical reasons. In addition, there are a vast number of individuals who are on weight reduction programs for aesthetic reasons.

It is estimated that 60–70 million American adults and at least 10 million American teenagers are overfat. Because millions of Americans have adopted unsupervised weight loss programs, it is the opinion of the American College of Sports Medicine that guidelines are needed for safe and effective weight loss programs. This position stand deals with desirable and undesirable weight loss programs. Desirable weight loss programs are defined as those that are nutritionally sound and result in maximal losses in fat weight and minimal losses of fat-free tissue. Undesirable weight loss programs are defined as those that are not nutritionally sound, that result in large losses of fat-free tissue, that pose potential serious medical complications, and that cannot be followed for long-term weight maintenance.

Source: American College of Sports Medicine. "Position Stand on Proper and Improper Weight Loss Programs." *Medicine and Science in Sports and Exercise* 15, no. 1:ix–x (1983).

Therefore, a desirable weight loss program is one that:

1. Provides a caloric intake no lower than 1200 kcal·d^{-1} for normal adults in order to get a proper blend of foods to meet nutritional requirements. (Note: This requirement may change for children, older individuals, athletes, etc.).
2. Includes foods acceptable to the dieter from the viewpoints of socio-cultural background, usual habits, taste, cost, and ease in acquisition and preparation.
3. Provides a negative caloric balance (not to exceed 500–1000 kcal·d^{-1} lower than recommended), resulting in gradual weight loss without metabolic derangements. Maximal weight loss should be 1 kg·wk^{-1}.
4. Includes the use of behavior modification techniques to identify and eliminate dieting habits that contribute to improper nutrition.
5. Includes an endurance exercise program of at least 3 d/wk, 20–30 min in duration, at a minimum intensity of 60% of maximum heart rate (refer to ACSM Position Stand on the Recommended Quantity and Quality of Exercise for Developing and Maintaining Cardiorespiratory and Muscular Fitness in Healthy Adults, (Appendix N).
6. Provides that the new eating and physical activity habits be continued for life in order to maintain the achieved lower body weight.

---

1. Since the early work of Keys et al. and Bloom, which indicated that marked reduction in caloric intake or fasting (starvation or semistarvation) rapidly reduced body weight, numerous fasting, modified fasting, and fad diet and weight loss programs have emerged. While these programs promise and generally cause rapid weight loss, they are associated with significant medical risks.

   The medical risks associated with these types of diet and weight loss programs are numerous. Blood glucose concentrations have been shown to be markedly reduced in obese subjects who undergo fasting. Further, in obese non-diabetic subjects, fasting may result in impairment of glucose tolerance. Ketonuria begins within a few hours after fasting or low-carbohydrate diets are begun and hyperuricemia is common among subjects who fast to reduce body weight. Fasting also results in high serum uric acid levels with decreased urinary output. Fasting and low-calorie diets also result in urinary nitrogen loss and a significant decrease in fat-free tissue (see section 2). In comparison to ingestion of a normal diet, fasting substantially elevates urinary excretion of potassium. This, coupled with the aforementioned nitrogen loss, suggests that the potassium loss is due to a loss of lean tissue. Other electrolytes, including sodium, calcium, magnesium, and phosphate have been shown to be elevated in urine during prolonged fasting. Reductions in blood volume and body fluids are also common with fasting and fad diets. This can be associated with weakness and fainting. Congestive heart failure and sudden death have been reported in subjects who fasted or markedly restricted their caloric intake. Myocardial atrophy appears to contribute to sudden death. Sudden death may also occur during refeeding. Untreated fasting has also been reported to reduce serum iron binding capacity, resulting in anemia. Liver glycogen levels are depleted with fasting and liver function and gastrointestinal tract abnormalities are associated with fasting. While fasting and calorically restricted diets have been shown to lower serum cholesterol levels, a large portion of the cholesterol reduction is a result of lowered HDL-cholesterol levels. Other risks associated with fasting and low-calorie diets include lactic acidosis, alopecia, hypoalaninemia, edema, anuria, hypotension, elevated serum bilirubin, nausea and vomiting, alterations in thyroxine metabolism, impaired serum triglyceride removal and production, and death.

2. The major objective of any weight reduction program is to lose body fat while maintaining fat-free tissue. The vast majority of research reveals that starvation and low-calorie diets result in large losses of water, electrolytes, and other fat-free tissue. One of the best controlled experiments was conducted from 1944 to 1946 at the Laboratory of Physiological Hygiene at the University of Minnesota. In this study, subjects had their base-line caloric intake

cut by 45% and body weight and body composition changes were followed for 24 wk. During the first 12 wk of semistarvation, body weight declined by 25.4 lb (11.5 kg) with only an 11.6-lb (5.3 kg) decline in body fat. During the second 12-wk period, body weight declined an additional 9.1 lb (4.1 kg) with only a 6.1-lb (2.8 kg) decrease in body fat. These data clearly demonstrate that fat-free tissue significantly contributes to weight loss from semistarvation. Similar results have been reported by several other investigators. Buskirk et al. reported that the 13.5-kg weight loss in six subjects on a low-calorie mixed diet averaged 76% fat and 24% fat-free tissue. Similarly, Passmore et al. reported results of 78% of weight loss (15.3 kg) as fat and 22% as fat-free tissue in seven women who consumed a 400-kcal·d^{-1} diet for 45 d. Yang and Van Itallie followed weight loss and body composition changes for the first 5 d of a weight loss program involving subjects consuming either an 800-kcal mixed diet, an 800-kcal ketogenic diet, or undergoing starvation. Subjects on the mixed diet lost 1.3 kg of weight (59% fat loss, 3.4% protein loss, 37.6% water loss), subjects on the ketogenic diet lost 2.3 kg of weight (33.2% fat, 3.8% protein, 63.0% water), and subjects on starvation regimens lost 3.8 kg of weight (32.3% fat, 6.5% protein, 61.2% water). Grande and Grande et al. reported similar findings with a 1000-kcal carbohydrate diet. It was further reported that water restriction combined with 1000-kcal·d^{-1} of carbohydrate resulted in greater water loss and less fat loss.

Recently, there has been some renewed speculation about the efficacy of the very-low-calorie diet (VLCD). Krotkiewski and associates studied the effects on body weight and body composition after 3 wk on the so-called Cambridge diet. Two groups of obese middle-aged women were studied. One group had a VLCD only, while the second group had a VLCD combined with a 55-min/d, 3-d/wk exercise program. The VLCD-only group lost 6.2 kg in 3 wk, of which only 2.6 kg was fat loss, while the VLCD-plus-exercise group lost 6.8 kg in 3 wk with only a 1.9-kg body fat loss. Thus it can be seen that VLCD results in undesirable losses of body fat, and the addition of the normally protective effect of chronic exercise to VLCD does not reduce the catabolism of fat-free tissue. Further, with VLCD, a large reduction (29%) in HDL-cholesterol is seen.

3. Even mild calorie restriction (reduction of 500–1000 kcal·d^{-1} from base-line caloric intake), when used alone as a tool for weight loss, results in the loss of moderate amounts of water and other fat-free tissue. In a study by Goldman et al., 15 female subjects consumed a low-calorie mixed diet for 7–8 wk. Weight loss during this period averaged 6.43 kg (0.85 kg·wk^{-1}), 88.6% of which was fat. The remaining 11.4% represented water and other fat-free tissue. Zuti and Golding examined the effect of 500 kcal·d^{-1} calorie restriction on body composition changes in adult females. Over a 16-wk period the women lost approximately 5.2 kg; however, 1.1 kg of the weight loss (21%) was due to a loss of water and other fat-free tissue. More recently, Weltman et al. examined the effects of 500 kcal·d^{-1} calorie restriction (from base-line levels) on body composition changes in sedentary middle-aged males. Over a 10-wk period subjects lost 5.95 kg, 4.03 kg (68%) of which was fat loss and 1.92 kg (32%) was loss of water and other fat-free tissue. Further, with calorie restriction only, these subjects exhibited a decrease in HDL-cholesterol. In the same study, the two other groups who exercised and/or dieted and exercised were able to maintain their HDL-cholesterol levels. Similar results for females have been presented by Thompson et al. It should be noted that the decrease seen in HDL-cholesterol with weight loss may be an acute effect. There are data that indicate that stable weight loss has a beneficial effect on HDL-cholesterol.

Further, an additional problem associated with calorie restriction alone for effective weight loss is the fact that it is associated with a reduction in basal metabolic rate. Apparently exercise combined with calorie restriction can counter this response.

4. There are several studies that indicate that exercise helps maintain fat-free tissue while promoting fat loss. Total body weight and fat weight are generally reduced with endurance training programs while fat-free weight remains constant or increases

slightly. Programs conducted at least 3 d/wk, of at least 20-min duration and of sufficient intensity and duration to expend at least 300 kcal per exercise session have been suggested as a threshold level for total body weight and fat weight reduction. Increasing caloric expenditure above 300 kcal per exercise session and increasing the frequency of exercise sessions will enhance fat weight loss while sparing fat-free tissue. Leon et al. had six obese male subjects walk vigorously for 90 min, 5 d/wk for 16 wk. Work output progressed weekly to an energy expenditure of 1000–1200 kcal/session. At the end of 16 wk, subjects averaged 5.7 kg of weight loss with a 5.9-kg loss of fat weight and a 0.2-kg gain in fat-free tissue. Similarly, Zuti and Golding followed the progress of adult women who expended 500 kcal/exercise session 5 d/wk for 16 wk of exercise. At the end of 16 wk, the women lost 5.8 kg of fat and gained 0.9 kg of fat-free tissue.

5. Review of the literature cited above strongly indicates that optimal body composition changes occur with a combination of calorie restriction (while on a well-balanced diet) plus exercise. This combination promotes loss of fat weight while sparing fat-free tissue. Data of Zuti and Golding and Weltman et al. support this contention. Calorie restriction of 500 $kcal \cdot d^{-1}$ combined with 3–5 d of exercise requiring 300–500 kcal per exercise session results in favorable changes in body composition. Therefore, the optimal rate of weight loss should be between 0.45–1 kg (1–2 lb) per wk. This seems especially relevant in light of the data which indicates that rapid weight loss due to low caloric intake can be associated with sudden death. In order to institute a desirable pattern of calorie restriction plus exercise, behavior modification techniques should be incorporated to identify and eliminate habits contributing to obesity and/or overfatness.

6. The problem with losing weight is that, although many individuals succeed in doing so, they invariably put the weight on again. The goal of an effective weight loss regimen is not merely to lose weight. Weight control requires a lifelong commitment, an understanding of our eating habits and a willingness to change them. Frequent exercise is necessary, and accomplishment must be reinforced to sustain motivation. Crash dieting and other promised weight loss cures are ineffective.

Appendix N

American College of Sports Medicine Position Stand: The Recommended Quantity and Quality of Exercise for Developing and Maintaining Cardiorespiratory and Muscular Fitness in Healthy Adults

This Position Stand replaces the 1978 ACSM position paper, "The Recommended Quantity and Quality of Exercise for Developing and Maintaining Fitness in Healthy Adults."

Increasing numbers of persons are becoming involved in endurance training and other forms of physical activity, and, thus, the need for guidelines for exercise prescription is apparent. Based on the existing evidence concerning exercise prescription for healthy adults and the need for guidelines, the American College of Sports Medicine (ACSM) makes the following recommendations for the quantity and quality of training for developing and maintaining cardiorespiratory fitness, body composition, and muscular strength and endurance in the healthy adult:

1. Frequency of training: 3–5 $d \cdot wk^{-1}$.
2. Intensity of training: 60–90% of maximum heart rate (HR_{max}), or 50–85% of maximum oxygen uptake (VO_{2max}) or HR_{max} reserve.[1]
3. Duration of training: 20–60 min of continuous aerobic activity. Duration is dependent on the intensity of the activity; thus, lower intensity activity should be conducted over a longer period of time. Because of the importance of "total fitness" and the fact that it is more readily attained in longer duration programs, and because of the potential hazards and compliance problems associated with high intensity activity, lower to moderate intensity activity of longer duration is recommended for the nonathletic adult.
4. Mode of activity: any activity that uses large muscle groups, can be maintained continuously, and is rhythmical and aerobic in nature, e.g., walking-hiking, running-jogging, cycling-bicycling, cross-country skiing, dancing, rope skipping, rowing, stair climbing, swimming, skating, and various endurance game activities.
5. Resistance training: Strength training of a moderate intensity, sufficient to develop and maintain fat-free weight (FFW), should be an integral part of an adult fitness program. One set of 8–12 repetitions of eight to ten exercises that condition the major muscle groups at least 2 $d \cdot wk^{-1}$ is the recommended minimum.

Rationale and Research Background

Introduction

The questions "How much exercise is enough," and "What type of exercise is best for developing and maintaining fitness?" are frequently asked. It is recognized that the term "physical fitness" is composed of a variety of characteristics included in the broad categories of cardiovascular-respiratory fitness, body composition, muscular strength and endurance, and flexibility. In this context fitness is defined as the ability to perform moderate to vigorous levels of physical activity without undue fatigue and the capability of maintaining such ability throughout life (167). It is also recognized that the adaptive response to training is complex and includes peripheral, central, structural, and functional factors (5,172). Although many such variables and their adaptive response to training have been documented, the lack of sufficient in-depth and comparative data relative to frequency, intensity, and duration of training makes them inadequate to use as comparative models. Thus, in respect to the above questions, fitness is limited mainly to changes in VO_{2max}, muscular strength and endurance, and body composition, which includes total body mass, fat weight (FW), and FFW. Further, the rationale and research background used for this position stand will be divided into programs for cardiorespiratory fitness and weight control and programs for muscular strength and endurance.

---

[1]Maximum heart rate reserve is calculated from the difference between resting and maximum heart rate. To estimate training intensity, a percentage of this value is added to the resting heart rate and is expressed as a percentage of HR_{max} reserve (85).

Fitness versus health benefits of exercise. Since the original position statement was published in 1978, an important distinction has been made between physical activity as it relates to health versus fitness. It has been pointed out that the quantity and quality of exercise needed to attain health-related benefits may differ from what is recommended for fitness benefits. It is now clear that lower levels of physical activity than recommended by this position statement may reduce the risk for certain chronic degenerative diseases and yet may not be of sufficient quantity or quality to improve VO_{2max} (71,72,98,167). ACSM recognizes the potential health benefits of regular exercise performed more frequently and for a longer duration, but at lower intensities than prescribed in this position statement (13A,71,100,120,160). ACSM will address the issue concerning the proper amount of physical activity necessary to derive health benefits in another statement.

Need for standardization of procedures and reporting results. Despite an abundance of information available concerning the training of the human organism, the lack of standardization of testing protocols and procedures, of methodology in relation to training procedures and experimental design, and of a preciseness in the documentation and reporting of the quantity and quality of training prescribed make interpretation difficult (123, 133,139,164,167). Interpretation and comparison of results are also dependent on the initial level of fitness (42,43,58,114,148,151,156), length of time of the training experiment (17,45,125,128,139, 145,150), and specificity of the testing and training (5,43,130,139,145A,172). For example, data from training studies using subjects with varied levels of VO_{2max}, total body mass, and FW have found changes to occur in relation to their initial values (14,33,109,112,113,148,151); i.e., the lower the initial VO_{2max} the larger the percentage of improvement found, and the higher the FW the greater the reduction. Also, data evaluating trainability with age, comparison of the different magnitudes and quantities of effort, and comparison of the trainability of men and women may have been influenced by the initial fitness levels.

In view of the fact that improvement in the fitness variables discussed in this position statement continues over many months of training (27,86,139,145,150), it is reasonable to believe that short-term studies conducted over a few weeks have certain limitations. Middle-aged sedentary and older participants may take several weeks to adapt to the initial rigors of training, and thus need a longer adaptation period to get the full benefit from a program. For example, Seals et al. (150) exercise trained 60–69-yr-olds for 12 months. Their subjects showed a 12% improvement in VO_{2max} after 6 months of moderate intensity walking training. A further 18% increase in VO_{2max} occurred during the next 6 months of training when jogging was introduced. How long a training experiment should be conducted is difficult to determine, but 15–20 wk may be a good minimum standard. Although it is difficult to control exercise training experiments for more than 1 yr, there is a need to study this effect. As stated earlier, lower doses of exercise may improve VO_{2max} and control or maintain body composition, but at a slower rate.

Although most of the information concerning training described in this position statement has been conducted on men, the available evidence indicates that women tend to adapt to endurance training in the same manner as men (19,38,46,47,49,62,65,68, 90,92,122,166).

Exercise Prescription for Cardiorespiratory Fitness and Weight Control

Exercise prescription is based upon the frequency, intensity, and duration of training, the mode of activity (aerobic in nature, e.g., listed under No. 4 above), and the initial level of fitness. In evaluating these factors, the following observations have been derived from studies conducted for up to 6–12 months with endurance training programs.

Improvement in VO_{2max} is directly related to frequency (3,6,50,75–77,125,126,152,154,164), intensity (3,6,26,29,58,61,75–77,80,85,93,118,152, 164) and duration (3,29,60,61,70,75–77,101,109, 118,152,162,164,168) of training. Depending upon the quantity and quality of training, improvement in VO_{2max} ranges from 5 to 30% (8,29,30,48,59, 61, 65, 67, 69, 75–77, 82, 84, 96, 99, 101, 102, 111, 115, 119, 123, 127, 139, 141, 143, 149, 150, 152, 153, 158,164,168,173). These studies show that a minimum increase in VO_{2max} of 15% is generally attained in programs that meet the above stated guidelines. Although changes in VO_{2max} greater than 30% have been shown, they are usually associated with large total body mass and FW loss, in cardiac patients. or in persons with a very low initial level of fitness. Also, as a result of leg fatigue or a lack of motivation, persons with low initial fitness may have spuriously low initial VO_{2max} values. Klissouras (94A) and Bouchard (16A) have shown that human variation in the trainability of VO_{2max} is important and related to current phenotype level. That is, there is a genetically determined pretraining status of the trait and capacity to adapt to physical training. Thus, physiological results should be interpreted with respect to both genetic variation and the quality and quantity of training performed.

Intensity-duration. Intensity and duration of training are interrelated, with total amount of work accomplished being an important factor in improvement in fitness (12,20,27,48,90,92,123,127,128,136, 149,151,164). Although more comprehensive inquiry is necessary, present evidence suggests that, when exercise is performed above the minimum intensity threshold, the total amount of work accomplished is an important factor in fitness development (19,27,126,127,149,151) and maintenance (134). That is, improvement will be similar for activities performed at a lower intensity-longer duration compared to higher intensity-shorter duration if the total energy costs of the activities are equal. Higher intensity exercise is associated with greater cardiovascular risk (156A), orthopedic injury (124,139) and lower compliance to training than lower intensity exercise (36,105,124,146). Therefore, programs emphasizing low to moderate intensity training with longer duration are recommended for most adults.

The minimal training intensity threshold for improvement in VO_{2max} is approximately 60% of the HR_{max} (50% of VO_{2max} or HR_{max} reserve) (80,85). The 50% of HR_{max} reserve represents a heart rate of approximately 130–135 beats·min^{-1} for young persons. As a result of the age-related change in maximum heart rate, the absolute heart rate to achieve this threshold is inversely related to age and can be as low as 105–115 beats·min^{-1} for older persons (35,65,150). Patients who are taking beta-adrenergic blocking drugs may have significantly lower heart rate values (171). Initial level of fitness is another important consideration in prescribing exercise (26,90,104,148,151). The person with a low fitness level can achieve a significant training effect with a sustained training heart rate as low as 40–50% of HR_{max} reserve, while persons with higher fitness levels require a higher training stimulus (35,58,152,164).

Classification of exercise intensity. The classification of exercise intensity and its standardization for exercise prescription based on a 20–60 min training session has been confusing, misinterpreted, and often taken out of context. The most quoted exercise classification system is based on the energy expenditure (kcal·min^{-1}·kg^{-1}) of industrial tasks

(40,89). The original data for this classification system were published by Christensen (24) in 1953 and were based on the energy expenditure of working in the steel mill for an 8-h day. The classification of industrial and leisure-time tasks by using absolute values of energy expenditure have been valuable for use in the occupational and nutritional setting. Although this classification system has broad application in medicine and, in particular, making recommendations for weight control and job placement, it has little or no meaning for preventive and rehabilitation exercise training programs. To extrapolate absolute values of energy expenditure for completing an industrial task based on an 8-h work day to 20–60 min regimens of exercise training does not make sense. For example, walking and jogging/running can be accomplished at a wide range of speeds; thus, the relative intensity becomes important under these conditions. Because the endurance training regimens recommended by ACSM for nonathletic adults are geared for 60 min or less of physical activity, the system of classification of exercise training intensity shown in Table 1 is recommended (139). The use of a realistic time period for training and an individual's relative exercise intensity makes this system amenable to young, middle-aged, and elderly participants, as well as patients with a limited exercise capacity (3,137,139).

Table 1 also describes the relationship between relative intensity based on percent HR_{max}, percentage of HR_{max} reserve or percentage of VO_{2max}, and the rating of perceived exertion (RPE) (15,16,137). The use of heart rate as an estimate of intensity of training is the common standard (3,139).

The use of RPE has become a valid tool in the monitoring of intensity in exercise training programs (11,37,137,139). It is generally considered an adjunct to heart rate in monitoring relative exercise intensity, but once the relationship between heart rate and RPE is known, RPE can be used in place of heart rate (23,139). This would not be the case in certain patient populations where a more precise knowledge of heart rate may be critical to the safety of the program.

Frequency. The amount of improvement in VO_{2max} tends to plateau when frequency of training is increased above 3 d·wk^{-1} (50,123,139). The value of the added improvement found with training more than 5 d·wk^{-1} is small to not apparent in regard to improvement in VO_{2max} (75–77,106,123). Training of less than 2 d·wk^{-1} does not generally show a meaningful change in VO_{2max} (29,50,118,123, 152,164).

Table 1 Classification of intensity of exercise based on 20–60 min of endurance training

Relative Intensity (%)		Rating of Perceived Exertion	Classification of Intensity
HR_{max}[*]	VO_{2max}[*] or HR_{max} reserve		
<35%	<30%	<10	Very light
35–59%	30–49%	10–11	Light
60–79%	50–74%	12–13	Moderate (somewhat hard)
80–89%	75–84%	14–16	Heavy
≥90%	≥85%	>16	Very heavy

Table from Pollock, M. L. and J. H. Wilmore. *Exercise in Health and Disease: Evaluation and Prescription for Prevention and Rehabilitation*, 2nd Ed. Philadelphia: W.B. Saunders, 1990. Published with permission.

[*]HR_{max} = maximum heart rate; VO_{2max} = maximum oxygen uptake

Mode. If frequency, intensity, and duration of training are similar (total kcal expenditure), the training adaptations appear to be independent of the mode of aerobic activity (101A,118,130). Therefore, a variety of endurance activities, e.g., those listed above, may be used to derive the same training effect.

Endurance activities that require running and jumping are considered high impact types of activity and generally cause significantly more debilitating injuries to beginning as well as long-term exercisers than do low impact and non-weight bearing type activities (13,93,117,124,127,135,140,142). This is particularly evident in the elderly (139). Beginning joggers have increased foot, leg, and knee injuries when training is performed more than 3 d·wk^{-1} and longer than 30 min duration per exercise session (135). High intensity interval training (run-walk) compared to continuous jogging training was also associated with a higher incidence of injury (124,136). Thus, caution should be taken when recommending the type of activity and exercise prescription for the beginning exerciser. Orthopedic injuries as related to overuse increase linearly in runners/joggers when performing these activities (13,140). Thus, there is a need for more inquiry into the effect that different types of activities and the quantity and quality of training has on injuries over short-term and long-term participation.

An activity such as weight training should not be considered as a means of training for developing VO_{2max}, but it has significant value for increasing muscular strength and endurance and FFW (32,54,107,110,165). Studies evaluating circuit weight training (weight training conducted almost continuously with moderate weights, using 10–15 repetitions per exercise session with 15–30 s rest between bouts of activity) show an average improvement in VO_{2max} of 6% (1,51–54,83,94,108,170). Thus, circuit weight training is not recommended as the only activity used in exercise programs for developing VO_{2max}.

Age. Age in itself does not appear to be a deterrent to endurance training. Although some earlier studies showed a lower training effect with middle-aged or elderly participants (9,34,79,157,168), more recent studies show the relative change in VO_{2max} to be similar to younger age groups (7,8,65,132,150,161,163). Although more investigation is necessary concerning the rate of improvement in VO_{2max} with training at various ages, at present it appears that elderly participants need longer periods of time to adapt (34,132,150). Earlier studies showing moderate to no improvement in VO_{2max} were conducted over a short time span (9), or exercise was conducted at a moderate to low intensity (34), thus making the interpretation of the results difficult.

Although VO_{2max} decreases with age and total body mass and FW increase with age, evidence suggests that this trend can be altered with endurance training (22,27,86–88,139). A 9% reduction in VO_{2max} per decade for sedentary adults after age 25 has been shown (31,73), but for active individuals the reduction may be less than 5% per decade (21,31,39,73). Ten or more yr follow-up studies where participants continued training at a similar level showed maintenance of cardiorespiratory fitness (4,87,88,138). A cross-sectional study of older competitive runners showed progressively lower values in VO_{2max} from the fourth to seventh decades of life, but also showed less training in the older groups (129). More recent 10-yr follow-up data on these same athletes (50–82 yr of age) showed VO_{2max} to be unchanged when training quantity and quality remained unchanged (138). Thus, lifestyle plays a significant role in the maintenance of fitness. More inquiry into the relationship of long-term training (quantity and quality), for both competitors and noncompetitors, and physiological function with increasing age is necessary before more definitive statements can be made.

Maintenance of training effect. In order to maintain the training effect, exercise must be continued on a regular basis (18,25,28,47,97,111,144,147). A significant reduction in cardiorespiratory fitness occurs after 2 wk of detraining (25,144), with participants returning to near pretraining levels of fitness after 10 wk (47) to 8 months of detraining (97). A loss of 50% of their initial improvement in VO_{2max} has been shown after 4–12 wk of detraining (47,91,144). Those individuals who have undergone years of continuous training maintain some benefits for longer periods of detraining than subjects from short-term training studies (25). While stopping training shows dramatic reductions in VO_{2max}, reduced training shows modest to no reductions for periods of 5–15 wk (18,75–77,144). Hickson et al., in a series of experiments where frequency (75), duration (76), or intensity (77) of training were manipulated, found that, if intensity of training remained unchanged, VO_{2max} was maintained for up to 15 wk when frequency and duration of training were reduced by as much as 2/3. When frequency and duration of training remained constant and intensity of training was reduced by 1/3 or 2/3, VO_{2max} was significantly reduced. Similar findings were found in regards to reduced strength training exercise. When strength training exercise was reduced from 3 or 2 d·wk^{-1} to at least 1 d·wk^{-1}, strength was maintained for 12 wk of reduced training (62). Thus, it appears that missing an exercise session periodically or reducing training for up to 15 wk will not adversely affect VO_{2max} or muscular strength and endurance as long as training intensity is maintained.

Even though many new studies have given added insight into the proper amount of exercise, investigation is necessary to evaluate the rate of increase and decrease of fitness when varying training loads and reduction in training in relation to level of fitness, age, and length of time in training. Also, more information is needed to better identify the minimal level of exercise necessary to maintain fitness.

Weight control and body composition. Although there is variability in human response to body composition change with exercise, total body mass and FW are generally reduced with endurance training programs (133,139,171A), while FFW remains constant (123,133,139,169) or increases slightly (116,174). For example, Wilmore (171A) reported the results of 32 studies that met the criteria for developing cardiorespiratory fitness that are outlined in this position stand and found an average loss in total body mass of 1.5 kg and percent fat of 2.2%. Weight loss programs using dietary manipulation that result in a more dramatic decrease in total body mass show reductions in both FW and FFW

(2,78,174). When these programs are conducted in conjunction with exercise training, FFW loss is more modest than in programs using diet alone (78,121). Programs that are conducted at least 3 d·wk^{-1} (123,125,126,128,169), of at least 20 min duration (109,123,169), and of sufficient intensity to expend approximately 300 kcal per exercise session (75 kg person)[2] are suggested as a threshold level for total body mass and FW loss (27,64,77,123,133,139). An expenditure of 200 kcal per session has also been shown to be useful in weight reduction if the exercise frequency is at least 4 d·wk^{-1} (155). If the primary purpose of the training program is for weight loss, then regimens of greater frequency and duration of training and low to moderate intensity are recommended (2,139). Programs with less participation generally show little or no change in body composition (44,57,93,123,133,159,162,169). Significant increases in VO_{2max} have been shown with 10–15 min of high intensity training (6,79,109,118, 123,152,153); thus, if total body mass and FW reduction are not considerations, then shorter duration, higher intensity programs may be recommended for healthy individuals at low risk for cardiovascular disease and orthopedic injury.

Exercise Prescription for Muscular Strength and Endurance

The addition of resistance/strength training to the position statement results from the need for a well-rounded program that exercises all the major muscle groups of the body. Thus, the inclusion of resistance training in adult fitness programs should be effective in the development and maintenance of FFW. The effect of exercise training is specific to the area of the body being trained (5,43,145A,172). For example, training the legs will have little or no effect on the arms, shoulders, and trunk muscles. A 10-yr follow-up of master runners who continued their training regimen, but did no upper body exercise, showed maintenance of VO_{2max} and a 2-kg reduction of FFW (138). Their leg circumference remained unchanged, but arm circumference was significantly lower. These data indicate a loss of muscle mass in the untrained areas. Three of the athletes who practiced weight training exercise for the upper body and trunk muscles maintained their FFW. A comprehensive review by Sale (145A) carefully documents available information on specificity of training.

[2]Haskell and Haskell et al. (71,72) have suggested the use of 4 kcal·kg^{-1} of body weight of energy expenditure per day for a minimum standard for use in exercise programs.

Specificity of training was further addressed by Graves et al. (63). Using the bilateral knee extension exercise, they trained four groups: group A, first ½ of the range of motion; group B, second ½ of the range of motion; group AB, full range of motion; and a control group that did not train. The results clearly showed that the training result was specific to the range of motion trained, with group AB getting the best full range effect. Thus, resistance training should be performed through a full range of motion for maximum benefit (63,95).

Muscular strength and endurance are developed by the overload principle, i.e., by increasing more than normal the resistance to movement or frequency and duration of activity (32,41,43,74, 145). Muscular strength is best developed by using heavy weights (that require maximum or nearly maximum tension development) with few repetitions, and muscular endurance is best developed by using lighter weights with a greater number of repetitions (10,41,43,145). To some extent, both muscular strength and endurance are developed under each condition, but each system favors a more specific type of development (43,145). Thus, to elicit improvement in both muscular strength and endurance, most experts recommend 8–12 repetitions per bout of exercise.

Any magnitude of overload will result in strength development, but higher intensity effort at or near maximal effort will give a significantly greater effect (43,74,101B,103,145,172). The intensity of resistance training can be manipulated by varying the weight load, repetitions, rest interval between exercises, and number of sets completed (43). Caution is advised for training that emphasizes lengthening (eccentric) contractions, compared to shortening (concentric) or isometric contractions, as the potential for skeletal muscle soreness and injury is accentuated (3A,84A).

Muscular strength and endurance can be developed by means of static (isometric) or dynamic (isotonic or isokinetic) exercises. Although each type of training has its favorable and weak points, for healthy adults, dynamic resistance exercises are recommended. Resistance training for the average participant should be rhythmical, performed at a moderate to slow speed, move through a full range of motion, and not impede normal forced breathing. Heavy resistance exercise can cause a dramatic acute increase in both systolic and diastolic blood pressure (100A,101C).

The expected improvement in strength from resistance training is difficult to assess because increases in strength are affected by the participants'

initial level of strength and their potential for improvement (43,66,74,114,172). For example, Mueller and Rohmert (114) found increases in strength ranging from 2 to 9% per week depending on initial strength levels. Although the literature reflects a wide range of improvement in strength with resistance training programs, the average improvement for sedentary young and middle-aged men and women for up to 6 months of training is 25–30%. Fleck and Kraemer (43), in a review of 13 studies representing various forms of isotonic training, showed an average improvement in bench press strength of 23.3% when subjects were tested on the equipment with which they were trained and 16.5% when tested on special isotonic or isokinetic ergometers (six studies). Fleck and Kraemer (43) also reported an average increase in leg strength of 26.6% when subjects were tested with the equipment that they trained on (six studies) and 21.2% when tested with special isotonic or isokinetic ergometers (five studies). Results of improvement in strength resulting from isometric training have been of the same magnitude as found with isotonic training (17,43,62,63).

In light of the information reported above, the following guidelines for resistance training are recommended for the average healthy adult. A minimum of 8–10 exercises involving the major muscle groups should be performed a minimum of two times per week. A minimum of one set of 8–12 repetitions to near fatigue should be completed. These minimal standards for resistance training are based on two factors. First, the time it takes to complete a comprehensive, well-rounded exercise program is important. Programs lasting more than 60 min per session are associated with higher dropout rates (124). Second, although greater frequencies of training (17,43,56) and additional sets or combinations of sets and repetitions elicit larger strength gains (10,32,43,74,145,172), the magnitude of difference is usually small. For example, Braith et al. (17) compared training 2 d·wk^{-1} with 3 d·wk^{-1} for 18 wk. The subjects performed one set of 7–10 repetitions to fatigue. The 2 d·wk^{-1} group showed a 21% increase in strength compared to 28% in the 3 d·wk^{-1} group. In other words, 75% of what could be attained in a 3 d·wk^{-1} program was attained in 2 d·wk^{-1}. Also, the 21% improvement in strength found by the 2 d·wk^{-1} regimen is 70–80% of the improvement reported by other programs using additional frequencies of training and combinations of sets and repetitions (43). Graves et al. (62,63), Gettman et al. (55), Hurley et al. (83) and Braith et al. (17) found that programs using one set to fatigue showed a greater than 25% increase in strength.

Although resistance training equipment may provide a better graduated and quantitative stimulus for overload than traditional calisthenic exercises, calisthenics and other resistance types of exercise can still be effective in improving and maintaining strength.

Summary

The combination of frequency, intensity, and duration of chronic exercise has been found to be effective for producing a training effect. The interaction of these factors provide the overload stimulus. In general, the lower the stimulus the lower the training effect, and the greater the stimulus the greater the effect. As a result of specificity of training and the need for maintaining muscular strength and endurance, and flexibility of the major muscle groups, a well-rounded training program including resistance training and flexibility exercises is recommended. Although age in itself is not a limiting factor to exercise training, a more gradual approach in applying the prescription at older ages seems prudent. It has also been shown that endurance training of fewer than 2 d·wk^{-1}, at less than 50% of maximum oxygen uptake and for less than 10 min·d^{-1}, is inadequate for developing and maintaining fitness for healthy adults.

In the interpretation of this position statement, it must be recognized that the recommendations should be used in the context of participants' needs, goals, and initial abilities. In this regard, a sliding scale as to the amount of time allotted and intensity of effort should be carefully gauged for both the cardiorespiratory and muscular strength and endurance components of the program. An appropriate warm-up and cool-down, which would include flexibility exercises, is also recommended. The important factor is to design a program for the individual to provide the proper amount of physical activity to attain maximal benefit at the lowest risk. Emphasis should be placed on factors that result in permanent lifestyle change and encourage a lifetime of physical activity.

References

1. Allen, T. E., R. J. Byrd, and D. P. Smith. Hemodynamic consequences of circuit weight training. *Res. Q.* 43:299–306, 1976.

2. American College of Sports Medicine. Proper and improper weight loss programs. *Med. Sci. Sports Exerc.* 15: ix–xiii, 1983.

3. American College of Sports Medicine. *Guidelines for Graded Exercise Testing and Exercise Prescription,* 3rd Ed. Philadelphia: Lea and Febiger, 1986.

3A. Armstrong, R. B. Mechanisms of exercise-induced delayed onset muscular soreness: a brief review. *Med. Sci. Sports Exerc.* 16:529–538, 1984.

4. Åstrand, P. O. Exercise physiology of the mature athlete. In: *Sports Medicine for the Mature Athlete,* J. R. Sutton and R. M. Brock (Eds.). Indianapolis, IN: Benchmark Press, Inc., 1986, pp. 3–16.

5. Åstrand, P. O. and K. Rodahl. *Textbook of Work Physiology.* 3rd Ed. New York: McGraw-Hill, 1986, pp. 412–485.

6. Atomi, Y., K. Ito, H. Iwasaski, and M. Miyashita. Effects of intensity and frequency of training on aerobic work capacity of young females. *J. Sports Med.* 18:3–9, 1978.

7. Badenhop, D. T., P. A. Cleary, S. F. Schaal, E. L. Fox, and R. L. Bartels. Physiological adjustments to higher- or lower-intensity exercise in elders. *Med. Sci. Sports Exerc.* 15:496–502, 1983.

8. Barry, A. J., J. W. Daly, E. D. R. Pruett, et al. The effects of physical conditioning on older individuals. I. Work capacity, circulatory-respiratory function, and work electrocardiogram. *J. Gerontol.* 21:182–191, 1966.

9. Benestad, A. M. Trainability of old men. *Acta Med. Scand.* 178:321–327, 1965.

10. Berger, R. A. Effect of varied weight training programs on strength. *Res. Q.* 33:168–181, 1962.

11. Birk, T. J. and C. A. Birk. Use of ratings of perceived exertion for exercise prescription. *Sports Med.* 4:1–8, 1987.

12. Blair, S. N., J. V. Chandler, D. B. Ellisor, and J. Langley. Improving physical fitness by exercise training programs. *South Med. J.* 73:1594–1596, 1980.

13. Blair, S. N., H. W. Kohl, and N. N. Goodyear. Rates and risks for running and exercise injuries: studies in three populations. *Res. Q. Exerc. Sports* 58:221–228, 1987.

13A. Blair, S. N., H. W. Kohl, III, R. S. Paffenbarger, D. G. Clark, K. H. Cooper, and L. H. Gibbons. Physical fitness and all-cause mortality. A prospective study of healthy men and women. *J.A.M.A.* 262:2395–2401, 1989.

14. Boileau, R. A., E. R. Buskirk, D. H. Horstman, J. Mendez, and W. Nicholas. Body composition changes in obese and lean men during physical conditioning. *Med. Sci. Sports* 3:183–189, 1971.

15. Borg, G. A. V. Psychophysical bases of perceived exertion. *Med. Sci. Sports Exerc.* 14:377–381, 1982.

16. Borg, G. and D. Ottoson (Eds.). *The Perception of Exertion in Physical Work.* London, England: The MacMillan Press, Ltd., 1986, pp. 4–7.

16A. Bouchard, C. Gene-environment interaction in human adaptability. In: *The Academy Papers,* R. B. Malina and H. M. Eckert (Eds.). Champaign, IL: Human Kinetics Publishers, 1988, pp. 56–66.

17. Braith, R. W., J. E. Graves, M. L. Pollock, S. L. Leggett, D. M. Carpenter, and A. B. Colvin. Comparison of two versus three days per week of variable resistance training during 10 and 18 week programs. *Int. J. Sports Med.* 10:450–454, 1989.

18. Brynteson, P. and W. E. Sinning. The effects of training frequencies on the retention of cardiovascular fitness. *Med. Sci. Sports* 5:29–33, 1973.

19. Burke, E. J. Physiological effects of similar training programs in males and females. *Res. Q.* 48:510–517, 1977.

20. Burke, E. J. and B. D. Franks. Changes in VO$_{2max}$ resulting from bicycle training at different intensities holding total mechanical work constant. *Res. Q.* 46:31–37, 1975.

21. Buskirk, E. R. and J. L. Hodgson. Age and aerobic power: the rate of change in men and women. *Fed. Proc.* 46:1824–1829, 1987.

22. Carter, J. E. L. and W. H. Phillips. Structural changes in exercising middle-aged males during a 2-year period. *J. Appl. Physiol.* 27:787–794, 1969.

23. Chow, J. R. and J. H. Wilmore. The regulation of exercise intensity by ratings of perceived exertion. *J. Cardiac Rehabil.* 4:382–387, 1984.

24. Christensen, E. H. Physiological evaluation of work in the Nykroppa iron works. In: *Ergonomics Society Symposium on Fatigue,* W. F. Floyd and A. T. Welford (Eds.). London, England: Lewis, 1953, pp. 93–108.

25. Coyle, E. F., W. H. Martin, D. R. Sinacore, M. J. Joyner, J. M. Hagberg, and J. O. Holloszy. Time course of loss of adaptation after stopping prolonged intense endurance training. *J. Appl. Physiol.* 57:1857–1864, 1984.

26. Crews, T. R. and J. A. Roberts. Effects of interaction of frequency and intensity of training. *Res. Q.* 47:48–55, 1976.

27. Cureton, T. K. *The Physiological Effects of Exercise Programs upon Adults.* Springfield, IL: Charles C. Thomas Co., 1969, pp. 3–6, 33–77.

28. Cureton, T. K. and E. E. Phillips. Physical fitness changes in middle-aged men attributable to equal eight-week periods of training, non-training and retraining. *J. Sports Med. Phys. Fitness* 4:1–7, 1964.

29. Davies, C. T. M. and A. V. Knibbs. The training stimulus, the effects of intensity, duration and frequency of effort on maximum aerobic power output. *Int. Z. Angew. Physiol.* 29:299–305, 1971.

30. Davis, J. A., M. H. Frank, B. J. Whipp, and K. Wasserman. Anaerobic threshold alterations caused by endurance training in middle-aged men. *J. Appl. Physiol.* 46:1039–1049, 1979.

31. Dehn, M. M. and R. A. Bruce. Longitudinal variations in maximal oxygen intake with age and activity. *J. Appl. Physiol.* 33:805–807, 1972.

32. Delorme, T. L. Restoration of muscle power by heavy resistance exercise. *J. Bone Joint Surg.* 27:645–667, 1945.

33. Dempsey, J. A. Anthropometrical observations on obese and nonobese young men undergoing a program of vigorous physical exercise. *Res. Q.* 35:275–287, 1964.

34. devries, H. A. Physiological efforts of an exercise training regimen upon men aged 52 to 88. *J. Gerontol.* 24:325–336, 1970.

35. devries. H. A. Exercise intensity threshold for improvement of cardiovascular-respiratory function in older men. *Geriatrics* 26:94–101, 1971.

36. Dishman, R. K., J. Sallis, and D. Orenstein. The determinants of physical activity and exercise. *Public Health Rep.* 100:158–180, 1985.

37. Dishman, R. K., R. W. Patton, J. Smith, R. Weinberg, and A. Jackson. Using perceived exertion to prescribe and monitor exercise training heart rate. *Int. J. Sports Med.* 8:208–213, 1987.

38. Drinkwater, B. L. Physiological responses of women to exercise. In: *Exercise and Sports Sciences Reviews,* Vol 1. J. H. Wilmore (Ed.). New York: Academic Press, 1973, pp. 126–154.

39. Drinkwater, B. L., S. M. Horvath, and C. L. Wells. Aerobic power of females, ages 10 to 68. *J. Gerontol.* 30:385–394, 1975.

40. Durnin, J. V. G. A. and R. Passmore. *Energy, Work and Leisure.* London, England: Heinemann Educational Books, Ltd., 1967, pp. 47–82.

41. Edstrom, L. and L. Grimby. Effect of exercise on the motor unit. *Muscle Nerve* 9:104–126, 1986.

42. Ekblom, B., P. O. Astrand, B. Saltin, J. Stenberg, and B. Wallstrom. Effect of training on circulatory response to exercise. *J. Appl. Physiol.* 24:518–528, 1968.

43. Fleck, S. J. and W. J. Kraemer. *Designing Resistance Training Programs.* Champaign, IL: Human Kinetics Books, 1987, pp. 15–46, 161–162.

44. Flint, M. M., B. L. Drinkwater, and S. M. Horvath. Effects of training on women's response to submaximal exercise. *Med. Sci. Sports* 6:89–94, 1974.

45. Fox, E. L., R. L. Bartels, C. E. Billings, R. O'Brien, R. Bason, and D. K. Mathews. Frequency and duration of interval training programs and changes in aerobic power. *J. Appl. Physiol.* 38:481–484, 1975.

46. Franklin, B., E. Buskirk, J. Hodgson, H. Gahagan, J. Kollias, and J. Mendez. Effects of physical conditioning on cardiorespiratory function, body composition and serum lipids in relatively normal weight and obese middle-age women. *Int. J. Obes.* 3:97–109, 1979.

47. Fringer, M. N. and A. G. Stull. Changes in cardiorespiratory parameters during periods of training and detraining in young female adults. *Med. Sci. Sports* 6:20–25, 1974.

48. Gaesser, G. A. and R. G. Rich. Effects of high- and low-intensity exercise training on aerobic capacity and blood lipids. *Med. Sci. Sports Exerc.* 16:269–274, 1984.

49. Getchell, L. H. and J. C. Moore. Physical training: comparative responses of middle-aged adults. *Arch. Phys. Med. Rehabil.* 56:250–254, 1975.

50. Gettman, L. R., M. L. Pollock, J. L. Durstine, A. Ward, J. Ayres, and A. C. Linnerud. Physiological responses of men to 1, 3, and 5 day per week training programs. *Res. Q.* 47:638–646, 1976.

51. Gettman, L. R., J. J. Ayres, M. L. Pollock, and A. Jackson. The effect of circuit weight training on strength, cardiorespiratory function, and body composition of adult men. *Med. Sci. Sports* 10:171–176, 1978.

52. Gettman, L. R., J. Ayres, M. L. Pollock, J. L. Durstine, and W. Grantham. Physiological effects of circuit strength training and jogging. *Arch. Phys. Med. Rahabil.* 60:115–120, 1979.

53. Gettman, L. R., L. A. Culter, and T. Strathman. Physiologic changes after 20 weeks of isotonic vs. isokinetic circuit training. *J. Sports Med. Phys. Fitness* 20:265–274, 1980.

54. Gettman, L. R. and M. L. Pollock. Circuit weight training: a critical review of its physiological benefits. *Phys. Sportsmed.* 9:44–60, 1981.

55. Gettman, L. R., P. Ward, and R. D. Hagman. A comparison of combined running and weight training with circuit weight training. *Med. Sci. Sports Exerc.* 14:229–234, 1982.

56. Gillam, G. M. Effects of frequency of weight training on muscle strength enhancement. *J. Sports Med.* 21:432–436, 1981.

57. Girandola, R. N. Body composition changes in women: effects of high and low exercise intensity. *Arch. Phys. Med. Rehabil.* 57:297–300, 1976.

58. Gledhill, N. and R. B. Eynon. The intensity of training. In: *Training Scientific Basis and Application*, A. W. Taylor and M. L. Howell (Eds.). Springfield, IL: Charles C. Thomas Co., 1972, pp. 97–102.

59. Golding, L. Effects of physical training upon total serum cholesterol levels. *Res. Q.* 32:499–505, 1961.

60. Goode, R. C., A. Virgin, T. T. Romet, et al. Effects of a short period of physical activity in adolescent boys and girls. *Can. J. Appl. Sports Sci.* 1:241–250, 1976.

61. Gossard, D., W. L. Haskell, B. Taylor, et al. Effects of low- and high-intensity home-based exercise training on functional capacity in healthy middle-age men. *Am. J. Cardiol.* 57:446–449, 1986.

62. Graves, J. E., M. L. Pollock, S. H. Leggett, R. W. Braith, D. M. Carpenter, and L. E. Bishop. Effect of reduced training frequency on muscular strength. *Int. J. Sports Med.* 9:316–319, 1988.

63. Graves, J. E., M. L. Pollock, A. E. Jones, A. B. Colvin, and S. H. Leggett. Specificity of limited range of motion variable resistance training. *Med. Sci. Sports Exerc.* 21:84–89, 1989.

64. Gwinup, G. Effect of exercise alone on the weight of obese women. *Arch. Int. Med.* 135:676–680, 1975.

65. Hagberg, J. M., J. E. Graves, M. Limacher, et al. Cardiovascular responses of 70–79 year old men and women to exercise training. *J. Appl. Physiol.* 66:2589–2594, 1989.

66. Hakkinen, K. Factors influencing trainability of muscular strength during short term and prolonged training. *Natl. Strength Cond. Assoc. J.* 7:32–34, 1985.

67. Hanson, J. S., B. S. Tabakin, A. M. Levy, and W. Nedde. Long-term physical training and cardiovascular dynamics in middle-aged men. *Circulation* 38:783–799, 1968.

68. Hanson, J. S. and W. H. Nedde. Long-term physical training effect in sedentary females. *J. Appl. Physiol.* 37:112–116, 1974.

69. Hartley, L. H., G. Grimby, A. Kilbom, et al. Physical training in sedentary middle-aged and older men. *Scand. J. Clin. Lab. Invest.* 24:335–344, 1969.

70. Hartung, G. H., M. H. Smolensky, R. B. Harrist, and R. Runge. Effects of varied durations of training on improvement in cardiorespiratory endurance. *J. Hum. Ergol.* 6:61–68, 1977.

71. Haskell, W. L. Physical activity and health: need to define the required stimulus. *Am. J. Cardiol.* 55:4D–9D, 1985.

72. Haskell, W. L., H. J. Montoye, and D. Orenstein. Physical activity and exercise to achieve health-related physical fitness components. *Public Health Rep.* 100:202–212, 1985.

73. Heath, G. W., J. M. Hagberg, A. A. Ehsani, and J. O. Holloszy. A physiological comparison of young and older endurance athletes. *J. Appl. Physiol.* 51:634–640, 1981.

74. Hettinger, T. *Physiology of Strength*. Springfield, IL: C. C. Thomas Publisher, 1961, pp. 18–40.

75. Hickson, R. C. and M. A. Rosenkoetter. Reduced training frequencies and maintenance of increased aerobic power. *Med. Sci. Sports Exerc.* 13:13–16, 1981.

76. Hickson, R. C., C. Kanakis, J. R. Davis, A. M. Moore, and S. Rich. Reduced training duration effects on aerobic power, endurance, and cardiac growth. *J. Appl. Physiol.* 53:225–229, 1982.

77. Hickson, R. C., C. Foster, M. L. Pollock, T. M. Galassi, and S. Rich. Reduced training intensities and loss of aerobic power, endurance, and cardiac growth. *J. Appl. Physiol.* 58:492–499, 1985.

78. Hill, J. O., P. B. Sparling, T. W. Shields, and P. A. Heller. Effects of exercise and food restriction on body composition and metabolic rate in obese women. *Am. J. Clin. Nutr.* 46:622–630, 1987.

79. Hollmann, W. Changes in the Capacity for Maximal and Continuous Effort in Relation to Age. *Int. Res. Sports Phys. Ed.* E. Jokl and E. Simon (Eds.). Springfield, IL: Charles C. Thomas Co., 1964, pp. 369–371.

80. Hollmann, W. and H. Venrath. Die Beinflussung von Herzgrösse, maximaler O_2—Aufnahme und Ausdauergranze durch ein Ausdauertraining mittlerer und hoher Intensität. *Der Sportarzt* 9:189–193, 1963.

81. No reference 81 due to renumbering in proof.

82. Huibregtse, W. H., H. H. Hartley, L. R. Jones, W. D. Doolittle, and T. L. Criblez. Improvement of aerobic work capacity following non-strenuous exercise. *Arch. Environ. Health* 27:12–15, 1973.

83. Hurley, B. F., D. R. Seals, A. A. Ehsani, et al. Effects of high-intensity strength training on cardiovascular function. *Med. Sci. Sports Exerc.* 16:483–488, 1984.

84. Ismah, A. H., D. Corrigan, and D. F. McLeod. Effect of an eight-month exercise program on selected physiological, biochemical, and audiological variables in adult men. *Br. J. Sports Med.* 7:230–240, 1973.

84A. Jones, D. A., D. J. Newman, J. M. Round, and S. E. L. Tolfree. Experimental human muscle damage: morphological changes in relation to other indices of damage. *J. Physiol. (Lond.)* 375:435–438, 1986.

85. Karvonen, M., K. Kentala, and O. Mustala. The effects of training heart rate: a longitudinal study. *Ann. Med. Exp. Biol. Fenn.* 35:307–315, 1957.

86. Kasch, F. W., W. H. Phillips, J. E. L. Carter, and J. L. Boyer. Cardiovascular changes in middle-aged men during two years of training. *J. Appl. Physiol.* 314:53–57, 1972.

87. Kasch, F. W. and J. P. Wallace. Physiological variables during 10 years of endurance exercise. *Med. Sci. Sports* 8:5–8, 1976.

88. Kasch, F. W., J. P. Wallace, and S. P. Van Camp. Effects of 18 years of endurance exercise on physical work capacity of older men. *J. Cardiopulmonary Rehabil.* 5:308–312, 1985.

89. Katch, F. I. and W. D. McArdle. *Nutrition, Weight Control and Exercise,* 3rd Ed. Philadelphia: Lea and Febiger, 1988, pp. 110–112.

90. Kearney, J. T., A. G. Stull, J. L. Ewing, and J. W. Strein. Cardiorespiratory responses of sedentary college women as a function of training intensity. *J. Appl. Physiol.* 41:822–825, 1976.

91. Kendrick, Z. B., M. L. Pollock, T. N. Hickman, and H. S. Miller. Effects of training and detraining on cardiovascular efficiency. *Am. Corr. Ther. J.* 25:79–83, 1971.

92. Kilbom, A. Physical training in women. *Scand. J. Clin. Lab. Invest.* 119 (Suppl.):1–34, 1971.

93. Kilbom, A., L. Hartley, B. Saltin, J. Bjure, G. Grimby, and I. Åstrand. Physical training in sedentary middle-aged and older men. *Scand. J. Clin. Lab. Invest.* 24:315–322, 1969.

94. Kimura, Y., H. Itow, and S. Yamazakie. The effects of circuit weight training on VO_{2max} and body composition of trained and untrained college men. *J. Physiol. Soc. Jpn.* 43:593–596, 1981.

94A. Klissouras, V., F. Pirnay, and J. Petit. Adaptation to maximal effort: genetics and age. *J. Appl. Physiol.* 35:288–293, 1973.

95. Knapik, J. J., R. H. Maudsley, and N. V. Rammos. Angular specificity and test mode specificity of isometric and isokinetic strength training. *J. Orthop. Sports Phys. Ther.* 5:58–65, 1983.

96. Knehr, C. A., D. B. Dill, and W. Neufeld. Training and its effect on man at rest and at work. *Am. J. Physiol.* 136:148–156, 1942.

97. Knuttgen, H. G., L. O. Nordesjo, B. Ollander, and B. Saltin. Physical conditioning through interval training with young male adults. *Med. Sci. Sports* 5:220–226, 1973.

98. Laporte, R. E., L. L. Adams, D. D. Savage, G. Brenes, S. Dearwater, and T. Cook. The spectrum of physical activity, cardiovascular disease and health: an epidemiologic perspective. *Am. J. Epidemiol.* 120:507–517, 1984.

99. Leon, A. S., J. Conrad, D. B. Hunninghake, and R. Serfass. Effects of a vigorous walking program on body composition, and carbohydrate and lipid metabolism of obese young men. *Am. J. Clin. Nutr.* 32:1776–1787, 1979.

100. Leon, A. S., J. Connett, D. R. Jacobs, and R. Rauramaa. Leisure-time physical activity levels and risk of coronary heart disease and death: the multiple risk of coronary heart disease and death: the multiple risk factor intervention trial. *J.A.M.A.* 258:2388–2395, 1987.

100A. Lewis, S. E., W. E. Taylor, R. M. Graham, W. A. Pettinger, J. E. Shutte, and C. G. Blomovisi. Cardiovascular responses to exercise as functions of absolute and relative work load. *J. Appl. Physiol.* 54:1314–1323, 1983.

101. Liang, M. T., J. E. Alexander, H. L. Taylor, R. C. Serfass, A. S. Leon, and G. A. Stull. Aerobic training threshold, intensity duration, and frequency of exercise. *Scand. J. Sports Sci.* 4:5–8, 1982.

101A. Lieber, D. C., R. L. Lieber, and W. C. Adams. Effects of run-training and swim-training at similar absolute intensities on treadmill VO_{2max}. *Med. Sci. Sports Exerc.* 21:655–661, 1989.

101B. MacDougall, J. D., G. R. Ward, D. G. Sale, and J. R. Sutton. Biochemical adaptation of human skeleton muscle to heavy resistance training and immobilization. *J. Appl. Physiol.* 43:700–703, 1977.

101C. MacDougall, J. D., D. Tuxen, D. G. Sale, J. R. Moroz, and J. R. Sutton. Arterial blood pressure response to heavy resistance training. *J. Appl. Physiol.* 58:785–790, 1985.

102. Mann, G. V., L. H. Garrett, A. Farhi, et al. Exercise to prevent coronary heart disease. *Am. J. Med.* 46:12–27, 1969.

103. Marcinik, E. J., J. A. Hodgdon, U. Mittleman, and J. J. O'Brien. Aerobic/ calisthenic and aerobic/circuit weight training programs for Navy men: a comparative study. *Med. Sci. Sports Exerc.* 17:482–487, 1985.

104. Marigold, E. A. The effect of training at predetermined heart rate levels for sedentary college women. *Med. Sci. Sports* 6:14–19, 1974.

105. Martin, J. E. and P. M. Dubbert. Adherence to exercise. In: *Exercise and Sports Sciences Reviews,* Vol. 13. R. L. Terjung (Ed.). New York: MacMillan Publishing Co., 1985, pp. 137–167.

106. Martin, W. H., J. Montgomery, P. G. Snell, et al. Cardiovascular adaptations to intense swim training in sedentary middle-aged men and women. *Circulation* 75:323–330, 1987.

107. Mayhew, J. L. and P. M. Gross. Body composition changes in young women with high resistance weight training. *Res. Q.* 45:433–439, 1974.

108. Messier, J. P. and M. Dill. Alterations in strength and maximal oxygen uptake consequent to Nautilus circuit weight training. *Res. Q. Exerc. Sport* 56:345–351, 1985.

109. Milesis, C. A., M. L. Pollock, M. D. Bah, J. J. Ayres, A. Ward, and A. C. Linnerud. Effects of different durations of training on cardiorespiratory function, body composition and serum lipids. *Res. Q.* 47:716–725, 1976.

110. Misner, J. E., R. A. Boileau, B. H. Massey, and J. H. Mayhew. Alterations in body composition of adult men during selected physical training programs. *J. Am. Geriatr. Soc.* 22:33–38, 1974.

111. Miyashita, M., S. Haga, and T. Mitzuta. Training and detraining effects on aerobic power in middle-aged and older men. *J. Sports Med.* 18:131–137, 1978.

112. Moody, D. L., J. Kollias, and E. R. Buskirk. The effect of a moderate exercise program on body weight and skinfold thickness in overweight college women. *Med. Sci. Sports* 1:75–80, 1969.

113. Moody, D. L., J. H. Wilmore, R. N. Girandola, and J. P. Royce. The effects of a jogging program on the body composition of normal and obese high school girls. *Med. Sci. Sports* 4:210–213, 1972.

114. Mueller, E. A. and W. Rohmert. Die geschwindigkeit der muskelkraft zunahme bein isometrischen training. *Int. Z. Angew. Physiol.* 19:403–419, 1963.

115. Naughton, J. and F. Nagle. Peak oxygen intake during physical fitness program for middle-aged men. *J.A.M.A.* 191:899–901, 1965.

116. O'Hara, W., C. Allen, and R. J. Shephard. Loss of body weight and fat during exercise in a cold chamber. *Eur. J. Appl. Physiol.* 37:205–218, 1977.

117. Oja, P., P. Teraslinna, T. Partanen, and R. Karava. Feasibility of an 18 months' physical training program for middle-aged men and its effect on physical fitness. *Am. J. Public Health* 64:459–465, 1975.

118. Olree, H. D., B. Corbin, J. Penrod, and C. Smith. Methods of achieving and maintaining physical fitness for prolonged space flight. Final Progress Rep. to NASA. Grant No. NGR–04–002–004, 1969.

119. Oscai, L. B., T. Williams, and B. Hertig. Effects of exercise on blood volume. *J. Appl. Physiol.* 24:622–624, 1968.

120. Paffenbarger, R. S., R. T. Hyde, A. L. Wing, and C. Hsieh. Physical activity and all-cause mortality, and longevity of college alumni. *N. Engl. J. Med.* 314:605–613, 1986.

121. Pavlou, K. N., W. P. Steffee, R. H. Learman, and B. A. Burrows. Effects of dieting and exercise on lean body mass, oxygen uptake, and strength. *Med. Sci. Sports Exerc.* 17:466–471, 1985.

122. Pels, A. E., M. L. Pollock, T. E. Dohmeier, K. A. Lemberger, and B. F. Oehrlein. Effects of leg press training on cycling, leg press, and running peak cardiorespiratory measures. *Med. Sci. Sports Exerc.* 19:66–70, 1987.

123. Pollock, M. L. The quantification of endurance training programs. In: *Exercise and Sport Sciences Reviews,* J. H. Wilmore (Ed.). New York: Academic Press, 1973, pp. 155–188.

124. Pollock, M. L. Prescribing exercise for fitness and adherence. In: *Exercise Adherence: Its Impact on Public Health,* R. K. Dishman (Ed.). Champaign, IL: Human Kinetics Books, 1988, pp. 259–277.

125. Pollock, M. L., T. K. Cureton, and L. Greninger. Effects of frequency of training on working capacity, cardiovascular function, and body composition of adult men. *Med. Sci. Sports* 1:70–74, 1969.

126. Pollock, M. L., J. Tiffany, L. Gettman, R. Janeway, and H. Lofland. Effects of frequency of training on serum lipids, cardiovascular function, and body composition. In: *Exercise and Fitness,* B. D. Franks (Ed.). Chicago: Athletic Institute, 1969, pp. 161–178.

127. Pollock, M. L., H. Miller, R. Janeway, A. C. Linnerud, B. Robertson, and R. Valentino. Effects of walking on body composition and cardiovascular function of middle-aged men. *J. Appl. Physiol.* 30:126–130, 1971.

128. Pollock, M. L., J. Broida, Z. Kendrick, H. S. Miller, R. Janeway, and A. C. Linnerud. Effects of training two days per week at different intensities on middle-aged men. *Med. Sci. Sports* 4:192–197, 1972.

129. Pollock, M. L., H. S. Miller, Jr., and J. Wilmore. Physiological characteristics of champion American track athletes 40 to 70 years of age. *J. Gerontol.* 29:645–649, 1974.

130. Pollock, M. L., J. Dimmick, H. S. Miller, Z. Kendrick, and A. C. Linnerud. Effects of mode of training on cardiovascular function and body composition of middle-aged men. *Med. Sci. Sports* 7:139–145, 1975.

131. No reference 131 due to renumbering in proof.

132. Pollock, M. L., G. A. Dawson, H. S. Miller, Jr., et al. Physiologic response to men 49 to 65 years of age to endurance training. *J. Am. Geriatr. Soc.* 24:97–104, 1976.

133. Pollock, M. L. and A. Jackson. Body composition: measurement and changes resulting from physical training. Proceedings National College Physical Education Association for Men and Women, January, 1977, pp. 125–137.

134. Pollock, M. L., J. Ayres, and A. Ward. Cardiorespiratory fitness: response to differing intensities and durations of training. *Arch. Phys. Med. Rehabil.* 58:467–473, 1977.

135. Pollock, M. L., R. Gettman, C. A. Milesis, M. D. Bah, J. L. Durstine, and R. B. Johnson. Effects of frequency and duration of training on attrition and incidence of injury. *Med. Sci. Sports* 9:31–36, 1977.

136. Pollock, M. L., L. R. Gettman, P. B. Raven, J. Ayres, M. Bah, and A. Ward. Physiological comparison of the effects of aerobic and anaerobic training. In: *Physical Fitness Programs for Law Enforcement Officers: A Manual for Police Administrators,* C. S. Price, M. L. Pollock, L. R. Gettman, and D. A.

Kent (Eds.). Washington, D.C.: U.S. Government Printing Office, No. 027–000–00671–0, 1978, pp. 89–96.

137. Pollock, M. L., A. S. Jackson, and C. Foster. The use of the perception scale for exercise prescription. In: *The Perception of Exertion in Physical Work*, G. Borg and D. Ottoson (Eds.). London, England: The MacMillan Press, Ltd., 1986, pp. 161–176.

138. Pollock, M. L., C. Foster, D. Knapp, J. S. Rod, and D. H. Schmidt. Effect of age and training on aerobic capacity and body composition of master athletes. *J. Appl. Physiol.* 62:725–731, 1987.

139. Pollock, M. L. and J. H. Wilmore. *Exercise in Health and Disease: Evaluation and Prescription for Prevention and Rehabilitation,* 2nd Ed. Philadelphia: W. B. Saunders, Co., 1990.

140. Powell, K. E., H. W. Kohl, C. J. Caspersen, and S. N. Blair. An epidemiological perspective of the causes of running injuries. *Phys. Sportsmed.* 14:100–114, 1986.

141. Ribisl, P. M. Effects of training upon the maximal oxygen uptake of middle-aged men. *Int. Z. Angew. Physiol.* 26:272–278, 1969.

142. Richie, D. H., S. F. Kelso, and P. A. Bellucci. Aerobic dance injuries: a retrospective study of instructors and participants. *Phys. Sportsmed.* 13:130–140, 1985.

143. Robinson, S. and P. M. Harmon. Lactic acid mechanism and certain properties of blood in relation to training. *Am. J. Physiol.* 132:757–769, 1941.

144. Roskamm, H. Optimum patterns of exercise for healthy adults. *Can. Med. Assoc. J.* 96:895–899, 1967.

145. Sale, D. G. Influence of exercise and training on motor unit activation. In: *Exercise and Sport Sciences Reviews,* K. B. Pandolf (Ed.). New York: MacMillan Publishing Co., 1987, pp. 95–152.

145A. Sale, D. G. Neural adaptation to resistance training. *Med. Sci. Sports Exerc.* 20:S135–S145, 1988.

146. Sallis, J. F., W. L. Haskell, S. P. Fortman, K. M. Vranizan, C. B. Taylor, and D. S. Soloman. Predictors of adoption and maintenance of physical activity in a community sample. *Prev. Med.* 15:131–141, 1986.

147. Saltin, B., G. Blomqvist, J. Mitchell, R. L. Johnson, K. Wildenthal, and C. B. Chapman. Response to exercise after bed rest and after training. *Circulation* 37, 38(Suppl. 7):1–78, 1968.

148. Saltin, B., L. Hartley, A. Kilbom, and I. Åstrand. Physical training in sedentary middle-aged and older men. *Scand. J. Clin. Lab. Invest.* 24:323–334, 1969.

149. Santigo, M. C., J. F. Alexander, G. A. Stull, R. C. Serfass, A. M. Hayday, and A. S. Leon. Physiological responses of sedentary women to a 20-week conditioning program of walking or jogging. *Scand. J. Sports Sci.* 9:33–39, 1987.

150. Seals, D. R., J. M. Hagberg, B. F. Hurley, A. A. Ehsani, and J. O. Holloszy. Endurance training in older men and women. I. Cardiovascular responses to exercise. *J. Appl. Physiol.* 57:1024–1029, 1984.

151. Sharkey, B. J. Intensity and duration of training and the development of cardiorespiratory endurance. *Med. Sci. Sports* 2:197–202, 1970.

152. Shephard, R. J. Intensity, duration, and frequency of exercise as determinants of the response to a training regime. *Int. Z. Angew. Physiol.* 26:272–278, 1969.

153. Shephard, R. J. Future research on the quantifying of endurance training. *J. Hum. Ergol.* 3:163–181, 1975.

154. Sidney, K. H., R. B. Eynon, and D. A. Cunningham. Effect of frequency of training of exercise upon physical working performance and selected variables representative of cardiorespiratory fitness. In *Training: Scientific Basis and Application,* A. W. Taylor (Ed.). Springfield, IL: Charles C. Thomas Co., 1972, pp. 144–188.

155. Sidney, K. H., R. J. Shephard, and J. Harrison. Endurance training and body composition of the elderly. *Am. J. Clin. Nutr.* 30:326–333, 1977.

156. Siegel, W., G. Blomqvist, and J. H. Mitchell. Effects of a quantitated physical training program on middle-aged sedentary males. *Circulation* 41:19–29, 1970.

156A. Siscovick, D. S., N. S. Weiss, R. H. Fletcher, and T. Lasky. The incidence of primary cardiac arrest during vigorous exercise. *N. Engl. J. Med.* 311:874–877, 1984.

157. Skinner, J. The cardiovascular system with aging and exercise. In: *Physical Activity and Aging,* D. Brunner and E. Jokl (Eds.). Baltimore: University Park Press, 1970, pp. 100–108.

158. Skinner, J., J. Holloszy, and T. Cureton. Effects of a program of endurance exercise on physical work capacity and anthropometric measurements of fifteen middle-aged men. *Am. J. Cardiol.* 14:747–752, 1964.

159. Smith, D. P. and F. W. Stransky. The effect of training and detraining on the body composition and cardiovascular response of young women to exercise. *J. Sports Med.* 16:112–120, 1976.

160. Smith, E. L., W. Reddan, P. E. Smith. Physical activity and calcium modalities for bone mineral increase in aged women. *Med. Sci. Sports Exerc.* 13:60–64, 1981.

161. Suominen, H., E. Heikkinen, and T. Tarkatti. Effect of eight weeks physical training on muscle and connective tissue of the m. vastus lateralis in 69-year-old men and women. *J. Gerontol.* 32:33–37, 1977.

162. Terjung, R. L., K. M. Baldwin, J. Cooksey, B. Samson, and R. A. Sutter. Cardiovascular adaptation to twelve minutes of mild daily exercise in middle-aged sedentary men. *J. Am. Geriatr. Soc.* 21:164–168, 1973.

163. Thomas, S. G., D. A. Cunningham, P. A. Rechnitzer, A. P. Donner, and J. H. Howard. Determinants of the training response in elderly men. *Med. Sci. Sports Exerc.* 17:667–672, 1985.

164. Wenger, H. A. and G. J. Bell. The interactions of intensity, frequency, and duration of exercise training in altering cardiorespiratory fitness. *Sports Med.* 3:346–356, 1986.

165. Wilmore, J. H. Alterations in strength, body composition, and anthropometric measurements consequent to a 10-week weight training program. *Med. Sci. Sports* 6:133–138, 1974.

166. Wilmore, J. Inferiority of female athletes: myth or reality. *J. Sports Med.* 3:1–6, 1974.

167. Wilmore, J. H. Design issues and alternatives in assessing physical fitness among apparently healthy adults in a health examination survey of the general population. In: *Assessing Physical Fitness and Activity in General Population Studies,* T. F. Drury (Ed.). Washington, D.C.: U.S. Public Health Service, National Center for Health Statistics, 1988 (in press).

168. Wilmore, J. H., J. Royce, R. N. Girandola, F. I. Katch, and V. L. Katch. Physiological alternatives resulting from a 10-week jogging program. *Med. Sci. Sports* 2:7–14, 1970.

169. Wilmore, J. H., J. Royce, R. N. Girandola, F. I. Katch, and V. L. Katch. Body composition changes with a 10-week jogging program. *Med. Sci. Sports* 2:113–117, 1970.

170. Wilmore, J., R. B. Parr, P. A. Vodak, et al. Strength, endurance, BMR, and body composition changes with circuit weight training. *Med. Sci. Sports* 8:58–60, 1976.

171. Wilmore, J. H., G. A. Ewy, A. R. Mortan, et al. The effect of beta-adrenergic blockade on submaximal and maximal exercise performance. *J. Cardiac Rehabil.* 3:30–36, 1983.

171A. Wilmore, J. H. Body composition in sport and exercise: directions for future research. *Med. Sci. Sports Exerc.* 15:21–31, 1983.

172. Wilmore, J. H. and D. L. Costill. *Training for Sport and Activity. The Physiological Basis of the Conditioning Process,* 3rd Ed. Dubuque, IA: Wm. C. Brown, 1988, pp. 113–212.

173. Wood, P. D., W. L. Haskell, S. N. Blair, et al. Increased exercise level and plasma lipoprotein concentrations: a one-year, randomized, controlled study in sedentary, middle-aged men. *Metabolism* 32:31–39, 1983.

174. Zuti, W. B. and L. A. Golding. Comparing diet and exercise as weight reduction tools. *Phys. Sportsmed.* 4:49–53, 1976.

Glossary

acclimatization　The ability of the body to undergo physiological adaptations so that the stress of a given environment, such as high environmental temperature, is less severe.

acetaldehyde　An intermediate breakdown product of alcohol.

acetic acid　A naturally occurring saturated fatty acid; a precursor for the Krebs cycle when converted into acetyl CoA.

acetyl CoA　The major fuel for the oxidative processes in the body, being derived from the breakdown of glucose and fatty acids.

acid-base balance　A relative balance of acid and base products in the body so that an optimal pH is maintained in the tissues, particularly the blood.

acidosis　A disturbance of the normal acid-base balance in which excess acids accumulate in the body. Lactic acid production during exercise may lead to acidosis.

acute exercise bout　A single bout of exercise that will produce various physiological reactions dependent upon the nature of the exercise; a single workout.

additives　Substances added to food to improve color, texture, stability, or for similar purposes.

adenosinetriphosphate　*See* ATP.

ADH　The antidiuretic hormone secreted by the pituitary gland; its major action is to conserve body water by decreasing urine formation.

adrenaline　A hormone secreted by the adrenal medulla; it is a stimulant and prepares the body for "fight or flight."

aerobic　Relating to energy processes that occur in the presence of oxygen.

aerobic walking　Rapid walking designed to elevate the heart rate so that a training effect will occur; more strenuous than ordinary leisure walking.

alanine　A nonessential amino acid.

alcohol　A colorless liquid with depressant effects; ethyl alcohol or ethanol is the alcohol designed for human consumption.

alcohol dehydrogenase　An enzyme in the liver that initiates the breakdown of alcohol to acetaldehyde.

alcoholism　A rather undefined term used to describe individuals who abuse the effect of alcohol; an addiction or habituation that may result in physical and/or psychological withdrawal effects.

aldosterone　The main electrolyte-regulating hormone secreted by the adrenal cortex; primarily controls sodium and potassium balance.

alpha-keto acid　Specific acids associated with different amino acids and released upon deamination or transamination; for example, the breakdown of glutamate yields alpha-ketoglutarate.

alpha-tocopherol　The most biologically active alcohol in vitamin E.

alpha-tocopherol equivalent　The amount of other forms of tocopherol to equal the vitamin E activity of one milligram of alpha-tocopherol.

amenorrhea　Absence or cessation of menstruation.

amino acids　The chief structural material of protein, consisting of an amino group (NH_2) and an acid group (COOH) plus other components.

amino group　The nitrogen-containing component of amino acids (NH_2).

aminostatic theory　A theory suggesting that hunger is controlled by the presence or absence of amino acids in the blood acting upon a receptor in the hypothalamus.

ammonia　A metabolic by-product of the oxidation of glutamine; it may be transformed into urea for excretion from the body.

anabolic steroids　Drugs designed to mimic the actions of testosterone to build muscle tissue (anabolism) while minimizing the androgenic effects (masculinization).

anabolism　Constructive metabolism, the process whereby simple body compounds are formed into more complex ones.

anaerobic　Relating to energy processes that occur in the absence of oxygen.

anaerobic threshold　The intensity of exercise at which the individual begins to increase the proportion of energy derived from anaerobic means, principally the lactic acid system. *Also see* steady-state threshold and OBLA.

android type obesity　Male type obesity, in which the body fat accumulates in the abdominal area and is a more significant risk factor for chronic disease than is gynoid type obesity.

anemia　In general, subnormal levels of circulating RBCs and hemoglobin; there are many different types of anemia.

angina　The pain experienced under the breastbone or in other areas of the upper body when the heart is deprived of oxygen.

anion　A negatively charged ion, or electrolyte.

anorexia athletica　A form of anorexia nervosa observed in athletes involved in sports in which low percentages of body fat may enhance performance, such as gymnastics and ballet.

anorexia nervosa　A serious nervous condition, particularly among teenage girls and young women, marked by a loss of appetite and leading to various degrees of emaciation.

antibodies　Protein substances developed in the body in reaction to the presence of a foreign substance, called an antigen; natural antibodies are also present in the blood. They are protective in nature.

antidiuretic hormone　*See* ADH.

antioxidant　A compound that may protect other compounds from the effects of oxygen. The antioxidant itself reacts with oxygen.

antipromoters Compounds that block the actions of promoters, agents associated with the development of certain diseases, such as cancer.

apoprotein A class of special proteins associated with the formation of lipoproteins. A variety of apoproteins have been identified and are involved in the specific functions of the different lipoproteins.

appetite A pleasant desire for food for the purpose of enjoyment that is developed through previous experience; controlled in humans by an appetite center, or appestat, in the hypothalamus.

arginine An essential amino acid.

arteriosclerosis Hardening of the arteries; *also see* atherosclerosis.

ascorbic acid Vitamin C.

atherosclerosis A specific form of arteriosclerosis characterized by the formation of plaque on the inner layers of the arterial wall.

athletic amenorrhea The cessation of menstruation in athletes, believed to be caused by factors associated with participation in strenuous physical activity.

ATP Adenosine triphosphate, a high-energy phosphate compound found in the body; one of the major forms of energy available for immediate use in the body.

ATPase The enzyme involved in the splitting of ATP and the release of energy.

ATP–PC system The energy system for fast, powerful muscle contractions; uses ATP as the immediate energy source, the spent ATP being quickly regenerated by breakdown of the PC. ATP and PC are high-energy phosphates in the muscle cell.

basal metabolic rate *See* BMR.

Basic Four Food Groups Grouping of foods into four categories that can be used as a means to educate individuals on how to obtain essential nutrients. The four groups are meat, milk, bread-cereal, and fruit-vegetable.

bee pollen A nutritional product containing minute amounts of protein and some vitamins that has been advertised to be possibly ergogenic for some athletes.

behavioral modification Relative to weight-control methods, behavioral patterns, or the way one acts, may be modified to help achieve weight loss.

beriberi A deficiency disease attributed to lack of thiamin (vitamin B_1) in the diet.

beta-carotene A precursor for vitamin A found in plants.

bile A fluid secreted by the liver into the intestine that aids in the breakdown process of fats.

bile salts Active salts found in bile; cholesterol is part of their structure.

binge-purge syndrome An eating behavior characterized by excessive hunger leading to gorging, followed by guilt and purging by vomiting. *Also see* Bulimia nervosa.

bioavailability In relation to nutrients in food, the amount that may be absorbed into the body.

bioelectrical impedance analysis (BIA) A method to calculate percentage of body fat by measuring electrical resistance due to the water content of the body.

biotin A component of the B complex.

blood alcohol concentration (BAC) The concentration of alcohol in the blood, usually expressed as milligram percent.

blood alcohol level *See* blood alcohol concentration.

blood glucose Blood sugar; the means by which carbohydrate is carried in the blood; normal range is 70–120 mg/ml.

blood pressure The pressure of the blood in the blood vessels; usually used to refer to arterial blood pressure. See also systolic blood pressure and diastolic blood pressure.

BMI *See* Body Mass Index.

BMR The basal metabolic rate; measurement of energy expenditure in the body under resting, postabsorptive conditions, indicative of the energy needed to maintain life under these basal conditions.

body image The image or impression the individual has of his or her body. A poor body image may lead to personality problems.

Body Mass Index An index calculated by a ratio of height to weight, used as a measure of obesity.

bread exchange One bread exchange in the Food Exchange System contains 15 grams of carbohydrate, 3 grams of protein, and 80 Calories.

brown adipose tissue A special form of body fat that is designed to produce heat; small amounts are found in humans in the area of vital organs such as heart and lungs.

bulimia nervosa Excessive hunger; the binge-purge syndrome.

bulk-up method A method of weight training designed to increase muscle mass; uses high resistance and moderate volume with many different muscle groups.

CAD Coronary artery disease; atherosclerosis in the coronary arteries.

caffeine A stimulant drug found in many food products such as coffee, tea, and cola drinks; stimulates the central nervous system.

calciferol A synthetic vitamin D; vitamin D.

calcium A silver-white metallic element essential to human nutrition.

caloric concept of weight control The concept that Calories are the basis of weight control. Excess Calories will add body weight while caloric deficiencies will contribute to weight loss.

caloric deficit A negative caloric balance whereby more Calories are expended than consumed; a weight loss will occur.

Calorie A Calorie is a measure of heat energy. A small calorie represents the amount of heat needed to raise one gram of water one degree Celsius. A large Calorie (kilocalorie, KC, or C) is 1,000 small calories.

calorimeter A device used to measure the caloric value of a given food, or heat production of animals or humans.

carbohydrate A group of compounds containing carbon, hydrogen, and oxygen. Glucose, glycogen, sugar, starches, fiber, cellulose, and the various saccharides are all carbohydrates.

carbohydrate loading A dietary method used by endurance-type athletes to help increase the carbohydrate (glycogen) levels in their muscles and liver.

carcinogenicity The potential of a substance to cause cancer.

carnitine A chemical that facilitates the transfer of fatty acids into the mitochondria for subsequent oxidation.

catabolism Destructive metabolism whereby complex chemical compounds in the body are degraded to simpler ones.

catalase An enzyme that helps neutralize free radicals.

cation A positively charged ion or electrolyte.

cellulite A name given to the lumpy fat that often appears in the thigh and hip region of women. Cellulite is simply normal fat in small compartments formed by connective tissue, but may contain other compounds that bind water.

cellulose The fibrous carbohydrate that provides the structural backbone for plants; plant fiber.

Celsius A thermometer scale that has a freezing point of 0 and a boiling point at 100; also known as the centigrade scale.

cerebrospinal fluid (CSF) The fluid found in the brain and spinal cord.

CHD Coronary Heart Disease; a degenerative disease of the heart caused primarily by arteriosclerosis or atherosclerosis of the coronary vessels of the heart.

chloride A compound of chlorine present in a salt form carrying a negative charge; Cl^-, an anion.

cholecalciferol The product of irradiation of 7–dehydrocholesterol found in the skin.

cholesterol A fatlike pearly substance, an alcohol, found in all animal fats and oils; a main constituent of some body tissues and body compounds.

choline A substance associated with the B complex that is widely distributed in both plant and animal tissues; involved in carbohydrate, fat, and protein metabolism.

chromium A whitish metal essential to human nutrition; it is involved in carbohydrate metabolism via its role with insulin.

chronic-training effect Physiological changes in the body, brought on by repeated bouts of exercise, that will help make the body more efficient during exercise.

chylomicron A particle of emulsified fat found in the blood following the digestion and assimilation of fat.

circuit aerobics A combination of aerobic and weight training exercises designed to elicit the specific benefits of each type of exercise.

circuit training A method of training in which exercises are arranged in a circuit or sequence. May be designed with weight training to help convey an aerobic training effect.

cirrhosis A degenerative disease of the liver, one cause being excessive consumption of alcohol.

cis The chemical structure of unsaturated fatty acids in which the hydrogen ions are on the same side of double bond.

clinical obesity Obesity determined by a clinical procedure.

cobalamin The cobalt-containing complex common to all members of the vitamin B_{12} group; often used to designate cyanocobalamin.

cobalt A gray, hard metal that is a component of vitamin B_{12}.

coenzyme An activator of an enzyme; many vitamins are coenzymes.

colon The large intestine.

complete protein A protein that contains all eight essential amino acids in the proper proportions. Animal protein is complete protein.

complex carbohydrates A term used to describe foods high in starch such as bread, cereals, fruits, and vegetables as contrasted to simple carbohydrates such as table sugar.

concentric method A method of weight training in which the muscle shortens.

conduction In relation to body temperature, the transfer of heat from one substance to another by direct contact.

convection In relation to body temperature, the transfer of heat by way of currents in either air or water.

copper A reddish metallic element essential to human nutrition; it functions with iron in the formation of hemoglobin and the cytochromes.

CoQ10 An advertised nutritional ergogenic aid that contains a number of purportedly ergogenic substances, such as inosine.

core temperature The temperature of the deep tissues of the body, usually measured orally or rectally; *also see* shell temperature.

coronary artery disease *See* CAD.

coronary heart disease *See* CHD.

coronary risk factors Behaviors (smoking) or body properties (cholesterol levels) that may predispose an individual to coronary heart disease.

cruciferous vegetables Vegetables in the cabbage family, such as broccoli, cauliflower, kale, and all cabbages.

cyanocobalamin Vitamin B_{12}.

cysteine A breakdown product of cystine. It is also a sulfur-containing amino acid.

cystine A sulfur-containing amino acid.

cytochromes Any one of a class of pigment compounds that play an important role in cellular oxidative processes.

deamination Removal of an amine group, or nitrogen, from an amino acid.

dehydration A reduction of the body water to below the normal level of hydration; water output exceeds water intake.

depressant Drugs or agents that will depress or lower the level of bodily functions, particularly central nervous system functioning.

diabetes mellitus A disorder of carbohydrate metabolism due to disturbances in production or utilization of insulin; results in high blood-glucose levels and loss of sugar in the urine.

diarrhea Frequent passage of a watery fecal discharge due to a gastrointestinal disturbance.

diastolic blood pressure The blood pressure in the arteries when the heart is at rest between beats.

dietary fiber Fiber in plant foods that cannot be hydrolyzed by the digestive enzymes.

dietary-induced thermogenesis (DIT) The increase in the basal metabolic rate following the ingestion of a meal. Heat production is increased.

2,3-diphosphoglyceride A by-product of carbohydrate metabolism in the red blood cell; helps the hemoglobin unload oxygen to the tissues.

disaccharides Any one of a class of sugars that yield two monosaccharides on hydrolysis; sucrose is the most common.

dispensable amino acids *See* nonessential amino acids.

diuretics A class of agents that stimulate the formation of urine; used as a means to reduce body fluids.

diverticulosis Weak spots in the wall of the large intestine that may bulge out like a weak spot in a tire inner tube. May become infected leading to diverticulitis.

DNA Deoxyribonucleic acid; a complex protein found in chromosomes that is the carrier of genetic information and the basis of heredity.

duration concept One of the major concepts of aerobics exercise; duration refers to the amount of time spent exercising during each session.

eating disorder A psychological disorder centering on the avoidance, excessive consumption, or purging of food, such as anorexia nervosa and bulimia nervosa.

eccentric method A weight training method in which the muscle undergoes a lengthening contraction.

electrolytes A solution that contains ions and can conduct electricity; often the ions of salts such as sodium and chloride are called electrolytes; *also see* ions.

electron transport system A highly structured array of chemical compounds in the cell that transport electrons and harness energy for later use in the process.

element Relative to chemistry, a substance that cannot be subdivided into substances different from itself; many elements are essential to human life.

EMR Exercise metabolic rate; an increased metabolic rate due to the need for increased energy production; during exercise, the BMR may be increased more than twenty-fold.

endocrine system The body system consisting of glands that secrete hormones, which have a wide variety of effects throughout the body.

energy The ability to do work; energy exists in various forms, notably mechanical, heat, and chemical in the human body.

English system A measurement system based upon the foot, pound, quart, and other nonmetric units; *also see* metric system.

enzyme A complex protein in the body that serves as a catalyst, facilitating reactions between various substances without being changed itself.

epidemiological study A study of certain populations to determine the relationship of various risk factors to epidemic diseases or health problems.

epithelial cells The layer of cells that covers the outside and inside surfaces of the body, including the skin and the lining of the gastrointestinal system.

ergogenic aid Work-enhancing agents that are used in attempts to increase athletic or physical performance capacity.

ergogenic effect The physiological or psychological effect that an ergogenic substance is designed to produce.

ergolytic effect An agent or substance that may lead to decreases in work productivity or physical performance. *See also* ergogenic effect.

essential amino acids Those amino acids that must be obtained in the diet and cannot be synthesized in the body. Also known as indispensable amino acids.

essential fat Fat in the body that is an essential part of the tissues, such as cell membrane structure, nerve coverings, and the brain; *also see* storage fat.

essential fatty acid Those unsaturated fatty acids that may not be synthesized in the body and must be obtained in the diet, e.g., linoleic fatty acid.

essential nutrients Those nutrients found to be essential to human life and optimal functioning.

Estimated Safe and Adequate Daily Dietary Intakes (ESADDI) Part of the RDA. Daily allowances for selected nutrients that are based upon available scientific evidence to be safe and adequate to meet human needs.

ethanol Alcohol; ethyl alcohol.

ethyl alcohol Alcohol; ethanol.

evaporation The conversion of a liquid to a vapor, which consumes energy; evaporation of sweat cools the body by using body heat as the energy source.

exercise frequency In an aerobic exercise program, the number of times per week that an individual exercises.

exercise intensity The tempo, speed, or resistance of an exercise. Intensity can be increased by working faster, doing more work in a given amount of time.

exercise metabolic rate *See* EMR.

exercise sequence Relative to a weight training workout, the lifting sequence is designed so that different muscle groups are utilized sequentially so as to be fresh for each exercise.

exercise stimulus   The means whereby one elicits a physiological response; running, for example, can be the stimulus to increase the heart rate and other physiological functions.

exertional heat stroke   Heat stroke that is precipitated by exercise in a warm or hot environment.

experimental study   Study that manipulates an independent variable (cause) to observe the outcome on a dependent variable (effect).

extracellular water   Body water that is located outside the cells; often subdivided into the intravascular water and the intercellular, or interstitial, water.

faddism   Relative to nutrition, the use of dietary fads based upon theoretical principles that may or may not be valid; usually used in a negative sense, as in quackery.

fasting   Starvation; abstinence from eating that may be partial or complete.

fast-twitch fibers   Muscle fibers characterized by high contractile speed.

fat exchange   A fat exchange in the Food Exchange System contains 5 grams of fat and 45 Calories.

fat-free mass   The remaining mass of the human body following the extraction of all fat.

fat loading   A term used to describe practices used to maximize the use of fats as an energy source during exercise, particularly a low-carbohydrate, high-fat diet.

fat patterning   The deposition of fat in specific areas of the human body, such as the stomach, thighs, or hips. Genetics plays an important role in fat patterning.

fatigue   A generalized or specific feeling of tiredness that may have a multitude of causes; may be mental or physical.

fats   Triglycerides; a combination, or ester, of three fatty acids and glycerol.

fatty acids   Any one of a number of aliphatic acids containing only carbon, oxygen, and hydrogen; they may be saturated or unsaturated.

female type obesity   *See* gynoid type obesity.

ferritin   The form in which iron is stored in the tissues.

fetal alcohol effects (FAE)   Symptoms noted in children born to women who consumed alcohol during pregnancy. Not as severe as the fetal alcohol syndrome.

fetal alcohol syndrome (FAS)   The cluster of physical and mental symptoms seen in the child of a mother who consumes excessive alcohol during pregnancy.

FFA   Free fatty acids; formed by the hydrolysis of triglycerides.

fiber   In general, the indigestible carbohydrate in plants that forms the structural network; *also see* cellulose.

First Law of Thermodynamics   The law that energy cannot be created nor destroyed; energy can be converted from one form to another.

flatulence   Gas or air in the gastrointestinal tract, particularly the intestines.

fluoride   A salt of hydrofluoric acid; a compound of fluorine that may be helpful in the prevention of dental decay.

folacin   Folic acid.

folate   Salt of folic acid.

folic acid   A water-soluble vitamin that appears to be essential in preventing certain types of anemia.

food additives   *See* additives.

food cultism   Treating a particular food as if it possesses special properties, such as prevention or treatment of disease or improvement of athletic performance, usually without scientific justification.

Food Exchange System   The system developed by the American Dietetic Association and other health groups that categorizes foods by content of carbohydrate, fat, protein, and Calories. Used as a basis for diet planning.

foot-pound   A unit of work whereby the weight of one pound is moved through a distance of one foot.

free fatty acids   *See* FFA.

free radicals   An atom or compound in which there is an unpaired electron. Thought to cause cellular damage.

fructose   A monosaccharide known also as levulose or fruit sugar; found in all sweet fruits.

fruit exchange   One fruit exchange in the Food Exchange System contains 15 grams of carbohydrate and 60 Calories.

fruitarian   A type of vegetarian who subsists solely on fruits, fruit products, and nuts.

galactose   A monosaccharide formed when lactose is hydrolyzed into glucose and galactose.

generally recognized as safe   *See* GRAS.

glucarate   A compound found in cruciferous vegetables that is thought to block the actions of cancer-causing agents.

glucogenic amino acids   Amino acids that may undergo deamination and be converted into glucose through the process of gluconeogenesis.

gluconeogenesis   The formation of carbohydrates from molecules that are not themselves carbohydrate, such as amino acids and the glycerol from fat.

glucose   A monosaccharide; a thick, sweet, syrupy liquid.

glucose–alanine cycle   The cycle in which alanine is released from the muscle and is converted to glucose in the liver.

glucose-electrolyte replacement solutions   A solution designed to replace sweat losses containing varying proportions of water, glucose, sodium, potassium, chloride, and other electrolytes.

glucose polymer   A combination of several glucose molecules into a more complex carbohydrate.

glucostatic theory   The theory that hunger and satiety are controlled by the glucose level in the blood; the receptors that respond to the blood glucose level are in the hypothalamus.

glutathione peroxidase An enzyme that helps neutralize free radicals.

glycemic index An index expressing the effects of various foods on the rate and amount of increase in blood glucose levels.

glycerol Glycerin, a clear syrupy liquid; combines with fatty acids to form triglycerides.

glycogen A polysaccharide that is the chief storage form of carbohydrate in animals; it is stored primarily in the liver and muscles.

glycogen-sparing effect The theory that certain dietary techniques, such as the use of caffeine, may facilitate the oxidation of fatty acids for energy and thus spare the utilization of glycogen.

glycolysis The degradation of sugars into smaller compounds; the main quantitative anaerobic energy process in the muscle tissue.

gout The deposit of uric acid by-products in and about the joints contributing to inflammation and pain; usually occurs in the knee or foot.

gram calorie A small calorie; *see* Calorie.

GRAS Generally recognized as safe; a classification for food additives indicating that they most likely are not harmful for human consumption.

gums A form of water-soluble dietary fiber found in plants.

gynoid type obesity Female type obesity; body fat is deposited primarily about the hips and thighs. *Also see* android type obesity.

HDL cholesterol High-density lipoprotein cholesterol; one mechanism whereby cholesterol is transported in the blood. High HDL levels are somewhat protective against CHD.

Healthy American Diet A diet plan based upon healthful eating principles that is designed to help prevent or treat common chronic diseases in the United States, particularly cardiovascular disease and cancer.

heat-balance equation Heat balance is dependent upon the interrelationships of metabolic heat production and loss or gain of heat by radiation, convection, conduction, and evaporation.

heat cramps Painful muscular cramps or tetany following prolonged exercise in the heat without water or salt replacement.

heat exhaustion Weakness or dizziness from overexertion in a hot environment.

heat stroke Elevated body temperature of 106° F or greater caused by exposure to excessive heat gains or production and diminished heat loss.

heat syncope Fainting caused by excessive heat exposure.

hematuria Blood or red blood cells in the urine.

heme iron The iron in the diet associated with hemoglobin in animal meats.

hemicellulose A form of dietary fiber found in plants. Differs from cellulose in that it may be hydrolyzed by dilute acids outside of the body. Not hydrolyzed in the body.

hemochromatosis Presence of excessive iron in the body resulting in an enlarged liver and bronze pigmentation of the skin.

hemoglobin The protein-iron pigment in the red blood cells that transports oxygen.

hemolysis A rupturing of red blood cells with a release of hemoglobin into the plasma.

hepatitis An inflammatory condition of the liver.

hidden fat In foods, the fat that is not readily apparent, such as the high-fat content of cheese.

high blood pressure *See* hypertension.

high-density lipoprotein A protein–lipid complex in the blood that facilitates the transport of triglycerides, cholesterol, and phospholipids. *See* HDL cholesterol.

high-fructose corn syrup A common high-Calorie sweetener used as a food additive; derived from the partial hydrolysis of corn starch.

histidine An essential amino acid.

homeostasis A term used to describe a condition of normalcy in the internal body environment.

hormone A chemical substance produced by specific body cells, secreted into the blood and then acting on some specific target tissues.

HR max The normal maximal heart rate of an individual during exercise.

human growth hormone (HGH) A hormone released by the pituitary gland that regulates growth; also involved in fatty acid metabolism.

hunger A basic physiological desire to eat that is normally caused by a lack of food; may be accompanied by stomach contractions.

hunger center A collection of nerve cells in the hypothalamus that is involved in the control of feeding reflexes.

hydrogenated fats Fats to which hydrogen has been added, usually causing them to be saturated.

hydrolysis A mechanism for splitting substances into smaller compounds by the addition of water; enzyme action.

hypercholesteremia Elevated blood-cholesterol levels.

hyperglycemia Elevated blood-glucose levels.

hyperhydration The practice of increasing the body-water stores by fluid consumption prior to an athletic event; a state of increased water content in the body.

hyperlipidemia Elevated blood-lipid levels.

hyperplasia The formation of new body cells.

hypertension A condition with various causes whereby the blood pressure is higher than normal.

hypertonic Relative to osmotic pressure, a solution that has a greater concentration of solute or salts, hence higher osmotic pressure, in comparison to another solution.

hypertriglyceridemia Elevated blood levels of triglycerides.

hypertrophy Excessive growth of a cell or organ; in pathology, an abnormal growth.

hypervitaminosis A pathological condition due to an excessive vitamin intake, particularly the fat-soluble vitamins A and D.

hypoglycemia A low blood-sugar level.

hypohydration Dehydration; a state of decreased water content in the body.

hypothalamus A part of the brain involved in the control of involuntary activity in the body; contains many centers for neural control such as temperature, hunger, appetite and thirst.

hypotonic Having an osmotic pressure lower than that of the solution to which it is compared.

incomplete protein Protein food that does not possess the proper amount of essential amino acids; characteristic of plant foods in general.

Index of Nutritional Quality *See* INQ.

indicator nutrients These eight nutrients, if provided in adequate supply through a varied diet, should provide adequate amounts of the other essential nutrients. The eight are protein, vitamin A, thiamin, riboflavin, niacin, vitamin C, calcium, and iron.

indispensable amino acids *See* essential amino acids.

initial fitness level The physical fitness level of an individual prior to the onset of a physical conditioning program.

inosine A nucleoside of the purine family which serves as a base for the formation of a variety of compounds in the body; theorized to be ergogenic.

inositol A member of the B complex, although its role in human nutrition has not been established; not classified as a vitamin.

INQ Index of Nutritional Quality; a mathematical means of determining the quality of any given food relative to its content of a specific nutrient.

insensible perspiration Perspiration on the skin not detectable by ordinary senses.

insoluble dietary fiber Dietary fiber that is not soluble in water, such as cellulose. *Also see* soluble dietary fiber.

insulin A hormone secreted by the pancreas involved in carbohydrate metabolism.

insulin response Blood-insulin levels rise following the ingestion of sugar and the resultant hyperglycemia; the insulin causes the sugar to be taken up by the muscles and liver, possibly creating a reactive hypoglycemia.

intercellular water Body water found between the cells; also known as interstitial water.

International Unit *See* IU.

International Unit System *See* SI.

interstitial water *See* intercellular water.

interval training A method of physical training in which periods of activity are interspersed with periods of rest.

intracellular water Body water that is found within the cells.

intravascular water Body water found in the vascular system, or blood vessels.

iodine A nonmetallic element that is necessary for the proper development and functioning of the thyroid gland.

ions Particles with an electrical charge; anions are negative and cations are positive.

iron A metallic element essential for the development of several chemical compounds in the body, notably hemoglobin.

iron deficiency anemia Anemia caused by an inadequate intake or absorption of iron, resulting in impaired hemoglobin formation.

iron deficiency without anemia A condition in which the hemoglobin levels are normal but several indices of iron status in the body are below normal levels.

ischemia Lack of blood supply.

isoleucine An essential amino acid.

isokinetic Literally meaning same speed; in weight training an isokinetic machine is used to control the speed of muscle contraction.

isometric Literally meaning same length; in weight training the resistance is set so that the muscle will not shorten.

isotonic Literally meaning equal tension or pressure; in weight training the resistance is set so there is supposed to be equal tension in the muscle through a range of motion, but this is rarely achieved owing to movement of body parts. Isotonic also means equal osmotic pressures between two solutions.

IU International Unit; a method of expressing the quantity of some substance, such as vitamins, which is an internationally developed and accepted standard.

jogging A term used to designate slow running; although the distinction between running and jogging is relative to the individual involved, a common value used for jogging is a nine-minute mile or slower.

joule A measure of work in the metric system; a newton of force applied through a distance of one meter.

KC Kilocalorie or Kcal; *see* Calorie.

ketogenesis The formation of ketones in the body from other substances, such as fats and proteins.

ketogenic amino acids Amino acids that may be deaminated, converted into ketones and eventually into fat.

ketones An organic compound containing a carbonyl group; ketone acids in the body, such as acetone, are the end products of fat metabolism.

ketosis The accumulation of excess ketones in the blood; as ketones are acids, acidosis occurs.

key-nutrient concept The concept that if certain key nutrients are adequately supplied by the diet, the other essential nutrients will also be present in adequate amounts. *Also see* indicator nutrients.

KGM Kilogram-meter; a measure of work in the metric system whereby one kilogram of weight is moved through a distance of one meter; however, the joule is the recommended unit to express work.

kidney stones Compounds in the pelvis of the kidney formed from various salts such as carbonates, oxalates, and phosphates.

kilocalorie A large calorie; *see* Calorie.

kilogram A unit of mass in the metric system; in ordinary terms, 1 kilogram is the equivalent of 2.2 pounds.

kilogram-meter See KGM.

kilojoule One thousand joule; one kilojoule (KJ) is approximately 0.25 kilocalorie.

Krebs cycle The main oxidative reaction sequence in the body that generates ATP; also known as the citric acid or tricarboxylic acid cycle.

lactic acid The anaerobic end product of glycolysis; it has been implicated as a causative factor in the etiology of fatigue.

lactic acid system The energy system that produces ATP anaerobically by the breakdown of glycogen to lactic acid; used primarily in events of maximal effort for one to two minutes.

lactose A white crystalline disaccharide that yields glucose and galactose upon hydrolysis; also known as milk sugar.

lactose intolerance Gastrointestinal disturbances due to an intolerance to lactose in milk; caused by deficiency of lactase, an enzyme that digests lactose.

lactovegetarian A vegetarian who includes milk products in the diet as a form of high-quality protein.

LDL Low-density lipoprotein; a protein–lipid complex in the blood that facilitates the transport of triglycerides, cholesterol, and phospholipids. *Also see* LDL cholesterol.

LDL cholesterol Low-density lipoprotein cholesterol; a mechanism whereby cholesterol is transported in the blood. High blood levels are associated with increased incidence of CHD.

lean body mass The body weight minus the body fat, composed primarily of muscle, bone, and other nonfat tissue.

lecithin A fatty substance of a class known as phospholipids; said to have the therapeutic properties of phosphorus.

legume The fruit or pod of vegetables including soybeans, kidney beans, lima beans, garden peas, black-eyed peas, and lentils; high in protein.

leucine An essential amino acid.

levulose Fructose.

lignin A noncarbohydrate form of dietary fiber.

limiting amino acids An amino acid deficient in a specific plant food, making it an incomplete protein, methionine is a limiting amino acid in legumes while lysine is deficient in grain products.

linoleic acid An essential fatty acid.

lipase An enzyme that catabolizes fats into fatty acids and glycerol.

lipids A class of fats or fatlike substances characterized by their insolubility in water and solubility in fat solvents; triglycerides, fatty acids, phospholipids, and cholesterol are important lipids in the body.

lipoic acid A coenzyme that functions in oxidative decarboxylation, or removal of carbon dioxide from a compound.

lipoprotein A combination of lipid and protein, possessing the general properties of proteins. Practically all the lipids of the plasma are present in this form.

lipoprotein lipase An enzyme involved in the metabolism of lipoproteins.

lipostatic theory The theory that hunger and satiety are controlled by the lipid level in the blood.

liquid meals Food in a liquid form designed to provide a balanced intake of essential nutrients.

liquid-protein diets Protein in a liquid form; a common form consists of predigested protein into simple amino acids.

liver glycogen The major storage form of carbohydrate in the liver.

long-haul concept Relative to weight control, the idea that weight loss via exercise should be gradual, and one should not expect to lose large amounts of weight in a short time.

lysine An essential amino acid.

macrominerals Those minerals essential to human nutrition with an RDA in excess of 100 mg/day: calcium, magnesium, phosphorus, sodium, potassium, chloride.

magnesium A white metallic mineral element essential in human nutrition.

major minerals *See* macrominerals.

male type obesity *See* android type obesity.

malnutrition Poor nutrition that may be due to inadequate amounts of essential nutrients. Too many Calories leading to obesity is also a form of malnutrition. *Also see* subclinical malnutrition.

maltodextrin A glucose polymer that exerts lesser osmotic effects compared with glucose; used in a variety of sports drinks as the source of carbohydrate.

maltose A white crystalline disaccharide that upon hydrolysis yields two molecules of glucose.

manganese A metallic element essential in human nutrition.

maximal heart rate *See* HR max.

maximal heart rate reserve The difference between the maximal HR and resting HR. A percentage of this reserve, usually 60–90 percent, is added to the resting HR to get the target HR for aerobics training programs.

maximal oxygen uptake *See* VO_2 max.

meat exchange One lean meat exchange in the Food Exchange System contains 3 grams of fat, 7 grams of protein and 55 Calories; a medium-fat meat exchange has an additional 2 grams of fat and totals 75 Calories; a high-fat exchange has 5 additional grams of fat and totals 100 Calories.

megadose An excessive amount of a substance in comparison to a normal dose of RDA; usually used to refer to vitamins.

metabolic aftereffects The theory that the aftereffects of exercise will cause the metabolic rate to be elevated for a time, thus expending calories and contributing to weight loss.

metabolic rate The energy expended to maintain all physical and chemical changes occurring in the body.

metabolic water   The water that is a by-product of the oxidation of carbohydrate, fat, and protein in the body.

metabolism   The sum total of all physical and chemical processes occurring in the body.

metalloenzyme   An enzyme that needs a mineral component, such as zinc, in order to function effectively.

methionine   An essential amino acid.

metric system   A method of measurement based upon units of ten.

METS   A measurement unit of energy expenditure; one MET equals approximately 3.5 ml O_2/kg body weight/minute.

MFP factor   Meat, fish, and poultry factor; an unknown property of meat, fish, and poultry that facilitates the absorption of nonheme iron found in plant foods.

microgram   One millionth of a gram (μg).

milk exchange   One skim milk exchange in the Food Exchange System contains 12 grams of carbohydrate, 8 grams of protein, a trace of fat, and 90 Calories. A low-fat exchange contains 120 Calories whereas whole milk has 150 Calories.

milligram   One thousandth of a gram.

millimole   One millimole is one thousandth of a mole.

mineral   An inorganic element occurring in nature.

mitochondria   Structures within the cells that serve as the location for the aerobic production of ATP.

mole   One mole is the gram molecular weight of a compound, which is the quantity of a substance that equals its molecular weight.

molybdenum   A hard, heavy, silvery-white metallic element.

monosaccharides   Simple sugars (glucose, fructose, and galactose) that cannot be broken down by hydrolysis.

monounsaturated fatty acids   Fatty acids that have a single double bond.

morbid obesity   Severe obesity in which the incidence of life-threatening diseases is increased significantly.

muscle glycogen   The form in which carbohydrate is stored in the muscle.

muscle hypertrophy   An increase in the size of the muscle.

myoglobin   An iron-containing compound, similar to hemoglobin, found in the muscle tissues; it binds oxygen in the muscle cells.

narcotic   Any agent that produces insensibility to pain.

natural, organic foods   Foods that are stated to be grown without the use of man-made chemicals such as pesticides and artificial fertilizers.

Nautilus   A brand of exercise equipment designed for strength-training programs; uses a principle to help provide optimal resistance throughout the full range of motion.

negative caloric balance   A condition whereby the caloric output exceeds the caloric intake, thus contributing to a weight loss.

negative nitrogen balance   A condition in which dietary protein is insufficient to meet the nitrogen needs of the body. More nitrogen is excreted than is retained in the body.

net protein utilization   See NPU.

neutron activation analysis   A sophisticated, noninvasive method of analyzing body structure and function.

newton   A unit of force that will accelerate one kilogram of mass one meter per second per second.

niacin   Nicotinamide; nicotinic acid; part of the B complex and an important part of several coenzymes involved in aerobic energy processes in the cells.

niacin equivalent   A unit of measure of niacin activity in a food related to both the amount of niacin present and that obtainable from tryptophan; about 60 mg tryptophan can be converted to 1 mg niacin.

nickel   A silvery-white metallic element.

nicotinamide   An amide of nicotinic acid; niacin.

nicotinic acid   Niacin.

nitrogen   A colorless, tasteless, odorless gas comprising about 80 percent of the atmospheric gas; an essential component of protein that is formed in plants during their developmental process.

nitrogen balance   A dietary state in which the input and output of nitrogen is balanced so that the body neither gains nor loses protein tissue.

nonessential amino acids   Amino acids that may be formed in the body and thus need not be obtained in the diet; also known as dispensable amino acids. See essential amino acids.

nonessential nutrient   A nutrient that may be formed in the body from excess amounts of other nutrients.

nonheme iron   Iron that is found in plant foods; see heme iron.

nonprotein nitrogen   Nitrogen in the body and foods that is associated with nonprotein compounds.

normohydration   The state of normal hydration, or normal body-water levels, as compared with dehydration and hyperhydration.

NPU   Net protein utilization; a technique used to assess protein quality.

nutrient   Substances found in food that provide energy, promote growth and repair of tissues, and regulate metabolism.

nutrient density   A concept related to the degree of concentration of nutrients in a given food; also see the related concept INQ.

nutritional labeling   A listing of selected key nutrients and Calories on the label of commercially prepared food products.

obesity   An excessive accumulation of body fat; usually reserved for those individuals who are 20–30 percent or more above the average weight for their size.

OBLA   Onset of blood lactate. The intensity level of exercise at which the blood lactate begins to accumulate rapidly.

octacosanol   A solid white alcohol found in wheat germ oil.

Olestra   A commercially produced substitute for dietary fat.

omega-3 fatty acids   Polyunsaturated fatty acids that have a double bond between the third and fourth carbon from the terminal, or omega, carbon. Found in fish oils and theorized to help in the prevention of coronary heart disease.

onset of blood lactic acid   *See* OBLA.

oral contraceptives   Birth control pills used to prevent conception.

osmoreceptors   Receptors in the body that react to changes in the osmotic pressure of the blood.

osmotic pressure   A pressure that produces a diffusion between solutions that have different concentrations.

osteomalacia   A disease characterized by softening of the bones, leading to brittleness and increased deformity.

osteoporosis   Increased porosity or softening of the bone.

overload principle   The major concept of physical training whereby one imposes a stress greater than that normally imposed upon a particular body system.

overweight   Body weight greater than that which is considered normal; *also see* obesity.

ovolactovegetarian   A vegetarian who also consumes eggs and milk products as a source of high-quality animal protein.

ovovegetarian   A vegetarian who includes eggs in the diet to help obtain adequate amounts of protein.

oxalates   Salts of oxalic acid, which are found in green leafy vegetables such as spinach and beet greens.

oxygen consumption   The total amount of oxygen utilized in the body for the production of energy; it is directly related to the metabolic rate.

oxygen system   The energy system that produces ATP via the oxidation of various foodstuffs, primarily fats and carbohydrates.

PABA   Para-aminobenzoic acid; although not a vitamin, often grouped with the B complex.

pangamic acid   A term often associated with "vitamin B_{15}," the essentiality of which has not been established. Often contains calcium gluconate and dimethylglycine.

pantothenic acid   A vitamin of the B complex.

para-aminobenzoic acid   *See* PABA.

PC   Phosphocreatine; a high-energy phosphate compound found in the body cells; part of the ATP–PC energy system.

peak bone mass   The concept of maximizing the amount of bone mineral content during the formative years of childhood and young adulthood.

pectin   A form of soluble dietary fiber found in some fruits.

pellagra   A deficiency disease caused by inadequate amounts of niacin in the diet.

pentose   A simple sugar containing five carbons instead of six as in glucose.

peptides   Small compounds formed by the union of two or more amino acids; known also as dipeptides, tripeptides, etc., depending upon the number of amino acids combined.

perceptual–motor activities   Physical activities characterized by the perception of a given stimulus and culminating in an appropriate motor, or movement, response.

pernicious anemia   A severe progressive form of anemia that may be fatal if not treated with vitamin B_{12}. Usually caused by inability to absorb B_{12}, not a dietary deficiency of B_{12}.

pesticides   Poisons used to destroy pests of various types, including plants and animals.

pH   The abbreviation used to express the level of acidity of a solution; a low pH represents high acidity.

phenylalanine   An essential amino acid.

phosphagens   Compounds such as ATP and phosphocreatine that serve as a source of high energy in the body cells.

phosphates   Salts of phosphoric acid, purported to possess ergogenic qualities.

phosphocreatine   *See* PC.

phospholipids   Lipids containing phosphorus that in hydrolysis yield fatty acids, glycerin, and a nitrogenous compound. Lecithin is an example.

phosphorus   A nonmetallic element essential to human nutrition.

phosphorus: calcium ratio   The ratio of calcium to phosphorus intake in the diet; the normal ratio is 1:1.

photon absorptiometry   An analytical, noninvasive technique designed to assess bone density.

phylloquinone   Vitamin K, essential in the blood clotting process.

physical conditioning   Methods used to increase the efficiency or capacity of a given body system so as to improve physical or athletic performance.

phytates   Salts of phytic acids; produced in the body during the digestion of certain grain products; can combine with some minerals such as iron and possibly decrease their absorption.

plaque   The material that forms in the inner layer of the artery and contributes to atherosclerosis. It contains cholesterol, lipids, and other debris.

polypeptides   A combination of a number of simple amino acids; *also see* peptide.

polysaccharide   A carbohydrate that upon hydrolysis will yield more than ten monosaccharides.

polyunsaturated fatty acids   Fats that contain two or more double bonds and thus are open to hydrogenation.

positive caloric balance   A condition whereby caloric intake exceeds caloric output; the resultant effect is a weight gain.

postabsorptive state The period after a meal has been absorbed from the gastrointestinal tract; in BMR tests it is usually a period of approximately twelve hours.

potassium A metallic element essential in human nutrition; it is the principal cation present in the intracellular fluids.

power Work divided by time; the ability to produce work in a given period of time.

power–endurance continuum In relation to strength training, the concept that power or strength is developed by high resistance and few repetitions, whereas endurance is developed by low resistance and many repetitions.

PRE Progressive Resistive Exercise.

pre-event nutrition Dietary intake prior to athletic competition; may refer to a two- to three-day period prior to an event or the immediate pre-event meal.

Pritikin program A dietary program developed by Nathan Pritikin, which severely restricts the intake of certain foods like fats and cholesterol and greatly increases the consumption of complex carbohydrates.

progressive-resistance principle A training technique, primarily with weights, whereby resistance is increased as the individual develops increased strength levels.

proline A nonessential amino acid.

promoters Substances or agents necessary to support or promote the development of a disease once it is initiated.

proof Relative to alcohol content, proof is twice the percentage of alcohol in a solution; 80-proof whiskey is 40 percent alcohol.

protein Any one of a group of complex organic compounds containing nitrogen; formed from various combinations of amino acids.

protein–Calorie insufficiency A major health problem in certain parts of the world where the population suffers from inadequate intake of protein and total Calories.

protein complementarity The practice among vegetarians of eating foods together from two or more different food groups, usually legumes, nuts, or beans with grain products, in order to ensure a balanced intake of essential amino acids.

protein-sparing effect An adequate intake of energy Calories, as from carbohydrate, will decrease somewhat the rate of protein catabolism in the body and hence spare protein. This is the basis of the protein-sparing modified fast, or diet.

proteinuria The presence of proteins in the urine.

provitamin A Carotene, a substance in the diet from which the body may form vitamin A.

psyllium A plant product that contains both water-soluble and insoluble dietary fiber.

purines The end products of nucleoprotein metabolism, which may be formed in the body; they are eventually degraded to uric acid.

pyridoxal A component of the vitamin B group.

pyridoxamine A part of the vitamin B group; an analog of pyridoxine.

pyridoxine A component of the vitamin B complex, vitamin B_6.

pyruvate The end product of glycolysis. Under aerobic conditions it may be converted into acetyl CoA, whereas under anaerobic conditions it is converted into lactic acid.

quackery Misrepresentation of the facts to deceive the consumer.

radiation Electromagnetic waves given off by an object; the body radiates heat to a cool environment.

rating of perceived exertion *See* RPE.

RDA Recommended Dietary Allowances; the levels of intake of essential nutrients considered to be adequate to meet the known nutritional needs of practically all healthy persons.

RE Retinol equivalent; a measure of vitamin A activity in food as measured by preformed vitamin A or carotene, provitamin A; 1 RE equals 5 IU.

recommended dietary allowances *See* RDA.

recommended dietary goals Dietary goals for Americans that have been established by a U.S. Senate subcommittee on nutrition; goals stress dietary reduction of fat, cholesterol, salt, and sugar, and increase of complex carbohydrates.

recuperation principle A principle of physical conditioning whereby adequate rest periods are taken for recuperation to occur so that exercise may be continued.

regional fat distribution Deposition of fat in different regions of the body. See also android and gynoid type obesity.

relative humidity The percentage of moisture in the air compared to the amount of moisture needed to cause saturation, which is taken as 100.

relative-weight method A method of determining obesity by comparing the weight of an individual to standardized height and weight tables.

repetition maximum (RM) In weight training, the amount of weight that can be lifted for a specific number of repetitions.

repetitions In relation to weight training or interval training, the number of times that an exercise is done.

resting energy expenditure (REE) *See* RMR.

resting metabolic rate *See* RMR.

retinol Vitamin A.

retinol equivalent *See* RE.

riboflavin Vitamin B_2, a member of the B complex.

ribose A five-carbon sugar found in several body compounds, such as riboflavin.

risk factor Associated factors that increase the risk for a given disease; for example, cigarette smoking and lung cancer.

RMR Resting metabolic rate; the energy requirement to drive all physiological processes while in a state of rest; also see BMR and EMR.

RPE Rating of perceived exertion; a subjective rating, on a numerical scale, used to express the perceived difficulty of a given work task.

running Although the distinction between running and jogging is relative to the individual involved, a common value used for running is 7 mph or faster.

saccharide A series of carbohydrates ranging from simple sugars (monosaccharides) to complex carbohydrates (polysaccharides).

salt-depletion heat exhaustion Weakness caused by excessive loss of electrolytes as in excessive sweating.

satiety center A group of nerve cells in the hypothalamus that responds to certain stimuli in the blood and provides a sensation of satiety.

saturated fatty acids Fats that have all chemical bonds filled.

scurvy A deficiency disease caused by a lack of vitamin C in the diet; symptoms include weakness, bleeding gums and anemia.

SDA Specific dynamic action; often used to represent the increased energy cost observed during the metabolism of protein in the body. *Also see* dietary-induced thermogenesis.

secondary amenorrhea Cessation of menstruation after the onset of puberty; primary amenorrhea is the lack of menstruation prior to menarche.

selenium A nonmetallic element resembling sulfur; an essential nutrient.

semivegetarian An individual who refrains from eating red meat but includes white meat such as fish and chicken in a diet stressing vegetarian concepts.

serum-lipid level The concentration of lipids in the blood serum.

set-point theory The weight-control theory that postulates that each individual has an established normal body weight. Any deviation from this set point will lead to changes in body metabolism to return the individual to the normal weight.

sets In weight training, a certain number of repetitions constitutes a set; for example, a lifter may do three sets of six repetitions per set.

shell temperature The temperature of the skin; *also see* core temperature.

SI Le Systeme International d'Unite, or the International System of Units; a system of measurement based upon the metric system.

silicon A nonmetallic element.

simple carbohydrates Usually used to refer to table sugar, or sucrose, a disaccharide; may refer also to other disaccharides and the monosaccharides.

Simplesse A commercially produced fat substitute derived from protein.

skinfold technique A technique used to compute an individual's percentage of body fat; various skinfolds are measured and a regression formula is used to compute the body fat.

sling psychrometer A device that incorporates both a dry-bulb and wet-bulb thermometer, thus providing a heat-stress index incorporating both temperature and relative humidity.

slow-twitch fibers Red muscle fibers that have a slow contraction speed; designed for aerobic-type activity.

sodium A soft metallic element; combines with chloride to form salt; the major extracellular cation in the human body.

soluble dietary fiber Dietary fibers in plants such as gums and pectins that are soluble in water.

specific dynamic action *See* SDA.

specific heat The amount of energy or heat needed to raise the temperature of a unit of mass, such as one kilogram of body tissue, one degree Celsius.

specificity of training The principle that physical training should be designed to mimic the specific athletic event in which one competes. Specific human energy systems and neuromuscular skills should be stressed.

sports anemia A temporary condition of low hemoglobin levels often observed in athletes during the early stages of training.

sports drinks Popular term for various glucose-electrolyte fluid replacement drinks.

sports nutrition The application of nutritional principles to sport with the intent of maximizing performance.

spot reducing The theory that exercising a specific body part, such as the thighs, will facilitate the loss of body fat from that spot.

standardized exercise An exercise task that conforms to a specific standardized protocol.

steady state A level of metabolism, usually during exercise, when the oxygen consumption satisfies the energy expenditure and the individual is performing in an aerobic state.

steady-state threshold The intensity level of exercise at which the production of energy appears to shift rapidly to anaerobic mechanisms, such as when a rapid rise in blood lactic acid exists. The oxygen system will still supply a major portion of the energy, but the lactic acid system begins to contribute an increasing share.

standard error of measurement or estimate A measure of variability about the mean. Sixty-eight percent of the population is within one standard error above and below the mean, while about 95 percent is within two standard errors.

standards of identity A list of ingredients that are specified for a particular food product, such as mayonnaise; food manufacturers need not label ingredients if the product conforms to such specifications.

sterols Substances similar to fats because of their solubility characteristics; the most commonly known one is cholesterol.

stimulus period In exercise programs, the time period over which the stimulus is applied, such as a HR of 150 for fifteen minutes.

storage fat Fat that accumulates and is stored in the adipose tissue; *also see* essential fat.

strength–endurance continuum In relation to strength training, the concept that power or strength is developed by high resistance and few repetitions and that endurance is developed by low resistance and many repetitions.

subclinical malnutrition A nutrient deficiency state in which no clinical signs of the nutrient deficiency are observable, but other nonspecific symptoms such as fatigue may be present.

sucrose Table sugar, a disaccharide; yields glucose and fructose upon hydrolysis.

sulfur A pale yellow nonmetallic element essential in human nutrition; component of the sulfur-containing amino acids.

sumo wrestling A form of wrestling in Japan.

superoxide dismutase An enzyme that helps neutralize free radicals.

systolic blood pressure The blood pressure in the arteries when the heart is contracting and pumping blood.

target heart rate In an aerobic exercise program, the heart-rate level that will provide the stimulus for a beneficial training effect.

testosterone The male sex hormone responsible for male secondary sex characteristics at puberty; it has anabolic and androgenic effects.

thiamin Vitamin B_1.

threonine An essential amino acid.

thyroxine A hormone secreted by the thyroid gland that is involved in the control of the metabolic rate.

tin A white metallic element.

tocopherol Generic name for an alcohol that has the activity of vitamin E.

total body electrical impedance A sophisticated method of measuring the resistance provided by water in the body as a means to predict body composition.

total body fat The sum total of the body's storage fat and essential fat stores.

trabecular bone The spongy bone structure found inside the bone, as contrasted with the more compact bone on the outside.

trace elements Those minerals essential to human nutrition that have an RDA less than 100 mg daily.

trans The chemical structure of unsaturated fatty acids in which the hydrogen ions are on opposite sides of double bond.

triglycerides One of the many fats formed by the union of glycerol and fatty acids.

triose A simple sugar having three carbon atoms.

tryptophan An essential amino acid.

type I muscle fiber The slow-twitch red fiber that provides energy primarily by the oxygen system.

type IIa muscle fiber The fast-twitch red fiber that provides energy by both the oxygen system and the lactic acid system.

type IIb muscle fiber The fast-twitch white fiber that provides energy primarily by the lactic acid system.

tyrosine A nonessential amino acid.

underwater weighing A technique for measuring the percentage of body fat in humans.

United States Recommended Daily Allowances See USRDA.

Universal Gym A brand name for exercise equipment, particularly weights for strength development.

unsaturated fatty acids Fatty acids that contain double or triple bonds and hence can add hydrogen atoms.

urea The chief nitrogenous constituent of the urine and the final product of the decomposition of proteins in the body.

uric acid A crystalline end product of purine metabolism; commonly involved in gout and the formation of kidney stones.

USRDA The United States Recommended Daily Allowances; the RDA figures used on labels, representing the percentage of the RDA for a given nutrient contained in a serving of the food.

valine An essential amino acid.

Valsalva phenomenon A condition in which a forceful exhalation is attempted against a closed epiglottis and no air escapes; such a straining may cause the person to faint.

vanadium A light gray metallic element.

vascular water The body water contained in the blood vessels; a part of the extracellular water.

vasodilation An increase in the size of the blood vessels, usually referring to the arterial system.

vegan An extreme vegetarian who eats no animal protein.

vegetable exchange One vegetable exchange in the Food Exchange System contains 5 grams of carbohydrate, 2 grams of protein and 25 Calories.

vegetarian One whose food is of vegetable or plant origin; also see lactovegetarian, ovovegetarian, ovolactovegetarian, and vegan.

very low-Calorie diet (VLCD) A diet containing less than 800 Calories per day.

very low-density lipoprotein See VLDL.

vitamin, natural Often referred to as vitamins derived from natural sources; i.e., food in nature; contrast with vitamin, synthetic.

vitamin, synthetic An artificial vitamin commercially produced from the separate components of the vitamin.

vitamin A An unsaturated aliphatic alcohol; fat soluble.

vitamin B_1 Thiamin; the antineuritic vitamin.

vitamin B_2 Riboflavin.

vitamin B_6 Pyridoxine and related compounds.

vitamin B_{12} Cyanocobalamin.

vitamin B_{15} Not a vitamin but marketed as one; usual composition is calcium gluconate and dimethylglycine (DMG).

vitamin C Ascorbic acid; the antiscorbutic vitamin.

vitamin D Any one of related sterols that have antirachitic properties; fat soluble.

vitamin deficiency Subnormal body-vitamin levels due to inadequate intake or absorption; specific disorders are linked with deficiencies of specific vitamins.

vitamin E Alpha-tocopherol, one of three tocopherols; fat soluble.

vitamin K The antihemorrhagic, or clotting vitamin; fat soluble.

vitamins A general term for a number of substances deemed essential for the normal metabolic functioning of the body.

VLDL Very low-density lipoproteins; a protein-lipid complex in the blood that transports triglycerides, cholesterol, and phospholipids; has a very low density; *also see* HDL and LDL cholesterol.

VO$_2$ max Maximal oxygen uptake; measured during exercise, the maximal amount of oxygen consumed reflects the body's ability to utilize oxygen as an energy source; equals the cardiac output times the arteriovenous oxygen difference.

waist/hip ratio The mathematical ratio of the waist girth to the hip girth, usually taken as the smallest waist measurement and the largest hip measurement.

warm-down A phase after an exercise session during which the individual gradually tapers the level of activity—for example, by jogging slowly after a fast run.

warm-up Low-level exercises used to increase the muscle temperature and/or stretch the muscles prior to a strenuous exercise bout.

water A tasteless, colorless, odorless fluid essential to life; composed of two parts hydrogen and one part oxygen (H_2O).

water-depletion heat exhaustion Weakness caused by excessive loss of body fluids such as through exercise-induced dehydration in a hot or warm environment.

watt A unit of power in the SI; one watt equals about 6 kilogram-meters per minute.

WBGT Index Wet-bulb globe thermometer index; a heat-stress index based upon four factors measured by the wet-bulb globe thermometer.

weight cycling Repetitive loss and regain of body weight; often called yo-yo dieting.

wet-bulb globe thermometer A device that takes into account the various factors determining heat stress: air temperature, air movement, radiation heat and humidity.

wheat germ oil Oil extracted from the embryo of wheat, high in linoleic fatty acid, vitamin E and octacosanol.

work Effort expended to accomplish something; in terms of physics, force times distance.

xerophthalmia Dryness of the conjunctiva and cornea of the eye, which may lead to blindness if untreated; caused by deficiency of vitamin A.

xylitol A sugar alcohol that may be obtained from fruits.

zinc A blue-white crystalline metallic element essential to human nutrition.

Index